THE COMPLETE MILITARY WORKING DOG MANUAL

by

Department of Defense
and
U.S. Army Veterinary Services

Post-Apocalyptic Fiction & Survival Nonfiction

The Complete Military Working Dog Manual

By Department of Defense and U.S. Army Veterinary Services

Cover Photo: Senior Airman Tariq Russell, a 21st Security Forces Squadron military working dog handler, shakes the paw of his partner, Paul, at Peterson Air Force Base, CO, June 14, 2016. (U.S. Air Force photo/Airman 1st Class Dennis Hoffman

ISBN13: 978-1-939473-98-1
Published by Prepper Press
www.PrepperPress.com

U.S. MILITARY'S DOG TRAINING HANDBOOK

OFFICIAL GUIDE FOR TRAINING MILITARY WORKING DOGS

Post-Apocalyptic Fiction & Survival Nonfiction

CHAPTER 2—PRINCIPLES OF CONDITIONING AND BEHAVIOR MODIFICATION

Motivation 54
Learning and Conditioning 56
Classical Conditioning 58
Instrumental Conditioning 60
Discriminative Stimuli 64
Inducive versus Compulsive Training 65
Application of Inducive Training 65
Application of Compulsive Training 68
Generalization of Classical and Instrumental Conditioning 70
Learning Transfer 71
Anticipation 71

CHAPTER 3—PATROL DOG TRAINING

Obedience Commands 73
Obstacle Course 78
Controlled Aggression 79
Agitation 80
Control 81
Scouting 84
Scouting Problems 85
Maintaining Proficiency 85
Security Problems 85
Building Search 86
Building Search Training 86
Tracking 89
Decoy Techniques 91
Proficiency Standards and Evaluations 96
SF Standardization & Evaluations 98

CHAPTER 4—CLEAR SIGNALS TRAINING METHOD

Introduction 99
Clear Signals Training Method 99
Obedience Training with CST 109
Controlled Aggression Training with Clear Signals Training 117
Gunshots 132

CHAPTER 5—DEFERRED FINAL RESPONSE (DFR)

DFR Background 134
Reward Not from Source Method 134
Deferred Final Response Method 135
Overview of the DFR Training Sequence 135
Liabilities of DFR 136

Slow or Reluctant Final Response in DFR Dogs 137
Stop and Stare in DFR Dogs 138
Issues with DFR Dogs 142

CHAPTER 6—DETECTOR DOG TRAINING VALIDATION AND LEGAL CONSIDERATIONS

Validation Testing 145
Legal Aspects 146

CHAPTER 7—THE MILITARY WORKING DOG (MWD) PROGRAM

Doctrine 148
Functional Area Responsibilities 148
Employment Areas 148
Understanding MWDs 150
The MWD Section 151

CHAPTER 8—ADMINISTRATION/MEDICAL RECORDS, FORMS, AND REPORTS

Administrative Records, Forms, and Reports 154

CHAPTER 9—FACILITIES AND EQUIPMENT

Kennel Facilities 158
Obstacle Course 158
Authorized Equipment 158
Maintenance of Equipment 160
Vehicle Authorization for Kennel Support 160
Shipping Crates 160

CHAPTER 10—SAFETY AND TRANSPORTATION PROCEDURES

Kennel Safety 161
Training Area 161
Safety in the Veterinary Facilities 162
Operational Safety 162
Vehicle Transportation 162
Aircraft Transportation 162
Military Air Transportation 163
Explosive Safety 163
Drug Safety 163

CHAPTER 11—OPERATIONAL EMPLOYMENT

Security Operations 164
Air Provost Operations 165

- Regular or irregular rhythm.
- Strong or weak strength.
- The normal pulse character is regular and strong.

Determine the Dog's Respiratory Rate and Character

Count the number of times the dog breathes to determine breaths per minute by counting the number of breaths taken in 60 seconds or count the number of breaths taken in 30 seconds and multiply by 2. The normal respiratory rate of a dog is from 10 to 30 breaths per minute.

Judge respiratory character based on the depth (shallow, deep or normal), the rhythm (panting, regular or forced). The normal respiratory character of a dog is a normal depth and regular rhythm.

Determine the Dog's Mucous Membrane Color and Mucous Membrane Moistness

The best place to check mucous membrane color and moistness is the tissue covering the gums in the mouth.

Expose the dog's gums by gently pulling the top lip up or the bottom lip down and note the color of the gums. The normal mucous membrane color of a dog is pink. Pink mucous membranes tell us that enough oxygen is making it into the blood stream. Abnormal mucous membrane color would be pale, white, blue, yellow or brick-red. Some breeds have black pigmented mucous membranes. If this is the case, place your thumb on the skin just under the lower eyelid and gently pull down and observe the color of the membranes of the inner lower eyelid.

Note the moistness of the gums by gently touching your finger to the exposed gums Mucous membrane moistness is one of several crude assessments of hydration status of the dog. Normal mucous membranes are moist or slippery. Mucous membranes dry or tacky to the touch are not normal.

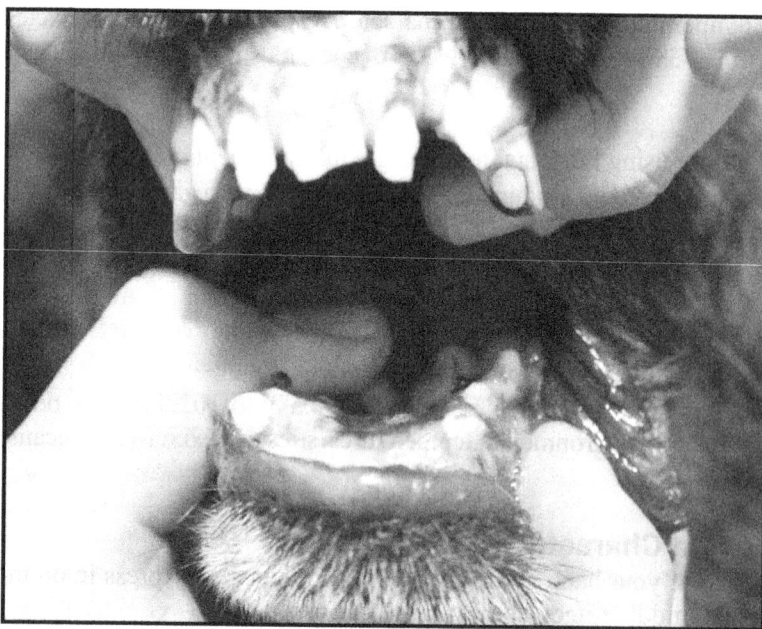

*Staff Sgt. Patrick Lau (not pictured opens Arek's mouth to show the damage this military working dog suffered when the convoy Arek was traveling in was hit by an explosive in Iraq. At the time of the incident, Arek clenched his jaw so hard that he shattered four teeth, three of which were reconstructed. Sergeant Lau and Arek are deployed to the 376th Expeditionary Security Forces Squadron at the Transit Center at Manas, Kyrgystan, from Hill Air Force Base, Utah.
(U.S. Air Force photo/ Staff Sgt. Carolyin Viss)*

Determine the Dog's Capillary Refill Time (CRT)

CRT is the amount of time, measured in seconds, that it takes blood to return to an area of the gum after it has been blanched by your finger. CRT assesses blood flow to tissues.

Expose the dog's gums by gently pulling the top lip up or the bottom lip down. Gently press your index finger into the gums to blanch the area. Release the finger and count in seconds how long it takes for blood to return to the area. The normal CRT of a dog is less than 2 seconds.

Determine the Dog's Skin Elasticity or Skin Elasticity
Skin elasticity is another of the crude assessment tools we have to evaluate hydration status of a dog.

Gently grasp a small area of skin on the back and pull it up into a "tent". Hold for a few seconds and then release. Note how long it takes the skin to return to normal. The normal skin elasticity in a dog is immediate return of tented skin to its normal position. Skin that remains tented more than 1 or 2 seconds is a crude indicator of dehydration.

Observe the Dog's Level of Consciousness, or Mental Alertness
Use one of the following terms to describe the dog's mental alertness:

- **Bright, alert, and responsive (BAR), or quiet, alert, and responsive (QAR):** The dog appears normal in all respects mentally.
- **Depressed:** The dog appears "down", lethargic, and not interested in normal activities (work, play), and may have a loss of appetite; the dog responds to verbal and physical stimuli but is slow to respond.
- **Stupor:** The dog acts "drunk" and "out of it"; the dog responds to physical stimulation but not verbal stimulation; responses are very slow.
- **Coma:** The dog is completely unresponsive to verbal and physical stimulation.
- **Agitated:** The dog can't sit still, moves rapidly and irregularly, and acts "disturbed".

Determine the Dog's Weight and Body Condition Score (BCS)
Do this by weighing the dog on the scale and observing the dog's physical appearance. BCS should be determined utilizing the Purina™ Body Condition Score chart as a reference, located at www.purina.com/dogs/health/bodycondition.aspx. The optimal BCS for a MWD is a score of 4 or 5. Any MWD that is above or below the optimal BCS range is possibly over- or underweight.

Record Vital Signs Using the Following Format:
- Body temperature: T - XXX.X° F
- Pulse rate: P - XX bpm (beats per minute)
- Pulse character: Regular or irregular; strong or weak
- Respiratory rate: R - XX breaths /min (or panting)
- Respiratory character: normal, shallow, or deep; regular, panting, or forced
- Mucous membrane color: MM - color observed
- Mucous membrane moistness: Moist or dry/tacky
- Capillary refill time: CRT - ≤2 (less than) or >2 (more than) seconds
- Skin elasticity: normal or slow.
- Level of consciousness or mental alertness: BAR, QAR, depressed, stupor, coma, or agitated
- Body weight: W-XX.X lbs. or XX.X #.
- Body condition score: X out of 9 or X/9

Make note of any other significant observations or abnormalities. Be as specific as possible. Notify the veterinary staff immediately of any abnormalities or significant findings.

PERFORM A PHYSICAL EXAM

To identify an illness or injury, you must recognize what is normal for your MWD. Sometimes the condition is so obvious that there is no question it is abnormal. Frequently, changes in your dog's health and disposition are subtle and it is important they are recognized. Early recognition of a serious problem can save your MWD's life.

Perform a Physical Exam of the Dog

- Note any external obvious signs of injury or illness.
- Prior to restraining your dog for physical exam, observe the animal in its natural state (that is, in the kennel or in the exercise yard). Look for things such as abnormal behavior, attitude, or level of consciousness, food and water intake, working or playing normally, vomiting or diarrhea, normal urination and defecation or lameness or any other obvious signs of injury or illness.
- Measure and record the dog's vital signs IAW chap 1, para 1.1, Taking Vital Signs.
- Examine the dog's head looking for abnormalities including but not limited to eye discharge, nasal discharge, areas of hair loss, swellings, masses, sores and obvious deformities.
- Evaluate the dog's eyes looking for foreign objects lodged in the eye, eye trauma or an eye out of its socket, masses, twitching or spasms, abnormal discharge such as blood or pus, and cloudiness of the clear part of the eye (cornea).
- Examine the dogs muzzle looking for obvious deformities, swelling, sores and discharge.
- Examine the lips looking for obvious deformities, warts or similar bumps, masses and redness or swelling.
- Remove the muzzle and examine the inside of the dog's mouth, if the dog will allow it. Look for obvious abnormalities such as broken teeth or a cut tongue, masses, cuts or sores, redness or swelling, foreign bodies and abnormal odor.
- Examine the ears for foreign substances or debris, a dark, dry, waxy debris (signs of ear mites), bacterial or yeast infections produce a moist, greenish-yellow substance and an abnormal odor.
- Examine the dog's hair coat and skin, looking for areas of hair loss, parasites (lice, fleas, and ticks), redness and swelling, crusts, scales, masses and matted areas.
- Examine the trunk and limbs by feeling the muscles and bones of the rib cage and front and hind legs. Note any swelling, masses and pain response.
- Flex and extend all the joints of the front and hind legs and note any swelling and pain response.
- Check the spaces between toes of the paws looking for foreign objects, cuts and scrapes, wounds, swelling or masses.
- Check the nails for proper trimming. Nails should not extend beyond the pad of the toes.
- Observe the genitalia. In both the male and female dog, look for inflammation, swelling, obvious deformities, abnormal discharge (A small amount of yellowish-green discharge from the prepuce is normal) and sores, especially of the scrotum in male dogs.
- Observe the rectum and anal area looking for inflammation, swelling, masses, sores or wounds.
- Examine the tail looking for wounds, sores and areas of hair loss.
- Make a note of all observations recording vital signs as trained in Chap 1, para 1.1 and specific information concerning any abnormalities.
- Notify the veterinary staff immediately of any abnormalities or significant findings.

PERFORM A PRIMARY SURVEY

Military Working Dogs can become seriously ill or injured in a very short period of time. It is critical to identify life-threatening problems immediately. A Primary Survey is a rapid examination that is designed to target the most critical body systems in order of importance to detect serious problems. The survey should be done quickly (less than two minutes).

Visually Assess the Dog from a Distance as You Approach It

Note the level of consciousness, responsiveness, and any unusual behavior or activity. Note unusual body or limb postures or positions that suggest bone fractures, joint dislocations, or other traumatic injuries. Listen for unusual breathing sounds and for any audible airway obstructions. Look for obvious blood, wounds, or other gross abnormalities. Immediately notify the Kennel Master or veterinary personnel if any abnormalities are noted.

Assess the Airway by Listening for Labored and Noisy Breathing that Suggests Something is Blocking the Airway

Feel the throat area and trachea (windpipe) in the front part of the neck. Look for obvious masses, wounds, swellings, or deformities that may cause airway obstruction. If possible, open the mouth and examine the inside and as far back into the throat area as you can see. Look for masses, foreign objects, swelling, or deformities that may cause airway obstruction. If possible, clear airway obstructions using a —finger sweep technique with 2 fingers to remove any large objects or blood clots or vomit.

Assess Breathing by Watching the Dog Breathe for Clues to the Location of Lung or Airway Trauma or Problems

Deep, labored breathing suggests lung trauma or lung problems, such as lung bruising. Shallow, rapid breathing suggests air, blood, or some other fluid in space around the lungs inside the chest cavity (air, blood, or fluid). If the dog is not breathing, he is in respiratory arrest; this is an emergency condition and you should seek immediate assistance from the vet. Irregular breathing may indicate brain injury. Look at the mucous membranes (gums). Blue, pale or white, yellow, or bright red gums are abnormal. Feel the chest rise and fall with each breath. If breathing is not effective, immediately contact veterinary personnel and request further guidance. Be prepared to provide basic cardiopulmonary life support if the dog is not breathing or not breathing well.

Assess Circulation by Determining the Dog's Pulse Rate and Character IAW Ch 1, Para 1.1.1

A very slow pulse rate or a very rapid pulse rate suggests major trauma or medical problem. Absence of pulse rate indicates cardiac arrest. Be prepared to provide basic cardiopulmonary life support if the dog's pulse rate is less than 60 beats per minute, there is no pulse detected or if the pulse is weak or irregular. Determine the dog's Capillary Refill Time (CRT). Prolonged CRT (> 2 seconds) suggests poor blood flow to tissues. Be prepared to provide intravenous fluid therapy for shock or basic cardiopulmonary life support if the CRT is prolonged.

- If you determine there is a problem with the heart or circulation, immediately contact the Kennel Master or veterinary personnel and request further guidance.
- Perform a brief, rapid examination of the rest of the dog.

- Quickly assess the dog's body for wounds, fractures, and evidence of trauma elsewhere (painful areas, swelling, bruising, skin abrasions). Pay particular attention to the spinal column, abdominal region, flank, and limbs for signs of trauma.
- If necessary, evacuate the MWD to the nearest veterinary facility.
- Make a written record of the treatment. Include the date, time and actions taken.
- Provide First Aid for a Bleeding Wound. Uncontrolled bleeding can be fatal or cause shock and lead to further complications. Serious bleeding, especially arterial bleeding, must be controlled immediately.
- Venous bleeding (bleeding from injured veins) is generally less likely to cause shock or death unless major veins are injured. Venous bleeding is more likely in skin wounds, lower leg, paw wounds, face and neck wounds. Venous bleeding is usually dark in color and usually oozes from the injury site. First aid for most venous bleeding involves applying immediate direct pressure and a pressure bandage.
- Arterial bleeding (bleeding from injured arteries) is much more likely to cause shock and death, and must be managed more aggressively than venous bleeding. Arterial bleeding is more likely in groin and armpit wounds, deep neck, leg and paw wounds. Arterial bleeding is usually bright red in color and usually spurts or flows rapidly from the injury site. First aid for arterial bleeding requires immediate direct pressure followed by application of a hemostatic clotting agent and application of a pressure bandage.

PROVIDE FIRST AID FOR A BLEEDING WOUND

Providing First Aid for MILD Bleeding

- Immediately apply pressure with your hand and continue to hold firm pressure while you or another person gathers your first aid supplies.
- Apply 5–10 sterile 4 X 4 gauze sponges to the bleeding wound. If sterile 4 X 4 gauze sponges are not available, use clean pieces of cloth, a field dressing, or similar material. The key is to control bleeding; dirty wounds and infections can be dealt with later.
- Continue to apply firm pressure to the wound with the bandage between the wound and your fingers.
- Using direct pressure to stop bleeding takes time. Do NOT lift the bandage or remove the bandage to look at the wound because this will break up the clot that is forming and bleeding will begin again.
- If the bleeding leaks through the gauze or cloth you applied, APPLY more gauze or cloth; do NOT remove the original gauze or cloth.
- Without removing the gauze sponges, apply a bandage to provide direct pressure and control bleeding. This allows you to do other things, such as coordinating a Medical Evacuations (MEDEVAC).
- Wrap the bleeding wound with 1–4 rolls of roll gauze. Usually, lower leg wounds require 1–2 rolls, and higher limb wounds and body wounds require 4 rolls. The roll gauze should be applied tightly to provide pressure to the bleeding wound. Wrap the area with 1 – 3 rolls of elastic conforming bandage.
- If your first aid kit is not available, use whatever it is you have to apply a protective bandage with pressure over the bleeding site. Field dressings cut or torn T- shirt or cloth material can be used. Either use medical adhesive tape to secure the bandage, strips of cloth or the field dressing tapes to tie the bandage in place.

Providing First Aid for MODERATE or SEVERE Bleeding
- Immediately apply pressure with your hand and continue to hold firm pressure while you or another person gathers your first aid supplies.
- Apply 1 full packet of the hemostatic clotting agent from the first aid kit directly into the wound.
- Immediately cover the wound with 10–15 sterile 4 X 4 gauze sponges as for mild bleeding. Continue to apply firm pressure to the wound with the bandage between the wound and your fingers.
- Using direct pressure to stop bleeding takes time. Do NOT lift the bandage or remove the bandage to look at the wound because this will break up the clot that is forming and bleeding will begin again.
- If the bleeding leaks through the gauze or cloth you applied, APPLY more gauze or cloth; do NOT remove the original gauze or cloth.
- Without removing the gauze sponges, apply a bandage as described for mild bleeding to provide direct pressure and control bleeding.
- Observe for signs of pain and discomfort. If the bandage is too tight, it may interfere with circulation to the point of requiring an amputation.

Inform the Kennel Master of the situation and immediately contact the closest veterinary staff and request further instructions.

Make a written record of the treatment. Include the date, time and actions taken.

PROVIDE FIRST AID FOR UPPER AIRWAY OBSTRUCTION

Recognizing signs of an upper airway obstruction is imperative. Typically, a dog playing with or chewing on an object, followed immediately by pawing at his face or throat, acting frantic, trying to cough and choke, with sudden onset of difficulty breathing with abnormal — snoring breathing sounds is a good indication the MWDs airway is blocked.

Upper Airway Obstruction is a Life-Threatening Situation
You must perform first aid as quickly as possible. **The following steps should be completed in less than 30 seconds.** The dog may or may not have lost consciousness.
1. Determine that the dog has an upper airway obstruction by checking the airway.
2. Gently tilt the head slightly back and extend the neck.
3. Look in the mouth and identify anything that is blocking the airway, such as vomit, a ball, a stick, clotted blood, bone fragments, or other object.
4. Use a gauze sponge to grasp the dog's tongue and pull it forward to improve visualizing the mouth.
5. If you are able to visualize a foreign object use the — 2 finger sweep technique to remove fixed objects. Run your index and middle fingers into the dog's mouth along the cheek and across the back of the throat, removing any foreign objects that are visualized or felt. If unable to dislodge the foreign object, immediately transport to the nearest veterinary treatment facility as the airway may have become blocked due to swelling.
6. You may also use the modified Heimlich maneuver to remove mobile foreign objects such as a tennis ball or Kong.

- Grasp the dog around the waist so that the rear is nearest to you, similar to a bear hug.
- Place a fist just behind the ribs.
- Compress the abdomen several times (5 times) with quick thrusts.

- Check the mouth to see if the foreign object is dislodged.
- Repeat the modified Heimlich maneuver 1-2 times if initial efforts are unsuccessful.
- If unable to dislodge the foreign object, immediately transport to the nearest veterinary treatment facility as the airway may have become blocked due to swelling.

7. If the dog has lost consciousness and you were able to successfully remove the foreign object, the dog may regain consciousness on his own or Cardio Pulmonary Resuscitation (CPR) may need to be performed. Immediately perform a primary survey and take appropriate action.

Report the event by immediately contacting supporting veterinary personnel for further instructions and notify the Kennel Master.

Even if you are successful in removing a foreign object, veterinary examination is required. Internal injury could have occurred that may not be evident.

Make a written record of the treatment. Include the date, time and actions taken.

PERFORM CARDIAC ARREST LIFE SUPPORT

Assess whether the dog is in cardiopulmonary arrest, cardiac arrest, or respiratory arrest **within 30 seconds**. Use the mnemonic, **"CAB"** to focus your attention on the Circulation, Airway, and Breathing as you assess the MWD.

- Cardiac arrest is determined when the heart has stopped beating, no pulse can be found but the dog is breathing voluntarily.
- Respiratory arrest is determined when the dog is not breathing voluntarily, but the heart is beating and a pulse is present.
- Cardiopulmonary arrest is determined when the heart has stopped beating, no pulse can be found and the dog is not breathing.
- Try verbally and physically to get the dog to respond. If the dog responds, it does not need Basic Cardiac Life Support (BCLS).
- If the dog is unresponsive, immediately call for help if others are nearby. Have someone request support from veterinary personnel. Although BCLS requires at least two people to be most successful, continue with the following steps even if you are alone.

Check for Blood Circulation
- **Look** at the dog's gums to assess the color of the mucous membranes and CRT.
- **Listen** to the chest for a heartbeat.
- **Feel** for a pulse at the femoral artery.

Clear the Airway
1. Gently tilt the head slightly back and extend the neck.
2. Look in the mouth and remove anything that is blocking the airway, such as vomit, a ball, a stick, clotted blood, bone fragments, or other objects.

Check for Breathing
1. **Look** for the rise and fall of the chest.
2. **Listen** to the dog's mouth and nose for signs of breathing.
3. **Feel** breath on your skin by placing your face or hand near the dog's mouth and nose.

Take Action Based on Your Findings

- If the dog is not breathing, but has a pulse or heart rate, the dog is in respiratory arrest. Begin rescue breathing immediately.
- If the dog has no pulse or heart rate, the dog is in cardiac arrest. If the dog is not breathing voluntarily and has no heartbeat or pulse, the dog is in cardiopulmonary arrest. Begin BCLS immediately.
- Be very careful not to get bitten! Even if the dog would not normally bite you, the dog may not have normal control of his actions. If your dog is conscious, it is NOT in cardiopulmonary arrest and does NOT need BCLS.
- Perform Assisted BCLS **within 2 minutes** of determining the dog has no pulse or heartbeat.

Determine with your assistant who will give chest compressions and who will give — mouth-to-snout breathing. BCLS on a large dog is physically demanding work. Be prepared (by practicing) to rotate positions with other personnel with minimal interruption of chest compressions and rescue breathing.

Position the Dog
1. Kneel next to the dog.
2. Place the dog on its side (lateral recumbency) with his spine against your body.
3. Bend the dog's front leg up so the elbow moves about 1/3 of the way up the chest; release the elbow and make a note of the area, as this is the spot to place your hands to perform chest compressions.

Position Your Hands
Position your hands by placing one hand on top of the other with all fingers closed together. Place your hands on the chest wall at the position you identified above.

Perform Chest Compressions
1. With partially locked elbows, bend at the waist and apply a firm, downward thrusting motion.
2. Compress the chest wall approximately 6 inches at a sustained rate of 100 compressions per minute, which is about 1 compression every half-second. Proper chest compressions are the most important part of BCLS. Do not stop chest compressions to direct or assist in other actions unless safety is an issue.
3. Clear the airway to remove upper airway obstructions and open the airway for better rescue breathing by removing the dog's collar, pull the tongue out in downward motion using gauze to hold onto it. Visually inspect the inside of the dog's mouth for obstructions and feel along the outside of dog's throat for obstructions. Using either the 2-finger sweep technique or the modified Heimlich maneuver, remove obstructions if possible.
4. Perform rescue breathing using the mouth-to-snout method within 30 seconds of clearing the airway.
5. Seal the dog's mouth and lips by placing your hands around the lips, gently holding the muzzle closed.
6. Place your mouth over the dog's nose and forcefully exhale into the nose.
7. Give 2 quick breaths first, then check to see if the dog is breathing without assistance.
8. If the dog does not breathe voluntarily, continue breathing for the dog at a rate of 20 breaths per minute (one breath every 3 seconds).
9. Check the dog's response after 4 minutes of BCLS, and every 4 minutes thereafter.
10. Check for voluntary breathing and for a heartbeat or pulse.
11. If there is no voluntary breathing or a heartbeat or pulse, continue BCLS.
12. If there is a heartbeat or pulse, but no voluntary breathing, stop chest compressions but continue rescue breathing. Every time BCLS is stopped, blood pressure drops and blood flow and ventilation stop. Frequent stopping results in poor survival rates. Stop only every 4 minutes and only long

enough to quickly check the patient's breathing, pulse, and heartbeat.

Perform UNASSISTED BCLS within 2 Minutes of Determining BCLS is Necessary
1. Kneel next to the dog, position the dog, and perform chest compressions exactly as you do for assisted BCLS.
2. Perform —mouth-to-snout breathing 2 times after every 15 chest compressions.
3. Maintain chest compressions and rescue breathing at a compression: breathing cycle of 15 compressions: 2 breaths.
4. Check the dog's response every 4 minutes as directed.
5. Continue BCLS as long as the dog does not have a pulse or heart rate or is not breathing on its own.

Discontinue BCLS under the Following Circumstances
1. The dog is successfully resuscitated (has a pulse and heartbeat and is breathing on its own).
2. The dog has not been resuscitated after at least 20 minutes of BCLS.
3. You are directed to stop BCLS by a more-senior handler, Kennel Master, or veterinary personnel.

Report your Actions and Initiate MEDEVAC
Immediately contact supporting veterinary personnel for further instructions, notify the kennel master, make a written record of the treatment. Include the date, time and actions taken.

PROVIDE FIRST AID TO MWD WITH AN ALLERGIC REACTION

Check with local resources to identify venomous snakes, arthropods, and insects in your area that could cause potential harm to your dog. Reliable resources would be the Kennel Master, local community health center's Preventive Medicine Department and supporting veterinary personnel.

It is best to know the venomous snakes and insects by sight or characteristic markings. After getting information about the snakes and insects, try to commit to memory their habits and behavior.

Recognize the signs of an allergic reaction to envenomation by an insect, arthropod, or snake. Mild signs may include any of the following:

- Apparent pain at the wound site. The dog may lick or bite the area; if the wound is to a paw or leg, he may hold it up and not put any weight on it.
- Fang marks, bite marks, or puncture wounds.
- Drops of blood or oozing blood at the wound site.
- Swelling.
- Excessive salivation (drooling).

Severe signs may include any of the following:

- Weakness, lethargy, disorientation.
- Muscle tremors.
- Slow, labored breathing.
- Vomiting.
- Diarrhea.
- Tissue necrosis (death) with open, draining wounds at bite site.
- Collapse or unconsciousness.
- Shock, including pale or blue mucous membranes, weak or absent arterial pulse, prolonged CRT,

collapse, increased heart rate.
- Death.

Not all snake and insect bites or stings will cause an allergic reaction. Your dog may not suffer an allergic reaction to a bite or sting, but still may require immediate treatment for envenomation by veterinary staff. The severity of symptoms your dog displays are based on the amount and type of venom injected through the bite or sting, the location of the bite or sting, and the size of the dog.

Typically, an allergic reaction is immediate, occurring within 5 minutes of envenomation. If there are no visible signs of a reaction after an hour, then it is unlikely that an allergic response to envenomation occurred.

You may or may not witness your dog being bitten or stung. However, if you see your dog bitten by an insect, arthropod or snake, take immediate action and provide first aid.

Provide First Aid for an Allergic Reaction to Insect, Arthropod, or Snake Envenomation

If the signs have progressed so much that the dog has ceased breathing, his heart has stopped beating, or shock is present, take immediate action to treat for these problems.

Administer drugs to reduce the allergic reaction. Give one (1) intramuscular dose of diphenhydramine (50 mg/mL), using the following dose chart.

Table 1. Diphenhydramine Dosage Chart

Body Weight (in pounds)	Volume of DIPHENHYDRAMINE to give INTRAMUSCULARLY (in milliliters)
30 to 35	0.7
36 to 40	0.7
41 to 45	0.9
46 to 50	1.0
51 to 55	1.1
56 to 60	1.2
61 to 65	1.3
66 to 70	1.4
71 to 75	1.5
76 to 80	1.6
81 to 85	1.7
86 to 90	1.8
91 to 95	1.9
96 to 100	2.0
101 to 105	2.1
106 to 110	2.2
111 to 115	2.3
116 to 120	2.4

Give one (1) intramuscular dose of dexamethasone sodium phosphate (4 mg/mL), using the following dose chart.

Table 2. Dexamethasone Sodium Phosphate Dosage Chart

Body Weight (in pounds)	Volume of DIPHENHYDRAMINE to give INTRAMUSCULARLY (in milliliters)
30 to 35	1.8
36 to 40	1.9
41 to 45	2.4
46 to 50	2.7
51 to 55	3.0
56 to 60	3.3
61 to 65	3.6
66 to 70	3.9
71 to 75	4.1
76 to 80	4.4
81 to 85	4.7
86 to 90	5.0
91 to 95	5.3
96 to 100	5.6
101 to 105	5.9
106 to 110	6.1
111 to 115	6.4
116 to 120	6.7

Keep the dog calm and quiet; cease operations with the dog. If possible, keep the affected area lower than the heart. Inform the Kennel Master of the situation, and contact supporting veterinary staff to request further instructions.

If the dog's condition deteriorates, initiate a MEDEVAC. If an open wound is present or develops, protect the wound with a bandage.

Do NOT do Any of the Following, as These Make the Allergic Reaction Worse:
1. Apply ice to the bite or sting area.
2. Exercise or have the dog move around. Movement causes the venom to spread more quickly.
3. Apply a tourniquet if the bite or sting was to an extremity.
4. Cut the area to squeeze or suction out the poison. Note: Rattlesnake Antivenin is the only definitive treatment for snakebite; this is only available from your supporting veterinary personnel. Specific treatments are going to vary with the type of snake, spider or insect involved.
5. For true anaphylactic reactions (collapse, increased heart rate, weak or absent pulses), initiate treatment for shock.
6. Make a written record of the treatment. Include the date, time and actions taken.

PROVIDE FIRST AID FOR DEHYDRATION

1. Dehydration is the excessive loss of fluids and electrolytes from the body through illness or physical exertion. Electrolytes (sodium, chloride, potassium) are salts needed by cells to control movement of water in the body and to control many body functions. Understand the definition of dehydration and common causes in MWDs.
2. Causes of dehydration include inadequate water intake or loss of water and electrolytes due to illness

(fever, diarrhea and vomiting) and environment (heat, humidity and cold).
3. Determine that the dog is dehydrated by observing signs of dehydration. The early signs of dehydration are very hard to recognize. You must know your MWD well in order to identify them. Signs of early dehydration:
   a. Reduced physical activity.
   b. Abnormal mental activity or level of consciousness (depressed, lethargic).
   c. Tacky gums (mucous membranes) and a dry nose.

Signs of Moderate Dehydration:
- Dry and tacky mucous membranes (nose, mouth, gums).
- Loss of skin elasticity/increased skin elasticity—the skin doesn't snap right back to place as it normally does.
- Slightly sunken eyes.
- Slightly increased CRT.

Signs of Severe Dehydration:
- Pale mucous membranes
- Prolonged CRT.
- Weight loss (5% or more).
- Sunken eyes.
- Weak arterial pulse.

Provide First Aid for Dehydration
1. If your dog is showing early signs of dehydration, offer fresh water. Unfortunately, if your dog is already dehydrated, sick, injured or cold, he may not want to drink.
2. If the dog does show an interest in drinking water, make sure he doesn't drink more than a few sips every few minutes. Overdrinking, or drinking quickly could lead to vomiting, dehydrating the dog further.
3. If the dog is vomiting, has diarrhea, is showing signs of heat injury or signs of moderate to severe dehydration, contact veterinary personnel immediately for possible emergency treatment.
4. If the environment is hot, humid, or sunny, move the dog to shade or indoors if air conditioning is available and allow the dog to rest.
5. If the dog is showing signs of moderate dehydration, administer 1 Liter of Lactated Ringers Solution (LRS) fluids (beneath the skin) in 4 separate locations.
6. If the dog is showing signs of severe dehydration, administer 1 Liter of LRS fluids over a two-hour period intravenously.
7. For all dogs with dehydration, monitor for shock and provide appropriate first aid if signs of shock develop.
8. Evacuate the MWD to the nearest veterinary facility if it is showing signs of severe dehydration or shock.
9. Make a written record of the treatment. Include the date, time and actions taken.

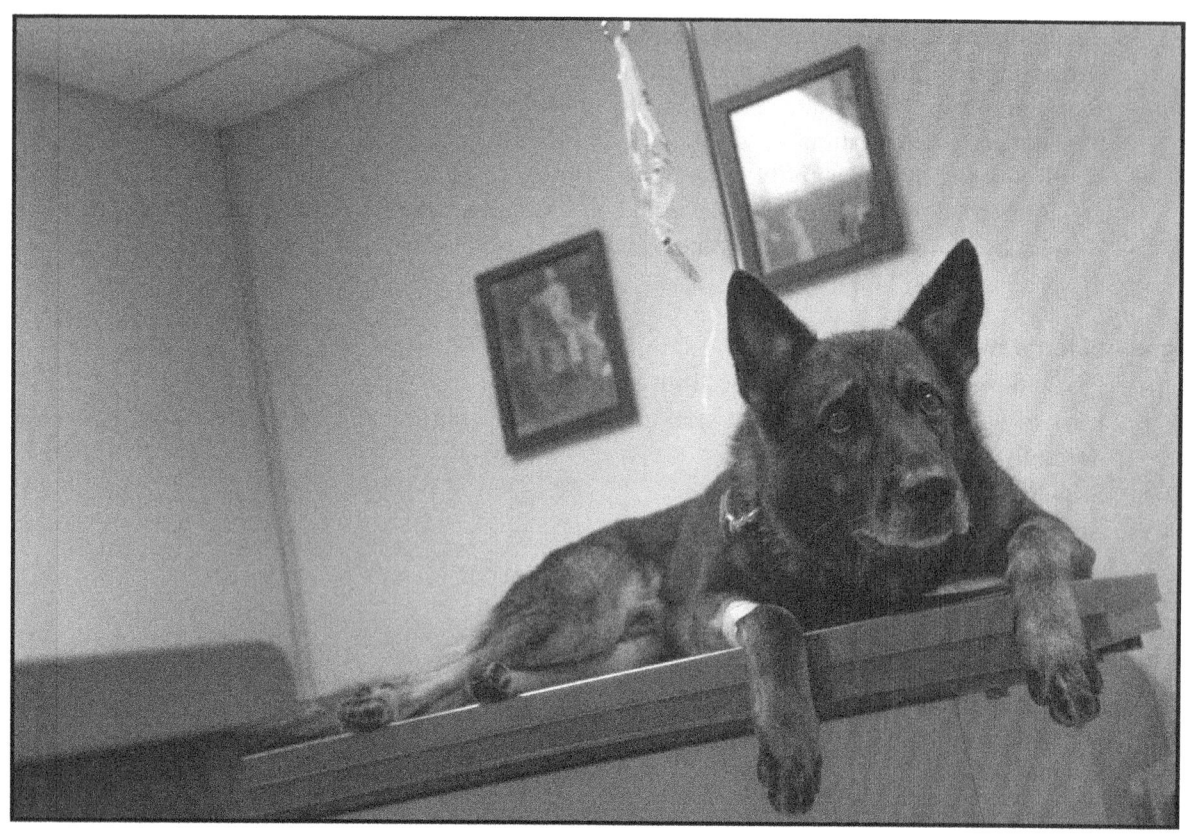

Military working dog Mex, assigned to the 822nd Base Defense Squadron, receives a vitals test during a routine checkup July 16, 2015, at Moody Air Force Base, GA. Mex's checkup ensured he was healthy and ready to perform the job of supporting base security. (U.S. Air Force photo/Airman 1st Class Dillian Bamman)

ADMINISTER SUBCUTANEOUS FLUIDS

Administering subcutaneous fluids is a method to provide water and electrolytes for dehydrated MWDs. Understand reasons for use of subcutaneous fluids.

Subcutaneous fluid administration is acceptable only for MWDs with mild dehydration due to inadequate water intake or excessive loss of body water and electrolytes (illness or environmental factors).

If moderate or severe dehydration is present, or if shock is present, use other methods for fluid administration. Subcutaneous fluids are not appropriate for dogs exhibiting signs of severe dehydration or shock.

Recognize Clinical Signs of Mild Dehydration or Historical Facts that Suggest Dehydration is Present
- Abnormal mental activity (depressed, lethargic).
- Decreased performance.
- Prolonged skin elasticity (prolonged skin —tenting).
- Prolonged CRT.
- Tacky mucous membranes (gums).

- Slightly sunken eyes.

Historical Facts that Suggest Dehydration is Present
- Three or more episodes of vomiting or watery diarrhea in the past 24 hours.
- Moderate or heavy work in hot and/or humid environment.
- Recent illness with decreased water intake.

Assemble Supplies and Prepare Equipment for Use
- One 1-Liter bag of sterile LRS.
- Fluid administration set.
- Four 18-gauge needles.
- 4-6 4X4 gauze sponges.
- Isopropyl alcohol.

Prepare Equipment
1. Remove the wrapper from the bag of LRS.
2. Remove the administration set from its packaging.
3. Close the flow regulator on the administration set. You must roll the flow regulator toward the end of the line to close it. This pinches the tubing closed so it won't leak.
4. Remove the cover from the injection port of the bag of LRS.
5. Remove the cap from the administration set spike and insert the spike into the injection port of the fluid bag. Maintain sterility at all times and avoid contaminating uncapped surfaces. Don't allow any uncapped surfaces to come in contact with anything.
6. Hang the bag or have someone hold the bag two to three feet above the dog. Put the bag under your armpit if there are no other options.
7. Squeeze the sides of the administration set chamber several times to force fluid into the chamber. Fill the chamber halfway or to the arrow mark or line on the side.
8. Remove one 18-gauge needle from its outer packaging. Do not touch the exposed end of the needle.
9. Remove the cap from the drip set line and attach the needle to the end. Twist the needle and make sure it's seated snugly on the line. Avoid contaminating either the needle or the line.
10. Move the flow regulator back to the open position to allow fluid to flow freely out the end of the line. Let fluid flow out until all air bubbles are gone from the line. Once the air bubbles are gone, stop the flow of fluid by rolling the regulator back down. Recap the exposed end.
11. Visually divide the bag of fluids into four equal parts, of about 250 mL each. You will be administering approximately one quarter of the bag (250 mL) in each subcutaneous location. Use the markings on the fluid bag to determine how much fluid you will administer to each site.

Administer Subcutaneous Fluids
Select an area of skin. You will be injecting fluids into the skin in four separate places, so you will need to select four areas.

Choose parts of the body where there is loose skin such as over the shoulder blades (above the front legs) and over the rib cage on each side.

1. Soak a 4X4 gauze sponge with isopropyl alcohol and vigorously scrub the skin over the injection site to remove dirt and skin oils.
2. Pinch up a fold of skin forming a "tent" or inverted V.
3. Uncap the needle from the fluid administration set and insert the needle quickly and firmly into the

center and towards the bottom of the tent at a horizontal angle. The needle should go in easily and should not hit any obstructions.
4. The needle should go in about 1/2" to 3/4" and should not go through the other side of the tent.
5. Release the skin while still holding onto the needle.
6. Roll the flow regulator to the open position, allowing fluid to flow through the tube and into the dog. It is normal to see large bumps appear in the areas when you are administering fluids. These are fluid pockets. These bumps will last for several hours as the fluid is slowly absorbed.
7. Administer one quarter (250 mL) of the bag of fluids at the first site.
8. Mark the LRS bag.
   - Tear a piece of tape approximately 12" long.
   - Place the tape on the bag vertically along one side next to the volume marks printed on the bag by the manufacturer.
   - Make marks on the tape to help you control how fast you give the fluid.
   - At the prescribed rate of administration (1 liter per hour for 2 hours), you will give 250 mL of fluid every 15 minutes.
   - Make marks on the tape at the 250 mL, 500 mL, 750 mL, and 1000 mL lines on the bag. These marks correspond to 15 minutes, 30 minutes, 45 minutes, and 60 minutes of time.
   - You will use the flow control dial to give the correct amount of fluid over time.
   - Mark a start line on the tape at the point where the fluid level and the tape meet. This is the start line. It should be at about the 1000 mL mark.
9. Stop the flow with the flow regulator when the appropriate amount of fluid is given.
10. Carefully remove the needle from the skin and apply pressure to site for a few seconds to prevent bleeding or fluid leakage.
11. Carefully recap the needle.
12. Change the needle and replace the used needle with a sterile needle.

Repeat steps three additional times at three separate sites, administering approximately one quarter (250 mL) of the bag at each site.

Contact supporting veterinary personnel for further instructions. Make a written record of the treatment. Include the date, time and actions taken.

PROVIDE FIRST AID FOR SHOCK

Understand Shock and Common Causes of Shock in MWDs

Shock is the body's response to a traumatic injury or severe illness in which blood flow to vital organs like the brain, heart, lungs, liver, and kidneys is not adequate for survival because of lack of oxygen delivery to these organs.

- Shock is progressive, meaning that if not treated quickly, shock may worsen. Even with effective treatment, shock can ultimately cause death.
- Shock is a life-threatening situation. Emergency first aid must be provided immediately to improve chances of survival.

In most cases of shock, fluid therapy is one of the most important treatment measures aimed at improving blood flow.

Common Causes of Shock in MWDs
- Trauma with blood loss (motor vehicle accident, gunshot injury, shrapnel wound, blast injury).
- Severe dehydration (vomiting, diarrhea).
- Heat injury.
- Allergic reactions to snake bites and insect stings.
- Poisoning.

1. Shock is always caused by something else. It is important to identify, if possible, the primary cause, because first aid for the primary cause is just as important as first aid for shock. You may have to provide first aid for shock at the same time you are providing first aid for the primary cause.
2. Perform a Primary Survey of the MWD to identify a primary cause for the shock.
3. Treat any other severe injuries such as respiratory arrest, cardiopulmonary arrest, arterial bleeding, heat stroke, allergic reaction to snake bite or insect sting, poisoning, severe dehydration or Gastric Dilatation-Volvulus Syndrome (GDV or bloat) while preparing to treat the shock.

Recognize Signs of Shock
- Panting or labored breathing.
- Bright red mucous membranes (gums) OR pale, gray, or blue mucous membranes.
- Increased heart rate.
- Weak or absent arterial pulse.
- Prolonged CRT >2 seconds.
- Low body temperature.
- Cold paws.
- Weakness, collapse.
- Depressed, acting "out of it", lethargic, coma.

Provide First Aid to Treat Shock
1. Place an 18-gauge intravenous catheter in a leg vein and administer intravenous fluids
2. Give 1 liter of Lactated Ringer's Solution each hour for 2 hours. Do not give more than 1 liter in an hour or more than 2 liters total.
3. If oxygen is available, use a face mask or tubing and blow oxygen into the dog's nose or mouth at a flow rate of 5-10 liters per minute.
4. If you must move the dog, do so very gently and try to keep the dog on a flat surface. The dog may have a spinal cord injury that is not obvious.
5. Cover the dog with something to keep it warm (e.g., blanket, towel, clothing, etc.).
6. Try to keep the dog calm by speaking calmly and reassuringly to it.

Monitor the Dog and Your Treatment
1. Continue to monitor vital signs and note whether the dog is responding to treatment.
2. Monitor the Intravenous Fluid (IV) catheter insertion site on the leg. If swelling is noted around the catheter or if the catheter is not working or becomes blocked, place a second intravenous catheter in another leg vein and use the new catheter.
3. Monitor the intravenous fluid therapy equipment. Look for:

- Disconnects anywhere in the set-up, kinks or blocks in the tubing and monitor fluid administration rate.
- Use the marks you created on the tape/bag and a timepiece to ensure the administration rate is correct. Adjust the drip rate by rolling the regulator up or down if the fluids are flowing too fast or too slow.

Continue to provide first aid for any medical problems found on the Primary Survey.
Make a written record of the treatment. Include the date, time and actions taken.

PROVIDE FIRST AID FOR HEAT INJURY

Heat Injuries Result when the Body's Natural Cooling Mechanisms Fail in Response to Internal Overheating

Humans regulate body temperature mostly by sweating. Since dogs do not sweat, they regulate their body temperature by panting. If a dog is unable to cool enough, its internal temperature will rise, and the dog may progress through different stages of heat injury.

Normal body temperature for a dog is 100.50 F to 102.50 F. As the dog's temperature rises to 1050 or 1060 F, the dog develops heat stress. If cooling measures are not taken immediately, the dog's body temperature will continue to rise, progressing to heat exhaustion, usually with a temperature of 1060 to 1080 F. Once the dog's body temperature rises over 1080 F, heat stroke is likely. All phases of heat injury are life-threatening situations.

The progression of heat injuries can be quite rapid, sometimes only taking a few minutes. Occasionally, there is little or no warning and the progression is so rapid the dog might already be suffering heat stroke when the situation is discovered.

Short term effects on a dog suffering from a heat injury may include shock, organ damage, or death. Long term effects may include brain damage and the increased possibility of recurrence of a heat injury.

Immediate first aid is required for any MWD with suspected heat injury.

Causes of Heat Injury Are Divided into Environmental Causes and Exertional Causes

Environmental causes are due to exposure to high environmental temperature and humidity or a combination of both, confinement to a small, hot space such as a crate, kennel run, or vehicle, poor acclimation to heat and humidity or inadequate water intake.

Exertional causes are due to increased body temperature that develops with strenuous exercise or work (worsened by hot, humid, or hot and humid environments), existing or undiagnosed disease or illness, medications or drugs, age and previous heat injury.

The combination of exposure to high environmental temperatures and exertion can markedly increase the risk of heat injury.

Heat Injury Prevention

MWDs rely on their handlers to take care of them and make decisions for them, especially in extreme environments. Take care of, monitor, and know your dog!

Acclimation

Follow the human rules of acclimation. Increase workload and exposure to the environment gradually over a 14-day period. Use an acclimation period if the dog is recovering from an illness, as well.

Hydration
1. Make sure your dog is properly hydrated by allowing for frequent water breaks.
2. Ensure your dog always has access to water whether in his kennel, exercising, or resting.
3. Initially, dehydration is undetectable. By the time you are able to detect your dog is dehydrated, it is already too late.
4. Dehydration makes your dog more susceptible to heat injury and causes decreased performance.
5. Allow your dog to drink when you drink—typically a small amount every 10-15 minutes in an extreme or high activity environment.
6. Use fresh water. Do not give your dog "Cool Blue", Gatorade®, Pedialyte® or similar fluids.
7. Fitness. Dogs need a physical training program to remain in shape. Out of shape dogs are more prone to heat injuries.
8. Do NOT confine a MWD in a small, poorly-ventilated, hot area at any time.
9. Use the human heat category work/rest cycles and Wet Bulb Globe Temperature (WBGT) guide. The local supporting Preventive Medicine team at your installation will keep this information updated and available. Additionally, if the dog has had a prior heat injury, consider ceasing exercise when the temperature reaches 90° F. For all other dogs, consider ceasing exercise when the temperature reaches 95° F.
10. Do not use muzzles unless required for safety reasons. Loosen muzzles when possible to allow the dog to pant easier. A dog's cooling mechanism is his ability to pant.

Recognize Signs of Heat Injury

Mild heat injury (—heat stress) can be recognized by heavy, controlled panting, high rectal temperature, usually 105° to 106° F, fast, strong pulse and slightly decreased performance. NOTE: Controlled panting means the dog can stop panting when an alcohol-soaked gauze is put in front of his nose or he becomes interested in something. Uncontrolled panting means the dog cannot stop panting even when offered a treat or exposed to alcohol-soaked gauze.

Moderate heat injury (—heat exhaustion) can be recognized by very high rectal temperature, usually 106° to 108° F, uncontrolled panting, fast, strong OR weak pulse, failure to salivate, tacky or dry nose and mouth, unwillingness to work or exercise; acts tired, loss of appetite, becoming unresponsive to handler and commands, staggering, weakness, depressed, or acting "out of it" or bright red mucous membranes (gums).

Severe heat injury (—heat stroke) can be recognized by extremely high rectal temperature, usually over 108° F, body is hot to the touch, vomiting, pale mucous membranes (gums), abnormal mental activity or level of consciousness—completely "out of it", seizures, or coma, diarrhea, sometimes with blood (bright red blood or dark, tarry feces), shock or death.

Provide First Aid for Heat Injury
1. First aid for mild heat injury (—heat stress) is to cease working the dog and to cool the dog externally.
2. Immediately cool the dog using one or more of the following methods.
3. Spray or pour cool water on the dog, or use soaked wet towels. Do NOT use ice or ice water, because this causes a serious rapid decrease in body temperature and results in hypothermia (dangerously LOW body temperature).
4. Move the dog to a shaded area if outdoors or into a cool building.
5. Circulate cool air near the dog using fans.
6. Loosen the muzzle and collar. Remove these if possible and safe.
7. Monitor and treat for shock, if shock develops.

8. Monitor vital signs every 5 minutes.
9. Discontinue cooling efforts when the rectal temperature reaches 1030 F.

First Aid for Moderate and Severe Heat Injury (—Heat Exhaustion and —Heat Stroke) is to Cease Working the Dog

1. Cool the dog as for mild heat injury.
2. Initiate intravenous fluid therapy.
3. Give 1 liter of LRS intravenously every hour for 2 hours. Do not give more than 1 liter of fluids every hour or more than 2 liters of fluid total.
4. Monitor the MWD and fluid therapy as directed.
5. Monitor and treat for shock, if shock develops. Monitor vital signs every 5 minutes.
6. Discontinue cooling efforts when the rectal temperature reaches 1030 F.

Notify the Kennel Master of the situation and contact supporting veterinary personnel.

ADMINISTER INTRAVENOUS FLUIDS

Prepare and Assemble Supplies for an Intravenous Infusion
Assemble Supplies
- One roll of 1" medical adhesive tape.
- Two 1-liter bags of LRS.
- Fluid administration set.
- 18-gauge X 1 ½ inch intravenous catheter.
- Injection port adapter.
- One roll of self-adhesive conforming tape.

Prepare Equipment
1. Maintain sterility at all times, especially avoiding contamination of uncapped surfaces.
2. Open the package of the intravenous catheter. Inspect the catheter to ensure serviceability (no burs, sterile, etc.). Flush with sterile LRS. Replace the catheter cap.
3. Flush catheter injection port with sterile LRS.
4. Tear three 12" strips of medical adhesive tape. Fold about ¼ of the end of each on itself to create a tab.
5. Open a package of self-adhesive conforming tape.
6. Remove the wrapper from the bag of LRS.
7. Remove the fluid administration drip set from its packaging.
8. Close the flow regulator on the tubing attached to the drip set. You must roll the flow regulator toward the end of the line to close it. This pinches the tubing closed so it won't leak.
9. Remove the cover from the injection port of the bag of LRS.
10. Remove the cap from the administration set spike and insert the spike into the injection port of the fluid bag.
11. Hang the bag or have someone hold the bag 2-3 feet above the dog. Hold the bag under your armpit if there are no other options.
12. Fill the drip chamber halfway by squeezing the sides of the chamber several times. If you over-fill the chamber, just flip the bag upside down and squeeze the drip chamber several times to force fluid back into the bag.

13. Remove the protective cover from the end of the administration set line. Set the cap aside and keep it uncontaminated.
14. Remove air bubbles from the line by moving the flow regulator back to the slightly open position. This will allow fluid to flow slowly out of the end of the line. Let fluid flow out until all air bubbles are gone. Once the air bubbles are gone, stop the flow of fluid by rolling the regulator back down. Recap the exposed end.
15. It is important to remove all air from the line so that air does not enter the dog's bloodstream. Air in the bloodstream can potentially travel to the heart and cause cardiac arrest.
16. Do not allow too much of the fluid out while clearing the line. Allow just enough out to remove air bubbles.

Mark the LRS bag.

1. Tear a piece of tape approximately 12" long.
2. Place the tape on the bag vertically along one side next to the volume marks printed on the bag by the manufacturer.
3. Make marks on the tape to help you control how fast you give the fluid.
4. At the prescribed rate of administration (1 liter per hour for 2 hours), you will give 250 mL of fluid every 15 minutes.
5. Make marks on the tape at the 250 mL, 500 mL, 750 mL, and 1000 mL lines on the bag. These marks correspond to 15 minutes, 30 minutes, 45 minutes, and 60 minutes of time.
6. You will use the flow control dial to give the correct amount of fluid over time.
7. Mark a start line on the tape at the point where the fluid level and the tape meet. This is the start line. It should be at about the 1000 ml mark.

Place an Intravenous Catheter

Direct another dog handler to position and restrain the dog.

1. Have the dog restrained in a sitting position or in sternal recumbency (chest on the ground) that eliminates movement.
2. Muzzle the dog.
3. Have the handler restrain the dog's head by wrapping his arm, farthest from the dog, around the dog's neck and cradling the dog's head and neck in his elbow.
4. Have the handler wrap his fingers around the back of the dog's elbow and push the dog's front leg slightly forward to stabilize it.

Prepare the catheter site over one of the front leg veins, located on the front part of the leg about halfway between the elbow and the wrist.

1. Wet the area with 2-3 alcohol-soaked gauze sponges to remove gross dirt and smooth the hair. If alcohol is not available, use water.
2. Have the handler place the thumb over the vein and the heel of the hand under the dog's elbow and apply resistance in a forward direction. This will make it easier to see the vein as it swells with blood and prevents the dog from pulling the elbow backwards.

Remove the catheter cover and hold the catheter in your dominant hand.

With your other hand, stabilize the leg and vein by placing your thumb directly alongside the vein and wrap your remaining fingers underneath and around the leg. It will appear that the leg is "cradled" in your hand.

Puncture the vein.
1. Pierce the skin with the catheter needle bevel (the angled tip of the catheter) facing up, at a 10 to 30-degree angle to the skin.
2. Advance the catheter to pierce the vein.
3. Confirm that you are in the vein by looking for a flash of blood at the hub of the catheter needle.
4. Decrease the angle of the catheter needle until it is almost parallel to the skin surface.
5. Advance the catheter needle approximately ¼-inch into the vein using a gentle forward motion.
6. Position the catheter.
7. Stabilize and hold the catheter needle hub with one hand.
8. Without moving the needle, advance the catheter into the vein as far possible with the other hand, only touching the hub of the catheter with the fingers.

Direct the dog handler to release the pressure on the vein but continue to hold the elbow in place.

Remove the needle from the catheter by pulling it back and out while stabilizing the catheter to keep it in the vein.

- Blood will immediately flow out of the catheter if you have placed it correctly.
- Do not attempt to reinsert the needle into the catheter if blood is not flowing, as this could result in the catheter being sliced in half and the free end flowing into the heart. If the first attempt at catheterization is not successful, try placing a catheter in the other front leg.

Quickly attach the injection port adapter to the hub of the catheter to stop the flow of blood.

Secure the catheter to the leg with the tape.

1. Wrap the tape around the hub of the catheter then wrap the tape around the leg just below and under the cap, ensuring that the tape is not so tight as to restrict circulation.
2. Wrap a second piece of tape over the catheter injection port and around the leg.
3. Wrap a third piece of tape over the site where the catheter pierces the skin and around the leg to provide protection and additional security.
4. Flush the catheter.
5. Draw out 3 mL of sterile saline from the fluid bag using a 6 mL syringe and a sterile 22-gauge 1-inch needle.
6. Gently insert the syringe into the catheter injection port and inject the sterile saline in short, gentle spurts to flush the catheter.
7. The saline should flow smoothly and there should not be any swelling developing around the catheter under the skin.
8. If the saline does not inject easily or swelling is noted around the catheter, the catheter is not placed correctly and should be removed. A new catheter should be placed in the other front leg.
9. Roll self-adhesive conforming tape around the leg and catheter for further stability, ensuring that the catheter injection port is easily accessible.

Administer Intravenous Fluids
1. Administer fluids.

2. Remove the caps from both the line and catheter. Be careful not to contaminate either end!
3. Attach the line to the catheter. Make sure the fit is snug.
4. Slowly move the flow regulator back up to start the flow of fluids.
5. Note the time. Mark the start time, at the start line, on the tape marking the bag.
6. Observe the catheter insertion site for swelling. If there is swelling, the catheter is not correctly placed in the vein and may need to be replaced.
7. Set the drip rate at approximately 1-2 drops into the chamber per second. The drip rate is adjusted by rolling the flow regulator up or down.

Secure the Administration Set in Place
1. Place a piece of tape around the dog's leg and the tubing, securing the tubing close to the catheter and tubing connection site. Create a courtesy tab at the end of the tape by folding the last ½ inch of tape onto itself.
2. Form a loop with the IV tubing and place more tape around the dog's leg and loop of the tubing, securing the tubing to the dog's leg. Create a courtesy tab at the end of the tape.

Continue Monitoring
Monitor the catheter insertion site. Look for:
- Swelling.
- Blood.
- Movement of the catheter.

Monitor the equipment. Look for:
- Disconnects anywhere in the set up.
- Kinks or blocks in the tubing.

Monitor the Dog
1. Make sure the dog doesn't bite or chew at the administration site. If the dog is conscious, you may need to keep the muzzle on to prevent chewing.
2. Monitor the dog's response to the fluid therapy. Be prepared to relay the information to the veterinary staff.
3. Monitor the fluid administration rate.
4. Use the marks you created on the tape on the bag and a timepiece to ensure the administration rate is correct.
5. Adjust the drip rate by rolling the regulator up or down if the fluids are flowing too fast or too slow.
6. The goal of therapy is the controlled administration of 2000 mLs of LRS over a 2-hour period.
7. Ensure that the MWD received 500 mLs in the first ½ hour, 1000 mLs by 1 hour, 1500 mLs by 1 ½ hours, and 2000 mLs by 2 hours.
8. Periodically reassess the MWD's vital signs.
9. Advise the Kennel Master and veterinary staff of the event and request further instructions. MEDEVAC any MWD that required intravenous fluid therapy.
10. Make a written record of the treatment. Include the date, time and actions taken.

PROVIDE FIRST AID TO MWD WITH GASTRIC DILATION-VOLVULUS (BLOAT)

A MWD has severe abdominal distention, retching or non-productive vomiting, and signs of pain (rapid and shallow breathing, anxiety, grunting, and weakness). Veterinary personnel are not available. You must initiate first aid for gastric dilatation-volvulus (bloat) for gastric dilatation-volvulus in a MWD without causing further harm to the dog.

Recognize the 3 hallmark signs of Gastric Dilatation-Volvulus (GDV, "bloat").

Varying degrees of abdominal distention from stomach filling with air, food, and fluid. NOTE: Many medical problems cause abdominal distention. It can be difficult to tell the difference between these and GDV/Bloat. However, if abdominal distention is present in addition to these other signs, assume GDV/Bloat is present and initiate first aid.

Nonproductive retching, attempted vomiting without result, retching a small amount of saliva, "dry heaves," excessive salivating.

Signs of pain, if the dog is conscious:

- Grunting, especially when the stomach or abdomen is palpated.
- Anxiety, which is commonly noted as pacing, anxious stares, and inability to get comfortable when lying down.
- Panting.

Recognize signs associated with shock such as weakness or collapsing, pale, grey, or blue mucous membranes, prolonged capillary refill time (CRT), rapid heart rate, weak, rapid pulse, change in level of consciousness, from agitated to depressed to semi-conscious, to unconscious.

Treat Shock
1. Administer intravenous fluids.
2. Place a 20-gauge intravenous catheter in a leg vein.
3. Give 1 liter of LRS each hour for 2 hours. Do not give more than 1 liter in an hour or more than 2 liters total.

If you don't have the necessary materials to give intravenous fluids, move on to decompress the stomach.

If oxygen is available, use a face mask or tubing and blow oxygen into the dog's nose or mouth at a flow rate of 5 - 10 liters per minute.

Decompress the Stomach to Relieve Gas Pressure
Lay the dog with its left side down and locate the insertion point.

- Feel the last rib on the right side of the dog.
- Find the point that is 2 finger-widths behind the last rib, halfway between the spine and the bottom border of the abdomen on the right side.

Wipe the area generously with gauze sponges soaked in alcohol.

Forcefully insert an 18-gauge intravenous catheter through the skin, abdominal wall, and stomach wall until you hit the hub at the end of the catheter.

- Leave the needle in the catheter.
- Ensure the abdominal wall and distended stomach is penetrated.
- The procedure is successful if gas or air comes through the trocar from the stomach. If no air or gas escapes, attempt the procedure one more time. If still unsuccessful, immediately transport the MWD

to veterinary care and **do not** attempt the procedure a third time.

Attach a 3-way stopcock and 60-cc syringe to the catheter and gently aspirate air from the stomach using the syringe until you can no longer remove any air.

Remove the catheter once no further air can be removed, because leaving it inserted may cause trauma to internal organs.

Keep the catheter clean and repeat trocarization if abdominal distension recurs during evacuation.

Monitor the Dog and your Treatment
Continue to monitor vital signs and note whether the dog is responding to treatment.

Continue to monitor the dog's abdominal area for further distention. Repeat stomach trocarization if significant abdominal distension develops.

Monitor the IV Catheter Insertion Site on the Leg
Look for:

- Swelling.
- Bleeding.
- Movement of the catheter. Once inserted, the catheter should not move.

Monitor the Intravenous Fluid Therapy Equipment
Look for:

- Disconnects anywhere in the set up.
- Kinks or blocks in the tubing.

Monitor Fluid Administration Rate
- Use the marks on the bag and a timepiece to ensure the administration rate is correct.
- Adjust the drip rate by rolling the regulator up or down if the fluids are flowing too fast or too slow.

Make a written record of the treatment. Include the date, time and actions taken.

PROVIDE FIRST AID TO MWD WITH AN OPEN CHEST WOUND

Open chest wounds can be caused by shrapnel, bullets, foreign objects (sticks, metal rods or pieces, etc.) or other objects that penetrate the chest wall. When an open chest wound is present, the lungs collapse, causing severe breathing problems and possibly death.

Recognize the Signs of an Open Chest Wound
- May be obvious or concealed by hair or blood.
- Probe any suspicious areas with a finger to see if the chest wall has been penetrated.
- Object impaled in the chest.
- Sucking or hissing sounds coming from a wound to the chest.
- Frothy blood coming from a wound on the chest.
- Labored or difficult breathing.

- Chest not rising as it should with a breath.
- Apparent pain with breathing.
- Signs of shock.

Provide First Aid for an Open Chest Wound by Immediately Covering the Wound as Described Below

1. Immediately place your hand directly over any chest wound to provide immediate protection.
2. If someone is available to help you, have that person place their hand over the wound.
3. Obtain a field dressing.
4. Check carefully for entry and exit wounds. If there is more than one wound, you will have to treat each wound separately.
5. Check for the presence of a penetrating object. If the penetrating object is still in the chest, do NOT try to remove it.
6. Treat for shock if indicated.

Apply an Air-Tight Cover to the Wound

1. Quickly cut a field dressing package all the way so that you have a flat piece of plastic. Place the paper-wrapped field dressing to the side. If a field dressing package is not available, try to find a similar item such as plastic sheet, cellophane, MRE wrapper, foil, or part of a poncho.
2. Squeeze some water-based lubricant on the plastic or other item, and spread it around.
3. Place the lubricant-covered, air-tight material directly over the wound to form a seal.
4. If there is more than one wound, use a separate plastic cover for each wound. If the penetrating object is still in the chest, do the best you can to form an airtight seal around the object.

Dress the Wound

1. Maintain pressure on the seal covering the wound.
2. With your free hand, shake the paper wrapper from the field dressing.
3. Place the dressing, white side down, directly over the seal covering the wound.
4. Secure the dressing by wrapping it around the dog's chest and tying the tails together.
5. Apply a bandage over the field dressing using non-adhesive conforming wrap that is wrapped around the entire chest. Apply this bandage with enough tension to keep the field dressing in place, but not so tightly that the dog has more difficulty breathing. NOTE: If the airtight seal is lost at any time during this process, start over. An airtight seal must be maintained at all times.

Notify the supporting veterinary personnel to request further instructions and contact the Kennel Master to advise him of the situation.

Make a written record of the treatment. Include the date, time and actions taken.

Provide First Aid to MWD with an Open Abdominal Wound

1. Major organs such as the stomach, intestines, spleen, kidneys, urinary bladder, and liver are located in the abdominal cavity of the dog. These critical organs are susceptible to serious injury from ballistic wounds (e.g., gunshot, penetrating foreign body, shrapnel), blunt trauma (e.g., vehicular injury, falls), and blast injury (e.g., explosive devices and munitions). You must recognize and know how to provide first aid if your dog has an open abdominal wound in order to protect these organs and their blood supply.
2. Obvious hole(s) in the abdominal area or an object impaled in the abdominal area.
3. Lacerations or cuts and scrapes on the abdomen that appear to penetrate the abdominal wall.

4. Exposed or protruding intestines or abdominal organs.
5. Signs of shock.

PROVIDE FIRST AID FOR AN OPEN ABDOMINAL WOUND

1. Treat for shock if present and cover the wound.
2. Immediately place your hand directly over the abdominal wound(s). If someone is available to help you, have that person place their hand over the wound.
3. Check for entry and exit wounds. If there is more than one wound, you will have to treat each wound separately.
4. Rinse the wound by pouring a liter of sterile LRS into the wound and over any exposed organs.
5. If there is a penetrating object still in the wound, do not remove it. Leave it where it is and work around it.
6. If internal organs have come out through the wound, do not try to push them back in. Wrap them in sterile gauze, dampen them with sterile LRS, and place them over the abdominal wound.
7. Apply a plastic cover to the wound.
8. Quickly cut a field dressing package all the way so that you have a flat piece of plastic. Place the paper-wrapped field dressing to the side. If a field dressing package is not available, use a similar item such as plastic sheet, cellophane, MRE wrapper, foil, or part of a poncho.
9. Squeeze some water-based lubricant on the plastic and spread it around.
10. Place the lubricant-covered plastic directly over the wound.

Dress the Wound
1. Maintain pressure on the plastic covering the wound.
2. With your free hand, shake second (paper) wrapper from the field dressing.
3. Place the dressing, white side down, directly over the plastic covering the wound.
4. Secure the dressing by wrapping it around the dog's abdominal area and tying the tails of the dressing.
5. Apply a bandage over the field dressing using non-adhesive conforming wrap that is wrapped around the entire chest. Apply this bandage with enough tension to keep the field dressing in place, but not so tightly that the dog has more difficulty breathing.
6. If the bandage becomes soiled by feces or urine, replace it immediately.
7. If your MWD is a male, try to avoid wrapping the prepuce in the bandage.

Notify the supporting veterinary personnel to request further instructions and contact the Kennel Master to advise him of the situation.

Make a written record of the treatment. Include the date, time and actions taken.

INDUCE VOMITING

1. An emetic is a drug that causes, or induces, vomiting. Emetics can be an important aspect in the treatment of orally ingested toxins. Determine if inducing vomiting is appropriate for your Military Working Dog.
2. Reasons to induce vomiting:
3. Ingestion of a toxic substance or training aid within the last 2 hours.
4. Ingestion of a substance that is not corrosive or petroleum based.

5. Reasons NOT to induce vomiting:
6. Ingestion of a toxic substance or training aid more than 2 hours ago.
7. Your MWD is unconscious.
8. Your MWD is unable to swallow.
9. Ingestion of a corrosive or petroleum-based product, such as gasoline, oil, tar, grease, paint, solvents, paint strippers, paint thinners, nail polish or removers, hair spray and batteries

Induce Vomiting
1. Retrieve 1 of the 2 milligram apomorphine tablets from the aid bag.
2. Determine how much apomorphine is needed for your dog, which is based on body weight.
3. If the dog weighs less than 66 pounds, administer ½ tablet.
4. If the dog weighs more than >66 pounds, administer 1 full tablet.
5. Crush the tablet up and dissolve with a few drops of water. Place the correct amount of tablet in a 3-cc syringe.
6. Administer the apomorphine by gently pulling down on the lower eyelid to expose the conjunctiva. Place the entire amount of liquefied apomorphine directly onto the conjunctiva of the dog. Never administer more than 1 dose of apomorphine, even if vomiting does not occur. Repeated doses are unlikely to induce emesis and may cause apomorphine toxicity.

Take Action after Vomiting has Started to Prevent Excessive Vomiting and to Monitor the Dog
1. Apomorphine will cause intense vomiting in about 10-15 minutes.
2. Excessive vomiting is dangerous to the dog.
3. 15 minutes after vomiting started, thoroughly rinse the eyelid of unabsorbed apomorphine with at least one-half of a bottle of sterile eye rinse.
4. Once the dog has vomited, DO NOT let the dog re-ingest the vomitus. If possible, save the vomitus for transport to the veterinary treatment facility for examination.
5. Monitor the dog for any adverse effects from the apomorphine. Successful induction of emesis does not signal the end of appropriate monitoring or therapy.

Adverse effects include:
- Prolonged vomiting
- Excitement
- Restlessness
- Respiratory depression.

Report your Actions
Notify the supporting veterinary personnel to request further instructions and contact the Kennel Master to advise him of the situation.

Make a written record of the treatment.
Include the date, time and actions taken.

APPLY A BANDAGE TO THE HEAD, NECK OR TRUNK

As a MWD handler, you should be prepared to provide first aid for an injury to the head, neck, or trunk of your dog. Wounds need to be protected during evacuation. Bandaging incorrectly can cause further injury to your dog, so it is important to properly apply a bandage.

Advantages of Bandaging:
- Speeds wound healing.
- Provides wound cleanliness.
- Controls bleeding.
- Reduces swelling and bruising.
- Eliminates hollow spaces under the skin where fluid pockets and infection can develop.
- Immobilizes injured tissue (splinting).
- Minimizes scar tissue.
- Makes dog more comfortable.

Disadvantages of Bandaging:
- May increase dog's discomfort.
- Dog's may self-mutilate bandage and wound.
- Bacterial colonization of wound is greater.
- Ischemic injury (cuts off circulation).
- Damage to healing tissues.

General Principles of Bandage Application
1. Direct an assistant to position and restrain the dog so that the area to be bandaged is accessible.
2. Apply the first layer.
3. The first layer is in direct contact with the wound.
4. Cover the wound with a non-adherent dressing (e.g., Telfa® pad).
5. Apply the second layer.
6. The second layer holds the non-adherent dressing in place, adds wound protection, and absorbs fluid that comes from the wound.
7. Wrap 1-2 rolls of roll gauze around the affected area. Use firm even pressure when wrapping, but do NOT wrap the gauze too tightly.
8. Apply the third layer.
9. The third layer provides support and additional protection.
10. Wrap conforming self-adhesive bandage (e.g., VetWrap) over the secondary layer without tension.

Bandaging the Head and Neck
- Do not restrict breathing, swallowing, eating, or the eyes (unless covering an eye injury).
- Ears may be left uncovered if not wounded.
- If the ear is covered, mark the outline of the ear flap or write "ear flap up" or "ear flap down" on the bandage. This prevents anyone who removes the bandage from accidentally cutting the dog's ear.
- Check tightness by placing 2 fingers under each side of the bandage. Your fingers should slip snugly under the bandage edges. If too tight, re-bandage with less tension
- Observe for difficulty swallowing, choking, or discomfort. If observed, re-bandage with less tension.

Bandaging the Thorax
1. The bandage must be wrapped in front of at least one of the front legs to prevent the bandage from slipping rearward.

2. Check tightness by placing 2 fingers under each end and observe for difficulty breathing or discomfort. If observed, re-bandage with less tension.

Bandaging the Abdomen
1. Leave the prepuce exposed in male dogs to prevent urine soiling of the bandage.
2. Check tightness by placing 2 fingers under each end and observe for difficulty in breathing or discomfort. If observed, re-bandage with less tension.
3. To prevent the bandage from slipping rearward, tape may need to be applied at the junction of the hair line and bandage material, along the leading edge of the bandage.

Monitor the Dog
1. Write the date and time the bandage was applied on the bandage.
2. Ensure that the bandage stays clean and dry. Replace if wet or soiled.
3. Observe for signs of pain or discomfort.
4. Observe for difficulty breathing. If a chest or abdominal bandage is too tight, it may interfere with respiration to the point of being life-threatening!
5. Check to see that the bandage has not slipped out of place.
6. Sudden chewing at a bandage that has been previously well-tolerated is usually a sign the bandage is too tight.

Notify the supporting veterinary personnel to request further instructions and contact the Kennel Master to advise him of the situation.

Make a written record of the treatment. Include the date, time and actions taken.

PROVIDE FIRST AID FOR A PAD OR PAW INJURY

MWDs are very active on their feet making their pads and paws susceptible to injury. Additionally, because their pads and paws are in contact with the ground, this area is open to all kinds of contaminants—especially if there is a wound. As a dog handler, it is an absolute necessity to learn how to give your dog first aid in case of a pad or paw injury.

Clean the Wound
1. Cleanse the wound with 250 mL of LRS. If LRS is not available, use sterile water, or as a last resort, tap water.
2. Cut the syringe port off the fluid bag and squeeze the fluid directly on the wound.
3. Dry the foot very well before bandaging.

Apply a Bandage to the Paw
1. Position and restrain the dog so that the area to be bandaged is accessible.
2. Apply the first, primary or contact layer by placing a non-adherent dressing (Telfa pad) in direct contact with the wound.
3. Apply the second, secondary or intermediate layer. Apply cotton cast padding starting at the end of the paw and working your way up the leg. Use firm pressure when wrapping and keep it smooth with no wrinkles. Overlap the previous roll by 1/2 each time and go all the way up to and include the accessory pad.

NOTE: Never pull the gauze roll tight as you are applying it. Unless the middle two toes are injured, the bandage is applied such that these two toes can be seen to check for swelling. The toenails should be close together (almost touching) and parallel. If the toes are spreading apart, the foot is swelling and the bandage should be changed or removed immediately.

Staff Sgt. Erick Martinez, a military dog handler, inspects Argo II's paws for damage March 4, 2011, at Hill Air Force Base, Utah. Dog handlers inspect their K-9 on a daily basis to ensure good health. (U.S. Air Force photo/Airman 1st Class Allen Stokes)

The Above Noted Care for Your Dogs Paws are Performed Under Ideal Non-threatening Conditions

The following can be followed when caring for your dog's pad/paw injuries in less desirable conditions and situations.

1. Cover the wound with some sort of bandage, preferably use 1" thickness of 4X4 gauze. If 4X4 gauze is not available try to find something sterile or clean (even a tee-shirt can work in a pinch).
2. Apply firm pressure to the wound with the bandage between the wound and your fingers.
3. Using direct pressure to stop bleeding takes time. Avoid lifting up the bandage to look at the wound while waiting for the bleeding to stop. Looking under the bandage to look at the wound pulls off the blood clot that is forming. When the blood clot gets pulled off, bleeding takes longer to stop.
4. If the blood flow is strong enough to bleed through the bandage, apply an additional inch of 4X4 gauze and continue applying pressure until bleeding stops.
5. Apply the third outer layer. Wrap with rolled gauze (Kerlix) over the secondary layer without tension followed by elastic wrap (Vetrap) and/or adhesive tape (Elastikon) without tension. Start the Elastikon where the Vetrap ends. Wrap the tape around the paw/leg, ensuring that it is covering the

top edge of the bandage and the dog's hair. Wrapping the tape too tightly will cause the paw to swell.

Monitor the Dog
- Ensure that the bandage stays clean and dry.
- Note if the dog's pain and/or discomfort level rises. If the bandage is too tight, it may interfere with circulation to the point of requiring an amputation.
- Check to see that the bandage has not slipped out of place
- Sudden chewing at a bandage that has been previously well tolerated is a sign of a problem.

Notify the supporting veterinary personnel to request further instructions and contact the Kennel Master to advise him of the situation.

Make a written record of the treatment. Include the date, time and actions taken.

APPLY A SPLINT OR SOFT PADDED BANDAGE TO A FRACTURE OF THE LIMB

The possibility always exists that your MWD may break his leg, and as a handler, it will be important for you to know how to prepare your dog for transport to the closest veterinary facility. In the instance of a broken bone, it will be important for you to know how to splint your dog's leg or apply a soft padded bandage to protect the leg during transport.

Recognize Fracture Type
Open Fracture or Compound Fracture
- A broken bone has gone through the skin and is poking out.
- Because of the open skin, there is an elevated risk of infection.

Closed Fracture or Simple Fracture
A closed fracture has no protruding bone. There are many other types of fractures, but open and closed are the basic two types with which you need to be familiar with.

Recognize Signs of a Fractured Limb
- The dog appears to be in pain.
- The dog will not put any weight on the affected limb.
- Swelling of the affected limb.
- The limb may look deformed, out of its normal shape.
- If the break is an open fracture, there will be a bone sticking out at the point of the break.
- The limb may be in an abnormal/awkward position.

Recognize Basic Dog Anatomy Requiring Splinting if Fractured
Only fractures below the knee and elbow need to be splinted.

Limb Anatomy
- Front legs—note elbow and wrist
- Upper leg or humerus. The humerus is the big bone at the top of the front leg.
- Lower leg has 2 bones, radius and ulna. These two bones are the smaller bones at the bottom of the

leg. The ulna is the bigger bone towards the back of the leg. The ulna includes the elbow. The radius is the smaller bone in front of the ulna.
- Rear legs—note stifle (knee) and hock (ankle).
- Upper leg/thigh or femur. The femur is the big bone at the top of the rear leg.
- Lower leg has 2 bones, fibula and tibia just below the knee. The tibia is the bigger bone in the front of the leg, and the fibula is the smaller bone towards the back of the leg.

Splinting Limbs
- The bigger bones, the humerus and femur, are self-splinting. If there's a lot of muscle around the bone, it will stabilize it naturally; if you try to add padding for a fracture above the knee or elbow, the extra weight of the padding on the end of the leg will act like a pendulum and make things worse.
- If broken, splint the bones below the knee and elbow: i.e. radius, ulna, fibula or tibia.
- Apply a splint or soft padded bandage to a fractured limb.
- Do not try to straighten a fractured limb and handle a dog with a fractured limb with extreme care and caution.

Splint
Only apply a splint if the dog is unconscious and for temporary stability while transporting the dog to the veterinary facility. Only splint the bones below the knee or elbow: i.e. radius, ulna, tibia, or fibula.

Field Expedient Splint
1. Wrap a magazine or section of newspaper around the fracture.
2. Secure the magazine or newspaper around the fracture with heavy-duty tape such as masking tape, packing tape, duct tape or "100 mile-an-hour" tape.

Two-tie Splint
1. Place a sturdy stick or similar object on each side of the fractured limb.
2. Gently tie the sticks in place with one tie a few inches above the fracture and one tie a few inches below the fracture. The tie should be tight enough to maintain the leg in the position it is in.

Robert Jones™ Bandage (Soft Padded Bandage)
If there is bone sticking out of the fracture, cover it with something sterile (preferably), or clean.
1. Position and restrain the dog so that that area to be bandaged is accessible.
2. Apply 1-inch wide tape stirrups to the inside and outside of the leg. Ensure that the ends of the tape extend about 4 to 6 inches below the foot. Fold the tape back on itself about 1/2 to 1 inch at the very end.
3. Place a tongue depressor between the two tapes where they extend beyond the paw. This will make it easier to handle the tape and to separate the tape later when it will be used in the bandage.
4. Apply roll cotton to the leg, starting from the paw end and working up the leg. Use a lot of padding. If you don't have roll cotton available, use towels, large first aid or medical dressings, or anything else you can think of to provide padding.
5. Apply conforming gauze to compress the cotton starting from the paw end and working up the leg. Ensure that you stabilize one joint above and below the fracture.
6. Remove the tape stirrups from the tongue depressor, twist 1/2 turn, and apply to the gauze on both sides of the leg.

7. Apply a layer of self-adhesive elastic wrap starting from the paw end and working up the leg.
8. Secure the elastic wrap with adhesive tape.
9. Test the bandage for firmness by thumping it with a finger. It should sound like a ripe watermelon.
10. Ensure the bandage is not too tight by slipping two fingers under the paw end of the bandage and loosen as necessary.
11. Write date and time on bandage.
12. Place an Elizabethan collar on the dog's neck if he is biting or licking the bandage.

Monitor the Dog
- Ensure that the bandage stays clean and dry. If the bandage becomes wet, replace it immediately.
- Note if the dog's pain and/or discomfort level rises.

Make a written record of the treatment. Include the date, time and actions taken.

ADMINISTER ORAL MEDICATION

Dogs get sick or injured and require medication just as humans do. It is unrealistic to assume that there will always be a veterinary staff member available to give your dog his required medication; therefore, learning how to administer oral medications to your dog is a necessary skill.

Obtain Prescribed Medication
Verify the medication is what was prescribed by the veterinarian by checking the bottle for type of medication, strength, dosage, etc.

Ensure the medication is not expired by checking the expiration date on the bottle.

Do NOT give the medication if the medication has expired or is not the medication that was prescribed for the MWD without first consulting with veterinary personnel.

Prepare Medication for Administration
Tablets or Capsules
- Check the label of the bottle for dose.
- Take out required dose.
- Wrap the tablet or capsule in a meatball. It is easiest and safest to give a dog a tablet or capsule this way as most dogs will eat a meatball. If high quality canned dog food is not available, wrap the tablet or capsule in a hot dog or a chunk of cheese.

Liquid Medication
1. Check the label of the bottle for dose.
2. Draw up the required dose in a syringe or applicator provided with the medication.
3. Position and restrain the dog in the down or sitting position to administer the medication.

Administer the Medication
Tablets or Capsules
Give the dog the prepared meatball. If the dog will not eat the meatball, then take the following steps:

1. Grasp the upper jaw with the palm of one hand resting on the dog's muzzle.
2. Lift and extend the dog's head.

3. Press the upper lips over the upper jaw teeth.
4. Apply gentle pressure directly behind the canine teeth.
5. Use the thumb and index finger. Do not cause harm to the dog by using too much force or pressure.
6. Pick up the tablet or capsule using the thumb and index finger or the index and middle finger of the free hand.
7. Open the dog's mouth by pushing downward on the lower jaw using the free fingers of the hand holding the tablet or capsule.
8. Place the tablet or capsule on the center, far back portion of the dog's tongue.
9. Hold the dog's mouth closed.
10. Ensure that the dog has swallowed the medication.
11. The meatball should be completely gone, as well as the tablet or capsule.

If manually administering the medication, massage the dog's throat with a gentle up and down motion until the dog swallows the tablet or capsule. If the dog does not swallow the capsule, try the following:

1. Gently tap the nose or under the chin to startle the dog into swallowing the capsule.
2. Blow sharply into the dog's nostrils to cause the dog to swallow. This is not advised on a highly unruly or aggressive dog.
3. Place 1 to 2 drops of water on the dog's nose.
4. Open the dog's mouth to ensure that the tablet or capsule was swallowed.

Liquid Medication
1. Tilt the dog's head so the nose and eyes are in one line (parallel to the floor).
2. Form a pocket by pulling out the dog's lower lip at the corner of the mouth.
3. Insert the syringe or applicator into the pocket using the free hand. Do not scrape the gums with the syringe.
4. Push the plunger of the syringe or applicator forward.
5. Administer the medication slowly in 3 to 5 mL increments.
6. Observe for swallowing while administering the medication. If the dog is wearing a muzzle, apply liquid oral medication the same as you would if dog is not wearing a muzzle. Pay extra attention to not scraping the gums with the syringe. Be aware that the dog may jerk their head suddenly. Ensure that if the dog jerks their head, your syringe and hand do not remove the muzzle.

Monitor the Dog Following Administration of Medication
Observe for possible side effects and inform the veterinary staff if any of the following symptoms appear:
- Drooling.
- Nausea.
- Vomiting.
- Depression.
- Diarrhea or change in stool.
- Coughing and gagging.
- Pawing at face.
- Any other reactions.

Make a written record of the treatment. Include the date, time and actions taken.

ADMINISTER EAR MEDICATION

As a dog handler, it may be up to you to administer oral ear medication in the event that your dog has an ear infection.

Obtain Prescribed Medication

Verify the medication is what was prescribed by the veterinarian by checking the bottle for type of medication, strength, dosage, etc. Otic medication is medication that is given in the ears. You may see "otic" rather than "ear" on a medication bottle. Remember that the two words mean the same thing.

Ensure the medication is not expired by checking the expiration date on the bottle.

Do NOT give the medication if the medication has expired or is not the medication that was prescribed for the MWD without first consulting with veterinary personnel.

Administer the Medication

1. Direct the dog handler to position and restrain the dog in the down or sitting position.
2. Expose the ear canal by holding the ear flap straight up.
3. Position the dispenser directly above the outside opening of the ear.
4. Do not touch any portion of the ear with the dispenser.
5. Administer the exact amount of the prescribed medication. It must go directly into the ear canal.
6. Gently massage the base of the ear.
7. Release the ear flap.
8. Repeat the procedure in the other ear, if applicable.
9. Make a written record of the treatment. Include the date, time and actions taken.

CLEAN THE EXTERNAL EAR CANALS

1. Clean the external canals of a MWD.
2. Position and restrain the dog in the down or sitting position.
3. Gently pull the ear flap straight up with one hand and hold it vertically. If the ear flap itself is extremely dirty, you will need to clean it.
4. Observe the ear canal for obvious deformities. Look for things such as lumps, sores, excessive debris or offensive odors. DO NOT attempt to clean the ear if there are wounds, masses, or ulcers until you have consulted your local supporting veterinary personnel.
5. Apply ear cleanser so that the entire external ear canal is filled with cleaning solution. Ensure the dog does not shake the cleanser out of the ear until you have massaged the ear. Do not use any other liquid other than a labeled otic cleanser to clean the ears.
6. Massage the base of the ear to break up debris in the ear.
7. Allow the dog to shake his head.
8. Blot any excess cleanser using cotton balls or 4X4 gauze. Do not scrub or push debris down into the ear canal. NEVER use Q-tips or other similar devices to clean the ears and DO NOT attempt to clean the vertical or horizontal canals.
9. Ensure the ear is clean.
10. Look in the ear to ensure it is clean
11. If the ear still appears dirty, clean the ear again until no further debris is observed on the cotton balls or gauze.
12. Make a written record of the treatment. Include the date, time and actions taken and inform the veterinary staff of any abnormalities.

TRIM THE TOENAILS

1. Routine care of your MWD may require occasional nail trimming. Nails allowed to grow too long can lead to breakage, bleeding, and lameness. Long nails can continue to grow so much that they curl up and grow back into the paw. This situation must be avoided by trimming the toenails.
2. Muzzle the MWD and position and restrain the dog on his side to allow for easy access to the paws.
3. Hold the nail trimmers with the handle in the fingers of one hand and hold the dog's paw in the other hand.
4. Position the nail in the trimmers as close to the quick as possible with the cutting blade away from the quick. The quick is the central portion of the nail that is very sensitive and contains small blood vessels. The quick is also known as the nail vein. Cutting the quick causes pain, bleeding, and in some cases, infection.
5. In light or white nails, the quick appears pink or darker than the nail. It is harder to see the quick in dark nails. If in doubt about the position of the quick, position only the very tip of the nail in the trimmers.
6. Cut the nail with the nail trimmers in one smooth motion.
7. Repeat the nail trimming process on every nail of each paw, as necessary.
8. Take immediate action to stop bleeding in the event you cut the quick.
9. Apply direct pressure to the bleeding nail tip with a 4X4 gauze.
10. If direct pressure does not stop the bleeding, apply a blood-clotting product IAW manufacturer's instructions.
11. If a blood-clotting product is not available, press the affected nail into a bar of mild soap.

EXPRESS THE ANAL SACS

1. Recognize signs that your dog has impacted anal sacs.
2. Scooting the hindquarters on the floor or ground, biting or licking the rectum or tail area, pain in the area of the tail or anus and holding the tail in a funny position are all indicators your MWD has impacted anal sacs.
3. To express the anal sacs, position and restrain the dog in a standing position.
4. Ensure the dog is muzzled and ensure the dog restrained in a standing position that prohibits movement.
5. Put on exam gloves and lubricate your index finger with water-based lubricant.
6. Insert the lubricated index finger into the rectum and locate the left anal sac. Anal sacs are typically found at the 4 and 8 o'clock positions. Each anal sac in a MWD is about the size and firmness of a small grape when filled with secretions.
7. Place 4X4 gauze or a folded paper towel over the rectum to catch secretions.
8. Gently squeeze the anal sac between the thumb and index finger, "milking" the fluid out toward the duct. It is possible to rupture an anal sac if you are not gentle. If you cannot manually express the anal gland, do NOT keep trying and immediately notify Veterinary Personnel.
9. Repeat this procedure for the right anal sac.
10. Inspect anal sac fluid on the gauze or paper towel and note if there is blood or pus present.
11. Notify the veterinary staff immediately of any abnormalities such as blood or pus.
12. Make a written record of the treatment. Include the date, time and actions taken.

INITIATE MEDICAL EVACUATION

The ability to properly initiate a MEDEVAC request is imperative for today's dog handlers. The following is the first aid and/or life-saving treatments that must be completed on your dog at your location prior to initiating a Medevac or more commonly referred 9-line evac.

1. Immediately contact the senior military member present. This individual determines the need to request a medical evacuation and assigns precedence for such an evacuation.
2. Contact the dog's attending veterinary or supporting veterinary unit. The veterinarian or veterinary staff will ensure that the MWD is in stable condition and provide other guidance.
3. The attending veterinary unit generally coordinates with the MWD owning unit for medical evacuation of the dog and handler. As the dog's handler, you will travel with your dog when medical evacuation is required.
4. Attend to the dog's medical needs as required or instructed. Relay important information to appropriate personnel as required, provide restraint as necessary, and follow instructions for medical evacuation given to you by your superiors and veterinary services personnel.
5. Prior to the actual evacuation, it is imperative that you as the handler have a clear understanding of where you and your MWD are going to be evacuated to. This will help you ensure that veterinary personnel are at your destination.

Collect all Applicable Information Needed for a MEDEVAC (9 Line) Request

1. Line 1 - Determine the grid coordinates for the pickup site.
2. Line 2 - Obtain radio frequency, call sign, and suffix.
3. Line 3 - Obtain the number of patients and precedence.
4. Line 4 - Determine the type of special equipment required.
5. Line 5 - Determine the number and type (litter or ambulatory) of patients.
6. Line 6 - Determine the security of the pickup site.
7. Line 7 - Determine how the pickup site will be marked.
8. Line 8 - Determine patient nationality and status.
9. Line 9 - Obtain pickup site nuclear, biological, and chemical (NBC) contamination information, normally obtained from the senior person or medic (only included when contamination exists).

Record the gathered MEDEVAC information using the authorized brevity codes. Unless the MEDEVAC information is transmitted over secure communication systems, it must be encrypted. You must inform MEDEVAC personnel that patient is a MWD and also include handler and veterinary personnel in line 5.

Transmit a MEDEVAC Request

1. Contact the unit that controls the evacuation assets.
2. Make proper contact with the intended receiver.
3. Use effective call sign and frequency assignments from the SOI.
4. Announce clearly "I HAVE A MEDEVAC REQUEST;" wait one to three seconds for a response. If no response, repeat the statement.
5. Transmit the MEDEVAC information in the proper sequence.
6. State all line item numbers in clear text. The call sign and suffix (if needed) in line 2 may be transmitted in the clear.
7. Line numbers 1 through 5 must always be transmitted during the initial contact with the evacuation

unit. Lines 6 through 9 may be transmitted while the aircraft or vehicle is en route.
8. Follow the procedures provided in the explanation column of the MEDEVAC request format to transmit other required information.
9. Pronounce letters and numbers according to appropriate radiotelephone procedures.
10. Take no longer than 25 seconds to transmit.
11. End the transmission by stating "OVER."
12. Keep the radio on and listen for additional instructions or contact from the evacuation unit.

PROVIDE FIRST AID TO MWD FOR VOMITING OR DIARRHEA

- Knowing causes of vomiting will assist you in diagnosing your dog's ailment. Digestive system problems, irritation or pain, drugs, toxic waste products (organ disease or failure), chemicals, inner ear problems, sudden change in diet and other diseases are common reasons your dog may be vomiting.
- Knowing causes of diarrhea is also very important. Irritation, infection, altered bacterial population, breakdown of the lining of the intestinal tract and sudden change are some common reasons your dog may have diarrhea.

Recognize Signs of Vomiting and/or Diarrhea
The signs of vomiting and diarrhea are usually obvious and visible. If the animal does not vomit or have an episode of diarrhea right in front of you, you may find evidence of it in his kennel.

Recognize Signs that Require Immediate First Aid or Attention from a Veterinarian
These signs include:
- Presence of fresh blood/blood clots in the stools or vomit.
- Black, tarry stools.
- Difficult or painful defecation. The dog will cry out in pain or stay hunched up trying to defecate for long periods of time.
- An abnormally swollen abdomen. This may indicate gastric dilatation or gastric dilatation-volvulus or some other abdominal disease or problem.
- The dog appears to be in pain or is depressed in addition to the vomiting or diarrhea.
- Increased body temperature.
- Profound dehydration.

Provide First Aid for Vomiting or Diarrhea
Vomiting
1. Take the vital signs and perform a physical examination of the dog.
2. Withhold all food for 24 hours after the last episode of vomiting.
3. Withhold all water for 12 hours after the last episode of vomiting.
4. Offer small amounts of water every thirty minutes after 12 hours.
5. After 24 hours, introduce small amounts of food several times a day over 2-3 days.
6. The dog's full diet can be fed after 2-3 days.
7. Notify the closest veterinary staff if vomiting persists or there are any abnormalities on the physical exam.

Diarrhea
1. Take the vital signs and perform a physical examination of the dog.

2. Withhold all food for 24 hours after last episode of diarrhea. After 24 hours, introduce small amounts of food several times a day over 2-3 days. The dog's full diet can be fed after 2-3 days.
3. Allow the dog to drink as much water as he wishes.
4. Notify the closest veterinary staff if diarrhea persists or there are any abnormalities on the physical exam.

Monitor the dog for signs of continued vomiting/diarrhea.
Make a written record of the treatment. Include the date, time and actions taken.

PROVIDE FIRST AID TO MWD FOR EYE IRRITATION OR TRAUMA

Dogs may have mild eye irritation or suffer significant eye trauma MWD handlers must recognize signs of eye irritation and trauma and know how to provide first aid for eye problems.

Indications and Signs of Eye Irritation
Tearing, rubbing of the eye or face are excessive tearing, rubbing of the eye or face, excessive squinting or holding the eyelids shut, excessive reddening of the white part of the eye, milky white discoloration of the outer clear part of the eye and excessive discharge (greenish, yellowish, bloody) from the eye.

Provide First Aid for Eye IRRITATION
If eye irritation is observed, immediately contact Veterinary Service personnel for guidance. If none can be reached, then administer first aid.
1. Have the dog muzzled, sitting or lying upright on chest. Ensure the dog's head is restrained enough to prevent sudden head movement.
2. Remove dry debris from around the eye using a dampened gauze sponge with sterile eye rinse. Gently stroke the eyelids and surrounding area. Do not rub the eye directly. Allow the dog to close the eye during this procedure.
3. Flush moist secretions, dirt, blood, and discharge from the eye with approximately one-fourth of a bottle of sterile eye rinse.
4. Use the heel of the hand holding the eye flush to pull the upper eyelid open.
5. Use the thumb of the hand holding the jaw to pull the lower eyelid downward, exposing the inside part of the lower eyelid.

Apply Sterile Antibiotic Eye Ointment to the Affected Eye
1. If the ointment has been used before, squirt a small amount onto a gauze sponge to remove possible contaminants.
2. Use the heel of the hand holding the medication to pull the upper eyelid open.
3. Use the thumb of the hand holding the jaw to pull the lower eyelid downward, exposing the inside part of the lower eyelid.
4. Administer the medication.
5. To prevent contamination or injury, do not allow the tip of the tube to touch the eye or any other surface.
6. Squeeze the ointment tube to lay a single ribbon of ointment (1/4 to 1/2-inch-long) directly on the inside part of the lower eyelid.
7. Allow the dog to blink. If the dog does not blink, gently move the eyelids together to spread the ointment over the eye.

Recognize the Signs of Eyeball Trauma
- Blood or bruising in or around the eyeball.
- Cuts or wounds to the eyeball or surrounding skin.
- Foreign object in or around the eyeball.
- Displacement of the eyeball from the socket.

Provide First Aid for Eyeball Trauma
1. Clean and rinse the eye as noted above.
2. Do NOT pull on the eye if it is displaced. Do NOT try to put the eyeball back in the eye socket if it is displaced. Do NOT try to remove any object that seems to be embedded in the eyeball. These actions may cause more damage to the eye.
3. Gently coat the eyeball with the entire contents of one tube of sterile antibiotic eye ointment.
4. Cover the eyeball with 5-8 gauze sponges that have been moistened with sterile eye rinse.
5. Apply a bandage over the gauze to protect the eye.

- When bandaging the head and neck, do not restrict breathing, swallowing, or eating.
- Ears may be left uncovered if not wounded.
- If the ear is covered, mark the outline of the ear flap or write "ear flap up" or "ear flap down" on the bandage to prevent anyone who removes the bandage from accidentally cutting the ear.
- Check tightness; you should be able to slide 2 fingers under each edge of the bandage. If too tight, re-bandage with less tension.
- Observe for difficulty swallowing and for choking or discomfort. If observed, re-bandage with less tension.

Inform the Kennel Master of the situation and contact supporting veterinary personnel to request further instructions.

Make a written record of the treatment. Include the date, time and actions taken.

ADMINISTER AN ANALGESIC INJECTION

Unfortunately, your dog may experience pain, whether due to a traumatic accident or some other medical reason. As the individual closest to your dog, it will be up to you to recognize when your dog needs pain relieving medication and give it to him without causing further harm.

Recognize the Signs of Moderate to Severe Pain
Pain in a MWD may be caused by trauma, injury, or significant disease. Any Military Working Dog with these signs may need to be treated for pain. Contact your nearest Veterinary Support personnel FIRST. If no Veterinary personnel can be reached than you must treat for pain by following the specific steps described in this task. These are signs of moderate to severe pain:

- Vocalizing (barking, howling, whimpering, crying out, groaning) continuously or intermittently, especially when touched or moved, or when the dog is trying to move.
- Change in behavior, usually becoming more aggressive than normal or becoming depressed, anxious, nervous, or obviously uncomfortable.
- Uncomfortable appearance, with the dog acting restless or avoiding certain positions.

- Not putting weight on a limb or affected part of the body or vocalizing when attempting to bear weight or use a body part.

Administer an Analgesic Injection

1. Assemble the needle and syringe.
2. Select a sterile 22-gauge X 5/8-inch needle and a sterile 3 mL syringe from the first aid kit.
3. Test the plunger for smooth, easy movement and a tight seal by pulling the plunger back and forth.
4. Connect the needle and syringe by screwing them together. Do NOT contaminate the needle or syringe—hold both only by the protective cap or covers, and do not touch the bare needle or tip of the syringe at any time.
   a. Open the package containing the needle.
   b. Screw the needle onto the syringe while holding the package.
   c. Once the needle is screwed into place, remove the outer package. The cap should remain over the needle.
   d. Draw the correct amount of pain medication (morphine, 15 mg/mL) into the syringe.
   e. Inspect the medication vial to ensure it is the proper medication and strength and that it is not expired.
   f. Check the dose chart and determine the volume of pain medication to give based on the MWD's known or estimated body weight.

Table 3. Analgesic Injection Dosage Chart

Body weight (in pounds)	Volume of morphine to give (in milliliters)
30 to 40	0.4
40 to 50	0.5
50 to 60	0.6
60 to 70	0.7
70 to 80	0.8
80 to 90	0.9
90 to 100	1.0

NOTE: A copy of this dose chart needs to be included in all medical kits. It is mandatory that all handlers know the weight of their MWDs and the appropriate dose.

Wipe the top of the medication vial with a gauze sponge soaked in alcohol.

Remove the needle cap and insert the needle into the medication vial and withdraw slightly more medication than necessary, while holding the needle, syringe and medication bottle vertically with the needle pointing up.

1. Work the air bubbles out of the syringe.
2. Hold the needle, syringe, and medication bottle vertically with the needle pointing up.
3. Tap the syringe with a finger to work air bubbles up toward the needle hub.
4. Push the plunger to expel the bubbles back into the medicine vial.
5. Push the plunger of the syringe forward until the prescribed amount of medication remains in the syringe.
6. Remove the syringe/needle from the vial.
7. Replace the needle cap.
8. As an alternative, a 10 mg morphine auto injector can be used if you are issued one of these for your canine.

Inject the Medication
1. Position and restrain the dog.
2. Have the dog restrained in a standing position that eliminates movement. If the dog cannot stand, it is ok to administer the injection with the dog lying down on their side.
3. Ensure the dog is muzzled.
4. Ensure the injection site is accessible. Intramuscular injections are administered in the muscle mass behind the femur bone in the upper, rear leg, avoiding the large nerve (sciatic nerve). NOTE: The sciatic nerve is a large nerve that runs parallel to the femur. If you do touch the sciatic nerve you will cause pain and possible paralysis.

Prepare the Intramuscular Injection Site
Isolate the muscle receiving the injection. There are two acceptable ways to do this.

Wrap your thumb around the front portion of the thigh with your hand on the inside of the leg from the front to the rear.

Use your fingers to push out the muscle from the inside to the outside.
1. With the tip of your thumb, cover the area where the sciatic nerve lies on the outside to protect it from the injection.
2. Wrap your hand around the rear portion of the thigh with your hand on the inside of the leg from the rear to the front.
- Use your hand to push the muscle up.
- Use your thumb to block off the sciatic nerve.

Apply alcohol to the injection site. With the free hand, apply alcohol using a gauze sponge soaked with alcohol to wet the skin. Gently rub the skin to remove dirt and skin oil.

Inject the Medication
1. Insert the needle into the muscle quickly and firmly.
2. Insert the needle at a 90° angle to the skin.
3. Insert the needle 1/2" to 3/4".
4. Pull back on the syringe plunger to ensure the needle is not in a blood vessel.
   a. Pull back on the plunger of the syringe.
   b. If the needle is in a blood vessel, blood will flash into the hub and syringe.
   c. If a blood flash appears, immediately remove the needle. DO NOT INJECT!
5. Press the plunger steadily forward while holding the syringe barrel steady.
6. When finished injecting the medication, withdraw the needle.
7. The drug's effects are usually felt within fifteen to thirty minutes and may last up to eight hours. These effects may include but are not limited to pain relief, sedation, apathy, reduced tension, anxiety, and/or aggression.

Dispose of the needle and syringe IAW local SOP.

How to Give the Auto Injector (Same Site as the Previous)
The U.S. military utilizes auto-injectors; the dosage is usually 1 auto-injector equals 10 mg. Auto-injectors come in multiple strengths. Make certain you always double-check the dosage on the auto-injectors.

- The dog handler will remove the safety cap; press the colored end into the proper injection location and press firmly. This will depress the black firing plunger.

- This action causes a release of gas within the injector that drives the hypodermic needle through the protective cap and about an inch into the thigh muscle. It also pushes 1.0 mL of the fluid, containing 10 mg of morphine, through the needle and into the muscle tissue.

Document the injection and the time administered.

Monitor the Dog Following Administration of Medication

Observe for possible side effects and inform the veterinary staff if any of the following symptoms appear: nausea/drooling, vomiting, depression, diarrhea or change in stool, change in breathing pattern, skin rash, swelling at the injection site and any other reactions.

Immediately contact the closest veterinary staff to request further instructions.

Make a written record of the treatment. Include the date, time and actions taken.

1. Note medication and dosage given to the dog and reason medication was administered.
2. Do not administer additional analgesic medication to your dog unless specifically directed to do so by your supporting veterinary personnel. Additional analgesic medication may cause life-threatening decreases in blood pressure or cause the dog to stop breathing.

PROVIDE FIRST AID FOR A BURN

It is important to determine what type of burn and the severity of that burn the dog has prior to initiating treatment.

There are many types of burns, but the following two are the typical burns affecting Military Working Dogs.

- Thermal burns are from radiation or some other type of heat source.
- Chemical burns are from a caustic chemical.

Determine Severity of the Burn

Burns are classified in degrees. The more layers of skin affected by the burn, the higher the degree classification. The higher the degree classification, the more serious the burn injury.

- First degree (superficial) burn—redness and pain, similar to a sunburn.
- Second degree (partial thickness) burn—red or mottled appearance, swelling, extreme hypersensitivity leading to pain. The area may appear wet and weeping due to fluid swelling up below the skin.
- Third degree (full thickness) burn—dark and leathery appearance. Skin surface is dry. There is no pain as the nerve endings are destroyed. If any hair remains, it will pull out easily.

Provide First Aid for a Burn

1. Perform a survey of the dog and take immediate action, if required.
2. Take the patient's vital signs.
3. Provide first aid for shock, if indicated from the vital signs.
4. Initiate appropriate burn treatment based on the type of burn.

Thermal Burn

1. Apply cold compresses made of sterile water or saline-soaked towels, lap sponges, or gauze for a

minimum of 30 minutes.
2. Submerge the dog in a cold-water bath if the burn covers a large surface area.
   DO NOT: use ice, ice water, or iced saline or attempt to clip hair from the burned skin.
3. Carefully flush the burned surface with chlorhexidine solution (i.e. Nolvasan®) to remove surface debris.
4. Thoroughly flush with saline solution after the chlorhexidine solution flush.
5. Apply a thin coating of silver sulfadiazine ointment. Make sure you are wearing sterile gloves, not exam gloves, or use sterile applicators.
6. Apply sterile non-stick pads (i.e. Telfa® pad) to all wounds and loosely bandage the affected area with dry, sterile bandage material.

Chemical Burn
1. Flush the burned area with sterile water or saline thoroughly for a minimum of 30 minutes to remove residual chemical.
   DO NOT attempt to clip hair from the burned skin.
2. Carefully flush the burned surface with chlorhexidine solution (i.e. Nolvasan) to remove surface debris.
3. Thoroughly flush with saline solution after the chlorhexidine solution flush.
4. Apply a thin coating of silver sulfadiazine ointment. Make sure you are wearing sterile gloves, not exam gloves, or use sterile applicators.
5. Apply sterile non-stick pads (i.e. Telfa® pad) to all wounds and loosely bandage the affected area with dry, sterile bandage material.

Immediately contact your closest supporting veterinary staff and request further instructions. Contact the Kennel Master immediately and inform him of the situation.

Continue to monitor the dog's vital signs. Be aware that pulmonary edema from smoke inhalation can occur after 24 hours, even if the dog shows no outward signs of being burned.

Make a written record of the treatment. Include the date, time and actions taken.

PROVIDE FIRST AID FOR A COLD INJURY

Identify Cold Injury Risk Factors
Always check your dog's records for a history of exposure to extreme cold. Several risk factors make a dog more susceptible to cold injury to include but not limited to, inadequate acclimation, previous cold injuries, fatigue, inactivity, geographic origin, medications, poor nutrition and dehydration.

Identify Individual Protective Measures Used to Avoid Cold Injuries
The military mission and situation may be such that you will not be able to incorporate all of these measures. In whatever situation you find yourself, take the best possible care of you and your dog. Avoid cold exposure, if possible. If mission dictates being out in the cold, take the following measures:

1. Avoid wind exposure. The wind chill factor should be considered if there is any wind. Wind combined with cold temperatures creates a wind chill factor which is actually colder than the temperature on the thermometer.
2. Avoid contact with frozen objects.
3. Avoid fatigue. Use work/rest cycles to allow for re-warming.

4. Allow the dog time to acclimate to the environment and workload gradually. Partial acclimatization takes approximately 4-5 days, whereas full acclimatization takes 7-14 days.
5. Gradually increase physical activity.
6. If your dog has had a previous cold injury or if the dog is on medication, discuss the situation with your supporting veterinary staff.
7. Address nutritional needs by providing hot fluids and/or increasing the dog's caloric intake. Always discuss food or water changes with your supporting veterinary staff beforehand.

Describe the Two Types of Cold Injuries and their Clinical Signs
Hypothermia—Below Normal Body Temperature
Preventing hypothermia must take place when the dog is still above 98°. Clinical signs of hypothermia include rectal temperature below 95° (Dog may also be cold to the touch), dog is unconscious or appears to be "out of it", slow breathing, slow pulse rate, shivering may be present or may have stopped, weakness and shock.

Frostbite—Frozen Body Tissues
Signs of frostbite include dog's tissues are very cold to the touch, skin appears gray, white or waxy instead of pink and blistering occurs in more advanced cases. The tips of the dog's ears, scrotum, tail, lower legs, paws, and toes are the most common areas affected by frostbite. Frostbite may be most noticeable at the toenail beds and/or the edge of the ear flaps.

1. Provide first aid for a cold injury. Cold injuries are progressive meaning that they get worse as time passes. Take immediate action as soon as you recognize the onset of a cold injury. The dog must be warmed as quickly as possible.
2. When treating for hypothermia warm the dog by wrapping the dog in blankets or towels or if available or place the dog on a circulating warm water heating pad, ensuring a water temperature of 85° to 103°F. Wrap the water pad in towels or a blanket and cover the dog and pad with a blanket. If a water pad is not readily available, old expired IV bags can be heated and used to warm the dog. Wrap the bag in a towel to prevent burns. Ensure you use a heater to warm the room and monitor the dog's rectal temperature every 15 minutes.
3. When treating for frostbite, warm the affected area by placing the injured part(s) of the dog in warm water (85° to 103°F) for 15 to 20 minutes or by applying warm wet towels to the affected area for 15 to 20 minutes, changing the towels every 5 minutes. Gently pat dry the injured area. DO NOT rub. To prevent self-trauma to the affected area or if it appears that the dog will not leave the area alone apply an Elizabethan collar, if one is available or muzzle the dog.
4. Inform the Kennel Master of the situation, and immediately contact the closest veterinary staff and request further instructions.
5. Make a written record of the treatment. Include the date, time and actions taken.

ADMINISTER ACTIVATED CHARCOAL

Activated Charcoal is administered to an MWD to induce vomiting should your dog eat a toxic substance. Ensure when administering the activated charcoal that the dog is conscious and is able to swallow.

Activated Charcoal would NOT be administered to an MWD if 1 hour has passed since the dog ingested the toxic substance.

Do not induce vomiting if the MWD ate a corrosive or petroleum-based product such as, but not limited to gasoline, oil, tar, grease, paint, solvents, paint strippers, paint thinners, nail polish or removers, hair spray or batteries.

Administer Activated Charcoal by Mouth
DO NOT attempt to administer activated charcoal orally if the dog is not conscious.
1. Determine how much activated charcoal your dog needs based on his body weight. For dogs weighing between 40-60 pounds, give 2 bottles of Toxiban™ (240 mL/bottle) orally. For dogs weighing more than 60 pounds, give 3 bottles of Toxiban™ (240 mL/bottle) orally.
2. You should have 3 bottles of Toxiban™ in your aid bag. Retrieve the proper number of bottles and use a 60 cc syringe to measure the required amount.
3. Administer the required amount of Toxiban™ in one of two ways, as an oral slurry or mixed with food.
4. Administer Toxiban™ as an oral medication (slurry).
5. Tilt the dog's head up so the nose is pointing mostly towards the sky.
6. Form a pocket by pulling out the dog's lower lip at the corner of the mouth.
7. Insert the syringe gently into the pouch using your free hand.
8. Do not scrape the gums with the syringe.
9. Push the plunger forward slowly to squirt the medicine onto the dog's cheek pouch.
10. Administer the medication in 3 to 5 mL increments.
11. Watch for swallowing between squirts and give your dog enough time to swallow each squirt of charcoal before giving him/her more.
12. Administer Toxiban™ mixed with a high-quality canned dog food.
13. Mix a small amount of Toxiban™ (1/4 of the bottle) with an equal amount of high-quality canned dog food (if available). Give it to the dog. If he consumes it, administer the rest of his dosage mixed with an equal amount of dog food.
14. If the dog does not consume the Toxiban™ mixed with dog food, you will have to administer the medication as an oral slurry.
15. Contact veterinary support for further instructions.
16. Inform Kennel Master of the situation.

Make a written record of the treatment. Include the date, time and actions taken.

TREAT A MWD FOR TRAINING AID TOXICITY

MWDs will frequently come in contact with explosive and narcotic training aids when conducting training. It is imperative that handlers be able to recognize and provide first aid to a MWD who is displaying signs and symptoms of training aid toxicity.

Symptoms of training aid toxicity for a nitrate and nitro based explosive training aid which has been ingest are salivation, dizziness, stumbling, nausea, convulsions, dark brown mucous membranes, cyanosis and death.

Symptoms of training aid toxicity for narcotic training aids are as follows:

- If a marijuana/hashish training aid is ingested, MWDs will show signs of confusion, hallucinations, dizziness, nausea and having breathing problems.
- If a heroin training aid is ingested, MWDs will have pinpointed pupils, slow heart rate, breathing problems and possibly go into a coma.
- If a cocaine or amphetamine is ingested, MWDs will have dilated pupils, shows signs of restlessness, aggression, hallucinate, have a rapid heart rate and convulsions.

Treat a MWD for training aid toxicity. If you witness your dog ingest a training aid, or the dog is displaying symptoms that he has recently ingested a training aid, take immediate action by inducing vomiting.

Try to keep the dog calm by speaking to them and reassuringly to and around him.
Immediately contact the closest veterinary staff to request further instructions.
Make a written record of the treatment. Include the date, time and actions taken.

PERFORM NUCLEAR, BIOLOGICAL, AND CHEMICAL DECONTAMINATION

The decision to decontaminate and treat a MWD or other military animal will be based on local SOP, theater restrictions, and other factors. These decisions will be directed by the theater commander, senior medical commander in theater, or senior veterinary commander in theater. The steps outlined in this task are generic in nature and are based on current available doctrine. Modifications to these steps may be necessary based on numerous factors, and the commander must direct the specific steps to be followed for a given situation.

Decontaminate for Nuclear Fallout
1. Remove radioactive particles from the hair coat and skin by brushing and bathing the animal in soap and water.
2. Decontaminate for biological agents. Wash the animal with soap and water or follow command directives or policies for specific agents.

Decontaminate for Irritant Agents
1. These agents have little effect on animals.
2. Flush the eyes with copious amounts of water or saline if liquid or solid agents come in contact with the eyes.

Decontaminate for Nerve Agent
1. Decontaminate hair and skin using the M291 skin decontamination kit. Protect the eyes by applying a generous amount of ophthalmic ointment or similar nonmedical ointment (e.g., petroleum jelly). Decontaminate using the M291 skin decontamination kit. Rinse the animal thoroughly to remove the decontamination solution. Bathe the animal with warm, soapy water, and rinse thoroughly.
2. Decontaminate the eyes by irrigating with copious amounts of water or saline until all agent has been removed. Avoid using any components of the M291 skin decontaminating kit in the eyes. Decontaminate collars, leashes, muzzles, cages, bowls, and other items using M291 or M295 decontamination kits prior to putting them back on the MWD or using them.

Decontaminate for White Phosphorus
Immediately cover the affected area with water by submersion or with water-soaked bandaging material. As quickly as possible, bathe the affected part in a bicarbonate solution to neutralize the phosphoric acid. Remove remaining white phosphorous fragments (these are visible in dark surroundings as luminescent spots).

Treat the animal for thermal burns once all phosphorus has been removed.
1. Decontaminate for blood agents using the M291 skin decontamination kit.
2. Decontaminate for blister agents (mustard, nitrogen mustard agent, or arsenical blister agents) should be carried out within 1-2 minutes after exposure using the M291 skin decontamination kit.
3. Decontaminate for incapacitating agents (BZ Type) by washing the hair coat and skin with warm soapy water.
4. Dispose of wastes IAW local SOP.

PERFORM LIFE-SAVING THERAPY FOR ORGANOPHOSPHATE OR CARBAMATE POISONING

If your MWD is exposed to chemicals and is now acting unusual, perform a primary survey and took the dog's vital signs and take the following measurements and record them.

- Body temperature.
- Pulse rate.
- Respiration rate.
- Capillary refill time.
- Mucous membrane color.

Signs of Organophosphate/Carbamate (pesticide) Toxicity are excessive salivation, drooling, muscle twitching (usually begins with the face and progresses over the entire body and becomes much more severe and attempts at walking becomes stiff and jerky, difficulties breathing, convulsions, urination, tearing, defecation/diarrhea and death due to respiratory failure.

Gather additional history from the person who has been with the dog for the past 12 hours. For example, were there unusual odors in the kennel or work environment, was the kennel area sprayed or fogged for insects recently, was the dog exposed to unusual dust or powder, was anything applied to the dog externally (i.e. shampoo, ointment, drops, etc.), is there any other situation that you can recollect that might have involved a chemical exposure?

Smell the hair coat for the odor of insecticides or to determine if the dog has any unusual odor. While wearing gloves use your hand to part the fur in several places on the dog's body and smell for chemicals. Inspect the dog's feet and legs and smell them for chemicals. Look at the fur to see if there are any dark, wet, or damp spots on the dog that might indicate the dog got something on it.

Initiate Life-Saving Therapy for Organophosphate/Carbamate Toxicity.

Administer atropine to your MWD intramuscularly using the dosing chart below (ensure that a copy of this chart is stored with the medication):

Table 4. Atropine Dosage Chart

Wt of Dog	Atropine Dose (15mg/mL)
50 lbs	.45 mL
60 lbs	.55 mL
70 lbs	.65 mL
80 lbs	.70 mL
90 lbs	.80 mL
100 lbs	.90 mL

NOTE: If after administering atropine, the dog's heart rate increases or the pupils dilate, DO NOT administer more atropine, as it is unlikely to be OP or carbamate toxicity.

Watch for improvement of the patient or disappearance of signs within 3 to 10 minutes.

1. Place an IV catheter.
2. Initiate an IV infusion.

3. Continue to monitor the MWD by:
   a. Take the dog's vital signs.
   b. Watch for muscular twitching to intensify.
   c. Watch for improved breathing and breathing pattern.
   d. Monitor mucous membrane color and how moist the gums and tongue are.
   e. Check eyes and note if pupils are dilated or pinpoint.
   f. Check capillary refill time (CRT).
4. Lower elevated body temperature if it is over 104°F by drenching the dog with cool water, wrapping the dog in wet towels and by placing a fan near the dog to keep it cool.
5. Reduce continued exposure to the toxic agent.
   a. If the exposure was through the skin or fur, bathe the dog with a mild shampoo (NOT a flea/tick shampoo) and rinse thoroughly with warm water.
   b. If the exposure was by mouth, administer activated charcoal.
6. Repeat atropine administration if clinical signs return or intensify using the same dose from your dose card given in the muscle every 4-6 hrs.
7. If you haven't determined it yet, continue to try to find the source of the chemical exposure.
8. Immediately contact the closest veterinary staff to request further instructions.
9. Evacuate the MWD to the nearest veterinary facility if the situation dictates.
10. Make a written record of the treatment. Include the date, time and actions taken.

SYMPTOMS AND CONTROL MEASURES OF DISEASES AND PARASITIC INFECTIONS

Parasitic Infections
Animal parasites survive by feeding from the dog's body and are harmful to the animal's health.

Hookworms
The most harmful intestinal parasite which live primarily in the small intestine and are typically 1-5–2-5 inches in length.
   1. **Symptoms.** Pale mouth and eye membranes, loose stools containing blood and weight loss.
   2. **Control.** Primarily by feeding rations with a chemical to prevent worms from completing a life cycle, and by keeping the dog's living area sanitary and free of stools.

Roundworms
An internal parasite that robs the infected animal of vital nutrients while living in the intestines and are can be up to 6 inches in length.
   1. **Symptoms.** Diarrhea, vomiting, loss of weight, and coughing. The worms (spaghetti like) may be noticed in the stool or vomitus.
   2. **Control.** Done by treating the infected animal and kennel sanitation.

Whip worms
Can be microscopic to 2 inches in length.
   1. **Symptoms.** Diarrhea, loss of weight, and paleness mouth and eye membranes.
   2. **Control.** Same as for roundworms.

Tapeworms
Long, flat, ribbon-like, and segmented. They infect intestines and are noticed in the dog's stool as tiny whitish objects approximately 1/4 inch in length.
   1. **Symptoms.** Not very noticeable but may include diarrhea (often with blood or mucus), loss of

weight, and decreased appetite.
2. **Control.** Treatment of infected animals, good sanitation and control of fleas.

Heart worms
Thread-like parasites, 6 to 11 inches long, are found in the heart and lungs and interferes with the dog's cardiovascular functions.
1. **Symptoms.** Coughing, loss of weight, difficult breathing, and loss of energy, or stamina. The veterinarian can diagnose the disease with a blood test.
2. **Control.** Feeding rations with a chemical that terminates the life cycle of a heart worm and controlling mosquitoes in the area.

Ticks
Common in many parts of the world, they attach themselves to the skin and suck the animal's blood and may transmit disease.
1. **Symptoms.** Small bumps on the skin. Take extreme care in their removal, they may carry diseases harmful to humans. Grasp the tick as close to the skin as possible (a pair of tweezers is recommended). Pull slowly and gently until the tick is removed. Examine the tick to make sure you removed the head and body from the dog, and not separated from the tick's body, remaining attached to the dog.
2. **Control.** Spraying the kennel runs and kennel areas with insecticide.

Fleas
Torment the dog and spread disease and tapeworms.
1. **Symptoms.** Found on the dog's skin and crawling in the hair.
2. **Control.** Individual treatment and kennel sanitation.

Lice
External parasites that fall into two categories: biting and sucking.
1. **Symptoms.** Small white or gray crescent-shaped objects fastened to the dog's hair.
2. **Control.** Treatment of infected animals.

Mites
Two types: ear and mange.
1. **Symptoms.** Ear mites--the dog will shake and/or scratch its head, and a brown (often dry) discharge from the ear(s) may occur. Mange mites-the dog may experience hair loss, scabbing/crusting skin lesions, and/or skin infections.
2. **Control.** Treatment of infected animals by the attending veterinarian.

CANINE INFECTIONS AND DISEASES

Microscopic organisms cause contagious diseases transmitted from animal to animal. Zoonotic diseases are contagious diseases transmittable from animal to man. The following diseases, symptoms, and control measures apply:

Canine Distemper
Widely spread, highly contagious, and usually fatal.
1. **Symptoms.** Elevated temperature, loss of appetite, depression, loss of weight and energy, diarrhea, vomiting, coughing, thick discharge from eyes and nose, muscle stiffness and convulsion.

2. **Control.** Proper sanitation and immunization.

Infections Canine Hepatitis
Found mostly in young dogs and spread through urine of infected animals.
1. **Symptoms.** Same as canine distemper.
2. **Control.** Immunization and sanitation.

Leptospirosis
Known commonly as "Lepto," is caused by a microorganism called a spirochete, transmittable to man.
1. **Symptoms.** Same as canine distemper.
2. **Control.** Immunization, rodent control, and thorough cleanup after treating infected animals.

Rabies
A disease that like Lepto, transmittable to man, but the transmission is through the saliva of an animal bite.
1. **Symptoms.** May include sudden change in temperament or attitude, extreme excitement, difficulty in swallowing water or food, a blank expression, slackened jaw, excessive drooling from the mouth, paralysis, coma, and eventually, death.
2. **Control.** Vaccination. Handlers must prevent contact between their dogs and wild or stray animals. Report contact resulting in bites or scratches to the veterinarian. Capture the biting animal and hold for observation until released by the veterinarian. Use extreme caution during the capture to prevent bites to personnel.

Other Contagious Infections and Diseases
Vaccine cannot treat upper respiratory infection, pneumonia, and gastroenteritis.
1. **Symptoms.** High temperature, loss of appetite, loss of energy, vomiting, diarrhea and coughing.
2. **Control.** Immediate diagnosis and treatment with antibiotics.

FIRST AID KITS

The local veterinarian will usually provide several first aid kits to a dog section. Use kits only when a veterinarian is not available. See attachment 2 for contents of recommended first aid kit. The items listed are specific in nature. Your local veterinarian approves items in first aid kits. They may add, delete, or change any item(s) in the kits. Replace items used immediately.

EMERGENCY VETERINARY CARE

Each MWD kennel facility must have a contingency plan for emergency veterinary care. Post the plan in the kennel facility and at the law enforcement desk. The plan must include:

- Procedures for emergency care during normal duty hours.
- Procedures for contacting military veterinarian during duty and non-duty hours.
- A list of local veterinarian emergency treatment centers approved by the military veterinarian.
- Telephone numbers and directions to the civilian treatment centers. Thoroughly familiarize all personnel associated with the MWD program with the Emergency Veterinary Plan.

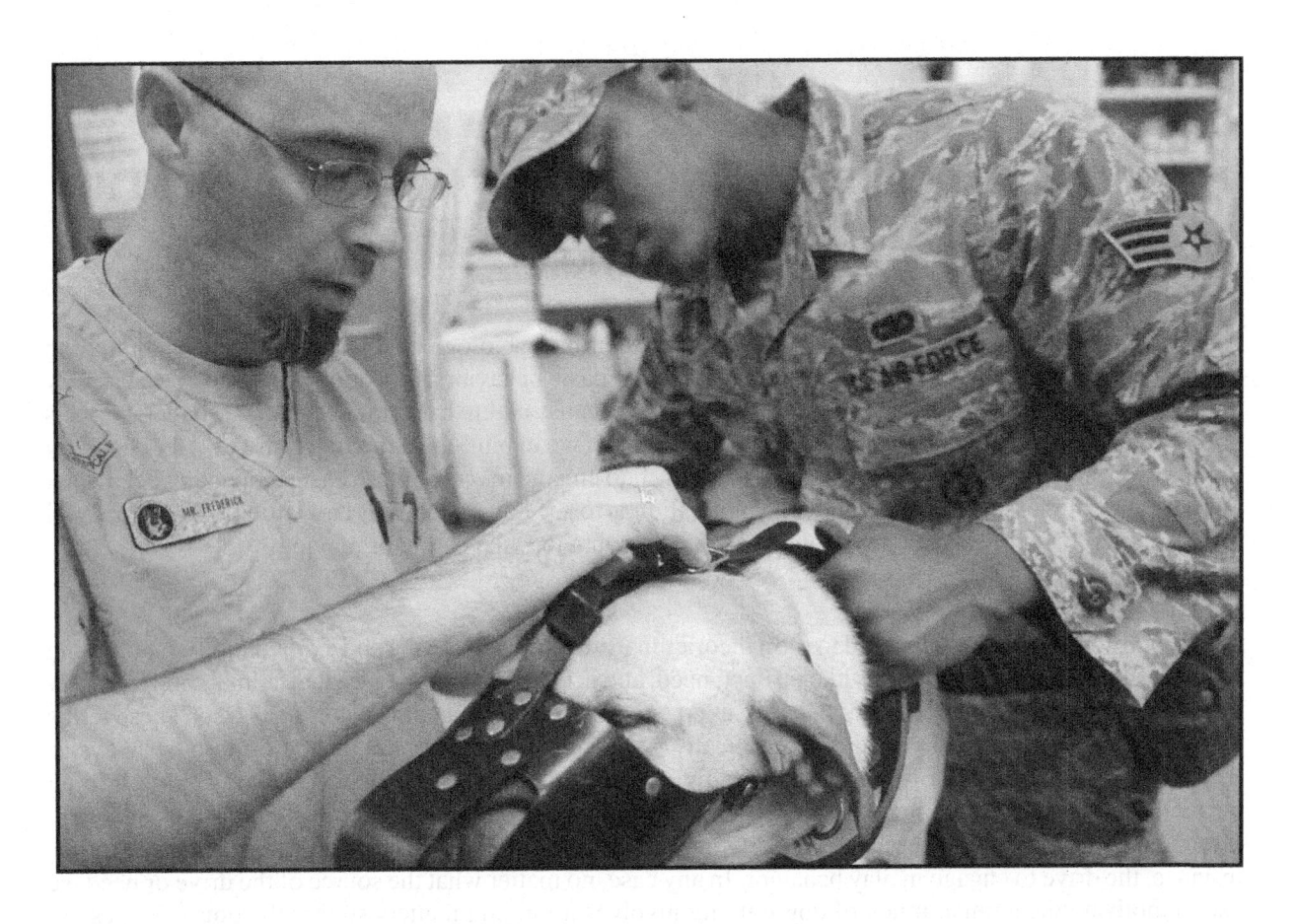

Mr. Rufus Fredrick and Senior Airman Tommy Carter conduct a weekly checkup on a military working dog at Lackland Air Force Base, Texas, recently. To reassure all military working dogs are in proper health, each dog is given a weekly checkup. (U.S. Air Force photo/Senior Airman Christopher Griffin)

CHAPTER 2

PRINCIPLES OF CONDITIONING AND BEHAVIOR MODIFICATION

MOTIVATION

Animals respond to the environment in order to fulfill their basic biological objectives, such as maintaining life and reproducing themselves. Animals do not perform basic behaviors like eating and mating because they feel the desire to maintain life or reproduce—they do so because nature has arranged matters so that it—feels good to engage in these behaviors. When we train animals, we exploit the animal's desire to—feel good by requiring the animal to do as we wish before we allow it to engage in one of these basic motivating behaviors. Our best way of measuring the strength of a motivation is to see how much effort and trouble an animal will go to in order to get the chance to engage in a specific behavior, like eating or playing.

Needs and Drives

Behavioral scientists have long tried to form theories that adequately describe and explain motivation. Along the way, they have employed terms like instinct, need, and drive to express the idea that animals preferentially engage in certain kinds of behavior, and even exert enormous effort to get the chance to do so. These terms are no longer considered to be valid, scientifically speaking, and science has moved on to other ways of dealing with motivation. However, it is perfectly adequate to speak of needs or drives when describing behavior for the purposes of dog training. Needs range from those that are clearly physiological, like thirst, to those that are a puzzle to us because they do not seem to fulfill any immediate biological requirement for instance, the drive to engage in play behavior. In any case, no matter what the source of the drive or need we use to motivate the animal, much of dog training involves arranging matters so that the dog's desires are gratified when it behaves in desirable ways. However, before expecting the animal to learn and work, the handler must ensure the dog's primary needs are adequately met. The dog must be healthy and happy and feel an emotional bond with its trainer. The dog's needs and drives include the following:

Primary Drives

We will use the expression—primary drives to refer to the motivations for those behaviors that function to prevent physiological or physical injuries.

1. **Oxygen.** Breathing is perhaps the dog's most immediate need. Exercise or excitement creates an increased oxygen requirement, which causes panting. Note that heavy panting may hinder the dog's olfactory ability. In addition, keep in mind that a dog that is panting heavily may be overheated and/or physically exhausted, and is not in a physiological state that is conducive to learning. Therefore, the trainer should avoid working on new lessons or problem behaviors when the dog is fatigued.
2. **Water.** The trainer must provide adequate quantities of water to prevent thirst from interfering with learning or task performance. Do not use water as a reward in dog training.
3. **Food.** The trainer must supply adequate quantities of food to prevent hunger from interfering with task performance. You may use food as a reward. The majority of dogs have sufficient appetite so that they will work strenuously for extra food rewards, particularly when these rewards are highly palatable—treat foods. Food deprivation is not required. Intense physical exertion, particularly in hot conditions, should be avoided when the dog has recently eaten.
4. **Pain avoidance.** A dog will avoid objects and actions that it has learned to associate with pain or

discomfort, and this behavior is frequently exploited by dog trainers. The use of a physical correction, however, does not necessarily teach a dog the correct response to any specific cue. The trainer cannot assume the dog knows what he did wrong. In addition, natural defensive responses to corrections may often interfere with the target behavior unless the dog already understands the desired response (e.g. pulling downwards on the choke collar to try to make the dog lie down may simply result in teaching the dog to brace its forelegs and strain upwards, unless the dog has previously learned how to lie down to earn a reward, and then learned to turn off collar pressure by lying down). The dog must know the correct response before the handler can use training that depends upon the dog's desire to avoid discomfort.

Secondary Drives

In addition to the primary needs like food and pain avoidance, the dog has other behaviors that can be exploited by providing the trainer with ways to reinforce and reward its behavior.

1. **Socialization.** Dog trainers sometimes speak of the dog's desire to socialize as the pack drive. The handler must keep in mind that one of the dog's strong drives is to enjoy a stable social relationship with one or more other beings, to belong to someone. A predictable and stable relationship in which the dog trusts (and has affection for) his handler is the basis of any effective system of training. This relationship does not form instantly—the handler must take the time and trouble to foster it. A period of socialization ("rapport-building") between dog and handler is required to establish this social relationship, and to render verbal and physical praise from the handler rewarding to the dog.

    a. **Dominant or "Alpha" Socialization.** In most cases, a dominant dog will strive to achieve rank in a pack or social group. This behavior is a normal part of the character of many working dogs. To work effectively with a highly dominant dog, the handler must gain the initiative in the relationship. However, this is not done simply by showing the dog who is boss. Attempts to physically punish a dominant dog into cooperative behavior normally only results in handler aggression and the dog and handler becoming suspicious of one another.

    b. **Subdominant or "Beta" Socialization.** A subdominant dog is driven to behave in affiliative ways that will establish its belonging in the pack. These affiliative responses are called submissive behavior. However, keep in mind that a dog's social rank or dominance with respect to its handler is not an index to its quality, even as a controlled aggression dog. Many strong patrol dogs are compliant and submissive with their handlers but are capable of very strong aggression towards outsiders when commanded. A submissive dog will often exhibit what is called willingness or eagerness to please. This behavior can greatly facilitate the dog's training if the handler has established a positive rapport with the animal. Especially in the case of a submissive dog, excessive corrections and compulsion, whether verbal or physical, can degrade rapport and decrease the dog team's proficiency in training and deployment.

    c. **Play socialization.** Play is difficult to define precisely, and although scientists argue about what its purpose is, play is a distinct and identifiable behavior that occurs in a very wide range of animals. We may presume that it is one of the dog's needs, and there can be little doubt that carefree and happy play between dog and handler is a vital part of a healthy and productive training relationship.

2. **Prey.** Prey drive is an expression that refers to the dog's natural tendency to chase, bite, and carry an item the dog perceives as prey. This applies to things that would, in the natural world, constitute prey items for a dog (e.g. a rabbit), as well as artificial objects (e.g. a thrown ball) that are also capable of triggering the dog's impulse to engage in predatory behavior. Prey behavior has enormous importance for the training of MWDs because it provides the reinforcement for nearly all substance detection training, and it also contributes very importantly to controlled aggression training. Many dogs display elements of social play behavior while retrieving balls and toys, and balls and toys can be thought of as play facilitators in addition to surrogate prey objects.
3. **Aggression.** Even though there is not much evidence that animals have a need to behave aggressively, dog trainers still tend to speak of aggressive behavior as being based on one or more drives. There are many different types of aggression, including dominant, defensive, and pain-elicited aggression. Aggression plays a vital role in MWD training and utilization because it is the foundation of patrol work. In addition, because MWDs are selected for a moderate to high level of aggressiveness, a MWD handler must at all times be aware of his or her dog's potential for aggressive behavior. The MWD handler must handle his/her dog responsibly and with care to prevent injuries to him/herself, to the dog, to other dogs, and to bystanders and co-workers. The handler must also help to prevent the development of handler-aggressiveness in his/her dog by:
    a. Treating the animal compassionately, humanely and fairly.
    b. Avoiding a reliance on strict or overly compulsive methods for training.
    c. Ensuring at all times that the dog clearly understands how to perform the desired skills.
    d. Renouncing emotionality—When you get angry and frustrated with your dog, put him/her up and think the situation over!

LEARNING AND CONDITIONING

Learning is a permanent change in the behavior of an organism as a result of interaction with the environment. This definition distinguishes learning-based behavior change from other short-term behavior changes such as sensitization, fatigue, and sensory adaptation. The terms learning and conditioning are synonymous. For the purpose of dog training, it is sufficient to discuss three types of learning—habituation, classical conditioning, and instrumental conditioning.

Habituation
Habituation is a gradual decrease in the strength of responsiveness to a stimulus as a result of repeated experience with that stimulus. Think of habituation as a mechanism by which organisms learn what to pay attention to and what to ignore. For instance, the first time a dog hears a door slam it may startle. In all likelihood, when it hears this slam again and again, it will gradually startle less and less until finally it exhibits very little response. This is adaptive because it allows the dog to save its energy and attention for more important events and stimuli, such as the noise of the lid coming off of the dogfood can. Habituation takes place continually during dog training, in ways that are both advantageous and disadvantageous to the dog trainer.

Advantageous Habituation
Dogs are normally to some extent frightened of, or interested in, things that are new to them. However, MWDs are expected to carry out their duties in environments that feature very distracting and sometimes intense stimuli, such as taxiing airplanes and marching formations of personnel. Through habituation a working dog can learn to respond minimally to irrelevant stimuli and pay attention to his/her—job.

Procedures for Advantageous Habituation

Habituation proceeds most effectively and rapidly with stimuli that are mild or moderate in intensity. (In fact, if a fearful dog is exposed repeatedly to a very intense stimulation, such as a running helicopter engine at close range, the animal is likely to respond more intensely to this stimulus over time instead of less intensely). Habituation is most efficient when the stimulus exposures and training sessions are distributed or well-separated in time. For example, a dog can learn more easily to stop being startled by gunshots when the gunshots are spaced out at intervals of 15 or 20 seconds, and when the training sessions are separated by 24 hours. The opposite procedure, exposing the dog to rapid series of gunshots several times a day, may lead to increased fear of the noise. When habituation is conducted with mild stimuli on a distributed basis, undesirable responses such as fear tend to disappear more or less permanently.

Hierarchies of Intensity

Sometimes the trainer needs to cause a decrease in undesirable responding (i.e. fear) to a very intense stimulus, such as gunshots or jet engines, yet repeated exposure to these stimuli at full-strength is likely to produce even more undesirable responding. In order to cause habituation to these intense stimuli, it is necessary to modify them so that they become milder. A practical way to decrease the intensity of noise stimuli is by exposing the dog to them at a great distance. For instance, once the dog exhibits little fear to a jet engine at 500 yards, then the animal can be brought a little closer, and so on. The scale of noise intensity, ranging from very mild to very intense, is called a hierarchy. By introducing the dog to the stimulus at a level of intensity that is so low that it provokes very little or no fear responding, and by moving very slowly and gradually from one stage on the hierarchy of intensity to the next, the trainer may be able to teach his/her dog to eventually exhibit little fear in the presence of even very intense stimuli.

Counter Conditioning

Habituation processes can be made more powerful by exploiting another stimulus (e.g food or ball) to offset the behavioral reaction (fear) caused by the stimulus we want the dog to be less sensitive to (e.g. jet engine). If we are far enough—down the hierarchy—far enough away from the jet engine—the dog will become oblivious to the noise and intent on eating or playing. The pleasant emotional reactions to the food or ball will counter condition the jet engine, reducing the fear response to it. However, if we are too far-up the hierarchy—too close to the frightening jet engine—we will instead find that the jet engine will counter condition the food or ball, reducing the dog's pleasurable response to these motivators. Note: Counter conditioning is actually a form of classical conditioning, but it is introduced here for the sake of clarity.

Spontaneous Recovery

Fear responses, especially, are very durable and persistent. They tend to re-emerge even after extensive training. In fact, because habituation includes certain short-term processes that wear off after a few minutes or hours, it is normal for a habituated response to re-appear to some extent between training sessions. Thus, a dog may exhibit no fear of a stimulus by the end of one day's training session yet show recovered fear at the beginning of the next day's session.

Disadvantageous Habituation

In some circumstances, effective performance in a working dog also depends upon a certain level of interest in, and responsiveness to, environmental stimuli and routines. A dog that is relatively new to detection work, or obedience, or patrol training, may deliver very animated and lively performance because it is still stimulated and excited by these situations. The disinterested and inefficient performance that a dog handler often describes by saying my dog is bored with the work may be the result of habituation to training and deployment scenarios. This is disadvantageous habituation. To some extent, we can retard and offset disadvantageous habituation by changing the training scenarios constantly and offering the MWD as much variety in its daily work as possible (in addition to effective and timely positive reinforcement).

CLASSICAL CONDITIONING

In this form of learning (also called Pavlovian conditioning) the dog learns that there is a relationship between two events, or stimuli. One of these stimuli is a neutral or unimportant stimulus like the ringing of a bell – something that a dog would normally pay little attention to. This stimulus is called the Conditioned Stimulus, or CS, because it can generate strong behavior only as a result of conditioning. The other stimulus is a biologically important stimulus that a dog naturally pays a lot of attention to—like food. This stimulus is called the Unconditioned Stimulus, or US, because it can generate strong behavioral responses without any conditioning. Thus, a dog normally responds to the ringing of a small bell by merely perking its ears or looking towards the noise. However, a piece of food can cause the dog to show a great deal of strong behavior like excitement, salivation, digging and pawing, chewing, and eating. This very strong behavior caused by exposure to a US like food is called the Unconditioned Response, or UR. Through classical conditioning, the CS and the US become associated in the dog's mind, so that the behavior that is naturally triggered by the US (the UR) comes to be triggered by the CS also. When a CS develops the ability to trigger behavior that is normally caused by a US, this learned response is called the conditioned response, or CR. In the classical example, the Russian scientist Ivan Pavlov taught dogs to salivate in response to the ringing of a bell. Pavlov did this by repeatedly pairing the bell (CS) and the food (US), presenting them close together in time. Eventually the dog learned that the bell predicted food, and then it began to salivate when he heard the bell (CR).

Figure 1. Before conditioning

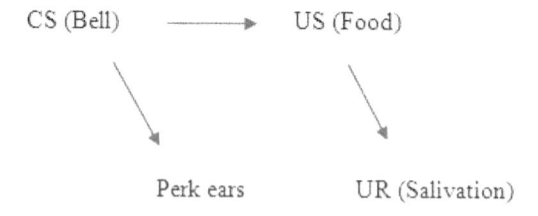

CS (Bell) ⟶ US (Food)
     ↓   ↓
 Perk ears   UR (Salivation)

Figure 2. After conditioning

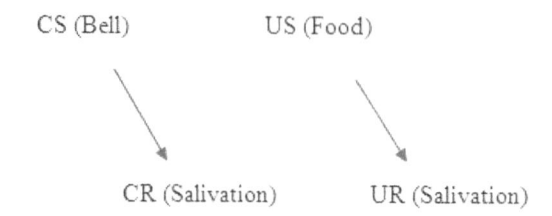

CS (Bell)   US (Food)
     ↓   ↓
CR (Salivation) UR (Salivation)

Classical Conditioning Procedures

Normally, the most effective way to condition a CS, to associate it with a biologically potent US, is to present the CS and then follow it very quickly (within a second or less) with the US. Thus, if the handler wishes to train his/her dog to feel startled and anxious in response to the word — No! then an effective method would be to wait until the dog engages in some misbehavior like sniffing the trash. The handler would then give the

— No! cue and throw a chain choke collar into the side of the trashcan so that it makes an unpleasant sound about ½ second after the — No! Originally the word — No! (CS) will mean little to the dog and produce little change in behavior. The unpleasant noise (US) will be potent and cause a strong startle or freezing response (UR). Pairing the No! with the unpleasant noise will condition startling to — No! (CR) within a very few CS-US pairings. Then, when the dog is engaged in misbehavior, the handler can use the — No! command, the dog will freeze or startle (which serves to interrupt the undesirable activity), and the handler can then call the dog to him/her and praise it. The dog will soon learn to shy away from behaviors and objects when he/she hears the — No! command (classical conditioning) and return to his/her handler for praise (instrumental conditioning).

Backward Conditioning

When the CS and the US are reversed, so that the US actually occurs before the CS, this is called a backward conditioning procedure. Little or no learning takes place during backward conditioning. Thus, in the above example, if you first startled the dog with a loud noise and then said — No! you would find that you could do this many times and still the dog would not show a startle response when — No! was given by itself.

Importance of Classical Conditioning

Very little of working dog training involves the deliberate creation of classically conditioned associations, like the above example. Most of the action in dog training has to do with the use of reinforcers and punishers in instrumental conditioning. However, it is still very important to understand classical conditioning processes because they underlie almost everything that takes place in dog training. Classically conditioned associations help the trainer and contribute positively to training in countless ways. For instance, if a handler makes an announcement (— This is SSGT Smith of the ....) prior to sending his/her Patrol MWD into a building to search for and find a hidden agitator, the dog will associate the sound of the announcement (CS) with the aggressive cues and behaviors that it experiences shortly thereafter (US) when it finds the agitator and bites. It will begin to exhibit aggressive responses to its handler's announcement—excitement and barking (CR)—that help to prepare it for the search and the bite. However, classically conditioned associations may also interfere with training. For instance, if the handler decides that his/her dog sits too slowly in response to the command, he/she may decide to hasten the sit by applying physical force. The handler gives the command — Sit! in a loud voice, watches for a moment to see if the dog is sitting, and then gives a strong jerk upwards on the choke chain. The handler intends to demonstrate to the dog the consequence of sitting slowly, but unwittingly he/she actually constructs a very effective classical conditioning trial — Sit! is immediately followed by a sharp jerk on the collar. Soon — Sit! develops the power to trigger responses that are normally only triggered by a sharp collar correction. These responses can range from pain-elicited aggression and biting to avoidance and cowering. More commonly, they involve anxiety and a reflexive stiffening of the body's muscles to defend against the sharp jerk on the collar. Thus, although the handler intends to speed the sit up, he/she is actually teaching the dog to respond to the — Sit! command with anxiety and stiffening. The physical stiffening hinders the dog's ability to sit quickly, with the result that it receives yet another jerk on the neck, which makes it even more anxious and stiff when it hears — Sit! and so on.

Extinction of Classically Conditioned Behavior

In order to make a classically conditioned behavior disappear, what we must do is present the CS repeatedly over and over again without pairing it with the US. The CR will gradually decrease in strength until it disappears. This procedure is called extinction. It is just like habituation procedures, except in habituation we are getting rid of an unlearned response, whereas in extinction we are getting rid of a learned response. Keep in mind that, just because a learned behavior has been extinguished, this does not mean that it has been unlearned or erased. There is much evidence that learning causes permanent changes in the brain that are not reversed by extinction.

Four-year-old Gina plays during her off-duty hours July 21, 2010, at the dog kennel at Peterson Air Force Base, CO. Gina served her first tour in Southwest Asia and suffered from post-traumatic stress disorder. Gina is a 21st Security Forces Squadron military working dog. (U.S. Air Force photo/Monica Mendoza)

INSTRUMENTAL CONDITIONING

Instrumental conditioning and operant conditioning mean almost the same thing, except that instrumental conditioning is a slightly more general and flexible term. Instrumental conditioning refers to the way that rewards and punishments change the strength, or probability of occurrence, of prior behavior. Another way to put this is to say that behavior is modified by its consequences. Thus, if a dog engages in a particular behavior such as investigating an odor, and then he encounters food, the odor-investigation behavior will be more likely to occur again in the future, and/or stronger when it does occur. This is an example of reinforcement. On the other hand, if a dog investigates an odor, and then he receives a jerk on the collar from his/her handler, the odor-investigation behavior will be less likely to occur in the future, and/or weaker when it does occur. This is an example of punishment.

Distinction Between Classical Conditioning and Instrumental Conditioning

For the purposes of dog training, it is adequate to think of classical and instrumental conditioning as separate processes that can be distinguished from one another in the following ways: Classical conditioning involves learning that there is a relationship between two environmental events, or stimuli, such as the ring of a bell and food, or the command — No! and an unpleasant event. Instrumental conditioning mainly involves the animal learning that there is a relationship between its own behavior and some stimulus, such as the act of sitting and praise from the handler, or the act of searching for odor and a ball. Classical conditioning affects mainly what are called autonomic responses; things like reflexes and feelings and emotions that are not under the dog's voluntary control. Instrumental conditioning affects mainly what are called skeletal responses; behaviors like sitting, running, standing, and biting that are under the dog's voluntary control.

Figure 3. Classical conditioning

Stimulus/CS (Bell) _____Association_____ Stimulus/US (Food)
CR—Salivation (involuntary behavior)

Figure 4. Instrumental conditioning

Response (Sit) _____Association_____ Stimulus/Consequence (Food)
Instrumental response--- Sit (voluntary behavior)

Response Contingency

Contingency is a term that refers to a relationship between two occurrences. When we say that one event is contingent on another that means that one event will not occur unless the other occurs. In instrumental conditioning there is a contingency between a particular behavior, or response, and a stimulus. Thus, a handler will not give his/her dog food unless the animal first sits. The relationship between sitting and food in this example is called a positive response contingency. This is a final and very important distinction between classical and instrumental conditioning—in classical conditioning there is no response contingency. Pavlov did not ring the bell and wait for the dog to salivate before rewarding the animal with food, he merely rang the bell and then presented food, regardless of what the dog did.

Positive Response Contingency

This is a relationship between a response/behavior and a specified event such that if the behavior occurs it will be followed by the event. For instance, if the dog sits, his/her handler will give it food. On the other hand, if the dog tries to bite another dog, his/her handler will give it a jerk on the leash. Even though this last example does not sound positive because it is not pleasant for the dog, it is still a positive response contingency. In the language of learning, positive is not used to refer to pleasantness. It is used to say that one thing will happen provided that another happens first.

Negative Response Contingency

A relationship between a behavior and specified event such that if the behavior occurs it will NOT be followed by the event. For instance, if the dog sits, his/her handler will not give him/her a jerk on the leash. Similarly, if the dog fails to find a hidden training aid, its handler will not allow it to have the ball. Although this last example does not sound negative because it does not involve anything unpleasant happening to the dog, it is still referred to as a negative response contingency. In the language of learning, negative is not used to refer to unpleasantness. It is used to say that one thing will not happen if another happens first.

Consequence

A consequence is an event that happens to the dog after it performs some instrumental behavior. There are two main categories of consequence (reinforcement and punishment). When we combine these two types of consequence with the two types of response contingency (positive and negative), we get four possible consequences that can result from any instrumental behavior—positive and negative reinforcement, and positive and negative punishment.

Reinforcement

A reinforcer is an event that encourages or strengthens prior behavior. Examples of reinforcers are food, access to a toy, or a pat on the head. Any of these, when given to the dog after it sits, tends to strengthen sitting behavior. Food, toys, and pats on the head are reinforcing because they are pleasant. However, unpleasant events can also act as reinforcers. The handler can reinforce a behavior with an unpleasant event like a jerk on the leash by withholding the jerk when the dog sits. In this example, there is a negative response contingency between sitting behavior and a jerk on the collar—if the dog sits, there will be no jerk. Although the jerk itself is unpleasant, the absence of the jerk is a satisfying state of affairs and will, under proper circumstances, serve to reinforce sitting behavior.

1. **Positive reinforcement or reward.** Positive reinforcement is the use of intrinsically pleasant stimuli like food, toys, and pats on the head to strengthen and encourage prior behavior. The word positive does not refer to the goodness or pleasantness of the stimuli, it instead refers to the positive response contingency between a target behavior (like sitting) and the reinforcing event—if the dog sits, he/she will be given food, toy, or a pat on the head. Positive reinforcement is synonymous with reward.
2. **Negative reinforcement.** Negative reinforcement is the strengthening of behavior by using the withholding or withdrawal of intrinsically unpleasant events like jerks on the collar. The word negative does not refer to the badness or unpleasantness of these stimuli, instead it refers to the negative response contingency between a target behavior (like sitting) and some event—if the dog sits, he/she will NOT be given a jerk on the collar.

Punishment

A punishment is an event that discourages or weakens prior behavior. Examples of punishers are jerks on the collar (collar corrections) or a bump on the nose. Either of these, when administered to a dog after he misbehaves by, for example, departing from the down-stay position without permission, will tend to weaken down-stay breaking behavior. Collar corrections and bumps on the nose are punishing because they are unpleasant. However, pleasant events can also act as punishers. The handler can punish an undesirable behavior by withholding or taking away a pleasant stimulus like praise and petting. Thus, if the dog tends to jump up on his handler when he/she is excited, seeking attention, this behavior can be punished by withholding praise and attention. In this example, there is a negative response contingency between jumping-up behavior and praise and petting—if the dog jumps up, he/she will not receive praise or petting. Although the praise and petting are themselves pleasant, their absence is an unsatisfying state of affairs and will, under the proper circumstances, serve to punish jumping-up behavior.

1. **Positive punishment or punishment.** Positive punishment is the use of intrinsically unpleasant stimuli like collar corrections to discourage or weaken behavior. The word positive does not refer to the pleasantness or unpleasantness of the stimuli, it instead refers to the positive response contingency between a target behavior (like breaking the down-stay) and the punishing event—if the dog breaks the stay, he/she will be given a collar correction. To simplify, we can use the simpler term punishment in place of positive punishment.

2. **Negative punishment, or omission.** Negative punishment is the weakening or discouragement of prior behavior by withholding pleasant events like food or praise and petting. The word negative does

not refer to the pleasantness or unpleasantness of these stimuli, instead it refers to the nature of the negative response contingency between a target behavior (like jumping up) and an event—if the dog jumps up, he/she will NOT be given praise and petting. To simplify, we can use the expression omission to refer to negative punishment.

Contingency Square

The contingency square is a table that graphically depicts the relationships between reinforcement and punishment (i.e. the effect the instrumental procedure has on behavior) and the nature of the response contingency (positive and negative—the handler gives something to the dog or the handler withholds something from the dog). Memorizing the table will help the trainer remember each of the four possible consequences of an instrumental behavior, and their definitions. For example, take negative reinforcement, normally the most difficult of the consequences for trainers to understand. The key is to take each of the words of the term negative reinforcement and analyze it separately in order to understand whether the consequence involves pleasant or unpleasant events for the dog. Negative means a negative response contingency—the handler will withhold something or take something away if the dog performs a target behavior. Reinforcement means that the outcome will be to encourage or strengthen the target behavior. What must I withhold or withdraw from a dog in order to encourage prior behavior? An unpleasant event. Therefore, to use negative reinforcement means to encourage a dog's behavior by removing or withholding from the animal something that it does not like. For instance, we can reinforce a dog for dropping a ball by releasing pressure exerted on his neck with a choke chain. Reward and omission DO NOT involve the use of force or discomfort to modify the dog's behavior. Negative reinforcement and punishment DO involve the use of force or discomfort to modify the dog's behavior.

Table 1. Nature of the response contingency

INDUCIVE	COMPULSION
POSITIVE (WITH) REINFORCEMENT Use of pleasant stimuli, such as food, toys, and petting	*POSITIVE (WITH) PUNISHMENT* Use of unpleasant stimuli, such as a collar correction
NEGATIVE (WITHOUT) PUNISHMENT Withholding or absence of pleasant events, such as food or praise	*NEGATIVE (WITHOUT) REINFORCEMENT* Reinforcement of behavior by withholding compulsion

Compulsive Training

"Compulsion" is a word that refers to forcing or coercing people or animals to do things. In compulsive dog training, the handler relies on unpleasant events to obtain desired behavior from the dog. Thus, compulsive training involves the use of negative reinforcement (encouraging desirable behavior by withdrawing or withholding unpleasant stimuli) and punishment (discouraging undesirable behavior by administering unpleasant stimuli). Although the training of working dogs often involves the use of some compulsive methods, it is important to understand that:
1. These methods are effective and humane only under certain circumstances—when the dog is well-prepared and already understands the desired response and how to avoid compulsion.
2. Excessive reliance on compulsion will damage the dog's rapport with his handler and cause it to dislike and avoid work.
3. Compulsion may stimulate defensive and aggressive responses in the dog and can in many circumstances be counterproductive and even dangerous for the handler.
4. Some phases of working dog training, most especially the detection phase, are incompatible with compulsive techniques.

Inducive Training
Inducive training is the opposite of compulsive training. The root word induce means to gently persuade. In inducive training the handler relies on the use of pleasant events and stimuli to obtain desirable behavior from the dog. Thus, inducive training involves the use of reward (encouraging desirable behavior by administering positive reinforcement) and omission (discouraging undesirable behavior by withholding or withdrawing positive reinforcement).

Primary and Secondary Reinforcement and Punishment
Many rewards and punishments are stimuli that are biologically powerful, such as food or pain. In the language of classical conditioning, they are called unconditioned stimuli (US's). In the language of instrumental conditioning, they are called primary reinforcers or primary punishers. Dogs respond readily and strongly to these stimuli without having to be taught to do so. However, some rewards and punishments are things, such as the words —Good! and —No! that originally have little effect on a dog's behavior. These are called secondary reinforcers and punishers because they do not become effective until they have been associated with primary reinforcers or punishers.

Secondary Reinforcers
Secondary reinforcers gain their pleasant value by being associated with primary reinforcers. For instance, puppies probably do not instinctively enjoy being spoken to. They learn to like being spoken to in a happy voice because this voice is associated (through classical conditioning) with physical petting and with the presentation of food. After enough of this conditioning, words like —Good! spoken in a happy voice become pleasant stimuli. Subsequently, the word —Good! has the power to reinforce prior behavior (if the handler says —Good! immediately after the dog executes the behavior).

Secondary Punishers
Secondary punishers gain their unpleasant value by being associated with primary punishers. For instance, the word —No! means nothing to an untrained dog. The word becomes unpleasant because it is associated (through classical conditioning) with unpleasant primary punishing events like a jerk on the collar. After enough of this conditioning, the command —No! spoken in a stern voice becomes an unpleasant stimulus. Subsequently, the word —No! has the power to punish prior behavior (if the handler says —No! immediately after the dog executes the behavior).

DISCRIMINATIVE STIMULI

Thus far in our discussion of instrumental conditioning we have described only the contingent relationship between a target behavior and a reinforcer or a punisher (e.g. sit-food or jump up —No!). However, in order to behave appropriately in training, the dog must know when these contingent relations are actually in force. The handler will not reward a sit anytime the dog sits, but only when he/she desires the dog to sit. The way he/she signals to the dog that he/she wants it to sit is with the command —Sit! This command tells the dog that now one or more response contingencies are in force—for instance, a prompt sit will result in petting and praise and the omission of a collar correction, while refusing to sit will result in no petting or praise and the administration of a collar correction. Thus, our full model for the use of instrumental conditioning can be symbolized as follows: Stimulus–Discriminative–Response–Consequence, or SD-R-C. SD is the command (—Sit!), while R is the dog's response (sitting or refusing to do so), and C is the consequence of the dog's behavior (reward, negative reinforcement, punishment, or omission—food, petting and praise, collar corrections, etc). This three-term model shows that the dog must actually learn at least two associations for any command skill—one between the behavior and the consequence, and one between the command and the behavior. In some types of animal training, these two associations are taught separately. For instance, first a killer whale is taught to jump for reinforcement, and then he/she is taught that the jump-reinforcement contingency is in force only after the trainer issues a command. If the whale jumps at any other time, no reinforcement will be forthcoming. However, in dog training both associations are normally taught simultaneously because the handler always includes the command in lessons.

INDUCIVE VERSUS COMPULSIVE TRAINING

Some compulsion is normally necessary in working dog training, especially in the controlled aggression phase. However, inducive methods are to be preferred whenever practical. In particular, inducive methods are most advantageous for the initial teaching of any skill. That is, to an untrained dog the SD/command (e.g. —Sit!) means nothing. Therefore, if the handler gives the command —Sit! and then administers a strong collar correction in the attempt to force the dog to sit, the dog will have no idea that it can avoid further unpleasantness by sitting. It will instead attempt to defend itself or avoid its handler. (More than anything else, such a method is a perfectly designed classical conditioning procedure that will condition fear and/or aggression to the command —Sit! by pairing the command closely together in time with physical discomfort.) However, if we first teach the dog to sit on command using inducive methods, and ensure that it understands what sit means and that it has learned to enjoy training, then we may constructively use compulsion to hasten the dog's sit or to teach it to sit even in distracting circumstances. Thus, the proper role of inducive training is to teach the dog skills, while the proper role of compulsive training is to enforce the performance of these skills (if necessary). In addition, another very important role for inducive techniques is during the early stages of handling any dog, even a well-trained dog. The optimal way for a handler to build rapport and a good working relationship with a new dog is to perform inducive training exercises with the animal (e.g. food-rewarded sits), even if the dog already knows these exercises, and avoid the use of physical compulsion.

APPLICATION OF INDUCIVE TRAINING

In inducive training, the handler employs gentle means to lead a dog to perform some target behavior, and then he/she reinforces this behavior. In the event that the dog does not execute the desired behavior, or executes it incorrectly, then the handler will omit reinforcement (negative punishment/omission). In the classical example, the handler teaches a dog to sit by drawing the dog's attention to a piece of food in his/her hand. Once the dog places its muzzle in contact with the handler's fist in the attempt to take the food, the handler then slowly raises his/her hand and moves it slightly backwards towards the dog's tail, simultaneously giving the command —Sit! In following the movement with its head, the dog is very likely to sit. The handler then opens his/her hand to feed the dog and administers praise. If the dog fails to sit, the handler withholds reinforcement and praise (omission) and continues attempting to finesse the sit. In such a stress-free setting, a dog can learn very rapidly to sit on command. In addition, it also learns to enjoy work, and it develops affection and trust for its handler. There are similar methods for teaching almost all of the exercises of obedience.

Successive Approximation and Shaping

Successive approximation is a practice in which animals are taught behaviors by rewarding responses that are progressively more and more like the desired target response. For instance, to teach a dog to sit through successive approximation, a handler would wait until he/she observed a tiny approximation of a sit on the dog's part, such as flexing of the hind legs, and then reinforce this movement. Once the dog was flexing its legs readily for reinforcement, then the handler would withhold reinforcement until the animal exhibited a flexing that was slightly greater than before, that approximated a little more closely an actual sit, and then he/she would reward this behavior, and so on. The entire process of extracting a trained response through successive approximation is called behavior shaping. Successive approximation and shaping are of vital importance in the training of exotic animals such as killer whales and sea lions, but they play comparatively little role in dog training, for the simple reason that a good dog trainer can usually think of a way to get the dog to offer the complete behavior, and then reward that, as described in relation to the sit above. However, particularly in the case of very complex or difficult behaviors, or behaviors for which the dog is handicapped or contra-prepared (i.e. when a dog has a history of problems with a particular exercise), it is very important to realize that often a good handler will reinforce his/her dog for a good effort in the direction of the desired target behavior. This will encourage the animal and lead it to continue trying to learn the lesson.

Otto, a Belgian Malinois, takes a quick break with his handler, Staff Sgt. Eric Morales, 100th Security Forces Squadron, after sniffing around the base passenger terminal Jan. 22, 2010, at Royal Air Force Mildenhall, England. (U.S. Air Force photo/Staff Sgt. Austin M. May)

Reward Schedules

A reward schedule is a rule that dictates how often a dog will receive positive reinforcement when it correctly executes a skill. It is very important to understand these schedules, because they produce different effects and are appropriate at different stages of the training of each skill. There are six types of reward schedule we should consider:

Extinction Schedule

To extinguish an instrumental response, we merely allow the behavior to occur again and again, without rewarding it. The behavior will gradually decrease in strength and frequency until it disappears. Thus, to extinguish an undesirable behavior like jumping-up, it is often sufficient to identify the reward for the behavior (it is usually some reaction given by the handler when the dog jumps up) and then make sure that this reward never follows the problem behavior. This is called—putting jumping-up on an extinction schedule. It is important to realize that some behaviors are intrinsically reinforcing—that is, just doing them is rewarding to the dog. If a behavior is intrinsically reinforcing, it will not extinguish even though we put it on an extinction schedule. Thus, if an anxious dog finds a way to release tension by barking in its kennel, it may not ever stop barking in the kennel, even if its handler is careful to never go to it when it is barking.

Continuous Reward Schedule (CRS)

Positive reinforcement is given immediately when the dog makes a correct (or sometimes a near-correct) response. Assisting the dog to assume the desired position or behavior is permissible (i.e. in the case of the sit, gentle pressure on the rump to encourage the animal to sit), but it is preferable to finesse the dog into the sit by baiting it with food or some similar technique. Inducing the animal to perform the desired behavior independently and then reinforcing the behavior will produce more rapid learning than pushing the animal into position and then rewarding it for allowing this to happen. CRS is the most effective reinforcement schedule for teaching a dog a skill.

Fixed Ratio Reward Schedule (FRRS)

Positive reinforcement is given to the dog after it makes two or more correct responses. It is most useful to think in terms of ratio schedules of reinforcement in the case of behaviors that are episodic like barks and scratches. To start a dog on the FRRS schedule, every second response is rewarded. When the dog consistently makes two responses to obtain a reward, require three responses. By increasing the number of responses, one at a time, and allowing the dog to perform at each level with 100% proficiency, you can work up to a high FRRS. If the proficiency falls below 100%, then decrease the number of responses required to obtain a reward until the dog recovers its proficiency. Then proceed as before, adding one response at a time. A fixed ratio reward schedule is the way that a handler can best train his/her dog to, for instance, bark or scratch repeatedly at a door to indicate the presence of an agitator in a building. Initially, while we are trying to teach the behavior, the handler will open the door and allow the dog to bite (reward) after one bark or scratch, then he/she will require two barks or scratches before rewarding the dog, then three, and so forth.

Variable Ratio Reward Schedule (VRRS)

Once the dog has learned to perform the maximum number of responses by this FRRS schedule, then use the VRRS. Select a range of responses (e.g. 5 to 10 correct responses) required and reward the dog on a random basis within this range (e.g. the dog has already learned to bark 15 times in order to obtain a bite on an FRRS). Now you should begin rewarding the animal somewhere between 5 and 10 barks--on a random basis, so that the dog never knows whether it will have to bark 5, 6, 7, 8, 9, or 10 times in order to get a bite. The dog will learn that it must correctly respond at least 5 times, and perhaps up to 10 times in order to obtain a desired reward.

Fixed Interval Reward Schedule (FIRS)

Reinforcement is given to the dog after he/she responds to a command for a given fixed period of time. It is most useful to think in terms of interval schedules of reinforcement in the case of behaviors that are continuous, such as staying in position, heeling, and searching. In initial training, select a short period. If the dog does not respond correctly, select a shorter period of time until the dog responds correctly to obtain a reward. As in the FRRS, add short periods of time (e.g. 5 seconds) to the interval and require the dog to attain 100% proficiency at each interval. If the dog fails to respond correctly for the required period of time, readjust the time requirement to a lower time requirement until the animal regains 100% accuracy, and then begin gradually again to increase the required interval. Excellent examples are staying in a position (like the down) and walking at heel. In each of these cases, a good trainer initially rewards the dog for just a few moments of good responding. With time and practice the handler gradually extends the period of time that the dog must remain in the down or walk at his/her handler's side. Gradual extension of the period of time a dog works before reinforcement plays a vitally important role in detection training. A good trainer arranges a search problem for a novice dog so that it can easily find the target odor and obtain reward in perhaps less than a minute, whereas he/she requires an advanced dog to work for 5 or 10 minutes or more prior to finding the target odor.

Variable Interval Reward Schedule (VIRS)
Once the dog has learned to perform a task for a period of time on a FIRS, use the VIRS. Select a time range (e.g. 1 to 2 minutes) and reward the dog on a random basis within this time period. For example, if the dog has already learned to hold a down-stay for 3 minutes on a FIRS, then begin rewarding it somewhere between 1 and 2 minutes on a random basis. The dog will learn that it must hold the down for at least 1 minute and perhaps for up to 2 minutes in order to obtain reward.

Application of Reward Schedules
Normally, in dog training it is not necessary to exactly follow the above steps to get good results. It is usually sufficient to follow these general rules: When teaching a dog to give an episodic response (e.g. bark) begin by rewarding it every time it barks (CRS), then reward it gradually for longer and longer sequences of barking, working your way up to the maximum number of barks that will be useful (FRRS). At any point that the dog shows hesitation or confusion, decrease the number of barks required so that the animal regains proficiency and then begin working back up again. Once the dog barks rapidly and confidently about the maximum number of times desired in order to obtain its reward, then begin giving it rewards randomly for some number of barks less than the maximum (VRRS). When teaching a dog to perform a continuous response (e.g. holding a down-stay), establish performance by rewarding it consistently after a very short period of time (FIRS). Then begin gradually extending the period of time that you require the dog to stay. Do not hesitate to decrease the duration requirement if the dog's performance deteriorates. Once the dog stays solidly for about the maximum desired period of time, then begin rewarding it randomly for stays of various durations less than the maximum (VIRS).

Advantage of variable reward schedules
You may ask —Why bother to use VRRS and VIRS schedules? Using FRRS and FIRS the animal has already learned to bark many times in succession or stay for several minutes. The reason is that variable schedules teach the dog to be persistent and stubborn in trying to obtain its reward through instrumental behavior. Many scientific studies have shown that variable reward schedules produce stronger and more persistent conditioned behavior than fixed schedules. The psychological basis of this persistence effect is well understood, but it is very complicated. So, a good simple way to think of the variable reinforcement phenomenon is this: when the dog never knows how many times or how long it will be required to perform before being rewarded, it loses track of how many and how long and just concentrates on performing persistently for reward, convinced that if it tries hard enough it will eventually get what it wants.

APPLICATION OF COMPULSIVE TRAINING

Just as it is important to understand certain basic principles (such as reward schedules) in order to perform effective inducive training, it is also important to understand certain basic principles in order to use compulsive training effectively.

Use of Positive Punishment
Positive punishment is used to teach a dog not to do something. Of course, this doesn't mean that the dog should do nothing, but that it should do something else, such as sit still. There are three major principles the trainer must understand in order to use punishment effectively and humanely:
1. The dog must have the ability to perform the alternative behavior. For instance, if a dog is breaking the down-stay because it is frightened of a jet engine, the dog's fear may render it unable to do what is necessary to avoid punishment. That is, if a trainer physically punishes a frightened dog for not staying, the punishment is likely to make the dog even more afraid and less capable of staying. This

is not fair nor humane nor effective dog training.
2. Do not ramp up corrections. That is, do not begin punishment by using a very soft correction, and then gradually increase it as needed. Dogs, especially very excited dogs' intent on working their way to a reward, adapt quickly to physical punishment and can learn in a short period of time to endure very uncomfortable events without altering their behavior. It is possible to, without meaning to, create a monster, a highly excited and stressed animal that can absorb enormous amounts of physical discomfort without changing its behavior into the desired path. Instead, begin punishment training with a correction of an intensity that is meaningful to that dog and sufficient to cause it to change its behavior immediately.
3. Do not use punishment if it is not working. That is, if you have tried to intervene with a problem behavior by using what you believe is a meaningful intensity of punishment for that dog, and the desired result is not achieved, think carefully before you apply stronger physical punishment. The dog may be, for any number of reasons, incapable of the alternative behavior. He/she may have a history of bad training that has rendered humane and reasonable levels of physical punishment ineffective. You may be making some errors in technique that are preventing a humane and reasonable level of punishment from having the desired effect. In any of these cases, it is inexcusable to continue to physically punish a dog.
4. Avoid emotion when administering punishment. If you are angry, or frustrated, or upset while administering punishment to a dog, you can be virtually certain that you are making mistakes and being unfair to the dog. Revenge and temper tantrums have absolutely no place in working dog training—you must not let training turn into a spectacle of one dumb animal hurting another.

Use of Negative Reinforcement

Negative reinforcement is the reinforcing of behavior by withholding compulsion. The classic example in military working dog training is the out, in which the dog releases an agitator on command. Although a clever handler uses whatever positive reinforcement he/she can to reward the dog for releasing cleanly (e.g. praise, immediate re-bite, etc.), the out is normally taught and maintained principally through the administration of negative reinforcement. Thus, if the dog releases cleanly on command, he will NOT be corrected with a jerk or pull on the choke collar. All of the principles stated above that apply to positive punishment apply to negative reinforcement as well. In addition, it is also vital to understand the following terms and definitions:

Escape Training

Escape is an initial stage of negative reinforcement training. During this stage, the command —Out! is meaningless. The dog does not yet understand that the command —Out! means that if it does not release it will receive a collar correction. On the first trial, when the handler gives the —Out! command and the dog continues biting, the handler then applies a collar correction until the dog releases the bite, praising the dog once it has released. In all likelihood one or several more trials will proceed much the same. Although the dog may not be releasing on command, it is learning all the same. During this stage the dog learns to expect the correction when it hears the command —Out!, and it also learns to turn off or terminate the correction once it is applied by releasing the bite. This escape learning is very important. A dog that does not know precisely how it can turn off compulsion will be stressed and upset by corrections and may engage in inappropriate behaviors to try and terminate discomfort, such as biting its handler. This point is especially important when the escape behavior, the behavior that we desire to teach the dog, involves a complex response like walking at heel or recalling to heel. If these exercises are taught using negative reinforcement, there must necessarily be a stage during which the handler teaches the dog to terminate collar corrections by placing itself at heel. If the animal does not know how to terminate compulsion by placing itself at heel, then collar corrections will only make it move more and more strongly away from its handler. In fact, this is why it is so important to patiently teach the dog as many skills as possible by means of positive reinforcement prior to polishing any of them with negative reinforcement—to make sure that the dog knows how to perform all behaviors on command. In this way the dog is well prepared to learn very quickly, with minimal stress or confusion, how to terminate compulsion by executing a commanded behavior.

Avoidance Training

Avoidance is the next stage of negative reinforcement training, during which the dog learns that, in addition to terminating compulsion by releasing the bite, it can also completely avoid compulsion. That is, if the dog releases the bite quickly on command, the collar correction will never occur. When avoidance is completely and cleanly taught, every time the dog releases on command, he/she is reinforced by the absence of the correction, as though he/she beat the rap. Note that sometimes the dog, especially if it has prior experience with the —Out! command, will go directly to avoidance (releasing on command) after only one correction, without a noticeable escape stage of learning.

Criterion Avoidance

The end goal of negative reinforcement training is to secure correct response to the command every time, without the need to use compulsion to escape the dog into the desired behavior. In working dog training, this goal has the additional dimension that the handler also is training towards the point at which he/she can discard the means of compulsion (i.e. collar and leash). That is, a dog that is fully trained to out not only releases cleanly on command, it also releases when the collar is not attached to the leash, and when the handler is 20 or 30 yards away. In these cases, the handler has given up his/her option to correct the dog effectively. If the animal fails to obey the command, the handler has no good options. This means that the handler must not discard the means of compulsion until the dog has achieved a good avoidance criterion— clean avoidance of compulsion by good response to command consistently and repeatedly over at least 4 or 5 training sessions. During these error-free training sessions the handler stands ready to correct the dog instantly, with all necessary things in place, but does not ever need to. On the other hand, if the dog still occasionally fails to respond correctly, testing to see if the handler is ready to apply the correction, then the dog has not yet achieved criterion avoidance and it is not yet ready to proceed further in training. The animal must continue to practice, with the handler standing by, ready to enforce obedience, until criterion avoidance is obtained.

Supporting Negative Reinforcement with Positive Reinforcement

Although behavior learned through negative reinforcement training can be very durable and reliable, it is advisable to, whenever possible, support negative reinforcement with positive reinforcement—give the dog rewards in addition to the reinforcement of not being corrected. For instance, after a clean, fast out from the agitator, you might praise your dog quickly and then immediately let it re-bite and take the sleeve away from the agitator. After the last out of the training session, after the agitator runs away, you can reward your dog for his good compliance by letting him bite and carry a section of rubber hose or some other toy.

GENERALIZATION OF CLASSICAL AND INSTRUMENTAL CONDITIONING

Generalization is a process in which behavior that is learned in response to one stimulus is expressed to some degree in response to another stimulus. Generalization takes place with both classically-conditioned and instrumentally-conditioned behaviors, and the more similarity there is between two stimuli, the more generalization there will be from one to the other. Thus, a dog that has learned a strong startle response to the —No! command may also startle and return to its handler when he/she says —Yo! loudly to a friend. A dog that has learned to sit in response to one explosive odor, such as ammonia dynamite, may also sit in response to a similar non-explosive odor, such as ammonia-based house-cleaning liquids. These are both examples of undesirable generalization, but generalization may also work in our favor. For instance, if you are incapacitated during a patrol deployment, but your well-trained dog also releases the bite in response to your partner's out command that is desirable generalization.

Context Generalization
Trained behaviors are not just controlled by CSs (classical) and SD's (instrumental). To some extent, they are also controlled by context. Context is the word psychologist's use to label all of the stimuli present in the conditioning situation other than the CSs and US's, the SD's and consequences. Context means the environment. Context definitely participates in learning, and generalization from one context to another is rarely perfect. As a result, a dog that has learned to search and detect in a warehouse may also do so when it is taken to an office building, but its search and/or detection behavior is liable to be substantially different in the office building. To a degree, much of dog training consists of teaching dog's skills, and then trying to make these trained behaviors as independent as possible of the context, so that the dog will perform correctly anytime and anywhere. The best way to make trained behavior independent of the context is to train in as many different places and situations as possible (after the initial learning phase).

LEARNING TRANSFER

Transfer of learning is what takes place when the learning of one skill or command affects the learning of another skill or command. Transfer can be positive (favorable) or negative (unfavorable).

Positive Transfer
In positive transfer of learning, the fact that the dog has already learned to do one thing actually helps it to learn to do another. Thus, learning to sit in response to the —Sit! command during obedience training transfers positively to detection training, helping the dog to learn to sit in response to odor. In fact, one of the main ingredients to good dog training is teaching each skill at such a time and in such a way that it helps the dog learn the next skill.

Negative Transfer
In negative transfer of learning, the fact that the dog has already learned to do one thing hinders it when it is trying to learn another. For instance, if your dog has already learned to scratch at a door in order to get through it and reach an agitator, this may transfer negatively to explosives detection training, making it more likely to aggress a training aid rather than sit cleanly.

ANTICIPATION

As a result of classical and instrumental conditioning, the dog learns to predict what will happen next during training. This knowledge of what is about to happen is accompanied by psychological and physiological changes that prepare the dog for upcoming action. Much the same thing happens to you when, riding in a car, you see the car ahead lock up its brakes. As a result of your anticipation of a collision, you brace yourself. When the dentist starts the motor in his drill, you will tend to wince and stiffen your body in anticipation of pain, even before you can feel the drill. The dog's anticipation of the events in dog training and its preparatory responses can help it learn. For instance, if your dog is having difficulty responding without assistance to odor during detection training, it sometimes helps to allow the animal to find a particular training aid two or three times running. Because the dog anticipates finding the same aid in the same place and sitting, he/she will be likely to respond quickly and completely without an assist, giving you the chance to reinforce this independent behavior. On the other hand, there are many circumstances in which anticipation can interfere with learning desired behavior. For instance, during the obedience exercises at the End of the Leash (EOL), the dog is normally commanded to change position a few times (e.g. sit-down-sit) without moving towards the handler, and then recalled to the heel position and rewarded. However, if we practice this complete sequence of exercises many times, we may find the dog's knowledge of the routine interfering with the changes of position—the animal's anticipation of returning to the handler and being rewarded will cause it to creep forward instead of staying in place while moving from sit to down and back to sit. Controlled aggression is a situation where anticipations can be particularly crippling to progress. When in the intensely motivated state that pertains during controlled aggression, the dogs' anticipations have tremendous power, and can create intense interference with ongoing exercises. So, for instance, if you have brought your dog to the line of departure for the biting exercises, it will tend to become very excited and tense and focus its attention completely on the agitator, ready to respond explosively to the first cue sending it to bite. Its powerful anticipation of the bite and its preparatory responses will make it very difficult to, for instance, ask it to pay attention to you and walk at heel away from the agitator. It is inappropriate and ineffective in many of these circumstances to use compulsion to overcome the dog's anticipation and rigidity—physical discomfort is likely to make the dog even more tense and rigid and aggressive. What is necessary is to find ways to offset the dog's anticipations so that they do not interfere so strongly with training—for instance begin teaching the animal that the command to bite will often come when it looks at its handler or walks at heel with its handler away from the agitator. When this anticipation is formed, the dog will naturally begin to ask for the —Git'em! command by looking at and moving towards its handler.

Compartmentalization

The single most useful technique for dealing with anticipation and interference is to separate, or compartmentalize, exercises that interfere with each other. Thus, in the EOL example above, the thoughtful trainer will seldom recall his/her dog from EOL. Instead the trainer will place the animal EOL, run it through a few changes of position, pause, and then go to the dog and release it and reward it. In this way the dog does not anticipate a recall at the end of the EOL exercises, and therefore does not creep forward. To practice the recall from EOL, on a separate occasion the trainer will place the dog EOL and make it stay for a while, and then recall it, in this way keeping the changes of position and the recall compartmentalized and preventing interference.

CHAPTER 3

PATROL DOG TRAINING

OBEDIENCE COMMANDS

Give voice commands sharply, crisply and in unison with the corresponding hand command. After the handler/dog team becomes proficient, you may give the commands and/or gestures independently. The commands start with the instructor, directed at the handler, (e.g., Instructor, "SIT DOG, COMMAND"; Handler, "SIT" with a hand gesture.)

Master At Arms 2nd Class David Nerling gives the hand command "down" to his military working dog Valerie during basic obedience training at Lackland Air Force Base, Texas, Aug. 29. MA2 Nerling is a Navy military working dog trainer with the 341st Training Squadron and works jointly with Air Force, Army, and Marine dog trainers. (U.S. Air Force photo/Robbin Cresswell)

Obedience Commands Beside the Dog

Teach all basic obedience commands first on leash with the dog at the handler's left side. These commands and correct responses start and end with the dog in the HEEL/SIT position.

Heel
The initial command and response is "HEEL." There are two HEEL positions for the dog, one is for marching and the other is for the stationary HEEL/SIT. Whether marching or in the HEEL/SIT position, ensure the dog's right shoulder is even with the handler's left leg, and the dog's body is parallel to the handler's body. The dog should not forge ahead or lag behind.

Give the Verbal and Manual
—HEEL when the handler starts forward movements, changes direction, and at one pace before coming to a halt. Give the hand gesture by slapping the left leg with the open left hand, while commanding —HEEL. When called to attention, give the command HEEL as the left foot strikes the ground. At the command "Forward MARCH," give the command —HEEL with the first step forward. If a dog lags behind, coax the dog into the HEEL position (NOT JERKED) by patting the left leg, snapping the fingers, calling the dog's name, or verbally encouraging the dog. On movements to the left, give the command —HEEL after the handler's right foot begins to pivot. This prevents the dog from blocking the pivot movement. On movements to the right and the rear, give the command —HEEL as the handler pivots. The dog can then assume the HEEL position before the movement is completed.

Heel/Sit
After the dog learns to walk in the HEEL position, it must learn to HEEL and then SIT in the HEEL position. Once the dog has learned the separate responses of HEEL and SIT, the next step is to teach the dog to SIT automatically in the HEEL position when stopped without further command.

1. When the instructor gives the command —SIT DOG, COMMAND, the handler gives the command —SIT, while grasping the leash several inches above the choke chain with the right hand. Place the palm of the left hand over the dog's hips with the fingers positioned at the base of the dog's tail, apply upward pressure on the leash while pushing down on the dog's hindquarters. As the training progresses, the dog should no longer require physical assistance.
2. In learning the command SIT, the dog may get slightly out of position. If this occurs gently reposition the dog. Every time the dog assumes the correct position praise the dog. Take care not to make praise excessive, since this may cause the dog to break position.

Down
When the instructor gives "DOWN DOG, COMMAND," and when the handler gives the command "DOWN," the dog must promptly lie parallel to the handler with its right shoulder in line with the handler's left foot.

1. The handler introduces the command —DOWN when the dog is in the HEEL/SIT position. Give the hand gesture along with the verbal command. Some dogs may resist going down because it places them in an unnatural position. Therefore, use caution since the dog could bite the handler. The handler first bends down and grasps the leash just behind the snap or the choke chain ahead of the snap depending on how much space is needed to apply downward pressure on the leash. Then, while giving the DOWN command, apply pressure firmly toward the ground until the dog lies down. If the dog assumes the DOWN position without resistance, the handler should praise verbally before returning to the position of attention. Take care not to make praise excessive; this may cause the dog to break position. Use the command "STAY" before returning to the position of attention.
2. To place a resisting dog in the DOWN position, the handler kneels down and grasps the leash just behind the snap with the left hand; then place the right arm behind the right front leg and grasp the

left front leg about 6 inches above the foot. While pressing down on the leash, command —DOWN and push the front legs forward until the dog is in the DOWN position.

3. Once the dog has learned the DOWN command, you may need to correct the dog's position. If this occurs, give the command "SIT"; and after the dog sits, repeat the down process. Take care not to move the left foot while correcting the position since the dog is trained to line up on the left foot/leg.

Stay
The stay command is introduced while the dog is in the HEEL/SIT position and used for any position you commanded the dog to assume. Ensure the hand gesture is distinct, decisive, and executed in the following manner:

Lock the Left Arm at the Elbow
Turn the hand until the palm faces rear and open it until the fingers are extended and together. Move the extended, locked arm forward until the arm and body make an angle of approximately 45 degrees. Bring the flattened palm smartly straight back toward the dog's face, stopping immediately in front of the nose. Drop the arm directly back to the left side.

Commands Away from the Dog
Once the team is proficient in movements with the dog in the HEEL position, progress to movements and positions with handler and dog separated by varying distances.

"End of the Leash, Move."
After giving this command, the handler gives the hand and voice command "STAY," then takes one step forward, right foot first, and pivots 180 degrees left to face the dog. As you make the pivot, transfer the leash from the right hand to the left. At the completion of the pivot, place the left hand in front of the belt buckle with the loop of the leash over the left thumb and the fingers curled around the leash as it continues down past the palm of the left hand.

"STAY" at end of leash.
When at the end of the leash with the leash in the left hand and in front of your belt buckle, give the command —STAY (verbal and hand).

With fingers extended and together, bring the right hand to shoulder level, palm toward the dog. Push the palm toward the dog's face smartly, commanding "STAY." Smartly drop hand and arm directly to the side.

"Return to the HEEL Position, Move."
After you give the verbal and manual command of "STAY," step off with the right foot to the right flipping the leash to the left so that the leash rests on the right side of the dog's neck. This will keep the leash from hitting the dog in the face. Walking in a small circle around the dog to the rear returning to the dog's right side. Take up the slack in the leash and transfer it back to the right hand. Praise the dog verbally and physically.

"DOWN" at EOL
With the dog in the HEEL/SIT position, give the command "STAY" and move to the end of the leash changing the leash to the left hand. Take one step forward with the right foot and grasp the leash about 6 inches from the snap. Exerting pressure downward on the leash, verbally command "DOWN." When the dog is in the DOWN position, give the command "STAY" and bring the right foot back to the starting position. At the point when the leash pressure is no longer needed, introduce the hand gesture for down. Lock

the elbow, extend the fingers and rotate the arm in a full circle to the rear, until the arm is at shoulder level and parallel with the ground, palm down. While the arm is making the circle, give the verbal command "DOWN."

"SIT" at End of LEASH

The command "SIT" is introduced when the dog has learned the command "DOWN/STAY." With the dog in the DOWN position, the instructor gives the command "SIT DOG, COMMAND." The handler steps forward one step with the right foot, grasps the leash about 12 inches above the choke chain, exerts upward pressure on the leash and gives the command "SIT." When the dog sits, give the command "STAY", give verbal praise, then return to the original position. When the dog is sitting, without using leash pressure, introduce the manual gesture as follows. Extend the fingers of the right hand and lock the elbow. Turn the flattened palm toward the dog. Smartly lift the extended arm to the horizontal shoulder position and command "SIT." Drop the arm smartly back to the side. Praise verbally but not excessively.

Commands and Moves for the Handler/Dog at End of Leash
Circle Dog

The handler gives the command "STAY" and steps off with the right or left foot depending on the direction of the command. As you make the circle around the dog, flip the leash around the dog's neck to the opposite side of the beginning direction of the circle. Take care during the circle movements not to stretch the leash taut causing the dog to break position.

Step Over the Dog

The same procedures apply as the Circle Dog, with the exception that the dog is in the DOWN position so that the handler can step over conveniently.

Straddle Dog

The handler gives the command "STAY," steps forward with the right foot, lowers the leash, steps over it with the left foot, and proceeds to straddle the dog that is in the DOWN position. When the handler gets to the rear of the dog, to the left 180 degrees, step over the leash with the left foot, straddle the dog, and return to the end of the leash. As the handler makes the turn to face the dog again, he/she returns the leash to the left hand.

Recall Dog

With the handler at the end of the leash, the instructor commands, "RECALL dog, COMMAND." The handler gives the verbal and manual command of "HEEL" and if necessary, calls the dog's name to get its attention. If the dog is reluctant to come on command, you may have to apply slight pressure on the leash with some verbal coaxing to get the dog to come. As the dog is returning, take up the slack in the leash and guide the dog into the HEEL position.

Military Drill

In all formations, the dog remains in the HEEL/SIT or marching HEEL position.

Attention

The position of attention is a two-count movement. At the preparatory command "SQUAD," the handler comes to attention. At the command "ATTENTION," the handler takes one step forward with the left foot and gives the command "HEEL." When the right foot is brought forward even with the left, the two-count movement is complete, and the dog should be in the HEEL/SIT position.

Parade Rest
At the preparatory command of "PARADE," the handler gives the command and manual gesture "DOWN." At the command of execution "REST," the handler gives the command and manual gesture "STAY," then steps over the dog with the left foot straddling the dog. The handler places his/her left hand behind his back. To resume the position of attention, use the preparatory command "SQUAD," at which time the handler gives the command "STAY." At the command of execution (—ATTENTION), the handler steps back over the dog and gives the command —HEEL.

At Ease/Rest
When given the command, keep the left foot in place while the dog remains in the HEEL/SIT position.

Fall Out
When given the command, the handler leaves ranks and puts the dog on break.

Fall In
The handler and dog resume their previous position in ranks at the position of attention with the dog in the HEEL/SIT position.

Right Face
"RIGHT FACE" is a four-count movement. At the command of execution "FACE," the handler takes one step forward with the left foot, commands "HEEL" and pivots on the balls of both feet 90° to the right. They then take one step forward with the right foot, bringing the left foot even with the right. The handler then commands "HEEL" and returns to the position of attention.

Left Face
"LEFT FACE" is a four-count movement. At the command of execution "FACE," the handler takes one pace forward with the right foot, pivots on the balls of both feet 90° to the left and commands "HEEL." They then take one step forward with the left foot, bringing the right foot even with the left and returning to the position of attention.

About Face
"ABOUT FACE" is a four-count movement. At the command of execution "FACE," the handler takes one step forward with the left foot, commands "HEEL," then pivots 180° and gives the command "HEEL." On the completion of the pivot, the handler takes one step with the left foot bringing the right foot beside it and returning to the position of attention.

Drill Formations
Four drill formations are used to teach basic obedience. Each is designed for a specific purpose yet is flexible enough for other phases of training. For safety, allow intervals of 15 feet between dog teams during initial obedience training. When handlers can control their dogs, you may reduce this distance.

Circle Formation
In this formation, the dog can learn the HEEL position. It requires walking at the handler's side without sharp turns. The instructor is usually in the center of the circle for better observation of the dog teams.

Square Formation
This formation is excellent for teaching the dog the HEEL position when the handler is making sharp turns.

Line Formation
The line formation is used effectively during basic, intermediate and advanced obedience.

Flight Formation
The flight formation is introduced after the dog teams demonstrate proficiency in the circle, line, and square formations. Use it for moving groups of dog teams from one location to another.

Intermediate Obedience
This training differs from basic obedience in distance only. In intermediate obedience, use the 360-inch leash instead of the 60-inch leash. Once the 360-inch leash is attached, the handler should start at the same distance as with the 60-inch, then gradually increase distance and time spent at the end of leash. During intermediate obedience, if the dog fails to perform any specific command, the handler should walk back to the dog and put the dog in the desired position. While approaching, give the command "STAY," only if the dog starts to break position. After making the correction, use shorter distances for later trials. Never run back to the dog or make threatening gestures. This may make the dog break position and run.

Advanced Obedience
Advanced obedience allows the dog to learn to execute commands given at a distance, off leash. To begin off-leash training, the handler must execute basic command and movements with the dog at his/her side. (This gives the handler an opportunity to test the dog's reliability and revert to using the long or short leash to correct deficiencies.) This obedience training at the handler's side should continue until the handler believes the dog will perform among other teams without hostility. As training progresses, the handler moves out in front of the dog a short distance and gradually increases the distance and time periods away from the dog. The dog's performance will determine distance from the handler. Normally, 50 feet is the maximum distance. When the handler moves back to the dog, the handler should circle around and step or jump over the dog. These movements teach the dog to remain in position until otherwise commanded. This stage of training should require only a minimum number of corrections. If the dog does not respond correctly and consistently to commands, the handler must return to the preliminary off-leash exercises and repeat them as often as required.

OBSTACLE COURSE

As an MWD team becomes proficient in basic obedience and associated tasks, introduce the obstacle course for the purpose of building the dog's confidence in negotiating similar obstacles the dog may encounter in the field. The obstacle course also conditions the dog and builds handler confidence in the dog's abilities. The determining factors for length of time spent and frequency of obstacle course use include dog's age, physical condition, and weather conditions.

Obstacle Course Training Procedures
The dog jumps or scales obstacles on the command "HUP," and when commanded, returns to the HEEL position. As in other training, first teach the dog to complete exercises on leash. This allows the handler more control while guiding the dog over obstacles. As the dog's proficiency increases, train the dog off leash. A dog may hesitate to jump over a hurdle. It is best to use a hurdle with removable boards and lower it so the dog can walk over it. Exerting pressure upward on the leash will cause the dog to balk or hesitate. When the hurdle is lowered, the team approaches it at normal speed, and the handler steps over it with the left foot and commands "HUP." If the dog balks, the handler helps it over by coaxing and repeating the command "HUP." After crossing the hurdle, the handler praises the dog, and gives the command "HEEL." As the dog

progresses, add boards until attaining a height of 3 feet. Thereafter, when the handler is two paces from the hurdle, give the command "HUP." Instead of stepping over, the handler passes around to the right of the obstacle while the dog passes over it. (Allow more than two paces from the hurdle if necessary.) As the dog's front feet strike the ground, the handler commands "HEEL," adjusting the distance in front of the dog so there is room to recover from the jump and assume the HEEL position. Immediately after the dog is in the HEEL position, give praise. Vary hurdle procedures somewhat for the window, scaling wall, catwalk, and stairs. For the window, the handler must transfer the leash from the right hand to the left and throw the leash through the window catching it on the other side. If the dog hesitates, put the front feet in the window and coax the dog through. For scaling the wall, the dog must have more speed on approaching and you must give the HUP command sooner. Adjust the wall to the dog's abilities during initial training gradually increasing the incline. For the catwalk, the handler may have to guide the dog onto it and steady the dog's balance while it crosses. The dog must walk up and down the stairs. If wet, remove the water from the stairs prior to use. The handler may have to walk over the steps with the dog if it hesitates.

CONTROLLED AGGRESSION

With exception of detection training, controlled aggression is the most intricate aspect of military dog training. Supervisors must ensure that each dog is trained and maintained at maximum proficiency.

Attack "GET 'EM"

Give the command only once. Give further encouragement if necessary. During on leash agitation, the handler must maintain position and balance by spreading the feet at least shoulder-width apart, one foot slightly forward of the other. Flex the knees and bend slightly at the waist. While extending the arms, unlock elbows. Not following this procedure could cause the handler to lose balance and cause serious injury to another handler or dog.

"HOLD 'EM"

Give command in an encouraging tone of voice while the dog is biting. If the dog releases the bite, repeat the command "GET 'EM," then repeat "HOLD 'EM."

"OUT."

Give this command to cue the MWD to cease attack. A properly trained dog will release the bite and on receiving the command "HEEL" return to the handler. Upon successful completion, the handler must physically and verbally praise the dog. If the dog does not release the bite, the handler should wait 3 seconds and repeat the "OUT" command or command "NO-OUT." If the dog does not release after the second command, the handler should repeat "NO-OUT" and apply a physical correction. NOTE: The dog must know the task before using the physical correction! You can teach the "OUT" command before the dog is actually biting the wrap. Do this with end of leash agitation. The handler should give the command "OUT, HEEL" and use the leash to guide the dog back to the HEEL position. The handler must physically and verbally praise the dog when it ceases aggression.

"STAY."

A properly trained MWD will remain in the stay position until you give another command. During controlled aggression exercises, use the command "STAY" to notify the agitator that you are ready for exercise initiation. You may find the DOWN position helpful in preventing some dogs from breaking position.

"WATCH 'EM."

Given in a very suspicious tone of voice to put the MWD on guard. If during agitation, the dog loses interest, repeat the command.

Senior Airman Jarred Uzeta, 9th Security Forces Squadron military working dog handler, commands his MWD Vvladimir to jump through an obstacle June 27, 2018 at Beale Air Force Base, CA. (U.S. Air Force photo by Airman 1st Class Tristan D. Viglianco)

AGITATION

Agitators Role

The agitator plays an important role in agitation exercises; therefore, thoroughly instruct persons acting as agitators on what to do. As an agitator, you may use a supple switch, a burlap bag, an arm protector, or a rag to provoke the dog without actually striking him. The dog's level of aggression will determine the need for using such training aids. The agitator's actions should replicate actions of real-life subjects, the dog may encounter. The dog is always the winner and never backed down.

Aggressiveness
To determine the degree of aggressiveness or develop aggressiveness of the dog, conceal the agitator upwind of the dog team. The handler, while maintaining a safety leash, approaches the area concealing the agitator. The agitator will attempt to attract the dog's attention through normal suspect/intruder actions. Weaker dogs may require the agitator to slightly increase movements and/or make additional noise to gain the dog's attention. Meanwhile, the handler must watch the dog closely to provide timely assistance by encouraging the dog in a low suspicious voice, to "WATCH 'EM." When the dog detects the intruder, the handler must encourage the dog immediately. If the dog shows no interest, the agitator should show himself/herself and move away suspiciously as the team gets within 10 feet.

Under Aggressive
This type dog will fail to exhibit interest in the agitator even as they move away suspiciously. To develop aggression in these dogs, use the chase method. The agitator provokes the dog. As the dog shows aggression, the intruder will run away while continuing to make noise, while the team gives chase. After running 20 yards or so, the agitator will throw up an arm to indicate the direction they intend to turn. The agitator will turn in that direction and the team will turn in the opposite direction. The handler should exercise care not to jerk the dog off the chase, causing an unintentional correction.

CONTROL

Building Control
To build control, give the dog "STAY" in the HEEL/SIT position and have the agitator move in from a distance of approximately 20 feet. The agitator may use a play rag, puppy tug, or arm protector. The agitator should approach the dog team in a manner that arouses the dog's suspicion. The handler should give the dog the STAY command and reinforce the command as necessary. The agitator will then retreat back to the starting position and cease movement. The handler should physically and verbally praise the dog. If the dog breaks position, the handler should command "NO-STAY", guide the dog back into position and repeat the command stay. If the dog continues to fail the STAY command, the handler must adjust the severity of the corrections to meet the level that will effectively change the dog's behavior. Once the dog is proficient in this scenario, the agitator will move in closer to the dog team and act in a more suspicious manner thus increasing dog stimulus to aggress. As the dog becomes proficient at this level, introduce the wrap and command the dog to bite. Use the same process to train the dog to release the wrap as you did in the initial scenario. You may need to increase the level of correction or revert to the previous method. If the dog fails to progress at this level, return to the initial scenario.

Commands of "OUT" or "NO-OUT."
After the dog demonstrates proficiency in biting and holding, the agitator can hold the rag/protector. The handler will command "OUT" or "NO-OUT" when the agitator ceases movement.

If for any reason the intruder is hurt or bitten, they should signal the handler by raising the free arm above their head. The handler should immediately give the "OUT" command and physically gain control of the dog.

False Run (MWDs Trained Under the Out and Guard Method--FIELD INTERVIEW)
The field interview is a practical replacement for the traditional false run and designed to demonstrate the MWD's ability to be tolerant of non-aggressive movements or situations dog teams can be exposed to throughout their tour of duty. Through this training exercise it enables the handler to gain complete control over the MWD while subjected to various non-suspicious actions by a subject. As the dog's proficiency increases, this exercise will be conducted off leash.

Training Procedure
Put the dog in the HEEL/SIT or DOWN position and give the "STAY" command. The subject, wearing the arm protector, starts at a distance anywhere from 15 to 100 feet from the dog team. MWD proficiency levels of each dog trained in this exercise scenario will determine the start distance for this portion of the exercise. Once the distance has been determined, the subject will start off by facing the dog team in a non-suspicious manner and will walk towards the team by taking an indirect route. The purpose of this type of movement is designed to simulate an individual who upon initial contact or observation is non-threatening to the dog team, others or resources. As the subject reaches the dog team's location, the subject reaches out (using the wrap protected hand first) and simulates shaking the handler's hand and engages the handler in a normal conversational tone of voice. After the non-threatening verbal interaction between handler and subject, the subject simply turns and walks away from the team. Again, the subject's intension/movements are non-threatening towards the dog team as they depart. Throughout all stages of this exercise the dog must remain in the HEEL/SIT or DOWN position and should not show any signs of aggressive behavior towards the handler or subject. Handlers and trainers should use caution not to misinterpret the dog's natural behavior to be interested or curious of the person, as they move closer towards the team as aggressive behavior. Some dogs may attempt to break the HEEL position as the subject approaches just because they are simply interested in a non-threatening sense of the approaching individual. Should a dog show this type of behavior and it is determined, as non-aggressive behavior the handler must reinforce the HEEL command, ensuring the dog returns and stays in the HEEL position. If the dog stays and doesn't exhibit aggressiveness, give the dog lavish praise. If the dog breaks position, correct it immediately and repeat the exercise. During repeat exercises, as the dog shows progress the subject should now take a more direct route towards the dog team. Take care to let the dog have a bite at irregular intervals to keep the dog from becoming too frustrated, and as an indirect form of praise. Correction must not be too harsh. Training in "STAND OFF" and "FALSE RUN" phases can be very difficult, especially for dogs with a high fight drive. Dogs demonstrating a high proficiency rate for this particular exercise will naturally have the distances and time ratios of dog team/subject interaction varied. Dogs with a lower proficiency rate for this exercise will need specific distances and time ratios closely monitor and controlled to build the MWD's proficiency level for this exercise.

Pursuit and Apprehension
Used to teach the dog, on command, to pursue, bite, and hold an individual.

Training Procedure
Proficiency in all phases of obedience and timely response to commands is required prior to starting controlled aggression training. Begin with the MWD in the HEEL position off leash and give the command "STAY." To begin the exercise, the subject should stand or move around suspiciously at a distance of 40 or 50 feet. Prior to releasing the dog, the handler will give a warning order "Halt or I will release my dog," (NOTE: Refer to your unit SF operating instructions for exact verbal challenging procedures/instructions.) and warn bystanders to cease all movement. When the handler commands "GET 'EM," the dog should pursue, bite and hold the subject until commanded to release from the bite. The handler follows the dog as closely as possible. If the subject stops or indicates surrender, the handler will immediately call the dog off the pursuit (stand-off). If the dog makes contact with the subject, the handler will call the dog —OUT once the situation is under control. DURING TRAINING ONLY, when the dog is biting, the handler provides encouragement and commands "HOLD 'EM." After a short struggle, the subject ceases movement, and the handler commands "OUT". Give praise when the dog returns to the HEEL position. There may be times were the dog will release from the bite but hesitates in returning to the handler. Should this be the situation the handler will use verbal encouragement to refocus the dog's attention back to the handler. As the handler gains the dog's attention and the dog is returning to the heel position the handler should cease verbal

encouragement/praise until the dog is in the HEEL position.

Training Realism
Conduct training in the dog's working environment when possible. Training problems must replicate—real-life scenarios as much as possible to include the frequent use of hidden arm protectors.

Search of a Suspect
Search apprehended personnel as soon as possible. In most instances, it is best to have another security forces person conduct the search with the dog team as back up. If no other police personnel are present, the handler may search the suspect with the dog in the GUARD position. Ensure the dog can observe the agitator/suspect at all times.

Training Procedure
The handler will position the suspect 6 to 8 feet in front of the dog, facing away from the dog. Prior to the search, place the dog in either the SIT or DOWN position and inform the agitator/suspect not to make any sudden or aggressive movements or the dog will attack. The handler gives the dog "STAY," moves forward (right foot first) to search the agitator. Do not pass between the agitator/suspect and the dog. After searching both sides, the handler positions themselves directly behind the suspect. If the dog attempts to bite again or shows undue interest in the agitator/suspect, issue an immediate correction. When the dog returns to the proper HEEL position, give lavish praise.

Re-attack
During a search, the MWD must learn to re-attack. If, during the search, the agitator/suspect attempts to run away or attack the handler, the dog must immediately pursue and bite and hold the agitator without command. In the early stages of or periodically during proficiency training, the handler may have to command "GET 'EM." Excessive training in this area may result in a dog anticipating the moves of the agitator/suspect, causing loss of control by the handler.

Escort
After apprehending and searching a suspect, you may find it necessary to escort the apprehended individual out of the immediate area to a vehicle. After recalling the dog to the heel position, directly behind the suspect, the handler takes control of the suspect by placing their hands on the suspect's shoulder and escorting the suspect. The dog may heel on the handler or slightly forward on the side of the decoy to ensure an effective escort.

Stand Off
The purpose of the standoff is to develop control needed by the handler to call the MWD back from a bite and hold command.

Training Procedure
The agitator moves toward the dog acting suspiciously. At a distance of 4 feet, the agitator turns and runs. When the agitator gets about 30 feet from the team, the handler commands "GET 'EM." When the agitator hears the command, they should stop and cease movement. The handler commands "OUT" and, if necessary, "NO-OUT." After the dog —OUTs, the dog must —SIT, —DOWN, or —STAND within the immediate area of the agitator.

Gunfire and Cover Command
The primary purpose of gunfire training is to condition the dog to perform all required tasks satisfactorily

when gunfire is introduced to the scenario. The dog should not react aggressively, unless commanded by the handler, nor should it display an avoidance behavior toward gunfire. Training should be conducted both with the handler and agitator/suspect firing the weapon individually and together depending on the various stages of training, however, gunfire associated with agitation or bite training should be kept to an absolute minimum, and then only to determine if the dog still performs satisfactorily in the presence of gunfire.

Training Procedure
Under no circumstances will a dog be backed down or defeated in gunfire training. Conduct gunfire training using only authorized blank ammunition. Ensure the muzzle of the firearm is always pointed in a safe direction.

Conduct Gunfire Training
It is best to use a small caliber weapon, casually and intermittently. Begin initial gunfire training from a distance of at least 70 yards and include it in all phases of training. As the dog performs satisfactorily, move gunfire gradually closer to the dog. Reward the dog when it ignores gunfire. Do not reward the dog when it shies away from or aggresses toward gunfire. As the dog accepts gunfire at varying distances, introduce advanced training. Progress to larger caliber weapons and, if possible, expose the dog gradually to mortar, artillery, and grenade simulators. When the dog is proficient in gunfire, introduce the command "COVER." This simply means that on the command of execution, the handler gives his dog "DOWN" and assumes the prone position. Great care and caution must be used to prevent a potential safety mishap during this phase of gunfire training. Training supervisors must understand during this phase of training the handler will be placed in a difficult position to protect themselves (from a dog attack) while in the prone position next to their dog. As in all initial stages of dog training, training supervisors and handlers need to remember there might be a period were the dog may not produce the desire behavior at first therefore, practice and patience is a must for the dog to master this task.

SCOUTING

Scouting is the most effective procedure to locate intruder(s) hidden in a large area. The following factors affect the MWD's ability to scout.

Wind
Wind is the most important and variable factor in scouting. It carries the scent either to or away from the dog; therefore, the handler must remain aware of direction and velocity at all times and must fully understand how this affects the dog's ability to successfully perform this task. Handlers must be capable of accurately identifying wind direction in all types of terrain and/or situations without outside sources. For example, at night or other limited visibility situations it may not be feasible to drop hair or a blade of grass to check wind direction. The best way to check the wind direction is to remove head gear and turn slowly until the breeze creates a cool feeling on the upper forehead. As mentioned earlier, not only is it important to know the proper wind direction it is equally important to know how wind speed will affect your scout. An ideal wind speed is difficult to pinpoint, but normally slight, steady and consistent wind conditions will produce the best scouting results for dog teams.

Terrain
The next important consideration is terrain. Besides manmade structures, there are trees, bushes, large rocks, high grass, and many other natural variations. Odor cannot pass through obstacles, so it must go over, under, or around them. Handlers must understand how these obstacles come into play when performing scouts with their MWDs.

Additional Factors
Additionally, the MWD trainer and agitator must remain aware of the wind direction and their route when walking within the area that the dog will search. Agitators should always approach the area from the upwind flank to ensure the dog does not cross the path and track the agitator. Trainers should also take the same precaution when training multiple dog teams. The agitator should be moved between scouting problems so dogs cannot track each other. Other factors that affect scouting abilities and conditions are rain, snow, sleet, temperature, and humidity. These factors affect the odor concentration or scent cone in numerous ways.

SCOUTING PROBLEMS

Set your scouting problems to match the proficiency of the dog team. For example, when quartering a field, an advanced dog may be able to consistently locate the decoy from 40 yards. This should be considered when bounding forward when quartering the terrain to locate decoy. Use chase agitation to build drive in weak dogs. Once teams are proficient in initial scouting problems, advance to realistic problems including vast areas of the installation. Vary the terrain to include wooded, as well as developed areas. Use your imagination and set real world scenarios, including the use of other flight members for back-up, and response forces. There should be an even balance of bite training incorporated into scouts.

MAINTAINING PROFICIENCY

When a team arrives at a proficient level to scout and clear an area, there are many ways to keep the dog team proficient.

Field Problems
Designed to evaluate use of scouting principles. The area should have a variety of terrain features, and the handler must know the area boundaries.

Patrolling Exercises
Usually consist of point-to-point posts; however, a specific or a designated area might need securing.

Training Procedure
The trainer places several intruders along the line of patrol 75 to 100 yards apart along the route the dog team takes. Position the agitators off the line of patrol, far enough to challenge the dog's detection capabilities, but not defeat it. Set up all three types of responses to include sight, scent, and sound. At the conclusion of the exercise, the handler indicates the number of agitators found.

SECURITY PROBLEMS

Set up realistic problems with the goal of extending the period of time the dog team remains alert on regular sentry posts. Supervisory personnel can use these problems to best evaluate the dog's training and the abilities of the handler to control the dog.
- Alternate teams between different types of posts as training progresses. Initially, each team is used on-post for about 30 minutes before the agitator hides on the post or tries to penetrate the post.
- At this advanced stage of training, do not use the command —FIND HIM to get the dog to respond unless it is absolutely necessary. Once the dog responds, replicate normal apprehension and escort

procedures.
- After a few nights of this training, the teams tour of duty is extended to either 4 or 6 hours, as determined by posts and training time. The extended training time is necessary to condition the dog to remain alert and watchful over a normal tour of duty. Vary the number of penetrations for each team in time and number. This variation keeps the dog alert for penetrations.
- Penetrations serve two purposes: to check the security of an area, and to maintain a patrol dog team's proficiency. The penetrator tries to enter the post undetected and, if successful, hides along the handler's route where he/she must allow the dog to detect the intruder.
- A patrol dog team gains no training benefit from an exercise in which the agitator/intruder penetrates a post with the intent to elude detection. The penetrator must not use the same route or time of approach. If he/she does, the handler and dog begin to anticipate arrival. The penetrator must use cover and concealment when penetrating a post, to avoid revealing the position before reaching the post perimeter.
- Raining emphasis is placed on developing the detection capabilities of the dog. Sometimes it is necessary for the penetrator to make his or her presence on the post more obvious.
- During the early stage of training, the penetrator must not use diversionary tactics because these tactics may confuse the inexperienced dog team.
- An effective penetrator must have the dog team's proficiency training in mind. He/she must employ sound judgment and adapt methods to the situation matched to the proficiency level of the team. These practices apply during training as well as under field conditions.

BUILDING SEARCH

Use a building search to locate an intruder hiding in a structure.

Factors Affecting Building Searches

Factors that influence an MWD's ability to scout also affect its ability to locate an intruder inside a building. A variety of air currents are common inside buildings just as they are outside buildings.

- Wind direction outside buildings correlates with the direction of air currents inside by filtering through any openings such as windows, doors, vents, and cracks in floors.
- Type and size of buildings and wind direction will affect the dog's ability to detect an intruder.
- Air conditioning units, fans, and heater blowers affect the speed and direction of airflow. Changing air currents can confuse the dog in its effort to locate the intruder.
- Temperature inside and outside a building may influence the concentration of odor. Cold temperatures will keep the odor closer to the surface, while warm temperatures will cause the odor to rise.
- Residual odor from personnel who recently departed the building may serve to distract the dog.

BUILDING SEARCH TRAINING

Set your building search problems to match the proficiency of the dog team. Use chase agitation to build drive in weak dogs. Conduct initial training with a 6 foot or a 30-foot leash. Make your problems more difficult as the dog progresses. Once your team is proficient in initial building search, conduct advanced searches in realistic environments. Use your imagination to set problems that challenge the capability of the team. Use other flight members to act as back-up, over watch and response forces. As in all training scenarios the safety of the handler, agitator and dog must be at the forefront of your scenario planning at all times.

Eric Smith, a military working dog handler, and Viola, a patrol explosive detector dog with the 550th Military Working Dog Detachment, 42nd Military Police Detachment, 503rd Military Police Battalion, search containers for explosives during detection training exercise Nov. 8, 2016 at Macomb Warehouse, Fort Bragg, N.C. (Photo Credit: Pfc. Hubert D. Delany III)

Initial Building Search Training Procedures

In initial building search training, allow the dog to see, hear, and smell the intruder just inside the building at the entrance door. Gradually move the intruder into a room, allowing the dog to detect by the use of intruder movement (vision and sound); then progress to the dog locating the intruder by odor. When the dog responds to the odor of the intruder, by barking, scratching, etc., ask the dog —WHAT YA GOT? Verbally reward the dog as it makes the required response and enter the room to allow the dog to bite the intruder. As the dog responds correctly to the following trials, move the intruder into the next room to teach the dog the intruder location was moved. Gradually lengthen the search, one room at a time until the dog searches the entire building. Then randomly position the intruder throughout the building. Conduct all building searches in a systematic manner, preventing duplication. The handler should always clear an area or room before passing it and maintain an avenue of escape. Dogs are trained to make one of the following final responses upon locating an intruder.

Vocal
Vocal (bark, growl, whine), scratching, biting, or ceasing movement at the intruder location.

Intermediate Building Search Training Procedures (on Leash)
Hide an intruder in the building for a designated period of time prior to the search. The trainer/supervisor should adjust the time based on dog's ability, building size and difficulty of search. The handler should cue the dog to start searching for the intruder with the command of "FIND 'EM" to begin a systematic search at the appropriate starting point. The handler allows the dog to clear the building observing any indication the dog detected the intruder. Tell the handler the location of the intruder during training to help identify responses. The trainer should accompany the team occasionally to give added advice and assistance as needed. When the handler is sure the dog has detected the intruder, reward the dog with a CRS using verbal and physical praise. You may use a bite reward if it enhances the dog's proficiency. Remember, the dog is also operating on a VIRS at this point. To assure the dog that the intruder is really present, you may find it necessary to reveal the intruder's presence by noise or even show a portion of the intruder's body. Eventually the dog develops proficiency on odor cues only. When possible, terminate all building search exercises by having the team escort the intruder from the building.

Advanced Building Search Training Procedures (off Leash)
Cue the dog to start a systematic search similar to the on-leash search. The handler must follow the dog as much as possible to keep it in view. The handler must react instantly when the dog responds. Conceal the intruder in a location not accessible to the dog. The intruder should remain quiet and allow the dog sufficient time to search out the hiding place. A dog that has performed well to this point, will have learned to search systematically and efficiently on its own without the handler close by. A dog should eventually search out the intruder without assistance from the handler. If the dog responds on an area where the intruder was previously hidden, make certain the area is cleared, then repeat the command "FIND 'EM" and continue the search. During actual (not training) searches, a single trial where no reward is given constitutes an extinction trial. This single trial will not degrade the dog's subsequent performance due to the fact the dog is on a VIRS. Once you have trained a dog on this schedule, you have proven behavior is highly resistant to extinction.

Actual Building Search Procedures
When conducting an actual building search, several factors must be considered:
- Potential danger to the handler and MWD.
- Type and size of building (speed of search).
- Time of day or night.
- Evidence of forced entry.
- Known or suspected contents of the building.
- Possibility of innocent persons inside.

After considering the advice of the handler, the on-scene commander will determine whether to search building on or off leash. The handler must announce in a clear, loud voice that he/she will release the dog to search the building if no one appears within a specified time. This allows intruders the opportunity to surrender or innocent persons the opportunity to make their presence known. If no one appears, the handler will allow the dog enough time to clear the immediate area before proceeding. The handler will then follow the dog to each unclear room until the building is cleared.
- If an intruder is located, recall the dog, challenge, and apprehend the intruder. Another security member should accompany dog teams. This individual should follow at a discreet distance to avoid interference with the search. This additional person is needed to provide over watch protection to the handler since the handler must focus his or her attention on the dog and not necessarily the threat

associated with the building search itself. If an intruder is found, the security forces person who accompanied the dog handler can perform a quick body search and remove the individual.
- Do not enter the building until backup units have secured all avenues of escape. If forced entry is indicated but search results are negative, consider using the dog's scouting or tracking capabilities. If the situation allows, the building custodian should be called to the scene prior to security forces members entering the facility. By having the custodian on scene, they should be able to provide more in-depth information of the facility and possibly identify what is out of place and what is not associated with the building.

TRACKING

Tracking selection and training. Some MWDs are completely unsuited for tracking and show no willingness to track. Nothing can be gained by continually trying to make one of these dog's track. Therefore, once a Kennel Master or trainer is able to document a dog's inability to track, further training in this task may be stopped. Dogs that demonstrate a definite ability to track must remain proficient by consistent training.

Tracking dogs are utilized during combat to locate enemy by the scent they leave on the ground. In law enforcement, tracking dogs are often used to search for fleeing felons, lost/missing persons, and evidence. Since MWDs are not trained to track during initial training at Lackland AFB, it is left to Kennel Masters to identify dogs with tracking potential. Therefore, it is important to have general knowledge and understanding of the tracking dog capabilities.

Before beginning training with your dog, you must understand some of the conditions that affect your dog's performance: Wind, Surface, Temperature, Distractions; and Age of the track.

Wind
The dog takes the human scent not only from the ground, but also from the air near the ground. A strong wind can spread the scent causing the dog difficulty in detecting the scent. A strong wind may also cause a dog to depend upon its scouting ability (track laid into the wind) to find the tracklayer instead of tracking. A wind blowing across a track (track laid crosswind) may cause the dog to work a few feet downwind of the track. To encourage the dog to pick up the scent directly from the ground, all initial tracks should be laid downwind from the starting point. Once the dog becomes proficient, use tracks that combine different wind conditions.

Surface
The ideal surface for tracking is an open field with short, damp vegetation. A hard-dry surface does not hold a scent well. Heavy rain can dissipate or mask the scent. In contrast, a damp surface will allow the scent to remain.

Temperature
The scent dissipates faster when the temperature is high. The early morning or late afternoon hours are more favorable tracking periods. Rain will quickly dissipate the scent.

Distractions
Some odors can mask the human scent the dog is following. Conflicting scents, animal odors, smoke fumes, chemicals, and fertilizers affect the dog's ability to detect and follow a track

Age
The age of the track is another factor that must be taken into consideration. It is more difficult for the dog to follow an older track.

Types of Tracks
For training purposes there are three types of tracks: Initial, Intermediate, and Advanced

Initial Track
The initial track is laid downwind and runs from one point to another for about 50 paces. The tracklayer leaves a scent pad approximately three-square feet by stepping in the entire section. After laying a scent pad, the tracklayer takes short steps closely together in a straight line downwind to the end of the track. This will place more scent on the track making it easier for the dog to learn the task. During initial tracking, encourage the dog to watch the tracklayer. Preplan the initial track so all personnel involved know the start and end points. The handler must know the exact location of the track. For all phases of tracking, establish records to document conditions. Furnish the handler a precise map and detail the length and age of each track. The area used for an initial track should have low vegetation (i.e., mown grass). There should be ample room to lay the track. Keep distractions to a minimum.

Initial Track Procedures
After the tracklayer finishes laying the track, have the dog team approach and stop six feet from the scent pad. During initial training, attach the 360 leash to the choke chain to control the speed and assist in keeping the dog on the track. You may use a collar or harness. At the scent pad, coax the dog to smell the scent pad, command the dog TRACK, pronouncing it in a slow, drawn-out, pleasant manner: T-R-A-A-A-A-CK. Casting is given by making a sweeping downward and out motion with the palm of the hand up. Keeping on the track, give the dog half leash and move along the track. Whenever the dog strays from the track, slow the pace until the dog recovers or returns to the track. If the dog strays off track, stop, call the dog back, have it smell the track and repeat the command, casting the dog out to half leash. To encourage the dog to track, use a mild form of enticement or small pieces of food at the scent pad and throughout the track. Allow the dog to track at a slow pace. Place several pieces of food to indicate the end of the short track. After the dog consumes the food, praise the dog lavishly as you exit the area. This may take several trails before moving on to the next phase.

Intermediate Track
The intermediate track includes turns the dog must follow and articles that must be found. Articles are small pieces of wool, leather, rubber, or cloth. As in any track, preplanning is a must so the handler can observe and assist the dog during turns and in locating articles.

Procedures
The starting scent pad is smaller than the scent pad used for the initial track. The length of the track is 100 paces and will include two 45-degree turns. Articles are placed to reinforce the tracklayers scent on the trail. They are also used to indicate change of direction in the track. The scent is placed on the articles by rubbing them between the hands. The dog is not required to pick up the articles, but should indicate the exact location. The dog should respond by lying down with the article directly in front of them. The response on the article serves as the point to reward the dog and a resting place. Give verbal praise and a small piece of food after the dog downs at the article (no more food is placed on the track itself). It must be emphasized that incentives are extremely important in getting the dog to follow a scent. The article can be used as a refresher scent if the dog loses the track. The down indication of the articles should be taught separately to avoid any pressure on the track. To create a new problem for the dog, lay the track crosswind. The dog may work a few feet downwind from the track to pick up the scent. Initially, the track should be fresh and increased in length and age as the proficiency of the dog increases. After making a scent pad, the tracklayer walks normally along a preplanned route, occasionally shortening the pace to put down more scent. Wherever an article is placed, the tracklayer stops and stands in that area to increase the scent. Going into and coming out of a turn, slowing

the pace makes small scent pads.

Advanced Track
Dogs that have shown a marked degree of proficiency in tracking will use the advanced track. Not every dog has the ability to track for long periods or follow old tracks. Notice that scented articles are used, the turns are sharper, and a diversionary track is used.

Advanced Track Procedures
The track should be approximately 1–2 hours old and about 1-mile long. The tracklayer lays a track by making a scent pad and then walking at a normal pace but occasionally breaking into a run. Increase turns to 90 degrees and include downwind, crosswind, and upwind scenarios. Use a diversionary track to teach your dog the difference between the primary and a cross track. To prevent confusing the dog, have a diversionary tracklayer quickly cross the primary track. Thus, to observe your dog's reaction, you must know exactly where the tracks cross. At every other turn, the tracklayer makes a scent pad if the trainer feels the dog still needs assistance. After the turns, place articles as a reward for accomplishing the turns. If articles are not used at the turns, make separate scent pads for the dog to follow. In planning this track, prepare a detailed map so the handler can help the dog when necessary. To ensure a successful performance, the handler and trainer must stay flexible in their approach to tracking and allow latitude to make necessary adaptations.

Regaining Lost Tracks
As the dog advances through the track, it may lose the scent and wander off track. The key handler action is to recognize the dog has lost the track and stop immediately. When the dog loses the track, the handler should recognize a change in the dog's mannerisms. The dog may regain the scent on its own. If your dog does not regain the track by itself, take it back to the last known location of the track. Command TRACK and follow your dog along the track. If this does not work, use a more advanced method to regain the track. These methods include the spiral, cloverleaf, and figure eight patterns. These methods involve walking your dog in a pattern so it has an opportunity to regain the track.

Maintain Tracking Proficiency by Performing at Least One Advanced Track per Week
Set up the tracks to exercise and reinforce the dog's capabilities and provide enough variety so the dog does not learn to anticipate the route of the track.

DECOY TECHNIQUES

The decoy (or Helper) plays a vital role in developing the drives of an MWD. Trainers, handlers, and decoys should know the dog's temperament and gear the training to build a solid balance of prey and defense drive. Decoys must always remember their ultimate goal is assisting in the building of the dog's proficiency levels and aside from the safety of themselves and other personnel involved in dog training this should always be at the forefront of training.

Temperament
Temperament is the combination of all of a dog's mental and emotional attributes, disposition, and personality. By understanding and evaluating temperament, we can predict trainability in any working dog. Experienced trainers can modify behavior and cover temperament flaws; however, you cannot completely change basic temperament.

Instinct
Instinct is a dog's innate response to certain stimuli, independent of any thought process such as chewing, vocalizing, digging, leg lifting and scratching. Instincts most often have their roots in survival or reproduction.

Drives
MWD drives is discussed later in chapter 4.

Imprinting
An initial impression on a dog that will evoke a lasting or permanent reaction or behavior, usually associated with the untrained dog's initial learned reaction to a given stimulus or set of stimuli.

Compulsion
Compulsion is using the application of pain or negative stimuli to extinct a behavior, evoke a response, or otherwise modify a dog's behavior. Use of compulsion in patrol dog training can adversely affect drives and ultimately result in undesired behaviors. One example includes a dog that avoids the handler after a bite. Through excessive use of compulsion, the dog has associated the handler with negative stimuli (correction), and therefore avoids the handler to delay or avoid the correction. Another example of the inauspicious effect of compulsion is a dog that slows his pursuit as he reaches the decoy and doesn't fully commit to the bite. In this case the dog has associated the decoy or the distance with a previous correction in "stand-off" training.

Anthropomorphism
Anthropomorphism is to place human characteristics, motives, or emotions on a dog. Example: "My dog is bored with training and will not work." This type of statement contradicts quality training and exemplifies a misunderstanding of the animal.

Shaping
Shaping is rewarding nearly correct responses as a dog is learning a task. As the training continues, reward only those responses that are more like the desired final response. Shaping is highly effective in teaching a task without compulsion.

Rewards
Rewards are born out of drives and used to evoke the desired behavior. The anticipation for the reward drives the dog more than the reward itself. The drive for the reward can help trainers predict trainability. Use the bite, slip, and carry as a reward to satisfy prey, defense, and fight drives.

Learning Curves
Learning Curves is an analytical theory that depicts fluctuations in an animal's ability to learn a task. The curve will depict the starting point, the peak, the drop off, and the flat areas of a dog's learning abilities. As the trainer begins to teach a task, the dog is eager to satisfy the drive--the starting point of the learning curve. As training progresses, the trainer can apply the learning curve using care to terminate the training session at the peak. Training beyond the peak will push the dog into the flat area. The dog is unable to properly learn a task in the flat area and will invariably respond incorrectly. At this point the trainer is counteracting the positive learning that occurred in the beginning of the trial. The ideal training session will flow through the incline of the curve and stop at or near the peak. By consistently following this routine, the trainer ensures that all training is conducted in a positive manner, ingraining an enduring desire for the dog to successfully

complete the tasks. Failure to understand and track learning curves is common among dog trainers and will lead them to assume that the animal is unable or unwilling to comprehend and complete a task.

Presenting for the High Bite (Decoy)

As the dog is in pursuit, the decoy waves the sleeve at shoulder height, ensuring that the dog targets high. As the dog leaps for the bite, the decoy pulls the sleeve in at chest level and forces the dog to fully commit to the bite. This method instills confidence and fight drive in the dog. This will transfer to the actual (suspect) bite. Failure to build this confidence will result in the dog failing to commit to the actual bite because he has anticipated the presentation of the sleeve.

Spc. Michael Coffey, a military working dog handler, and Max, a patrol explosive detector dog with the 550th Military Working Dog Detachment, 42nd Military Police Detachment, 503rd Military Police Battalion, practice-controlled aggression training Nov. 8, 2016 at Macomb Warehouse, Fort Bragg, N.C. (Photo Credit: Pfc: Hubert D. Delany III)

Working the High Bite

The decoy works the sleeve at chest level while standing in an upright position. This forces the dog to give a harder and fuller bite. While working the dog, the decoy gives as the dog attempts to bite deeper and pulls as the dog lets up. This conditions the dog to maintain a hard and full bite. A dog that is trained with the high bite is less likely to nip a suspects clothing and more likely to fully bite and hold the individual.

Pull Down in the Bite

If the bite is weak or mouthy, the handler and decoy work together to build the dog's bite. With the dog on a 6-foot leash and leather collar, the handler applies backward and downward pressure on the leash while the dog is on the sleeve. The decoy works the dog in the high bite. The handler and decoy must apply pressure when the bite is weak causing the dog to fight harder for the full mouth bite. Then simultaneously release the pressure and allow the dog to readjust the bite. Do this two or three times to build the dog's bite. As the dog takes a fuller and stronger bite, reward the behavior by slipping the sleeve and allowing the dog to carry or parade with it in a circle.

Confidence Bite

Used as a stress relief for the animal. Because the presence of a decoy causes stress in the dog, you can use this technique to release the stress before a training session. Simply allow the dog to attack the decoy and take the sleeve. Let the dog carry the sleeve in a wide circle at a medium gait. Do not let the dog thrash or manipulate the sleeve, and do not use verbal or physical corrections with the dog. Once the dog has calmed down, the decoy can entice him with a second sleeve.

Reward Bite Method
The reward bite develops a willingness to release the sleeve and return to the handler by using positive motivation. This method has helped solve several long-standing problems in military working dog training, including failure to release a bite, attacking during a stand-off, hesitation in the attack, handler avoidance, and handler aggression. The reward bite is divided into three progressive steps, all of which are conducted with the dog on a 30-foot leash.

Double Ball Method (Step 1)
This technique teaches a willingness to release while the animal is in a low state of drive. It also produces willingness for the dog to return to the trainer. The trainer uses two identical prey reward items such as balls, kongs, tug toys, jute rolls, or play rags. The trainer throws one of the items and the dog is sent to retrieve it. Once the dog returns to the trainer, he is enticed with the second item. This creates a conflict within the animal between the desired item and that which he already possesses. The conflict leads to a willingness to release the possessed item, which has no movement, and rewarded with the desired item. The trainer must add enough movement to the second item to build the desire to release. Do not reach for the item that the dog possesses, let it drop to the ground, and immediately reward the dog with the second item. To end this training session, provoke the release and escape the dog away from the area. Do not progress to the next step until the dog willingly releases the prey item.

Double Decoy Method (Step 2)
This technique follows the same principle as the double ball method, releasing the dead object (no movement) for the one with life (movement). Adding the presence of the decoy in this step evokes aggression in the form of fight drive and makes it more difficult for the animal. Step 2 is comprised of three phases.

Phase I
The dog is sent for a bite and the first decoy slips the sleeve. The trainer should then walk the dog in a circle. Do not allow the dog to drag, thrash, or manipulate the sleeve, these behaviors degrade the training. To prevent this, increase the gait causing the dog to lift the sleeve high for the carry. The second decoy evokes the dog by adding life to the other sleeve. The dog's focus will shift from the dead sleeve to the one with life. The trainer should not correct the dog or interfere. Let the natural drive dictate the dog's behavior! He will release and transfer to the sleeve with life. The second decoy rewards the dog with the slip of the sleeve. End your session by evoking a release and escape the dog away from the area. Once the dog shows consistency on this phase, progress to PHASE II.

Phase II
Begin as in PHASE I by sending the dog for a bite on the first decoy while the second decoy is out of the dog's view. The first decoy will not slip the sleeve, after the bite he must freeze and offer no fight or life. The second decoy is introduced and moves close to the dog. Once in position he provides life in the second sleeve, this stimulates the dog's prey drive. The dog will release the first sleeve and take the one with life. There is a period of conflict at this point which will vary from dog to dog. Allow the dog time to make the transition! The handler should not interfere. The key is to let the dog accomplish the tasks through positive reinforcement. Verbal or physical corrections will void this training process and detract from the dogs learning ability. When the dog transfers, the second decoy slips the sleeve providing the reward. Let the dog carry the sleeve in a circle as in PHASE I.

Phase III
Once the dog consistently releases the sleeve in PHASE II, increase the distance between the two decoys, and add the verbal cue "OUT". Give the cue in a moderate tone of voice and time it with the dog's natural release. At this point the trainer should know the dog well enough to predict the release. Use successive approximation to add distance between the two decoys, allowing the dog to run back and forth for each bite. Locate the trainer between the decoys and encourage the dog as he makes the transfer. The goal in PHASE III is to have your trainer, dog and decoy positioned as in a standard controlled aggression training session. The second decoy is located behind the dog team out of sight. As the first decoy freezes, the handler commands "OUT" the dog should release cleanly and return to the handler with enthusiasm because he anticipates the reward bite. As the dog is returning to the handler, he is redirected to the second decoy. From this point begin to extinct the second decoy by commanding the dog to "HEEL" follow the proper heel with a reward bite on the same decoy. As in all aspects of dog training, vary the routine to prevent anticipation on the dog's part.

Obedience Bite
This training principle is an extension of the reward bite; it consists of the same techniques but is employed differently. The dog is cued to conduct an obedience task and rewarded for the correct behavior with a bite, slip, and carry. Use of this training method will create positive focus on the handler and higher drive in obedience. The end result provides a more reliable and confident animal. This method also helps to eliminate hesitation problems.

Continuation Training
Employ the reward bite method intermittently throughout training. Use it to build the dog in all aspects of patrol training, including building search and scouting. When you use the reward bite in these scenarios, the decoy should work the dog to get a full hard bite and then release the sleeve. The training supervisor predetermines the level of "fight" the decoy uses, always striving to build the dog's confidence and reliability.

False Run (Decoy)
The objective of this exercise is to condition the dog to remain in position and not bite unless commanded to. Conduct initial training on leash. When the handler commands the MWD to stay, begin to suspiciously advance towards the dog. Use successive approximation and move toward the dog from the starting position. The dog's actions will dictate how many trials it will take to completely train the dog. If the dog attempts to bite, or fails to remain in position, the handler must immediately correct the dog. To prevent the dog from becoming deficient in aggression and attack, the agitator and handler should decide when to give the dog a bite. To maintain aggressiveness, you may allow the dog to bite on a random basis during this type of training. To fully condition the dog, the decoy should mimic provocative behavior encountered in real-world situations.

Controlled Aggression
Used to teach the dog to pursue, bite, and hold on command. The team starts in the HEEL/SIT position off leash. Wearing the arm protector, move around suspiciously about 40 to 50 feet in front of the team. The handler will order the agitator to halt and place their hands over their head. The agitator ignores this order, turns, and attempts to run away. The handler commands the dog "GET 'EM." When the handler calls the dog —OUT, the decoy ceases all resistance and agitation.

Standoff
This training enables the handler to gain complete control over the dog after commanded to pursue. The starting position is the same as with the attack and apprehension. Approach the dog making provocative

gestures. When you get within a few feet, turn and run away. After you're about 30 feet from the team, the handler will command "GET 'EM." When you hear this command, cease all movement. The dog will be called "OUT." This training may become confusing to the dog; therefore, to keep it at an acceptable level of aggressiveness, allow it to bite at irregular intervals. NOTE: You may vary time and distance in all aspects of stand- off training depending on the dog's proficiency level.

Double Decoy Attack
This exercise requires an additional decoy. The purpose of this exercise is to teach the dog to ignore one of the decoys while pursuing, biting, and holding the other. The dog starts off leash in the HEEL/SIT position. Position the decoys approximately 30 feet from the dog team. The handler challenges by ordering them to halt. One decoy obeys the command while the other ignores it and runs away. The handler immediately commands "GET 'EM." The dog ignores the decoy that halts and pursues, bites and holds the second decoy. During the early stages of this training, attract the dog's attention by making provoking gestures and noises.

Scouting
The primary mission of the MWD is to detect and warn the handler of the presence of an intruder. The team is placed in a semi-cleared area facing into the wind. The terrain features in front of the team should allow the decoy to run and crouch behind bushes and trees. Before the decoy starts to run, the handler tells the dog to "WATCH 'EM," the decoy will run from one point to another, acting suspicious, and hide at a pre-designated position of cover. The decoy will leave cover and run when the team is within 15 feet. This exercise is concluded with a short chase and bite.

Building Search
On-Leash Building Search
Introduce the building search on leash as an agitation exercise ends in such a way that it will seem a natural extension of agitation training. For example, as an agitation exercise ends, the agitator runs away from the dog and hides behind the doorway to an adjacent building. The team will pursue to the doorway. The agitator continues to provoke the dog to illicit a desire to pursue. The procedures remain the same until the dog is ready to advance to the next step, which is to enter a building and actually seek out an intruder while concealed on floor level. To assure the dog of the agitator's presence, you may need to provide a faint noise or an obvious movement for the dog. The noise and/or actions should cause the dog to bark or produce a response. The decoy may have to agitate or act afraid of the dog to get a favorable response. Conclude this exercise with the team escorting the agitator out of the building.

Off-Leash Building Search
During off-leash building search, perform exercises in the same manner as on leash. Conceal the agitator in a location inaccessible to the dog--either floor level or an elevated position. The agitator must remain quiet and motionless allowing enough time for the dog to detect and respond. The agitator(s) may need to make noise or partially reveal themselves to ensure success. The ultimate goal is for the dog to detect and respond to the agitator while separated from the handler.

PROFICIENCY STANDARDS AND EVALUATIONS

The Kennel Master is responsible for establishing an effective training and evaluation program to maximize the dog and handler's proficiency. The post certification standards establish minimum proficiency standards the dog team must maintain. These standards must be met within 90 days of team assignment and validated annually thereafter. Certification standards are a combination of dog training scenarios conducted within the controlled environment of the MWD section's dog training area and within the actual working environment the dog team performs their duties. Certifications are documented on the AF Form 321/Military Working Dog Training and Utilization Record. Should a team fail to meet the minimum proficiency standards; the Kennel Master will immediately initiate remedial training. If, after remedial training, it is determined the poor performance of the team is due to the dog and not its handler contact the 341 TRS Dog Training Section for further guidance.

Obedience Commands

Dog's must respond to the handler's commands of "SIT," "DOWN," "HEEL," and "STAY" at a distance of 50 feet with no more than one correction per five commands. The dog must on the command of "STAY," remain either in the SIT or DOWN position for 3 minutes.

Controlled Aggression

Evaluations should be a combination of scenarios conducted within the controlled environment of the MWD training area and on post.

False Run (off Leash)

Given the command "STAY," when confronted by an individual who approaches no closer than 3 feet, the dog must not break position.

Stand-off

When commanded to bite and hold the intruder(s), the dog must pursue until commanded "OUT" and "HEEL" by the handler. The dog must not bite the intruder regardless of the intruder's actions.

Bite and Hold

When commanded "GET 'EM," the dog must pursue, bite, and hold an intruder for a minimum of 15 seconds. The dog must not release until commanded "OUT." Dogs must demonstrate proficiency in this task with either an exposed or concealed arm protector.

Search and Escort

The handler positions the suspect at a distance of 6 to 8 feet from the dog, facing away from the dog and advises the suspect not to move. The handler then moves up and conducts a search of the suspect. Once the search is conducted, the handler positions themselves directly behind the suspect(s) and calls the dog to the heel position. The handler then puts the dog on leash, takes control of the suspect by placing their non-leash hand on the suspect's shoulder and then conducts the escort. Prior to initiating the escort, the handler will instruct the suspect to only move when told to do so, and that any sudden movement of the suspect may result in the dog breaking the heel position and biting. The dog may heel on the handler or slightly forward and to the side of the suspect to ensure an effective escort. During training, re-attack scenarios should be conducted periodically to ensure that the dog will perform the task without command.

Building Search

The dog finds an intruder with or without an arm protector hidden in a building and indicates to the handler the presence/location of the intruder.

Scouting

The dog finds an intruder hidden in an open area or field by scent at 50 yards, sight at 35 yards downwind, or sound at 35 yards downwind. Consider terrain and weather conditions when evaluating by these standards.

Vehicle Patrol

The MWD rides in a vehicle driven by the handler without showing aggression towards handler or other passengers.

Gunfire

The MWD successfully performs basic obedience, and controlled aggression tasks, during gunfire. Gunfire during aggression phases of training must be kept to a minimum.

Obedience Course

The dog negotiates the obstacle course at a moderate rate of speed on or off leash in the HEEL position.

SF STANDARDIZATION & EVALUATIONS

The Kennel Master should work closely with the unit's STAN-EVAL section to assist in the coordination of practical/performance evaluations of dog handlers being formally evaluated as an MWD patrolman.

CHAPTER 4

CLEAR SIGNALS TRAINING METHOD

INTRODUCTION

Dog training methodology is not static. Instead, as a result of new insights and new information, dog training methods evolve, becoming more effective and more powerful. This chapter is meant to provide a brief review of new techniques that are available for training Military Working Dogs for obedience and controlled aggression. These techniques are currently used at the 341 TRS, Lackland AFB, TX.

CLEAR SIGNALS TRAINING METHOD

In the last 10 years, enormous technical progress has been made in the methods used to train working dogs for obedience and controlled aggression. The most important advances were made by amateur trainers who compete in obedience competition. The method developed for use by the DoD MWD Program is called Clear Signals Training (CST).

CST is founded on three very important ideas:
1. Teach skills with rewards, not physical force;
2. Establish clear communication;
3. Use compulsion only when necessary, and use it in a fair and effective fashion.

Teach Skills with Rewards, not Physical Force
As much as possible, MWDs should be taught and motivated to work using rewards to induce desired behavior, rather than using force to compel the dog to do as the trainer wants (see discussions of inducive versus compulsive training methods).

Establish Clear Communication
One of the most critical aspects of dog training is the development of clear communication between handler and dog, so that the dog knows what the trainer wants, and it fully understands the relationships between its behavior and various consequences.

CST makes sure the dog understands what the trainer wants by breaking training into stages, the first of which is a teaching phase in which the dog performs for rewards in a very low-stress atmosphere.

CST makes sure that the dog understands the relationships between its behavior and specific consequences (the response contingencies—see Ch 2) by using conditioned signals or—markers (the words —Yes, —Good, and —No) to help the dog realize exactly which of its behaviors resulted in a particular reward or a particular punishment. This approach has only recently become established in the working dog world, but for many years it has been extremely influential in the training of exotic animals like killer whales and big cats. In more recent years the response marking approach has also influenced trainers that work with dogs assisting deaf persons, and otherwise disadvantaged populations. When combined with the use of positive reinforcement techniques, response-marking methods are the most powerful available technology for shaping behaviors, and they should become a basic part of the DoD MWD Program skill set.

Use Compulsion Only when Necessary, and Use it in a Fair and Effective Fashion
CST assumes for the dog trainer to use physical force or compulsion (see Ch. 2) in a way that is effective and fair, the dog must first pass through two stages of learning. It must first be taught the skill (e.g. sitting or lying down), so that it understands what is required before it is subjected to any physical or psychological pressure. Then the dog must also go through another stage in which it is taught about the correction that will be used to apply the pressure (e.g. the jerk on the choke collar). In this stage the dog learns that it can terminate the correction by using a certain behavior, and it learns not to fear the correction (here we are discussing a very gentle version of escape learning). Only when the dog understands the skill and understands the correction and how to respond to it is it fair and effective for the handler to apply strong pressure (to generate avoidance learning).

Teach, Train, and Proof. CST Breaks MWD Training into a Three-Stage Process
Each skill is first taught, then trained, and then proofed. Not all skills that we teach working dogs participate in all three of these phases, but many of them do, especially obedience skills like sit, down, and heel.

Teach
The initial stage is called teaching. During this stage the dog learns what is expected of it in a given situation. As a rule, teaching proceeds best when the dog works for a reward like food or a ball/kong, and is not stressed or anxious. Earlier we described this kind of training as—inducive and pointed out that the two inducive tools available are positive reinforcement and negative punishment (also called omission). During teaching we concentrate on motivating and teaching the dog in a low-stress atmosphere, giving it rewards when it performs correctly (positive reinforcement) and withholding rewards (negative punishment) when it makes mistakes.

1. For example, we teach the dog to sit by holding food over its head. In the effort to reach the food, the dog lifts its head and rocks backward, accidentally assuming the sit position, and then we reward this action by allowing the dog to have the food.
2. For example, we teach the dog to maintain eye contact with the trainer by making a noise so that the dog looks at the trainer's face, and then we allow the dog to have the ball/kong.
3. During teaching we avoid the use of any physical force or input designed to compel the dog to perform a specific behavior. Instead the dog is given the freedom to experiment with its own behavior and learn what responses bring reward and which responses do not bring reward. Errors are seen as desirable because it is by making mistakes that the dog sharpens its understanding of correct behavior.
4. During initial teaching we normally rely on continuous reinforcement in which we reward every correct repetition of the exercise.
5. Teaching normally involves the use of obvious gestures and body language cues that the trainer uses to lure the dog into position with the reward—moving the hand upwards for the sit, bending at the waist and placing the hand on the ground for the down, etc. These gestures are called prompts, and with further training they are normally faded out.

Train
The next phase of CST is called *training*. During the training phase we take the practiced skill that the dog has learned to use to obtain reward and we put it under the influence of some form of physical correction. In dog training, it is very common to use the term correction for physical inputs that are meant to pressure the dog into certain actions. Thus, correction refers to the other two response contingencies described earlier, negative reinforcement and positive punishment. This does not mean that during training we use heavy psychological and physical pressure on the dog. Far to the contrary, during training our main objective is to keep the dog

comfortable and positively motivated, while showing it the meaning of each specific correction, teaching the animal that it has the power to control this correction, and teaching it how we wish it to behave under the correction.

For example, we train the dog to associate a tug on the leash/choke collar with sitting by asking the dog to sit in the presence of food, much like before, but after we give the sit command we give a soft correction on the collar by popping the leash. The pop does not make the dog execute the sit; the animal is already sitting because of habit and its desire for reward. The pop does not hurt the dog. The procedure connects the correction to the sit, it puts the sit skill under the control of the collar correction.

For example, we train the dog to maintain eye contact (attention) by bringing the dog into focus on the handler and keeping it there for a moment. An assistant provides a soft distraction like tapping a foot so that the dog looks away from the handler for an instant. At that moment the handler says the dog's name and an instant later gives a soft pop on the leash/collar. The pop does not make the dog look back at the handler. The dog looks back simply because it hears its name and it wants reward. But the procedure connects the pop to attention so that the dog's attention comes under the control of the leash correction.

Proof

The last phase of CST training is called proofing. During proofing the handler reduces the frequency of reinforcement (moving into intermittent and random reinforcement schedules), begins to fade out gestures (prompts) that have been used to assist the dog to execute skills, and begins asking the dog to perform the skills in different, distracting environments. As a result of these changes, the dog's performance is disrupted. To put it another way, the animal makes mistakes, and these mistakes may be corrected (to generate avoidance learning).

Corrections administered during proofing of a particular skill, like sitting under distraction or holding the down-stay, must be fair. Another way to say that a correction is fair is to say that it is effective, and the dog learns very quickly to avoid any future corrections. Providing that we have done a good job of teaching and training a skill, proofing of that skill normally proceeds efficiently (i.e. results in avoidance responding), and without any particular upset or stress on the dog's part.

Table 1. Teaching, Training, And Proofing Phases of Various MWD Skills

	Teaching Phase	**Training Phase**	**Proofing Phase**
Skill	Dog learns to perform a skill for reward—errors are permitted and even encouraged so that the dog learns which behaviors are successful and which behaviors are errors.	Dog learns that the skill terminates or turns off a gentle correction, and that an error (such as breaking attention or breaking the sit-stay) —turns back on the correction See *escape learning.*	Dog learns that, even though the skill still earns reward, this reward is less frequent, and the skill is mandatory—Refusal and errors—turn on sharp corrections, and compliance to first command avoids corrections altogether. See *avoidance learning.*
Attention	Teach dog to look at the handler on cue (usually the dog's name) for food, then transition to ball/kong reward.	Train dog to turn off mild collar corrections by looking at handler on cue, or by continuing to look at the handler.	On first command, dog must pay attention to the handler, and maintain this attention despite distractions, in order to avoid sharp collar

			correction--Initially dog given food, ball/kong frequently to reduce stress; later these primary rewards to some extent—weaned out.
Down	Teach dog how to lie down for food, then transition to ball/kong reward.	Train dog to turn off mild collar correction and social correction (see 4.2.7.3.3) by lying down, or by holding the down.	On first command, dog must lie down quickly and hold the down, in order to avoid a sharp collar correction or strong social correction (see 4.2.7.3.3)—Initially dog given food, ball/kong frequently to reduce stress; later these primary rewards to some extent—weaned out.
Heel	Teach dog to move to heel position for food, then transition to ball/kong reward.	Train dog to turn off mild collar corrections by moving to heel position, or by staying at heel and in attention.	On first command, dog must move to heel position, establish attention (looking at handler's face), and maintain heel position and attention, in order to avoid sharp collar correction. Initially dog given food, ball/kong frequently to reduce stress; later these primary rewards to some extent—weaned out.
Out	Teach dog to release grip on—dead object to earn another bite and —fight – Not always practical. Normally begun using a less motivating object such as PVC pipe.	Train dog to turn off collar corrections by releasing bite. If necessary, dog forced to release with collar correction. Performed with more motivating bite object like rubber hose or jute tug toy.	Dog must release bite immediately on first command in order to avoid sharp collar correction. Performed on decoy with bite sleeve, suit, etc.
Stand-off	Teach dog to earn bite by lying down on command—Decoy comes to the dog to give reward (see 4.4.5.8.1.1).	Train dog to turn off mild collar corrections by stopping forward movement, and then lying down.	Dog must stop forward movement on command in order to avoid sharp correction—Down maintained by positive reinforcement—I.e. once dog stops moving

			forward, tends to lie down voluntarily to earn bite.
Odor recognition	Teach dog that target odor is associated with ball/kong.		
Final response	Teach dog to sit in order to gain access to a blocked ball/kong (—blocked = held in hands, wedged between furniture and wall, etc.).	Sit in response to odor supported by the use of mild cues (pressure on rump, mild pops on collar) that are turned off by the sit.	

The Escape Training Method

We should compare CST to more traditional methods in which the dog is not taught skills inducively, but instead has to learn what is expected under physical force. In this situation, because the skills are associated from the beginning of training with psychological pressure and discomfort, the dog learns to dislike its work and to resist the trainer, which makes the animal difficult to train. More importantly, the dog also becomes defensive. What we mean by defensive is this: When we expose an animal time and again to something unpleasant like a jarring collar correction, or choking with a chain collar, and we have not previously taught the animal how to understand this correction, then the first thing that the animal begins to do when it anticipates a correction (e.g. when it hears the —sit command) is protect/defend itself by stiffening its neck and bracing its legs. Obviously, a dog that is physically stiff and tense has great difficulty sitting quickly (or doing anything quickly), so the dog tends to make more mistakes, and receive more corrections; which makes the animal even more stiff and tense, and so on. For these reasons, traditional escape methods for obedience and patrol tend to generate very high levels of resistance, fear, and confusion on dogs' part.

In contrast, CST is directed at preventing fear and confusion by first teaching the dog exactly what to do on command to get a reward (teaching), then teaching it how to use this action to turn off' a correction (training), and finally showing it that sometimes it has no choice but to do what its handler commands (proofing). When training is approached this way, even if the trainer finds it necessary to apply physical force to the dog, the animal is not excessively frightened or stressed; because it knows what to do and how to control the correction it receives (respond quickly to terminate the correction, and then in future the behave so as to avoid the correction completely).

The Clear Signals part of CST

The division of MWD training into teaching, training, and proofing phases is a new idea in the DoD MWD program, but it is not cutting-edge theory. Teach-train-proof is a version of what the best dog trainers have been doing for decades now. But the next part of CST is more revolutionary—it involves the use of conditioned cues to communicate with the dog, to give it very precise information about the relationship between its behavior and rewards and punishments. These conditioned cues are called markers, and often bridges, because they perform two very important functions—marking responses for reward or correction, and bridging delays to reward or correction.

Response (or Behavior) Marking

Most skills in dog training feature a critical aspect, a point in the course of the skill when the trainer's requirement is fully met. This can be the moment the dog locks its eyes on its handler's in response to the —look command for attention, or the moment the dog's elbows touch the ground in response to the —down command. If we can make the dog understand that it is these critical aspects, these core requirements of the skill, that earn reward, then we can become very effective trainers.

In traditional training we try to make the dog understand by following the old rule—in order for the dog to understand why it is being rewarded or corrected, reward and correction must follow immediately after the desired behavior. The problem is that in many situations it is very difficult to reward a desired behavior without accidentally rewarding some behavior that comes after the desired behavior. To choose just one of very many examples, if I am teaching my dog to march/heel while maintaining attention on my face, and I start to reward this behavior with the kong in my right pocket, when the dog sees me move my hand towards my right pocket it looks at my hand instead of my face, and often it crosses in front of me to follow the hand to where it knows the reward is. Therefore, when I produce the ball and give it to the dog, I am not rewarding the behavior I want (clean heeling at the left side with eye contact) but other behaviors (looking at my right hand, forging ahead, crossing in front, and interfering with my movement) which are detrimental to my goal.

The —Yes release marker. The use of a marker solves this problem for us. The marker we most commonly use is the word —yes said in a distinctive way. In order to use the —yes, we must first condition it—turn it into a secondary reinforcer by pairing it with the reward (see classical or Pavlovian conditioning and secondary reinforcers). Most often we use —yes with ball reward. We can condition the marker by saying —yes and then giving the dog the ball about a dozen times, with about ½ to 1 second between —yes and the ball. Once the —yes marker is conditioned, then it has gained the power to act as a reward. The word has become significant, and when I say —yes immediately after some behavior on the dog's part, the dog notices what it has done—the behavior is marked.

In order to produce rapid learning of the desired behavior, you need to let the dog have the primary reinforcer, the ball. And here is the advantage to using the —yes—Because I have marked the desired behavior with the word —yes you are no longer under pressure to get the reward to the dog quickly, and you do not need to worry about any behaviors the dog engages in between the behavior you want to reward and when the dog actually receives the ball. The:

- —Yes marker does three critical things for the trainer.
- —Yes marks a specific desired behavior (e.g. making eye contact while moving in heel position).
- —Yes releases the dog from the behavior—when the dog hears —yes it knows it's finished with its job.
- —Yes bridges the delay to reinforcement (hence the term bridge, often used interchangeably with marker). Even though it may take me 10 seconds to get the ball out of my pocket and give it to the dog, and the whole time the dog is dancing around me and jumping up and down in anticipation of getting its reward, when the dog actually gets the ball it will associate this reward with what it was doing right before it heard —yes instead of what it was doing right before it got the ball.

Because the dog can release after hearing —yes, because the job is ended when the —yes is given, this cue is called a terminal marker. Saying —yes is just like saying —OK, in that the dog can do anything it wants after it hears —yes.

The good marker. However, sometimes we don't want to release the dog, we want to encourage it but keep it performing. In this case we need a different kind of marker. Because the skill is not done when we use this marker, it is called an intermediate marker (as opposed to the terminal marker, —yes). In CST the intermediate bridge is usually the word —good, said in a distinctive and encouraging voice.

The sequence runs like this—While the dog is performing the skill it receives one or two good markers at critical moments, then when it has finished the skill to the trainer's satisfaction it receives the —yes, and then the primary reward. Because the dog hears —good before receiving the —yes cue and then receiving the reward, after a number of repetitions the —good also becomes associated with reward (this is called second-order conditioning) and —good also takes on the power to reinforce and mark behaviors.

The two methods of marking and rewarding behavior. We have now described two different ways of rewarding the dog with markers —yes-release, and —good-marker followed by —yes-release.

—Yes-release. When the dog has completed the skill, the trainer rewards it with the —yes cue. On hearing —yes the dog breaks from position, and the trainer provides the primary reward. Yes-marking is used to teach the dog to respond swiftly to commands.

—Good-marker followed by —yes-release. When the dog is doing well, the trainer encourages it with the —good cue, the dog continues to perform, and then when the skill is complete, the handler releases with —yes, and then provides the primary reward. —Good-marker then —yes-release is used to encourage the dog and keep it performing.

Reward in position. A special kind of —good-marker followed by —yes-release is used to stabilize the dog into certain positions, such as the sit and down at the end of the leash, sit at heel position, and the field interview. These skills are all characterized by one problem—the dog is supposed to stay in a particular place and position, but it will be rewarded from another location. For instance, after sit and down EOL, the dog is recalled to heel and then released and rewarded. Because the dog anticipates this reward, it begins to creep forward towards the handler while moving from down to sit or vice-versa, and many difficulties can follow. To prevent these difficulties with anticipation, the handler can follow this procedure: When the dog accomplishes a correct transition (e.g rising from down to sit without moving towards the handler), the handler marks this behavior with —good! Then the handler walks to the dog, removes the primary reward from his/her pocket, and holds the reward very close to the dog's nose while the dog maintains position (obviously some preliminary training is required to gain good control of the dog's behavior in the presence of the reward). When the dog is steady the handler gives the —yes cue; the dog normally first takes the reward and then breaks from position. Because the dog receives the reward in position, the animal is not encouraged to creep while performing EOL. Because the handler used the —good to mark the correct transition from down to sit, the dog knows what it is being rewarded for. As a result, with repetition the dog will become more and more proficient at performing EOL without creeping toward the handler. This method of providing reward while the dog is in position and using —good to make sure it knows what it is being rewarded for, is called reward in position.

—OK. Another method of releasing the dog from work. For clarity of communication, it is extremely important that the dog know when a particular skill is finished. The verbal cue that the trainer uses to tell the dog that a skill is finished is called the release. We have already discussed how the —yes marker serves as both a behavior marker and a release cue. The trainer can also release the dog with the cue —OK. The difference between —yes and —OK is that while —yes is a promise to the dog that it will be rewarded after a delay, —OK is used to release the dog from work when the trainer does not intend to give the dog a primary reward. This can be the case when the dog will merely be praised, or when the dog has made a mistake, and the trainer intends to make it repeat the exercise correctly before providing a reward.

Rewards Used in Obedience Training

CST (like virtually every effective system for teaching obedience to working dogs) relies heavily on positive reinforcement to teach lessons and motivate performance. Sources of positive reinforcement are praise, food, tug toys, and ball or kong.

Praise

Praise and social reinforcement are vital ingredients to working dog training, and some dogs can be obedience trained with nothing but praise as a positive reinforcer, combined with corrections to discourage disobedience. The problem is that few of the dogs that DoD procures are trainable with this method—they are not socialized in the way that pet dogs or sport dogs are socialized, and without a background of proper socialization, praise alone is often not sufficient to support efficient training. In addition, praise suffers from one great disadvantage. Praise does not provide us with a focal point or goal that we can use to attract, lure, and manipulate the dog, the way we can with, for instance, a handful of food.

Food
Food is a very effective positive reinforcer for many dogs, but eventually we must wean the dog off of food and find other sources of motivation that are more operationally practical. In addition, a substantial number of the dogs procured by DoD do not have enough desire for treat food to perform useful training.

Tug Toy
Many dogs work well for the opportunity to play with a tug toy, but not all. Dogs that are bought for detection only may exhibit little desire to bite and tug on an object.

Ball
This leaves one remaining source of motivation, ball or kong (hereafter referred to as ball). This is just as well, because the ball is cheap, easily carried and used, and every military dog is selected especially for its intense desire to chase, carry, and play with balls. Many DoD trainers (educated in the escape method of obedience training) never allow an MWD to play with its ball except in the course of detection training, for fear that ball-play will de-value the dog's primary reward for detection training. However, as long as the dog has high levels of retrieve/play drive, this is an outmoded and unnecessary practice. Countless highly effective detector dogs are allowed to play with the ball in obedience and sometimes just for exercise and the sheer fun of it, and they do not lose their effectiveness in detection. On the contrary, ball play keeps their enthusiasm for the ball high, and their physical condition and stamina high as well.

Corrections Used in Patrol Training
CST resembles traditional methods of dog training in that it makes extensive use of physical inputs called corrections. Corrections are designed to do three things for the trainer:
1. Increase the dog's precision of performance;
2. Reduce dependency on primary rewards (food, ball/kong, and tug toy);
3. Ensure that the dog performs correctly regardless of distractions.

Fundamentally, corrections accomplish these functions by exerting punishment and negative reinforcement effects, which means that by definition effective corrections are unpleasant for the dog. The responsibility of the trainer is to use this unpleasantness for proper effect, while treating the animal fairly and humanely, and ensuring that, although moments of the dog's training are unpleasant, on the whole it enjoys training, and has affection and trust for the trainer rather than fear.

Humane Versus Inhumane Corrections
Barring techniques that are likely to produce physical injury, it is not possible to categorize certain forms of correction as humane and others as inhumane simply on the basis of the physical parameters of the corrections. The primary concerns in judging whether a given correction technique is humane in a certain situation are:

Will the correction cause physical injury?
A correction procedure that causes physical injury to the dog, or is likely to cause physical injury, is inhumane.

Does the dog understand what behavior is required of it in this situation?
If the dog does not understand what behavior is required, or cannot very quickly learn the required behavior, then the procedure is inhumane.

Is the dog capable of executing the desired response in this situation?
The dog may be incapable of executing the response, even though it understands the response (i.e. it may not be able to sit quickly, because it is too physically tense and apprehensive to do so, or it may not be able to release a bite object on command because severe treatment has conditioned biting to the pain of collar corrections). If the dog is incapable of executing the desired response, then the procedure is inhumane.

Does the dog learn from the correction, so that it quickly changes its behavior and thereby avoids further corrections?
If the procedure does produce learning, with the result that the dog continues to experience correction in training session after training session, then it is inhumane.

By the above definitions, procedures involving rather mild corrections may be inhumane, because they are not effective for one reason or another and the dog never learns to prevent them. Even mild events, if they are chronic and unpleasant and uncontrollable, can cause significant suffering. By the same token, procedures that appear rigorous and severe may be eminently humane because they do not injure the dog, and because they result in rapid learning and no more corrections. These are subjective judgments best made by experts in dog training, but these experts must always be prepared to justify their procedures and practices on the basis of above. Ultimately, perhaps the best indicator of what is humane and what is not is the dog. Is the animal eager for work and eager for contact with its trainer at all times? Then it is likely that this dog's training is conducted humanely. Or does it consistently show inhibition, avoidance behavior, and fear in training contexts? Then it is likely that at some point the dog was treated inhumanely.

Tools and Methods for Correction
Choke Collars
Choke collars may be made of nylon webbing, light or heavy chain, or nylon cord, connecting two metal rings. In general, the thinner and smaller the chain or cord, and the more efficiently it runs through the rings, the more severe a collar it is, because forces exerted through the collar on the dog's neck are distributed over a smaller area. The choke collar is used either to make a jerking correction followed by an immediate release of pressure (i.e. a pop), or by exerting a steady pull to produce a choking sensation. Choke chains are very well-accepted in American life and are sold wherever pet supplies are sold.

Pinch (or Prong) Collars
Pinch/prong collars are assemblies of heavy, bent wire links arranged with a chain yoke, so that when the leash attached to the yoke is pulled, the links tighten on the dog's neck and the dull ends of the wire links exert pressure on the dog's neck. They produce a sharper sensation than choke collars do and can be used with a lighter touch and more precise timing, because less force is needed to get an equivalent effect. Pinch collars are generally used by jerking or popping the attached leash. They are also very well accepted in American life and are sold wherever pet supplies are sold.

Social corrections
Slaps or cuffs of the foot, hand, or leash-end, or pokes of the fingers. In many circumstances, the quickest and most efficient correction is made by gently slapping the dog with hand, foot, or leash-end, or by poking the dog with stiffened fingers, especially when the handler's intent is to stop the dog from moving forward or biting. Such corrections have the advantage that they do not depend upon the presence of leash and collar, and therefore if used properly give the handler greater control over the dog in a wider range of situations.

Appropriate, effective, and humane examples are:

The handler commands the dog to lie down while the MWD team is heeling rapidly forward (as when an MWD team is running from one position of cover to another in a fire zone). The dog does not lie down quickly, and the handler slaps the dog on the back or neck or ears with the hand or the leash end. The handler then heels forward again rapidly and repeats the command and, if the dog complies rapidly, it is praised and petted and given food reward while in down position.

The handler commands the dog to release a ball, the dog does so, and the ball drops to the ground and comes to rest. The handler commands the dog to —stay and reaches to take the ball, but as he/she does so, the dog attempts to bite the ball, and thereby the handler's fingers. The handler says —no and cuffs the dog sharply on the side of the muzzle with the open palm of the other hand. As a result, a moment later the dog is somewhat tentative in taking the ball from the handler's hands, even when invited to do so, and the handler praises and encourages this respect for his/her hands/fingers.

The handler holds the dog on a 6-foot leash and gives the —heel command, but the dog is distracted by nearby activity and reluctant to obey, and keeps turning its head and forequarters away and pulling into the leash, making it difficult for the handler to get enough slack on the leash to give a popping leash correction; so the handler uses the instep of his/her foot to slap the dog sharply on the big muscle at the back of the thigh. The dog, startled, turns to look at the handler, and the handler instantly encourages the dog to come by praising it and running backwards, and then gives the dog a ball reward.

Electronic/electric collars. Electronic collars are devices that deliver a high-voltage but very, very low-amperage electric shock to the skin of the dog's neck through electrodes. They are operated remotely by means of a hand-held transmitter on which there are intensity settings and buttons which trigger continuous or momentary shocks through the collar and sometimes beeps and tones (markers) that aid the dog in understanding what is required of it. This electrical shock is like a static electrical discharge from the carpet; it is similar to, but much weaker than, the shock delivered by a livestock fence. This shock may be uncomfortable, but it does not cause injury, because injury is a result of the amperage of an electrical shock, not the voltage.

Electronic collars are common and well-accepted instruments, not only among the pet-owning American public but also by Federal agencies (e.g. United States Secret Service) and very many state, county, and city law enforcement agencies.

Electronic collars provide the ability to deliver electrical stimulation that is finely calibrated to the individual dog's level of sensitivity, over long distances and with very precise timing. However, electronic collars demand a very high level of technical knowledge and ability from the trainer, for a number of reasons:

Because the onset and offset of electrical stimulation is so precise and clean, the electronic collar magnifies the effect of any errors of timing on the trainer's part. A satisfactory analogy is razor blade—it cuts clean, but it had better be handled with expertise and care, or accidents will happen.

Without prior teaching and training to show the dog how to respond to it, electrical stimulation of the dog's neck produces something like a startle response—the dog throws its head up, or bends its neck and perhaps jumps forward or up, precisely as you would do if you were momentarily shocked on the back or neck by a prank buzzer. This means that the dog's natural reaction to electrical stimulation of its neck does not help it do any of the things that we might be interested in training an MWD to do—recall to the handler, lie down, or release a bite. Therefore, the dog must be very expertly prepared through teaching phase (teach it what to do and how to do it in order to earn reward) and training phase (show it how to use this behavior to turn off very mild levels of electrical stimulation) of CST, before the proofing phase (convince it that it must perform the behavior to avoid uncomfortable levels of electrical stimulation) is accomplished with electronic collar. Otherwise even the most well-meaning trainer can completely fail the humaneness test. The dog may not understand what it is supposed to do, be unable to do what it is supposed to, and be unable to learn what it is supposed to do. With even mild levels of shock this is inhumane and unacceptable.

As of this writing, the only arm of the United States Air Force that is authorized to employ the electronic collar is 341 TRS, Lackland AFB, Texas. The electronic collar is utilized only in particular cases with special authorization, under the supervision of specially-trained personnel, to solve severe training problems in high-value MWDs.

OBEDIENCE TRAINING WITH CST

Sit and Down
Teaching Sit and Down
1. Sit and Down are best taught by luring the dog into position with soft, appetizing food. This food must be something like small pieces of meat or specialty dog food that the dog is eager for and that it swallows quickly without chewing. Crunchy treats do not work well. The dog is first taught to eat from the hand and then taught to maintain soft contact with the hand and follow the hand until it is allowed to eat. Then the handler uses the closed hand to lure the dog into position (square, erect sit; or sphinx-like down position with both elbows in contact with the ground), and then loosens the hand so that the dog can lick and nibble the food out of it while holding position. Then, before the dog breaks position the handler releases the dog by saying —OK and enticing the dog out of position. Through a number of steps, this is developed into sit and down on command with stay (for 5 or 6 seconds), using the dog's food motivation only.
2. The same method can be used with the ball, but because the dog's level of excitement will be much higher than in the case of food, the technique requires more skill and experience. In addition, prior to luring the dog into position using the ball, the animal must be taught to release it cleanly on command (—out), to refrain from biting the reward until given permission, and to respect (i.e. not bite) the trainer's hands. The handler must be able to hold the ball/kong in his/her hand an inch or two from the dog's head without having the dog take the ball until it is given permission. In addition, the dog must learn to follow the hand closely, the way a dog would naturally follow a hand in which food is held, but without snapping at or biting the hand.
3. —Sit and —Down commands are given as the dog is lured into position.
4. —Good is used when the dog is holding position well, before the dog is fed. The dog is fed in position, without being released. —OK and enticement are used to release the dog from position. —No is used to mark errors, and to tell the dog that it will not be rewarded. For instance, the dog is in down position, the trainer moves the hand towards its nose to feed it, the dog begins to crawl towards the hand to eat, the trainer says —No and stands upright, withdrawing the hand and the food until the dog re- stabilizes in down position. —Stay may be used to steady the dog in position, once longer sits and downs are introduced.
5. The —yes-release marker is not employed until the dog is proficient at sit and down, stays in position until it hears the —OK cue, and has had many rewards in position. —Yes is introduced by having the dog sit or lie down, saying —yes, enticing the dog out of position (so that it releases), and then feeding the dog. —Yes may be used with food reward or ball reward interchangeably.

Training Sit and Down
1. The first training of sit and down begins with the stay component rather than the actual sitting or downing motion—That is to say, when we begin to prepare the dog for the experience of being forced to sit or lie down, we apply the force to make the dog stay in sit or down position, rather than sit or lie down in the first place. The handler uses a handful of food to lure the dog into position and then rewards the animal. Then he/she tells the dog to —stay and waits for a mistake. In fact, the handler does whatever is necessary to cause the dog to break the stay—stands upright, holds the stay an unusually long time, etc. When the dog attempts to break (prematurely release from) the stay the

handler applies a very quick but rather gentle pop on the leash (up and away from the handler in the case of the sit, and directly backwards along the dog's spine in the case of the down), sufficient to stop the dog from breaking, and then the handler quickly brings the food hand back and feeds the dog and repeats the exercise. When this is done skillfully it is not clear what keeps the dog in position, the collar correction or the dog's fixation on the food-bearing hand. With time the dog comes to associate the leash correction with sit and down position. Now we can begin to use collar corrections to enforce the —sit and down motions, in addition to the —stay.

2. Alternate mode of correction for the down. For the down, especially, it is very advantageous for the handler to use a—social correction—a slapping correction rather than a collar correction-- because a slap is normally faster and if done well a slap is more effective in pressing the dog into the down position. But we cannot just suddenly slap a dog with leash or hand and expect it to understand. The animal must learn the meaning of this correction and connect it to the previously understood skill. The handler stands with food in hand and signals the dog into the down with a long hand movement towards the ground and past the dog's nose, with food in the hand. This is merely an exaggeration of the movement the handler normally uses to lure/signal the dog into down position with food. Once the dog is down, it is fed in position, then given the —sit command, enticed up to the sitting position, and then signaled back into the down. This sequence of sit-down-sit-down is repeated several times. After this repetition, the dog will anticipate the next —down command and it will be waiting eagerly to lie down. As the handler again makes the long downward hand gesture combined with the command —down, he/she clips or cuffs the dog rather gently on the muzzle with the ends of the fingers. The dog will notice the contact, perhaps blink or flinch away, and then quickly lie down because both force of habit and the near proximity of the food will guide it into this well-rehearsed behavior. We must be clear—We are not forcing the dog to lie down. The animal is lying down voluntarily to obtain the food. Before it even feels the contact of fingers on its' muzzle it is already beginning the down motion. But we are preparing the dog (training phase) for the experience of being forced to lie down (proofing phase).

Proofing Sit and Down
1. During proofing of the sit and down skills we begin to challenge the dog's understanding, with more distracting surroundings and longer stays, less frequent food or ball reinforcement, and more praise reinforcement instead. When the dog performs correctly it is rewarded and encouraged, and when it refuses commands or becomes distracted, the corrections that were introduced and attached to the exercises during training are used in a stronger form, to ensure compliance. For instance, if the dog refuses to sit it is given a quick, popping collar correction upwards. If it refuses to lie down the handler slaps it lightly but sharply on top of the neck or skull with the flattened hand or with a loop of the leash.
2. As a rule, early in the proofing process, to keep the animal motivated and reduce stress, we tend to give the dog rewards after a correction—For instance, if the trainer gives a —sit command, but the dog is distracted by another dog nearby and therefore does not sit, the handler delivers a quick, popping correction on the leash/collar, the dog sits, and then the handler rewards (either with —yes and release, or —good, —yes, and release, see this Chapter). Rewards after corrections help to reduce stress, and help the dog keep trying even under a little bit of pressure.
3. Later in proofing we raise our standard—If the dog must be corrected to secure compliance, then the animal does not receive any reward beyond a bit of praise and petting. Then the dog is released and immediately asked to repeat the exercise. If this repetition is correct, then the dog is rewarded.
4. We should always keep in mind the difference between a mistake on the dog's part, where the animal is trying to do as the trainer asks but just makes an error, and disobedience or refusal. As a rule, we do not often correct simple errors, instead we punish them with the word —No and we withhold

reward (omission). Sharp corrections (positive punishment and negative reinforcement) are normally reserved for disobedience or refusal.

5. During proofing of sit and down, the motivation is normally supplied by ball—The dog is initially taught using food if possible and then once it understands the exercises the ball is introduced. Introduction of the ball will result in the dog becoming much more excited than it did when working for food. Ball motivation is thus a good way to challenge the dog so that it makes a few mistakes, and also it helps the dog to shake off any discouragement or stress it feels as psychological pressure gradually becomes a part of training.

Communication During sit and Down

1. While initially teaching the sit and down with food, verbal cues are of relatively little importance—the handler's gestures as he/she lures with food are most important. However, we normally give the —sit or —down command as we lure the dog into position, praise the dog with —good before and during reward, and release with the cue —OK. Later, as we move into training and proofing stages and begin to use ball reward, these verbal cues become very important, and we also begin to make use of the markers, —yes, and —no.

2. Reward in position for sit and down. Our first concern with sit and down is establishing stability—making the dog understand that its job is to stay still without fidgeting or creeping. The best way to do this is to make sure that the animal receives its reward while it is still holding the sit or down. This is called a reward in position (see this Ch). For both sit and down, reward in position is performed as follows—The handler, with the ball in pocket, gives the —sit or —down command. When the dog moves swiftly and correctly into the appropriate position, then the handler marks this behavior with the —good cue (intermediate marker). This cue tells the dog that it performed well and earned reward, but that it must not break position yet. Then the handler gets the ball out of his/her pocket and holds the ball very closely in front of the dog's nose. Some care and a bit of training is required so that the dog does not creep or break position as the ball is brought out and does not try to take the ball before given permission. After a moment in which the handler makes sure the dog is steady, he/she gives the —yes cue (terminal bridge) which is the dog's authorization to take the ball. If this technique is done well, the dog takes the ball while still in position and then releases from the position. Use of —good and —yes cues, combined with reward in position, achieves the twin goals of making sure we mark and reward the correct movement into sit or down position, yet also keep the position stable and prevent creeping, fidgeting, or breaking towards the handler and reward. Reward in position (using "good' then "yes"-release) teaches the dog to hold a position.

3. —Yes-release for sit and down. Once we have a stable sit or down, our next concern is making sure that the dog understands that the correct response to the commands —sit or —down is a rapid, crisp movement. To do this we must reward the sit or down movement, rather than the stay. What is important here is that we pick out and mark the critical aspect of the skill—in the case of the sit, the moment the dog fully sits, and in the case of the down, the moment that the dog gets both elbows in contact with the ground. Using the down as our example, the handler does this by giving the —yes cue the instant both elbows are in contact. When it hears —yes, the dog will release from position and wait to be rewarded. The handler then breaks position and retrieves the ball from his/her pocket and gives it to the dog. The handler must not be in a hurry to get the ball out, and it is extremely important that the handler not break his/her position until after he/she has said —yes. The critical aspect of timing here is when the handler says —yes. The —yes must be timely, but the delivery of the ball can be and should be done deliberately and without hurry. Remember that the function and value of the —yes terminal marker is that it bridges delays to reward. Therefore, if the —yes is properly conditioned and well-timed, there is no need to hurry in delivering the ball. Reward at completion of a movement (with "yes"-release) teaches the dog speed in assuming a position.

4. —No marker. —Good and —yes are not the only markers we can use, nor is the power of marking technique limited to rewards. We can also mark behaviors we want to punish, by using the word —no. —no is used much like —yes, in the sense that it is used to mark a behavior and bridge a delay—in this case a delay to punishment. Earlier we covered two kinds of punishing response contingencies, positive punishment (giving the dog something that it dislikes) and negative punishment (or omission, taking away from the dog something that it likes). —No can serve to signal both of these response contingencies. —No is also used like —yes in the sense that it tends to be a terminal cue—when the dog does something that earns a —no, the animal often has to start the whole exercise again and therefore it can break when it hears —no.

5. We can use the —no to gently punish the dog (through omission) for overeager or careless mistakes. For instance, if we are working the dog through a sit- down-sit sequence, and the dog does not wait for the sit command but pops up without permission, then the handler gives the —no and makes the dog go back into the down again and wait for the command before rising up into sit. If the animal rises to the sit correctly, it can be rewarded in position with —good and —yes, or it can be rewarded with —yes and allowed to break immediately. Here the —no gives us the ability to improve performance without killing the enthusiasm of an eager dog.

6. We can also use the —no more forcefully as a predictor of physical (positive) punishment. Let us say the handler leaves the dog on a down-stay and steps a few feet away, and the dog breaks position and moves toward the handler without permission. If the handler then simply corrects the dog, the animal will be corrected in the act of approaching the handler, which can be hopelessly confusing for an eager dog. What is needed is a tool to tell the dog exactly what critical behavior earned it the punishment. Therefore, the handler gives the —no immediately when the dog's elbows lift from the ground. Then the handler calmly approaches the dog and administers a correction of appropriate strength for the dog, normally by popping the leash two or three times, then takes the dog back to the exact place where the dog was lying and commands it to lie down. Then the handler steps away and, if the dog holds position correctly, the handler performs a reward in position—first —good to reinforce the act of holding position, then approach and placement of the ball directly in front of the dog's nose, and —yes to release the dog into the ball.

Advanced Sit and Down Exercises
1. To meet certification standards, the dog must eventually learn to transition from sit to down and back up to sit again at heel position, and while at EOL. For these exercises, the dog must not only understand sit and down, but also how to move from one position to the other without creeping forward or changing its alignment. This is where —good and —yes and —no cues come into their own, because they give the handler the power to teach the dog to understand the difference between a perfectly correct down (in which the dog does not creep forward) and an incorrect down (in which the dog lies down every bit as fast, but creeps forward as it does so).

2. For sit and down EOL, —good is used to let the dog know immediately when it has performed a correct sit or down, and then the handler approaches and delivers reward in position (by putting the ball close to the dog's head and releasing the dog into it with —yes). If the dog creeps as it transitions from sit to down or vice versa, then the handler marks the mistake with —No, and either makes the dog repeat the skill or calmly delivers a correction and then makes the dog repeat the skill.

3. For sit and down at heel, —good is used in the same way to mark a correct transition. Reward in position is performed by taking the ball from the pocket and holding it directly in front of the dog's nose at heel position, and then releasing the dog into it with —yes. If the dog creeps forward or slews sideways at heel while performing the transition, the handler marks the error with —no, (perhaps followed by a correction) and sends the dog back to correct heel in the original posture (sit or down). Then the handler makes the dog repeat the exercise, rewarding the dog in position if it is executed

correctly.
4. For real-world operations/utilization, the down has greater importance than the sit. The down is the dog's most stable position. When given the —down command the dog must drop immediately no matter where it is and what speed it is travelling, and then lie still and silent until given another command or released, even under intense distraction (gunshots, decoys carrying bite equipment and cracking whips, etc.). Accordingly, substantial psychological pressure must often be applied to achieve this level of obedience. In order for such treatment to be fair and effective, corrections used for the down must be thoroughly trained, and —good, —yes, and —no must be properly applied so that the dog understands what it is being corrected for and can adjust its behavior to avoid corrections.

Heeling (Marching)

1. Heeling is an attention-based exercise in which the dog walks at its handler's left side (personnel who carry weapons on the left side often teach the dog to heel on the right) with the shoulder even with the handler's knee, keeping pace and position no matter what the handler's pace or direction, and sitting automatically when the handler halts. The primary functions of heeling are to refine the dog's obedience to its handler, and to provide the ability to transport the dog under close control through hazardous or distracting circumstances with both hands free. A well-trained dog concentrates completely on its handler while heeling, and heeling is therefore very fatiguing and not an appropriate way to transport the dog long distances. For mere transportation, where all that is important is that the dog remains under control, does not pull against the leash, and does not use any more energy than necessary, a walk easy skill is used instead. Walk easy (the command is normally —easy) is much less strict and demanding than heeling.
2. It is traditional in DoD to use the verbal command —heel, and also slap the left hip with the left hand, and to repeat these verbal and gestural commands at each change of pace or direction. However, if we view heeling as a tactical tool rather than a parade-ground skill, then we must realize that, a) slapping the hip is unnecessary and inadvisable, because the left hand should be left free (for weapon-handling, for instance), and b) repeated commands are also unnecessary and inadvisable, because the verbal command —heel is all that is necessary to tell the dog that it should place itself at heel position and remain there, no matter what the handler's movement or direction, until released. Accordingly, in the discussion of heeling that follows, the left-hip slap and repeated commands are not used. The CST method for teaching heeling described below normally results in a dog that positions itself for marching close to the handler's left knee and hip, with the handler's left hand hanging or swinging outside of the dog's head. In effect, the dog positions itself "between" the handler's left hand and hip and looks directly up at the handler's face, rather than positioning itself "outside of" the handler's hand and arm and looking around the handler's elbow at the handler. This close positioning is in most situations advantageous because it gives better and closer control of the dog and results in fewer training problems and less stress for the dog. Weapons retention is not normally an issue for law enforcement applications because the dog works on the handler's non-weapon-carrying side and the handler need not carry the left arm pinched close to the body (a left-handed handler normally trains the dog to heel on the right side and so can carry the right arm loosely while holding the left arm tight to the body for weapons retention).
3. The CST method of teaching heeling concentrates on teaching the dog to understand the exact position that it must maintain at heel, how to move its body in order to reach that position, and on making sure that the dog is highly motivated for the work. This is the best way to prepare the dog for the physical corrections that may later be necessary to render heeling—fail safe for real-world tactical scenarios, in which handler safety depends on his/her control of the dog.

Teaching Heeling

1. The finish. The dog first learns to heel not by walking at the handler's left side, but instead by learning to finish. —Finish is an expression used by competitive obedience trainers to describe a skill in which the dog moves from position in front of the handler to heel position. In DoD, the dog does not normally walk around behind the handler, passing to the handler's right—instead the dog passes by the handler's left hand, turns in place and sits at heel (called the military finish).

2. To teach the finish the dog is lured with food or the ball (in the left hand) from position in front, past the handler's left side, and behind the handler about 2 or 3 feet (the handler normally takes one long step back with his/her left foot). Then the handler turns the dog in towards himself/herself (the dog turns counter-clockwise) and leads the dog forward into heel position and asks the dog to —sit. When using food, the handler then allows the dog to eat from the left hand while in heel position. When using the ball, the handler holds the ball in the left hand just in front of the dog's nose, gives the —yes, and flicks the ball into the dog's mouth. Initially the handler leads the dog through the entire path, covering nearly as much ground as the dog does. With time the handler moves less and less, taking a smaller step backward and shortening the circle he/she makes with the left hand and the reward. Eventually the handler does not step backward with the left foot, simply commanding the dog to —heel and making a long gesture with the left hand to send the dog past the left side and behind, and turn the dog and bring it back up into heel position. The amount of room the dog is given to accomplish the movement is gradually decreased, and when the entire teaching sequence is performed well, the dog begins flipping or swinging to heel position (rather than walking behind the handler, turning around, and walking up into heel position). A wall or barrier is often used initially, to help the dog reach a straight heel position at the conclusion of the movement. If the dog sits crookedly or too far forward, the handler gives the —no cue and makes the animal repeat the whole exercise correctly before rewarding.

3. In the next step the dog's attention is shifted from the left hand to the handler's armpit. When the dog reaches heel position, the handler marks this behavior with —good, and then carefully moves the left hand and the ball up above the dog's head to a position just in front of/under the armpit. Then he/she gives the —yes and drops the ball into the dog's mouth.

4. After a few repetitions, the handler actually places the ball in his/her armpit prior to rewarding the dog. The movement begins as before. The dog is led through the finish with the ball in the left hand, concluding with the dog at heel position and the ball held directly in front of the dog's nose or on the left side of the dog's head. The handler then marks the correct completion of the exercise with —good, and then raises the left hand above the dog's head, transfers the ball to the right hand, and places the ball in the left armpit, clamping it there with the bicep. Then the handler drops both hands to natural positions, with the left as always hanging just outside of the dog's head. The dog should stare straight up towards the ball from heel position. The handler rewards the dog by saying —yes (the dog will normally release and rear straight up towards the ball) and delivering the ball directly into the dog's mouth by unclamping the bicep so that the ball drops free.

5. Reward in position at heel. Eventually, the handler begins leaving the ball in his/her pocket until the dog correctly finishes. We now expect the dog to complete the finish in order to obtain the ball reward, but without seeing or following the ball reward. The handler makes the same motion with the left hand, and even cups the hand as though he/she is holding a ball, but the ball remains in the right pocket (at this point the leash is normally transferred to the left hand for the first time and held in a manner similar to holding the ball). When the dog reaches correct heel position, the handler marks with —good,' and reaches with his/her right hand into the right pocket, withdraws the ball, reaches across the body and places the ball in the left armpit, and then says —yes and drops the ball. This is a type of reward in position technique.

6. Another technique for reward in position at heel. In a variation on this procedure, the handler does

not place the ball in his/her armpit after the —good cue, but instead places the right hand with the ball directly in front of the dog's head, or to the left of the dog's head (to bend the dog's head away from the handler and straighten the animal's spine) and then gives the —yes release and rewards in position. Once the dog can correctly complete this skill, it has learned a specific position and a specific movement that will become the basis of heeling/marching.

7. Eventually the gesture of the left hand (the prompt) that is used to send the dog to heel is faded out, so that the dog swings into correct heel position and into attention on the word —heel alone.

8. Now we are ready to teach heeling proper, actual marching with the dog at heel position. Initially the handler keeps the ball in the left armpit to give the dog a focal point. Holding a very, very short leash in the left hand (from 3 to 8 inches, but without any tension on the leash between hand and the dog's collar), with the hand outside of and just behind the dog's head, the handler gives the command —heel and shuffles very carefully forward a few feet. When the dog moves well, between the handler's left hand and hip while looking straight up at the ball held in the handler's armpit, then the handler marks this behavior with —good, and comes to a halt carefully so that the dog does not lose position (initial heeling is often performed along a wall or fence). Once the dog is in sit-halt position, then the handler gives the —yes release and drops the ball into the dog's mouth. It is important to remember that in the initial stages of marching, the dog is rewarded after only a few steps, and normally always in the sit halt—That is, when the dog moves well, the handler marks this with —good and then comes to a halt and performs reward in position.

9. With further practice the trainer can leave the ball in the right pocket, asking the dog to move at heel while looking up at the handler's face or armpit rather than the ball. Once the dog moves well, then the handler marks this behavior with —good, comes to a halt, takes the ball out of the pocket with the right hand and then performs reward in position in one of the two ways described. Place the ball in the left armpit and drop it to the dog after saying —yes, or transfer it to the left hand and hold it near the dog's head while it is sitting in heel position, and then flicking it into the dog's mouth after saying —yes. Gradually the dog is taught to heel for longer periods with the ball in sight and without the ball in sight, depending on the circumstances.

10. Eventually, the heeling pattern is made longer, with turns and halts and changes of pace, and the dog is made to work for extended periods for the —good and the —yes and the reward. If, while moving, the dog loses position by running wide or forging forward or swinging out into a crabbing motion, then the handler marks this error with —No, halts, and re-commands the dog to finish to heel. Once the dog is back in correct position, the handler encourages with —good and resumes heeling again. If the dog this time maintains correct position it is given —good, sit-halt, and reward in position.

11. Up until this point, the —yes has normally been given only after the —good, as a way of releasing the dog into the ball. This practice has been advantageous because it served to make sure that the dog always got its reward while holding the desired position. Such rewards in place are optimal for making sure that reward anticipation does not interfere with steadiness in the sit and down and correct position while heeling. However, they do not make full use of the power of the well-conditioned —yes, to instantaneously identify to the dog, and reward, very specific aspects of performance. But now we are ready to begin using the full potential of the —yes.

12. Once the dog shows that it understands how to finish quickly and efficiently to heel position, maintain focus on the handler by looking up towards the handler's face while maintaining correct heel position, move at heel without losing position, and correct itself back to the proper position when it happens to lose position, then we are ready for the final step, in which the handler begins rewarding directly out of heel with the —yes marker. At any moment that the handler judges the dog should be rewarded, either after the finish, while heeling, or after the dog corrects itself back into position in response to the —No, then the handler rewards the dog by saying —yes. The dog will release from heel and show that it expects reward, and the handler can then withdraw the ball from

the pocket and give it to the dog.
13. Use of the —yes marker in this way enables the handler to bring to the dog's attention and selectively reward very fine-grained aspects of performance, such as small differences in speed of movement, angle, or posture. Competitive trainers find this useful because they are interested in polish and speed and precision, because these are the things that win trophies. However, MWD trainers should also be interested in polish and speed and precision, because these are the hallmarks of a dog that fully understands commands and skills: Only when the dog has full understanding is it fair and effective to apply pressure to the dog in order to make sure that it always performs correctly, even under real-world conditions where failure to perform is dangerous for dog and handler and those personnel that depend upon the MWD team.
14. Note that the —heel' command is given only in order to finish the dog, and when the handler first goes into motion. The handler may re-command —heel after a —no also. In finished form the command for finish and for heeling is the verbal command —heel only—there is no gesture of hand or body.

Training Heeling

We begin training the heeling skill when the handler no longer has to hold the ball in the left hand to signal/lure the dog to heel position. Now, instead of the ball, the handler holds the leash with no more than 12-18 inches of slack. After saying —heel,' the handler delivers a slight popping correction on the leash. As always during the training, the leash input does not force the dog to finish. The dog is already on its way to heel position, because of habit and its desire for the ball. This technique merely serves to connect heeling and the leash input and bring the finish under the control of the leash input. Similarly, slight pops can also be given as the dog arrives at heel position to encourage it to stop in the correct place, as it sits, and while it is sitting to encourage it to keep its eyes focused up at the handler. All of these movements are thus brought under the control of leash inputs, so that subsequently the dog will not be confused if it receives a correction (see proofing heeling) for failing to complete any of them quickly enough or correctly.

Proofing Heeling

1. Once the finish and heeling, the halt, and attention to the handler have all been trained/connected to leash inputs, then we are ready to begin making the —heel command an obligation for the dog rather than request. This is done by sharpening the leash inputs so that the dog begins to deliberately avoid errors in order to avoid the corrections. Plenty of ball reward is provided during proofing to keep the dog's drive up and ensure that it still enjoys heeling work. Most corrections are preceded by the marker —no (given exactly when the dog goes wrong), to make absolutely sure that the dog associates the correction with what it did wrong rather than some other behavior. The handler must realize that if the —no is used properly to mark undesirable behaviors, the correction need not be delivered immediately. In fact, in many cases the technique works better if the handler is very deliberate and takes his/her time delivering the correction in a calm and measured manner (as long as the no has been delivered at exactly the right moment).
2. Corrections for attention—to bring the dog's focus to its handler—are made by lifting the leash-hand quickly directly toward the handler's face. Once the dog comes into proper attention, then the animal receives —good and reward in position, or simply the —yes. Almost all other corrections are made directly towards the dog's tail, jerking backwards with the leash held in the left hand, directly behind the dog's head, over its back, with only a few inches of leash held between the hand and the dog's collar. In this way the hand hangs in a natural position just behind and outside of the dog's head, and any input with the leash serves to stop the dog from coming too far forward past the handler's knee. When a dog is taught to heel using the ball (and generating prey/retrieving drive), most of the errors

are related to the dog wanting to move too far forward while heeling and come across the handler's body, in anticipation of receiving the ball. The leash corrections just described are ideal for counteracting this tendency and encouraging attention, when combined with proper rewards in position as described above.
3. Once left turns are begun, the same correction will help to prevent the dog from bumping or riding against the handler. When right turns are begun, if necessary the left hand holding the leash is brought from behind the dog's head across the handler's front and up, to generate a correction that brings the dog's head towards the handler's centerline and up towards his/her face.
4. During the proofing stage, the handler reduces the frequency of ball reward (substituting praise and petting) and asks the dog to heel for longer and longer periods, and with greater and greater distractions. The eventual goal is tactical heeling capability—meaning that the dog finishes to heel from any distance on verbal command, and remains at heel after one command no matter what the handler's pace or direction, off-leash, and under intense distraction (such as gunfire and stimulation from decoys dressed in bite gear cracking whips, etc.).

CONTROLLED AGGRESSION TRAINING WITH CLEAR SIGNALS TRAINING

Definitions
Decoy or Agitator
The trainer who plays the role of suspect or aggressor for the dog and gives the dog bites. The decoy's skill and ability are critical to success in training, accounting for at least 50% of the finished product.

Agitation
The art and practice of provoking aggression and biting behavior from working dogs as performed by the decoy or agitator.

Civil Agitation
Agitation performed by a decoy or agitator who does not wear any bite equipment; hence—in civil.

Rag
A piece of jute or burlap, often in the form of a feed bag, used to excite and provoke the dog, and allow it to practice biting.

Sleeve
An arm protector worn by the decoy on which the dog bites. In DoD, the sleeve is often referred to as a wrap, from the days in which bites were given by wrapping the arm with fire hose or similar materials.

Bite-Bar Sleeve
Hard sleeve made with plastic and/or leather barrel, equipped with upper arm protector, and with a blade-like—bite bar projecting from the forearm area and meant for the dog to bite.

Soft Sleeve
A soft arm protector made of padding and synthetic or jute fabric. Often used to strengthen or build the dog's bite for harder sleeves. Also, sometimes referred to as a puppy sleeve.

Intermediate Sleeve
A firm sleeve of padding and synthetic or jute fabric, often patterned after Belgian bite sleeves used for training Ring Sport. In DoD intermediate sleeves have traditionally not been used—instead the bite bar sleeve was emphasized. Clear signals patrol training makes extensive use of intermediate sleeves for several reasons:
 1. The intermediate sleeve has a better bite building effect with many dogs than the bite-bar sleeve.
 2. The intermediate sleeve is more versatile; appropriate for soft biting dogs through very hard biters, and also enabling bites on the upper arm and the insides of the arm.
 3. The intermediate sleeve is safer for the dog; protecting it against impacts, collisions, and twists that break teeth and injure necks and spines when they occur on hard bite-bar sleeves.

Hidden Sleeve
A firm sleeve resembling a very small intermediate sleeve, made so that the hand is exposed, and meant to be worn under the sleeve in a concealed fashion. The hidden sleeve is designed to render the biting dog less equipment dependent.

Bite Suit
A heavy, padded suit with a synthetic fabric outer surface on which the dog can bite anywhere on the arms, legs, or body.

Whip
A short-handled whip with a lash that is used by the decoy to create motion and noise (by cracking it) in order to provoke and excite the dog. Reed sticks and split bamboo batons are used in a similar fashion. All of these instruments may be used to test the dog's nerve and prepare it for combat (use of the whip does not include striking the dog).

Full Bite
A manner of biting in which the dog employs its entire mouth, rather than just the front teeth, while biting. In general, a dog that bites full is more confident and reliable than a dog that bites shallow.

Commitment
The habit of biting without hesitation or prudence, and with full force. A dog that bites with commitment flings itself into the decoy with impact and shuts its mouth instantly with all of its strength.

Equipment-Oriented
The habit or tendency to pull towards, bark at, and try to bite decoys wearing visible bite equipment, or bite equipment itself lying on the ground, rather than the decoy—in civil.

Man-Oriented
A dog showing a great deal of man interest.

Man Interest
The habit or tendency to pull towards, bark at, and try to bite the (unprotected) decoy—in civil as opposed to a decoy wearing bite equipment, or bite equipment itself lying on the ground. Can also be called civil aggression, but man interest is a better general term for a dog that tries to close with unprotected agitators, whether it does so because it is hunting them (prey drive) or because it likes to fight (active aggression or dominance drive), or because it has the habit of offensively defending itself when provoked (defense drive).

Transfer
A skill in which a dog voluntarily releases a piece of bite equipment that the decoy drops and re-directs its

attention to the decoy. The dog may transfer because it is a very civil aggressive animal (for which the transfer comes very easily, because the dog's man interest is strong), or because it has been carefully taught to do so. Transfer is used to denote the shift of attention only, not an ensuing bite. Thus, when we say —transfer the dog, we mean that the dog is induced to release the bite equipment and shift its focus back to the decoy. A second bite may or may not then be delivered.

Drives
A term used by dog trainers to describe the intensity and the quality of a dog's goal-motivated behavior.

Prey Drive
The motivation said to cause the dog to search for, chase, and bite objects (including people) that—remind it of prey animals like rabbits. In prey drive the dog is relatively unstressed. It seems to enjoy itself and does not growl or snarl or show its teeth—it merely chases or approaches and bites. Prey drive is associated with full-mouth biting. The very prey-oriented dog tends to be very equipment-oriented and does not transfer easily from equipment.

Defense Drive
The motivation said to cause the dog to defend itself aggressively from other animals (including people) that threaten or frighten it. When behaving defensively, the dog is stressed, it does not appear to enjoy itself and it growls, snarls, and displays its teeth prominently. A very defensive dog exhibits pronounced signs of fear and stress. The defensive dog is normally very man-oriented and transfers easily from equipment.

Fighting Drive
The motivation said to cause the dog to perform work (like search for prolonged periods) in order to close with, and fight, a person. The behavioral signals said to indicate fighting drive are somewhat indistinct and poorly defined—The term is used mainly to denote a dog that combines characteristics of prey and defense—The animal works with the intensity and man interest typical of self-defense, and appears to be very man-oriented, but does not exhibit the stress and fear typical of a very defensive dog. Also referred to as active aggression, and sometimes as dominance drive.

Nerves
A term used to describe the degree of emotional stability or calmness the dog appears to show while engaged in bite work. A very nervous dog appears anxious and stressed while working, is prone to snarl and growl, and tends to bite with a small or shifting mouth. A very steady or clear-headed dog appears un-stressed while working (although perhaps very excited), is not prone to snarl and growl, and tends to bite with a full mouth without shifting. Dog trainers express these ideas with remarks like—the dog is nervy, for undesirable behavior, or—the dog has good nerves, or—is clear-headed, for desirable behavior. For dogs that are extremely stressed while biting, normally as a result of excessive or poorly-applied compulsion, the term (from German) hectic is frequently used.

Flat Collar
A flat, buckled collar made of nylon webbing or leather and meant for the dog to pull against comfortably. The flat collar should fit loosely and sit low on the dog's neck to provide for comfortable pulling without choking.

Correction Collar
A choke collar made of light chain or of nylon cord, or a pinch collar. The correction collar should fit snugly

and ride high on the dog's neck above the flat collar.

Back-Tie
A technique, and the line used for it, in which the dog is anchored by means of a line or rope attached to a secure point (fence or post, or bolt anchored in a wall) and clipped to the dog's flat collar. Depending on the need and the situation, the back-tie is often equipped with an elastic section made of bungee cord or bicycle inner tube that allows the back-tie to stretch and give a few inches, encouraging the dog to pull, and protecting its spine against shocks.

Airman 1st Class Darren Raines, 22nd Security Forces Squadron military working dog handler, participates in a MWD demonstration at McConnell Air Force Base, KA, May 2, 2019. (U.S. Air Force photo by Senior Airman Alan Ricker)

Basic Bite Work
MWDs are selected for DoD purchase by means of a consignment test. The patrol portion of this test emphasizes the dog's willingness and ability to defend itself (i.e. defense drive) rather than its raw desire to engage in bite work (prey drive or active aggression). Training for patrol certification and also most types of patrol MWD utilization/deployment (e.g. scouting, building search, and pursuits) require that the dog enjoy bite work (either through hunting/prey behavior, or because the dog likes to fight active aggression) rather than just be self-defensive. Accordingly, the first order of business with a green MWD is basic bite work, in which the dog's desire to bite, physical condition and power, and bite-targeting skills are developed. In addition, either in the course of basic training or in the course of more advanced training in the field, the dog must learn to bite any area of the decoy's body though training on the bite suit, and also learn to bite concealed/hidden sleeves. Exceptionally strong dogs also benefit from attack-work on civil decoys in the agitation muzzle. The objectives for basic bite work are:

- The dog should confront, with barking and lunging and attempts to bite, an agitator—in civil that approaches and threatens the animal.
- The dog should bite with commitment, power, and as full a mouth as possible on intermediate sleeves, and if possible, on hard sleeves.
- The dog should transfer (release bite equipment when the decoy drops it) and attempt to approach and bite the decoy in preference to the equipment.
- The dog should continue to bite, without excessive growling or shifting of the bite, when threatened and struck with a whip/stick.
- The dog should pursue a decoy at full speed over a distance of at least 50 yards, bite with commitment and power, and continue to bite without disturbance as the handler approaches and takes the leash and praises it.
- The dog should perform all of the above skills indoors on slick surfaces as well as outdoors.

Basic Bite Work Session

All of the above objectives are achieved through training sessions resembling the following:

The Dog Wears Two Collars

1. A flat leather nylon collar and a correction collar is attached to a short back-tie anchored well above its back and 5 to 8 feet long. The handler stands near the dog holding the leash (attached to the correction collar). The decoy stands out of sight behind some obstacle, —in civil with or without whip/stick.
2. The session begins with the —watch'em command from the handler, then the decoy steps into view and begins to work, provoking and exciting the dog with threats and aggressive postures and movements. Initially, the dog may have very little reaction when hearing the —watch'em cue, but after a few sessions, the dog will learn the association between —watch'em and the appearance of the decoy (classical or Pavlovian conditioning) and it will become excited and aggressive on command. This is called—alerting the dog.
3. In real-world law enforcement and military patrol dog applications, the alert is critically important, because the dog's aggression and biting must be under the control of the handler's command rather than under the control of the decoy's appearance or behavior. A high percentage of patrol dog deployments in which the dog is called upon to engage/bite personnel involve passive subjects, or subjects that may not be moving as vigorously or shouting as loudly as non-target personnel in the area. Accordingly, the handler must have the capability of cuing the dog's drive, so that it wants to bite, and then telling it who to bite.
4. The decoy works by alternately threatening the dog (by moving directly at the animal, staring into its eyes, pretending to hit or strike at it, and vocalizing angrily), and by yielding to the dog (turning away from the dog, taking a step back, running away, pretending to be afraid). The object of the exercise is to make the dog more resistant and confident in the face of threats, and therefore the decoy must yield when the dog reacts powerfully to threats (i.e. counter-threatens) by lunging forward, barking, or attempting to bite. The handler's role is to encourage the dog (not too loudly) and praise it when the decoy runs away, but the handler should not intrude too much into the situation. The primary trainer in this situation is the decoy and we must let the dog concentrate on him/her.
5. The decoy has another means of relieving stress, which is to—channel the dog's energy and emotion from aggression (defensive or active) into prey. The decoy accomplishes this channeling by reacting to a counter-threat with rapid, exciting lateral movement. This rabbit-like motion stimulates prey impulses, brings the dog forward offensively, and unloads stress.
6. After a brief passage of civil agitation, the decoy retreats to the hiding place and puts on a pair of

intermediate sleeves, one on each arm (see note about intermediate sleeves versus bite-bar sleeves). The handler again alerts the dog with —watch'em, and the decoy appears and re-agitates the dog. This time, when the dog counter-threatens by lunging and/or barking, the decoy delivers a bite on one of the intermediate sleeves. If the dog is very powerful and appears confident, then the decoy can deliver the bite by moving directly into the dog. If the dog appears less powerful and confident, then the decoy moves laterally, coming close enough for a bite by zig-zagging right and left, approaching diagonally.

7. Note that the quality of the dog's behavior is likely to change noticeably from aggression (defensive or active) to predatory when the decoy wears sleeves, and the result may be that the dog becomes less sensitive and reactive in response to threats from the decoy, instead merely lunging toward the decoy in efforts to engage the equipment.

8. The bite is delivered by holding the arm high and across the chest or upper abdomen and encouraging the dog to jump up and strike the sleeve, rather than by swinging the arm into the dog's mouth. Once the dog bites, the agitator struggles with the dog and yells and vocalizes, always being careful not to overwhelm or frighten the dog. If the dog takes a shallow bite or shifts its bite nervously, then the decoy puts tension on the backtie by leaning backwards, threatening the dog with having the sleeve pulled from its mouth. This should cause the dog to bite harder and, if the agitator suddenly reduces tension on the back-tie and pauses for a moment, it may cause the dog to bite in and take a fuller bite. This act of biting-in is often rewarded by resuming movement or yielding to the dog by pretending to stagger or fall back. Sometimes the bite-in is rewarded by letting the dog take the sleeve off of the decoy's arm.

9. When the agitator allows the dog to pull the sleeve off of the arm, he/she steps back out of range of the dog's bite, and immediately begins to agitate the dog. The dog should lose interest in the sleeve and transfer, dropping the loose sleeve and lunging to bite the decoy again. Once the dog transfers, then the decoy delivers a bite on the other intermediate sleeve.

10. If the dog does not transfer voluntarily, then the handler makes the dog release the sleeve by lifting up on the collar(s). During this process, the decoy stands passive. Once the dog has released the sleeve, then the decoy agitates and delivers the next bite.

11. While struggling with the dog on the second bite, the agitator uses the free hand to pick up the first sleeve and put it back on. At a moment when the dog is biting well, he/she releases the second sleeve, transfers the dog again, and gives another bite on the first sleeve. The session proceeds like this for three to six bites. On the last transfer, the decoy does not give a bite, instead he/she attracts the dog to the side, away from the grounded sleeve, the handler gets control of the dog, and the decoy runs away with the sleeve. The dog is left victorious, having bitten several times, transferring each time, and finally chasing the decoy away.

12. This basic session is designed to:
    a. Teach the dog to alert powerfully on command (by lunging and barking when given the —watch'em cue, even though it cannot yet see the agitator);
    b. Strengthen the dog's man interest;
    c. Build the bite;
    d. Teach the dog to drop dead training equipment and shift its attention back to the decoy (transfer).

Intermediate Bite Work Session

The intermediate bite work session progresses much like the basic session, except in three respects:
1. The decoy conditions the dog to withstand and fight back against stick-threats;
2. The dog is expected to transfer to the decoy in civil;
3. The session's end with off-leash pursuit bites.

a. Counters to stick-threats. During the bites, the decoy begins to threaten the dog more vigorously. The decoy does this by looking strongly into the dog's eyes and moving the hands and the stick/whip sharply at the dog's face and body without striking the dog. Initially these threats are relatively weak, but as training proceeds they become more violent and longer in duration, finally concluding in a simulated fight between dog and decoy. If these threats are performed correctly, the dog does not avoid, or —back off of its bite, instead it counters powerfully by biting in and pulling and headshaking. The decoy rewards these counters by yielding, and sometimes letting the dog take the sleeve. The result is a dog that knows how to fight a person, and feels confident that it can win the fight, even when the decoy exerts considerable psychological and physical pressure.

b. The handler's role during this process is to encourage the dog, but not so loudly that he/she distracts or disturbs the animal. At least 90% of the responsibility for training at this point is the decoys.

c. Because serious fighting, even victorious fighting, causes accumulated stress, the trainers must not pressure the dog during every bite work session. Some sessions are easy, even fun, some sessions are slightly more serious, and very rarely the trainers design a session to test and strengthen the dog's nerve.

d. Transfer to the decoy in civil. When the decoy drops the first sleeve and transfers the dog, and then allows the animal to bite the second sleeve, he/she does not put on the first sleeve again. Instead the agitator leaves the first sleeve on the ground, and then releases the second sleeve to the dog and steps back out of range (i.e. the decoy is now—in civil. By now the dog should have learned a very automatic transfer) the moment it recognizes that the decoy has dropped the sleeve it should release the sleeve and re-direct its focus to the decoy. In this case, the dog is transferring to the man rather than to the equipment. The moment the dog transfers, the decoy rewards the dog for this behavior. How the decoy accomplishes this reward depends upon the type of dog.

e. If the dog is a dog with very high man interest (presumably because it is very high in defense drive or fighting drive) then all the decoy needs to do is to react to the dog by vocalizing and moving vigorously, and then running away. A defensive dog will be gratified because it has chased away the enemy that is causing it stress. An actively aggressive dog (with abundant fighting drive) will be reinforced because it has won possession of the battle ground and increased its sense of dominance. Of course, if either of these types of dog have ample prey drive as well, when the decoy runs away this rapid movement will also stimulate hunting behavior, which is reinforcing for the dog.

f. If the dog has a higher degree of equipment orientation, so that it tends to be reluctant to transfer from the dead sleeve, or it tends to return to the sleeve after releasing it (presumably because it is a dog in which prey drive predominates) then the decoy must provide a bite reward. If this type of dog does not receive a bite reward of some sort when it transfers to the civil agitator, then it will be disappointed, or punished (by omission of the bite) for the transfer and soon it will stop transferring to the civil decoy and continue biting the sleeve when the decoy drops it.

g. In the case of a very strong-biting dog of this type, the decoy can provide this bite on an arm- or leg-sleeve hidden under the outer clothes. The opportunity to transfer to a decoy that appears to be in civil, and then bite that decoy, teaches the dog a very important lesson—the man IS prey. At the conclusion of the bite the decoy drops prone, and the handler removes the dog from the bite physically by lifting upward on the collar(s), and then the decoy runs away.

h. In the case of a less powerful dog, that may not have the necessary drive and confidence to bite the hidden sleeve, the decoy can pull a jute rag from its hiding place in the waistband at the small of the back and let the dog suddenly bite it. This is not as powerful a technique for producing man interest in a prey/equipment-oriented dog, but it does reward the dog for directing its energy and attention at a civil decoy. After a few seconds of biting and a vigorous fight with the rag, the decoy releases the rag to the dog, transfers the dog from this rag (usually by picking up one of the sleeves), and runs away.

i. Pursuit bites. Following a session of bites and transfers to the decoy as above, the decoy runs away in civil and picks up two more intermediate sleeves lying on the ground at the desired distance for the pursuit bite. The handler unhooks the dog from the back-tie and releases the dog to pursue and bite. The decoy takes this bite and keeps the dog occupied with fighting while the handler runs up, being careful not to disturb or frighten the dog, and praises and pets it enthusiastically while it bites. Once the handler has the leash, then the decoy drops the first sleeve and steps back out of range. The dog will transfer, and then the decoy runs back towards the original back-tie location. Again, the handler releases the dog for a pursuit bite, follows the dog up and praises it and regains the leash. The session can end in one of two ways:

j. If the dog has very high man interest and transfers easily to a civil decoy, ignoring the sleeve after the transfer, then the decoy drops the sleeve, the dog transfers, and the decoy runs away with the dog, restrained by the leash, in hot pursuit. The handler gradually brings the dog to a stop, and the decoy escapes.

k. If the dog has lesser man interest, so that it is not clear that the dog prefers the decoy to equipment, then during the bite the decoy picks up and puts on one of the original sleeves. Then he/she drops the sleeve the dog is biting, transfers the dog by letting it see the sleeve he/she is wearing, and then the decoy runs away with the dog, restrained by the leash, in hot pursuit. The handler gradually brings the dog to a stop, and the decoy escapes.

Controlled Aggression

There are two crucial points in the career of any practical patrol K9 or MWD. One of these, of course, is when the dog is first called upon to engage a subject. The other is when the handler for the very first time begins to exert control over the dog during bite work. When we say —control we mean verbal commands enforced with physical corrections. Depending upon how this stage of the dog's training is performed, it is more or less stressful for the dog, and it is the first acid-test of the dog's quality. Many dogs cannot withstand the stress and do not satisfactorily evolve into well-controlled but hard-biting patrol dogs. Therefore, as in any phase of Clear Signals Training, the trainer's main concern is minimizing the degree of stress the dog suffers by ensuring that the animal understands the skills it is taught, and as much as possible avoiding the use of any substantial corrections until it is clear that the dog understands the target skill and is fully capable of executing the skill. However, in controlled aggression training (as opposed to obedience), because it is often difficult to withhold the reward from the dog in order to punish it (i.e. prevent it from biting), we are necessarily more dependent upon physical correction and compulsive training. Therefore, the emphasis in controlled aggression training is on the training phase (in which the dog learns what corrections—mean and how to handle them) and the proofing phase (in which the dog learns that it must obey certain commands or it will receive meaningful correction).

Out and Guard Versus Recall

The modern DoD patrol dog is trained to meet an out and guard standard. This means that the dog is trained to release the bite on command (or out) and then remain near the decoy, guarding intently (silently or while barking), as opposed to releasing the bite and returning to heel position as was taught during the era of six phases of controlled aggression. Similarly, when the dog is called out prior to the bite, while it is running downfield after the decoy (i.e. the stand-off), it is supposed to halt and remain guarding the decoy. In contrast, the six phases dog was taught to return to heel position after being called out during the stand-off.

The Out and Guard Approach
The out and guard approach is technically more sound from a training standpoint than the out and recall approach. It is a better platform for teaching the dog to understand the out, and adapt to being controlled by the handler during bite work. However, from a liability point of view, it is inadvisable to have a law enforcement K9, or an MWD used in a law enforcement role, guard a suspect/subject closely, because of the risk and likelihood of unwarranted bites. Similarly, from a tactical point of view, it is extremely dangerous for the handler to have the dog guard the subject unless the handler has the ability to recall the dog to heel from the guard position, because in order to recover the dog, the handler must approach the subject while the dog guards, and potentially leave a position of cover for an exposed position to do so.

Therefore, at some point in its career and training, the out and guard patrol MWD should be taught to recall to the handler from the guard, over any distance at which the dog might be sent to engage a suspect.

Out and guard standard. In order to be certified as an out and guard patrol MWD, the dog must perform the following exercises:
1. **Field interview**—In which the dog remains at heel and under control while the decoy approaches the handler, converses with him/her, and then departs at a walk.
2. **Attack**—In which the dog pursues the decoy on command, bites and holds, outs on command, and then guards while the handler approaches and places himself/herself at heel position.
3. **Search and escort**—In which the dog guards the decoy while the handler searches him/her, and then walks under control with the handler while escorting the decoy back to the starting point.
4. **Search and re-attack**—In which the dog bites the decoy without being commanded when the decoy attacks the handler during the search.
5. **Stand-off**—In which the dog is called out in mid-pursuit and stops in a standing, sitting, or lying position and guards the decoy while the handler approaches and places himself/herself at heel position.
6. The essential aspects of all these skills are taught to the dog in the course of sessions in which the dog is back-tied, with the back-tie attached to the flat collar and the handler holding the correction collar.

Communication During Clear Signals-Controlled Aggression Training
If anything, use of clear communication cues is even more important in controlled aggression than it is in obedience, because the dog is intensely excited and therefore easily confused, and because controlled aggression can be extremely stressful for the dog if it becomes confused about what the trainers want, and how to obtain reward and avoid punishment. Fundamentally the same cues/response markers are used in controlled aggression training as in obedience:
1. —Yes—Signals to the dog that it may release from control and bite the decoy or try to bite the decoy by pulling against the leash. Often in bite work a trainer will use a word like —get'em instead of— yes, but this word is conditioned and used in controlled aggression exactly as the —yes is used in obedience, as a terminal bridge (in addition to an alert cue).
2. In controlled aggression, the bite can be signaled by the handler with —yes/get'em, or by having the decoy move so as to deliver a bite (i.e. simulating either an attack on the dog, or an attempt to escape). Which approach is used depends on the dog and the specific situation, but as a rule very powerful dogs that are difficult to control receive their bites after a —yes from the handler (so that they think about their handlers, and their responsibilities to their handlers, all the time during controlled aggression), whereas softer dogs, that do not guard as powerfully and worry continually about where their handlers are, receive their bites after a movement by the decoy (so that they think about the decoy all the time and as a result guard more intently).
3. —Good—Intermediate marker that signals to the dog that it is performing correctly, and it will be rewarded with a bite or a chase, but it must continue to perform until released.

4. —No—Signals to the dog that it has made a mistake and it will be punished. The punishment can take two forms—negative punishment (or omission) in which we withhold reward (the bite) from the dog, and positive punishment, in which we apply some more or less uncomfortable input to the dog (usually a collar correction). The —no also tends to be a terminal marker in the sense that any time the dog hears a —no, it means that the animal has made a mistake and the last exercise will have to be repeated.
5. The clear signals —no versus the traditional DoD —no. This manner of employing the —No is utterly different than the traditional DoD method of using —no. Typically in DoD the handler was taught to say —no (perhaps many times while giving a continuous correction) and correct the dog simultaneously. This makes the —no nothing more than part of the punishment, and it gives the dog very little information. As it is used in CST the —no is a much more powerful tool that enables the handler to identify for the dog exactly what it did to —get in trouble and, if the handler allows, self-correct in order to —get out of trouble.
6. Out (release bite on command). The out is seemingly the simplest of skills for the dog to execute—simply opening the mouth. But, in releasing the decoy, the dog is relinquishing its grip on the single most motivating object it knows. This means that tremendous psychological currents and emotional turbulence can be caused by the out, especially when strong physical force is used on the dog to accomplish the release. In short, although the out is simple, it is far from easy for the dog, and the better and more powerful the dog, the more difficult it can be for the animal to learn to control itself sufficiently to obey commands. This means that the trainer is under a tremendous obligation to be patient, skilled, fair and humane with the dog in this phase of training. CST methods assist us to meet this obligation by giving us powerful tools for showing the dog what we want it to do, and also by giving us a hierarchical method of adjusting the dog's level of motivation, and hence the difficulty of the exercise for the animal.

Hierarchy of bite objects and motivation. To adjust the dog's level of motivation, the trainer chooses from an assortment of possible bite objects, ranging from very unappealing objects like hard wood and plastic, to more motivating objects like rubber hoses and tug toys, to the most motivating bite objects such as decoys wearing sleeves and suits. This range of objects, and the range of motivation they produce—from low to high—is called a hierarchy. The basic approach to instructing the out in clear signals training is to manipulate this hierarchy so that the dog learns the skill in a situation of the lowest possible stress (using a bite object that the dog likes enough to bite but not enough to be stubborn about keeping hold of), and then gradually moving up the hierarchy to the target situation in which the dog is fighting and biting a decoy.

Teaching/Training the out. Because many green dogs procured by DoD already have extensive experience at the time of procurement in being choked off of bites with choke collars, and struggling against handlers who are trying to physically control them, often it is not possible to persuade these dogs to perform an entirely inductive, or voluntary, out. Such dogs have already been taught to be resistant and anxious while biting. Therefore, in many cases some sort of physical input or correction is needed to cause the animal to release on command, so that it can be rewarded with another bite. For this reason, because corrections may be involved in even the earliest stages of instructing the dog to out, teaching and training stages are often not distinct, and they are here discussed as one.

The out is best taught during play with the handler (low on the hierarchy of motivation), rather than during bite work on a decoy (extremely high on the hierarchy of motivation), because during bite work the dog becomes extremely excited and therefore may require heavy (and stressful, even potentially injurious) corrections, unless it has already been taught at a lower level of the hierarchy how to release the bite on command for a reward.

1. An object is chosen that generates low to moderate motivation. For a somewhat low-drive dog this

might be a tug toy; while for a high-drive or problem dog it might be an object like a piece of hard wood or plastic. In the case of the latter type of dog, the goal is to find an object the dog likes enough to bite, but not enough to cause it to stubbornly fight the handler in order to retain the object.
2. The handler entices the dog with the bite object, holding it in both hands by the ends, allows the dog to bite it, and then provides a brief fight with praise. Then the handler freezes, holding the bite object still, with the leash (with some slack) held in the left hand along with the end of the object.
3. The handler gives the —out command, and then causes the dog to release. Ideally, this is done very gently, either by waiting for the dog to become frustrated by the handler's refusal to play tug of war, or by crowding the dog's mouth off of the bite object with hands and fingers. When neither of these options is practical, a correction is applied, as lightly as possible, by leaning backwards against the back-tie and exerting tension on the correction collar with the leash held in the left hand. Once the dog releases, it is told —good, and a moment later —yes/get'em and enticed to bite the object again.
4. The exercise is practiced several times during a session. On the last out of the session, the dog is rewarded by being allowed to take the bite object from the handler (equivalent to the decoy dropping a bite sleeve). The handler then entices the dog with a second bite object, induces a transfer and a bite, gives the dog that bite object, picks up the first object, and transfers the dog back to the first object again. After a few rewarding transfers, the handler ends the session by using the object in his/her hand to entice the dog to the side, away from the object lying on the ground (that the dog has just transferred from), throws the bite object behind him/her to keep the dog's attention away from the other object lying on the ground, and then steps in and regains control of the dog with the leash. In this way the session ends with drive and with pursuit activity, rather than ending with an out and guard followed by no reward bite.
5. The emphasis here is not on trying to cause the dog to out cleanly on command—it is on teaching the dog to release calmly and willingly in order to escape a collar correction, then to guard (rather than back away or otherwise avoid) and confidently re-bite when rewarded with the —yes/get'em cue. At this point we are not especially concerned if the dog ignores the —out command and waits for the correction to be applied before it releases. However, typically this stage of training, in which the dog is allowed to practice escaping corrections rather than avoiding them is relatively brief—one or two sessions for a powerful dog that has unshakeable persistence under correction, and several sessions for a softer dog that is more easily upset and put into avoidance behavior.
a. Proofing the out. To proof the out, we must drive the dog from escape responding, in which it tends to wait until it feels the correction before it releases the bite object, to avoidance responding, in which it releases on command in order to avoid the correction entirely. This is done by:
   a. Moving up one or two levels on the hierarchy of motivation so that the dog begins to disobey the out command reliably;
   b. Applying a sharper correction.
6. Once the dog has become skilled and comfortable in releasing the bite in order to escape/avoid correction, at a low level on the hierarchy of motivation, we increase the motivation by choosing another object for the dog to bite a little higher on the hierarchy. For a very compliant dog we may move directly to the decoy and bite sleeve. For a more powerful and resistant dog we may continue to practice the out only during play with the handler, and merely move one small step up the hierarchy of objects, for instance from a PVC pipe to a firm rubber hose.
7. In either case, if the dog fails to release on the —out command, the handler applies a sharp correction with the leash and collar, pulling towards himself/herself so that the dog's mouth is pulled into the bite object. When the dog releases under this correction, the handler gives the —good cue (which now takes on the meaning of a safety signal telling the dog that discomfort is over and will not re-occur so long as it continues to obey). After a moment of stable, guarding the handler (or decoy, if we

are training on the decoy) delivers another bite and immediately freezes, and the —out command is given again. If the dog releases cleanly on command, the handler says —good (the safety signal reassures the dog, telling it that it has done the right thing and the danger of a correction is past), and then —yes/get'em, and gives the dog a rewarding bite.

8. In early training, the handler does not say —no before correcting. The dog simply receives a rapid correction after the —out if it does not release. In later training, especially when the handler is at some distance and is unable to deliver a correction immediately (so there will be some delay between disobedience of the command and the correction), then the handler marks disobedience of the —out command (continuing to bite) with the —no. Then the handler approaches the dog and calmly and methodically administers the correction.

9. The —good cue as a safety signal. When we introduce corrections to obedience and patrol training, the —good takes on two meanings—It now tells the dog that no correction is coming, that by choosing the right behavior it avoided correction, and it also predicts for the dog that, if it continues to perform well, reward in the form of —yes/get'em is on the way. The purpose of this safety signal is to reduce the dog's stress and anxiety—instead of waiting to see if it will be corrected, it learns immediately that it has found safety from discomfort, and thereby it also learns exactly which behavior earned that safety.

10. The dog is taught not to re-bite until the handler signals reward with the —yes/get'em release. If the dog attempts to re-bite without permission, the handler gives the —no. After the —no, in most cases the handler proceeds to calmly and methodically deliver the correction. However, at some points in training it is advisable to omit the correction if the dog exhibits a very respectful response to the —No by recoiling from the bite. If the dog self-corrects in this way and the handler decides not to correct, he/she then gives the —good cue (signaling safety for the dog), pauses a few moments, and then the dog is rewarded.

Guarding the Decoy
Once the dog has learned to reliably out from the decoy on command, then we begin the process of developing the dog's skill and persistence in guarding the decoy. This guarding will be the foundation for nearly all the exercises of controlled aggression such as field interview, search, stand-off, and so forth.

Teaching/Training the Dog to Guard
1. The dog is still trained on the back-tie, and it learns the first stages of these exercises while working on the back-tie.
2. In DoD the most frequent cause of severe training problems in patrol, and eliminations from patrol training, is failure to guard—the dog leaves the decoy when it should be guarding, waiting for its next opportunity to bite. This problem is most often caused by faulty training, by handlers pressuring and correcting dogs while guarding until the animals' drive is overcome by their anxiety, and they avoid the situation. This behavior is not disobedience, it is avoidance behavior fueled by anxiety and confusion. In order to guard well the dog must be confident that it knows how to guard without biting, confident that it knows when a re-bite will be safe because it is authorized, and it must trust its handler. Accordingly, CST takes a great deal of trouble teaching the dog to guard while still on the back-tie, by breaking the guarding into steps.
3. At all times, it is the decoy who causes the dog to guard by enticing the dog subtly and delivering bites at the right times. The handler does not make the dog guard by pressuring it to —stay! However, if while guarding the dog re-bites without permission, then the handler may deliver the —no and correction.
4. Guard during handler movement. The first step is to teach the dog to continue guarding while the

handler moves. While standing near the dog, holding the leash, the handler takes one step away from the animal. The dog should continue to guard, and then the decoy rewards this behavior by delivering a bite. After the next out the handler takes two steps, and the dog receives a bite, and so on. Eventually we condition the dog to guard intently while the handler walks and even runs about— around the decoy, to the dog and away, behind the dog, etc. If the dog becomes distracted for a moment by the handler and looks away from the decoy, or tries to leave the decoy, then the decoy punishes the animal by jumping away out of range and agitating the dog to produce frustration. If the dog on the other hand becomes unsettled by handler movement and bites the decoy prematurely, then it receives a —no and perhaps a correction. If it recoils obediently form the bite on hearing the —no, then the handler may elect to reassure it with —good and continue the exercise.

5. Guard during decoy movement. In the second phase of teaching guarding, the handler steps to heel position on the guarding dog, tells the animal calmly to —stay in a reassuring but forceful voice, and uses his/her right arm to wave or push the decoy back one small step. This must be done carefully to avoid triggering a premature bite. When the dog allows this step away and continues to quietly guard, the handler rewards with the —good marker, and then waves the decoy back close to the dog. Once the decoy has stepped up close, with the dog still guarding, then the animal is rewarded with a bite (either after a —yes/get'em from the handler or after a sharp movement from the decoy, depending on whether we want to emphasize the dog's attention to the decoy or to the handler).

6. If at any point the dog attempts to re-bite prematurely or move away from the decoy, these errors are handled as above—re-bite is met with —no from the handler, while avoidance is met by an escape from the decoy.

7. With additional training the dog is taught to remain in a stable guard position on the backtie while the decoy steps backwards, turns and walks up to 100 feet away; or steps backwards and turns and runs in place; or steps backwards and then turns and runs rapidly away; or steps backwards and stands while the handler searches him/her. (Note that the only situation in which the dog is allowed to bite without command is when the decoy attacks the dog or the handler. If the dog merely sees a person running, this is not authorization to bite).

8. Reinforcing guarding with reward in position. When the dog obeys the handler by guarding intently while the decoy makes the above-described movements, the handler marks this compliance with —good and then signals the decoy to approach the dog very closely and stand, and then give the reward bite. The reward bite may be delivered after a —yes/get'em from the handler, or in response to the decoy attacking (moving suddenly at) the dog or the handler. In the early stages of teaching the dog to guard, the exercise does not conclude with the dog running downfield and biting; it normally ends with dog being rewarded in the original place on the backtie where the animal was given the —out command, released the bite, and began to (and continues) to guard. The alert reader will recognize that this is a reward in position procedure, identical to the procedure used during obedience to help the dog understand how to remain in place without anticipating or breaking position.

9. Reinforcing the dog for vigilant guarding with a reward out of (i.e. breaking from) position. If the trainer judges it advisable to bring up the dog's intensity or attention to the decoy, the dog can also be given a bite occasionally at any point in any of the exercises by having the decoy suddenly attack or threaten the dog or handler. In response the dog will release from guarding and lunge to the limit of the back-tie (which has a rubber inner tube or bungee cord insert to absorb shock). The decoy can move quickly to the dog and deliver a bite. This is how the dog learns to bite without command when the decoy attacks the handler during a search.

10. Punishing the dog for inattention or looking/moving away from the decoy. If the dog becomes anxious or distracted during any of the guarding exercises, the decoy can punish the dog (through negative punishment, or omission of reward) by suddenly becoming aggressive (but without letting

the dog bite), running away to a hiding place, and then pausing for 30 seconds or a minute before coming back and resuming the exercise. After a few such escapes followed by a frustrating time out period, the dog will guard more intently.

11. From this basic out and guard exercise performed on the back-tie, with rewards delivered in guard position, we develop:
    a. the field interview;
    b. the false run (in which the dog remains under control at the handler's side while the decoy walks or runs away);
    c. the search of the decoy by the handler while the dog guards;
    d. the re-attack during the search.

    Most importantly, we teach the dog to guard confidently and calmly while the handler approaches and places himself/herself at heel. In order to increase the dog's confidence and steadiness during handler approach, the handler often gives the —yes after arriving at heel, or the decoy delivers a bite without —yes by attacking dog or handler.

12. At the end of the session, the dog is normally unhooked from the back-tie and allowed to perform one or two pursuit bites concluding with transfers. However, these bites are not practiced from the guard. The animal is not released (given the —yes/get'em command) from the guard to run downfield and bite, because these thrown attacks develop tremendous anticipation for the run and make the dog difficult to control in the guard position. Before the handler begins to sending the dog downfield from guard position, we must first do extensive work to make the dog steady at heel, and teach it to guard quietly, without barking, whining, bouncing or lunging, even when the decoy moves off to a distance of 25 or 50 yards. Therefore, all bites from the guard are practiced by having the decoy return to the dog (reward in position), and if the dog is turned loose for a pursuit this is not done from the guard. Instead the handler holds the dog by the flat collar (the dog is encouraged and allowed to lunge and bark so that it knows that it is not under control), the decoy runs away, and the dog is released.

Proofing the Guarding Exercises

All the exercises involving guarding, whether the decoy is nearby or at a distance, are proofed after extensive and patient teaching/training, so that the dog becomes very confident and stable in guard position, and very accustomed to the —No and appropriate collar corrections. This way the dog will not be tempted to avoid the decoy when corrected during a guarding exercise, but instead will resume guarding confidently after it makes a mistake.

Proofing is accomplished by increasing the intensity of correction so that the dog begins to avoid mistakes, so as to avoid corrections. If the dog makes a mistake (i.e. breaks guard position or attempts to rebite without permission) when the handler is at a distance, then the handler marks the misbehavior with a —no and approaches the dog calmly to correct. If the dog has learned what —no means and has been given plenty of practice to understand how to correctly guard, then this procedure will make it afraid of making a mistake again, not make it afraid of its handler approaching.

The stand-off. When the stand-off is correctly taught and performed, the dog drops into a down in mid-flight on the command —out, down and guards from this remote position. The dog should not follow up after the out command—that is, it should not run all the way to the decoy and then guard him/her from nearby.

Teaching/training the dog to perform the stand-off. A good stand-off depends on recruiting the dog's cooperation with the —out, down command, so that the dog is eager to lie down in order to get its bite. If we begin the stand-off exercise by forcing the dog to lie down, it will be much more difficult to teach.

The first step is to teach the dog to earn the bite by lying down. In essence we are teaching the dog to change positions on command while guarding, in order to be paid. The exercise begins on the back-tie as always, with the dog guarding in sitting position and the decoy standing at a distance from 10 to 35 feet. The handler asks the dog to lie down, by giving the —down command plus whatever additional gestures (kneeling and tapping the ground in front of the dog, etc.) will help the dog to lie down even though it is very interested in the decoy. Once the dog's elbows touch the ground, the handler marks with —good. Then the handler signals the decoy to come in and stand very close to the dog, and then the dog receives a bite (reward in position). This exercise is repeated until the dog is trying eagerly to lie down (even before it is commanded) anytime the decoy steps back and stands.

1. In the next phase the exercise is repeated in much the same way, but the dog is not commanded —down when in a sitting guard position, but instead when it is on its feet watching the decoy or even pulling somewhat on the back-tie. In this situation the —out, down command begins to interrupt ongoing activity, rather than just moving the dog from sit-guard to down-guard.

2. Then the dog is taken off of the back-tie and held on leash. Ideally, for the first exercises the dog is walking forward towards the decoy while leaning a bite against the leash, or some similar low-intensity activity, rather than pulling against the leash and lunging and barking with all its strength. The handler commands —out, down, helps the dog to lie down, and then gives the —good and brings the decoy in to stand close to the dog and deliver the bite, providing the dog guards calmly from the down. With repeated exercises, the dog is allowed to move faster or become more excited, pulling harder against the leash until given the —out, down command. In this way, the —out, down command begins to take on the power to interrupt the dog as it moves forward vigorously (but not off- leash) towards the decoy. At this point we are ready to begin allowing the dog to run free of restraint towards the decoy.

3. Preventing hesitation. Simultaneously with the work described above (teaching the dog to lie down to earn a bite), we have also been preparing the dog in another way, to prevent problems with hesitation. The dog is set up at heel position next to its handler, with a decoy about 50 to 60 feet away. The dog is not back-tied. Normally the handler holds a 6-foot leash which he/she will drop when he/she gives the —get'em command. An assistant stands mid-way between the handler/dog team and the decoy, holding a long line attached to the dog's correction collar. The dog is sent to bite with the command —get'em, but the decoy stands passive (although he/she will provide slight enticement if necessary to help the dog bite), so that the dog bites on command alone rather than in response to decoy movement. This procedure is repeated until the dog is thoroughly accustomed to the —stand-off set-up and shows no hesitation in biting a passive decoy on command.

4. Once the dog downs readily for bite reward even when it is moving vigorously on leash, and when there is no trace of hesitation when the dog is commanded to bite a passive decoy with the assistant standing mid-way, then we are ready to run the stand-off proper. The set-up is with handler and decoy 50-60 feet apart and an assistant at the midpoint holding a long line attached to the dog's correction collar. The dog is sent with the —get' em command, but at the half-way point the handler commands —out, down. The assistant uses the long line to rather gently check the dog and bring it to a stop. Once the dog is down, the handler gives the —good marker, advances to heel position, and then signals the decoy to come forward, stand near the dog, and deliver the bite (either after —yes from the handler or by attacking dog or handler, depending on the needs of the dog). Note that again we are using the reward in position command; to steady the dog in the down and teach it that, once it hears the —out, down command, reward will no longer be earned by running forward towards the agitator, but instead through dropping immediately into the down and guarding.

5. In alternating exercises, set up identically, the dog is sent with —get'em, but —out, down is not given. The dog is allowed to continue and bite the passive decoy. The mixture, or balance of bite trials versus stand-off trials is arranged to keep the dog from hesitating (i.e. anticipating the —out, down command and running out slowly when told to —get'em). The decoy never varies his/her behavior, always standing passive until the dog either bites or is called —out, down.

6. Soon the dog should be lying down quickly and eagerly once checked, although it may be necessary for the assistant to use the line to check/stop the dog's forward movement.

Proofing the Stand-Off
1. Proofing is performed by making the checking correction sharper and more uncomfortable, so that the dog begins to check on its own when commanded —out, down in order to avoid the checking correction.
2. Once the dog begins responding reliably to the command —out, down instead of waiting for the assistant to check with the line, then we increase the difficulty of the exercise. The decoy begins stimulating the dog more at the beginning of the exercise, by walking or running away before the dog is sent. The decoy freezes when the —out, down command is given. Now the decoy's behavior begins to provide a clue that helps the dog to perform the stand-off correctly. When the dog performs the exercise correctly at full speed and in full drive, with the line on and an active decoy, then we are ready to take the line off.
3. Initial off-line stand-offs are performed with the decoy standing still. The dog is sent and called —out, down. If it performs correctly it is rewarded as before, with a —good marker and reward in position. If it does not lie down immediately, continuing towards the decoy or even biting, then the handler gives the —no command (we often have a short, light leash on the dog's collar so that the agitator can reach up and take this leash if the dog bites). Then the handler advances to the dog and delivers a correction, and then we repeat the exercise. It is useful with a dog that is difficult to control to have an escape hatch for the decoy (such as a gate or door very, very close by) so that, if the dog disobeys the —out, down and continues towards the decoy, the decoy can quickly escape through the gate and stand passive. In this way we can prevent the dog from stealing reward after disobeying the —out, down.
4. Eventually, the stand-off is run with an active decoy, and the dog can be rewarded for a good —out, down by being given the —yes as soon as it touches its elbows, allowing it to release forward from the down, and finish its run to the decoy and bite.

GUNSHOTS

A well-trained patrol MWD reacts in a neutral way to gunfire—meaning that it is neither frightened nor aggressive. For both handler safety and mission effectiveness, in almost every case the best thing for the dog to do is to continue doing whatever it was doing before gunfire or explosions and be ready to obey the next command. If, on the other hand, the dog becomes extremely excited and aggressive under gunfire or detonations, this response is highly dangerous for handler and dog. However, this mission requirement is problematic, because the vast majority of MWDs have already been taught prior to procurement to become excited and look for someone/something to bite when they hear gunshots.

If MWD trainers attempt to teach a dog not to become excited under gunfire by using strong corrections to compel the dog to remain in a sit or down or heel position during gunshots, this procedure can and often does back-fire in two ways—we can inadvertently teach the dog to be afraid of gunshots (because they become associated with corrections and pain), or we can teach the dog to bite the handler.

Normally, the best approach to teaching a dog to behave calmly under gunfire is counter-conditioning the gunshots with ball reward.
1. In the initial procedure, dog and handler are placed at about 100 yards from an assistant with the weapon. The assistant is protected in some way in case the dog runs to him/her and attempts to bite. The handler throws the ball across the field and sends the dog in pursuit, and two or three gunshots are fired while the dog chases, but before it picks up the ball. Then the shots are fired after the dog

picks the ball up and is returning to the handler. Next, shots are fired while the dog is close to the handler and moving about with the ball in its mouth. Then shots are fired after the handler has commanded the dog to release the ball, while the dog is waiting for the next throw. In the next stage, the dog is asked to respond to simple commands like sit, down, and heel while occasional shots are fired. Eventually, the dog is required to sit at heel with the ball out of sight in the handler's pocket while a series of shots is fired at 100 yards' distance. After each series the dog is rewarded with a throw of the ball.

2. In the next phase, the assistant/gunshots are gradually brought closer. The dog sits at heel and in attention while the shots are fired nearby. If it attempts to break position, it is leash-corrected. When it holds position and maintains attention, it receives ball reward. When the dog is proficient in this skill, then the handler begins to hold the weapon and dry-fire it while the dog remains at heel. Eventually, the handler heels the dog to the gun lying on the ground, picks the gun up with the dog at attention in heel-sit position, fires a series of shots, puts the gun down, heels away, and then rewards the dog. Eventually ball reward is provided less and less often, until finally the dog no longer needs any more than praise reward.

3. Trainers must keep in mind that loud gunshots and heavy concussions hurt, and cause injury to hearing organs. In addition, dogs appear to be especially sensitive to muzzle blast. Therefore, attempts should be made to protect the dogs' ears, and to place them out of muzzle blast and far enough away from the weapons fire to meet local safety standards.

Rexo waits for his handler Senior Airman John Spearing to get instructions before participating in a Brave Defender training scenario Oct. 23 at Eglin Air Force Base, FL. (U.S. Air Force photo/Staff Sgt. Mike Meares)

CHAPTER 5

DEFERRED FINAL RESPONSE (DFR)

DFR BACKGROUND

This chapter discusses the DFR method for training substance detector dogs that is now in use in the MWD course at 341 TRS. Because Deferred Final-trained dogs are taught to look at source when indicating odor, rather than at their handlers, this method is frequently referred to as—focus training. This paper is provided to assist MWD users in understanding and troubleshooting DFR Dogs.

In order to become proficient in substance detection, the dog must acquire two main conditioned associations, or lessons. First, the dog must learn to recognize the target odor, meaning that it must begin to expect reward when it smells that odor. Second, the dog must learn that, in order to receive the reward, it has to sit. This sit is, of course, called the—final response in DoD terminology.

REWARD NOT FROM SOURCE METHOD

The traditional DoD method for teaching odor recognition and final response was called Reward Not From Source (or Reward NFS). The dog is encouraged to investigate an area or a scent box, commanded/helped to sit, and then given a reward (ball/kong). Over the course of many trials the dog learns to sniff a series of locations and sit on the location that smells of target odor, without sitting on any locations that do not smell of target odor. Although it appears procedurally simple and therefore practical for students and non-experts, the Reward NFS method in reality relies upon great experience and skill on the part of the trainers. Furthermore, Reward NFS often builds into the dog's undesirable behaviors which present long-term challenges to trainers and users. This is because the method:
1. Attempts to teach the dog odor recognition and final response simultaneously.
2. Makes no attempt to associate reward with odor source.

These two factors interact to bring the dog's attention to its handler during the crucial period when it should be learning to pay attention to odor. The process by which this learning occurs is as follows: During the initial trials, of course, the target odor has no meaning for the dog. In Reward NFS the animal is persuaded to more or less accidentally sniff the odor, normally by having the handler use hand presentations to get the dog to place its nose near the training aid. Then, hoping that the dog has noticed the odor, the handler manipulates the dog into a sit position, most often with a combination of verbal commands and physical prompts such as leash tugs and/or pressure on the hindquarters. In the course of this intervention, the dog's attention becomes focused on the handler and, once in the sit position, this attention to the handler is rewarded by presentation of the reward.

Because the dog is rewarded while looking at the handler rather than while sniffing odor, the dog is very slow to learn that odor predicts reward (often requiring more than 150 trials). In addition, it learns that handler behavior also predicts reward. It begins to watch its handler closely during detection problems; it tends to rely upon presentations to make it sniff; and it learns much about the cues (stutter steps, etc.) a handler gives when a training aid is nearby. As a result, the dog often develops a false response tendency based on handler cues, and very much time and effort is expended in trying (often unsuccessfully) to work out the cues.

In addition to slow acquisition of odor recognition and high false response tendency, the most common deficiencies in dogs trained with Reward NFS are handler- dependence/lack of independent search behavior, weak change of behavior in response to odor (the dogs tend to simply sit when encountering odor, making it difficult for the handler to discriminate between false responses and hits), and poor localization (many Reward NFS dogs have a fringing tendency). All of these weaknesses are consequences of a system that encourages the dog to look to its' handler for reward and guidance early in training, before the dog's behavior has come under strong control by target odor.

DEFERRED FINAL RESPONSE METHOD

The DFR method differs from the Reward NFS method in three critical ways:
1. First, during initial training of odor recognition, the final response is not required. Instead we defer teaching of the final response until later, when the dog has mastered some critical pieces of learning. On initial trials, the dog is prompted to search a given area, normally by pretending to hide the reward in that area. When the dog investigates, sniffing for the reward, and sniffs target odor instead, then the reward is provided. Thus, we provide the dog with a very clean and simple pairing of target odor and reward, without any cues from the handler to compete with odor for the dog's attention. As a result, the dog learns to recognize odor extremely quickly. Dogs trained with DFR normally exhibit strong changes of behavior in response to target odor after 5 or 6 trials.
2. Second, DFR is a reward-from-source method, meaning the dog is taught that reward originates from odor source. There are many ways to provide reward from source, including simply placing the reward with the odor, but in DFR we rarely place the reward with the training aid. Instead, we lob the reward in from behind the dog when it is sniffing odor, so that the reward appears without any warning and falls as softly as possible directly on odor source.
3. Third, during early stages of DFR training, the role of the handler in making presentations and guiding the dog's search is greatly reduced. In fact, the handler gives the dog as little information as possible. The dog searches off-leash in a confined area or works on leash with an absolute minimum of influence from the handler. We are not concerned if the dog walks the training aid. We operate from the principle that the worst thing the handler can do in detector dog training is show the dog where the aid is by stopping the animal on the aid. It is the dog's job to stop the handler on the training aid, and if it fails to do so it learns two important lessons:
   a. No one will help it to find odor;
   b. Leaving odor is a mistake to be avoided, because it results in more work and greater delay to reinforcement.

OVERVIEW OF THE DFR TRAINING SEQUENCE

The first step is to teach odor recognition by paying on sniff' without any requirement for final response. The dog is not paid unless it is clear that it is sniffing and that it has noticed the smell of the training aid. Normally within 1 day of training and no more than 10 trials the dog exhibits vigorous changes of behavior when encountering target odor. These changes include bracketing to source, perhaps freezing behavior, and sometimes scratching or biting (i.e. aggression) at the source. Aggression is not desirable and efforts are made to control it, but all recent experience in the Specialized Search Dog and other dog Courses indicate that, in a focus-trained dog, a degree of aggressive responding early in training is common and does not necessarily indicate that the animal will develop into a persistent aggressive responder.

During the first 6 to 8 days of training and perhaps 30 to 50 trials, the dog works on one odor, with a minimum of handler presentations and interference, with pay on sniff rather than final response. Efforts are made to encourage the dog to look/focus/point at odor source, because when the dog focuses on odor it is not observing its handler and learning about handler cues. The dog is desensitized to people in the search area and taught to ignore physical contact and interference from personnel while it is searching. At the same time, it is taught to focus on odor for 2 or 3 seconds at a time and taught to check back to odor on command when focus is broken.

Simultaneously with odor recognition training, the final response (sit) is pre-trained. The sit is not performed in obedience mode, and corrections are not used. Instead the dog is induced to sit with food or a reward. Ideally the dog learns to sit when it is pointing at a reward (such as a kong held by the handler) that it cannot take because it is blocked by a barrier (in this case the handler's hand enclosing the reward). The dog is never forced to sit. Instead it is kept interested in the reward until it chooses to sit voluntarily, and then it is rewarded. Initially, the use of a —Sit command or any other cue to sit is avoided, so that the sit is not dependent on a command. Ideally, the dog perceives a blocked reward and learns to spontaneously sit in order to unblock the reward. Once the dog sits quickly and easily to unblock a reward, then we may attach a cue to the sit, such as a light touch on the dog's rump, or a slight tug on the collar, or even the verbal command —Sit.

When the dog recognizes target odor, stops on it and stares, can be made to check back, and when the pre-trained sit is fluent, then we begin to require the animal to give the final response on odor. This stage is normally reached on day 6 to 10 of training. Initial final response training can be accomplished in a number of different ways, but in the most straightforward method, the aid is placed in a piece of furniture at about nose height. Rather than paying on sniff, the handler cues the dog into the sit using one of the cues (tug on leash from behind, touch on rump, verbal command —sit) that was taught during pre-training of the sit. It is important to realize that this use of the word cue is not identical to the common use of the word cue in DoD terminology. When we speak of a handler cue in Reward NFS, we are referring to a piece of information that the handler gives the dog to help it sit on/find the training aid (normally the handler cue is a mistake or an accident). In DFR we never deliberately cue the dog to help it find the training aid. The dog must always find the training aid and stop on it without assistance. The cue in DFR is merely help from the handler in completing the final response. One way to think of it is if the dog independently detects and localizes the training aid, then it earns help with the final response.

The dog is introduced to additional odors, beginning with pay on sniff. Once the dog begins to show recognition of the new odor (normally within three to five trials or even less), then we add the final response to the new odor. The dog also is taught to perform search exercises in new training areas (vehicles, aircraft, etc.). Finally, as one of the last important lessons the dog acquires, the handler for the first time encourages the dog to look to him/her for help in finding the training aid (i.e. the dog is trained to accept guidance in the form of handler presentations of productive areas).

LIABILITIES OF DFR

Above we reviewed the significant liabilities of the standard DoD (Reward NFS) method. DFR also has liabilities—it can produce certain undesirable behaviors. However, these undesirable behaviors are not as harmful and difficult to correct as the handler-dependence, weak change of behavior and localization, and high false response tendency so common in Reward NFS dogs. In a word, the kinds of problems associated with Deferred NFS are the kinds of problems we would rather have.

DFR-trained dogs can be excessively independent while searching and may sometimes be reluctant to accept presentations. This shortcoming is offset by the fact that these dogs are often extremely accurate and effective when scanning and working independently.

The most common problem in DFR dogs is a tendency to stop/stand and stare at odor rather than sit. It is worth noting that this is not a functional problem from the standpoint of detecting narcotics or explosives. A distinct change of behavior followed by localization and then a stop and stare is every bit as recognizable to the handler as a sit. In fact, the DoD Specialized Search Dog Program officially authorizes the stop and stare as a final response.

The first thing to realize about stop and stare is that it is the result of physical and psychological tension rather than disobedience. For the DFR dog, an odor source is like a magnet that draws the dog's attention. The dog orients to odor in the same way it looks at the reward—with great excitement. As a result, the dog carries much more physical tension in its body than a Reward NFS dog. This tension makes the final response more difficult because, in order to sit, the dog must relax major muscle groups in its back and hindquarters.

The expression —stop and stare is used to describe a wide range of difficulties with the final response, ranging from a dog that delays its' sit for 5 or 6 seconds, to an animal that exhibits a classic locked up stop and stare, in which its' body goes completely rigid. The classic locked up stop and stare is a comparatively rare problem with DFR dogs. More common final response issues are:

1. Slow sit.
2. Not completely reliable sit (stops/stands and stares sometimes).
3. Refusal to sit unless cued somehow.

SLOW OR RELUCTANT FINAL RESPONSE IN DFR DOGS

1. If the dog's sit is slow or delayed, but all that is needed is to wait a few seconds for the final, we advise that you leave well enough alone. There is no compelling reason to pressure the dog for a rapid or crisp sit; so long as the animal stops on odor without any help from the handler, will not leave source, and sits on its own without assistance given a few seconds.
2. If the dog sometimes does not complete the final response (this may happen when the footing is difficult, or the aid is very low to the ground, or the dog is tired, etc.), then it is important not to over-react. A stop and stare error is not equivalent to critical errors like missing an aid or false responding. Keep in mind that the dog has completed the most important part of the job: it has found and indicated the drug or explosive hide. Now we just need the animal to fulfill the statutory requirement for the final response. Strong verbal corrections (—No!) and physical corrections (jerk on choke collar) are normally not helpful because they increase the dog's stress and tension and make it all the more difficult for the animal to relax enough to finish the final response. Likewise, simply trying to force the dog's hindquarters down to the ground should be avoided, because it generates resistance and makes the dog lock its' legs.
3. The first corrective action for a dog that stops and stares should be familiar, because it is a fundamental part of handling any DoD-trained detector dog. When the dog stops on the training aid, the handler should keep moving away from the dog and present the next location in the search area. If the dog neither leaves the training aid nor sits, then the handler should put more pressure on the dog with slight leash tension or a tug on the leash. If the dog is not actively working the odor, or sitting, then it needs to move on and actively sniff the next location. This procedure is no different than handling a Reward NFS dog, but still many handlers need to be reminded of it. In this situation, many dogs will react by completing the final because they do not want to be taken away from the aid. Some dogs will allow themselves to be taken away from odor but then they immediately realize this was a mistake. They begin trying to cut back to it, and if they are allowed to do so (on their own—the handler does not bounce them back to the aid) they will complete final when they get to source.
4. If the above procedure is not effective, and still the dog stops and stares, then the next thing for the handler to try is to simply give a —Sit! command from behind the dog. Very many animals will comply. In preparation for this procedure, it is a good idea to practice and fine tune the dog's response to the —Sit!' command during obedience training.
5. If the dog does not complete the final response with the verbal command, then the handler can try

two other types of assist. First, he/she should use the leash to administer light snaps or tugs on the choke collar, straight back towards the dog's hindquarters. If this is not effective, then the handler should try lightly tapping or pushing downwards against the dog's rump, just ahead of its tail and behind the hips. The handler should NOT push against the dogs back ahead of the hips, because this normally causes the dog to brace against the pressure. Most dogs know one of these assists for the final, or a combination of them may be most effective, and will respond by executing the sit. Once the dog has completed the final response, then the handler praises with —Good! and prepares to provide the reward.

6. The reward should be given while the dog is focused on odor, from straight behind or some other blind spot, and it should be lobbed in as softly as possible. Ideally, it goes dead at odor source, so that the dog can simply pick it up, rather than chase it frantically around the room. SSD trainers and other specialists in DFR sometimes arrange nets or even pillows near the training aid, or use a spiked tennis ball or something similar, so that the reward lands at source and stays there without bouncing. If the assist distracted the dog, then focus on the odor source should be re-established prior to reward.

7. If the sit is consistently assisted as described above, the dog's final response normally improves, and no other special efforts are required. Sometimes it may happen, however, that the dog becomes dependent upon the assist it will not sit unless it is given some cue. In this case, it is often effective to allow the dog to make repeated finds of the same training aid. This procedure removes the search element from the exercise and allows us to concentrate the dog's energy on the final response. Also, because the dog is asked to sit repeatedly in the same location, the animal's anticipation works in our favor to produce a fluent (relaxed, easy, prompt) sit. The first time the dog finds the aid, it is assisted into the sit and paid. After the reward is recovered from the dog, the animal is allowed to go right back to the aid. On the second indication of the aid, if the dog does not complete the final response, then it is assisted, but the dog is not paid. Instead it is praised for the sit, then gently pulled backwards off of the training aid. (Keep in mind here that a well-trained focus dog will not allow itself to be easily taken away from a training aid. Instead it will fight to check back to the aid.) Once the dog is pulled away, it is encouraged by praising it, and then allowed to go to the aid again. If the cue is still necessary to produce the sit, then the dog is again praised for the sit verbally and physically, then pulled gently away from the aid, and allowed to go back again. The procedure is repeated as many times as necessary (within reason). When the dog eventually sits without the assist, the handler praises it and pays. Once they understand that they must sit without the assist in order to be paid, most dogs quickly improve their final response.

8. A word of caution is necessary here. Unless the dog is well-trained in checking back, pulling the animal off of the aid repeatedly can produce some undesirable side-effects. Some dogs may become discouraged or frustrated and begin to leave the odor source. If a cage is used (after a bit of basic training to establish good focus on the visible aid), then the dog is less likely to leave the visible aid. On the other hand, the dog may not leave the aid, it may instead become more tense and resistant, and begin stopping and staring more. However, the resistance may be specific to the aid that it has encountered again and again. If we move the aid to another location and surprise the dog with it, the animal may show one of its' best unassisted sits. Similarly, if we have a session one day in which we hammer the sit with many repetitions, even though the dog may conclude the session looking as though it has regressed, sometimes we find that on the first aid of the next training session, the dog will give a crisp, perfect final.

STOP AND STARE IN DFR DOGS

If the dog's sit is extremely slow, or unreliable, or if the dog has become very tense, locking up and going rigid on the training aid, then we must take a more patient and multi-pronged approach to improving the final response. Probably the most important part of this approach is making sure that the dog knows how to sit in order to gain access to a blocked reward. This process is referred to as—pre-training the sit. It was mentioned briefly above, but now we will discuss it in detail.

Pre-Training the Sit

1. First, the dog is taught to sit when the handler holds a reward in the air above its' head. If possible, it is better to avoid use of the verbal cue —sit. Instead just keep the dog's attention and let it experiment with various behaviors until it hits the right one. When the dog sits, the handler gives the reward, preferably by simply handing it to the dog calmly or dropping it into the animal's mouth. The reward should NOT be vigorously thrown or bounced. With many dogs it is more constructive to begin pre-training the sit with food rather than ball/kong reward, because food produces a more manageable level of drive. In addition, in the process of taking and eating food, the dog can more easily be taught to respect (i.e. not bite) its' handler's hands.

2. In the next step, the reward is held lower, where the dog can reach it, but the handler blocks the reward by enclosing it in his/her hands. The dog can see the reward, smell it, even get nose and teeth on it, but not take it. We use the hands to block the reward rather than a physical barrier because most dogs respect their handler's hands—they do not aggress a reward that is held in the hands the way they would a reward held in a drawer. In this situation, with the reward just inches away, nearly every dog falls into stop and stare behavior very similar to the behavior we see in detection. The handler does not try to hurry the dog into the sit. Instead he/she provides time for the dog to think, just keeping the dog's attention on the reward by moving it slightly when necessary. When the dog eventually sits, it receives the reward (i.e. is paid).

3. As time passes, the handler holds the reward lower and lower, trapping it against the legs or body, waiting until the dog sits and then paying the animal calmly. Once the dog is very fluent with this behavior, easily and quickly offering a relaxed sit in order to unblock the reward, then the handler begins to hold the reward against the wall or against furniture, teaching the dog to give the sit whether the reward is held six feet up the wall or on the ground. Low placements of the reward, like low placements of a training aid, are particularly difficult for the dog. Note: Blocking the reward by holding it against walls and furniture should be performed sparingly because the dog can confuse this gesture with hand presentations, causing a tendency to sit or false respond on hand presentations that will then have to be extinguished.

4. Next the handler gives the reward to another party. The handler holds the dog on leash while the assistant shows the dog the blocked reward and pays the dog for the sit. The assistant begins with the reward held high, but then quickly passes through all the steps of holding it trapped against the body and then legs, and then against a wall or furniture at various heights.

5. Eventually, the reward is not held by a person. Instead it is trapped--jammed between a piece of furniture and the wall, or between a car door and its frame, etc. The exact situation does not matter, only that the dog can see and smell the reward but not touch it or take it. The moment the dog sits, then the door is pulled open or the furniture pulled away from the wall to liberate the reward. If the dog responds aggressively rather than sitting, then you wait until the dog becomes discouraged, stops scratching/biting, and sits, and then you pay. The most important factor is not whether the dog is allowed to aggress a reward or aid—it is whether the dog achieves some result with the aggression. With most dogs, if aggression does not produce any result such as opening a drawer or moving furniture or making the handler react, then alternative behavior (i.e. sitting) will quickly take over if it is rewarded. Occasionally, it may be necessary to pay the sit not by liberating the trapped reward, but instead by lobbing another reward in from behind the dog.

6. As a last step, the fluent and relaxed sit is placed under the control of some cue. This cue can be a

voice command, a tug on the leash, or a touch on the hindquarters, whatever works best with that dog—but the cue must be given from behind the dog while it is facing a blocked reward. The exercise is set up as before, with a reward trapped in a suitable location. The dog watches the reward placed, and then is allowed to move forward on leash until it is stopped by the barrier blocking the reward. The handler gives the cue as the dog is assuming the sit position. This means that the cue does not cause the sit—the sit is voluntary. But by pairing the cue with the voluntary sit, you can gradually give the cue the ability to trigger the sit. Most importantly, the sit we obtain is the relaxed, fluent sit the dog has learned in pre-training, rather than a tense, resistant sit.

Re-Teaching the Final Response

Once the sit is adequately pre-trained, with a cue that enables the handler to sit the dog from behind when it is facing a blocked reward, then we bring odor into the situation. We choose a location in which the dog has been extensively drilled on sitting to unblock a reward a trap between a cabinet and a wall, or between a car door and its' frame, etc. We place both the reward AND a training aid in the trap. We must be careful to place the reward and training aid at a height that facilitates the sit—normally at about nose height.

The dog associates the particular location of the trap with sitting. It also associates a blocked reward with sitting. These conditioned associations help to overcome the dog's tendency to respond to odor by freezing and staring.

The dog is allowed to see the reward and the training aid being placed in the trap. When the dog approaches and sniffs at the reward, it also catches target odor. Depending on the individual dog and the preferences of the trainers, we can then do one of two things.

1. Wait until the dog sits. We wait as long as necessary without giving the dog any input or cue. We watch for the sit and ignore anything else that the dog does, except that, when the dog becomes so frustrated it leaves odor, the handler may entice it back to the trap again. This process may take a very long time (up to 5 or 10 minutes) and it may get ugly, in the sense that the dog may stand and stare for minute after minute, or begin looking around, even leave odor and return, or it may begin scratching or biting at the trap. However, nothing produces so much learning as a problem independently solved, and if we allow the dog to choose the sit in its own time and in its own way, just a few trials can result in dramatically less stopping and staring and a faster and faster final response.

2. Once the dog sits, then it is rewarded--not by unblocking the trapped reward but instead by lobbing another reward in from behind. After a bit of reward- play, then the dog is immediately sent back to the exact same trap to practice the final response again. In fact, the dog is sent back to this same trap several times in a row. This is not a search exercise, it is a final response exercise, and knowing the location of the aid only helps the dog.

For the second session the exercise can be moved to another location, so that the dog has to search a little before finding the trap. This will revive the animal's sniffing behavior so that on the first trial or two we can be sure that it is smelling the training aid (and reward), rather than using eyes alone.

Cue the sit. If the dog's sit (to unblock a reward) is controlled by a cue, then the trainers can also cue the sit rather than wait for it. This method has the advantage that it results in a faster sit and less ugly behavior like leaving odor or aggressing, but it has the disadvantage that the cue will eventually have to be extinguished, which may involve a surprising amount of repetition and work.

As before, the dog is sent to a trap containing a reward and a training aid. The moment the dog sniffs, it is cued by the handler into the sit. The handler does not wait to see if the dog will stop and stare; he/she immediately cues the sit without any pause, almost hurrying the dog into the sit. Also, once the handler begins to ask for the sit with the cue, they make sure that the sit is obtained, even if in the process the dog loses focus on the training aid. When the dog completes the sit a reward is thrown in so that it lands at odor source (training aid odor + trapped reward odor).

This exercise is repeated many times, sometimes leaving the trap in a familiar location so that associations with that location help the dog to sit, but moving it often enough so that sniffing behavior is from time to time re-established. Every now and again, the handler tests the dog by waiting a moment to see if the dog begins to sit before being cued. Then for the next few trials, the handler returns to immediately cuing the sit again without waiting to see what the dog will do on its own. Once we find that during the test trials the dog has begun to reliably initiate the sit without waiting for the cue, then we move to the next step.

Throughout the trials described above, the dog was paid once it reached sit position whether a cue was necessary or not. Now we raise the criterion—if a cue is required to obtain the sit, we will not pay the dog. The dog is allowed to find the reward/training aid, and the handler watches to see if the dog gives the final. If not, the handler cues the sit, then praises the dog verbally and perhaps physically while in the sit, then pulls the dog by the leash away from the aid 5 to 10 feet, and then allows the dog to go back to the trap. This procedure is repeated again and again, cuing the sit if necessary but never paying the dog for the sit if a cue was used. When the dog finally sits on its own without the cue, we give the reward.

Eventually, once the dog is very fluent with the sit when presented with reward and training aid together in a trap, then we omit the reward and present the training aid alone. We follow the rules described in the last paragraph, giving the dog only praise and encouragement if it requires the cue in order to sit, but giving the reward if the dog sits without a cue.

Waiting the Dog Out vs. Cuing the Sit

Choice of strategy is guided by trainer inclinations and dog characteristics. If the dog has a very rigid, — locked up stop and stare, but will not leave the aid and does not tend to aggress, then the waiting approach is often best. Attempting to cue such a dog often stimulates more tension and resistance. Instead the animal just has to be given the time to learn that stop and stare does not produce reward but sitting does. It is not unknown to wait 10 or 15 minutes.

If the dog has a very prompt, fluent, unresisting sit when cued, and if the dog is not extremely tense when indicating a training aid, then the cued approach is likely to be quick and effective, and has the additional advantage that it will prevent the dog from aggressing the aid, leaving it, looking around, etc.

Use of a Cage to Contain the Training Aid

1. Rather than the trap, DoD's Specialized Search Dog Course often places the training aid inside a sturdy cage of some sort that allows the dog to see the training aid. Although being able to see the aid may decrease sniffing somewhat, visual access to the aid helps to establish and maintain focus. This is helpful because maintaining focus can be very difficult while re-training the final response, because we may leave the dog on the aid for long periods of time while we wait for the sit, or subject the dog to strong physical influences in order to cue the sit.
2. The addition of visual information to the situation can have a beneficial effect on many dogs that have difficult habits when working—hidden training aids. Dogs that are very aggressive to aids in other situations fall into staring behavior when they are caged; dogs that walk away from hidden aids in frustration stay with them when they are visible inside a cage.
3. Initially the cage is placed on the ground in an empty corner. A few introductory cage trials are performed to establish the dog's focus in this unique situation. The dog is paid on sniff, which may seem puzzling in view of the fact that the goal is to cure a stop and stare problem. However, a few pay on sniff trials will help us establish focus on the caged aid, and they won't make the stop and stare problem any worse than it already is.
4. An assistant shows the dog the reward and pretends to place the reward on/in the cage. The dog is released from a distance of 15 or 20 feet away. As the dog moves in to investigate the cage the assistant fades away slightly so that, just as the dog reaches the cage and sniffs, he/she can drop the reward in on top of the cage without the dog seeing where the reward came from.

5. After two or three trials like this, the dog's sense of sight will assert itself. The animal will begin sniffing less and looking more. It may do any number of things. The dog may stop short of the cage and stare at it, or it may go to the cage and check it and then turn away or begin to look around. In response, the assistant encourages the dog to investigate the cage, often by presenting it with his/her hand, and then drops the ball in on top of the cage when the dog checks it. The most important consideration is to pay the animal when it is focusing on the caged aid.

6. After several trials, when the dog's sniffing has been reduced because it has begun to look at the training aid/cage instead of smelling it, then you can wake the dog's nose up again by moving the cage to a new location. You can move it to another corner of the room--or you can place it inside a chest of drawers, replacing one of the drawers with the cage. In this location, the cage and training aid will be easy to find, but the dog will still have to sniff to find it. In addition, once found, there are plenty of visual cues to help the dog stay with the training aid. The dog will go to the familiar corner, find the cage is gone, and begin sniffing for it. When it finds the cage, it will check the aid closely and sniff, and you can pay for this sniffing and checking. After a few trials like this, you should obtain good—focusing and—checking back and sniffing behavior on the cage. Now, if you withhold the reward, you should see the dog's stop and stare behavior in full force. At this point you can adopt one of the two strategies described above:

   a. If you choose to wait for the sit, then the visual cues of the training aid inside the cage will help to keep the dog with the aid while it—thinks the problem over. In addition, the cage will protect the aid and prevent the dog from getting any result should it become frustrated and begin scratching and/or biting at the aid.

   b. If you choose to cue the sit, then again the cage will help keep the dog focused on the training aid while you use the cue. This is especially important if the dog loses focus while you are cuing the sit. Once in the sit, with a little encouragement the dog can be induced to look back at the training aid and then be paid for checking it. You assume you will have to assist the dog many times. Initially you pay the dog even if you have to assist it with the cue. Later you pay only if the dog completes the final response without assistance.

ISSUES WITH DFR DOGS

Disrupted Focus

In order to understand the importance of maintaining focus in the DFR dog, you must again consider the common shortcomings of the Reward NFS dog. Two of the cardinal faults of a conventionally-trained Reward NFS dog are that the animal:
1. Tends to sit on fringe odor rather than going to source.
2. Tends to stop working odor/sniffing after the final response.

These two faults, both rooted in the fact that the dog expects reward from the handler rather than from source, interact in the following way to produce final responding on handler cues rather than on odor. When the dog smells odor, it final responds and looks at the handler. If the dog is not as close to source as you desire, then the handler asks the dog to leave the final and continue to sniff/search. The dog normally does not do so effectively, because once it has smelled odor it quite rightly expects reward to come from the handler, and so it looks at the handler, its' mind on visual cues rather than sniffing. The handler normally makes a hand presentation or gives some other sort of encouragement; the dog makes a token head movement while looking at the handler, moves in the direction the handler has gestured, and then immediately sits again. If the dog has moved closer to source, the dog is then paid. However, from the moment the dog first gave final, it has not done any further sniffing or processed any more odor. It has merely oriented at and responded to a series of handler cues, and then been rewarded.

In contrast, a DFR dog needs absolutely no encouragement to go directly to source. In addition, if the dog is well-trained, it continues to work odor and investigate source even after first final. This is the basis of the checking back behavior that is so valuable to the detector dog handler. When the dog checks back, it points at, or crowds, or drives into the odor source, normally in response to some attempt on the handler's part to take it off of odor. This checking back behavior is extremely useful because it allows us to:
1. Refocus the dog's attention on odor after it has been disrupted by, for instance, cuing the final response. This enables the handler to pay the dog for sniffing odor rather than looking at its handler.
2. Ask the dog to confirm a find. You ask the dog to confirm by trying to pull it away from something it is interested in, either before final or after final. A well-trained DFR dog must be physically dragged away from odor and will exert strenuous efforts to get back to odor and repeat the final. This makes the dog extremely easy to read and simplifies the problem of telling the difference between interest in a distracting odor and a change of behavior in response to a bomb or drug hide.

When a DFR dog has lost focus on training aids, when it no longer checks back when asked, this is normally as a result of damage done while teaching the final response. However, note that many dogs lose focus while learning the final and have to be rebuilt once the final is fluent. This is not difficult as long as the dog was taught to check back to odor prior to introduction of the final response.

The first thing to do in re-establishing focus is to run a few pay on sniff trials. It is very helpful to have a visible training aid (in a cage) so that the dog has a visual fixation point. Next, allow the dog to find the aid again but wait for the final response. Once the dog has completed final, then the handler can attempt a variety of different techniques to induce the dog to check back.

Stand behind the dog and wait for a few seconds, encouraging the dog verbally to —check! Be extremely alert for a head movement towards the training aid and be ready to pay on odor source.

Exert a slight backwards pull on the dog's collar, as though to pull the dog straight back off of odor. At the moment the dog feels this traction, it is likely to head-poke back at the aid, and at this instant the handler or an assistant must pay by dropping the reward on source.

If slight pressure does not cause the dog to check back to source, then the handler can pull harder and actually pull the dog backwards out of the sit. Praise and encourage and excite the dog and then release it to go back to source. Initially, you pay the dog for checking back to odor without demanding the sit. Later you withhold the reward until the dog checks back and then completes the second final response. (Note: The decision about whether it is safe to reward the dog on sniff without the final response depends on how fluent the dog's final response is—If the dog has a very fluent, relaxed sit, then it is normally not harmful to sometimes pay on sniff. If, on the other hand, the dog has a resistant, tense sit, then paying on sniff may quickly result in stop and stare.) If the dog completes the second final but loses focus again, then give the slight pull (as above) to try and re-establish focus during the final. However, it may be impossible to obtain both focus and final at the same time, so alternately reward one and then the other until the dog unites them both.

If the dog has completely lost focus on the aid so that none of the above produces the check-back, then the handler can attempt a hand presentation to bring the dog's attention back to the aid. Do not pay the dog while the hand is still on source. This merely rewards the dog for looking at a part of the handler's body. Instead tap on source to draw the dog's attention, and then attempt to fade the handout and pay for focus on source.

One trick used by the SSD Course is to place a radio with the training aid. When the dog is in final, the radio is keyed. The dog looks at source and is paid.

Another trick to re-establish focus is to use a reward system to deliver the reward from odor source. There are very, very many of such devices—some complicated and elaborate and some very simple. In one version used by the SSD Course a training aid is placed in a box that opens towards the dog. Poised two or three feet above the aid is a reward in a PVC pipe, held there by a piece of thin bungee cord stretched from one side of the tube to the other. The reward rests on top of the bungee. Another piece of bungee cord or string is tied to the middle of the first so that if someone pulls sideways on it, the reward can slip past the first bungee and down the tube and land on the odor source. The important elements of such a reward system are that the reward is separate from odor prior to payment; that the dog is paid by someone other than the handler actuating the reward system, and that the reward lands as directly and softly as possible on odor source.

As a final note, keep in mind the purpose of focus on the aid—It is to make sure that the dog does not learn handler cues by watching the handler, and to make sure the dog can be rewarded on odor source for approaching source. If both of these conditions are met, then you are likely to produce a dog that shows strong independent search behavior, an obvious change of behavior, good bracketing to source before final, and a desire to check back to odor if walked or pulled off of it. If you have these elements in place, then exactly where the dog focuses while in the final response is not especially important as long as the animal does not look directly at the handler during payment. In fact, many DFR dogs learn a sort of superstitious staring behavior in which they do not focus on source (especially when it is high overhead and well-hidden); instead they stare generally upwards or away from the handler. This behavior still serves the most important purpose of focus on odor source—it keeps the dog from being paid for focusing on the handler.

Refusal to Accept Presentations

Because early in training they were never encouraged to look to their handlers for any help or information, DFR dogs tend to be very independent while searching. Many of them work very effectively on loose-leash scans, and handlers find that this is often the best way to begin a search. They make presentations only when the dog misses a productive area. Eventually, if the dog is unable to make the find independently, or when it becomes tired and needs some guidance and encouragement, then the handler becomes more active and supplies more guidance.

If a DFR dog is excessively independent and will not accept its' handler's presentations, this is normally because the dog has simply not yet learned that the handler can be a help in finding the aid. (Note that this is to some extent deliberate--you do not want the dog to learn to use presentations by its' handler until late in training, after it has already become completely independent, aid-focused, and self-reliant.) In working with such a dog, the two most important factors are: The handler should give few presentations and the handler must make sure that these presentations are productive from the dog's standpoint.

Set up a search problem with one training aid. Begin the search with the dog working independently, without presentations, but stay away from the area where the training aid is hidden. Wait until the dog tires substantially and becomes more receptive to the handler's influence. Then move the dog into the area of the training aid and make a careful presentation in a productive area near the training aid, so that the dog catches the odor and completes the find and receives reward. Repeat this sort of search exercise a few times--Run the dog on a long problem without any possibility of finding the training aid until the dog wears down somewhat, then take the dog into the vicinity of the training aid and make a presentation or two that put the dog —into odor. The animal will quickly learn to look for presentations, because they indicate an area in which odor can be found. Once the dog becomes very receptive to that initial presentation, then the handler can begin carefully adding a few more presentations here and there, very gradually building up the number of presentations the dog will eagerly accept before finding the training aid.

When teaching the dog to accept high presentations, it is especially important to make sure that the first few presentations are productive for the dog—that they help the animal find odor. Otherwise the dog quickly learns to merely rear up against anything that is presented, but without sniffing.

CHAPTER 6

DETECTOR DOG TRAINING VALIDATION AND LEGAL CONSIDERATIONS

VALIDATION TESTING

The Kennel Master conducts validation tests on each detector dog team annually (not to exceed 180 days from last certification) and prior to initial team certification. These tests are intended to verify the detection accuracy rates annotated on training and utilization forms. Conduct validation testing in a non-task related environment. Kennel Masters and Commanders will ensure handlers are provided sufficient dedicated time to complete all validation trials. Make every effort to complete validation within 5 duty days. If a team fails to meet the minimum accuracy rate, the Kennel Master will immediately initiate remedial training. Retest previously identified remedial teams in unsatisfactory areas only when deemed appropriate by the Kennel Master. If the team fails upon retest, consider those actions outlined in AFI 31-202/Military Working Dog Program.

Since validation testing is intended to verify accuracy of the entries on training and utilization forms, the rating for each training area and odor will reflect GO or NO GO. The minimum standard, however, will be an overall accuracy rate of 90 percent for drug dogs, and 95 percent accuracy rating for explosive dogs. (NOTE: Percentage rates are based on total number of training aids planted/found, and not the individual percentage rate of each substance/odor planted/found. Should the team achieve the overall standard but demonstrates difficulty in accurately detecting a particular substance/odor, proficiency training must increase for this particular odor). All available odors must be used during validation testing; any training aid/odor not used during validation testing period must be reflected in the validation report with a general statement explaining why they were not used. Forward this report to the Chief Security Forces (CSF) who will endorse it and return it to the Kennel Master. File the report with other probable cause documents and document validation testing on AF Form 323.

Conduct at least two trials per odor and one negative test (no training aids planted) per validation for both drug and explosive dogs. Drug dogs are also required to conduct 2 residual odor tests. Validation testing must be conducted in at least three of the below areas, but efforts should be made to conduct testing in as many areas possible:

- Vehicles.
- Aircraft.
- Luggage.
- Warehouse.
- Buildings/Dormitories.
- Open Area.

Validation reports must include date of each validation trial, start time of each validation trial, location of each validation trial, type of area used for each validation trial, aids planted/found for each validation trial, total search time of each validation trial. List each validation trial separately in the report. Validation testing will be documented on the AF Form 323 as well. Document validation testing on the AF Form 323 in the same manner you would for your normal detection proficiency training. Ensure annotation reflects,

"Validations conducted by (Grade/Name)".

Conduct out-of-cycle validation trials if there is any reason to suspect a dog's detection capability has significantly diminished. Out-of-cycle validation and certification trials will also be conducted whenever a detector dog has not received detection training with 1.1 munitions or drug training aids for 30 or more consecutive calendar days

For clarification purposes of this manual the term deployment is considered when a team is operationally forward deployed in support of contingency or humanitarian operations. When a home station certified team deploys for more than 179 days and returns to their home station within their current home station certification window, conduct out-of-cycle validation trials within 20 duty days of team being reassigned to home station operational detector dog duties. If required accuracy percentages rates are achieved, the team retains its current home station certification status. Should validation standards not be achieved, the team's current home station certification status is revoked, and the Kennel Master will reinstitute a new validation and certification process, thus establishing a new validation/certification cycle for the team. Teams deploying for less than 179 days are not required to re-validate unless, while the team was deployed, they did not receive detection training using 1.1 explosive training aids or narcotic training aids for 30 or more consecutive calendar days. Deploying handlers are required to document their animal's utilization and training on AF Form 321 and AF Form 323 while TDY/deployed. Handlers will turn in their TDY/deployed AF Form 321 & AF Form 323 to the Kennel Master upon return.

LEGAL ASPECTS

Prior to using the response of a detector dog as probable cause to grant search authority, the team will demonstrate their ability to detect the presence of all substances (odors) the dog is trained to detect. The individual(s) having search granting authority over the installation is encouraged to witness this demonstration. The search granting authority may delegate his/her responsibility to witness this demonstration to the CSF. After being satisfied with the team's detection capabilities, the CSF prepares and forwards a memo to the search granting authority describing the conduct of the demonstration to include the odors used and the accuracy rate of the team. The CSF will include a copy of the most current validation report, training and utilization records (covering the period since the last validation), and a resume of training and experience for each team being considered for certification. If the search granting authority concurs with the findings and recommendations of the CSF, he/she will endorse the memo indicating concurrence and return it to the CSF. File this memo with the most current validation report in the dog team's probable cause folder. A similar memo will be prepared for search granting authority signature if he/she personally witnesses the demonstration and filed in the probable cause folder as well.

1. Installation commanders and military magistrates appointed IAW AFI 51-201, para 3.1, are encouraged to periodically assess the reliability of detector dogs in a controlled test environment. Such assessments will bolster any probable cause search authorization based on an alert by the dog(s) observed. These assessments are not required and the failure to perform them will not, by itself, invalidate a search authorization made by these officials.
2. Conduct a recertification demonstration annually or whenever a handler change occurs.
3. SF supervisors and commanders responsible for managing and employing MWD assets must understand home station certifications are only valid under the purview of the search granting authority for that particular installation. For example: A dog team assigned to Lackland AFB, TX is certified with the search granting authority for Lackland AFB. This certification is only valid at Lackland AFB. Should this team go TDY to Randolph AFB, TX to perform probable cause searches, regardless of the TDY length, the team must certify under the search granting authority for Randolph AFB prior to conducting searches.

a. There may be instances such as mission time constraints, non-availability of training aids at the TDY or deployed location, etc. that may prevent an actual certification demonstration to take place. Should this be the case, ensure a copy of the team's probable cause folder is sent with the team along with an official memorandum with the search granting authority's signature block (TDY/deployed location). This memorandum must indicate the TDY/deployed search granting authority has reviewed the team's probable cause folder and finds the documented performance and training of the dog team satisfactorily, and the team is authorized to perform probable cause searches within their jurisdiction. The TDY/deployed search granting authority will retain this memorandum.

b. SF MWD teams must at a minimum meet validation standard at home station prior to going TDY or being deployed where it is anticipated the team will perform detector dog duties. Once at the TDY or deployed location, it is the responsibility of the gaining unit to conduct the certification process with the gaining search granting authority if required. If so, home station validation trials can be used in-lieu-of TDY or deployed location validation testing.

c. USAF MWD support to sister Services. In today's ever-increasing inter-service cooperation and support it is not uncommon for SF MWD assets to be called upon to assist sister services' and vice versa. Should this occur, MWD teams will validate and certify (if necessary) under the Air Force standard and not the validation and certification standard of the supporting Service while being operationally assigned to another service. US Army, US Navy and US Marine Corps dog teams supporting USAF operations using an USAF search granting authority will validate and certify under their respective service requirements. In most cases, these sister service teams will have already met their home service MWD certification standards prior to departing their home station. Should a sister service dog team be required to conduct probable cause searches under the purview of an USAF search granting authority, follow the guidance outline in this Manual. All DoD MWD teams maintain certification or probable cause folders. Use the USAF MWD probable cause folder as guidance, but not as an all-inclusive baseline when reviewing sister service dog team documentation.

CHAPTER 7

THE MILITARY WORKING DOG (MWD) PROGRAM

DOCTRINE

The MWD is a highly specialized piece of equipment that supplements and enhances the capabilities of security forces personnel. It is a unique force multiplier and provides security forces another level on the "use of force" continuum.

FUNCTIONAL AREA RESPONSIBILITIES

Every level of command must ensure the MWD program is efficiently managed and develop expertise to properly employ MWDs. If not properly maintained, MWDs lose their skills rapidly; therefore, any planning for long term use of MWDs must always have the training of the dog teams kept in mind. When employed as an integral part of the security forces team, the entire security forces effort is enhanced.

Installation Commander
AF wing commanders are normally an AF installation's search granting authority since they exercise overall responsibility and control of an installation's resources and its personnel. Wing Commanders may delegate their search granting authority to lower echelon commanders such as the Mission Support Group Commander. Consult with your installation's Staff Judges Advocate (SJA) for clarification of your particular installation's search granting authority to ensure all legal parameters associated with the MWD detection certification process are met.

Chief of Security Forces
Ensures MWDs are properly employed. The CSF establishes guidelines to ensure MWDs are properly trained and integrated into the unit's mission.

Flight Chief
Ensures MWD assets are properly employed working hand-in-hand with the Kennel Master to maintain team's proficiency at optimal levels. Flight Chief will ensure adequate time is provided for assigned handler(s) to accomplish daily required activities including but not limited to dog team proficiency training, kennel care and annotating MWD records when providing supervision and management of their flight operations.

EMPLOYMENT AREAS

The MWD team is a versatile asset to a Security Forces unit and can be effectively employed in almost every aspect of a unit's security, Air Provost and contingency operations. Local unit operating instructions address the use of dog teams. Consider them in the following areas:

Nuclear Security Operations

The MWD can be an invaluable asset in the protection of nuclear weapons and critical components. An MWD team may be used in weapon storage areas to replace or augment sensor systems, as a screening force in support of aircraft parking areas or in support of convoy and up/download operations. Explosive detector dog teams are highly effective in searching and clearing nuclear operation work and support areas and related equipment.

Air Provost

MWDs detect, locate, bite/hold, and guard suspects on command during patrol activities. They assist in crowd control and confrontation management and search for suspects both indoors and outdoors. Dog teams should not be used as the initial responding patrol for drunk driving traffic stops or dispatches, domestic violence responses, or disturbance responses, if possible. These types of responses require SF members to have direct contact with either the subject/suspect(s). Because of this close proximity to the suspect/subject during the initial response phase, handlers would be left with the choice of either focusing their full attention on the subject/suspect or their dog. Should the handler choose to focus their attention on the subject/suspect, rather than the dog, this could result in a lack of effective control over the MWD with the MWD inadvertently biting the subject/suspect or put the handler at risk should the subject/suspect become violent. In most potentially dangerous law enforcement responses, dog teams are well suited to provide back up or as a secondary response patrol. In many cases, just the mere presence of a dog team within the immediate area as an over watch will deter most hostile or violent acts.

Drug Suppression

MWD teams specially trained in drug detection support the Air Force goal of drug-free work and living areas. Their widely publicized capability to detect illegal drugs deters drug use and possession and is a valuable adjunct to a commander's other primary tools such as urinalysis and investigations.

Explosive Detection

MWD teams specially trained in explosive detection are exceptionally valuable in antiterrorism operations, detection of unexploded ordnance, and bomb threat assessment. Units will refrain from public demonstrations of their explosive detector dog capabilities.

Contingency Operations

In war fighting roles, MWD teams are tasked to bring enhanced patrol and detection abilities to perimeters, Traffic Control Point (TCP), Cordons, Dismounted Combat Patrols, and point defense in bare-base operations; they are a rapidly deployable and effective sensor system. A well-trained and effectively placed MWD team can augment and enhance current contingency operations.

Perimeter Defense

An MWD team can detect intruder(s) several hundred yards out from the team's position. Teams should be posted in such a manner as to allow the MWDs senses to be effectively utilized.

TCP Operations

MWD team's explosive detection capabilities make them a necessity to all TCP operations. MWD teams participating in TCP operations will remain out of sight in a vehicle or building until needed. Choke points and search area should be placed in such a manner as to allow the MWD team to safely maneuver around the vehicle(s). Once vehicle(s) are chosen, all personnel will exit the vehicle and all compartments will be opened for inspection by the team. Driver and any passengers should be removed or turned away from the immediate area while the team is searching and should not be allowed to observe the team while searching. MWD team will have an over watch at all times.

Flash TCP Operations
Same as TCP operations, but MWD Team is a member of a Convoy/Mounted Patrol. MWD team will remain out of sight within assigned vehicle until needed. Once vehicle(s) have been chosen, a Mounted Patrol will entrap the vehicle and safely get it stopped and positioned in such a manner as to allow the MWD team to safely maneuver around the vehicle(s). Once vehicle(s) are stopped, all personnel will exit the vehicle and all compartments opened for inspection by the team. Driver and any passengers should be removed and turned away from the immediate area while the team is searching and should not be allowed to observe the team while searching. MWD team will have an over watch at all times.

Aerial TCP Operations
Generally, the same as a Flash TCP Operations, but MWD team is part of a squad traveling and conducting TCPs by helicopter. Once vehicle(s) have been chosen, and stopped, get all personnel out of the vehicle(s) and all compartments will be opened for inspection by the team. MWD team will be the first on and last off of the helicopter. MWD team will remain out of sight until needed. Driver and any passengers of the vehicle being searched should be removed from the immediate area while the team is conducting the sweep. MWD team will have an over watch at all times.

Dismounted Combat Patrols
MWD team and security member(s) will be located in the middle of the patrol when traveling within villages. One of the security member's purpose is to mitigate any threat to the MWD team during the combat patrol since the handler's attention must remain on the dog making him/her unable to scan for threats. MWDs can be positioned in front of the patrol if in an open field, walking from downwind if possible. This will maximize the MWD team's explosive detection capabilities.

Cordon and Search (Raids) Operations
Initial entry team will clear all occupants from building as quickly as possible. Security member will escort the MWD team to the identified building. When the facility is cleared of personnel and hazards have been removed and/or identified the handler will initiate a search of the facility.

Physical Security
They augment in detection roles, replace inoperative sensor systems, patrol difficult terrain, and deter potential aggressors. Depending on what particular role MWD teams will serve determines the manner in which teams are posted. If the dog team's primary function is to provide direct security over the resource, its proximity may limit the team's ability to follow up on any alerts the dog gives its handler. If the dog team is to provide security from a greater distance than other SF patrols, their immediate response to the resource will be slower therefore should not be factored into any time sensitive initial response requirements. Remember, to gain the maximum use of the dog team's capability, handlers must be able to work their animals in such manner to take full advantage of the dog's keen sensory abilities.

UNDERSTANDING MWDS

Advantages
MWDs have distinct advantages over a lone SF member. MWD's have superior senses of smell, hearing, and visual motion detection. The MWD is trained to react consistently to certain sensory stimuli--human, explosive, drug--in a way that immediately alerts the handler. The MWDs reaction to this stimulus is always rewarded by the handler which reinforces the MWDs behavior and motivates the MWD to repeat the actions. People react to what they "think" a stimulus means. MWDs simply "react" to the stimulus and let the handler decide what it means.

Superiority of Senses

Though hard to quantify under almost any given set of circumstances, a trained MWD can smell, hear, and visually detect motion infinitely better than Security Forces personnel and, when trained to do so, reacts to certain stimuli in a way that alerts the handler to the presence of those stimuli. It is important to remember that MWDs are "biological" pieces of equipment having good and bad days, which is why training is crucial to their proficiency. Therefore, the continuous training of an MWD team must be kept at the forefront of any SF operation. Without proper training a dog team's capabilities will quickly diminish. Eliminating the "bad" days is important to the success of an installation's MWD program which is why every level of command's participation is paramount.

Evaluation of Desired Tasks

The MWD can enhance operations throughout the entire spectrum of security forces roles and missions. The most important question a supervisor should ask is "Where should we post the MWD to enhance the mission?" You have a dynamic force multiplier that tremendously enhances an SF member's ability. They have an asset that smells, hears, and detects better than anything else on flight. If this asset is left at the kennels, mission degradation is dramatic. The most important considerations are tasks required, the time of day to use the team, and the post environment. Consider these tasks:

1. **Deterrence**. If the desired task is to deter unauthorized intrusion, vandalism, attacks on personnel etc., use the team on a post and at a time of day when those you wish to deter can see the MWD. MWD demonstrations are also beneficial in accomplishing this as well. People do not know if an MWD is a patrol dog, detector dog, or both. This is one benefit of public visibility of a MWD. Security Forces benefit from the deterrence effect of every type of dog we train based on the presence of one MWD.
2. **Detection**. If the desired task is to detect unauthorized or suspect individuals, assign the team to a post at a time of day when visual, audible, and odor distractions are at a minimum. Examples include the flight line when operations are minimal, nuclear weapon storage areas, convoy operations and walking patrols in housing, shopping, or industrial areas after normal duty hours, WSAs and other priority restricted areas.
3. **Narcotic Detector Dogs (NDDs)/Explosive Detector Dogs (EDDs)**. NDDs and EDDs are trained to detect specific substances under an extremely wide range of conditions which make post selection and time of day less critical.

THE MWD SECTION

The base CSF develops and is responsible for the MWD program supporting the installation.

MWD Logistics

Air Force Instruction 23-224(I), DoD Military Working Dog Program set policies and procedures governing logistical aspects of the USAF MWD program. It assigns responsibilities for budgeting, funding, accounting, procuring, distributing, redistributing, and reporting of MWDs and specifies procedures for submitting dog requirements and requisitions. When preparing and submitting MWD requisitions, consult with your installation Logistics Readiness Squadron for assistance.

Obtaining Support Equipment

Use AF Form 601, Equipment Access Request, to order equipment to support the MWD program. A leash, choke chain, collar, and muzzle are shipped with the MWD to the gaining unit. Units must order other support items through supply channels or through use of the Government Purchase Card. SF units are authorized to pursue purchases of MWD support items outside the AF Form 601 channels, providing they comply with all USAF budgeting and requisition policies and guidelines. Consult with your unit Resources Advisor first.

MWD Section Organization

Most MWD sections are authorized a Kennel Master, a trainer (if five or more MWDs are assigned), and enough MWD handlers to meet the patrol standard of MWD teams. Refer to AF 31-202, Military Working Dog Program, for additional guidance.

Duties and Responsibilities

The basic organizational structure of an MWD section consists of a Kennel Master and a trainer.

Kennel MASTER

The Kennel Master exercises management and supervision over the MWD program. The Kennel Master reports to the operations flight. The Kennel Master will:
1. Know unit mission.
2. Match dog to handler.
3. Assist in identifying MWD team posts and prepare operating instructions for team employment.
4. Ensure an adequate MWD training program is developed, implemented, and maintained.
5. Validate proficiency of MWD teams and prepares dog teams for certifications.
6. Ensure the health, safety, and well-being of MWDs are maintained by working closely with military veterinarian.
7. Ensure handlers understand basic principles of training and conditioning, physical and psychological characteristics, and the capabilities/limitations of their MWDs.
8. Obtain equipment and supplies needed for the unit's MWD program.
9. Advise the commander on effective MWD utilization.
10. Ensure unit and flight-level supervisory personnel are familiar with proper MWD team utilization and employment standards.
11. Perform duties as trainer if fewer than five MWDs are assigned.
12. Assume duties as primary custodian for narcotics and explosive training aid accounts.
13. Ensures handlers are properly trained on safety and security procedures associated with narcotics and explosive training aids.

Trainer

The trainer is directly responsible to the Kennel Master for managing and implementing an effective MWD training program. They must be capable of performing all Kennel Master functions when necessary. The trainer should:
1. Schedule and conduct daily proficiency training following established Optimum Training Schedule (OTS) requirements.
2. Schedule and conduct periodic intensive or remedial training for teams with special problems and training deficiencies.
3. Identify and correct deficiencies of handlers and MWDs in all phases of MWD operations.
4. Ensure MWD records are current and accurate.
5. Act as alternate custodian for the narcotic and explosive training aids.

Kennel Support

Kennel support personnel need not be qualified handlers, although it is desirable. If not qualified, the Kennel Master must make sure support personnel are given local training in MWD care and feeding, kennel sanitation, disease prevention, symptom recognition, kennel area safety, and first aid/ emergency care. Kennel support personnel who are not qualified handlers will not handle MWDs. Do not assign personnel who have been relieved from duty for cause as kennel support.

MWD Handlers. MWD handlers are SF personnel trained to use a specialized piece of equipment. Because of the time and effort required to keep a team proficient, employ the handler and MWD as a "team" and assign appropriate posts and duties. Avoid posting an MWD handler without their dog except for medical reasons. While unit manning shortfalls may require this as a last resort, keep it to a bare minimum, as it could rapidly create an adverse effect on MWD proficiency. NOTE: SF supervisors with dog teams in their charge must coordinate, with the MWD supervisory staff, MWD training and kennel well-being & sanitation duties handlers are required to perform while on duty.

Accurately document all training and utilization of assigned MWD as directed by the Kennel Master and trainer.

U.S. Army Sgt. Adam Serella, a narcotics patrol detector dog handler with the 3rd Infantry Division, takes time to bond with his dog, Nero, as local children look on during Operation Clean Sweep conducted in districts throughout Kandahar City, Afghanistan, Oct. 3 2002. (U.S. Army photo by Spc. Tyler Meister)

U.S. MILITARY WORKING DOG TRAINING HANDBOOK ★ 153

CHAPTER 8

ADMINISTRATION/MEDICAL RECORDS, FORMS, AND REPORTS

ADMINISTRATIVE RECORDS, FORMS, AND REPORTS

The MWD staff maintains the following:

MWD Training Record Folder
A repository for MWD training records contains the following documentation:

DD Form 1834, MWD Service Record
Initiated when MWD is first procured and entered the DoD MWD Inventory and kept current by Kennel Masters throughout the MWD's service life. Annotate unit of assignment as well as assignment of new handlers on the reverse side of the form. Do not change information pertaining to MWD's national stock number without prior coordination with the MAJCOM, and the 341 TRS.LAFB Form 375, MWD Status

Report
Provides a record of training on the MWD after it graduates from a course.

AF Form 321, MWD Training and Utilization Record
Provides complete history of patrol training, utilization, and performance. Handlers annotate each duty day and sign at the end of each month. The Kennel Master, as the reviewing official, will also sign it at the end of each month.

AF Form 323, MWD Training and Utilization Record for Drug/Explosive Detection
Record of training, utilization, and performance of detector dogs. It serves as the basis for establishing probable cause. Annotate and sign the same as the AF Form 321.

Optimum Training Schedule
Used to outline training requirements for each individual MWD. The OTS should concentrate on tasks that each particular MWD is trained to perform. Adjust OTS as a team's performance improves or deteriorates. If the team performance deteriorates, consider increasing training requirements within that area. If the team performs with little or no difficulty, consider decreasing training requirements in that area. Once a schedule is established, follow it! Place optimum training schedule in the MWD training records. Document training records to reflect any deviation from the OTS and the reasons why.

Controlled Substance Accountability Folder
Used to provide a record of accountability for controlled substances. A separate folder is established for each substance and kept active until all controlled substances from that shipment are returned for final disposition. Once all substances from that shipment are returned, the folders are placed in an inactive file and retained for 1 year. The controlled substance accountability folder consists of the following documentation:

DEA Form 225, Application for Registration
The person assigned direct responsibility for control and safekeeping of narcotic training aids signs as the

applicant. Refer to Title 21, Code of Federal Regulations (CFR), Part 1300, for specific details. DEA Form 225 is only needed for CONUS, Hawaii, Guam, and Puerto Rico SF units.

DEA Form 225a, Application for Registration Renewal (Type B)
Required to maintain DEA registration. The form is mailed directly to the unit approximately 60 days prior to expiration of current registration. DEA Form 225a is only needed for CONUS, Hawaii, Guam, and Puerto Rico SF units.

DEA Form 223, Controlled Substances Registration Certificate
Valid for 1 year, unless withdrawn sooner by DEA. DEA Form 223 is only needed for CONUS, Hawaii, Guam, and Puerto Rico SF units.

DEA Form 222, Controlled Substance Order Form (Type B)
Accountable forms used to order drug training aids from the drug distribution center. Forward copies one and two to the drug distribution center; the unit maintains copy three. Upon receipt of the drug training aids annotate the number of training aids and date received. DEA Form 222 is only needed for CONUS, Hawaii, Guam, and Puerto Rico SF units.

AF Form 1205, Narcotics Training Aid Accountability Record
All SF units possessing narcotic training aids will record and account for these items using this form regardless whether they are registered with DEA or not.

Drug Training Aid Issue/Turn-in Log
Used to document the issuing and return of MWD drug training aids. AFI 31-202, Military Working Dog Program outlines specific instructions on annotating the Drug Training Aid Issue/Turn-in Log. CSF authorizes, in writing, individual access to the drug storage container and those personnel who are authorized to possess drug training aids. This authorization letter must be posted within the area/room containing the storage container, but not on the storage container itself. Primary custodian must ensure personnel who are authorized to sign for and/or possess drug training aids are properly trained on their control and security. Document this training in the person's OJT records. For those who do not have OJT records (MSgt or above), document their training via official memorandum. Primary custodian will maintain a record of those personnel who have been trained, whether the individual reports to the Kennel Master or not. Only MWD personnel who have attended the MWD supervisor's course will be assigned duties as primary training aid custodian.

Probable Cause Folder
Used to provide search granting authority an overview of the detector dog team's performance. Probable cause folders should reflect only the current team's performance. Maintain AF Forms 321 and 323 in the probable cause folder for 12 months. Upon removal, place AF Forms 321 and 323 in MWD training record folder. The probable cause folder should consist of the following documentation and provided to the search granting authority for review on a quarterly basis.

Search Granting Authority Record Review Sheet
The search granting authority signs and dates a signature page certifying concurrence with the contents of the probable- cause folder and recertification of the team. Conduct this review/recertification quarterly within the calendar year.

Certification Letter
Discusses details of the certification demonstration to include search granting authority, or designee, witnessing of the demonstration. Conduct the certification annually as needed and when handler change occurs.

Quarterly Summary Report
A report detailing training and actual search utilization conducted by the team during the previous calendar quarter. The training summary consists of a breakdown of detector dog training by times, numbers of training aids planted and found, and by areas which training was conducted. The actual search summary consists of search times in each area searched including all non-training aid substances found by the dog Validation Results. A summary of results from validation testing.
 MWD Team's Resume of Training and Experience. A summary of training and experience for both the handler and MWD.

Medical
The servicing veterinarian maintains all MWD medical records. Only veterinarian staff personnel make annotations to medical records. Medical records are made available for deployments. Servicing veterinarians are responsible for initiating the following forms:

DD Form 1743, Death Certificate of Military Dog
Required for the death of all MWDs. Includes a brief statement identifying the cause of death and used to close out accountability for a MWD through the base supply system.

DD Form 2209, Veterinary Health Certificate
Should accompany the MWD during interstate travel, depending on state requirements, or to foreign countries. Required for all commercial and military travel and may be required for military airlift. Certificate is valid for 10 days from date issued. The Kennel Master must ensure all health, customs and agriculture requirement associated with MWD travel to foreign countries are satisfied prior to allowing MWDs to depart CONUS. Should problems arise in meeting a foreign country's animal entry requirements contact your AF MWD Program Manager immediately. For missions requiring a United States Department of Agriculture health certificate consult your supporting veterinarian for guidance. Your local travel management office is another good source for interstate and foreign travel requirements of animals.

Forms
The following are forms used within the MWD program:
1. **AF Form 68, Munitions Authorization Record.** Used to document approval to procure explosive training aids. Updated every 6 months or whenever changes occur. Keep the form current in order to procure explosive training aids. Refer to local munitions account supply office (MASO) personnel for further information concerning completion of the form. Maintain most current AF Form 68 within the munitions accountability folder. Your local MASO provides guidance on maintaining this folder.
2. **AF Form 321, MWD Training and Utilization Record.** Used to document the MWDs patrol training and utilization.
3. **AF Form 323, MWD Training and Utilization Record for Drug/Explosive Detector Dogs.** Used to document the MWDs detection training and utilization.
4. **AF Form 324, MWD Program Status Report.** Prepared by units and used by USAF Program Manager and HQ AFSFC/DOD MWD Program Management Office to effectively manage the USAF and DOD MWD program(s). Units provide original copy of report to USAF Program Manager quarterly, which in turns forwards reports to HQ AFSC/DOD MWD Program Management Office.

MWD Status Reports are due to the
5. **USAF MWD Program Management Office NLT** the 5th of the month following the quarter.
6. **AF Form 601, Equipment Action Request.** Used for major equipment acquisition to include MWDs. Contact unit resources personnel for assistance in completing this form. Consult AFI 23-224(I), DOD Military Working Dog Program and AFMAN 23-110/USAF Supply Manual, Vol 2, Part 2, Chap 22.138 when submitting acquisition request for dogs.
7. **AF Form 1996, Adjusted Stock Level.** Completed on an annual basis to establish yearly levels and re-supply increments for explosive training aids. Due to sensitivity and transportation factors, accomplish a 5-year forecast for explosives. Consult with your local MASO and AF Catalog 21-209, Volume 1, Ground Munitions, Chapter 1.
8. **AF Form 2005, Issue Turn-in Request.** Used for small, expendable items that do not require approval above base level. Maintain all pending action copies of AF Form 2005 in munitions accountability folder along with other related accountability documents. Your local MASO provides guidance on maintaining this folder.
9. **DD Form 1348-6, DoD Single-line Item Requisition System Document.** Used for local procurement of munitions/equipment items when no national stock number (NSN) is available. Consult your local MASO prior to using this form for munitions requisition.
10. **DD Form 2342, Animal Facility Sanitation Checklist.** Completed on a quarterly basis. Includes standard of sanitation maintained, the adequacy of insect and rodent control, and the general health of MWDs judged by their appearance and state of grooming. The CSF reviews and signs completed forms which will be maintained at the MWD section.

CHAPTER 9

FACILITIES AND EQUIPMENT

KENNEL FACILITIES

Some existing facilities may not meet current construction guidelines. If they conform to health and safety requirements, they do not require modification. See the Kennel Design Guide for guidance regarding any new kennel construction located on the Headquarters Air Force Security Forces Center website (https://afsfmil.lackland.af.mil) under the DoD MWD Program Management Branch tab.

Kennel Maintenance
MWD supervisory staff will inspect kennel facilities and dog runs continuously to ensure safety and security of MWDs and personnel. Inspect all latches, hinges, and fences for signs of rusting or breakage. Free all surfaces of sharp objects that could cause injury.

Sanitation Measures
Sanitation is one of the chief measures of disease prevention and control and can't be overemphasized. MWD supervisory staff in conjunction with supporting veterinarian establishes and enforces stringent kennel sanitation standards in and around the kennel area. An effective, continuous sanitation program is the result of cooperation between handlers, supervisors, kennel support personnel, and the attending veterinarian. The Kennel Master, with consent of supporting veterinarian, approves all cleaning products and solutions used to sanitize kennel runs and dog feeding preparation area.

Food Preparation and Storage
Keep all kitchen surfaces and food preparation utensils always clean. Store dog food in rodent proof containers with excess food awaiting use stored off the floor. Ensure new food bags/containers are inspected before feeding. Do not use feed from containers if the manufacture's product packing seal is broke or punctured. Dispose of uneaten food immediately after the feeding period. Empty all trash containers as needed, at least daily, to preclude attracting pests into the facility

OBSTACLE COURSE

Construct the obstacle course IAW guidance provided by HQ AFSFC. Variations in construction material are authorized with attending veterinarian concurrence. Cover surfaces with nonskid material and cover all sharp edges. The Kennel Master ensures the obstacle course is maintained in a safe condition consistent with guidance from the servicing veterinarian. All military working dog sections will have a serviceable obstacle course.

AUTHORIZED EQUIPMENT

Kennel Masters must ensure all equipment is available and serviceable. Kennel Masters may establish local purchase programs through base supply to acquire additional equipment.

Choke Chain
The choke chain is the basic collar used for all MWDs.

Leather Collar
Use the leather collar when securing an MWD to a stationary object (stakeout). Tighten the collar to the point that the handler can slip two fingers snugly between the collar and the MWD's neck.

Kennel Chain
Use the 6-foot kennel chain with the leather collar when securing the MWD to a stationary object. Attach the kennel chain to the D-ring of the collar with the snap facing away from the buckle. Never tie/loop the kennel chain around the MWD's neck.

Muzzle
Use the leather muzzle, safety muzzle, or suitable plastic replacement to prevent the MWD from injuring the handler, other MWDs, and people. Use muzzles during veterinary visits or first aid treatment, and when numerous MWDs are assembled, in transit, or in crowded confined areas. When properly fitted, the muzzle will not restrict breathing. Check the fit by grasping the basket of the muzzle and lifting straight up until the MWD's front feet are off the ground. If the muzzle comes off, adjust accordingly. MWDs supporting US Secret Service, Department of State and/or Department of Defense explosive detector dog missions will be muzzled when traveling (on foot) to and from search locations or any other public area not directly associated with search activity.

Leashes
The 60-inch leather leash is the standard leash for MWD operations. Use the 360-inch nylon or web leash for intermediate obedience, attack training, and tracking operations. Kennel Masters may approve other leashes, such as heavy-duty retractable models, to meet operational requirements. Since the leash is the most used piece of MWD equipment handlers will inspect the serviceability of their leashes daily. DO NOT WORK MWDs WITH NONSERVICEABLE OR DEFECTIVE LEASHES.

Equipment Holder
Use the equipment holder to secure items to the handler's belt.

Combs and Brushes
Use the assorted combs and brushes listed in the TA to maintain MWD grooming standards as prescribed in Chapter 4.

Feed Pan
Use the 3-quart stainless steel feed pan for MWD feeding.

Water Bucket
The water bucket is steel or galvanized metal and holds at least 3.5 gallons. Use feed pans for small breed MWDs. If this type of bucket is used ensure drain holes are punched into the side of the bucket to prevent overfill. Punch drain holes approximately at the one-third full point of the bucket.

Immersion Heater
The immersion heater is automatic and has a thermostat to keep 12 quarts of water at 500 F. To work effectively, submerge in at least 2 inches of water. Inspect the power cord before each use. Don't use if the cord is unserviceable.

Leather/Nylon Harness

The MWD wears the harness while scouting or tracking. It enables the handler to control the dog's ranging distance but still allows the dog to breath normally. To fit the harness, place the leash in the left hand and the harness in the right hand, thread the loop end of the leash through the center of the harness. With the harness resting on the left forearm, change the leash to the right hand. Slide the harness over the MWD's head and shoulders and buckle the stomach strap behind the MWD's front legs. Then grasp the center of the back strap with the left hand, unsnap the leash from the choke chain and snap to the D-ring of the harness with the snap facing downward.

Arm Protector

The agitator uses the arm protector during aggression training. Use a leather gauntlet under the arm protector when training those dogs that bite hard.

Attack Suit

Consider using the full body attack suit acquired at the Kennel Master's discretion for advanced training. One major advantage of the suit is the ability to train dogs to bite and hold a suspect who does not present the attack sleeve. Some dogs become reliant on the sleeve and will not bite an actual suspect unless a target is presented. Using the suit properly will aid in correcting this behavior.

MAINTENANCE OF EQUIPMENT

Safety and extension of serviceability are primary objectives of all equipment maintenance plans.

Leather Items

Apply saddle soap or Neats Foot Oil to preserve the strength of the leather and prevent drying or cracking. Ensure surfaces are clean and dry prior to application. Never apply Neats Foot Oil to inside surfaces of the leather muzzle.

Metal Parts

Remove rust by rubbing with fine steel wool or sandpaper. Use a light coat of oil if necessary. Replace badly rusted items. Inspect snaps routinely to ensure they are working properly.

Care of Fabrics

Wash web leashes with a mild soap and dry slowly to prevent shrinkage. Do not wash the arm protector with soap and water. When this item becomes dirty clean by rubbing briskly with a coarse brush. To ensure safety, frequently check the arm protector. Make minor repairs with a needle and heavy thread.

Storage of Equipment. Keep all equipment dry when not in use. When in storage, inspect and treat as needed to ensure that it is clean, soft and in good condition.

VEHICLE AUTHORIZATION FOR KENNEL SUPPORT

Kennel support requires a suitable vehicle for transporting explosives as well as MWD teams.

SHIPPING CRATES

Shipping crates are authorized for each MWD in a Unit Type Code (UTC). Smaller airline approved plastic shipping crates are also authorized to support TDY's requiring transport via commercial aircraft or ground transportation. Plastic commercial shipping crates are not to be used for long term kennels. Refer to applicable UTC LOG DET.

CHAPTER 10

SAFETY AND TRANSPORTATION PROCEDURES

KENNEL SAFETY

Following sound safety procedures in kennel and training areas is very important. Personnel must always follow safety practices. Maintain positive control or a dog may get loose and injure a person or itself. Safety practices begin as soon as a person enters the kennel area. Personnel must ensure they secure all gates after use, avoid sudden movement when passing MWDs, and not speak or move in any threatening way. Personnel must not run or horseplay in or near MWDs. This activity agitates MWDs and could result in a dog mistaking it for hostility and provoke attack and cause injury to the dog.

One-Way System
Setup one-way traffic patterns in kennel areas to keep dogs from meeting head-on. Ensure the one-way system is clearly marked.

Loose Dog Procedures
If a dog gets loose, the first person observing the MWD calls out "LOOSE DOG!" Everyone except the handler should cease all movement until the dog is secured. Once the MWD is under control, the handler must sound off with "DOG SECURED!" SF units must develop local procedures to protect the public should an MWD escape the kennel area.

Verbal Warnings
Handlers with MWDs will give verbal warnings upon entering or leaving the kennel area or when vision is obstructed by calling out "DOG COMING THROUGH, AROUND, BY" whichever is appropriate.

Dog Fight Procedures
If a dog fight occurs, never attempt to stop it alone and never pull MWDs apart. Pulling may cause greater damage. If on-leash, keep the leash taut and work your hands toward the snap of the leash. Hold the leash firmly with one hand, grasp the MWD's throat with the other hand, and squeeze with the thumb and forefinger to cut off the air supply. When the dog gasps for air, move them away from each other. If off leash, grasp the choke chain, leather collar, or nap of the neck with one hand. With the other, squeeze the dog's throat using the thumb and finger to cut off the air supply.

TRAINING AREA

The following safety precautions are required in the training areas:
1. Keep a safety leash on the right wrist while moving to and from training areas.
2. Keep a minimum safety distance of 15 feet between MWD teams in the areas. When approaching another MWD team, keep dog in the heel position using a short leash.
3. Never use a leash to secure a MWD to any object. Never leave a MWD staked out unobserved and never secure a MWD to a vehicle.

SAFETY IN THE VETERINARY FACILITIES

When a MWD is taken to the clinic, it is around unfamiliar surroundings and people and may behave unexpectedly. The handler must control the dog while at the clinic. Get clearance from veterinary staff prior to entering the clinic.

Before entering the veterinary clinic, the handler will muzzle the MWD, unless instructed otherwise by the veterinarian staff.

The handler must give a verbal warning "DOG COMING THROUGH" before entering. In the treatment facility, the handler controls the MWD with a short leash.

OPERATIONAL SAFETY

Safety considerations are of paramount importance. Always apply safety practices for the protection of the handler, other handlers, MWDs, and the general public. When dog teams interact with the public, handlers must be in the mindset that it is the handler's responsibility to be safe around the public, not the public's responsibility to be safe around the dog team.

Static Posts
While working a static post, handlers must remain aware of their surroundings. Do not allow anyone to pet their MWD.

Mobile Patrol
While riding in a vehicle, avoid sharp turns and sudden stops whenever possible since they could result in injury to the MWD. Train MWDs not to attack personnel riding with the team. Do not allow the dog to ride with its head outside the vehicle window. Do not leave MWDs unattended in a vehicle except in an emergency situation that necessitates the handler responding without the MWD. However, if you must leave a MWD in a vehicle, ensure the vehicle is secure so the MWD cannot escape. Also, ensure proper ventilation so the animal does not overheat. The handler must always have full view of the vehicle. This ensures the handler can assist the MWD if he becomes distressed.

DoD and Civilian Law Enforcement Support Agency Operations
The same principles of safety that apply when using MWDs on the installation also apply when deployed in support of outside agencies. Handlers and trainers must remain aware of the potential danger of MWDs that are trained to attack. Whenever necessary, advise personnel on the safety procedures.

VEHICLE TRANSPORTATION

Use the hindquarter or abdominal lift when loading MWDs on a vehicle. To place a MWD in a vehicle for patrol purposes, begin with the MWD in the HEEL position. Open the door and command "HUP" and then "SIT."

AIRCRAFT TRANSPORTATION

Use commercial and military aircraft when shipping MWDs interstate or to overseas commands. Do not route MWDs through countries with quarantines. Consult the TMO office for details.

Commercial Air Transportation

When MWDs are shipped unaccompanied, attach detailed instructions for feeding and watering to the crate. Mark the top of the crate with the name and tattoo of the dog as well as special instructions noting the kennel should only be opened by a qualified handler or not at all. Specific instructions on contacting a point of contact for the dog will also be noted in case of emergency. Verbiage should be large enough to read from a safe distance. The top and sides of the crates should be labeled—DANGER – MILITARY WORKING DOG.

- Stay with the MWD until loaded. If there is a delay, remove the dog from the crate for exercise and water.
- Always place the crate in a cool spot when waiting for loading. Unload the MWD as soon as possible and make sure it has water.
- Never place the crate on top of other baggage.
- Do not lock shipping crates! They must be able to be opened in an emergency. Do make sure, however, they cannot be opened inadvertently.
- If shipped accompanied, ship the MWD as excess baggage. Check with the local carrier for an exemption to the excess baggage fee. Refer to AFI 31-202, para 2.7.5. for further guidance.

MILITARY AIR TRANSPORTATION

MWD handlers are required to escort MWD movements on military aircraft. Escorting handlers can make recommendations to aircraft crew personnel on the best way to load the dog, but ultimately the aircrew will have the final decision. Ensure however that load plan does not block ventilation to the crate furthermore, cargo and other equipment should not be placed on top of the crate. Handler must have ready access to the crate door in the event of dog distress or injury.

EXPLOSIVE SAFETY

Refer to AFMAN 91-201, Explosive Safety Standard and AFI 31-202, Military Working Dog Program

DRUG SAFETY

If an animal ingests a training aid, contact the veterinarian immediately to determine whether the animal was poisoned and what actions to take to ensure the dogs safety.

CHAPTER 11

OPERATIONAL EMPLOYMENT

SECURITY OPERATIONS

Mission
The MWDs primary mission is to deter, detect, and detain intruders in areas surrounding Air Force resources. Use MWD teams on almost any security post. Include the Kennel Master in planning use of MWDs in security operations.

The greatest advantage of an MWD team is their detection capabilities and their ability to cover a large area, particularly during periods of limited visibility. The presence of a MWD team may also discourage attempts by intruders to gain access to resources. MWDs detection capabilities are degraded in areas with a large number of people and constant activity. When used on a post where there is little room to maneuver to take advantage of wind direction, the MWD must depend mostly on its sense of sight and sound. When working on a post where the handler must concentrate on tasks other than working the MWD such as entry control, the MWDs abilities are largely wasted.

Post Selections
Ensure MWD posts are free of distractions such as excessive noise and numerous personnel. If deterrence is the objective for assigning a MWD team to a particular post, you will sacrifice detection ability for the higher degree of visibility. Wind direction, the location of priority resources, size of the area, condition and type of terrain, and likely avenues of approach dictate the best location for a MWD post. Under ideal conditions, the average MWD can detect and respond to intruders at 250 yards or more. Make efforts to keep MWDs working downwind, since this is where their sense of smell and hearing is best used. Keep post selection and limits flexible enough to meet varied conditions. If you must use an MWD team in a lighted area, allow it to patrol on a more varied route, remain in the shadows, or stand stationary in a concealed downwind position. Using MWD teams in lighted areas reduces the team's ability to remain undetected. This permits intruders to observe their movements and increases the possibility of successful penetration. Also, lights may cause the MWD to rely more on sight than its other senses. Since there are no steadfast rules on the number and location of MWD posts, make post selections with common sense in relation to environmental factors.

Close Boundary (CB) Post
A MWD team on close-boundary foot patrol provides security that far exceeds the capabilities of the lone security forces member. This is especially important when considering a sentry's effectiveness is limited by darkness due to poor visibility. The MWD team's objective is to detect and apprehend intruders before they can damage or destroy the protected resources. Consider these other factors:
1. Posting the MWD team inside a fenced area allows the team to patrol close to the resource, physically checking it periodically. On the other hand, if the MWD detects an intruder attempting entry, the fence will prevent the team from following in the response, possibly preventing or delaying apprehension. If an additional MWD is not available, take the MWD team with the response outside the area and allow it to follow-up the response. Personnel posted inside the area should increase their vigilance as well as observe the team's post until the situation returns to normal.
2. Posting MWD teams outside a protected area creates the advantage of using the wind, cover and concealment, and the opportunity to follow responses to the source. The team can effectively cover approaches to the area and detect odors from within the area by using the wind to their advantage.

3. Give consideration to using a flexible posting system. This permit using the MWD in or out of the area to meet varying conditions and increases psychological protection by preventing a routine patrol pattern.

Supplementing Intrusion Detection Equipment (IDE)
When planning MWD posts, consider using electrical or mechanical detection devices. Since these devices usually activate only when detecting intruders within the surveillance area, use the MWD more effectively as a back-up for these systems.

Position the team inside the protected area so it can patrol the whole area around the resource without setting off an alarm. The MWD handler should maintain close contact with the alarm monitor. The MWD team can then approach from the downwind side and make contact with the intruder.

Mobile Security Patrols
Vary duties of a mobile patrol to include building checks, area surveillance, and identification and apprehension of personnel. MWD teams on internal or external security response teams (SRTs) are effective force multipliers, cover large areas, and present both a physical and psychological deterrent.

Response Forces (RFs)
Enhance the effectiveness of a RF by using an MWD team during open-area searches, scouting, tracking, building searches, and apprehensions. The MWD is an integral part of the team, and you should not separate it from other members. Familiarize all RF members with the MWD's capabilities and procedures to follow. The team must discuss the situation and decide upon the approach route and what to do upon arrival. There is no set rule for deploying an RF area patrol when an MWD is used; therefore, circumstances will dictate each response. If the team leader decides not to use the MWD team in the deployment, they should have the handler remain with the vehicle and operate the radio.

After the situation is neutralized and declared safe, use explosive detector dogs to sweep areas for unexploded ordnance, explosive devices, weapons, and ammunition.

AIR PROVOST OPERATIONS

Psychological Impact
MWD teams in law enforcement activities offer a tremendous psychological deterrent to potential violators and should work in all areas of the base. Psychological advantage is complemented by conducting periodic public demonstrations. Keep these demonstrations as realistic as possible and include obedience, attack under gunfire, and drug detection techniques. Using local news media and conducting special demonstrations are excellent ways to enhance community relations (both on and off base), local Drug Abuse Resistance Education (DARE) programs, and deterrence of unlawful acts on Air Force installations. Supervisors should limit the number of demonstrations—MWDs are working dogs and not show dogs. Discourage public demonstrations by explosive detector dogs as this may tend to generate prank or hoax bomb threat calls.

Use
MWD teams can perform in all SF functions. Include the Kennel Master in planning the use of MWDs in SF operations. It is the flight leader's/sergeant's responsibility to ensure MWD teams are posted in areas that will capitalize on their capabilities. Do not post handlers without their MWDs except in extremely rare situations (i.e., MWD is ill, back- up force response when time is of the essence). MWD teams will discourage unruly and/or unlawful conduct and increase the probability of apprehension. A properly trained MWD can pursue, attack, and hold a suspect providing an alternative to the use of deadly force.

Resources Protection
Consider using MWD teams in AA&E storage areas during hours of darkness.

Military Housing and Billets
MWDs are especially effective in and around military housing and billet areas. Their mere presence can deter thefts, burglaries, drug use, and vandalism. Use teams both day and night in these areas.

Protection of Funds
Using MWD teams to escort and safeguard funds may deter a robbery. A MWD does not fear an armed or unarmed person and, if fired upon, will pursue and attack--an important characteristic to emphasize during demonstrations and in news releases.

Confrontation Management
Use MWD teams judiciously in confrontation situations since their presence could escalate the situation. Do not deploy MWD teams on front lines in riot control situations; keep them out of sight and use as necessary.

Narcotics/Explosives Detection
A trained detector dog can detect drugs or explosives regardless of efforts to mask the scent. Publicity on the presence and effective use of drug detector dogs may help reduce criminal activities involving drugs. Do not make public information on limitations and effectiveness of a detector dog.

Patrols
Walking Patrols
1. MWD teams should perform various duties such as checking buildings, parking lots, military housing, and billet areas. When used in this capacity, consider several factors:
2. Use MWD teams as much as possible during both day and nighttime hours in areas where one can easily see them. They should be tolerant of people, and the presence of crowds should not significantly reduce their usefulness. MWD teams should walk among people, stand guard mount, and show no outward sign of aggression. Extremely hot weather may restrict the MWD's abilities. In this case, divide the MWD team's time between mobile patrol and walking patrol.
3. When working among the public, handlers should keep in mind the MWD is a valuable tool and not a pet. Maintain a safe distance and do not let anyone pet the MWD.
4. The MWD's ability to detect individuals is more effective during darkness or limited visibility when there are fewer distractions. Therefore, give nighttime use in areas with few people, but high value resources the highest priority.
5. A MWD team can check or search a larger number of buildings and parking lots more efficiently than a single person.
6. Periodic use of MWD teams around on-base schools (especially when school is starting and dismissing) may deter potential vandals, child molesters, exhibitionists, and illegal drug activities.
7. Use MWD teams to provide security for such resources as aircraft, munitions storage areas, communications facilities, equipment, or command posts. When assigning walking patrols, one restriction to keep in mind is the lack of mobility. Like any security forces foot patrol, this could prevent a rapid response to a distant incident where time is essential.

Mobile Patrols
Mobile MWD teams increase their potential area of coverage but decreases MWD effectiveness. Teams are usually unaccompanied; but since MWDs can work in the proximity of people, other security forces personnel may accompany them. Assign the mobile MWD team a sedan or other passenger-type vehicle--air

conditioned in hot climates. If using a pickup truck, placing portable kennels in the beds of pickups for transporting MWDs while on patrol is prohibited.
1. When mobile patrolling, allow the MWD ride off leash. (If the leash is kept on, drape it over the dog's back to prevent it from getting caught on anything). Use a vehicle kennel insert or a specially designed platform when a MWD is on mobile patrol. Cover the surface with rubber matting or some other nonskid surface. The MWD should remain in the "SIT" position as much as possible. Do not allow the MWD to place its head out of the window while the vehicle is moving.
2. MWD teams should not remain mobile during the entire tour of duty. MWD patrols are more effective when the team uses the ride-a-while, walk-a-while method. The team can cover a larger area, and the exercise keeps the dog responsive.

Building Checks and Searches
MWD teams are especially effective in checking and searching buildings such as commissaries, base exchanges, finance offices, banks, and warehouses. With the MWD on leash, approach the building from the downwind side to take advantage of the MWD's olfactory senses. The responding patrolmen secure the surrounding area to avoid contamination by a fresh scent. This could serve to confuse the dog in the event tracking is required.

If a facility is found unsecure, the team should request backup. Upon arrival of the back-up patrol, the MWD team should approach from the downwind side and first check the exterior before entering the building. The on-duty supervisor, after conferring with the MWD handler, determines whether the MWD should search on or off leash. Generally, the MWD is most effective when worked off leash since the dog's movements are not restricted, and it can search a larger area in a shorter period of time. Before a handler releases a MWD inside the building, announce in a loud clear voice the intention to release the MWD, and anyone inside the building should exit within a set period of time (1-5 minutes). Before releasing the MWD, the handler should consider the following factors: danger to the handler, type and size of building, time of day or night, indication of forced entry, and the possibility of innocent persons. The handler must check and clear the immediate area before proceeding. As the handler follows the MWD, they should use the same precaution for each room or area. One suggestion includes turning on lights as the handler progresses. However, keep in mind turning on lights will silhouette the handler when entering/exiting the room. Also, consider the consequences of turning on lights if there is an explosive device with a light sensitive switch in one of the rooms. If the MWD responds, it is recalled, placed on leash, and the intruder is challenged, and apprehended. For an on-leash search, the handler enters and loudly announces that a MWD is being used to search. Another security forces member should always accompany the team. The assisting SF follows at a distance to avoid interfering with the search. If it is determined the suspect has exited the building, the MWD team should attempt to track the suspect from the scene. Tracking may result in additional evidence or information for a subsequent investigation.

Vehicle parking lots
Use MWD teams to detect and apprehend thieves and vandals in parking lots. The mere presence of the team may deter potential acts of theft and vandalism. The MWD team should approach from the downwind side.

Military housing and billet areas
Proper use of MWD teams in military housing areas will deter and decrease unlawful acts. During foot patrols, MWD team contact with area residents helps in the reinforcement of community relations. Outline clear procedures governing release of MWDs in military housing or billet areas in local operating instructions.

Alarm responses
Use the MWD team to search and clear the exterior and interior of alarmed buildings and surrounding areas. They may also assist in apprehensions. Limit the number of personnel allowed into the area to preclude contaminating the area with unnecessary scents.

Funds Escort
When escorting funds custodians on foot, position MWD team slightly to the rear of custodian to observe any potential hostile acts. MWD handlers should brief fund custodians on actions to take during an attempted robbery. If local procedures allow the carrier to ride in the security forces vehicle, position the MWD where the handler will have positive control.

Moving Traffic Violations
When a traffic stop is made, the MWD should accompany the handler on leash. The presence of the MWD will convince most offenders to remain cooperative.

Identification and Apprehensions
When conducting identification checks or effecting apprehension, the handler must inform the person(s) that any display of hostility could result in the MWD biting without command. If an apprehension is made, conduct a search with the dog in the guard position. If available, use a back-up to transport persons taken into custody. When circumstances require a MWD team to transport personnel taken into custody, and the vehicle is not equipped with a vehicle insert or platform, position the MWD between the offender and the handler.

Riot and Crowd Control
Normally, do not use MWDs for direct confrontation with demonstrators. In fact, the presence of MWDs could aggravate a situation. During the peaceful stages of a confrontation, hold MWD teams in reserve and out of sight of the crowd.

If the situation deteriorates, move MWD teams up to within sight of the crowd, but still well away from the front lines. Only when actual physical confrontation erupts, consider employing MWD teams on the front lines. Once committed, use MWD teams as a back-up force, integrated into the front line of forces, or use to assist apprehension teams.

Employment
When engaged in direct confrontation, keep MWDs on leash and allow biting only under specific circumstances authorized by the on-scene commander. Position other riot control force personnel approximately 15 feet from MWD handlers. Do not release MWDs into the crowd.

In an open area, chemical riot control agents will not normally adversely affect the MWD's capability to act as a psychological or physical deterrent. However, handlers should watch their dog closely under such conditions. If a MWD shows any signs of distress, have it examined by a veterinarian as quickly as possible.

Support Duties. In large areas such as open fields, position MWD teams on the outer perimeter to contain the crowd while other forces make apprehensions. Post MWDs around holding areas and processing centers to prevent the escape or liberation of prisoners. Use MWD teams to assist teams in apprehending and removing specific individuals within a group of demonstrators. In this role, use the MWD team to protect members of the apprehension team not to affect the apprehension. Exercise extreme caution in these situations. The MWD could become extremely excited and agitated and could mistakenly bite a member of the apprehension team. The handler must maintain positive control over the dog.

Civil Disasters
Provisions exist to provide MWD teams to a civilian community to assist in humanitarian or domestic emergency roles. For example, MWD teams may help locate lost children or search an area or building which has received a bomb threat. Exercise extreme caution in these situations to ensure the Posse Comitatus Act is not violated. Coordinate all requests for assistance with the base Staff Judge Advocate. Refer to AFI 10-801, Assistance to Civilian Law Enforcement Agencies, for additional guidance.

Protecting Distinguished Visitors
Employ MWDs around quarters and conference locations or for searching and clearing buildings. Used as a foot patrol, the MWD can use all its detection senses.

Fixed Post (Stake-Out)
The primary function of a MWD team on a fixed post is surveillance over an area or building. If used outdoors, locate the team downwind where the dog can detect a person by scent. If this is not possible, locate the team where the MWD may detect by sound or sight. When used indoors, the MWD must rely primarily on its sense of hearing. Other security forces personnel may accompany MWD teams on fixed posts.

Installation Entry Control
Use of MWD teams as entry controllers for extended periods of time seriously degrades their operational effectiveness. If circumstances warrant the posting of the MWD team on a base entry control point, the duration of posting should be kept to a minimum consistent with flight manning. Posting of MWD handlers without their assigned MWD is misuse of assigned resources. While performing as entry controllers, the MWD's primary function is psychological deterrence and handler protection. Permit the MWD to sit or lie down, but do not confine where it can't respond when needed.

Confinement Facilities
The CSF must authorize the use of MWD teams to augment inmate control procedures. MWD teams may be used to search for escaped inmates and conduct facility contraband searches but will not be used to guard inmates. MWDs will NOT be used in the interrogation or interview of prisoners, EPWs or detainees.

Tech. Sgt. John Mascolo and his military working dog, Ajax, await a helicopter pickup outside Forward Operating Base Normandy, Iraq, on Feb. 28, 2006. (U.S. Army photo/Pfc. William Servinski II)

U.S. MILITARY WORKING DOG TRAINING HANDBOOK ★ 169

CHAPTER 12

CONTINGENCY OPERATIONS

MWDS ROLE IN CONTINGENCY OPERATIONS

An MWDs excellent sensory skills coupled with their psychological deterrence make them a vital part of base defense and force protection missions. When establishing ground defense operations, MWD teams should be used to enhance the detection capabilities of the ground defense force and provide a psychological deterrent to hostile intrusion. Properly positioned, MWD teams can provide an initial warning to the presence of hostile intruders. Experience has shown that MWD teams often provide warning of attacks early enough to allow response forces time to deploy and prevent enemy forces from reaching their objectives. MWD teams can also be used to clear protected areas of hostile personnel, explosives and weapons after an attack as well as prevent the introduction of explosives to an installation.

BACKGROUND

History has shown the enemy strategy in guerilla or terrorist attacks against Air Force installations has been based on surprise and concentration of forces against weak points. The aggressors rely on advanced planning, preparation, concealment during approach, sudden attack and swift withdrawal. Therefore, effective early detection and warning systems are critical. Use of MWDs has proven their effectiveness in helping fulfill this role and compliment technology gaps. MWDs used on tactical perimeter posts can provide warning of an impending attack early enough to allow for the deployment of the response force, thus preventing the enemy from reaching their objective.

MWD ORGANIZATION

QFEBP:

Consists of an NCOIC (must be a graduate of the MWD Trainer/Kennel Masters Course No. L8AZR3P0710K1A) deployed in support of nine to fifteen MWDs when there is no in-place kennel support at deployed locations.

Responsibilities:
1. Coordinate in the planning of defense and posting of MWD teams.
2. Advise leadership and defense force personnel on MWD capabilities, limitations and effective employment of MWD teams.
3. Coordinate veterinarian support at deployed location. Train handlers on any unique health care concerns at deployment location.
4. Coordinate with Defense Force Commander (DFC) in planning kennel location.
5. Establish kennels and support areas.
6. Develop and implement SOPs for the MWD section.
7. Conduct orientation training to evaluate MWD teams.
8. Once the area is secure, conduct validation training immediately.
9. Develop and implement a training program to maintain MWD teams' proficiency.

QFECP:
Consists of one MWD trainer who is a graduate of the MWD Trainer/Kennel Masters Course No. L8AZR3P0710K1A11.
Responsibilities:
1. The trainer is directly responsible to the Kennel Master for managing and implementing an effective MWD training program. They must be capable of performing all Kennel Master functions when necessary.
2. Schedule daily proficiency training following established OTS.
3. Schedule and conduct periodic intensive or remedial training for teams with special problems.
4. Identify and correct deficiencies of handlers and MWDs in all phases of MWD operations.
5. Ensure MWD records are current and accurate.
6. Act as alternate custodian for the narcotic and explosive training aids.

QFEBR:
1. Consists of one MWD and one handler. All MWDs will be qualified patrol explosive detector dogs.
2. The QFEBR can be tasked to perform duties as mounted/dismounted patrols, fixed positions or perform explosive detection missions.

QFEDD:
1. Consists of one MWD and one handler. MWD team is qualified only for explosive detection.
2. The QFEDD can be tasked to perform duties based solely on its explosive detection abilities.

QFEND:
1. Consists of one MWD and one handler. All MWDs will be qualified patrol narcotic detector dogs.
2. The QFEND can be tasked to perform duties as mounted/dismounted patrols, fixed positions or perform narcotic detection missions.

QFEPD:
1. Consists of one MWD and one handler. All MWDs will only be qualified patrol dogs.
2. The QFEPD can be tasked to perform duties as mounted/dismounted patrols or fixed positions.

Chain of Command
The alignment of the MWD teams within the chain of command should be based upon how the Defense Force Commander intends to utilize the MWD teams within the defense. Example: If MWD teams will be tasked with a variety of missions such as mounted/dismounted patrolling, detection searches and other related duties, the centralized alignment would be beneficial to allow the Kennel Master to select the most suitable MWD team for each mission. At a deployed location where MWD teams will be doing primarily the same duties every day, such as explosive detection at ECPs, the decentralized alignment may be more effective.

Centralized Alignment
The QFEBP reports directly to the S3/Operations. The assigned MWD teams reports directly to the Kennel Master. All requests for MWD support are made through the S3 who in turn coordinates with the Kennel Master. Once the MWD team is tasked to a sector, that sector maintains OPCON (operational control) over the MWD team while the team is assigned.

Decentralized Alignment
Under this alignment, MWD teams are assigned directly to a sector command post and directly support sector defense operations.

PRE-DEPLOYMENT

Planning must be started upon initial notification of deployment. This planning must include acquiring needed equipment, veterinarian support, how teams will be transported to the deployed location, kenneling at en route stops and the final destination, and how the teams will be employed in the deployed AOR (Area of Responsibility).

Administrative
All MWD handlers will deploy with:
1. Copies of the most recent four months training records;
2. Most recent validation letter;
3. Copy of the MWDs health records.

Equipment
A number of considerations must be taken into account when planning the equipment requirements for the deployment. The length of the deployment, terrain and weather at the deployed location, as well as the amount of time it will take to establish re- supply channels. A minimum of a 30-day supply of food and medication must be taken on all deployments. If the MWD team deploys with a LOGDET (QFE4R), some items may need to be added depending on the terrain and weather at the deployment location. An example of this would be box fans for a hot climate or cloth booties for the dogs' paws in rugged terrain.

Transportation
The mode of transportation will determine the type of kennel that will be used for shipment. Unless specifically tasked otherwise, when traveling by military aircraft, teams will deploy with a suitable approved portable kennel. When traveling by commercial aircraft the plastic vari-kennel type container will be used. When deploying to a location that does not have a finished kennel facility, arrangements must be made to have suitable kennel crates shipped to the deployed location to allow for the establishment of a field kennel. Plastic transport kennels are unsuitable for temporary kenneling and will not be employed in this manner. The home station Kennel Master is responsible to check for any quarantine requirements at stops en route to the deployed location.

Veterinarian Support
Veterinarian support will be required prior to deployment, during deployment and upon redeployment. Upon initial notification of deployment, the Kennel Master must coordinate with the home station veterinarian to get health certificates issued; copies of the MWDs health records to deploy with the MWD team and identify any medical threats to the MWD at the deployed location as well have an MWD first-aid kit unique to the deployed location prepared. The home station Kennel Master is responsible to ensure that the deploying handler is competent in emergency first aid and MWD lifesaving skills. Prior to deployment, the home station veterinarian will be consulted as to the need of any insecticides that should be acquired to treat the area for insects such as mosquitoes and ticks. The handler must know how and when to use items deployed in the first-aid kit. It is the deployed Kennel Master/senior handlers' responsibility to coordinate veterinarian support at the deployed location.

Kenneling
The type of base the teams will be deployed to will determine the type of kennel used: main base, stand-by base, or bare base.

Main Base
A main base will have adequate facilities in place for maintaining MWD operations.
Stand-by Base
A stand-by base or en route stop may or may not have adequate facilities for maintaining MWD operations. In these cases, a temporary field kennel may have to be established.

Bare Base
A bare base will not have any facilities established. Under these circumstances, a field kennel will have to be established.

Qualifications
Although teams do not need to be certified at home station prior to deploying, the Kennel Master/trainer must ensure each team is fully qualified in all required tasks, e.g. patrol disciplines, detection and be subject of a current validation.

DEPLOYMENT

The QFEBP should be in place at the deployed location to establish the kennels prior to the arrival of any MWD teams. The UTCs required equipment should arrive with them at the Area of Operation (AO) to allow the kennel facilities to be operational in the minimum amount of time. If airflow does not allow for the full LOGDET to be shipped with the UTC, each MWD team must deploy with the following as a minimum:

Equipment for Deployment
1. Two (2) full sets of MWD gear
2. Suitable MWD shipping crate or K-9 mobility container
3. One (1) feed pan
4. One (1) water bucket
5. One (1) five-gallon water can
6. 30-day supply of prescribed dog food per dog

Upon Arrival at the AO, Security is the First Priority
The operations section will determine how the MWD teams will be integrated into the base defense.

Kennel Site
The initial kennel site should be determined during the leaders' recon or by a map recon prior to actual deployment. The actual site will most likely be determined when the Kennel Master arrives in the AO. When selecting a site, the following guidelines must be considered:

1. The ground should be graded or have a natural slope to prevent standing water.
2. The area should be generally quiet to allow MWDs to rest when not working.
3. Adequate shade and ventilation must be provided. This can be provided by natural cover such as trees or constructed by using camouflage netting or tents. The use of fans can help with the ventilation of the kennel area.
4. An adequate potable water supply must be available at the kennels. Each MWD team will require a minimum of ten gallons of water per day.
5. If a veterinarian is deployed, he/she must be consulted for any possible health hazards.

Construction of Kennels

There are numerous ways a field kennel can be designed when there are no permanent facilities available. The actual site and terrain as well as the number of dogs and materials on hand will be the determining factors. The kennel area should be located in a relatively quiet area with minimal traffic to allow the MWDs to rest. If the kennels must be located in a congested area to ensure safety, a temporary screen or fence will be needed.

1. Shipping crates can be used to construct a field kennel. The crates must have holes (approximately one-inch diameter) on the top of the crate. The crate is placed upside down and raised 4 to 6 inches off the ground to allow drainage and to reduce parasite-breeding places. Place duct boards in the crate to prevent the MWD from injuring their feet or legs in the air holes. Small smooth gravel should be placed under and around the crate to allow for drainage and easy removal of solid waste. Place the crates under some type of cover, either natural such as trees or artificial such as a tent or camouflage netting to keep the MWD out of direct sunlight and provide some protection from inclement weather.
2. K-9 Mobility Containers are another type of kennel that may be used. Although these kennels are more modern, the same requirements for establishing the field kennel apply.
3. Based on the local threat, a satellite site may be needed to kennel MWDs at two or more locations to reduce the threat of losing all assets in one attack.

Support Facilities

1. Within the kennel area numerous support facilities and MWD specific areas must be established.
2. When circumstances dictate, a bivouac area should be established within the kennel area but located separately from the actual kennels. At no time while under field conditions will MWDs and personnel be housed in the same tent.
3. A food preparation/utensil cleaning area must be established. In this area rodent prevention measures must be taken to prevent the contamination of MWD food and feeding utensils. MWD food will not be stored in the same area with the MWDs.
4. An area must be established to maintain supplies and extra equipment.
5. A designated break area must be established. This area should be away from the kennels and must always be kept clean of MWD waste. A bucket or plastic bag can be used to store the waste until it can be disposed of properly. This will help prevent parasitic infestation within the kennel area.

Security Measures Must be Taken within and Around the Kennel Area

A perimeter must be established around the area to prevent unauthorized personnel from entering. Rope or fence with signs stating —Keep Out in English and host nation language will be used. When establishing the perimeter, remember that using items such as concertina wire to keep people out will also keep you in during an emergency. Determine if there may be a need for rapid egress when constructing the perimeter. If kennels are within a hostile fire/combatant zone, defense-fighting positions should be integrated into the overall kennel construction. Ensure adequate protective shielding is constructed to protect the MWD kenneling area from fragmentation debris. SF leadership must have in place procedures to protect MWDs in the event of chemical or biological attacks. Refer to USAF Manual 10-2602, Nuclear, Biological, and Conventional (NBCC) Defense Operations and Standards, dated May 03, Chapter 4, paragraphs A4.13 (Security Forces) through A4.13.6 for SF/MWD operations within a chemical/biological environment.

Standard Operating Procedures (SOP)

The Kennel Master must establish SOPs for the kennel operations to run smoothly. The following are only the minimum areas that must be addressed:

Work/Rest Schedule
The mission will determine how the work/rest schedule will be designed. MWDs are fully capable of working 12-hour shifts with the understanding that they will need intermittent breaks. Alternating duties during a shift will also help keep the MWD fresh and alert. An example of this would be starting a shift at an ECP and after 2 hours rotate the team to a walking/mobile patrol in the cantonment area and then to a mobile reserve team later in the shift. Another example would be posting on an LP/OP, and after a (suggested time/no more than 4 hours, etc.) period of time, have a patrol with an assigned MWD team swap posts with the LP/OP team. Time must also be set aside to conduct training.

1. Frequency of kennel checks and procedures for reporting incidents, accidents or breeches of security in the kennel area must be established in the SOP.
2. Establish procedures for the feeding of MWDs at least two hours before and not sooner than two hours after working. This schedule must be available for all personnel conducting CQ duties to view. The SOP must also outline procedures for the removal and cleaning of the feed pans. In austere environments, MWDs will need fresh water more often than the standard four hours due to contamination by insects and other debris. Water buckets will be cleaned and disinfected as needed. Guidelines must be in place to ensure that MWDs are only given small amounts of water immediately following a hard workout, such as patrolling or conducting aggression training. As a minimum, clean pans and buckets with hot soapy water, rinse and air-dry.
3. Kennel Sanitation. In field conditions it is imperative the entire kennel area be kept clean. This includes cleaning and disinfecting each kennel and removing all trash from the area. Employ rodent control procedures for both discarded and stored food areas. If veterinary support is deployed, they will be consulted concerning how areas and items will be cleaned and disinfected.
4. Safety. Establish safety standards applicable in the kennel area and around other personnel. Ensure these standards are strictly adhered to.
5. Stray animals. MWD teams will not be used to capture stray animals nor will stray animals be kept in or around the kennel area. Local procedures must be established covering the use of service weapons to defend an MWD team from stray or wild animals.
6. The Kennel Master or trainer will attend all Operations Group meetings to answer any questions pertaining to the capabilities, limitations and employment of MWD teams.

Orientation Training
After arriving at the deployment site and ensuring site security has been established, the Kennel Master along with the trainer will conduct orientation training with all deployed teams. This training allows the deployed Kennel Master the opportunity to evaluate all deployed MWD teams. This training will give the Kennel Master the information needed to advise the Ground Defense Force Commander on the best employment of each team. Orientation training also gives the Kennel Master the opportunity to establish rapport, control and discipline with deployed handlers. This training consists of field problems, obedience, gunfire, aggression and detection problems. Once security has been established, the Kennel Master/trainer must validate all detector dogs on all available odors to ensure environmental conditions have not degraded the MWDs ability to detect all trained odors. This does not need to be a full validation, merely a test of the MWDs abilities to detect required odors under the deployed conditions.

Contingency Plan
The Kennel Master must establish procedures to disperse MWD teams in case of indirect fire. A plan must also be made in the case of natural disasters.

Re-Supplies
The Kennel Master must coordinate with the S-4 to establish re-supply of food, water and equipment. Do not wait until supplies are exhausted to initiate this process.

CAPABILITIES AND LIMITATIONS

Capabilities. An MWD teams' detection and warning capabilities are a combined result of the dogs' superior faculties of sight, sound and smell all of which far exceed those of a human.

Limitations:
1. Terrain. Trees, bushes, heavy underbrush, thick woods, jungles, hills, ravines and other terrain features can obscure an intruder's scent pattern. Obstructions and high winds often split and divert the scent pattern making it much more difficult for the dog to locate its source.
2. Smoke and dust are also limiting factors in detection because they reduce the MWDs ability to use its senses.
3. Wind, temperature and humidity can affect the scent pattern and the dog. High winds and low humidity quickly disperse the scent pattern while hot temperatures and high humidity will cause fatigue in the MWD. Rain and fog will also reduce the MWDs ability to use its senses.
4. There is no standard set time an MWD is capable of working, your operations tempo and type of mission, the dog's fitness level all impact work/rest cycles. A physically fit dog with adequate rest and intermittent breaks should be able to work as long as needed.

Training is the most important limitation that can be controlled. It starts at home station in the pre-deployment phase. MWDs must be proficient in all required tasks prior to deploying. Once security has been established at the deployed location, training should be initiated. The type of training should be geared toward the intended mission of the MWD team. Failure to conduct this training will decrease the effectiveness of the team. Initial training also allows the Kennel Master to validate the teams' efficiency and in turn select the best team for the required duties.

EMPLOYMENT

Patrolling

MWD teams can be used on both mounted and dismounted patrols to detect enemy presence, avoid discovery, and locate enemy outposts.
1. Dismounted Patrol: The MWD team must join the patrol in time to receive the warning order and participate in all phases of planning, preparation and execution.
2. The handler gives recommendations for employment of the team.
3. The MWD team must participate in patrol rehearsals.
4. The rehearsal allows the patrol members to become familiar with the MWDs temperament and the teams method of operation. It also allows the MWD to become familiar with the scents of the patrol members as well as the noises and motions of the patrol on the move.
5. When taking cover, patrol members must avoid jumping close to the MWD team. When approaching the MWD team always approach from the handler's front-right side since the MWD is normally on the handlers left. This should be covered in the handlers' patrol brief.
6. At least one patrol member must be designated as security for the MWD team.

    a. Working the MWD requires the handler's full attention on the dog and does not allow the handler to scan the surrounding area for any threat.
    b. Handling an MWD severely reduces the handlers' ability to effectively use a weapon.
    c. The proximity of the security person to the MWD team will be determined by the handler. The handler must ensure the security person does not distract the MWD.

d. The handler must ensure the security person is knowledgeable of the MWD teams' responsibilities and able to perform their duties in the close proximity of a MWD.
e. Prior to departing on a patrol, handlers must brief all members on the MWD team's capabilities, limitations and safety issues. This briefing must include actions the patrol must take if the handler is injured, killed or incapacitated.
f. Since wind is a key factor in the MWD's ability to detect; the team will normally be positioned on the point or flank depending on the wind direction. If the wind is coming from behind the patrol the team should be placed in the position that is most advantageous to the patrol.
g. When speed is essential, the team should be placed in the rear to allow the patrol to proceed as quickly as need be without the MWD posing a threat to the members.
h. The length of the patrol and the weather conditions will determine the actual amount of equipment and supplies that will be needed. As a minimum; a muzzle, first aid kit and extra water for the MWD must be taken. The muzzle will be used if the handler or MWD are injured to prevent the MWD from biting any of the patrol members. Patrol members may be needed to assist carrying the extra water for the MWD.

Mounted Patrols

1. MWD teams may be attached to mounted patrols. When assigned these duties, the preparation for the patrol is the same as dismounted patrols. MWD teams should be assigned to a vehicle large enough to allow room for the handler to safely control the dog.
2. MWD teams may be used to search vehicles along routes and at roadblocks for explosives.
3. MWD teams can be used to provide security for convoy vehicles if attacked or for any reason there may be to dismount.
4. After the all clear is given, MWD teams can be used to assist with search and clear operations after an attack.
5. In some locations it may be beneficial to have an MWD on a mounted patrol to deter host nation personnel from approaching and reaching into the patrol vehicles.

Observation Post/Listening Post

MWD teams are most effective on these posts during the hours of darkness and times of limited visibility.
1. Team must have a member assigned to act as a security person. Ample time should be spent with the security person prior to assuming post to associate them with the dog and to provide a patrol briefing.
2. The team is located forward of the tactical area of operation to reduce distractions, preferably downwind of avenues of approach to allow the MWD to use its sense of smell. If the wind direction is not favorable, the MWD may still provide early warning using its sense of sight and hearing.
3. The Kennel Master should be consulted when selecting sites for MWD teams. One or more alternate positions covering the same avenue of approach should be determined to allow the team to periodically change locations. This will maximize the MWDs tentativeness and reduce the chance of the MWD becoming complacent.
4. As a minimum, each team posted on an LP/OP post will have a muzzle, first- aid kit and extra water for the MWD.

Support Capabilities

MWD teams can be used in several ways within the AO both as a psychological and physical deterrent. Using MWD teams at different locations for short periods of time can give the perception that MWDs can be anywhere. The fear of dogs alone may prove to be an effective deterrent.
1. MWD teams offer both a physical and psychological deterrent in enemy prisoner of war (EPW) and

detainee operations. MWD teams can be used at collection points, holding areas, during movement and enhancing perimeter security at a compound or camp. MWDs can help locate and capture escaped EPWs. Under no circumstance will MWDs be used in the interrogation or interview of EPWs or detainees.

2. MWD teams can be used to patrol, both mounted and dismounted, assigned areas within the cantonment area to conduct security checks, respond and clear unsecured buildings, and assist at roadblocks controlling personnel and detecting contraband.
3. MWD teams placed at entry control points can search all incoming vehicles and cargo for contraband as well as provide a psychological deterrent.
4. When assigned to a response force element, MWD teams can provide a quick response. In this capacity they can be used to investigate alarm, sensor and tripwire activations as well as possible sightings in unauthorized areas.
5. When using MWDs in confrontation management situations, the presence of an MWD may provide a psychological deterrent, however, the mere sight of an MWD may escalate the situation.
    a. MWDs will not normally be used for direct confrontation with demonstrators.
    b. During peaceful stages, MWDs should be held in reserve and out of sight of demonstrators.
    c. If the situation deteriorates, MWD teams should be moved up within sight of the crowd, but still at a distance.
    d. Only when actual physical confrontation erupts should using an MWD team be considered. When a team is committed, all other personnel should be positioned at least 10 feet from the MWD team due to the dog not being able to distinguish between friend or foe.
    e. MWDs should never be released into a crowd.

RE-DEPLOYMENT

1. The same considerations apply when making pre-deployment travel arrangements. Ensure there are no animal restrictions or quarantines at any en route stops.
2. MWDs are subject to inspection at ports of entry and may be denied entry into the United States if they have evidence of an infectious disease that can be transmitted to humans. If a dog appears to be ill, further examination by a licensed veterinarian at handler's expense might be required at the port of entry. MWDs must have a certificate showing they have been vaccinated against rabies at least 30 days prior to entry into the United States as well as a health certificate. There are no restrictions on who (nationality) can sign a health certificate or rabies vaccination certificate, provided the individual is licensed to practice veterinarian medicine in that country. Dog's medical records must also contain evidence of a favorable FAVN test.
3. Each handler must ensure they have an adequate supply of dog food in case of any unforeseen stops en route to their home station. In addition, handlers must hand carry any MWD medication, MWDs medical records and at least one set of dog gear.

CHAPTER 13

MILITARY WORKING DOG FORMS

1. **AF Form 321.** *MWD Training and Utilization Record.* Provides complete history of patrol training, utilization, and performance. Handlers annotate each duty day and sign at the end of each month. The Kennel Master will sign as the reviewing official at the end of each month.
2. **AF Form 323.** *MWD Training and Utilization Record for Drug/Explosive Detection.* Record of training, utilization, and performance of detector dogs. It serves as the basis for establishing probable cause. Annotate and sign the same as the AF Form 321.
3. **AF Form 324.** *MWD Program Status Report.* Prepared by units and used by USAF Program Manager and HQ AFSFC/DOD MWD Program Management Office to effectively manage the USAF and DOD MWD program(s). Units provide original copy of report to USAF Program Manager quarterly, which in turns forwards reports to HQ AFSC/DOD MWD Program Management Office. MWD Status Reports are due to the USAF MWD Program Management Office NLT the 5th of the month following the quarter.
4. **AF Form 1205.** *Narcotics Training Aid Accountability Record.* All SF units possessing narcotic training aids will record and account for these items using this form regardless whether they are registered with DEA or not.
5. **DD Form 1743.** *Death Certificate of Military Dog.* Required for the death of all MWDs. Includes a brief statement identifying the cause of death and used to close out accountability for a MWD through the base supply system.
6. **DD Form 1834.** *MWD Service Record.* Initiated when MWD is first procured and entered the DoD MWD Inventory and kept current by Kennel Masters throughout the MWD's service life. Annotate unit of assignment as well as assignment of new handlers on the reverse side of the form. Do not change information pertaining to MWD's national stock number without prior coordination with the MAJCOM, and the 341 TRS.
7. **LAFB Form 375.** *MWD Status Report.* Provides a record of training on the MWD after it graduates from a course.
8. **Forms Prescribed.**
   LAFB Form 375, *MWD Status Report*
9. **Forms Adopted**
   AF Form 68, *Munitions Authorization Record.*
   AF Form 601, *Equipment Action Request.*
   AF Form 1996, *Adjusted Stock Level.*
   AF Form 2005, *Issue Turn-in Request.*
   DEA Form 225a, *Application for Registration Renewal (Type B).*
   DD Form 1348-6, *DoD Single-line Item Requisition System Document*
   DD Form 2209, *Veterinary Health Certificate.*
   DD Form 2342, *Animal Facility Sanitation Checklist.*

LOREN M. RENO, Lt Gen, USAF
DCS/Logistics, Installations and Mission Support

ATTACHMENT 1

GLOSSARY OF REFERENCES AND SUPPORTING INFORMATION

References
AFI 31-202, *Military Working Dog Program,* 16 May 2009
AFI 51-201, *Administration of Military Justice*, 21 Dec 2007
AFI 10-801, *Assistance to Civilian Law Enforcement Agencies*, 15 Apr 1994
AFMAN 23-110, *USAF Supply Manual*, Vol 2, 1 Apr 2009
AFMAN 33-363, *Management of Records*, 1 Mar 2008
AFMAN 91-201, *Explosive Safety Standard*, 17 Nov 2008
AFJI 23-224, *DOD Military Working Dog Program*, 1 Dec 1990

Abbreviations and Acronyms
AFSFC — Air Force Security Forces Center
AO — Area of Operation
AOR — Area of Responsibility
BAR — Bright Alert and Responsive
BCLS — Basic Cardiac Life Support
BCS — Body Composition Score
BPM — Beats per Minute
CAB — Circulation, Airway, Breathing
CFR — Code of Federal Regulations
CPR — Cardiopulmonary Resuscitation
CR — Conditioned Response
CRS — Continuous Reward Schedule
CRT — Capillary Refill Time
CS — Conditioned Stimulus
CSF — Chief, Security Forces
CST — Clear Signals Training
DEA — Drug Enforcement Agency
NDD — Narcotic Detector Dog
DOD — Department of Defense
DFC — Defense Force Commander
DFR — Deferred Final Response
EDD — Explosive Detector Dog
EOL — End of Leash
FIRS — Fixed Interval Reward Schedule
FRRS — Fixed Ratio Reward Schedule
GDV — Gastric Dilatation Volvulus
IAW — In Accordance With
IV — Intravenous Fluids
LP/OP — Listening/Observation Post
LRS — Lactated Ringers Solution
MASO — Munitions Account Supply Office

MEDEVAC — Medical Evacuation
ML — Milliliters
MRE — Meals Ready to Eat
MWD — Military Working Dog
NCOIC — Non-Commissioned Officer in Charge
NFS — Not from Source
NSN — National Stock Number
OPCON — Operational Control
OJT — On the Job Training
OTS — Optimal Training Schedule
QAR — Quiet, Alert and Responsive
RF — Response Force
SD — Stimulus Discriminative
SJA — Staff Judge Advocate
SOP — Standard Operating Procedures
SRT — Security Response Team
SSD — Specialized Search Dog
TCP — Traffic Control Point
TDY — Tour of Duty
TMO — Traffic Management Office
UR — Unconditioned Response
US — Unconditioned Stimulus
UTC — Unit Type Code
VIRS — Variable Interval Reward Schedule
VRRS — Variable Ratio Reward Schedule
WBGT — Wet Bulb Globe Temperature

ATTACHMENT 2

MILITARY WORKING DOG FIRST AID KIT

Figure A2.1. Military Working Dog First Aid Kit

Proponent: DoD Military Working Dog Veterinary Service, Lackland AFB, TX 78236

- Bag, MWD first aid kit (any source/size/type/configuration that meets tactical and logistical requirements; suggested NSN is 6545-00-912-9870 for *case, medical instrument and supply set*)
- Bandage and dressing material
  - Non-adherent dressing (Telfa® pad or equivalent), 3-inch X 8-inch, (NSN 6510-00-986-2942), 4 pads
  - Roll gauze, 3-inch width, (NSN 6510-ST-509-6001), 3 rolls
  - Conforming bandage, self-adherent (VetWrap® or equivalent), 4-inch width, (NSN 6510-LP-734-3001), 2 rolls
  - Adhesive tape, 1-inch width, (NSN 6510-00-926-8882), 1 roll
  - Gauze sponge, 4-inch X 4-inch square, sterile, (NSN 6510-ST-429-0001), 50 squares
  - Dressing, first aid, field, camouflaged, 11.5-inch width X 11.5-inch long, absorbable (NSN 6510-00-201-7425), 1 each
  - Pad, povidone-iodine impregnated, sterile, cotton/rayon, 2-inch X 1.375-inch, brown, 100/box, (NSN 6510-01-010-0307), 5 pads
  - Pad, isopropyl alcohol impregnated, nonwoven cotton/rayon, white, 200/box, (NSN 6510-00-786-3736), 5 pads
  - Roll cotton, 1-pound roll, (NSN 6510-00-201-4000), 1 roll
  - Cast padding, 4-inch roll, (PART NUMBER 9044), 2 rolls
  - Elastikon® tape, 2-inch roll, (PART NUMBER JJ1574), 1 roll (Johnson & Johnson™)
  - Laparotomy sponges, (NSN 6510L101174), 2 sponges
  - Hemostatic biopolymer clotting agent granules, 0.5 oz/15 gram package (NSN 6510-01-549-6058; CELOX,® available from SAM Medical Products,® www.sammedical.com, 800-818-4726), 1 package
- Miscellaneous items
  - Thermometer, digital, with case, (any source), 1 each
  - Bandage scissors, 7.25-inch length (NSN 6515-00-935-7138), 1 each
  - Splint, universal, aluminum, 36-inch length X 4.25-inch width, reusable, (NSN 6515-01-149-1951), 1 each
  - Endotracheal tube, 10 mm id, hi-low cuff, silicone-base (Part Number: 86117 Mallinckrodt), 1 each
  - Glove, patient examining and treatment, size 10/large, purple, 4.3 mil, 100/box (NSN 6515-01-491-5719), 6 pair
  - Lubricant, surgical, 5-gram packets, 144/box, (NSN 6505-00-111-7829), 4 packets
  - Syringe, 60 mL, dosing tip (NSN 6515011643061PV), 1 each
  - Syringe, 60 mL, luer lock tip, sterile, (NSN 8881560125), 1 each
  - Stopcock, 3-way, sterile, (NSN 6515010357962), 1 each
  - Needles, hypodermic, 18-gauge (NSN 6515007542834), 4 each
  - Syringe, 6 mL, disposable (NSN 8881516911), 2 each

- Syringe and needle, hypodermic, safety, 3 mL, 22 gauge, sterile, disposable, 25/box (NSN 6515-01-519-5872), 4 each
- Catheter, over-the-needle, 14-gauge X 3 inch, sterile, (Purchase at Miller Vet # 1- 800-880-1920, part # 0208-0451), 1 each
- Ambu-bag (Purchase at Vital Signs, 1-800-932-0760, government accounts), 1 each
- Laryngoscope (Purchase at WelchAllyn; www.welchallyn.com), 1 each
- Nail trimmer, (6515-00-291-8398), 1 ea

- Medications
  - Toxiban,® (Purchase at MWI 888-223-8690; Part Number 010745], 2 bottles
  - Atropine sulfate for injection, 15 mg/mL bottle, (NSN 6505-00-582-4735), 1 bottle
  - Apomorphine tablets, 6mg, (Purchase at MWI 888-223-8690; Part Number 022196], 2 tablets
  - Morphine, 15mg/mL or auto injector 10 mg (NSN 00641234541), 1 vial (20 mL) (NOTE: Provided by in-theater veterinary assets ONLY)
  - Antibiotic ointment, sterile, (Purchase at Webster 800-872-3867 as ANIMAX®;
  - Part Number 078360601), 1 tube
  - Diphenhydramine for injection, 50 mg/mL, 1 mL vial, (NSN 00641037625), 2 vials
  - Dexamethasone sodium phosphate, (NSN 6505014926420), 1 vial
  - Ophthalmic irrigating solution (NSN 6505-01-119-7693), 1 each
  - Puralube® ophthalmic ointment (NSN 00168015038), 1 tube
  - Otic cleansing solution (many options; no specific recommendations), 20 mL
  - Silver sulfadiazine cream, (NSN 49884060057), 1 tube
  - Chlorhexidine solution, (NSN 6515LP2029050), 50 mL

- Fluid therapy supplies
  - Catheter injection port, sterile (many options; no specific recommendations), 2 each
  - Balanced electrolyte solution for injection, sterile, (Lactated Ringer's Solution), 1000 mL, (NSN 6505000836537JT), 2 bags
  - Administration set, sterile, (6515-ST-9234001, B-Brawn, Cardinal Health Part # 352049), 1 each
  - Catheter, intravenous, Introcan,® safety, 18 gauge X 1 ¼-inch length, winged needle guard, radiopaque, sterile, 50/box (NSN 6515-01-484-1327), 3 each.

U.S. Army's Guide to Veterinary Care of Military Working Dogs

U.S. ARMY VETERINARY SERVICES

PrepperPress

Post-Apocalyptic Fiction and Survival Nonfiction

U.S. Army's Guide to Veterinary Care of Military Working Dogs

U.S. Army Veterinary Services

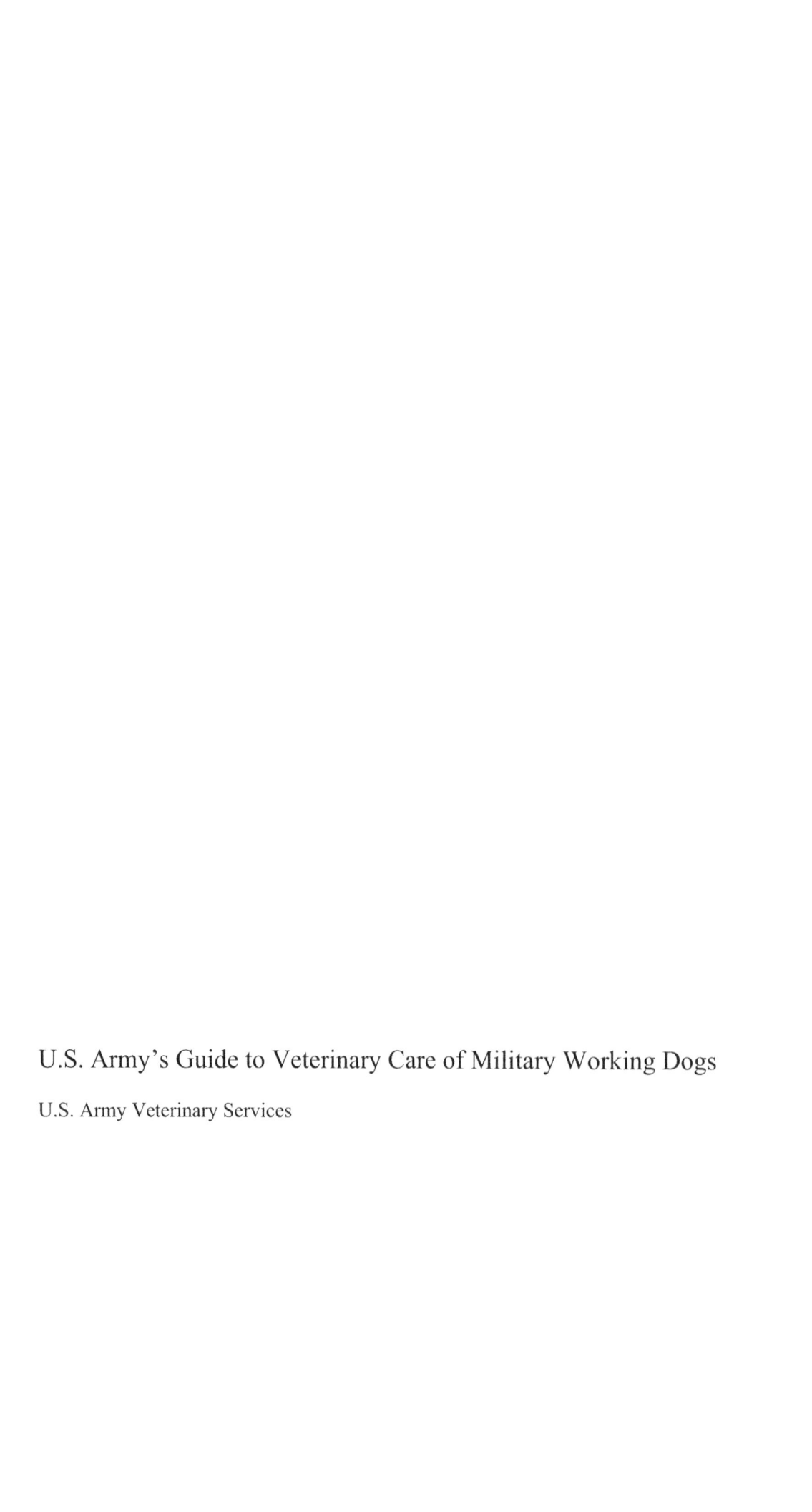

CONTENTS

CHAPTER 1. INTRODUCTION 1
Purpose and Scope 1
References 1
Abbreviations and Terms 1
Overview of THE Dod Mwd Program 1
Other Working Dogs 6

CHAPTER 2. EQUIPMENT AND FACILITIES 7
Purpose 7
Tiering Standards 7
Equipment Requirements 8
Programs and Funds 9
Special CONSIDERATIONS 10
Medical Supplies 10
Textbooks 11
Periodicals 12

CHAPTER 3. PREVENTIVE MEDICINE, DEPLOYMENT ISSUES, AND STANDARD PROCEDURES 14
Handling of Mwds 14
MWD Records 14
Preventive Medicine—Examination, Assessment, Vaccination, and Prophylactic Care 18
Annual Submission OF MWD Blood and Serum FOR Archival Banking 22
Laboratory 22
Nutrition Issues 25
Exercise and the Obstacle Course 35
Working Bite Quarantine 36
CBRN Considerations with MWDS 36
MWD Case Consultation with DODMWDVS 36
MWD Referral to DODMWDVS 37
MWD Referral for Civilian Care 37
Euthanasia or Death of MWDS 38

CHAPTER 4. EMERGENCY MEDICINE 40
Overview of Emergent and Critical Care 40
Emergency Preparedness Is Critical for Success 40
Cardiopulmonary Resuscitation (CPR) Guidelines 41
(See MWD CPGS Chapter 5) 41
Gastric Dilatation-Volvulus (GDV) Syndrome 42
(See MWD CPGs Chapter 8) 42
Mesenteric Volvulus 43
(See MWD CPGs Chapter 8) 43
Heat Related Injuries 44
(See MWD CPGs Chapter 9) 44
Hemorrhagic Shock 45
(See MWD CPGs Chapter 6) 45
Upper Airway Obstruction 46
(See MWD CPGs Chapter 3) 46
Blunt Chest Trauma 46
(See MWD CPGs Chapter 4) 46
Blunt and Penetrating Abdominal Trauma 48
(See MWD CPGs Chapter 7) 48
Anaphylactic Shock 49
Insect and Snake Envenomation 50
(See MWD CPGs Chapter 11) 50

CHAPTER 5. COMMON MEDICAL PROBLEMS 52
Skin 52
Ears 57
Eyes 59
Infectious Diseases of Military Working Dogs 60
Gastrointestinal Disease 64
Cardiac Disease 68
Respiratory Tract Disease 71
Urogenital Disease 72

CHAPTER 6. DIAGNOSTIC IMAGING 75
Radiation Safety 75
Digital Radiography 75
Technique Charts 78
Abdominal Radiography of MWDS 81
Elbow Radiography of MWDS 82
Pelvic Radiography of MWDS 82

ii ★ CONTENTS

Thoracic Radiography of Mwds 83
Spine Radiography of Mwds 84
Radiographic Contrast/Special Procedures 85
Ultrasound 90
Computed Tomography (CT) vs. Magnetic Resonance Imaging (MRI) 93
Computed Tomography 94
Magnetic Resonance Imaging 96
Radiographic Referral Procedures and Practical Teleradiology 99

CHAPTER 7. SURGERY 102
Overview of Common Surgical Procedures for the Mwd 102
Tail Amputation (CAUDECTOMY) 102
Scrotal Ablation 103
Exploratory Laparotomy 104
Intestinal Resection and Anastomosis 104
Gastropexy 105
Partial Gastrectomy 106
Splenectomy 107
Guide to Ordering MWD Videos 107

CHAPTER 8
DENTISTRY 108
Overview of Dental Care for Mwds 108
Dental Examinations 108
Dental Records 108
Dental Fractures 108
Periodontal Disease 110
Dental Prophylaxis 110
Handler Level Dental Care 111

CHAPTER 9. PHYSICAL CONDITIONING 112
Overview 112
Physical Demands on MWDS 112
Musculoskeletal Injuries 112
Physiological Responses to Conditioning 113
Principles of Conditioning 114
Exercise Prescription: Duration, Frequency, Intensity and Progression 118
Conditioning and Injury Prevention in MWDS 119

CHAPTER 10. BEHAVIORAL MEDICINE 120
Background 120
Overview of Diagnosis and Treatment of Behavior Disorders 120
Common Problems 122
Evaluation of Behavioral Disorders 122
Medical Causes for Behavior Problems 123
Diagnosis and Initial Treatment 123
Preventative Strategies 124
Consultation and Referral Information 127

CHAPTER 11. DISPOSITION 129
Definition 129
Process 129
Documentation Requirements 131
MWD Transfer/Adoption Guidelines 133

CHAPTER 12. NECROPSY AND PATHOLOGY SUPPORT 135
Actions Prior to Necropsy 135
Necropsy 136

APPENDIX A. REFERENCES 140
Section I. Required Publications 140
Section II. Related Publications 140
Section III. Referenced Forms 141
Section III. Selected Bibliography 142

APPENDIX B. SEQUENCE OF FORMS FOR MWD VETERINARY HEALTH RECORD 144

APPENDIX C. CARDIOPULMONARY RESUSCIATATION (CPR) ALGORITHM FOR MWDS 146

APPENDIX D. STEP-BY-STEP MRI GUIDELINES 147

APPENDIX E. INFORMATION FOR UPLOADING FILES FOR TRANSFER TO VIA AMRDEC SAFE 149

APPENDIX F
   EXAMPLE OF ATTENDING VCO DISPOSITION MEMORANDUM 151

APPENDIX G. EXAMPLE OF 64F DISPOSITION MEMORANDUM 152

APPENDIX H. EXAMPLE OF MWD MEDICAL DEPLOYMENT CATEGORY MEMORANDUM
.... 153

APPENDIX I. CANINE – TACTICAL COMBAT CASUALTY CARD (CTCCC) 155

GLOSSARY
   Section I 157
   Acronyms 157

CHAPTER 1

INTRODUCTION

PURPOSE AND SCOPE

1. The purpose of this document is to provide basic information pertinent to successfully managing the health and welfare of Department of Defense (DOD) Military Working Dogs (MWD). The material is directed toward Army Veterinary Corps veterinarians and animal care technicians, both military and civilian, that have primary responsibility for the care of these animals. However, it may be useful to others who work within the working dog community such as handlers, kennel masters (KM), dog-owning unit commanders, MWD program managers, and civilian veterinarians not employed by the Army providing care for MWDs and other federal working dogs.
2. This publication attempts to consolidate medical information, policies, procedures and regulatory directives specific to the medical management of MWDs into one document. This document is not, however, intended to be a veterinary medical text, therefore relevant applicable technical resources are essential. Army Veterinary Corps Officers have researched, extracted, and compiled the material from a variety of references from all services and standards of veterinary practice within the United States. In consonance with the Army Veterinary Medical Standardization Board (VMSB) process, information is evidence-based whenever possible.

REFERENCES

See appendix A.

ABBREVIATIONS AND TERMS

See the glossary.

OVERVIEW OF THE DOD MWD PROGRAM

1. Role of Services, Agencies and Organizations. The DOD MWD Program has the participation of all the branches of the Armed Forces. The United States Air Force (USAF) is the largest user of MWDs and has been designated as the DOD Executive Agent (EA) for the MWD program. The Army is the DOD Lead Agent for veterinary public and animal health services and as such, works closely with all services to support their respective programs. Specific roles of the various service elements include:
    a. Office of the Director, USAF Security Forces (USAF/A7S). USAF/A7S acts as the DOD Executive Agent for Military Working Dogs, represents MWD program interests at the Joint Service level, and designates the DOD MWD Program Manager (PM) as Chair of the Joint Services Military Working Dog Committee (JSMWDC). This office is also responsible for ensuring appropriate coordination between DOD and other federal agencies for utilization of canine resources to meet security and resource protection requirements.
    b. U.S. Army Veterinary Service (AVS). Provides veterinary support to all services and is responsible for ensuring MWDs receive full medical care irrespective of installation assigned or facility location. Veterinary Corps Officers (VCO) and Civilian Department of the Army General

Service Veterinary Medical Officers (GS-VMO) perform requisite exams, treatments and surgery as necessary, specify diets to be fed, advise on operational use, and, in concert with the owning unit, are responsible for the health and welfare of MWDs at the unit level in accordance with (IAW) applicable service regulations. Civilian Non-Appropriated Fund Veterinary Medical Officers (NAF-VMOs) may provide care to MWDs when VCOs or VMOs are not available on a reimbursable basis. Within this guide, "VCO" means VCOs and GS-VMOs and "technician" means both military Animal Care Specialists (MOS 68T) and Civilian Department of the Army veterinary technicians.

 c. Joint Services MWD Committee (JSMWDC). This committee, chaired by the DOD MWD Program Manager, is comprised of MWD program representatives from each military service branch. It meets semiannually to discuss MWD policy and operational issues to include training requirements, inventory management, unfilled MWD requisitions, certification procedures, veterinary support, etc. The JSMWDC is the policy development arm of the overall MWD program. The Director, Department of Defense Military Working Dog Veterinary Service (DODMWDVS), serves on the committee as a voting member.

 d. Air Force Security Forces Center (AFSFC). Headquartered at JBSA-Lackland, TX, this office administers the DOD and USAF MWD Programs and coordinates activities with AF major commands (MAJCOMs) and the other services. DOD taskings to support other federal agencies in National Special Security Events and Presidential protection missions originate from U.S. Secret Service (USSS) through this office and are passed on to the services for execution. This office is also responsible for ensuring appropriate coordination between DOD and other federal agencies for utilization of canine resources to meet security and force protection requirements.

 e. Service/Command MWD Program Managers. These individuals are senior personnel with MWD program experience designated at the headquarters level of their respective services to oversee MWD activities. They coordinate and advise on distribution and disposition of MWDs within their respective service branch or major command. The Program Managers are extremely important in their role of coordinating taskings for their MWD teams.

 f. 341st Training Squadron (341 TRS). This is the unit designation for the DOD MWD Training Center (commonly referred to as "the Dog Center") at JBSA-Lackland, TX. It is a subordinate unit of the 37th Training Group of the 37th Training Wing. Most DOD MWDs and handlers are trained through this unit. The 341 TRS procures, trains, distributes and manages disposition of dogs. The Operations Flight is composed of personnel from all services and is responsible for all dog and handler training. The Logistics Flight is charged with procuring dogs, conducting training evaluations on prospective dogs, shipping and receiving MWDs, and performing kennel care functions (feeding, grooming, cleaning, etc.) to support the dogs at JBSA-Lackland.

 g. Department of Defense Military Working Dog Veterinary Service (DODMWDVS). This Army unit is part of the Army Medical Command, but functions operationally as the 341 TRS Veterinary Service Flight (341 TRS/SGV). It has the mission of providing full veterinary support to the MWD Training Center and for comprehensive referral and consultation service to the MWD program worldwide. The Director, DODMWDVS advises the Defense Health Agency Veterinary Services (DHAVS) on veterinary aspects of MWD issues and drafts MWD policies for issue by DHAVS.

2. Interaction with other Federal Agencies. There is much interaction between the DOD MWD programs and other Federal Agencies, particularly with the Department of Homeland Security; specifically, the Transportation Security Agency (TSA), Customs and Border Protection (CBP), and the United States Secret Service (USSS). These groups may work together with the military services operationally on joint missions, participate in procurement and/or training with the 341 TRS, and utilize Army Veterinary Services. Provision of veterinary medical care by VCOs is defined by

Interagency Agreements (IAG), Memoranda of Understanding (MOU) or Agreement (MOA) between Army Medical Command (MEDCOM) and the specific federal agency. VCOs should be familiar with currently applicable care and reimbursement standards for federal non-DOD working dogs in their area. Every effort should be made by veterinary units to support these federal canine programs IAW published agreements in the interest of sharing government resources; however, this support should be appropriately prioritized with other military responsibilities. These dogs may be referred to the DODMWDVS for definitive care based on the IAG, but transportation is the responsibility of the respective agency. Generally, agreements will not be created locally by any veterinary organization. However, exceptions may apply so discuss potential new agreements with the chain of command prior to entering into any.

    a. Transportation Security Agency. TSA canines are evaluated, procured, medically processed and trained at the TSA Canine Training Center, JBSA-Lackland, TX. The TSA National Explosives Detection Canine Program trains and deploys both TSA-led and state and local law enforcement-led canine teams in support of day-to-day activities that protect the transportation system. TSA trains canine teams to operate in the aviation, multimodal, maritime, mass transit, and cargo environments. Considered the "center for excellence" for explosives detection canine training, the program is the largest explosives detection canine program in the Department of Homeland Security and the second largest in the federal government after the Department of Defense. The TSA has canine teams located at various major transportation facilities within and outside CONUS to assist in security and explosive detection.

    b. U.S. Secret Service. The USSS's Canine Detection Training Program provides the highest level of explosive detection training and produces canine teams that are able to protect the President and our nation's leaders, visiting heads of state and government, and National Special Security Events, in all environments and under all conditions. Many times, USSS works with DOD MWD teams to perform their mission.

    c. United States Customs and Border Protection. The CBP is the unified border agency of the United States Department of Homeland Security (DHS). CBP Canine Program is headquartered in El Paso, Texas and oversees two training delivery sites in El Paso, Texas and Front Royal, Virginia. The primary goal of the CBP Canine Program is terrorist detection and apprehension. The working CBP canine team has become the best tool available to detect and apprehend persons attempting entry to organize, incite, and carry out acts of terrorism. Their secondary goal is detection and seizure of controlled substances and other contraband. The CBP agriculture detector dog teams are trained at the USDA's National Detector Dog Training Center in Atlanta.

3. Functions of MWDs. Since the end of the Vietnam conflict, the operational use of MWDs within the DOD has essentially been vested in military police/security forces units. In this capacity, MWDs have performed primarily law enforcement and security functions. The concept of training MWDs for proficiency in two tasks was implemented in the mid-1970s and led to the development of the dual trained "patrol-detector dog." However, conflicts in Iraq and Afghanistan brought other types of dogs into the inventory to serve with non-law enforcement/security personnel and units. Further, some programs have considerable contractor involvement and are quite different in how they operate from the standard MWD which belongs to DOD law enforcement/security units. The following categories of MWDs have been trained and are in the DOD inventory:

    a. DOD-owned and DOD-operated program dogs (current programs).

        i. Patrol Dogs (PD). MWDs that are trained for the single purpose of performing security and law enforcement functions such as controlled aggression, scouting, resource protection, building searches, etc. These dogs are not trained or certified to detect drugs or explosives. They are utilized for foot patrol in high crime areas and perimeter patrol to augment security programs for resource and personnel protection. These dogs are handled on-leash except when released to interdict a suspect.

ii. Patrol/Drug Detector Dogs (PDDD). In addition to patrol capabilities, these dogs are trained to detect illegal drugs.

iii. Patrol/Explosive Detector Dogs (PEDD). In addition to patrol capabilities, these dogs are trained and certified to detect many different explosive substance odors. PEDDs are used to search and secure areas for explosive devices, particularly aircraft/terminals, VIP offices, vehicles, etc. They are frequently called on to assist the USSS in providing security and have been used extensively in other counter-terrorism missions.

iv. Patrol/Explosive Detector Dogs - Extended (PEDD-E). In addition to PEDD capability, these dogs have been trained to perform their detection function off leash at variable distance from the handler. This is an "add on" capability trained at the Advanced MWD Course. These dogs are trained through periodic use of the electronic collar. Within the Army, use of the electronic collar is restricted by ALARACT 070/2017 to use by/for dog teams specifically trained at the Advanced MWD Course. Note: VCOs should consider discussing host nation regulations addressing electronic collar use with KMs or MWD PMs. Technically, this is outside the responsibility of the VCO but is important for situational awareness.

v. Explosive or Drug Detector Dogs (EDD or DDD). A small number of single-purpose detector dogs are trained each year. Sporting breeds and occasionally small terriers may be used for this category of MWD. The dogs are only trained for detection of either explosives or narcotics. These dogs are handled on-leash to search.

vi. Specialized Search Dogs (SSD). These dogs are trained to detect explosives and generally are handled off-leash to search. Currently they are found in the United States Marine Corps (USMC) only.

vii. Mine Detection Dogs (MDD). These dogs are trained to detect explosives (mines) in a minefield and are handled on-leash to search. The method employed for searching is generally in a straight line clearing a narrow path. Currently they are found in the Army only.

viii. Combat Tracker Dog (CTD). These dogs are trained to track human scent and are handled off-leash. Currently they are found in the USMC only.

ix. Multi-Purpose Canine (MPC). These dogs can perform patrol and detection duties and are utilized within Special Operations Forces. The MPCs procurement and disposition process is through the SOF and not through the 341 TRS. The SOF unit's VCO provides much of their medical care, but they can be seen at a VTF and are authorized care identical to traditional MWDs.

b. DOD-owned, contractor-operated program dogs. (Note that these programs have been deactivated and no dogs currently exist in the inventory. These programs may be reactivated if needed in the future to meet surge requirements)

i. Improvised Explosive Device Detector Dogs (IDD). This USMC program utilized Labrador Retrievers trained to detect explosives and generally handled off-leash to search. The difference from SSD is that the dogs are not handled by professional dog handlers, but rather infantrymen or engineers given training and temporarily assigned as handlers. These dogs were dispositioned from the inventory as they

redeployed from the CENTCOM Theater and no replacements will be trained.
  ii. Tactical Explosive Detector Dogs (TEDD). This Army program utilized a variety of sporting and shepherd breeds. Similar to the IDD program, these dogs were trained to detect explosives and generally handled off-leash to search. These dogs were also handled by infantrymen given training and temporarily assigned as handlers. These dogs were dispositioned from the inventory as they redeployed from the CENTCOM Theater and no replacements will be trained.
4. Procurement, Training, and Inventory Management
   a. Procurement. MWDs are obtained by the 341 TRS from vendors primarily in the United States and Europe. The majority of the dogs considered for purchase are Belgian Malinois and German Shepherd Dogs. A lesser number of Dutch/Belgian Shepherd dogs are presented for evaluation and a few sporting breeds and small breeds are purchased for use as single-purpose detectors. The procurement process is conducted by the Consignment Section of the 341 TRS Logistics Flight and the DODMWDVS. The Veterinary and Consignment sections perform the medical and temperament evaluations to ensure prospective MWDs meet specific criteria. Standard criteria has been developed from years of observations of performance and analysis of training data in order to meet the objective of maximizing the functional life span of MWDs. When dogs are purchased and trained for DOD, they are expected to work to approximately 10 years of age. It is very important financially and ethically to accept dogs into the DOD MWD program that can be easily trained and can remain serviceable for many years. However, the most important factor is that the dog can do the job required, so some dogs showing great aptitude that are imperfect physically (e.g. mild orthopedic dysplasia) may still be procured. Final determination of whether a dog is acquired rests with the Air Force and not DODMWDVS. Specifically, the procurement process involves:
      i. Medical Evaluation. This evaluation is oriented toward checking for conditions that may be debilitating or will likely compromise the functional life span of the potential MWD. Dogs with poor conformation, poor dental health, lameness, evident heart murmurs or indications of chronic dermatological, otic, ophthalmic, renal, or gastrointestinal disease are eliminated based on physical examination, hematology, serum biochemistry, urinalysis, heartworm testing and fecal exam. Other diagnostics (ECG, echocardiogram, special serum chemistry or immune testing, etc.) may be conducted in some cases as indicated.
      ii. Radiographic Evaluation. Vendors are required to provide recent radiographs of dogs offered for procurement for veterinary assessment. If none are provided, local veterinarians or AVS personnel will perform required survey radiographs under sedation to include evaluation of pelvis, lumbosacral spine, and elbows. While sedated a complete oral exam and palpation for coxofemoral laxity is indicated. Prospective MWDs are recommended for rejection if there is evidence of hip or elbow dysplasia, transitional vertebrae, or past orthopedic or dental injury that may compromise future MWD service.
      iii. Temperament Evaluation. Consignment section personnel from the 341 TRS conduct a temperament evaluation on dogs that are medically acceptable for MWD service.
      iv. Consignment period. A timeframe for trainers to objectively evaluate search behavior, detector ability, aggressiveness, and potential trainability.
      v. Final Acceptance. Dogs meeting medical and training criteria are officially accepted, given a permanent tattoo number and assigned an ideal weight range. Intact females

and cryptorchid males are neutered at this time, any necessary dental care is performed, and all dogs receive a prophylactic gastropexy. Dogs enter training following recovery.

  vi. Training. New MWDs are entered into training as soon as possible. They are assigned to a training team and a specific trainer within the Operations Flight. Time in training is approximately 80-120 training days with dual trained dogs taking longer than single purpose dogs. MWDs are certified against established standards for the tasks trained.

 b. Distribution and Inventory Management. All distribution and inventory management of MWDs is the responsibility of the Logistics Flight Inventory Manager. Upon certification, MWDs are designated available for shipment to fill official requisitions from DOD customers. Each branch of service requests MWDs based on need and their requisitions are maintained by the Logistics Flight Inventory Manager. MWDs are distributed to the units at the direction of each service/branch MWD coordinator. Dogs may be moved from one installation to another by the respective service program managers as missions dictate; excess dogs may also occasionally be returned to JBSA-Lackland for redistribution. All movements are coordinated with the 341 TRS MWD Inventory Manager who maintains a listing of all MWDs and their locations.

OTHER WORKING DOGS

1. Interaction with other Nations. MWDs belonging to allied nations (NATO, etc.) are key assets in deployed environments and are often supported by US AVS personnel, and current strategic policy makes these interactions increasingly likely. The issues these allied MWDs face are similar to MWDs so this document can assist supporting them as authorized as well as provide proficiency-building opportunities for AVS personnel. VCOs must coordinate with their command to ensure protocols are followed to ensure US government reimbursement, and future AVS resourcing as necessary.

2. Contract Working Dogs (CWDs) are not specifically addressed in this MWD Handbook but must be mentioned as they are common assets in deployed environments. The issues these CWDs face are similar to MWDs so this document can assist supporting them as authorized as well as provide proficiency-building opportunities for AVS personnel. VCOs must coordinate with their command to be aware of which dogs they are authorized to treat on a routine/preventive and/or emergency basis due to contract agreements, and ensure protocols are followed to ensure government reimbursement and future AVS resourcing as necessary. CWDs will be seen as a lower priority than MWDs, though authorized emergency cases may be triaged as a higher priority subject to contract agreements. If any ambiguity exists as to the appropriateness of treating a CWD that is presented to a veterinary care team, treat the dog while ascertaining the status of contract agreements.

CHAPTER 2

EQUIPMENT AND FACILITIES

PURPOSE

The purpose of this chapter is to clarify capabilities among the various DOD veterinary facilities around the world that provide veterinary care to MWDs at the installation level. Additionally, this chapter will convey information regarding obtaining medical equipment for MWD care. The Director of DODMWDVS establishes the following minimum standards for MWD care. Veterinary care of MWDs requires that VCOs are able to:
1. Conduct physical examinations
2. Obtain and interpret the results of routine clinical pathological tests
3. Prescribe, administer and dispense medications
4. Safely perform anesthesia and surgery
5. Perform Comprehensive Oral Health Assessment and Treatment (COHAT)
6. Expose, process, and interpret radiographs (including dental radiographs)
7. Confine MWDs for short-term hospitalization
8. Provide emergency care
9. Conduct necropsy examinations
10. Maintain Veterinary Health Records (VHR) in an electronic medical record or deployment hard-copy VHR (see Chapter 3).

TIERING STANDARDS

All veterinary facilities across the DOD do not possess the same capabilities, staffing, and equipment. Installation mission requirements, number of MWDs supported, and various other factors play into how a facility is equipped and/or staffed. The following tiers (in order of increasing capability) have been established by the VMSB:
1. Veterinary Clinic (VC). No permanent active duty military assigned at these facilities with an emphasis on providing wellness/preventive medicine services. Surgical/dentistry services will not be readily available at these facilities. An equivalent to this type of facility in civilian veterinary practice would be what is generally considered to be a satellite clinic.
2. Veterinary Treatment Facility (VTF). Most veterinary facilities are tiered as a VTF with at least one permanently assigned VCO, and at least a 2:1 technician to doctor ratio, with in-house surgical/dentistry capabilities as well as laboratory analysis and radiology capabilities.
3. Veterinary Activity (VETAC). Same as VTF capabilities with the additional staffing of a Veterinary Clinical Specialist (64F). Have an increased surgical capability and hospitalization capability.
4. Veterinary Center (VETCEN). Same as VETAC with the additional staffing of a Veterinary Preventive Medicine Specialist (64B) and may have a First Year Graduate Veterinary Education (FYGVE) training program. They have the ability to perform advanced surgical/medical procedures, referrals, and consultations.

EQUIPMENT REQUIREMENTS

Equipment standards for each tier are also published by the VMSB and can be accessed via the Army Veterinary Services' milSuite site at:
https://www.milsuite.mil/book/community/spaces/armyveterinaryservices,
under VMSB. These standards provide guidance on what equipment is required, recommended model, and sourcing information for each veterinary facility based on tier. When submitting purchase requests for facilities, one should ensure that equipment purchases are commensurate with the tiering of that particular facility. All commanders are responsible for allocating resources and aligning personnel and equipment to provide full care to MWDs. For example, within MEDCOM, Public Health Command (PHC) Regional Commanders allocate resources for MWD care. Each Public Health Activity Commander (PHA) has responsibility for aligning their resources (equipment, facilities, and personnel) to ensure that consistently high-quality veterinary care is available for all MWD's within their area of responsibility. Below are the minimum equipment requirements that meet the standard of care:

1. Conduct physical examination. Exam table, stethoscope, thermometer, exam light (fixed or portable), scale, otoscope and ophthalmoscope.
2. Obtain the results of routine clinical pathological tests. Microscope, refractometer, microhematocrit centrifuge, stain kit for cytology, reagent dipsticks for screening blood/urine tests, CBC, and basic clinical chemistry. The capability to obtain more sophisticated diagnostic testing (endocrinology, serology, immunology, detailed urinalysis, and clinical microbiology) may be met by submitting samples to an outside laboratory. Some laboratory support can be obtained from a local Military Medical Treatment Facility (MTF) laboratory but many of the tests conducted on MWDs are not valid when completed in a lab equipped and calibrated for examination of human samples; therefore, the use of a commercial veterinary reference laboratory is necessary and use of human laboratories should be avoided (See Chapter 3 for more information).
3. Prescribe, administer and dispense medications. Properly stored controlled drugs (GSA approved safe) should be available for anesthetic induction, analgesia and euthanasia. The VMSB formulary dictates the current inventory of products available for procurement and use in its most currently published document which can be found on the Army Veterinary Services' milSuite site. MWDs are considered Service members for the purpose of receiving prescription medications from MTF pharmacies. This option should be used when appropriate for generic or non-veterinary labeled medications are indicated in a therapeutic regimen for an MWD. When veterinary label medications are available, use of human (near) equivalents from the MTF may not be in compliance with current veterinary standards of practice and FDA extra label drug use directives. It is recommended that a joint SOP for MTF prescriptions be completed by the responsible VCO and MTF Pharmacist so that prescriptions can be filled in a timely manner. Most commonly, a requirement exists for the VCO to register with the MTF pharmacy as a provider and for the MWD to be entered into the medical system database. To input an MWD into the database, access the non-human registration (NHR) field. Last Name should be "MWDOG", First Name should be the actual name of the MWD (i.e. "Rex"), followed by a space and the tattoo number. Enter sex and date of birth. Under SSN, enter the final 9 digits of the microchip number. Patient Category should be listed as K99 (patient not elsewhere classified). This non-human patient can now be "arrived" and procedures selected as with a normal patient. For veterinary specific medications not available through the MTF, or if the need for medications through a compounding pharmacy arises, consult with the supporting 64F for guidance.
4. Safely perform anesthesia and surgery. Pre-anesthetic medications, properly-sized endotracheal tubes/anesthetic mask, laryngoscope, bag valve mask (BVM), gas anesthetic machine with oxygen source and isoflurane vaporizer, waste anesthetic gas scavenging capability, anesthetic monitor (at a minimum the vital signs monitor should have continuous ECG trace, pulse oximetry, capnography,

non-invasive blood pressure measurement, and core temperature sensor), surgery lights (fixed or portable), scrub sink, surgery preparation area, surgery table capable of "V" positioning, general elective surgery packs, autoclave, patient warming system (i.e., forced air heating blanket or conductive fabric blanket), suction apparatus with sterile tips/tubing, and electrosurgical system.
5. Perform comprehensive oral health assessment and treatment. Clean teeth, perform extractions and evaluate dental health. Chapter 8 Dentistry and the VMSB COHAT guidelines clarify MWD dental procedures as well as supplies and equipment standards based on tier which can be found on the Army Veterinary Services' milSuite site and Remote Online Veterinary Record (ROVR) system.
6. Expose, process, and interpret radiographs. 300mAs/125kVP digital radiology machine (DR), dosimetry badges (or equivalent radiation monitoring program if required through local MTF), radio-opaque markers, radiolucent positioning devices, and personal protection apparel (lead-lined aprons, thyroid shield, gloves, partitions).
7. Confine MWDs for short-term hospitalization. Large cage and/or separate run in a climate- controlled room/kennel, which is separate from hospitalization areas for privately owned animals.
8. Provide emergency care. Emergency crash cart which contains emergency drugs and supplies to aid in hemorrhage control, airway management to include supplemental oxygen, intravenous access supplies, orogastric tube (foal-sized nasogastric tube), and wound management (casting material, cast cutter, splints, and bandage material). Additionally, crash carts fully stocked with emergency medications should be present before performing surgical procedures on MWDs.
9. Conduct necropsy. Exam light, table (prefer wet table), knives/scalpels, scissors, forceps, electric bone saw, various sized-containers, 10% neutral buffered formalin, specimen cassettes, and a digital camera to capture pictures of lesions (See Chapter 12 and see TB Med 283).
10. Maintain Veterinary Health Records. Internet connection to access the electronic veterinary medical record database, access to appropriate references, forms, documents, and policies for upkeep of the VHR.

PROGRAMS AND FUNDS

1. Medical equipment used in care of MWDs is purchased with appropriated funds. Usually such equipment (if it is of sufficient dollar value and durability) will also be entered on the supporting MTF or PHC Region Property Book and accounted for on the facility's hand-receipt. The PHC Region budget includes funding for medical equipment. Historically, Regional Commanders receive a share of the funding and must carefully prioritize the equipment requests submitted by their Public Health Activity (PHA) Commanders in order to purchase the most critical equipment first. Equipment requests should be well justified by documenting any significant clinical risks to personnel or compromise MWD care.
2. The most common mechanism to obtain medical equipment is the capital expense equipment program (CEEP). This program is a centralized program designed to approve and acquire equipment required to support health care activities. Thresholds for these particular programs are for items costing less than $100,000 (CEEP), $100-$250,000 (Super-CEEP), and those items greater than $250,000 (MEDCASE). Given that nuances may exist as per the specific steps for requesting equipment from one command to another, it is prudent to coordinate with the supporting command for further details. A generic description of steps the end user takes in this process is as follows:
    a. End user identifies the need for equipment through equipment lifecycle replacement program
    b. Research options through VMSB for equipment solutions.
    c. Submit requirement through the CEEP process.
    d. Send receiving documentation to command POC once items are received.
3. Non-Appropriated Fund (NAF) Equipment. Medical equipment that was purchased by the NAF for

use on privately owned animal patients is also used for MWD care. In the past, some large equipment items (usually x-ray machines and anesthesia machines) that were originally justified for privately owned animal care and purchased by the NAF were transferred to the appropriated fund hand receipt so that the local MTF Logistics branch could more reliably accomplish ongoing medical maintenance. With the Global Veterinary Medical Practice (GVMP), certain equipment may be acquired through central contracts. With a central contract, durable equipment is leased and maintained by the vendor. This equipment will not be transferred to the APF hand receipt and will not be maintained by medical maintenance.

SPECIAL CONSIDERATIONS

1. Equipment requests must include the specifications of a particular item of equipment and a suggested source. In some cases, there may be unique requirements for installation of the equipment item in a facility. These include specific electrical power requirements (voltage and amperage which varies per country), other utilities requirements (water, drains, temperature range, etc.), minimum space requirements and necessary structural modifications that should also be addressed. Another important consideration is the anticipated maintenance requirements – will the MTF Medical Maintenance service the equipment or will a contractor service it? The latter requires budgeting for future maintenance costs. Also consider whether the equipment will need connection to the communications network. Coordinate with local Information Technology (IT) support elements to ensure necessary certificates of net worthiness are obtained. Coordinate with the command to determine the documentation requirements.
2. The supporting Region or MTF maintains the property book accounting for all equipment on the facility's hand receipt and also assumes responsibility for performing certain preventive maintenance and calibration procedures on medical equipment. Each item of equipment should be labeled with the equipment control number (ECN) and a due date for scheduled maintenance. Typically, the facility's NCOIC assumes responsibility for both accountability of equipment as well as ensuring that scheduled maintenance is performed on time. Inhalant vaporizers typically must be shipped back to the manufacturer for annual calibration. For this reason, even small VTFs should have a minimum of two vaporizers on hand so that when one is shipped for maintenance, the remaining vaporizer will be available for use. Initial durable equipment necessary to meet the MWD mission is to be purchased with APFs. Associated expendable supplies and additional equipment may be purchased with NAFs.
3. All equipment items have an anticipated duration of serviceability. When formulating a list of equipment for purchase it is recommended to plan for turnover of equipment as a part of its life cycle. Example: if a dental unit is scheduled to reach its end date of serviceability, submitting for a replacement item prior to reaching that end date would be prudent in ensuring there is no lapse in equipment coverage. Once items reach their anticipated end date, medical maintenance personnel will typically no longer repair or maintain these items. Equipment end date of serviceability information can be furnished by medical maintenance personnel.

MEDICAL SUPPLIES

1. Medical supplies and commonly used pharmaceuticals are purchased and stocked in the VTF by NAF for POA care. When drugs and supplies are used for MWD care the NAF is reimbursed for their costs. Drugs and supplies used to treat a government-owned animal (GOA) must be linked to an individual treatment plan. Reimbursement is performed centrally. To ensure accurate accounting, a GOA transfer between activity (TBA) report must be completed and submitted to NAF Financial

Services or Central Accounting Office at the end of each calendar month. GVMP furnishes guidance on performing this end of month report, but a summary of the steps involved are as follows:
   a. On the first working day of the month, print a Transaction Summary Report in ROVR.
   b. Open the GOA TBA excel spreadsheet to generate the report for each respective location.
   c. Enter information from the report in the corresponding areas as applicable.
   d. Review the report for accuracy.
   e. Print, verify, and sign the TBA report.
   f. Submit the report to NAF Management Analyst to get PHC Region approval.
   g. Submit invoice to PHA supporting budget office for payment to GVMP.
2. Medical supplies (e.g. compounded medications, orthopedic devices) or services (specialized laboratory testing) used solely for the purpose of MWDs must be purchased with appropriated funds. These may either be obtained through the supporting MTF or PHA.

TEXTBOOKS

Below are the suggested reference materials that should be available to the VCO who is caring for MWDs listed in no particular order, alternatives are acceptable. These textbooks and periodicals listed as "Primary References" may be ordered with appropriated funds as essential references for MWD care. Reference books may also be ordered through the NAF, but they must be justified as supporting the privately-owned animal mission. Additionally, consulting the "AMEDD Virtual Library" (https://medlinet.amedd.army.mil/vetmed.htm) is encouraged as this site contains electronic texts and journals that may be accessed with CAC log in.

1. Primary References (latest edition)
   a. Veterinary Drug Handbook, Plumb (Iowa State University Press)
   b. Atlas of Radiographic Anatomy of the Dog and Cat, Schebitz & Wilkens (Verlag/Saunders)
   c. Atlas of Small Animal Ultrasonography, Penninck (Wiley)
   d. Canine and Feline Cytology: A Color Atlas and Interpretation Guide, Raskin & Meyer (Elsevier)
   e. Clinical Behavioral Medicine for Small Animals, Overall (Mosby)
   f. Clinical Textbook for Veterinary Technicians, Miller & McCurnin (Saunders) FM 8-52
   g. Control of Communicable Diseases in Man, Bennison (American Public Health Association) FM 8-33
   h. Essentials of Veterinary Ophthalmology, Gelatt (Wiley)
   i. Five-Minute Veterinary Consult, Tilley & Smith (Williams & Wilkins)
   j. Handbook of Veterinary Anesthesia, Muir et al (Mosby)
   k. Handbook of Veterinary Neurology, Lorenz & Kornegay (Saunders)
   l. Handbook of Veterinary Procedures and Emergency Treatment, Kirk, Bistner, & Ford (Saunders)
   m. Infectious Diseases of the Dog and Cat, Greene (Saunders)
   n. Muller & Kirk's Small Animal Dermatology. Scott, Miller & Griffin (Saunders)
   o. Small Animal Clinical Diagnosis by Laboratory Methods, Willard, Tvedten & Turnwald (Saunders)
   p. Small Animal Critical Care Medicine, Silverstein & Hopper (Elsevier)
   q. Small Animal Dental Equipment, Materials and Techniques: A Primer, Bellows (Wiley-Blackwell)
   r. Small Animal Internal Medicine, Nelson & Couto (Mosby)
   s. Small Animal Surgery, Fossum (Mosby)
2. Additional Recommended References

a. Behavior Problems of the Dog and Cat, Landsberg & Huinthausen (Saunders)
   b. Canine and Feline Skin Cytology, Albanese (Springer)
   c. Canine Rehabilitation and Physical Therapy, Mills et al (Saunders)
   d. Manual of Small Animal Soft Tissue Surgery, Tobias (Wiley-Blackwell)
   e. Merck Veterinary Manual
   f. Miller's Anatomy of the Dog, Evans & de Lahunta (Elsevier)
   g. Small Animal Clinical Nutrition; Hand, Thatcher, Remillard, & Roudebush (Mark Morris Institute)
   h. Small Animal Clinical Pharmacology and Therapeutics, Boothe (Saunders)
   i. Small Animal Oral Medicine and Surgery, Bojrab & Tholen (Lea & Febiger)
   j. Small Animal Medical Diagnosis, Lorenz, Neer, DeMars (Lippincott Williams & Wilkins)
   k. Textbook of Veterinary Internal Medicine, Ettinger & Feldman (Saunders)
   l. Veterinary Dental Techniques for the Small Animal Practitioner, Holstrom, Frost & Eisner (Saunders)
   m. Veterinary Surgery Small Animal, Johnston & Tobias (Elsevier)
   n. Withrow & MacEwen's Small Animal Clinical Oncology, Withrow & Vail, (Saunders)

PERIODICALS

Like textbooks, subscriptions for periodicals may be obtained through the MTF library, many of these journals are accessible via the AMEDD Virtual Library (AVL), with a My Athens Account. The veterinary periodicals which contain articles on small animal clinical medicine with potential application to MWDs, include:

1. Primary Periodical References
   a. Clinician's Brief
   b. Journal of the American Veterinary Medical Association
   c. Today's Veterinary Nurse
2. Additional Recommended Periodicals
   a. American Journal of Veterinary Research
   b. BMC Veterinary Research
   c. Canine Practice
   d. CDC Emerging Diseases
   e. DVM 360
   f. FDA Veterinarian Newsletter
   g. Journal of the American Animal Hospital Association
   h. Journal of Small Animal Practice
   i. Journal of Veterinary Emergency & Critical Care
   j. Journal of Veterinary Internal Medicine
   k. Journal of Veterinary Medicine
   l. Journal of Veterinary Science
   m. Seminars in Veterinary Medicine & Surgery (Small Animal)
   n. Transboundary & Emerging Diseases
   o. Vector-Borne and Zoonotic Diseases
   p. Veterinary Clinical Digest
   q. Veterinary Clinics of North America: Exotic Animal Practice
   r. Veterinary Clinics of North America: Equine Practice
   s. Veterinary Clinics of North America: Food Animal Practice
   t. Veterinary Clinics of North America: Small Animal Practice

u. Veterinary Medicine International
v. Veterinary Pathology
w. Veterinary Practice News
x. Veterinary Radiology and Ultrasound
y. Veterinary Surgery
z. Veterinary Technician
aa. Zoonoses & Public Health

CHAPTER 3

PREVENTIVE MEDICINE, DEPLOYMENT ISSUES, AND STANDARD PROCEDURES

HANDLING OF MWDS

All MWDs, regardless of breed or capabilities, should only be handled by individuals who have received handler training via an official military working dog handler course. All MWDs MUST be on leash and MUST be wearing a properly fitted and secured basket muzzle whenever they are in a Veterinary Facility unless hospitalized and impossible/impractical due to patient's medical condition. A certified handler will be present at all times in these cases. All handlers trained through JBSA - Lackland learn this practice as standard procedure. Bite incidents have occurred where dogs were able to extract themselves out of inadequate or poor-fitting muzzles. The fact that an MWD is not certified as a patrol dog does not mean that the dog will not bite or did not receive attack training. In fact, there are dogs in the inventory that did not certify as patrol dogs because they would not consistently release a bite or end an attack on command.

MWD RECORDS

1. Electronic Veterinary Health Record (VHR). In the spring of 2014, the Remote Online Veterinary Record (ROVR) web based veterinary record application came online. As per DODVSA/DHA policy, its use is mandated for all MWDs. Be aware that under the "Web Help" tab under the left-hand navigation pane there are several documents available and may serve as a useful resource for questions with ROVR. Whenever a specific form is mentioned throughout this document an electronic equivalent form is acceptable within the VHR.
2. When newly assigned MWDs arrive or return from deployment, the permanent hard copy record should be reviewed by the attending VCO or 68T and stored at the responsible VTF. The electronic VHR in ROVR must be updated to document the current status of the following items as described below:
    a. Master problem list (MPL): all problems must be transcribed with start and end dates if available.
    b. Current medications
    c. Vaccination records: transcribe all vaccine history.
    d. DD 1829, Record of Military Working Dog Physical Examination: transcribe most recent date into ROVR registry.
    e. FAVN test results: transcribe most recent date and results into ROVR registry and import the lab report.
    f. MWD monthly record review: performed and documented at time of arrival
    g. Laboratory results: import most recent CBC, chemistry, urinalysis, etc.
    h. Other documents associated with specific diagnosis, chronic illness or problem on MPL should be imported for electronic reference such as SF600s, SF519b for imaging results, and laboratory test results.
    i. Deployment medical history (all documents related to a dog's deployment will be scanned into ROVR as necessary).
3. Once these items have been uploaded/transcribed into the dog's record in ROVR, the following statement will be entered into the last SF 600 entry: "From this date forward, medical information for

this MWD is maintained in the ROVR". A signature will be entered by the provider following this statement.
4. Permanent VHR. With the advent of the ROVR and its mandated use for all privately-owned and government-owned animals, guidelines in this document relevant to hard copy MWD VHR are still relevant. Until the foreseeable future, MWDs coming out of procurement and initial training will still be assigned a hard copy, four-part VHR (AF Form 2110A). Additionally, when MWDs transition to a new duty station, the permanent VHR will accompany that dog and will be maintained by the new responsible VTF. Another instance of utilization of the permanent VHR may be if an MWD is seen by a civilian veterinary provider who will not have access to ROVR.
    a. Sequence of forms should be adhered to as outlined in Appendix B. A copy of this sequence of forms document typically is placed in the back of part four of the VHR for reference.
    b. ALL documents in the VHR must be identified with the MWD's Name and tattoo number, and with the location that care was provided.
5. Forms should be completed to report results of clinical pathology testing (CBC, chemistry panel, etc.) clinical or histological pathology samples (SF 515 or equivalent), surgery reports (SF 516 or equivalent) and radiological or other imaging reports (SF 519b or equivalent). These should be filed appropriately in sections 3 or 4 of VHR and imported if not already a part of the electronic VHR and must be referenced/assessed in the ccSOAP on the SF 600s.
6. SF 600-Chronologic Record of Medical Care (eNote). As the title states, the SF 600 should describe all medical care. This means that all care must be assessed, or at least cross-referenced, on the SF 600. The objective evaluation of laboratory, imaging, and other support documents should be filed appropriately and must be initialed or signed by the responsible VCO, but the assessment and plan must be written on the SF 600. The existence of DD Form 1829s, or other support documents for a given date should also be noted on the SF 600. This allows a reviewer to identify when another document is present without requiring a complete rewrite of that document's contents on the SF 600. Key aspects of SF 600 use include: MWD identification, location of care, proper ccSOAP format, notation of all prescription medications provided including parasite control medications issued to the handler, notation of Temperature/Pulse Rate/Respiration Rate/Weight (TPRW), body condition score (BCS), MWD diet, fitness for duty and deployment status statement on all patient care entries, presence of a treatment plan with checklist or other means of recording when a plan item is completed, and signature and stamp identifying the provider of care.
7. DD 1829 (MWD SAPE eNote). A DD Form 1829 will be used for documentation of semiannual physical examinations (SAPE) of MWDs and when a dog is being considered for disposition. Utilization of the DD form 1829, Record of Military Working Dog Physical Examination was replaced by the MWD SAPE eNote template found on ROVR. Selection of the "DD Form 1829" links in the Exam/Assessment/Diagnosis section of the eNote will prompt the user to insert data historically captured on the hard copy DD 1829 such as diet, handler concerns, behavior/temperament, etc. Completion of this form is self-explanatory.
8. DD Form 2619 (Master Problem List) or electronic equivalent. Any illness or injury that is recurrent, severe, or has impact on MWD performance or fitness for duty should be listed on the MPL. A recurrent problem should retain the original number but be assigned a new "date entered" and "date resolved." If the nature of the problem is nonspecifically recurrent or permanent the "date resolved" block may be lined out or left blank. Problems may be renamed or combined as appropriate. Bite quarantines will be added to the MPL. Surgical procedures should be added to the MPL usually as a resolution to a medical problem. Review of a VHR may reveal that a problem that previously existed warrants listing on the MPL and in the Surgeries\Significant Interventions section; in these cases the "date entered" should reflect the date the problem is first reported on the SF 600 and/or DD Form 1829 not necessarily the date it is entered on the MPL. Problem numbers need not be in direct

chronological order as record review may warrant addition of problems in a retroactive manner. The MWD Name and tattoo number must be entered on the MPL Form even though a designated space is not provided.

9. The Problem Oriented Medical Record or Chief Complaint, Subjective, Objective, Assessment, Plan (POMR/ccSOAP) System is used in MWD VHRs. The use of the ccSOAP format and POMR process is required by AR 40-905. Standardized ccSOAP format is necessary to promote quality and continuity of care, address special concerns, and fulfil records requirements for MWDs. While specific location and format may change in the eNote compared to the SF 600, these guidelines also apply to eNotes.

   a. Date and Vitals: When using a paper SF600 the date, weight, temperature, pulse and respirations will be recorded on the first line of each SF 600 VHR entry or under the date in the left column of the SF 600. When using ROVR a vital signs entry will be documented inside of the ccSOAP on the eNote when the MWD is physically examined.

   b. Chief Complaint (cc): The cc is brief identification of the reason that the patient was brought to the VTF by the handler. This section may be completed by the technician or clerk.

   c. Subjective (S): The technician may record the initial history from the handler before turning over the VHR and MWD to the VCO. The VCO will record additional history as appropriate, and brief observations of general progress, appearance, and mentation, e.g. BAR, dull, depressed.

   d. Objective (O): This section includes reports of significant findings, including body condition score and hydration status, from the VCO's physical examination. Normal status must be reported. In this section, a comment on all diagnostics performed and the primary findings, including negative tests and no clinical findings, will be completed. The technician should only make entries in the objective portion if they are transcribing for the VCO or no VCO is available to complete the examination.

   e. Assessment (A): This section must include a list of specific problems or a statement that there are none. Problems may be assessed individually or listed and then assessed as a group. Assessment may be in sentence format or in short bullets, but must identify the primary differential diagnosis for each problem along with key rule-outs and a brief explanation of each. If a definitive diagnosis is made, additional rule-outs need not be listed or discussed. If no problems are noted this must be specifically noted, e.g. "appears healthy, no problems identified or reported."

   f. Plan (P): The diagnostic and therapeutic plan for each problem must be updated or if no change is necessary, this must be stated. Actions taken at the time of examination and evaluation will also be recorded in this section, e.g. client education. (The use of check-boxes or other positive control measures are recommended to assure that plans are implemented correctly). The final entry in the plan for all MWDs must address fitness for duty (return to full, limited duty, or unfit) and medical deployment category.

   g. Addenda: will be dated and identified "Add:" and with the letter of the entry section being altered or completed. Addenda may only be used to report routine care previously prescribed, e.g. completion of a treatments or administration of heartworm medication, to modify the ccSOAP for that date, or to report routine monthly body weight reported by an MWD handler.

   h. Entries: will be signed and stamped with the signature block of the person making the entry. eNotes will be titled with type of note +/- chief complaint on signature page, ex. MWD Red SAPE or Sick Call Note – Diarrhea. This makes viewing specific eNotes regarding recurring problems easier in the future.

   i. Animal Care Specialists may complete entries, including ccSOAP format, if a VCO is

unavailable. If this is necessary, the technician should sign with his/her own signature block.
   j. Entries continued onto a second page will begin with the date and the word "continued."
   k. Lines should not be skipped within an entry.
   l. Each SF 600 and the first entry from a new treating VTF must list the VTF by name.
10. Deployment VHR. Deployment VHRs were created in the wake of working dogs not returning from deployment with their VHR. The concept of having both a permanent and a deployment VHR is no longer relevant now that an online repository of the dog's record can be found on ROVR. Updates to the deployment VHR should continue to be made in order to stay current with significant medical events in the life of the working dog. This is crucial so that the deployment VHR contains the most up to date medical information for that working dog. It should not be assumed that network connectivity will be sufficient in an austere, deployed setting and therefore the deployed military veterinary care team may not have access to ROVR. For this reason, the deployment VHR will be given to the handler for use in a deployed setting. Prior to giving the deployment VHR to the handler, ensure all sections of the record have been uploaded and/or transcribed into the dog's electronic record.
    a. The more complete the VHR, the better equipped the deployed VCO will be when providing care for the MWD. The handler is not always aware of the complete medical history of the MWD. The minimum requirements in a deployment VHR include the following: an up-to-date MPL, most current SAPE medical note to include the DD1829 overlays, results of most recent FAVN, vaccine history, copy of the two most recent rabies immunization certificates with a signature in blue ink, all veterinary visits over the past 90 days to include all pre-deployment evaluation and documentation of current medications and management of any chronic conditions, and health certificate at time of departure.
    b. Upon redeployment, the permanent station's veterinary team should ensure the MWD's ROVR record is brought up to date by transcribing relevant medical information into the record. This includes transcribing all problems on the MPL that occurred while deployed and closing the deployment date in the deployment section.
    c. Documents completed during the deployment such as SF 600s, SF 519B, DD2208, etc. should be uploaded into the dog's ROVR record and/or transcribed as applicable.
    d. Vaccine information (if any) should be transcribed into the immunizations history. If a rabies immunization is given during a deployment an original rabies certificate will be created by the attending VCO and signed in blue ink.
11. Elimination from Service. When an MWD has been eliminated from service through either adoption or death, the following steps should be performed in order to properly process the MWD's VHR (both hard copy and ROVR records):
    a. The Green Hard Copy Medical Record (AF Form 2110A) will be forwarded to DODMWDVS as described below in section 3-17, paragraph d. A copy of the adoption covenant or death certificate and necropsy report form (DD Form 1626, Veterinary Necropsy Report Checklist and Guidelines) will be placed in section II on top of the Master Problem List. Please ensure all forms are filed in the proper sections, chronologically, with newest on top as outlined in Appendix B.
    b. In the ROVR medical record, the following should be performed:
        i. WDMS Registry: enter EXCESS in the "WDMS Registry Comment" with effective date of the excess memo; also, enter the date the MWD was eliminated from service (due to adoption/euthanasia/death) in measure "Retirement Date."
        ii. Upload elimination documents, i.e., adoption covenant or death certificate and gross necropsy report forms.
        iii. Mark MWD patient as "INACTIVE" and email DODMWDVS Records Repository

(341TRS.SGV.MWDMedicalRecords@us.af.mil) the MWD Name, tattoo and new owner name or deceased. Once the hard copy records are received at DODMWDVS, then the record will be made "ACTIVE" to initiate the transfer of the electronic medical record to DOD Military Working Dog VS. Once transfer is complete the MWD will be marked as "INACTIVE"
    iv. Consult the supporting 64F for further questions about this process.
  c. Upon adoption, MWDs will not be converted from MWD (GOA) to POA as far as organization type is concerned. Once this rate plan is selected it cannot be undone. A new medical record will be created for this animal if the owner elects to take the retired MWD to a DOD veterinary facility. Relevant historical data from the former MWD's record, such as vaccine information, MPL, and surgeries/significant interventions will be transcribed into the new record.

PREVENTIVE MEDICINE—EXAMINATION, ASSESSMENT, VACCINATION, AND PROPHYLACTIC CARE

The most important part of a successful working dog health program is preventive medicine. Preventive medicine has the largest effect on MWD service life and performance by preventing disease and/or detecting conditions and diseases early in their course, often allowing more successful management of the disease. The ultimate goal is to ensure MWDs are medically fit for mission requirements and to remove unfit animals from the program. The different aspects of the preventive medicine program can be divided by frequency of care: daily to weekly, monthly, quarterly, semiannually, and annually. Maintenance of proper veterinary records should be a continuous activity to document the preventive medicine program.

1. Daily to Weekly Preventive Medicine Activities. These aspects of preventive medicine fall under the supervision of the KM and handlers to include appropriate care, feeding, and work practices. The kennel should maintain a record of MWD feed intake and stool characteristics, and abnormal behavior if present. Kennels often record body weights on a weekly basis even though they report it to the VTF only monthly. Unless a problem occurs, the VCO generally does not need to worry about these functions, but should be aware of and review the kennel records when conducting quarterly inspections and when otherwise medically appropriate.

2. Monthly Preventive Medicine Activities. These aspects generally involve interaction of the MWD unit and VCO or 68T. Depending on local SOPs, the MWD may or may not be presented to the VTF for care, which includes parasite prophylaxis, body weight/nutrition reporting, and optional monthly handler training and kennel sanitary inspection. These activities can be combined into a "Spot Day" by having the veterinary team conduct the weight checks, administer the preventatives, and verify diet at the MWD kennels or VTF.
    a. All MWDs are required to be administered monthly heartworm, gastrointestinal (GI) parasite and ectoparasite (flea and tick) prevention. Monthly preventatives are prescribed by DODMWDVS and currently include oral ivermectin/pyrantel for heartworm prevention and topical imidacloprid/permethrin/pyriproxyfen. Use of insecticide products not approved by Director, DODMWDVS is NOT authorized for MWDs. The use of long-acting supplemental tick collars containing deltamethrin is recommended in areas of high tick infestation or Leishmaniasis-endemic areas and when deployed, but the collar may cause problems as a foreign body if ingested. Judgment should be used on whether or not to apply or not in dogs which appear bothered by the collar or demonstrate other characteristics which the VCO feels would put the dog at risk of losing/ingesting the collar. If prophylactic

medications are dispensed to the MWD handler for administration, this prescription must be documented in the VHR and the handler or KM should keep a record of when the medications are administered, which should be reviewed by veterinary personnel at monthly visits to the kennel.

b. Each month, the MWD's body weight must be recorded and charted in the VHR. The KM may communicate this to the VTF, or the MWD may be presented for weighing and administration of the parasite preventatives at the VTF. Body weight is measured and recorded monthly in order to monitor body condition and detect important trends in weight loss/gain that may indicate illness or loss of condition. Body weight in MWDs can fluctuate dramatically due to various factors such as operational tempo, climate, life stage, or presence of gastrointestinal or metabolic disease. Periodic adjustment of type and quantity of rations is indicated to maintain an MWD within their ideal weight range (IWR). If an MWD is out of IWR a VCO must document a plan for weight loss/gain or adjustment to IWR in the VHR. The KM/handler documents food intake, stool consistency, vomiting, etc. and notifies veterinary personnel as necessary.

c. Monthly medical deployment category status will be provided by the VCO to the KM. Generally, categories will not change significantly month to month; however, at a minimum, monthly updates are necessary to ensure the KM has a record of all category changes when they do occur. There is no prescribed manner/format for category status updates, but there is a template that can be used in Appendix H.

d. Monthly kennel inspections by a 68T or VCO are optional but highly recommended, as it helps identify problems early and develop a positive relationship between kennel and veterinary service personnel.

e. Every month, each MWD's veterinary medical record should be opened and reviewed by a member of the supporting VTF's veterinary care team (68T/GS Vet Tech/VCO/VMO) and updated as well as checked for accuracy. Particular attention should be paid to ensure that the deployment category and status are correct. The Animal Medicine Division at the Army Public Health Center (APHC) regularly monitors the database and compiles the data for the Quarterly Portfolio Brief regarding: Deployability status, Semiannual Physical Exam, Record Review. Common problems in MWD records include:

  i. Not reviewing electronic VHR every month.
  ii. Not updating MPL and closing out items as appropriate.
  iii. Not entering a reason in the "Comments" block for Category 3 or 4 status. Be brief but as specific as possible.
  iv. Not entering a date in an Estimated Release Date (ERD) from Category 3.
  v. Current date is after the ERD from Category 3 date. Keep track of the estimated release date and update it as necessary. It is only estimated, so change it as the clinical situation warrants.
  vi. Not having correct dates and location entered when "Deployed" button is clicked. This is primarily a problem when the MWD has been previously deployed because when the "Deployed" button is clicked, the data from the previous deployment comes up and must be changed.
  vii. Entries in the "Comments" block with no date reference. All comments should be dated to aid reviewers in determining if the comment is current or not.
  viii. Past due for a semiannual physical without a comment. If the database shows an MWD as past due for its semiannual physical, make a comment as to the reason.

ix. If an MWD's deployability category changes, make the change in the database immediately. Do not wait a couple days to update the database.
x. Verify that the MWD's sex is correct (particularly Male-Intact and Male-Castrated) and be sure to change it if the MWD is castrated at his duty location.
   f. Check for MWDs requiring Semi-Annual Physical Exam (SAPE).
3. Quarterly Preventive Medicine Activities.
   a. Mandated quarterly activities include the completion of a Kennel Sanitary Inspection using DD Form 2342 by the responsible VCO. A signed copy of the DD Form 2342 should be provided to the KM within 72 hours of conducting the inspection with a courtesy copy provided to the MWD unit commander. Recurrent findings should be addressed with the MWD unit commander.
   b. Quarterly handler training by the VCO/68T is required as it assures timely training of handlers after initial assignment to an MWD unit as well as providing new skills and sustainment of others. It is not necessary that all handlers attend each training event as they work shifts, are deployed, on leave or TDY. However, all handlers should attend at least one training event per year with focused training (e.g. pre-deployment, needs additional training for a particular topic, etc.) provided as needed. The DODMWDVS is the proponent for all veterinary medical training of MWD handlers and they have developed the Medical Care of MWDs by Handlers: Handler Training Manual and supporting training resources. Training resources and materials are available directly on the Army Veterinary Services milSuite webpage (https://www.milsuite.mil/book/docs/DOC-580669) and through supporting Veterinary Clinical Specialists (64F). KM and handlers can access the training via Working Dog Management System (WDMS) by logging onto WDMS website, selecting "Library" link at top center of page, and selecting "MWD Handler Training". Work with the KM to coordinate this type of training. The VMSB has established the state of the art Trauma FX Diesel dog or Hero dog medical trainer as the realistic MWD skills trainer which allows learners to perform critical life-saving tasks such as maintaining an airway, needle decompression, thoracocentesis, hemostasis, IV insertion, intraosseous infusion, CPR, tracheostomy, and bandaging on a simulator in addition to other procedures on an MWD. These mannequins should be used to train MWD handlers on the canine – tactical combat casualty care tasks, human healthcare providers on the Clinical Practice Guidelines, and veterinary personnel for sustainment of emergency skills.
4. The Semiannual Physical Examination (SAPE). A complete medical evaluation is performed every 6 months. At procurement, each MWD is assigned two months for semiannual physical examinations. Red and yellow stickers attached to the right side of the hard copy record indicate the months for each exam. Responsible VCOs have the authority to change/update SAPE when early exams are performed due to deployments or other circumstances. SAPEs are recorded on the MWD SAPE template in the electronic VHR or utilizing DD Form 1829. Taking a thorough history and performing an extensive physical examination are the most important procedures that are performed. Ensure the handlers know the importance of their input on such things as food and water intake, stool and urine production and character, lameness, behavioral changes, exercise intolerance, cough, and skin abnormalities. Ensure that a history is recorded and that all physical examination findings are appropriately assessed and recorded in the VHR. Every SAPE must include an assessment of MWD Fitness for Duty and Deployment Category (see below). The specific actions required during the Red and Yellow SAPE are summarized in Table 3-1. These are minimums; it is the VCO's responsibility to assess the patient and perform additional examinations/diagnostic tests when appropriate.

Table 1. Semi-Annual Physical Examination and Health Evaluation

RED Semiannual Evaluation	YELLOW Semiannual Evaluation
Physical Examination (ROVR template or DD Form 1829)	Physical Examination (ROVR template or DD Form 1829)
Heartworm Antigen Test & Tick-transmitted pathogen tests such as SNAP 4Dx Plus®	
Vaccinations	
Fecal Flotation for parasite identification	
*Complete Blood Count: minimum of HCT, WBC with differential, Platelet Count or estimate	Will also be performed on dogs > 8 years of age and all dogs with chronic conditions or on chronic medications at YELLOW SAPE
*Comprehensive Serum Chemistry Panel: minimum of Creatinine, BUN, ALT, ALP, t.bili., glucose, Na+, K+, CL-, Calcium, Phosphorus, Albumin, Total Protein.	Will also be performed on dogs > 8 years of age and all dogs with chronic conditions or on chronic medications at YELLOW SAPE.**
*Urinalysis: Urine Specific Gravity by refractometer, dipstick, sediment examination	Will also be performed on dogs > 8 years of age and all dogs with chronic conditions or on chronic medications at YELLOW SAPE.
Blood and serum to FADL for Banking	
COHAT (if needed), ECG w/anesthesia	
Additional Exams/Tests as clinically appropriate (such as T. cruzi testing in endemic areas)	Additional Exams/Tests as clinically appropriate
Written Assessment, Plan and Fitness for Duty Statement (SF 600 and DD Form 1829)	Written Assessment, Plan and Fitness for Duty Statement (SF 600 and DD Form 1829, or equivalent)
*Clinical Pathology tests must be run in-house using veterinary-specific equipment, or submitted to a commercial veterinary clinical pathology laboratory. Use of a human commercial lab or human military MTF is not authorized except when veterinary lab facilities are not available ** Thyroid panel should not be performed unless clinical signs of hypothyroidism are present regardless of MWD age. Thyroid panel (if clinically indicated) must be submitted to a Veterinary Referral Clinical Pathology Laboratory as in-house equipment and human laboratories have been shown to provide invalid results for required indices. A thyroid panel consists of total T4, free T4, and thyroid stimulating hormone (TSH). Free T4 must be run by the equilibrium dialysis method as the RIA is not clinically valid.	

5. Annual Preventive Medicine Activities. In addition to the physical examination and assessment, the Red SAPE includes complete laboratory evaluation (CBC, chemistry panel, urinalysis, examination of feces for parasite ova, heartworm antigen test, and tick-transmitted pathogen tests such as SNAP 4Dx Plus), vaccination, serum and whole blood specimens for banking, and COHAT if required. The laboratory evaluations to include urinalysis sediment and fecal flotation, should be performed in the VTF unless there are no in-house lab capabilities or specific lab values are being monitored. Use of MTF clinical laboratories is not endorsed unless no veterinary laboratory is available. Serum and whole blood in EDTA must be collected during the Red SAPE and submitted to the DOD Food Analysis Diagnostic Laboratory (FADL). If a COHAT is warranted, it should be performed at the time of the Red SAPE, but only after assessment of the patient (exam and lab results) documents

healthy status and fitness for general anesthesia. ECGs must be performed on all MWDs at every anesthesia, in accordance with VMSB Anesthesia and Pain Management Guidelines, and reviewed to detect abnormalities. ECG abnormalities should be documented and worked up appropriately to ensure the best standard of care for the MWD patient. As such, it is imperative that VCOs ensure they have working ECG equipment and know how to obtain a good trace without artifact.

ANNUAL SUBMISSION OF MWD BLOOD AND SERUM FOR ARCHIVAL BANKING

1. Sampling. Yearly specimens of both serum and EDTA whole blood will be drawn from each MWD at each Red SAPE. At least 2 mL aliquots of both serum and whole blood in EDTA should be collected and placed in either a 2.0 mL, externally threaded, polypropylene cryotube vial or a conventional vacutainer tube. Utilize FADL Form D-127, MWD Banked Annual Blood and Serum Submission, available on the FADL website (https://phc.amedd.army.mil/topics/labsciences/fad/Pages/FADLFormsandDocuments.aspx) under the "DOD FADL Forms and Documents" tab. Vials must be clearly marked (using fine-point permanent marker) with MWD's name, tattoo and date of draw. If a dog is deployed during the time it would normally have had a Red SAPE performed, sample collection will be deferred until the next Red SAPE is conducted. Specific sampling will not be done pre/post deployment as each Red SAPE sample will serve as pre/post deployment sampling respectively.
2. Packing samples. Both blood and serum samples should be shipped refrigerated, not frozen. The samples should be placed in plastic, zip lock bags, with the paperwork (see below) in a separate plastic bag. The bags should then be put in a Styrofoam container with ice packs.
3. Shipping. Military Working Dog Banked Sample Form, Vet Lab Sample Form D-127 should be filled out completely and annotated for each MWD. Samples will be stored at the FADL for future testing as necessary for periodic surveys and comparison with serum from sick dogs. Testing of dogs with illness suggestive of arthropod- borne diseases will be done on a case-by-case basis at the request of the attending VCO. Coordination with the lab prior to shipping samples would be indicated for patients that are critical and need their results quicker than samples submitted for surveillance purposes. For those MWDs showing clinical signs consistent with arthropod-borne infections, the DOD Food Analysis & Diagnostic Laboratory will retrieve and test the latest banked submission from that dog for comparison with the results from current submission from the sick dog when appropriate. The DODMWDVS may direct collection of samples in conjunction with major deployments. The completed form and packaged samples should be submitted to:

   DOD Food Analysis and Diagnostic Laboratory
   2899 Schofield RD, Suite 2630
   Ft Sam Houston, TX 78234-7583
   210-295-4605/4010/4387; DSN: 312-421-xxxx

LABORATORY

1. General. Laboratory tests are routinely done as part of complete veterinary medical care provided to MWDs, either as part of an annual or semi-annual exam or clinical case. Complete blood counts (CBCs), blood chemistry panels, urinalyses (UAs), heartworm antigen tests, tick-transmitted pathogen tests, and fecal flotations for parasite identification are routinely performed. Other tests may be needed as part of a diagnostic work-up in sick animals. These tests can either be run in-house or

sent to an outside laboratory. Generally, for best practices, in-house testing should be performed on all emergent patients, patients that the results would impact or change treatment plan and tests that are easily performed (i.e. fecal flotations, heartworm antigen tests, UAs, to include sediment exams, etc.) Those that require more technical expertise, specialized equipment or reagents can be sent to outside diagnostic laboratories specialized in these techniques. If the VCO sends tests out, the tests must be sent to a commercial veterinary diagnostic lab, unless one is unavailable or specific exemption is given through the command chain. Veterinary diagnostic labs have the advantage of equipment that has been calibrated, validated methodologies for animal species, and trained personnel in identifying changes and conditions unique to different animal species. Each lab will have established normal reference intervals for each species and will be able to provide these reference intervals with sample results. Reference intervals vary considerably from lab to lab, and are dependent on methodology, reagents and instrumentation utilized. Do not compare one laboratory's results to another laboratory's reference intervals.

    a. CBC. As a minimum, hematocrit, a WBC count with differential, platelet count or estimate and slide review.

    b. Serum chemistry panel. As a minimum, include measures of renal, liver, and endocrine function, gastrointestinal health, and electrolytes (BUN, creatinine, ALT, ALP, total bilirubin, albumin, total protein, blood glucose, calcium, phosphorus, sodium, chloride, and potassium).

    c. Urinalysis. As a minimum, include urine specific gravity by refractometer, visual assessment of turbidity and color, chemical reagent evaluation of urine glucose, bilirubin, ketone, hemoprotein, pH, protein; and a sediment examination.

2. In-house laboratory testing. Every VTF should have equipment and supplies to perform at least a minimal amount of laboratory tests. These include:

    a. Manual packed cell volume (PCV).

    b. Manual plasma total protein and urine specific gravity.

    c. Manual WBC estimate.

    d. Blood smear. When reviewing the blood smear be sure to evaluate all components of the CBC; hemogram including RBC morphology, leukogram to include differential and morphology, and thrombogram including count and morphology. Abnormalities include:

        i. RBC: Moderate poikilocytosis (any type or combination), reticulocytosis (require special staining techniques to perform in-house) (>60,000/µl), Heinz bodies, basophilic stippling, RBC parasites, nucleated RBCs>5, anisocytosis, spherocytosis

        ii. WBC: Left shift >1000 bands, or with metamyelocytes or myelocytes, leukocytosis (>20,000/µl), neutrophilia (>15,000/ µl), lymphocytosis (>5,000/µl), monocytosis (>2500/µl), eosinophilia (>2000/µl), basophilia (>500/µl), unclassified cells

        iii. PLATELETS: thrombocytopenia (<200,000/µl), thrombocytosis (>500,000/µl)

        iv. BACKGROUND: Any odd discoloration or stippling

    e. Routine urinalysis to include visual assessment (color, turbidity, specific gravity by refractometry), chemical reagent strip ("dipstick") analysis (glucose, bilirubin, ketone, hemoprotein, pH, protein), and sediment examination (cells, casts, crystals, bacteria, other).

        i. Prolonged air exposure on the urine dipstick can result in false positive glucose test and false negative hemoprotein

        ii. Alkaline urine can cause a false positive protein test (the dipstick mainly tests albumin)

        iii. Protein greater than trace on a dipstick in concentrated urine (>1.045) or present at all in less concentrated urine (<1.030) should undergo additional diagnostic testing which may include, but is not limited to, a urine culture, sulfosalicylic acid test, or a

              urine protein-creatinine ratio
        f. Fecal flotation examinations and direct fecal smears.
3. External laboratory testing
    a. As previously mentioned, veterinary clinical laboratories are required unless unavailable. If the VCO does not have access to these facilities, the VCO may want to perform as much lab work as can be done in-house. The VCO can get a reasonable estimate of a CBC by doing a packed cell volume (PCV), total protein by refractometer, manual WBC, and by examining a blood smear to get a platelet estimate, manual WBC differential, and confirming RBC and WBC parameters visually by estimates. Also, by examining the blood smear, the VCO can evaluate RBC, WBC and platelet morphology, evaluate for hemoparasites or other inclusions. Complete reliance on human medical facilities in a deployed setting to meet all clinical pathology requirements, while forsaking use of organic laboratory equipment for a perceived convenience is entirely inappropriate, and utilizing human clinical laboratories should be performed only by exception.
    b. If sending samples to the local MTF is the only option, VCOs must be careful about interpreting the results.
        i. Hematology analyzers in human medical laboratories are not calibrated and validated for veterinary species and most medical technologists are not familiar with the unique morphological differences in normal and abnormal blood cells from different animal species. In general, cell counts from these analyzers in dogs (other species are variable) will be a reasonably good estimate. WBC differentials should not be used. The VCOs should make a blood smear at the same time the sample is drawn and perform a manual WBC differential on the smear, then using differential percentages, apply the WBC count obtained from the lab to calculate the individual absolute WBC values. By reviewing a blood smear the VCO should also be able to verify whether the cell counts obtained from the lab seem reasonable (very low, low, normal, high, very high). Another caution, do not use "normal values" provided by the MTF; these are for humans and are not valid for dogs. The VCOs will need to use the more generic reference intervals provided in veterinary medicine textbooks for comparison.
        ii. Blood chemistry panels are of even more concern. The VCO may be able to utilize in-house portable chemistry analyzers that can provide immediate partial chemistry panel results (electrolytes, some blood gas parameters, possibly BUN or creatinine). Again, samples should be submitted to the local MTF with caution. Methodologies and instrumentation will vary from hospital to hospital and not all methodologies have been validated for animal species. Certain methodologies have been recognized as not being valid in animals. For example, many human medical laboratories utilize bromcresol purple as a dye to measure albumin. Bromcresol purple does not reliably bind to animal albumin and results are therefore unreliable. Likewise, many antibody-based tests may have limited cross-species reactivity; this includes most thyroid function tests. These must be submitted to a veterinary diagnostic lab so that species specific tests can be run. Human thyroid tests are invalid in dogs. Also, the linearity of tests is designed for expected human values and may not accommodate values commonly obtained with animal species.
        iii. UAs (to include sediment exams) can usually be performed in-house relatively easily and quickly. Use caution if sending UAs to the MTF for evaluation. Many crystals commonly found in animal urine are not common in human medicine and may not be properly identified.

iv. Microbiological cultures are often sent to the MTF; however, the preferred analytical laboratory would be a commercial veterinary lab offering microbiology/bacteriology services. Again, caution is advised if utilizing MTF laboratories. Many veterinary pathogens are not routine isolates in human labs, and the labs may not be familiar with them. Additionally, most human microbiological labs test sensitivity against commonly encountered human drugs but not for many of the commonly used veterinary drugs.

c. If sending samples to The Joint Pathology Center see chapter 12 and TB Med 283 for complete details.
   i. The JPC does not accept fluid samples, any type of sample for culture, or stones.
   ii. The JPC does accept the following diagnostic material: Formalin fixed tissue specimens, paraffin- embedded tissue specimens, stained histologic sections, cytologic preparations, metal fragments, radiographs, photographs, and other forms of digital imaging.

NUTRITION ISSUES

1. Standard Diet. AR 40-905 requires that all MWDs be fed a standard diet unless a special diet is medically required. The standard diet selection is based on nutrition standards established by the DODMWDVS in consultation with veterinary nutrition specialists and is approved by the Joint Services MWD Committee. Though nutritional standards are set by DODMWDVS and the Joint Committee, the actual brand and manufacturer are based on solicitations to manufacturers for bid. A manufacturer must provide a diet that meets the criteria set, but the brand may change with each solicitation, which currently is every 5 years. The standard DLA MWD Diet is identified as NSN 8710-01-679-9480 with the nomenclature, "Dog Food"; the current standard diet is Hill's Science Diet Active. The 7-gallon pail, NSN 7240-01-411-0581, may be used for storage of food during deployment, but the food is delivered in bags. The use of the correct standard diet and appropriate means of procurement should be evaluated at each quarterly kennel sanitary inspection. MWD units are required to maintain a minimum one-month supply of food for their MWDs.
   a. Medical justification for a standard diet. Use of a standard diet (brand and type) minimizes the risk of diarrhea and gastroenteritis developing due to diet changes associated with deployments, TDYs, or PCSs. It also assures that healthy MWDs eat a diet appropriate for their athletic lifestyle, e.g. high digestibility, high energy density, fixed formula, American Association of Feed Control Officials (AAFCO) certified feeding trial, high protein content, high fat content, and controlled calcium: phosphorus ratio.
   b. Justification for purchase of the standard diet through DLA. In general, the DLA procurement will be least cost to the MWD unit. Even if the same food can be procured through other sources, DLA must be considered by regulation. DLA is likely the only option for contingency operations outside the US. Shipping costs through DLA will likely be much less than if units use commercial shipping of food bought locally. Regardless of the source of procurement, the standard diet must be fed to MWDs unless otherwise required by medical condition (see below).
   c. Reporting Problems with DLA Supplied MWD Diet. Occasionally MWD units have problems with late, poor condition, or out-of-date (expired/close to expired) food deliveries. This food should not be accepted. MWD diet is required to be properly palletized and in good condition at the time of delivery. If problems occur (e.g. wet, clumped, abnormal color or consistency), the DLA Customer Service should be notified so that they can correct the problem. The responsible KM should notify the local Supply Officer and the DLA Customer

Service Center: 1-877- 352-2255, (269) 961-7766 (DSN 661), dlacontactcenter@dla.mil.
   d. Use of non-standard diets for medical conditions. The only reason a dog should be fed a nonstandard diet is a medical condition as determined by the VCO, on a case-by-case basis. Such conditions might include congestive heart failure, chronic kidney disease, food allergies, hepatic disease, or inflammatory bowel disease. Compliance with the requirement to feed only this diet must be checked at least quarterly during kennel sanitation visits, but should be confirmed monthly. It is the responsibility of the MWD unit to purchase and feed medical prescription diets IAW veterinary prescription after the initial period of approximately 30 days for all long-term diets.
   e. In general, MWDs on special diets should not automatically be categorized as Category 2 limited deployment. If an adequate supply of the special diet can be sent with the MWD at initial deployment and in quantity sufficient to last an entire deployment, or if the ration can be obtained in theater utilizing the established logistical channels, these "special diet" dogs may be deployed as Category 1, as long as the diet allows the animal to perform at a Category 1 level.
2. Quantity and Frequency of Feedings. The MWDs ideal weight range (IWR) and daily diet are set at the DODMWDVS at the time of procurement and observed throughout the training of the dog. Most MWDs at the DODMWDVS start with 2.5 cups standard diet twice daily. This diet is adjusted as appropriate throughout training to maintain the MWD in its IWR. The IWR and diet amount may be changed by the local VCO, if required. Energy requirements may be dramatically altered due to environment, different training and operational requirements, and as the dog's metabolism changes throughout life. An estimate of a dog's caloric requirements (kcal/day) can be calculated as shown:

Science Diet Active Formula contains 560 kcal/cup.
Basal Energy Requirement (BER) = 30 kcal/kg + 70
Maintenance Energy Requirement (MER) = BER X Stress Factor.

As an example, a 37kg GSD requires (30 kcal/kg X 37 kg) + 70=1,180 kcal X stress factor 2.0=2,360 kcal/

Stress factors can be quite variable even among athletic dogs (1.8-11 X BER) and should be considered as a starting point. Most canine exercise studies relating to nutritional requirements have been performed with racing greyhounds or sled dogs, and MWDs should be considered intermediate athletes somewhere between these two extremes. Additionally, be advised of the different caloric density of the different rations. For example, when switching from Science Diet Active to Hill's d/d ® Potato and Duck formula, you are going from a diet with 560 kcal/cup to 368 kcal/cup, and the volume of food the handler is instructed to provide should be adjusted accordingly. Consult with the manufacturer to review relevant nutritional information for diets.

---

3. Body Condition and Ideal Weight Range. The IWR for MWDs is set based on a body condition score (BCS) using the Nestle-Purina BCS System. The IWR should be a 5-pound range centered at BCS 4-4.5/9. MWDs that become too thin (BCS <4) are at increased risk of skin disease (e.g. decubital ulcers), gastrointestinal disease, and may have decreased immune function and stamina. Working dogs with excessive body fat may be at higher risk of musculoskeletal injury resulting from a given level of work or exercise. In general, a valid IWR is established at DODMWDVS prior to a new MWDs first assignment, but the VCO can make adjustments when appropriate. MWD weight must be measured and recorded in the VHR at least once monthly. Observation of changes in weight and BCS can be a key signal to evaluate for illness or injury.
4. Monitoring and reporting of MWD food intake. It is important that the MWD's current diet (type and

quantity per day) be noted at each semi-annual examination. Whenever an MWD presents with an illness or injury associated with change in body weight or BCS or any changes are made in an MWD's diet, it must be recorded in the VHR. In most units the KM has authority to increase or decrease MWD diet quantity to keep a dog in IWR; the VCO should not interfere with this authority unless a clear problem exists; however, the KM must inform the VTF of any changes made so they can be recorded in the VHR. Be sure to get clear descriptions of how food is measured and make sure they measure in standard units, e.g. cups or ounces (from a measuring cup not a coffee cup, etc.), or ounces (from a scale). Do not let the kennels measure food as "scoops" or estimate weight; food must be portioned precisely and in standard units of measure.

5. Feeding Frequency and Gastric Dilatation Volvulus (GDV) prevention. The DODMWDVS mandates that MWDs be fed at least twice daily. Eating several smaller meals rather than one large meal decreases risk of GDV. This can be difficult as MWDs should also not be fed immediately before or immediately after strenuous exercise, but most MWD units can accommodate twice daily feeding. Meals need not be 12 hours apart. For example, at the Dog Center standard feeding times are at 1600 (roughly 4 hours after daily training ends) and at 2400 (4-6 hours before training begins). Once a day feeding must be avoided as this increases the risk of gastrointestinal disturbances.

VACCINATION PROTOCOLS

Vaccination should be completed at the time of the Red SAPE. MWDs will be vaccinated with Core Vaccines (see below) to ensure they remain operationally ready. Additional vaccinations or altered immunization frequency may be required based on local risk, operational requirements, or to meet specific import/home station requirements. Approval of these alterations can be approved by the supporting 64F. The director of DODMWDVS will be notified of the use of non-core vaccines. **Country specific requirements supersede published MWD immunization guidelines.** It is the home station VCO's responsibility to ensure dogs are vaccinated appropriately prior to deployment. Location of vaccination is standardized and will be administered IAW guidelines published by the VMSB. Rabies immunizations will be administered in the right rear/hip area, and the distemper, adenovirus (type 2), parvovirus with or without leptospirosis combinations will be administered in the right shoulder. Leptospirosis alone will be given in the upper portion of the left front limb.

1. Core Vaccines. Core vaccines are typically considered to be those vaccines that all dogs should receive regardless of lifestyle. MWDs will receive core vaccination against rabies virus, canine distemper (CDV), canine adenovirus (CAV-2), and canine parvovirus (CPV-2) every three years, except in locations where local jurisdiction requires increased frequencies by law. The need to maintain worldwide operational readiness and for MWD units to respond rapidly to operational requirements far outweighs any other concerns regarding vaccination frequency, therefore, MWDs assigned to high OPTEMPO units may be vaccinated on an annual basis. Additionally, the lifestyle and working conditions of MWDs dictate that Leptospirosis (quadrivalent) be considered core and administered annually. The Leptospirosis vaccine may be administered more often than annually if deemed appropriate for a particular MWD or location and following consultation with the supporting 64F.

2. Non-core Vaccines. Given the lifestyle and living conditions of MWDs, these vaccines are not currently recommended or required for MWDs. In the event that a vaccine is believed to be necessary in a particular circumstance, the supporting 64F should be consulted. The director of DODMWDVS will be notified of their utilization.
    a. Parainfluenza, Coronavirus, Bordetella. These vaccines are not currently recommended or required for MWDs.
    b. Lyme Disease. Lyme disease (Borrelia burgdorferi) vaccines generally will not be used in

MWDs without prior consultation with the supporting 64F. Preventive measures directed at prevention of tick exposure remain the cornerstone of Lyme disease prevention.

c. Canine Influenza. Canine Influenza immunization of MWDs is not currently recommended for MWDs. Given the lifestyle and living conditions and the fact that a risk/benefit assessment does not justify immunization all make a case for currently withholding this vaccine from the MWD population. This may be subject to change if the epidemiology of this disease dictates that immunization is warranted.

d. Other vaccinations. IAW AR 40-905, other vaccinations may be administered to prevent an epizootic. Authorization must be obtained from the Director, DODMWDVS. Request for authorization along with a justification statement should be sent through the supporting 64F to Director, DODMWDVS by email (dog.consult@us.af.mil) for review and approval.

MEDICATION AND MWD PERFORMANCE

The true impact of anticonvulsant, antibiotic, steroid, and antihistamine drugs on MWD performance, particularly detection capabilities, is not fully known. A recent study demonstrated degradation in olfaction in 50% of trained explosives detection dogs after a 10-day trial of metronidazole, with affected dogs not returning to baseline detection capabilities until 10 days post cessation of the drug. Anecdotal reports, and clinical signs reported by people on these classes of medication, suggest that they may affect some MWDs' ability to perform, either through altered scent sensation or other neurologic mechanism. Be advised that not all MWDs taking these drugs will have altered performance and there is NOT a standard policy from the 341 TRS or DODMWDVS limiting duty status or certification of MWDs while on medication. VCOs should use metronidazole only when medically indicated (rather than prophylactic use), and use the lowest dose for the shortest duration necessary. With respect to ability to work, each MWD must be evaluated as an individual. If an individual dog "hits" the training aides while on medication and the KM allows, it can work. If another dog has decreased performance, the effect of the medication must be considered and the treatment should be altered or the dog's duty and certification changed; a 10-day washout period after cessation of metronidazole is recommended. The larger implication may be that dogs temporarily on these medications may experience a transient degradation in olfaction that could possibly put both the dog and Service members at risk while the MWD is on metronidazole.

1. Anticonvulsants. The most common reason to prescribe anticonvulsants to MWDs is to control idiopathic epilepsy. Appropriate medications for seizure control maintenance include but not limited to phenobarbital, zonisamide, levetiracetam (extended and non-extended release), and potassium bromide. New medications and formulation may be appropriate as developed or researched. Some human medications/formulations are inappropriate for veterinary patients, such as primidone and oral benzodiazepines. Consultation with the supporting 64F or DODMWDVS prior to initiating anticonvulsants is recommended. Although the few MWDs receiving medication for the control of seizures have seemingly retained the ability to maintain certification standards, there are no controlled studies to ascertain the potential quality or quantity of cognitive decrement. If anticonvulsants impair performance, the greatest risk to force protection is clearly in explosives detection. There is no policy from the 341 TRS which categorically states that trainers and KMs must decertify an explosives detector dog once placed on anticonvulsant medication; however, the DODMWDVS recommends that any MWD diagnosed with recurrent seizures be downgraded to at least Category 2.

2. Steroids and Antihistamines. The most common reason to prescribe steroids and antihistamines is to control signs of allergic dermatitis. Appropriate medications include oral prednisone (on a short term, tapering dose), dexamethasone, diphenhydramine, chlorpheniramine, trimeprazine, and hydroxyzine. Both anti-histamines and steroids are reported to cause degradation of olfaction in humans, but the

impact on working dog performance is unclear. High doses of dexamethasone and hydrocortisone caused diminished olfactory performance in laboratory dogs after 7 days of use (without apparent clinical signs); effects of antihistamines on canine olfaction has not yet been studied. Prolonged utilization of immunosuppressive doses of systemic steroids may be justification to initiate the disposition process in certain MWDs. VCOs should consult with the supporting 64F for guidance with these cases. Inappropriate drugs for use in MWDs generally include ultra-long-acting preparations of steroids.

MEDICAL DEPLOYABILITY GUIDELINES

MWDs are frequently deployed to austere environments with high operational tempos and limited veterinary care. Consequently, it is important that all VCOs and KMs continually evaluate and prepare MWDs in a consistent manner to meet medical readiness requirements. This ensures the MWD arrives fit for duty. It is the joint responsibility of the VCO and the KM to meet no less than quarterly to discuss medical conditions, training proficiency, and physical fitness status of each MWD. VCOs advise and support KMs and MWD unit commanders on MWD medical issues affecting readiness and fitness for duty; however, the dog-owning unit commander has final authority regarding deployment of their MWDs.

1. MWDs will be assigned a medical deployment category as defined herein by the attending VCO in consultation with the KM. This deployment categorization serves as a valuable management tool to define current medical readiness for each MWD and is intended for use by the KM, unit commanders, major commands, and Service Program Managers to apportion MWD assets based on medical readiness and fitness for duty. Only the attending VCO assigns the medical deployment category. The medical deployment category is a reflection of medical readiness only. Lack of an assigned handler, failure to certify, or other non-medical limitations will not be considered in assignment of deployment category. Frequent and open communication between the VCO and KM will ensure a medically ready MWD population. VCOs must ensure that the medical deployment categories of all MWDs are updated at least monthly, at every routine exam or sick call, or any time a medical condition develops that warrants a change in the deployment category, and that this information is concurrently documented in the VHR and provided to the KM and MWD unit commander.
    a. Category 1 (CAT 1). Unrestricted Deployment:
        i. Medically fit for any contingency or exercise.
        ii. Can handle extreme stresses and environments.
        iii. No limiting or compromising factors (lack of stamina, etc.).
        iv. No existing or recurring medical problems that limit performance or will worsen by stress or increased demands. Note: The MWD may have chronic or minor medical problems currently undergoing treatment, but they do not limit performance, nor do they require intensive monitoring. Medications or special diets are not considered limiting factors unless unavailable.
        v. Summary: This means that the MWD is healthy or has well-managed minor illness or injury that does not affect duty performance or stamina, and the current medical condition is not likely to be made worse by the stress of deployment. The MWD is certified and is maintained at a physical fitness level that will allow strenuous duty while deployed. A good rule of thumb is that if the handler can carry a 6-month supply of required medication in his cargo pocket, the MWD is probably category 1, e.g. dogs with minor or radiographic evidence of arthritis but with no lameness or pain while on NSAID and Glucosamine-Chondroitin or hypothyroid in good body condition on supplements.

b. Category 2 (CAT 2). Restricted Deployment:
   i. Medically fit for regions/missions after consideration of known medical problems and consultation with KM.
   ii. No significant limiting or compromising factors.
   iii. Medical problems may exist which slightly limit performance but are controlled.
   iv. Reason for restriction must be reported in the Veterinary Health Record (VHR) and to the KM, MWD unit commander and program managers.
   v. Summary: This is generally considered a permanent status so a release date is not required, but a specific reason for CAT 2 status must be reported. Examples of CAT 2 dogs could include those on special diets or dogs with medical conditions requiring frequent monitoring by veterinary personnel. This category could also include dogs with mild arthritis, which improves with therapy, but is still clinically apparent and diminishes operational employment. In some cases in which the condition warranting CAT 2 status resolves, the VCO may consider returning the MWD to CAT 1 status as appropriate.
c. Category 3 (CAT 3). Temporarily Nondeployable:
   i. Medical condition exists that precludes daily duty performance and is under diagnosis, observation, or treatment. MWD may still be allowed to work at home station, but in a limited capacity.
   ii. Reason for non-deployability must be reported in the VHR and to the KM/MWD unit commander.
   iii. Estimated Release Date (ERD) from CAT 3 must be reported in the VHR. ERDs will be no longer than 90 days from change to CAT 3 status. After the problem is identified and a diagnostic/therapeutic plan is implemented, the MWD will ultimately be assigned CAT 1, 2, or 4 status pending the outcome of the diagnostic/therapeutic plan. A physical examination is required on or before the ERD in order to release the dog or to extend the duration of the CAT 3 status. For cases where assigning the proper deployment category is ambiguous, consult the supporting 64F.
   iv. An MWD in CAT 3 requires periodic follow-up exams, further consultation with clinical specialists and consistent reevaluation of the diagnostic and therapeutic plan for return to duty.
   v. Summary: There is no such thing as a permanent CAT 3 dog. A CAT 3 designation means the MWD cannot deploy because illness or injury significantly affects daily duty and is currently under evaluation & therapy. The MWD will eventually be upgraded to CAT 1 or 2, or downgraded to CAT 4. The MWD may still be capable of working in limited capacity at home station, but the VCO should be actively working up the medical problems so it can be moved to a permanent status. Additionally, a dog may not be considered CAT 3 due to non- medical issues, e.g. has not certified, has no handler, etc. Status will be determined solely on the dog's medical condition.
d. Category 4 (CAT 4). Nondeployable:
   i. Unresolved medical or physical problems exist that frequently or regularly impede daily duty performance and ERD cannot be given. VCOs will obtain concurrence for CAT 4 status designation from the supporting 64F.
   ii. Medical or physical conditions warrant submission to the MWD Disposition Process with subsequent replacement. CAT 4 MWDs are authorized to perform limited missions within their medical condition and training proficiency capabilities at the

            discretion of the KM and MWD unit commander.
       iii. The reason for non-deployability must be reported in the VHR.
2. It should be noted that some determinations are and will remain subjective; thus there remains the need for prudent judgment by all individuals involved in these assessments. This is particularly true regarding the effect of age on an individual MWD. Old age is not a disease and MWDs are not downgraded solely due to age, but with increased age comes increased incidence of illness or disability. The concomitant problems that may arise with age (i.e., lack of stamina or drive, exacerbation of osteoarthritis, etc.) could warrant a change in deployability status.
3. The list of MWDs assessed as CAT 4 (nondeployable) serves as a management tool for program managers and KM in determining programmed replacements. Dogs that are in the CAT 4 status for >90 days need to have their records evaluated to determine why their disposition packet has not been processed completely. Note that temporarily nondeployable (CAT 3) MWDs must have an ERD to assist commanders and program managers in their planning, and CAT 2 MWDs must have the restrictive reason reported to assist program managers and the DODMWDVS in identifying problems among the deployable MWD population. Although criteria listed for assessment addresses medical conditions, evaluations of the MWD at work can be used to help determine a deployability category. For example, a particular dog may be CAT 2 in that it is restricted from performing patrol work, but is unrestricted in detector work.
4. Medical readiness status is determined after the VCO examines the MWD. The KM determines training and proficiency status. The VCO and KM should discuss their findings and each dog's status should be forwarded through the KM to the unit commander. For example, an MWD who is medically ready (CAT 1 or 2) may not be certified and therefore is non-deployable. Updates to medical deployability status will be performed at least monthly or as changes occur in an individual dog's status. Anytime an MWD presents for "sick call" or has a SAPE, the medical deployability status must be addressed in the SOAP. Changes in the medical deployability status must also be updated in the registry section of the MWD electronic VHR. VCOs may utilize the template located in Appendix H for reporting to the KM and dog owning unit commander the monthly medical deployability status for all MWDs.

DEPLOYMENT

Unlike civilian police dogs, MWDs are frequently called on to travel extensively. Current and anticipated future OPTEMPO has increased everyone's concern about deployment. We not only must maintain the dogs and their veterinary records in a condition fit for travel, but we must also be familiar with travel and disease risks in areas that are distant to our own area of responsibility.
1. Local diseases will vary, depending on the region and how well the country is developed, and administrative requirements for international travel varies country to country. Information regarding potential medical capabilities and disease threats within a foreign country may be obtained through the Operations Section of the National Center for Medical Intelligence (NCMI), DSN 343-7574, https://www.intelink.gov/ncmi/index.php; the theater veterinarian; or DODMWDVS. The DODMWDVS may publish definitive guidance for larger-scale or sustained deployment areas which would be distributed through command channels.
2. Deployment Category. MWDs should be in CAT 1 (or CAT 2 with consideration to theater capability) status to be eligible for deployment OCONUS or outside their home theater of operation. Final deployment authority resides with the MWD commander.
3. All MWDs must have physical examinations and evaluations prior to deployment or TDY in order to confirm fitness for duty and to issue a health certificate. The most important aspect of deployment medicine is keeping routine care and SAPEs up to date. If this is done well, there should be few

surprises when MWDs arrive for pre- deployment evaluation or at their temporary duty station. See figure 1 for Predeployment Processing Algorithm.

Figure 1. Predeployment Processing Algorithm

When is Deploying MWD Red SAPE due?

Within 9 months	Greater than 9 months
1. Perform RSAPE[1,2] 2. Administer quadrivalent Leptospirosis vaccine 3. Administer Rabies and DA2P if due within the next 12 months[3]	1. RSAPE not required. Perform during deployment if possible or upon redeployment.[1] 2. Do not administer quadrivalent 3. Leptospirosis vaccine 4. Administer Rabies and DA2P if due within the next 18 months[3]

NOTES:
[1] Blood banking will be performed at every RSAPE. Specific sampling will not be done pre/post deployment as each RSAPE sample will serve as pre/post deployment sampling respectively.
[2] Dental prophylaxis should be performed, if necessary.
[3] It should be remembered that specific country importation requirements could supersede these vaccination guidelines; responsible VCO/VMO should thoroughly research these country-specific guidelines prior to deployment.

a. The ideal schedule is to perform a pre-deployment evaluation as soon as the KM and handler are notified of a possible deployment. This allows more time to correct problems that may have arisen (like dental cleaning) since the time of the last SAPE. If a SAPE has not been completed within the last three months, all routine medical care associated with the next scheduled SAPE should be completed at this time, to include any required vaccinations and COHAT. Dental cleaning prior to deployment is NOT an absolute requirement. Though desired, due to vagaries of deployment notification, personnel availability, etc., not all dogs will receive dental cleaning prior to deployment. Calculus in and of itself is NOT disqualifying for deployment unless the dog also has significant disease or dental/oral conditions which render the dog otherwise not deployable (CAT 3 or 4).

b. In some cases, this evaluation may occur too early for issuing the health certificate (HC). In those cases, a very brief second exam can be scheduled, just before departure, so the HC can be signed, giving maximum leeway for delays en-route. Key areas of concern for the pre-deployment examination include getting a good history of work performance and general health, updating the VHR to make sure everything is clear and legible for the receiving VCO, and checking that all vaccinations and SAPE are up to date. It is very important to research and understand importation requirements, as some countries require annual rabies vaccination and that the most recent vaccination to be at least 30 days old at time of arrival. Finally, the pre-deployment exam is also the VCO's opportunity to brief the handler on preventive medicine concerns in the anticipated AO, e.g. heat or cold injury, parasites and infectious diseases, and to issue preventative medications. A pre-departure examination must be completed within 10 days of DEPARTURE to issue a HC and make a final check for problems that may prevent deployment. However, be prepared for changes in schedules as MWD transport can take considerable time and delays in transit sometimes occur. If a HC is signed 10 days before departure, it may expire before the MWD reaches final destination. A rule of thumb is to issue the HC close to the actual departure date, but not more than 10 days before planned date of ARRIVAL at final destination.

c. Prophylactic therapy for vector-borne and parasitic diseases. Historically, the Army Veterinary Service has had a large concern with tick-borne infections and their effect on MWD health and performance. Many MWDs were lost to rickettsial infections during the Vietnam conflict and these infections continue to be a concern. Disease and vectors of most concern include: mosquitoes and heartworm disease, ticks and rickettsial disease, sand flies and Leishmaniosis, gastrointestinal parasites, and ectoparasite-associated allergic or irritation related skin disease. The NCMI and DODMWDVS can be consulted to identify vector-borne disease risks for different areas of operation. If in doubt, err toward more cautious prophylaxis. Send enough medications with the dog team to last the duration of the anticipated deployment plus 1-2 additional months. Make sure all medications sent have an expiration date after the planned completion of the mission, and that the handler knows how to store and administer/apply each medication.

The DODMWDVS recommends:

a. Ectoparasite control
   i. Tick and Flea Control:
   - Imidacloprid/permethrin/pyriproxyfen is the only approved "spot-on" formulation for MWDs at this time and should be re-applied every 30 days. The most common cause of medication failure is under-dosing. If the MWD is at the high end of the weight range for the application, the VCO should double the dose. One or more of the below supplemental treatments may also be warranted or necessary.
   - Deltamethrin collar is recommended as an additional tick/leishmania preventive. The handler should be warned that the collar is a potential foreign body hazard if eaten.
   - Permethrin Sprays and other insect repellants/insecticides should NOT be used on MWDs.

   ii. Sand Fly (Leishmania) Control: Particularly important in Southern Europe, SW Asia, Africa, and South America. The use of a 4% Deltamethrin Collar is recommended in Leishmania endemic areas and should be maintained throughout their time in the endemic areas. Use of a collar may be discontinued for collar-intolerant MWDs after consultation with the assigned clinical consultant and the unit KM. The reason for discontinuation must be recorded in the VHR. The collar may pose a potential foreign body hazard if ingested.

b. Endoparasite Control (heartworm and parasites). The use of a monthly heartworm preventative (avermectin type) that also helps control GI parasites is required. It should be administered every 30 days throughout the year, regardless of climate or geographic location. MWDs with food allergies/dietary hypersensitivities should be supplied with the unflavored option. Handlers should be instructed to monitor for dogs that may spit out the preventative or vomit up to four hours post administration. It is important that the dog chew the preventative rather than swallow it whole.

d. Prophylactic Antibiotics. The prophylactic administration of doxycycline is no longer authorized. Given concerns about antibiotic resistance, compliance, and more effective and easier to administer flea/tick preventatives, the benefits of prophylactic doxycycline administration do not merit continuation.

5. Other Medications. In addition to the prophylactic medications above, a supply of any other

medication the MWD routinely receives (e.g. thyroid supplements, NSAIDs, chrondroitin-glucosamine supplement, etc.) must be sent. Ensure potency-dated items have expiration dates good through the deployment period, and advise handlers as to proper storage and administration. Do not send more than a 30-day supply of any controlled drug with the handler. Have the handler notify the deployed VCO responsible for the MWD care that they will need to obtain refills to ensure the medication is available prior to running out.

4. Vaccinations. As noted above, if a Red SAPE has not been completed in the previous nine months it should be completed prior to deployment. This includes updating all appropriate vaccinations (see fig 1). Access to vaccines may be limited in deployment areas. MWDs' vaccinations must be current through the end of the planned deployment so they cover requirements for the return health certificate. It is the responsibility of the home station VCO to determine entry requirements of potential countries where the dog will work or transit through and ensure the dog has appropriate vaccinations to meet those requirements to avoid delays/problems with entry.

5. Handler Training. Handlers should be receiving training from the supporting VTF on a quarterly basis utilizing the Training Support Package (TSP). However, whenever possible, deploying handlers should receive refresher training on tasks considered most important for the particular handler and/or AO shortly before deployment. See paragraph 3 for more information.

6. MWD First Aid Kits. Historically, VCOs dispensed first aid supplies/equipment to deploying dog teams at their discretion. Efforts to standardize an MWD handler first aid kit have resulted in the adoption of a three- component MWD medical bag with a unique NSN that may be ordered by the MWD unit. The durable, expendable and potency dated components of the MWD Handler First Aid Kit are linked to the 36 tasks in the MWD Handler Veterinary Medicine Training Package. Simply stated, if an item is required to perform 1 of the 36 tasks, then it is listed in the kit contents, including specific medications that handlers are authorized to give and must be trained to administer to their MWD. The component packing list is a template for packing the three-component MWD medical bag (urban patrol chest rig, drop-leg kit and aid bag) in order of precedence for Canine-Tactical Combat Casualty Care (cTCCC) and non-combat emergency medicine. Handlers, with VCOs, can adjust the packing template based on mission analysis and unit SOPs or TTPs. VTFs will provide resupply of expendable class VIII items consumed in treatment (medications, bandaging material, syringes/needles, etc.); however, units are responsible for replacement of durable and non-expendable items. Kit components are listed in the training manual at https://www.milsuite.mil/book/docs/DOC-580710. Kits are available through the logistics system, NSN: 3770- 01-614-0683. All MWD handlers will be given a copy of the cTCCC card (see appendix I) to be utilized to record all combat medical care provided to the MWD at the point of injury through role II. This card will be filled out by the personnel performing the initial first aid which may be the handler or a combat medic. The cTCCC card (role I), along with the Canine Treatment and Resuscitation Record (role II/III), must be added to the MWD Trauma Registry (once development is completed) and the VHR. The completed cTCCC card and Canine Treatment and Resuscitation Record will be emailed to DODMWDVS until the MWD Trauma Registry is completed. Instructions on use and completion of these forms can be found on the JTS website, https://jts.amedd.army.mil/index.cfm/documents/forms_after_action and in the most current Clinical Practice Guidelines. See Chapter 4 for link to the Clinical Practice Guidelines.

7. For Deploying/Deployed Veterinary Staff.
    a. Work with theater/local aeromedical evacuation personnel to review evacuation policies for MWDs. MWDs are authorized evacuation on medical assets according to medical priority. Generally, the theater 64F will facilitate Aeromedical Evacuation (AE) procedures for working dogs that may require transport to Veterinary Medical Center Europe in Germany or CONUS based veterinary facilities.

b. It is beneficial to establish rapport with local MTFs in order to benefit from all the assets they can provide to include:
   i. Imaging, to include teleradiology capabilities, and advanced imaging such as CT, MR and ultrasound.
   ii. Pharmacy services
   iii. Central Material and Sterilization
   iv. Medical maintenance
   v. Logistics (supply items)
   vi. Surgical assistance
   vii. Endoscopic assistance
   viii. Dental assistance
c. Reach back consultation. Utilize Advanced Virtual Support for Operational Forces (ADVISOR) by calling 1-833-238-7756 or DSN 312-429-9089 and select option 5 for Veterinary Consults. This will ensure your call is directed to the appropriate veterinary personnel. In the event that ADVISOR is not working you can contact the following:

Veterinary Medical Center Europe:
DSN: 314-493-4529/4444/4475 (during duty hours)
68T on call: +49(0)162-297-1228
VCO on call: +49(0)162-297-1231
DSN Operator to connect to commercial number: 314-480-1110

DODMWDVS, Holland Memorial MWD Hospital, JBSA-Lackland:
Comm: (+1) 210-671-3992/3; DSN: 312-473-3992/3993
VCO on call: Commercial (+1) 210-421-3879 dog.consult@us.af.mil

EXERCISE AND THE OBSTACLE COURSE

MWD activity levels will vary greatly depending on duty status and location. At home station, many MWDs spend most of their time in the kennel or in a patrol car. When deployed, many MWDs experience a rapid increase in activity. More of their time is spent patrolling on foot and doing frequent vehicle and structure searches. In order to maintain a fitness level that will accommodate this rapid change in duty requirements, MWDs need a physical training program just like other Service members. Physical conditioning should be integrated into daily training and duty, and guidelines for conditioning programs are discussed in Chapter 9. Although MWDs have sufficient drive that they may perform extended work without prior conditioning, maximum performance and minimal injury risk can only be achieved through conditioning the dog to a performance standard. VCOs should work with the KMs and canine training NCOs to identify work requirements expected during deployments and installation support.

1. Although usually considered an integral part of conditioning and training in most dogs, exercise on the obstacle course may exacerbate joint problems in some older dogs and therefore may need to be limited or omitted.
2. The responsible VCO has the authority to limit the MWD's activities on the obstacle course (such as "no A- frame"), yet still allow the dog to perform all other aspects of its mission. Contact the DODMWDVS if further guidance is required.
3. Training of MWD handlers is very important. In addition to appropriate information on diseases present in the region, such things as hot and cold weather injuries, exercise induced injuries, and administration of preventative medications should be discussed. For cold weather, tell the handler to ensure the dogs have plenty of water to drink when working outside, keep them dry, and get them

into some type of protection (house, kennel, and building) if the weather becomes bad or if they are required to remain inactive for prolonged periods. For hot weather, they should ensure there is plenty of water to drink, provide shade, and ensure that they follow work/rest cycles. Some dogs may develop mild to moderate muscle and joint pain soon after arriving at busy overseas duty sites. The most likely reason is increased exertion while searching or patrolling. Remind the handler that the use of portable platforms, or ramps (vs. jumping in and out) will reduce MWD fatigue and injury when searching cargo trucks and other items/locations otherwise requiring the dog to jump up/down. Also remind them not to administer human medications to their MWD without talking to the responsible VCO for the deployment area.

WORKING BITE QUARANTINE

1. If a skin puncture occurs due to an MWD bite, the person bitten should be referred to the local MTF for treatment. It is expected that the dog's rabies vaccination will be current. The dog should be examined as soon as possible after the bite and placed on a "working bite quarantine." During which the dog may be employed in the normal manner but is under close observation by the handler for any abnormal behavior or signs of illness. If practical, the MWD should not come in direct physical contact with other dogs during the quarantine period. The dog is then reexamined at the end of 10 days and released from the quarantine. In deployed settings where veterinary care teams are not co-located with the MWD, telephonic communication with the KM in addition to medical record documentation fulfills this requirement.
2. The MWD's record will be annotated regarding the bite incident, circumstances of the bite event, and examination findings (SF600/eNote and reflect on MPL). The bite should also be annotated in local bite report log after receiving the DD 2341, Report of Animal Bite, from local MTF emergency room personnel.

CBRN CONSIDERATIONS WITH MWDS

MWD Handler Medical Care Task #28, Perform Nuclear, Biological and Chemical Decontamination of a Military Working Dog specifies treatment steps necessary to decontaminate an MWD potentially exposed to nuclear, biological, and/or chemical agents. Also refer to the appropriate Army Techniques Publications regarding CBRN.

MWD CASE CONSULTATION WITH DODMWDVS

Case consultation for MWDs should always start with the local supporting 64F. However, if they are not available or none are assigned, consult with the DODMWDVS specialists. The clinical specialists provide a valuable resource when assistance is needed in the workup, management, or disposition of an MWD. The DODMWDVS has clinical specialists in surgery, internal medicine, emergency and critical care, radiology, sports medicine/rehabilitation, and animal behavior.
1. Consult requests may be made by telephone (DODMWDVS: 210-671-3992/3; DSN 312-473-3992/3) or e-mail. E-mail is the preferred route using dog.consult@us.af.mil. Please do not directly email one of the DODMWDVS 64Fs directly unless directed to do so as this may delay the response. Ensure MWD name and tattoo are included in subject line for each correspondence about the dog. If the consult is of an urgent nature, please type URGENT in the subject line and follow up with a phone call. When consulting, the VCO must give animal identification (name and tattoo number), signalment, chief complaint, appropriate medical/surgical and dietary history, synopsis of workup

and results to date, and the specific questions. This information should be provided on the DODMWDVS referral form, DA Form 7593. Pertinent e-notes/SF 600s, test results/reports, images or other forms/documents will accompany the DA Form 7593. Use of AMRDEC SAFE should be used when large files need to be transferred. AMRDEC SAFE is a web-based file transfer system available to all DOD email users, and can be found at the following web link: https://safe.amrdec.army.mil/SAFE/. See Appendix E for instructions for utilizing AMRDEC SAFE. Always send the DA Form 7593 via email even if submitting other documentation through AMRDEC or mail to ensure the proper department receives the consult.
2. Consultation is required prior to:
   a. Non-emergent euthanasia of all MWDs
   b. Non-emergent cases being referred to civilian facilities
   c. Referral of MWDs to DODMWDVS (see below)
3. For radiology consultation and teleradiology consults see chapter 6.

MWD REFERRAL TO DODMWDVS

1. Pre-Shipment Consultation. Telephone and/or e-mail consultation and approval of a DODMWDVS clinician is required prior to referral of an MWD (Medical TDY). A unique email address has been created for consultations and referrals: dog.consult@us.af.mil. The DODMWDVS may be able to assist the VCO in making a disposition/diagnosis without having to transport the dog. When an MWD is sent to JBSA-Lackland, the Veterinary Health Record and pertinent images (hard copy or electronic) must accompany the dog.
2. Completion of a DA Form 7593. A referral form summarizing the dog's problem for referral and including name of approving DODMWDVS Clinician (that is, the DODMWDVS clinician the referring VCO discussed the case with), local POCs with current DSN and civilian phone and FAX numbers must accompany the record. This form should be placed on the top of the MPL in the VHR.
3. When an MWD is referred to the DODMWDVS for medical evaluation or treatment, transportation arrangements are made by the owning unit for MWD travel at the owning unit's expense. The unit will contact their installation Transportation and Movement Office (TMO) and request arrangements be made to ship the MWD to the 341 TRS, JBSA-Lackland. When transportation is arranged, the itinerary is to be provided to the 341TRS at e-mail: mwd.transportation@us.af.mil; however, call the 341TRS MWD Shipping Manager at DSN 473-7166/3125 or Commercial (210) 671-7166/3125 first. All MWDs sent for referral are considered to be TDY and return. The owning unit is required to provide a transportation fund cite to the 341 TRS so return transport can be arranged.
4. Updates. Referring VCOs will be kept updated by DODMWDVS staff regarding status of their MWDs. However, it is not DODMWDVS responsibility to provide status updates to the MWD's KM/handler. Referring VCOs must ensure the MWD's KM and handler are kept updated of their dog's condition as well as expected return date, etc.

MWD REFERRAL FOR CIVILIAN CARE

If the local VTF is unable to provide the needed emergency veterinary services, then a local civilian veterinary facility may be utilized IAW AR 40-3 and AR 40-1 and as described in MEDCOM Policy 17-062, Delivery of Veterinary Medical Care for GOAs 21 Dec 2017. This will be at no cost to the owning unit only with prior approval and coordination with the supporting PHA Command, or the owning unit risks responsibility for all civilian veterinary facility charges. Please refer to local SOP establishing policy for emergent and non-emergent civilian care. In general, the steps for approval and utilization of civilian care is

as follows:
1. Attending VCO communicates the MWD's relevant medical history and current condition to the supporting 64F.
2. In the event that the 64F is unavailable or they determine that a higher echelon of care is required, the Director, DODMWDVS is contacted to discuss referral. If the DODMWDVS is unavailable to accept the referral or determines that care at a local civilian specialty hospital will be more beneficial, the 64F will refer the MWD.
3. The attending VCO obtains a written estimate for care from the civilian facility and forwards that, along with the 64F's recommendation to the PHA approval authority. The VCO briefs both the PHA commander and the owning unit commander on the MWD's medical history, treatment, prognosis, and referral within two hours.
4. If extended hospitalization for recovery is required, the MWD should be transferred to the responsible VTF as soon as appropriate for continued care by military personnel, dependent on capability and staffing. Care for hospitalized patients is a critical skill for all military veterinary personnel that should be exercised at every opportunity.
5. While hospitalized under civilian care, the attending VCO will update the 64F on the MWD's condition daily to facilitate determination of appropriate care transfer or discharge.
6. Once the MWD is discharged, the VCO will complete the online Civilian Care of DOD Animals survey at: https://tiny.army.mil/r/1T2WJ/MWDCIVCARE.
7. The VCO will ensure all documentation from the civilian facility are imported into the MWD's electronic VHR.
8. An EXSUM will be completed for all admissions of MWDs to civilian facilities.
9. The VCO will work closely with their command to ensure the invoice is promptly paid utilizing appropriated funds.

EUTHANASIA OR DEATH OF MWDS

Since the passage of Public Law 106-446 in 2000 (also known as "Robby's Law"), Congress now has the authority to request documentation and justification for all dogs not considered for adoption and reasons for euthanasia.
1. Emergent euthanasia. When an MWD is experiencing undue suffering, or in an emergency situation from which recovery is not expected, any veterinarian is authorized to euthanize the dog in the most humane manner possible in accordance with the most current AVMA Guidelines for the Euthanasia of Animals. Following an emergency euthanasia, a letter of explanation/EXSUM and copy of the death certificate (DD Form 1743) must be sent to the Provost Marshal, Chief of Security Forces, or appropriate authority. In the event of an unexpected or emergent MWD death or euthanasia, the veterinary unit commander and the supporting 64F will also need to be informed immediately. The DODMWDVS Director (dog.consult@us.af.mil) must be notified by the supporting 64F and the MWD electronic VHR updated by the attending VCO or VMO within 24 hours. The death certificate should clearly read, "Emergent euthanasia due to (state condition/situation)". A complete necropsy will be performed on all MWDs IAW AR40-905 and TB MED 283 with tissue specimens sent to the Joint Pathology Center.
2. Non-emergent euthanasia. Usually performed on CAT 4 dogs with significant non-lethal medical conditions (e.g. debilitating arthritis) or those that have a poor prognosis (e.g. metastatic neoplasia). Such euthanasia might also be performed on very aggressive dogs or those with other behavioral issues which render them unadoptable as determined by the unit commander. If the VCO in consultation with supporting 64F or DODMWDVS consultant decides that the dog is not medically eligible for adoption due to conditions as mentioned above, authorization for euthanasia is granted

and may proceed after notification/coordination with the dog-owning unit. If however, the dog is not thought to be behaviorally eligible for adoption, a consultation with the DODMWDVS Behaviorist is indicated to complete the disposition process. A letter (MFR format) requesting/consenting euthanasia must be obtained from the owning unit commander and imported into the VHR. If after consultation the dog is deemed behaviorally ineligible, euthanasia can proceed. A complete necropsy will be performed on all MWDs IAW AR40-905 and TB MED 283 and tissue specimens sent to the Joint Pathology Center.

　　a. It is imperative that all disposition and adoption documents be completed and filed in the VHR. This documentation includes copies of the following:
　　　　i. Disposition authorization letter declaring dog "excess" to the needs of the DOD.
　　　　ii. Copy of the "Adoption Suitability Checklist" completed by the VCO and KM with the commander's signature.
　　　　iii. Copy of the Regional Clinical Specialist Consultation Letter.
　　　　iv. Copy of the Behavioral Testing Video consultation form.
　　　　v. Copy of the authorization letter from the MWD chain of command.
　　b. If euthanasia and necropsy are to be performed locally, the dog must be euthanized with an approved euthanasia solution at the prescribed dosage. Premedication with a sedative prior to euthanasia is recommended.

3. DD Form 1743. The Death Certificate of a Military Dog (DD Form 1743) must contain a brief statement explaining the reason for euthanasia and whether the death resulted from fault or neglect. "Euthanasia" alone is not an acceptable reason for death on the DD Form 1743. Summarize the medical or behavioral conditions leading to euthanasia or removal from service and statement why dog was not adopted.

　　a. An example summary would be similar to the following:
　　　　i. "Dog not fit for duty due to severe stifle arthritis and unmanageable pain, not an adoption candidate due to aggression."
　　　　ii. "Dog unfit for duty due to severe lumbosacral stenosis disease with neurological deficits, not considered for adoption due to medical condition."
　　　　iii. "Dog unfit for duty due to severe aggression, not considered for adoption due to aggressive behavior/temperament."
　　　　iv. "Dog found dead in kennel. Necropsy showed hemoabdomen secondary to ruptured splenic mass."
　　　　v. "Euthanasia performed at time of surgery due to extensive intestinal necrosis secondary to mesenteric volvulus."
　　　　vi. Provide the original DD Form 1743 to the KM, retain a copy in the dog's medical record, and email a copy to the DODMWDVS with an EXSUM (dog.consult@us.af.mil).
　　b. Without awaiting necropsy histopathology results from the Joint Pathology Center (JPC), the following items are then forwarded to the DOD MWD VS Record Repository, DODMWDVS, 341TRS/SGV, 1219 Knight Street, Bldg 7602, JBSA-Lackland, TX 78236:
　　　　i. Completed Veterinary Health Record (hard copy mailed and ROVR record electronically transferred). Ensure all forms are filed in the proper sections, chronologically, with newest on top as outlined in Appendix B.
　　　　ii. Copy of the DD Form 1626, Gross Necropsy Report
　　　　iii. Copy of the DD Form 1743, Death Certificate
　　　　iv. Complete radiographic file clearly stating that dog is deceased.

CHAPTER 4

EMERGENCY MEDICINE

OVERVIEW OF EMERGENT AND CRITICAL CARE

This section outlines treatment of common emergency situations that occur in MWDs.

1. The *Military Working Dog Clinical Practice Guidelines* (CPGs) provide quick reference for veterinary personnel regarding emergency and critical care management of MWDs. The CPGs were developed under the auspices of the Joint Trauma System to provide human healthcare providers (HCPs) specific and detailed medical and surgical management guidelines for deployed MWDs in austere situations, when veterinary personnel may not be available.
2. The CPGs are comprehensive, detailed, and directed towards human medical personnel, but also provide the essentials for emergent and critical care management for MWDs by veterinary personnel. Extensive use is made of treatment algorithms, charts, and photographs. Rather than repeat the CPGs here, veterinary personnel are directed to the JTS website for access. This serves two purposes. Firstly, it consolidates all guidance by veterinary personnel in a standard document used globally. Secondly, because veterinary personnel are required to provide training to HCPs on these CPGs, it enforces use of the definitive source document by veterinary personnel, which will additionally serve to reinforce familiarity with these guidelines.
3. The MWD CPGs are also open-source, and can be found at the Joint Trauma System website, at https://jts.amedd.army.mil/index.cfm/PI_CPGs/cpgs.
4. The MWD CPGs will be updated annually, with revisions released around January of each year. The CPGs are authored by military board-certified emergency and critical care specialists, and thus offer the most definitive source for MWD care in emergency and critical care medicine. The CPGs are extensively referenced with the most current information available for each topic. Veterinary personnel should have immediate access to the CPGs in the workplace.
5. The CPGs are best-practice clinical guidelines and do not serve to direct exact actions to be applied for every situation. Veterinary personnel should use sound clinical judgement when addressing each patient and modify management based on unique situations.
6. In addition to the select topics that will be addressed in this handbook, appendices are provided in the CPGs that discuss diagnostic imaging guidelines and protocols, and management of long bone fractures, wounds, traumatic brain and spinal cord injury, and canine post-traumatic stress disorder. Additional information is provided for management of blast, burn, and crush injuries, snake and scorpion envenomation, ocular injuries, and toxicoses.

EMERGENCY PREPAREDNESS IS CRITICAL FOR SUCCESS

1. Emergency care for MWDs is a mission priority. A rapid, appropriate response is essential to afford the MWD the best opportunity for return to duty. A VCO or 68T should be available at all times for handlers to contact for MWD emergencies.
2. Equipment and drugs to treat emergent ill or injured MWDs must be available at all duty sites where a VCO or technician is permanently assigned. Refer to the Veterinary Medical Standardization Board (VMSB), Formulary Section, Emergency Crash Cart Drugs for a list of emergency drugs that must be available in each VTF.

3. An organized method to store emergency drugs, equipment, and supplies is essential to facilitate response in an emergency. Emergency drug dosage and CPR charts should be readily available in high risk areas (e.g. surgery room/prep area). Conduct monthly inventory of emergency drugs and supplies. It is emphasized that emergency supplies are placed in an accessible location and are logically organized.
4. Emergency procedures and actions for common emergency situations must be in place and rehearsed. All veterinary personnel and MWD handlers must conduct periodic emergency training using likely scenarios. Animal Care Specialists (68T) assigned to duty sites that support MWDs but without direct supervision of an attending VCO should receive additional training that covers common emergency situations to ensure appropriate response and treatment are provided to the MWDs.
5. Standard Operating Procedures outlining MWD emergency procedures and how to obtain civilian veterinary care must be in place and be current.
6. In some circumstances, emergent or critical care measures may not be possible or may not be appropriate. Euthanasia should be considered in these situations, but only after careful assessment by the attending VCO in collaboration with the MWD handler, KM, and dog-owning unit commander. Follow procedures outlined in section 3-17.

CARDIOPULMONARY RESUSCITATION (CPR) GUIDELINES
(See MWD CPGS Chapter 5)

1. Consider CPR of MWDs in cases of non-traumatic cardiopulmonary arrest (CPA) such as anesthesia-related, hypothermia, near drowning, and electrocution. If resources permit, consider CPR in MWDs with CPA due to blast injury, blunt trauma, or penetrating trauma, although successful resuscitation in these cases is unlikely. Overall, survival with acceptable function is about 5% for dogs.
2. A recent veterinary evidence-based review of CPR, The RECOVER Initiative, updates clinical recommendations and guides canine CPR. Initiate 2-person, closed-chest CPR if a dog is noted unresponsive or with apneic breathing. Immediately begin sustained, forceful chest compressions with the MWD in lateral recumbency at a rate of 100 compressions per minute. Sustain compressions for at least 2-3 minutes per cycle. Hand placement should be over the widest part of the chest for most MWDs (>15kg). Consider hand placement over the heart for small dogs (<15kg). Ensure adequate relief of downward pressure during the relaxation phase of the compressions to allow for complete chest recoil. As for humans, "PUSH HARD and PUSH FAST." Establish an airway as rapidly as possible and as soon as possible; however, start chest compressions first. Intubate the MWD or perform an emergent tracheostomy. Ventilate the patient at a rate of 8-10 breaths per minute. Avoid hyperventilation. Oxygen is preferred when ventilating MWDs during CPR, but room air is acceptable if oxygen is not available.
3. Initiate advanced life support as soon as feasible, with ECG monitoring to guide actions. In the dog, sinus bradycardia often progresses to pathologic arrhythmias, and atropine is indicated if noted. The most common arrest rhythms in dogs are pulseless electrical activity (PEA) and ventricular asystole. Atropine or low-dose epinephrine are best choices for these rhythms or for empiric use if ECG capability is not available; vasopressin may be used instead of low-dose epinephrine. In most settings, there is no role for transthoracic pacing in MWDs with PEA or asystole. Ventricular fibrillation often develops during resuscitation, or may be the primary rhythm in some arrests. Perform external defibrillation if possible and as rapidly as possible if VF is noted; biphasic defibrillation is ideal. Apply paddles to either side of the chest at the level of the heart with the MWD in dorsal recumbency, or place a flat paddle under the MWD lying in lateral recumbency and a standard paddle on the upper chest wall. Defibrillate up to 3 times, performing aggressive chest

compressions for at least 2 minutes between each subsequent defibrillation. Staff should be properly trained in the use of the defibrillator to ensure its safe and proper use. After each defibrillation attempt, wait 2-3 minutes (1 cycle) before reassessing the ECG. IV access is critical; place multiple peripheral or IO catheters or perform venous cut-downs. Follow all drugs with at least a 20 mL sterile saline push. Place a central venous catheter when feasible. Do not give large volumes of fluids to MWDs during CPR, unless severe hypovolemia is thought to be present; only give fluids during CPR to facilitate drug delivery.
4. Resuscitated dogs will require intensive care. Many dogs arrest again, and most do so in the first 4 hours after resuscitation. Successful resuscitation in subsequent arrests becomes less likely. Key management issues for MWDs in the post-resuscitation phase are summarized in the CPGs. Some unique aspects of care in dogs are detailed. There is a limited role for open-chest CPR in most situations, however, it may be necessary in cases of pleural space disease or thoracic trauma. In the absence of specialty care/consultation, euthanasia should be considered.

GASTRIC DILATATION-VOLVULUS (GDV) SYNDROME
(See MWD CPGs Chapter 8)

1. GDV, commonly called "bloat" by handlers, is a multifactorial, rapidly progressive, life-threatening surgical emergency, common in large breed dogs. The mechanism of action is poorly understood but under certain circumstances, the stomach will rapidly dilate with ingested air, food, and water. This dilatation predisposes to development of a volvulus, with the stomach 'flipping' on its long axis. Fermentation of food, retention of gastric secretions, and influx of fluid exacerbates the dilatation. Given the volvulus, there is no way to empty the stomach. The dilatation is dramatic and rapid, often progressing to life-threatening shock in less than 4 hours. Death in the short-term period is due to shock; the dilated stomach prevents venous return from the abdomen and hind limbs, ultimately leading to decreased cardiac output. Death in the long-term period is due to the myriad of complications in this extreme form of ischemic shock.
2. GDV was a major cause of death in MWDs for decades; however, GDV is a rare occurrence in DOD MWDs now, since performance of a prophylactic gastropexy was instituted in 2009 for all new DOD MWDs. In this procedure, a permanent surgical adhesion between the stomach and inner peritoneal wall is created during an elective procedure that prevents volvulus and has dramatically reduced the incidence of GDV and gastric dilatation in the MWD population. However, veterinary personnel may still encounter emergently ill working dogs with GDV, because most Special Operations Forces, contractor and allied working dogs have not been prophylactically gastropexied. Although rare, failure of the surgical adhesion site after a gastropexy has been reported.
3. GDV is a surgical emergency and can be diagnosed based on a right lateral radiograph. Intervention is required, ideally within 4 hours of presentation, to correct the volvulus, assess gastric and splenic viability, and perform a gastropexy. In some cases, a partial gastrectomy or splenectomy may be necessary. Provide initial resuscitation and stabilization, and then prepare the dog for definitive surgical management.
4. Initial management of a dog presenting with GDV centers on gaining intravenous catheter access to initiate immediate shock therapy, followed rapidly by gastric decompression, with intensive monitoring for and management of potential complications. The most rapid and effective method of gastric decompression for GDV is trocarization of the tympanic stomach using a large-bore over-the-needle catheter. Briefly, after the insertion point is identified and prepared for aseptic procedure, a 14-gauge decompression device (commonly used for needle thoracocentesis) is forcefully inserted through the skin and body wall and advanced firmly into the stomach lumen to relieve gas pressure.

Decompression may need to be repeated if tympany recurs while the dog is prepared for evacuation or surgery.
5. Multiple complications can occur during GDV to include shock, cardiac arrhythmias, coagulopathy, electrolyte and acid-base disturbances, gastroparesis, gastric necrosis, gastric rupture, peritonitis, hypoproteinemia and hypoalbuminemia, and recurrent dilatation with or without volvulus. Thus, intensive monitoring is necessary.

MESENTERIC VOLVULUS
(See MWD CPGs Chapter 8)

1. Mesenteric or intestinal volvulus is a rare, often fatal condition that appears to be over-represented in MWDs. Several breeds are affected and the condition has been reported in all dog breeds currently employed by the DOD. German Shepherds appear over-represented in veterinary literature and a recent study examining risk factors in MWDs also found that German Shepherds have a higher risk for developing this condition. While the underlying cause is unknown, an increased risk of volvulus has been associated with concurrent GI disease including parvoviral enteritis, intussusception, exocrine pancreatic insufficiency, intestinal neoplasia, parasites and GDV. Dogs of virtually any age can be affected. Rapid presentation by the handler, diagnostics, stabilization and early surgical intervention are all related to survival. Dogs with mesenteric volvulus will decompensate within a matter of minutes, therefore emergent surgical intervention may be necessary (prior to full patient stabilization).
2. Clinical signs can vary from mild to severe depending on duration of the condition. Common signs are similar to many other acute abdomen cases, and include lethargy or collapse, persistent restlessness, abdominal pain, abdominal distension, tachycardia, hemoconcentration, severe hematochezia, and shock (tachycardia, hypotension, pale or injected mucous membranes, prolonged CRT). However, some of the recent MWD cases have presented with mild, nonspecific signs and were only diagnosed after radiographs and exploratory surgery. Body temperature can be variable with both hypo- and hyperthermia reported. Some patients are found dead. Differential diagnoses include any causes of acute abdomen, to include GDV, pancreatitis, acute hemorrhagic diarrhea syndrome (formerly HGE), GI foreign body, septic peritonitis, bile peritonitis, trauma, splenic torsion, urinary obstruction, and neoplasia.
3. The diagnostic workup for these cases includes blood biochemistry panel with electrolytes, complete blood count, lactate if available, fecal exam, abdominal radiographs, and an AFAST exam. While some animals have vague signs, the following signs are indicators for radiographs in all acute cases: severe or persistent abdominal pain or rigidity, abdominal distension, any indication of shock, hypothermia, hematochezia, and unexplained or refractory tachycardia with any abdominal discomfort.
4. Initial treatment is aimed at correcting shock. Upon diagnosis or suspicion of a surgical abdomen, anesthesia is initiated using the VMSB Compromised Patient protocol. Abdominal exploratory with resection of devitalized tissue and anastomosis is the definitive treatment. The necrosis can extend from distal to the left limb of the pancreas through much of the colon, but can also be less severe (i.e. segmental). The volvulus must first be derotated in order to fully assess the extent of the resection. This is a point where many toxic cytokines are released, causing the dog to become more hemodynamically unstable. Be prepared to address significant hypotension and cardiac arrhythmias following derotation. Pre-emptively, a lidocaine bolus of 2 mg/kg IV, followed by 50 mcg/kg/min, should be implemented prior to derotation to mediate reperfusion injury.
5. Post-operative care is very laborious, and referral may be the best course of action. Maintain

perfusion with appropriate fluid therapy, with balanced isotonic crystalloids as first choice. Often patients are severely hypoalbuminemic and nutritional support should be implemented as soon as possible. If plasma or albumin transfusion is necessary, the supporting 64F should be consulted prior to transfusion. Patients may also become coagulopathic, monitor coagulation and platelet count and administer plasma or whole blood as needed. Monitor for ventricular arrhythmias, and treat if hemodynamic instability is present (heart rate >180, hypotension, pulse deficits, syncope). Pain management is critical. Gut protection is beneficial.

HEAT RELATED INJURIES
(See MWD CPGs Chapter 9)

1. Heat injury is the leading non-trauma cause of death in deployed MWDs. Well-acclimated dogs working in hot, humid environments routinely have core body temperatures of 1050 ± 10 F. However, with cessation of work and access to shade and water, dogs that do not develop heat injury rapidly cool to normal body temperature (101- 1030 F). Since dogs do not sweat significantly, panting is the most critical method for cooling, to expose the highly vascular tongue for evaporative cooling. There is no cut-off temperature that denotes heat injury; temperatures as low as 1060 F have been associated with pathology. However, dogs with moderate to severe heat injury usually have sustained rectal temperatures of 1070 F or higher. The ability to compensate is more readily overwhelmed if the ambient air is humid. Most dogs develop heat injury due to heavy exertion in hot, humid environments, especially if inadequately acclimated. Rarely, dogs are treated for heat injury secondary to partial airway obstruction or inadvertent enclosure in vehicles.
2. Heat injury in dogs is described as mild ("heat stress"), moderate ("heat exhaustion"), and severe ("heat stroke"). MWD handlers are trained to recognize and treat heat injury in the field; thus, dogs may be hypothermic on arrival if treated before presentation. Dogs with moderate to severe heat injury frequently develop multi-organ complications and have a high case fatality rate.
3. If poorly managed or untreated, heat injury is a progressive process. Distinguishing between controlled versus uncontrolled panting is a reliable means of crudely assessing severity of heat injury. Controlled panting means the dog retains some voluntary control over its breathing and will temporarily stop panting if exposed to a noxious stimulus (such as an alcohol-soaked cotton ball). A dog with uncontrolled panting will not stop breathing even in the face of noxious stimuli, because inherent survival mechanisms drive panting continuously.
4. The progression of heat injury in dogs is well-described. Dogs with mild heat injury have increased thirst, are reluctant to work, seem uncomfortable, seek shade, and have controlled panting. Dogs with moderate heat injury demonstrate the signs of mild injury, but also become weak and more distressed, and have uncontrolled panting; some may present with petechiae or ecchymosis (best noted on the ear pinna, mucous membranes of the mouth, and skin over the abdomen), and vomiting or diarrhea. Dogs with severe heat injury show all of the signs of moderate heat injury, but classically demonstrate some degree of central nervous system (CNS) involvement, collapse, and shock. The most common CNS signs are ataxia, blindness, seizures, and stupor or coma. Dehydration frequently accompanies heat injury, and many dogs will require volume resuscitation with IV crystalloids.
5. The fundamental treatment for any dog with signs consistent with moderate to severe heat injury is to cool the dog as rapidly as possible – without causing other problems – until the rectal temperature is 1050 F or lower. The best ways to emergently cool MWDs are to soak the dog to the skin with room temperature water (and continue soaking the dog until the temperature decreases), giving room temperature IV fluids, and directing fans on the dog. Do not use cold or iced IV fluids, ice water immersion, ice water enemas, peritoneal lavage, or surface cooling with ice packs or alcohol, as these

methods cause peripheral vasoconstriction and shivering that actually may increase core temperature, and dogs appear very prone to rebound hypothermia that can be extremely difficult to correct. Reduce the rate of cooling when the rectal temperature reaches 1050 F; cease cooling efforts and dry the dog when the temperature reaches 1030 F to prevent rebound hypothermia. Be prepared to provide passive warming if the rectal temperature is less than 1000 F.
6. Monitor and manage common complications of heat injury, to include hypotension, glucose and electrolyte abnormalities, coagulopathy and thrombocytopenia, cardiac arrhythmias, and gastroenteritis.

HEMORRHAGIC SHOCK
(See MWD CPGs Chapter 6)

1. The majority of MWDs managed for shock have trauma-induced hemorrhagic shock; some are managed for heat injury or severe dehydration. Treatment by handlers and combat medics may have been performed, with varying degrees of success; expect dogs to arrive with pressure dressings, hemostatic gauze packed into wounds, and improvised tourniquets. Expect inadequately controlled bleeding, and suspect "hidden" hemorrhage in the chest and abdomen. When managing severe limb injuries and traumatic amputations, note that dogs have excellent collateral circulation, and major vessels can be ligated without long term adverse consequences. Use TFAST and AFAST to rapidly screen for intracavitary hemorrhage; assume any intracavitary fluid in a traumatized dog is due to bleeding until proven otherwise.
2. Shock management in dogs is similar to that in people. Provide immediate fluid therapy targeted to specific endpoints, provide supplemental oxygen, and identify and treat the underlying cause. Use multiple large-bore IV or intraosseous (IO) catheters or venous cut-downs. Intraosseous catheters are reliably placed on the lateral proximal humerus or the medial proximal tibia. Crystalloid fluid challenges, as needed based on response to therapy, are better than large volume fluid administration. For simplicity, use the "10-20-10-20 Rule". For example, a 40 kg MWD might need 3.6 L of fluids in the first hour to treat shock, but should be given "quarter-shock" volumes of 900 mL every 10-20 minutes during initial resuscitation, based on response. In most cases, MWDs in shock can be successfully stabilized with 2-3 bolus challenges.
3. Synthetic colloids and hypertonic saline can be used in dogs with refractory shock. While very limited data suggest increased risks, dogs do not seem to develop the many complications seen in people, so colloid use in dogs with refractory shock is warranted – the benefits are deemed to outweigh the risks in these cases. Hydroxyethyl starch (hetastarch, vetstarch, voluven, etc.) can be used as a bolus at 5 ml/kg IV, repeated as needed based on resuscitation endpoints up to 20 ml/kg/day. Hypertonic saline (HTS) can be used as a small volume resuscitation bolus, using 7.0-7.5% HTS at 4-6 ml/kg/bolus. No more than two HTS boluses should be given to correct intravascular volume deficits. Synthetic colloids and HTS should be used in conjunction with crystalloid fluid therapy. Do not use human serum albumin in dogs; although some reports suggest benefit in a very specific subset of canine patients with severe hypoalbuminemia, immediate and delayed life-threatening complications are reported, and the risks outweigh the benefits in the management of shock.
4. Canine blood products should be considered in cases of severe blood loss or hemolytic anemia. Prior planning and consultation is required to either have these products available when needed, or to develop a donor program locally. In most instances, plasma, packed red cell units, and whole blood cannot be ordered and delivered in time for true emergencies, and 'walking blood donor' programs are not available in a timely manner for emergent use. So, if deemed indicated, prior purchase and

storage of blood components may be authorized. In most instances, however, veterinary personnel will have to manage hemorrhagic shock with crystalloid and colloid therapy.
5. There is limited, but promising, data to guide use of tranexamic acid (TXA) and epsilon aminocaproic acid (EACA) in dogs with severe hemorrhage or suspected acute traumatic coagulopathy. Doses and guidelines for use of TXA and EACA in dogs with refractory hemorrhagic shock, limb amputation, penetrating torso trauma, and ongoing severe bleeding are provided in the CPGs, but discussion with clinical specialists is critical before use.

UPPER AIRWAY OBSTRUCTION
(See MWD CPGs Chapter 3)

1. While upper airway obstruction is an uncommon problem in MWDs, immediate action is required. The most common causes of obstruction are laryngeal paralysis, lodging of 'rewards' used by the handler (balls, Kongs™), and facial trauma.
2. Typically, dogs with upper airway obstruction present with severe respiratory distress with labored inspiration and abnormal upper airway noise (e.g., stertor, stridor). Dogs may be conscious but extremely agitated due to air hunger; thus, extreme care is necessary. Provide immediate oxygen therapy; however, because of the danger of working with an agitated dog, face mask or 'blow by' oxygen supplementation, in which the end of the oxygen tubing from the source is held as close to the face as possible at high oxygen flow rates, may be all that is possible. These methods are not ideal, but do provide inspired oxygen concentrations from 40-70% until the airway is secured.
3. Rapid sedation or general anesthesia is likely necessary for definitive management. If the obstruction can be removed, oral intubation is ideal. If the obstruction cannot be removed, emergent tracheostomy is indicated.
4. Perform emergent tracheostomy if safe, rapid airway access cannot be obtained by orotracheal intubation.

BLUNT CHEST TRAUMA
(See MWD CPGs Chapter 4)

1. Dogs in respiratory distress are fighting to get oxygen: they are anxious, have obvious labored breathing efforts, usually have their head and neck extended and elbows and upper legs held out from the chest, don't want to lie down, and fight restraint and handling. MWDs in respiratory distress typically have characteristic breathing patterns that help localize the problem; detailed descriptions of these patterns are provided in the CPGs.
2. Provide 100% oxygen to all trauma patients and any dog that is showing signs of respiratory distress, until proven unnecessary. Use a face mask or "blow by" technique for conscious dogs. Use orotracheal intubation or tracheostomy for unconscious, sedated, or anesthetized dogs. Thoracic radiography and serial TFAST are useful during management of the emergency patient, especially in the diagnosis and treatment of pneumothorax (PTX), hemothorax (HTX), pleural effusion, pulmonary contusions, and pulmonary edema.
3. Up to 50% of traumatized dogs have some form of thoracic injury. Pneumothorax and pulmonary contusions are most common. Rib cage trauma includes "flail chest," rib fractures, intercostal muscle rupture, and penetrating wounds. Usually the defect is obvious, especially if "paradoxical" chest wall motion is noted. Adequate management usually involves careful handling, laying the patient with affected side down (which may require sedation), minimizing restrictive chest bandaging, and providing analgesia. External splinting or surgical management is usually not necessary unless injury

is severe or extensive or chest wall is compromised and prolonged interference with gas exchange and ventilation are evident. Pain can substantially interfere with gas exchange and ventilation. Alleviate pain once the patient is stabilized to improve oxygenation and ventilation, using systemic and local analgesia. Note that compared to humans, dogs are generally not overly sensitive to the respiratory depressant effects of opioids. Local nerve blocks and intrapleural analgesia administration work well and are readily accomplished; short-acting opioids as a constant rate infusion (CRI) also provide excellent analgesia.

4. Pleural space trauma includes open, closed, and tension PTX, HTX, and diaphragmatic hernia. Open PTX requires immediate action. Rapidly clip hair from around the wound, and apply an occlusive seal over the wound. Apply a chest bandage to secure the seal. Delay wound closure until the MWD is stable. The presence of decreased lung sounds in a trauma patient with signs of respiratory distress, or rapid clinical deterioration in an MWD with respiratory distress is sufficient justification for needle thoracocentesis. Thoracocentesis is rapidly performed and safe when performed properly – "When in doubt, tap it!" Use an 18-gauge, 1-1.5 inch hypodermic needle attached to sterile tubing, attached to a stopcock that is attached to large syringe to aspirate air and fluid. Do not use needle decompression devices typically used in humans (e.g., 3.25-inch over-the-needle catheters) or insert the needle deep into the chest, because dogs have narrow thoracic cavities, and use of these devices or deep insertion markedly increases the risk of internal major vessel and cardiac injury. With the dog in lateral or sternal recumbency, insert the needle on the mid-lateral thorax in the 6th - 7th or 7th - 8th intercostal space. Count forward from the last rib (#13) to locate the insertion site. The intercostal artery, vein, and nerve run on the caudal aspect of each rib; thus, thoracocentesis is obtained by inserting the needle or catheter in the center of the intercostal space or at the cranial aspect of a rib. The mediastinum in dogs is thin and typically ruptures; therefore, always tap both sides of the chest, even if a positive tap is achieved on one side of the chest, as air pockets and fluid can migrate. Record the amount of air/fluid removed and save fluid samples (EDTA, red top) for later analysis. Repeated thoracenteses may be required to stabilize the patient. A negative chest tap doesn't always mean there's not an abnormal accumulation of air or fluid in the pleural space – it may mean you just couldn't find it! "When in doubt, tap it again!"

5. A thoracostomy tube is indicated if negative pressure cannot be achieved with needle thoracocentesis, if large amounts of blood are aspirated, or if repeated thoracocenteses are required to maintain negative pleural pressure. The tube should be the largest size that comfortably fits in the intercostal space. For most MWDs, use fenestrated tubes that are 24-36 Fr. As dogs are flattened laterally, compared to people, chest tubes are generally inserted through the skin high on the lateral chest wall at the 9th-11th intercostal space, tunneled cranioventrally toward the point of the elbow, and passed through the chest wall 2-3 intercostal spaces cranial to the skin insertion site. The chest tube will ideally be oriented cranioventrally in the pleural space, to maximize removal of air and fluid. Anesthesia or deep sedation and local anesthesia (intercostal nerve blocks) will likely be necessary for the thoracostomy procedure. Patients with chest tubes in place MUST be monitored continuously and intrapleural analgesia should be performed. Continuous suction or intermittent aspiration by personnel are management options.

6. There may be instances in which emergent thoracotomy is necessary. Thoracotomy in dogs is generally best done through a lateral thoracic wall approach, generally at the 4th - 5th or 5th - 6th intercostal space to afford optimal visualization. A median approach is more difficult and has higher incidence of post-operative complications.

7. Pulmonary contusions are common in traumatized dogs. Auscult the chest for decreased lung sounds, which suggest either fluid (blood) or air in the pleural space, or pulmonary contusions. A patchy distribution of altered lung sounds may be noted, which helps differentiate parenchymal injury from pleural space trauma. A negative thoracocentesis suggests the presence of pulmonary contusions.

Radiographic signs (mixed interstitial-alveolar infiltrates) may lag by 12-24 hours. Hemoptysis, especially of arterialized blood suggests significant pulmonary vessel trauma that typically carries a very guarded prognosis. Management of pulmonary contusions in dogs involves minimizing stress (patient rest and restricted activity), providing oxygen supplementation, cautious intravenous fluid administration to prevent progression of contusions and/or development of pulmonary edema, and addition of colloids to fluid therapy plans to decrease the amount of pulmonary edema that may accumulate during shock resuscitation. Diuretics and steroids are not indicated in treatment of pulmonary contusions. Severe, life- threatening major pulmonary vessel hemorrhage may require resuscitative thoracotomy, as discussed. Ventilatory support may be required for animals that fail to respond to correction or stabilization of the primary respiratory problem and supplemental oxygen support.

BLUNT AND PENETRATING ABDOMINAL TRAUMA
(See MWD CPGs Chapter 7)

1. Suspect significant intra-abdominal injury in any MWD that presents with abdominal rigidity or sensitivity to palpation, increasing abdominal size over time, visible bruising of the abdominal wall, or failure to respond to or deterioration in face of aggressive trauma resuscitation. Wounds involving more than the skin and superficial subcutaneous tissues dictate detailed examination to determine if the body wall was penetrated. Conservative medical management is usually indicated for MWDs with blunt abdominal trauma (BAT); most working dogs with BAT can be managed without surgery. Urgent exploratory surgery is recommended for MWDs with penetrating abdominal trauma (PAT) or ruptured viscus organs.

2. Perform an AFAST exam during the initial evaluation phase of every MWD presented for care with a history of trauma or acute collapse or weakness. AFAST is extremely reliable in detecting free abdominal fluid and can be performed rapidly during resuscitation. Refer to section 6-10f for a detailed description of AFAST examination technique. Examine all four quadrants. Perform serial AFAST exams every 4-6 hours and compare results: Exploratory surgery may be necessary for MWDs with progressive fluid accumulation, failure to respond, or clinical deterioration. Additional diagnostic tests that are helpful in differentiating abdominal injuries include abdominocentesis, diagnostic peritoneal lavage, computed tomography, and detailed ultrasonography.

3. The usual organs in MWDs subjected to blunt trauma are the spleen, liver, and urinary bladder, in this order of frequency. Most hemoperitoneum cases in MWDs suffering trauma are due to splenic and hepatic fractures, which can vary markedly in severity, with a significant difference in quantity of blood lost into the abdomen. The majority of MWDs with BAT and intra-abdominal hemorrhage that survive to admission can be successfully managed conservatively. These organ injuries usually will spontaneously cease bleeding given time and conservative fluid therapy. Monitor the MWD closely, as some will require exploratory laparotomy and surgical correction of hemorrhage, especially those that do not respond or deteriorate. Do not apply an abdominal counter- pressure bandage on an MWD. Patients with massive intra-abdominal bleeding need surgery to find the site of bleeding and surgically correct the loss of blood. There may be instances in which emergent laparotomy is necessary to afford a chance at patient survival.

4. Urinary bladder rupture, with uroperitoneum, is fairly common. Abdominocentesis fluid creatinine or potassium concentrations will be greater than serum values when uroperitoneum is present. MWDs with acute urologic trauma and uroperitoneum should be stabilized for other injuries and managed for shock. Repair of urologic injuries must wait until the patient stabilizes. In many cases, urologic injury is not apparent for several days after trauma, so a high index of suspicion must be maintained;

ultrasound and excretory urography studies may be necessary. In patients with known urologic tears and urine leakage, an indwelling urinary catheter can facilitate safe management and even healing of the bladder. Strict aseptic technique as well as daily cleaning of the catheter are required to minimize the occurrence of urinary tract infections. Abdominal drains may be necessary for proximal or severe urinary tract damage. Some sort of drain is often indicated, especially if surgery is delayed for several days. This allows removal of urine, which will minimize chemical peritonitis and electrolyte and acid-base imbalances. Fluid therapy to correct or prevent electrolyte and acid-base imbalances is often necessary, especially if several days have passed since traumatic injury.
5. Patients with a ruptured gastrointestinal viscus are candidates for emergent exploratory surgery. Broad-spectrum antibiotic therapy is vital, especially against anaerobic and gram-negative bacteria. Shock management is of special importance. Every attempt must be made to stabilize the patient as much as possible before definitive repair.
6. Exploratory laparotomy as a diagnostic and therapeutic modality is clearly indicated in trauma patients if penetrating trauma is highly suspected or known, and if the patient's status deteriorates despite aggressive resuscitation attempts and major organ hemorrhage is suspected or known. Surgical management includes an approach through the ventral midline under general anesthesia, with the dog in dorsal recumbency, to expose the abdominal cavity. A complete abdominal exploratory is necessary to define all injuries. Surgical management will depend on the injuries noted.

ANAPHYLACTIC SHOCK

Anaphylactic shock is a medical emergency and typically occurs after exposure to insect and snake venoms, antimicrobial agents, NSAIDs, opiates, vaccines, blood-based products, radiocontrast agents, and food. Anaphylaxis usually involves the skin, respiratory system, cardiovascular system, and gastrointestinal system. Cutaneous signs – if noted – (e.g., urticaria, angioedema) tend to be precursors to more severe responses; these dermal signs may be absent in rapidly-progressing systemic anaphylaxis.
1. Clinical signs vary depending upon the severity of anaphylaxis. Signs may include angioedema, urticaria, dermal erythema, restlessness, vomiting, diarrhea, labored breathing, and signs of shock (e.g., hypothermia, hypotension, tachypnea, tachycardia, altered mentation); severe cases may progress to coma and death. The major organ system involved in acute anaphylaxis for dogs is the liver, specifically the hepatic veins, and the gastrointestinal tract. Dogs typically demonstrate initial excitement followed by vomiting, defecation, and urination. Constriction of the hepatic vein causes portal hypertension and pooling of blood in the viscera, associated with signs of shock. Bowel edema and fluid translocation often occur, resulting in diarrhea (which may be hemorrhagic). Note specifically that a biphasic response may be noted, in which the original clinical signs abate, only to be followed by recurrence of signs; this typically occurs within 8-10 hours.
2. Diagnosis. Clinical signs of shock with appropriate history.
3. Treatment of mild allergic reactions. Mild allergic reactions are typically characterized by urticaria, angioedema, restlessness, and pruritus. Use antihistamines; avoid glucocorticoids. Most cases resolve rapidly. The key to remember when treating mild cases is that these cases may represent early anaphylaxis; therefore, monitor closely for at least 12 hours for progression, and be prepared to intervene if progression is noted.
4. Treatment of systemic anaphylaxis. Anaphylaxis is a true medical emergency. Delay in treatment can be life-threatening.
5. Administer epinephrine. Dose at 0.01 mg/kg using 1 mg/mL (1:1,000) epinephrine, given intramuscular initially. Current recommendations suggest a maximum dose of 0.5 mg in patients >40 kg and 0.3 mg in patients <40 kg. If signs persist, repeat this dose every 5-15 minutes as needed, based on response. In MWDs with clinical signs of shock on presentation, give epinephrine IV by

slow infusion at 0.05 mcg/kg/min to effect.
- a. Aggressive fluid therapy: Following IV catheter placement, provide an isotonic crystalloid fluid bolus using graduated bolus challenges, as discussed under shock treatment earlier in this chapter. Consider hydroxyethyl starch if shock persists, as discussed for refractory shock.
- b. Give oxygen to any patient with respiratory signs or hypoxemia. Use a face mask, nasal cannullae, or an oxygen cage, or intubate or perform a tracheostomy if signs are severe.
- c. Use bronchodilators for patients with respiratory distress believed to be secondary to bronchoconstriction. Use aminophylline at 5-10 mg/kg IM or by slow IV administration, or albuterol at 0.5 mL of the 0.5% solution in 4 mL of saline by nebulizer every 6 hours; if appropriate equipment is available, use a metered-dose inhaler (90 mcg/puff) every 15 minutes for up to 3 doses (1-2 puffs).
- d. Do not give glucocorticoids. Current recommendations discourage use of glucocorticoids in severe shock.
- e. Refractory anaphylaxis may require vasopressor support.

INSECT AND SNAKE ENVENOMATION
(See MWD CPGs Chapter 11)

MWDs are infrequently envenomated by spiders, scorpions, and snakes. Given the infrequent occurrence, detailed discussion of this topic is beyond the scope of this handbook; refer to the very detailed appendix in the MWD CPGs for guidance.

1. Clinical Signs. Severity is determined by amount of venom received and may develop within minutes.
   a. Heat, pain, puncture wounds, and swelling at envenomation site
   b. Persistent or heavy bleeding from bite wound
   c. Vomiting/ diarrhea
   d. Cardiovascular collapse/shock
   e. Snakebite associated coagulopathy – a typical DIC is not usually seen, but dog may experience coagulation delays and thrombocytopenia.
   f. Tissue necrosis at envenomation site
2. Diagnosis. Clinical signs with appropriate history. Echinocytes may be detected on blood smears in venomous snake bite cases.
3. Treatment. The majority of envenomations are mild, and supportive care is often all that is necessary. Arthropod bites especially may not be witnessed. An acute swelling of an extremity in the absence of trauma or fever may be the result of an insect/arthropod bite/sting. Treatment of mild insect and snake envenomations is not standardized, and references are often contradictory. Anecdotal use of antihistamines (diphenhydramine) is favored by some, while questioned by others. Likewise, use of corticosteroids and non-steroidal anti-inflammatory agents is also controversial; most recommend against their use, even in mild cases.
4. In moderate-to-severe snake envenomation, however, aggressive therapy is recommended, and includes use of antivenin.
   a. Specific treatment with geographic area-specific antivenin is optimal for patients with moderate-to-severe clinical signs. Although data are limited, antivenin decreases morbidity and may reduce mortality (especially for bites to the trunk and upper limbs, which have the highest mortality rates).
   b. Antivenin supply may be problematic. VCOs should plan ahead and coordinate with local

suppliers to ensure antivenin availability in areas in which envenomation is common. In deployed settings, antivenin is typically only available in select Role 2 and Role 3 facilities because antivenin use – for humans and dogs – is highly regulated and governed by theater policy; refer to theater policy for guidance, availability, and procedures to obtain antivenin.

c. Antivenins, especially those that contain whole immunoglobulin components, must be used with caution, due to the potential to induce allergic reactions. Although dosing in dogs is empiric, if used, antivenins should be given to effect to control clinical signs.

d. Most references suggest that corticosteroids and non-steroidal anti-inflammatories are contraindicated in the treatment of severe snake envenomation.

CHAPTER 5

COMMON MEDICAL PROBLEMS

Military Working Dogs are susceptible to the same illnesses as any other dog, but by virtue of travel, work, kennel and athletic stresses, they may be more prone to some injuries and illnesses than other non-working dogs. Rather than attempt to serve as a replacement for a textbook on canine disease, this section will attempt to outline some of the more common medical problems and appropriate therapies that may be unique or common to the MWD population. Clinicians should not hesitate to consult other resources in treating these conditions in MWDs, but this chapter may be a succinct starting point.

SKIN

Skin lesions/infections anecdotally account for approximately 50 percent of all MWD sick call complaints. Most are minor and easily treated, but some may be signs of chronic or systemic illness that may affect duty or deployment status. Any of the below problems can occur in dogs not housed in a kennel, but a kennel environment (hard floors and walls, tendency toward moist surfaces and humidity) increases the risk in MWDs. In many cases, paying close attention to husbandry issues in the kennel environment and advising the KM accordingly can assist in mitigating such problems. Ensuring an appropriate air exchange (10-15/hour), "squeegeeing" kennel floors after hosing them out, and adhering to proper tenets of kennel sanitation are some of the major areas where kennels typically have deficiencies.

1. Superficial Pyoderma/"Hotspots". Skin infections can be a primary problem, but most are secondary to another underlying disease that disrupts the skin or its defense mechanisms. This is especially true in the case of "hot spots" (acute moist dermatitis, superficial pyoderma), which are almost always secondary to some other irritation. Most of these cases are also complicated by secondary trauma as the dog scratches or bites at the affected area in an effort to relieve pruritus or pain. In MWDs, the most likely underlying problems are kennel moisture and heat, poor grooming and matted fur, or chronic abrasion against walls, gates, or fences. Other common primary problems may include inhalant (atopy) or food allergic dermatitis, primary seborrhea, and immune-mediated disease. In pets, ectoparasites, other infectious dermatopathy (esp. rickettsial) and flea allergy dermatitis (FAD) are common underlying causes of superficial pyodermas, but these should not be common problems in MWDs due to our aggressive preventive medicine program. Staphylococcal hypersensitivity and primary immunodeficiency disorders are rare causes. Primary endocrinopathies generally do not cause secondary superficial pyoderma.
    a. Diagnosis. Superficial pyoderma can generally be diagnosed based on history and appearance with confirmatory cytology.
    b. Treatment. The most important part of treatment is to identify the underlying insult and address it. This may require review of kennel sanitation and MWD grooming procedures. The affected area should be clipped and gently cleaned with dilute chlorhexidine solution and then treated with a drying agent. Daily treatment may be needed for a week or more. Some hotspots are quite painful and inflamed and treatment with a topical steroid or steroid-antibiotic combination cream may be necessary for 5-7 days. Systemic antibiotic therapy is generally not required.
2. Methicillin-Resistant Staphylococcus pseudintermedius (MRSP). MRSP infections are of major clinical importance in hospitalized patients as well as community-acquired pyoderma and otitis externa cases. These infections are becoming increasingly recognized in the MWD population, as well. The most significant implication in receiving a culture and susceptibility report with MRSP is

the likelihood that this organism is resistant to our most commonly used antimicrobials, namely the beta-lactam antibiotics (penicillins and cephalosporins). Additionally, these infections are often multi-drug resistant.
- a. Diagnosis. An in vitro culture and susceptibility report received on a patient with appropriate clinical signs from a veterinary commercial laboratory is ideal to confirm the diagnosis. MRSP does not appear to be any more virulent than Methicillin-Susceptible Staphylococcus pseudintermedius (MSSP) and it should be noted that a very large percentage of healthy dogs are colonized with MRSP yet show no clinical signs.
- b. Treatment. Many infections are secondary to an underlying primary disease which must be considered in the therapeutic plan for recurrent or persistent infections. For cutaneous infections, topical treatments are preferred over systemic antimicrobials to prevent multi-drug resistance. Examples include chlorhexidine, povidone iodine, benzoyl peroxides, fusidic acid, mupirocin and miconazole. Topical antimicrobials can be used in concentrations that overcome antimicrobial resistance associated with systemic therapies. Shampoos, lotions, rinses, sprays, andconditioners are appropriate for generalized or extensive cutaneous disease. Gels, creams ointments, lotions, and wipes may be appropriate for more focal or localized infections. Topical therapy may also be used in conjunction with systemic antimicrobials only when deemed necessary. Systemic antimicrobial selection should be based on susceptibility patterns and only used in cases when topical therapy alone is either not deemed appropriate or is ineffective. Treatment should be continued for a minimum of 7 days beyond clinical signs. If rapid improvement is not seen within the first 2 weeks of therapy then the antimicrobial choice should be reevaluated. Empirical therapy should be reserved for first time infections and limited to first tier antimicrobials as defined by the International Society for Companion Animal Infectious Diseases (ISCAID). First tier antimicrobials include clindamycin, first generation cephalosporins, amoxicillin-clavulanate, and trimethoprim-and ormetoprim-potentiated sulphonamides. To help prevent the emergence of multidrug resistant strains the selection of second tier drugs should be based on antimicrobial resistance patterns. The use of third tier drugs; i.e., linezolid, teicoplanin, and vancomycin is strongly discouraged, due to their use in people for serious MRSA infections.

3. Elbow, hock, and sternal callus. Many MWDs develop cutaneous callus associated with living in a concrete kennel. These usually form along bony prominences of the lateral elbow and hock, but may also form on the sternum in deep-chested dogs. Callus development is not generally harmful to the dog and treatment is not necessary unless inflammation or infection occurs (Callus Dermatitis – see below). These lesions should be noted on DD Form 1829 or equivalent, and are mainly cosmetic issues.
    - a. Diagnosis. Calluses can generally be diagnosed based on their appearance, alopecic, hyperpigmented, hyperkeratotic plaque (thickened "tough" skin) and is often unilateral but on both fore and hind limbs (e.g. the MWD tends to sleep lying on that side) and located over bony prominences.
    - b. Treatment. Use of elevated covered kennel racks (pallet/crate/grill) or other soft bedding may reduce callus formation. Caution should be exercised in furnishing such bedding options as some MWDs will attempt to ingest these materials.
4. Callus Dermatitis and Pyoderma. In some MWDs, callus may become inflamed, ulcerated, or fistulated, and occasionally deeply infected. This may be due to abrasive ulceration and trauma or in many cases it occurs due to irritation from broken hair and damaged hair shafts. These calluses do require therapy.
    - a. Diagnosis. Based on appearance. Diagnosis and response to therapy monitored with cytology.

b. Therapy. The most important treatment is to try and relieve pressure by adding an elevated kennel rack plus padding or bedding to the kennel. Be aware that many MWDs will chew and destroy soft bedding and pads so they should be used cautiously and removed if the MWD is destructive. The use of hydrotherapy, especially with Epsom salts, is often beneficial to reduce irritation and inflammation. Topical cleansing, drying, and antibiotic-steroid ointments may be helpful (as with superficial pyoderma). If deep infection occurs, systemic antibiotic therapy for 4-6 weeks may be necessary. Antibiotic therapy should continue for 1-2 weeks beyond the time of clinical and cytologic resolution.

5. Elbow, hock, and sternal hygromas. Any pressure point susceptible to callus development may also develop hygroma. A hygroma is a fluid-filled false or acquired bursa that develops in the subcutis. They are initially soft to fluctuant but may become abscessed, granulomatous, or infected.
   a. Diagnosis. Based on appearance and location. Supportive cytology may be needed to rule out abscess and/or infection, although introducing a needle into a hygroma should be performed very cautiously under aseptic conditions. Aspiration should not be performed upon initial exam or on a repeated basis.
   b. Treatment. Ideal treatment includes the use of elevated kennel racks, bedding and padding the kennel, and application of padded bandages for 2-3 weeks. Commercially available neoprene leg wraps are another option which may be effective. Recurrent aspiration/drainage of the hygroma is not recommended. Surgical drainage and resection should NOT be attempted in MWDs, at least at the VTF level, as the risk of dehiscence and other complications is very high. Systemic antibiotics should be administered if infection is present. Many cases improve over time and become chronic lesions that pose no significant detriment to the MWD in the long run.

6. Tail Lesions. Some MWDs may suffer trauma to the tail tip or tail shaft due to circling or spinning in the kennel, or occasionally due to "aggressive" tail wagging in the transport cage/kennel. Typical lesions appear as a crack in the tail tip with bleeding; often blood is flung on the walls by the moving tail. Sometimes the tail tip will become alopecic and develop a thick callus which may crack and bleed less severely, heal, then crack again. Linear deep abrasions along the tail shaft may also be seen. Less common, but more serious conditions may include severe inflammation/fasciitis of the tail shaft.
   a. Diagnosis. Based on appearance.
   b. Treatment. Short-term management of tail lesions may include the use of topical antiseptic and "skin toughening"/artificial bandage medications, reducing the amount of time the dog is in the kennel by altering work and training shifts, moving the dog into a larger run or exercise area for temporary housing and use of environmental enrichment (e.g. bowling ball) to reduce spinning behavior. Additionally, moving the dog to a less trafficked area may decrease stimulation for the repetitive behavior. Shaving the tail tip and applying bandages often makes the problem worse. At DODMWDVS there has been some success with utilizing 0.75in foam plumbing pipe insulation which can be purchased at the local home improvement store in 6ft sections for only $1-2. The tube should be cut to size (approximately 6in) and secured with elastic cloth tape beginning approximately 4.0in proximal to the tube. The tube should extend just distal to the tail tip with the end open to allow for air circulation. With some chronic cases, the tail tip may become infected thereby necessitating topical and systemic antimicrobial therapy. Severe or recurrent tail tip and shaft lesions should be addressed with amputation of the tail (caudectomy). When indicated, caudectomy should be completed so that the remaining tail is approximately 3-4 inches long, just enough to cover the anus and enough that the tail can be lifted to take a temperature. Behavioral evaluation for hyperactivity or repetitive behavior may be appropriate in some of

these MWDs.
7. Soft Foot Pads. The normal canine pad has a thick epidermis with a papillated and irregular surface, and a rough texture due to thick keratinization. In some dogs, especially those living or working on rough, hard surfaces or consistently damp surfaces, the keratinized layer of the pad may be worn down leaving a very soft, and often tender, pad surface. Spinning in the kennel may exacerbate this problem. On occasion the dog may actually wear the pad down thru the epidermis and in rare cases erosion and ulceration may occur into the subcutis.
    a. Diagnosis. Soft pads are easily recognized during physical examination because of their smooth, soft appearance. Many of these dogs will present with mild lameness, which may only be apparent on rough surfaces such as dry grass, gravel, or asphalt.
    b. Treatment. Treatment should be directed at toughening the pad using topical products such as tincture of benzoin, applied in small amounts for a 7-10 days, or commercially available pad tougheners. If the insulting surface can be identified, it should be avoided or repaired. Kennel surfaces with a highly abrasive surface can predispose to this problem.
8. Pododermatitis. There are many possible causes of pododermatitis, and, in many cases, more than one factor contributes to injury. Foot trauma, living or working on wet surfaces, stepping in irritating chemicals such as kennel sanitizer or spilled fuel and oil on roadways, and other injury or irritation are the most common factors in MWDs.
    a. Diagnosis. Based on appearance and clinical history. Extensive workups for allergic, immune mediated, and other systemic diseases may be appropriate in advanced or recurrent cases.
    b. Treatment. Once pododermatitis occurs, treatment must be aggressive and prolonged as the disease is often self-perpetuating. Systemic and topical antibiotics, daily cleaning and soaks in povidine-iodine or chlorhexidine solutions, and application of protective bandages may all be appropriate presumptive therapy.
9. Pad Laceration. Foot injuries are quite common in the MWD. They may include simple lacerations, bites, punctures, degloving injuries, pad avulsions, and fractures. The goals of therapy for foot injuries are proper diagnosis, prevention of infection, proper wound care striving for rapid healing, and early return to duty. To establish a diagnosis, thorough examination of the foot is necessary. Examination also aids in determining the extent of injury, a diagnostic protocol, and a treatment plan.
    a. Realistically, it takes 14 to 21 days for abrasions or lacerations of the foot to completely heal. Suturing of lacerations and especially pads can be very challenging and frustrating. The tension placed on sutures during normal ambulation, not to mention running and jumping, along with a damp environment make a perfect situation for failure. Keeping the foot and wound clean and dry along with the use of proper bandaging techniques and ancillary medications are extremely important for a rapid, successful resolution. Many times, a splint is required to decrease motion and allow for healing. All foot wounds should be thoroughly cleaned and flushed (debrided if necessary) prior to definitive treatment.
    b. When a flap is present upon presentation, but viability is questionable, it may be necessary to suture the flap in place and monitor the viability daily each time the foot is cleaned. The flap may be excised later if necessary and then allow second intention healing to take place. Suturing of any laceration on the foot or pad will bring tissue planes into apposition and a bandage will aid in decreasing the contamination of the injury while acting as an aid to preventing tension on the sutures.
    c. After the injury has been assessed and cleaned, the DODMWDVS uses two different topical medications to provide scaffolds for cellular matrix, to form a seal to prevent contamination, provide cellular stimulation, and in general provide an environment to enhance the healing process. Current topical medications used are a medical hydrolysate of type I collagen, and

maltodextrin N.F, a hydrophilic compound.
- i. Medical hydrolysate of type I collagen acts as a matrix in the wound. Because collagen is used as a matrix for fibroblast movement into a wound, it is probably most effective in the late inflammatory and early repair stages. It should be applied, allowed to dry, and then bandaged with a non-adherent bandage. It is absolutely necessary to change foot bandages anytime they become wet.
- ii. Maltodextrin N.F. The mode of action of maltodextrin is as a hydrophilic compound. Following wound debridement and lavage, the powder should be applied over the wound to a depth of approximately ¼ inch. A nonadherent primary bandage pad should be placed over the powder, followed by an absorbent wrap and an outer tertiary bandage layer, and changed daily. Based on its modes of action, the powder will have an effect from the early inflammatory through the repair stages of healing.
- iii. Foot injuries are a challenge to manage and bandage but with monitoring and proper care, a successful outcome can be accomplished.

10. Scrotal Dermatitis. The condition has been associated with infectious and immune mediated disease, especially Lyme disease and other vasculitides, but in MWDs it is almost exclusively a disease due to chronic moisture or contact irritation in the kennel. It may appear as mild erythema, swelling, and pain on palpation of small sections of scrotal skin. More severe cases may involve severe erythema, erosions and ulcerations, and exudation of serous and serosanguinous fluid. Serum adhering to the irritated skin creates a self-perpetuating irritation and propagation of the injury.
   a. Diagnosis. Based on appearance.
   b. Treatment. Focus is on keeping the scrotum clean and dry with gentle antimicrobial and drying agents (pre-mixed otic solutions work very well). Short-term (3-7 day) treatment with topical antibiotic-steroid creams may be necessary to reduce painful inflammation in severe cases. Kennel sanitation procedures should be addressed as part of therapy. Severe or recurrent cases should be addressed through castration and scrotal ablation. Systemic antibiotics may be needed for particularly severe cases.

11. Allergic Dermatitis. MWDs may develop allergic dermatitis and secondary pyodermas. These reactions may be triggered by due environmental, food, and/or microbial allergens. An organized, systemic diagnostic and therapeutic plan is essential to the proper treatment and management of these dogs. The International Committee on Allergic Diseases of Animals publishes guidelines for the diagnosis, treatment, and management of canine atopic dermatitis and is a valuable resource. Common signs include pruritus, recurrent or seasonal dermatitis and pyodermas, recurrent otitis externa, and self-trauma due to pruritus.
   a. Diagnosis. Diagnosis of canine allergic dermatitis is based on the patient's history, clinical signs, and disease history, not the results of a laboratory test. Diagnostic criteria are further described in the above-mentioned guidelines. It is important to rule out other dermatoses that can mimic atopic dermatitis through appropriate diagnostic tests and treatment trials. Regarding food hypersensitivity, enzyme-linked immunosorbent assays (ELISA), radioallergosorbent tests (RAST), and intradermal skin testing are not recommended. Dietary elimination trials are often a key component in workup of allergic dermatitis. Given that both Labrador Retrievers and German Shepherds have an increased predilection for food allergy, an appropriate food trial with a hypoallergenic (hydrolyzed or novel protein) diet is indicated to rule out food hypersensitivity as a cause of allergic dermatitis. Food trials should be performed for a minimum of 8 weeks (and in some cases 10-12 weeks) and it should be stressed that no other food items be furnished to the dog other than the prescribed ration. This includes beef flavored heartworm preventive products; monthly subcutaneous

ivermectin injection (0.1mL/dog of 1% solution) or administration of a non-flavored oral heartworm preventive is indicated for these dogs. For atopic dermatitis, if based on seasonal nature of the dermatitis and/or if a food trial proves to be ineffective, empiric therapy should be performed. Hyposensitization has arbitrarily been considered the gold standard and most preferred therapy for allergic skin disease when skin testing indicates efficacy. Anywhere from 50-80 percent of patients benefit from this therapeutic option. Commercial in vitro serum allergy testing is most likely inferior to skin testing performed by a veterinary dermatologist, however, in the absence of referral and if empiric therapy has failed to achieve an acceptable response, this option is viable. MWDs requiring chronic hyposensitization therapy should be placed in CAT 2.

    b. Treatment/Therapy. The goal of therapy is to reduce inflammation, pruritus, and self-trauma such that secondary infections and scratching do not impact MWD work performance or systemic health. The principles of therapy for allergic dermatitis in MWDs are the same as in other dogs, e.g. use of medicated or soothing antipruritic shampoos, topical corticosteroids for localized disease, antibiotic therapy of secondary pyodermas, supplementation of vitamin E and fatty acids, antihistamines, and ultimately hyposensitization. Supplementation of above therapies with the short-term administration of a steroidal anti-inflammatory, generally prednisone at 0.5 – 1.0 mg/kg q24 to q48 hours, may be necessary for limited duration. While cyclosporine certainly has a role in atopic dermatitis, newer therapies such as oclacitinib and monocolonal antibody therapy can rapidly reduce skin lesions and pruritus in dogs and may replace the need for glucocorticoids in many patients. See the above referenced guidelines for more information regarding treatment in acute and chronic cases.

12. Cutaneous Neoplasia. MWDs are susceptible to the same cutaneous neoplasias as other dogs. Superficial masses are common; a few can be diagnosed by their appearance. Most superficial tumors should be examined cytologically, aspirated or impression smear, prior to excision and must be submitted for histopathology after excision to the Joint Pathology Center. Human MTFs should NOT be relied on to diagnose veterinary cytologic lesions as most MD pathologists are not trained to identify or assess specific lesions in nonhuman species.

13. Bacterial Dermatitis/ Pyoderma. Generalized bacterial dermatitis/pyoderma should be considered a sign of some primary/underlying cutaneous, metabolic or immunologic disease. Principles of diagnosis and therapy are the same as in pet dogs with the following exceptions: kennel environment must be considered a risk factor, aggressive ectoparasite control reduces risk of flea allergy or irritation as a component, MWDs travel and may be exposed to infectious agents that cause atypical cutaneous disease and which must be added to the normal list of differential diagnoses, e.g. Leishmaniasis.

    a. Diagnosis. Must include good history of seasonality of signs, travel history, physical examination with special attention to evidence of pruritus, alopecia, seborrhea, etc. Skin scrapes, dermatophyte culture, skin cytology and biopsy, allergy testing and endocrine testing may be necessary.

    b. Treatment. In general, the therapy for bacterial dermatitis includes systemic antibiotics, and topical shampoos. The underlying disorder must be identified and addressed.

EARS

1. Otitis externa. Three factors are associated with otitis externa: primary, predisposing, and perpetuating. The following lists are limited to those factors that are common in MWDs. Other factors (see textbook references) should also be considered in atypical, nonresponsive or severe cases. Primary factors include foreign bodies or other ear trauma, allergies, endocrine disease and idiopathic

seborrhea. Common predisposing factors include increased environmental temperature and moisture, thermal insult due to exercise induced hyperthermia or associated with fever, iatrogenic irritation (e.g. overzealous ear cleaning), obstructive lesions associated with muzzle use or past ear injury. Common perpetuating factors include bacterial infections (Staphylococcus spp, Streptococcus spp, Pseudomonas aeruginosa), yeast infections (Malassezia pachydermatis), otitis media, proliferative changes due to chronicity, and treatment error or lack of treatment compliance.

    a. Diagnostics. Most otitis externa is relatively routine and will respond to trial therapy with ear cleaning and drying agents and or topical antibiotic-antimycotic-steroid solutions. Diagnostic workup should include history, physical examination, and ear cytology.

        i. Superficial and otoscopic exam. Assess type of exudates (color, moisture, smell) and presence or absence of inflammation, blood, visible parasites, or foreign bodies, and integrity and appearance of tympanic membrane. If the dog is too painful and fights otoscopic evaluation, consider sedation or short-acting anesthesia. Additionally, for swollen, painful ears, a short tapering course of an anti-inflammatory dose of prednisone could be prescribed in order to lessen inflammation and pain prior to commencing treatment.

        ii. Ear swabs (two types): 1) mix with mineral oil to look for mites; 2) dry, heat fix and stain with Wright- type stain to look for inflammatory cells, bacteria, yeast.

        iii. Culture (if it does not respond to standard therapy, the VCO should culture).

    b. Treatment.

        i. Clean and dry the canal. If the ear canal is not too inflamed or occluded by debris and exudates, treatment can be initiated without extensive cleaning of the ear canal, but in many MWDs sedation or anesthesia for thorough canal cleaning and debridement is required.

        ii. Initial cleaning. The canal must be thoroughly cleaned and dried (cotton tipped applicators, suction) to allow topical medication to reach the affected tissue. The job is not complete until the tympanic membrane can be visualized. The best cleaning solutions are pre-mixed chlorhexidine, acetic acid, boric acid, and/or salicylic acid solutions. Dilute betadine or chlorhexidine solution [NOT scrub], 1:10 with water, may also be used.

        iii. Maintenance cleaning. Long term: Application of ear cleaning and drying agents by the handler and/or 68T two to three times per week may be necessary to maintain the health of the ear canal in dogs with unresolved primary or perpetuating factors. Treatment should be tapered to the minimum effective frequency once efficacy has been shown and a healthy ear is obtained.

        iv. Topical medication. Usually a combination of antibiotics, antifungals, and steroids. Treatment with these medications is generally only required for 3-10 days and newer formations only require one application. If results are not obtained in this time it is likely that underlying factors have not been adequately addressed, that treatment compliance is suspect, or that an inappropriate medication was selected.

        v. Systemic therapy. If the lesions are very severe, systemic therapy is advised. Indications for systemic treatment include marked canal changes (if it's already calcified then there is evidence of chronic change that will not resolve with medical therapy), otitis media, and severe acute problems. Systemic therapy may include: antibiotics- use for marked changes, otitis media, antifungals – use for nonresponsive yeast infection, and less commonly anti-inflammatory dose of steroids – use for marked changes, or severe acute problems.

        vi. Surgery. If there are severe changes in the ear canal, total ear canal ablation and lateral bulla osteotomy is indicated. MWDs that have undergone this procedure retain some hearing via bone conduction and do not have significant problems in responding to commands. This is probably because hearing via the tympanic membrane and internal acoustic window has been gradually diminished by chronic otitis externa/media. Consult with the supporting 64F for consultation/referral.

EYES

1. Pannus. Refers to the specific clinical syndrome of chronic superficial pigmentary keratitis primarily seen in German Shepherd Dogs. An immune-mediated basis is suggested, and the disorder has a positive correlation to increased altitude and ultraviolet radiation. It involves superficial corneal vascularization and infiltration of granulation tissue. The condition is progressive, usually bilateral and may result in blindness if left untreated. Clinical signs include corneal edema, corneal vascularization and corneal pigmentation.
    a. Diagnosis. Signalment and bilateral lesions of neovascularization and/or pigmentation originating at temporal limbus are usually sufficient to warrant the diagnosis.
    b. Treatment. With any pannus, treatment must be continued for life. If the treatment is stopped, it will recur and handler compliance with medication administration is crucial. If the pannus is not under control within 2 weeks, call the supporting 64F or the DODMWDVS for suggestions. Once it is under control and the dog is able to work, decrease to the lowest frequency needed to keep it under control.
        i. Corticosteroids. Potent corticosteroids such as 0.1% dexamethasone, 1% prednisolone acetate and 1% prednisolone sodium phosphate are preferred. Medication must be applied 4-6 times per day during initial therapy. After medication takes effect, frequency of administration may be decreased to every 8-12 hours if this frequency is still effective.
        ii. Commercially available Cyclosporine A ophthalmic ointment is inadequate for most pannus cases as it is in a fairly low concentration (0.2%). A veterinary compounding pharmacy's 1-2% ophthalmic cyclosporine product is indicated in cases that do not respond to corticosteroids alone. The dose is 1-2 drops per eye every 6-8 hours until remission, then reducing to the lowest effective daily dose. Pay close attention to the expiration date of these preparations, as they can have fairly short shelf lives. Use gloves, as this is a chemotherapeutic agent. Subconjunctival injection may be applied for advanced cases or those where topical is not working or is not possible due to MWD behavior. Sedation and topical anesthesia is usually enough for subconjunctival injection, although short general anesthesia can be used. Injectable medications and doses include methylprednisone 5 mg per eye; betamethasone 1 mg per eye; triamcinolone 5 mg per eye. VCOs should discuss this method of treatment with their supporting 64F prior to administering to the MWD. Follow with topical treatment every 8 hours; this should be effective for 1-6 months, then repeat as needed.
2. Corneal Abrasions/Lacerations. Although primary corneal defects occur, most corneal problems are secondary to trauma, foreign body, entropion or other lid defects, and keratoconjunctivitis sicca. Clinical signs include blepharospasm, epiphora, and mucopurulent ocular discharge.
    a. Diagnosis. A comprehensive ophthalmic exam will give the diagnosis; however, it may require topical anesthesia. A Schirmer tear test should be conducted first followed by fluorescein dye stain of the cornea.

 b. Treatment. Topical broad-spectrum antibiotics are applied every 8-12 hours. One percent atropine drops at 8-12 hours (generally required for no more than 72 hours) are instilled if the pupil is miotic (i.e. pain). Use e- collar if needed and recheck in 1 week. Do not use steroids.
 c. If the lesion is not healing, or a deep or extensive ulcer develops, carefully debride the ulcer utilizing sterile cotton swab. If surgical intervention may be necessary, consult supporting 64F for guidance.

INFECTIOUS DISEASES OF MILITARY WORKING DOGS

Historically Ehrlichiosis was a disease of major importance in working dogs during and immediately after the Vietnam conflict. With the advent of easy to administer, effective topical ectoparasite products, this disease is less of a concern in the MWD population of today. However, there are certain diseases of significance that can affect MWDs that are unique to this population that VCOs should be aware of. Any MWDs that have tested positive for a blood-borne infectious disease should not be used as blood donors even if treatment was completed. Their Deployment VHR and electronic VHR should be clearly marked with "DO NOT USE AS BLOOD DONOR".

1. American Trypanosomiasis (Chagas disease). Chagas disease is caused by the organism, Trypanosoma cruzi. This parasite is primarily spread through fecal deposition into an open wound or mucous membrane by Triatomine species of bugs (reduviid, "kissing", "assassin" or "cone-nosed" bugs). These bugs are endemic to Bexar County, Texas in which the Dog Center is located and research indicates that the disease is spreading throughout the southern United States and affecting approximately 2% of the MWD population.
 a. Transmission to MWDs is thought to be primarily through ingestion of the insect vector, the reduviid bug. Transmission also occurs congenitally, via blood transfusion, or by deposition of the vector's fecal products onto mucous membranes, breaks in the skin, etc. Infection with T. cruzi is lifelong and avoiding contact with an infected MWD's blood through needle stick, cut with a necropsy knife, etc. should be a precaution the veterinary team should take care to implement.
 b. Dogs infected with T. Cruzi can be asymptomatic or develop acute or chronic infections. Once infected, a dog may exhibit symptoms during the acute phase, including lethargy, fever, inappetance, and lymphadenopathy, as the parasite replicates within its new host. Specifically, in dogs, there have been cases of sudden death, acute myocarditis, and congestive heart failure associated with new infection. However, these cases are rare.
 c. Both acute and chronic forms of Chagas disease exist in the dog with typically younger dogs suffering from the acute form. In most cases of infection, the parasite enters a chronic phase during which the individual may not experience any clinical signs. If signs materialize, they may not appear for years after initial infection. Clinical signs of chronic trypanosomiasis are indistinguishable from those signs associated with other cardiac disease including DCM, CHF, and other primary cardiac disease. MWDs in endemic areas should be screened annually (T. cruzi IFA and PCR) during the RSAPE. The DOD FADL conducts testing for T. cruzi. The cardiac form of Chagas disease in dogs can remain silent, but generally leads to clinical signs in some dogs such as lethargy, exercise intolerance, weakness, fainting, inappetance, abnormal cardiac rhythms, congestive heart failure, and sudden death. Ultimately, the cardiac form of Chagas disease in dogs results in DCM. A T. cruzi IFA and PCR should both be submitted in any MWD that exhibits signs clinical signs listed above and has resided in an endemic area.

d. Dogs that develop the cardiac form of Chagas disease will be considered Unfit for Duty and processed for elimination from the MWD Program. Asymptomatic MWDs will undergo treatment and monitoring for T. cruzi with Itraconazole and Amiodarone (See protocol). MWDs that remain asymptomatic will be retained and continue to work.

e. T. cruzi Treatment Protocol. See Figure 1. This protocol outlines the care and follow-up for asymptomatic T. cruzi dogs. Dogs with clinical signs will need to have more frequent assessment and management and will likely require additional therapy. Please contact the supporting 64F who will notify the Medicine Clinic at DODMWDVS when an MWD tests positive for T. cruzi.

2. Leishmaniasis. To date there have been very few cases of Leishmaniasis. However, given the worldwide deployability of working dogs, the fact that dogs serve as a reservoir for this organism, and the near global distribution of the disease, Leishmaniasis is a disease of concern in the MWD population.

   a. Dogs are considered the main reservoir for Leishmania infantum, the causative agent of Leishmaniosis. Although other species of Leishmania have been known to infect the dog, L. infantum is the primary organism of interest in canine leishmaniasis.

Figure 1. T. cruzi Treatment Protocol

MWD is identified as IFA or PCR positive for T. cruzi*

⬇

Initial Work-up for T. cruzi
1. CBC, Chemistry, UA, Troponin I
2. ECG, +/- 24 hour Holter
3. Chest Radiographs and Echocardiogram
4. Blood Pressure
5. T. Cruzi IFA and PCR (if >21 days since last test)

⬇

Start Treatment
1. Itraconazole 10mg/kg PO every 24 hours
2. Amiodarone is done on a loading schedule:
   a. Amiodarone 15 mg/kg PO every 12 hours x 7 days
   b. Amiodarone 15 mg/kg PO every 24 hours x 14 days
   c. Amiodarone 7.5 mg/kg PO every 24 hours for maintenance

These medications are continued for at least one year and with at least two negative PCRs and stable to decreasing titer prior to discontinuing. Dogs are typically CAT II if asymptomatic while on medications due to follow-up requirements. It is recommended that they do not deploy during this time.

⬇

Follow-up Medications

1. Recheck Physical Examination and Chemistry at 2 weeks. If the liver enzymes are elevated, Denamarin is started and liver enzymes are rechecked in 1-2 weeks. If they continue to rise or are not improved, the itraconazole dose is reduced by 25% and rechecked.
2. Recheck Physical exam at 1 month
3. Itraconazole level at 45-60 days done through an approved lab such as Auburn (Goal = 1- 2ug/ml) and 45-60 days after any adjustment to the itraconazole dose
4. T. cruzi rechecks every 3 months
    a. T. cruzi IFA and PCR to FADL
    b. CBC, Chem, UA, Troponin
    c. ECG
    d. Blood Pressure
    e. Physical exam
    f. Chest radiographs (+/- recheck echo if changes are noted)

Once the MWD has completed 12 months of therapy on a correct itraconazole level and if the last two T. cruzi PCRs have been negative, the medications may be discontinued. A T. cruzi IFA and PCR should be resubmitted at 1 month and 3 months after cessation of medications. If the IFA remains stable/decreased and the PCR remains negative, the IFA/PCR should then be monitored at every SAPE along with Chest radiographs, ECG and Troponin I.

*At the time of this writing, this protocol is considered experimental. Studies are ongoing to determine if this protocol will ultimately become the standard for treating MWDs diagnosed with T. cruzi.

    b. The Mediterranean basin, deserts in western Asia and the Middle East and rainforests in Central and South America are the primary geographic areas of concern.
    c. Transmission occurs through the bite of an infected phlebotomine sand fly which is most active at dusk and dawn (crepuscular) and at night (nocturnal). Transmission by other means, such as blood transfusion, in utero, venereal, etc. are possible, however, sand fly vector borne transmission is the most common, natural form of transmission.
    d. The degree to which Leishmaniasis is manifest in the infected host is dependent on such factors as nutritional support, stress levels, and immune competency. Dogs typically display both cutaneous and visceral components of infection with clinical signs such as:
        i. Skin lesions such as ulcers (especially over bony prominences) and exuberant scale/crusts especially on the face and limbs, or generalized
        ii. Localized/generalized lymphadenopathy
        iii. Splenomegaly
        iv. Emaciation/muscle atrophy
        v. Polyuria/polydipsia
        vi. Epistaxis
    e. Diagnosis usually starts with performing Leishmania antibody titers when clinical signs are

consistent with the disease. The titers are available through FADL. A cut-off titer for positive samples is considered 1:64, if positive this is diagnostic for the disease. Cytology of skin lesions, fine needle aspirates of organs, histopathology of organs or lesions and whole blood PCR are other diagnostics that can be performed in conjunction or if titers are negative and still highly suspicious of the diagnosis. If titers are negative, it is very unlikely that the MWD is infected with Leishmania.

   f. Prevention is primarily through the use of vector avoidance and implementation of deltamethrin- impregnated flea/tick collars as well as spot-on products containing permethrin. These factors play heavily in the decision to utilize deltamethrin collars and imidacloprid/permethrin/pyriproxyfen spot-on products for MWDs.

   g. The USDA and CDC do not prohibit patients with positive Leishmania titers from entry to the USA. If they have external clinical signs of Leishmania (skin lesions, uveitis, epistaxis…) then it would preclude the health certificate because they have clinical signs of an infectious or contagious disease.

3. Infective endocarditis (IE). Historically referred to as bacterial endocarditis, this infection of the endothelial surface of the heart valves (primarily aortic and mitral) in dogs is a particularly devastating disease. MWDs are rarely affected with infective endocarditis.

   a. Prerequisites for the disease are a transient or persistent bacteremia (due to cystitis, prostatitis, periodontal disease, pyoderma, etc.) coupled with damage to the endothelial surface of the heart valves. Colonization of the affected heart valve(s) ensues with sequelae such as immune-mediated polyarthritis and glomerulonephritis, thromboemboli formation, and sepsis culminating in acute congestive heart failure.

   b. The typical signalment of a patient suffering from IE is a young, large breed dog. German Shepherds have shown a predisposition toward this disease.

   c. Clinical signs include acute onset of a heart murmur, with a diastolic component being especially typical if the aortic valve is involved. Most common signs that a handler would notice are lethargy, inappetance, and lameness. Lameness can be a common presenting complaint for working dogs, but the presence of a fever coupled with these other signs should increase the clinician's suspicion for IE.

   d. Diagnosis is made by the presence of clinical signs in conjunction with aerobic and anaerobic blood culture (venous samples collected aseptically from a minimum of three different sites in an amount of 5-10 ml each) prior to administration of any antibiotics and 16S PCR. Samples should be collected 30 minutes to one hour apart, and ideally timed with a fever spike if possible. Negative culture rates even in positively affected cases of IE are fairly common (up to 70%), and this could result from previous antibiotic administration or difficult to culture organisms such as Bartonella. Both serology and PCR testing for Bartonella should be performed concurrent with blood culture. Laboratory samples may be submitted to Galaxy Diagnostics (http://www.galaxydx.com). Their testing method includes proprietary enrichment culture [BAPGM (Bartonella Alpha Proteobacteria Growth Medium)] with highly sensitive PCR methods to increase the sensitivity of Bartonella spp. detection.

   e. Treatment consists of long term bactericidal intravenous antibiotics ideally based on culture and susceptibility results and minimum inhibitory concentration testing. Symptomatic treatment of the secondary signs of congestive heart failure is also indicated.

   f. Prognosis with IE is notoriously poor and is typically contingent on which heart valve is affected. Consultation with the supporting 64F is recommended for guidance on which cases may benefit from long term therapy, and which cases should receive humane euthanasia.

4. Ebola Virus. Much attention is being directed to the role (if any) that domestic animals may have

played in the Ebola Virus outbreak in West Africa in 2014 after the disease spread to other continents/countries. At this point there is no evidence to show that dogs are susceptible to the disease, but their role as to the potential to spread the virus either through fomite transmission or directly through viral shedding is unknown. The Centers for Disease Control and Prevention report that there have been no reports of dogs becoming sick with Ebola or developing a capability to transmit the virus to people or animals. The following recommendations have been published through Defense Health Agency Veterinary Services (DHAVS) regarding deployment and redeployment of MWDs from Ebola outbreak areas:
   a. DHAVS does not endorse the deployment of MWDs into Ebola outbreak areas.
   b. If MWD-owning units do deploy MWDs to Ebola outbreak areas, these units should be prepared for the possibility that animal importation requirements may preclude the ability to redeploy these assets from endemic areas.
   c. MWDs should not be utilized in locations where there is a possibility of coming into contact with infected carcasses (human or animal). Positive control should be maintained with all dogs being on leash. MWDs should not be employed in hospitals, morgues, body collection points, etc.
   d. Physical exams are required upon redeployment.
   e. Upon redeployment, MWDs will be quarantined in isolation for 21 days under the supervision of a veterinarian.

GASTROINTESTINAL DISEASE

Non-GDV gastrointestinal disease is the cause of approximately 10% of MWD sick calls.
1. Apparently healthy MWD with weight loss and or anorexia. Weight loss or a lack of appetite are common reasons that MWD handlers seek veterinary care. Most of these dogs are not sick; in fact they are often in excellent health. Common causes of weight loss in an otherwise healthy MWD include:
   a. Anorexia may occur due to hot/humid weather, stress, travel or a new environment, and diet changes or poor food quality (should not happen with standardized diet). Mild transient anorexia associated with these problems should not be of sufficient severity or duration (less than a few days) to cause clinically significant weight loss (more than a few pounds). If anorexia persists more than a few days or significant weight loss occurs, assess the dog as outlined in section 5-5b.
   b. Increased energy expenditure associated with increased work or environmental extremes (e.g. cold weather), or activity in the kennel, e.g. agitation and more movement or "spinning" due to stress with PCS/TDY/Deployment. These dogs will generally be eating all the food provided, not anorectic, but some MWDs that are VERY active (or possibly clinically hyperactive) will not eat due to agitation and kennel activity or behavioral disorders.
   c. Inappropriate Feeding due to miscalculation of dietary needs and inadequate meal size, or incorrect measurement of the specified meal size. Science Diet Active (SDA) is very high in calories. When using prescription diets such as Hill's Z/D, bear in mind that the caloric density of these rations is much less than SDA and the volume of ration fed needs to be adjusted accordingly.
   d. Behavioral disease. Some hyperactive or repetitive activity MWDs may be so "distracted" by their behavior that they spill their food and can't eat it or essentially "forget" to eat.
2. Apparently sick dogs with weight loss and/or anorexia. If the animal is sick, more aggressive workup is warranted. A very important first step is determination of whether the dog is losing weight and not eating well (inability to eat or anorexia), or losing weight despite good appetite and food intake.

Specific categories of illness are discussed in more detail in later sections. The following rule-outs and diagnostic approaches are provided to help direct the workup:
- a. Weight loss plus not eating well/poor appetite. It is often difficult to tell if a dog wants to eat, but cannot or if it has true anorexia, a lack of desire to eat. A careful history from the handler may be helpful, but observation of the dog during feeding is often necessary.
- b. Weight loss plus wants to eat but can't/doesn't due to:
    - i. Orodental disease – won't eat due to dental pain (esp. fractured teeth), other oral trauma, or inability to prehend and chew food (e.g. tongue disease/injury, masticatory myositis). Of these, dental pain or mild oral pain associated with bite wrap use is most likely. Masticatory myositis should be suspected if MWD was recently anesthetized. A good cranial nerve, oral, and dental exam should aid diagnosis.
    - ii. Oropharyngeal disease – tries to eat but has difficulty swallowing and possibly prehending food. This may occur after oral or neck trauma (including heat injury, excessive choke chain use, other) and may be associated with upper respiratory tract distress or stridor. These problems are uncommon in MWDs but may occur. A good cranial nerve exam and observation of oropharyngeal function under anesthesia and or with fluoroscopy may be needed for diagnosis, as examination of the oropharynx of awake MWDs is hazardous to the VCO.
    - iii. Esophageal disease – Megaesophagus, esophagitis, and esophageal stricture are all uncommon causes of poor food intake in dogs. Most of these dogs will be hungry and want to eat but have signs of pain during swallowing or history of desire to eat/adequate food intake followed by regurgitation of undigested food. Esophagitis should be of particular concern in MWDs receiving tetracycline medications. These medications must be taken with food and water as they are potent esophageal irritants (they may also cause anorexia due to gastritis). Presumptive diagnosis may be made by observation and history and physical examination, but endoscopic and or fluoroscopic examination may be needed for definitive diagnosis.
- c. Weight Loss and Anorexia. There are too many causes of anorexia to specifically discuss in this document. Most problems likely to cause anorexic weight loss in MWDs will be associated with other signs of gastrointestinal disease, e.g. nausea and vomiting, diarrhea, etc. General causes may include inflammatory gastroenteritis (e.g. primary Inflammatory Bowel Disease (IBD), food allergy/intolerance, Antibiotic Responsive Enteritis (ARE), infectious), pancreatitis, hepatobiliary disease, and large bowel inflammatory disease (primary IBD, antibiotic responsive colitis/stress colitis), gastric ulceration and neoplasia. Some specific differential diagnoses are discussed in later sections. The key to diagnosis lays in getting a good history and physical examination, assessment of appropriate clinical pathologic indices, and trying to identify which area is most likely the problem. Trial therapy is often a key part of the diagnostic process. As with allergic dermatitis, trial hypoallergenic diet use is often a key to diagnosis, but long-term use may compromise deployability and this must be a consideration in management of MWD gastrointestinal disease if other therapeutic options are present.
    - i. Gastric and Small Intestinal Disease. Most MWDs with these problems will have anorexia, vomiting, weight loss, and small bowel diarrhea. Most will respond to basic GI management of no food for 24 hours, and non- antimicrobial treatment (e.g. Diagel®, Endosorb® or loperamide). If the dog is febrile or showing signs of general malaise diagnostics are warranted prior to considering treatment with antibiotics (e.g. amoxicillin, doxycycline, tylosin, metronidazole), gastric protectants

and antacids, and short term easily digested diet. If signs persist beyond 48 hours or recur, extensive workup is needed.
ii. Large Bowel Disease. Most MWDs with these problems will have signs of large bowel diarrhea, straining during defecation, hematochezia, etc. but not weight loss and anorexia. If majority of signs are related to large bowel disease but anorexia or weight loss are present, additional problems are likely. Most of these cases will resolve with non-antimicrobial therapy (e.g. Diagel®, Endosorb® or loperamide). However, if clinical signs persist, short-term antibiotic therapy and addition of dietary fiber are indicated.
iii. Hepatobiliary and pancreatic disease will often be associated with enteritis. It is often difficult to identify which problem is primary and which is secondary; however, in MWDs enteric disease is more commonly the underlying problem. Careful abdominal palpation and clinical pathology evaluation may help identify hepatic disease (acute vs. chronic/failure) and signs of pancreatitis.
iv. Other. Renal failure, neoplasia, heart disease, infection and other systemic disease may cause anorexia associated with nausea, vomiting, etc. Physical and clinical pathologic examination should help identify these problems if they are present.
d. Weight loss plus eating well. In general, the causes of weight loss despite adequate food intake are due to (NOTE: these are often multifactorial):
i. Inadequate absorption/utilization of consumed nutrients: Maldigestion/Malabsorption disorders such as Exocrine Pancreatic Insufficiency (EPI), ARE, intestinal inflammation (as above), etc.
ii. Excessive caloric expenditure: Increased metabolic rate due to behavioral hyperactivity, fever, infection/sepsis, malignancy, congestive heart failure, post-operative or post-trauma recovery.
iii. Loss of ingested nutrients: due to Protein Losing Nephropathy (PLN – glomerulonephritis with less likely amyloidosis), Protein Losing Enteropathy (PLE – inflammatory, infectious, lymphangiectasia or neoplasia), or Protein Losing Dermatopathy, diabetes mellitus, parasite infestation, chronic blood loss, etc.
3. Gastroduodenal ulcers (GDU). GDU are fairly uncommon in MWDs but may occur, especially when associated with NSAID therapy (inappropriate dosing or combination of different NSAIDs) or glucocorticoid administration, foreign body ingestion, hypotension, and liver disease. Other potential causes include primary gastroduodenal neoplasia, gastrinomas or mast cell tumors. Helicobacter infection is an unlikely cause of GDU in dogs, but may be a concern in some. Only NSAIDs approved for use in dogs should be used in MWDs.
a. Clinical signs. These signs may include melena, abdominal pain, hematemesis, anorexia, weight loss, decreased exercise tolerance, pale mucous membranes.
b. Diagnosis. Clinical signs, CBC/chemistry panel/UA, gross fecal and vomitus exam, radiology (barium series), endoscopy. Chronic gastrointestinal blood loss typically results in nonregenerative anemia with hypochromic and microcytic RBC indices.
c. Treatment options and deployability. The standard treatment should be use of an antacid combined with sucralfate for 1-2 weeks. Sucralfate may be discontinued 3-5 days prior to the antacid. If longer therapy is needed to control signs the supporting 64F should be consulted. During evaluation MWDs should be placed in CAT 3.
i. Mucosal binding protectants such as sucralfate bind to damage at the site of ulceration/developing ulcer in the acidic stomach. It should be administered at 1 gram/dose (MWD under 20 kg 500 mg per dose) at least every 12 hours, and every 8 hours may be optimal. Avoid giving with other medications as it may hinder

        absorption.
- ii. Acid reducers including H2 receptor antagonists or proton-pump inhibitors. Omeprazole a proton pump inhibitor is the preferred medication for acid reduction. Famotidine is the preferred H2-blocker; however, this medication should be reserved for cases in which only short term use is required. Famotidine and Omeprazole should not be used concurrently.
- iii. Misoprostol is a synthetic prostaglandin analog which can be used as a potent anti-ulcer medication in MWDs with history/risk of NSAID toxicity or severe or chronic ulceration not responsive to other medication. It is expensive and very hazardous to female personnel as it is a potent abortifacient and may cause severe uterine contractions. If used, it must be handled in the same manner as a chemotherapy drug and latex gloves must be worn. Due to the potential for adverse effects, it should generally not be the first choice for a newly diagnosed patient with GDU. This medication is better used as a preventative rather than a treatment of GDU.

4. Diarrhea. Diarrhea is a very common presenting complaint with MWDs. Large bowel signs include hematochezia, mucus, tenesmus, small amounts of stool, and frequent bowel movements. Small bowel signs include weight loss, large volumes of stool, melena, and vomiting. Potential etiologies include stress, dietary intolerance, bacterial overgrowth or imbalance (dysbiosis), inflammatory bowel disease (IBD), obstruction (foreign body, mass, etc.), parasites, and neoplasia. Parasitic diarrhea should be uncommon in MWDs as they receive monthly preventatives and have a standard diet but remain a concern (e.g. whipworms).
    a. Large bowel vs. Small bowel. Large bowel vs. Small bowel differentiation is integral to developing a diagnostic and therapeutic approach to the problem of diarrhea.
        i. Large bowel differentials include bacterial (Clostridium spp. especially), stress colitis, IBD, neoplasia, parasites and fungal. Diagnostics and treatment include fecal parasite examination, empiric deworming, non- antimicrobial therapy (e.g. Diagel®, Endosorb® or loperamide) in addition to dietary fiber are often all that is needed. If these do not resolve the problem, or if it recurs frequently and the MWD appears clinically ill then more aggressive workup is appropriate including: CBC/chemistry/UA, rectal exam, cytology, stool culture (usually not helpful unless really sick), colonoscopy, and radiographs.
        ii. Small bowel differentials include IBD, obstruction/intussusception, EPI or other malabsorption/maldigestion conditions, neoplasia, fungal, and parasites. If mild and no weight loss has occurred, fecal examinations, short-term bland/easily digestible diet and non-antimicrobial therapy (e.g. Diagel®, Endosorb® or loperamide) are often all that is needed. If these do not resolve the problem, it recurs frequently and/or the MWD appears clinically ill more aggressive workup is appropriate including: CBC/chemistry/UA, Pancreatic and Trypsin- like immunoreactivity (PLI and TLI), serum fasting cobalamin and folate levels, abdominal radiographs/abdominal ultrasound, and endoscopy or abdominal exploratory with biopsies (consult with supporting 64F).
    b. Treatment options and deployability. During evaluation MWDs should be placed in CAT 3.
        i. Diet-standard GI upset treatments. Rest the gut for 24 hours; feed easily digestible, low residue diet for 3-5 days such as I/d or I/d Low fat. Long-term use of a hypoallergenic diet (at least 8-12 weeks) may be necessary to rule out diet allergy or inflammatory bowel disease as a source of inflammatory enteritis.
        ii. Fiber. Psyllium (1-3 tsp/20 lb every 12 hours with food) or high fiber diet (W/D, R/D) or add canned pumpkin to the current diet (1-4 tsp per meal).

iii. Non-antimicrobial therapy (e.g. Diagel®, Endosorb®) – anti-microbial resistance is a significant challenge for the human and veterinary medical fields. Overzealous prescribing of antibiotics for conditions that either have alternative non-antimicrobial therapies (stress colitis) or antimicrobials are not indicated (viral infections) are leading contributors to the evolution of antimicrobial resistant bacterial strains. Diagel® (Van Beek Natural Science) and Endosorb® (PRN Pharmacal) are two examples of veterinary products that can be used in cases of simple diarrhea. Antibiotics should be reserved for non-responsive cases and for situations where an antimicrobial is clearly indicated.

iv. Motility modifiers - increase segmental contractions. Loperamide HCL 0.1-0.2 mg/kg PO every 8-12 hours. Use motility modifiers only if significant GI disease has been ruled out and if the diarrhea is duty or comfort limiting for the MWD and/or handler. Keep in mind that these drugs will stop almost all diarrhea but does not treat the underlying disease, and it should not be used to merely mask the diarrhea without investigating and treating the underlying problem. They should only be used for 1-3 days and concurrent workup should be initiated.

v. Antibiotics – 7-14 day trial therapy is appropriate to help determine the contribution of Small Intestinal Dysbiosis/Antibiotic Responsive Diarrhea and bacterial enteritides. Appropriate antibiotics include metronidazole (10 mg/kg PO every 12 hours), and tylosin (25-44 mg/kg PO every 12 hours). Trial therapy is the most accurate means of diagnosing bacterial colitis, although the immune modulating effects of some antibiotics may complicate the true cause of enteritis in certain cases. If bacterial enteritis is the only problem it should resolve quickly on antibiotic trial therapy. If it does not improve, or frequently recurs look for other causes of disease as well.

vi. Anti-inflammatories - without biopsies, use the ones with least systemic effects first such as sulfasalazine (10- 30 mg/kg every 8-12 hours) or olsalazine (5-10 mg/kg every 6-12 hours). If there is histopathological evidence of inflammatory infiltrates, steroid therapy (prednisone 1-2 mg/kg every 12 hours tapering to lowest effective dose) may be necessary to control IBD. Alternative immunosuppressive options to control IBD are azathioprine, cyclosporine, leflunomide and budesonide. Consult with the supporting 64F in treating these cases.

CARDIAC DISEASE

Although a major concern, cardiac disease is an infrequent cause of MWD morbidity and mortality. It is uncommon to encounter an MWD with a congenital cardiac defect due to the screening examinations performed on these dogs at procurement and the fact that many MWDs are purchased at approximately two years of age.

1. Chagas' Disease. Chagas' disease is caused by the hemoflagellate protozoan, Trypanosoma cruzi. See American Trypanosomiasis (Chagas Disease) for more information regarding epidemiology, transmission, and treatment of asymptomatic MWDs.

    a. Clinical signs generally follow either an acute or chronic course. The majority of patients suffering from acute signs are young dogs and can consist of sudden death, generalized lymphadenopathy, anorexia and diarrhea. Dogs that survive acute stage may become clinically normal, or undergo an indeterminate period of "latency" with no untoward effects. Some dogs with signs of chronic disease typically develop arrhythmias (ventricular premature contractions, heart block, etc.). Signs of congestive failure develop in many dogs

and may be clinically indistinguishable from dilated cardiomyopathy. Any MWD presenting with signs of right sided heart failure, cardiomegaly, and/or ECG abnormalities should have current T. cruzi serology performed.
- b. Diagnosis. Serology via IFA may be performed through the FADL. Older methodologies to test for Chagas cross-reacted with Leishmania spp, however newer methodologies employed by the FADL are much more specific for Chagas. In addition, the FADL also has the ability to run PCR testing on whole blood samples. Theoretically, the higher titer denotes the incriminating organism; however, performing PCR analysis for Leishmaniasis may be indicated to further rule it out. Given that most MWDs begin their working lives at JBSA-Lackland in San Antonio, TX (an endemic area for Chagas' disease) most cases that are positive for T. cruzi represent true exposure to this organism.
- c. Treatment. Two components of therapy are critical: control of arrhythmia and managing signs of dilated cardiomyopathy (DCM). Anti-arrhythmic medication options include sotalol (as a monotherapy if effective) or in conjunction with mexilitine (if available) or amiodarone. Currently the DODMWDVS is treating Chagas patients with amiodarone and itraconazole. Consult the supporting 64F or the DODMWDVS for guidance on management of individual Chagas patients. Obtaining a holter monitor analysis prior to and approximately one month after initiation of therapy are indicated to assess response to therapy. Regarding controlling signs of DCM, see section below.

2. Congestive Heart Failure. Congestive heart failure (CHF) may occur secondary to myocardial disease (Dilated Cardiomyopathy, Chagas-induced myocarditis), valvular disease, conduction disturbance, or pericardial disease. The most common cause in the aged MWD is mitral valve insufficiency (MVI). Although acute CHF may occur due to a ruptured chordae tendinae, or acute pericardial effusion, the most common presentation is one of slowly progressive weakness or exercise intolerance.
   - a. Clinical signs. These include weakness (often primarily evident in the hind limbs) exercise intolerance, cough, respiratory distress, ascites, hepatosplenomegaly, and syncope.
   - b. Diagnosis. Diagnosis is made by auscultation, pulse quality/rate, venous distention, jugular pulse, three view thoracic radiographs (essential for complete diagnosis), ECG, and blood pressure. Other diagnostic procedures that may be required to make a diagnosis include echocardiography, pericardiocentesis, CBC, chemistry profile and urinalysis.
   - c. Treatment and Deployability. CHF is a progressive disorder with the hallmark of decreased cardiac output and commensurate degradation in exercise capacity. Given the exercise demands of MWDs, the long-term utility of an MWD even in the early stages of CHF is questionable at best. Consultation with supporting 64F should be performed to assess deployability status of these patients as well as whether or not disposition should be considered.
   - d. Because of breed dispositions both for right atrial hemangiosarcoma and idiopathic pericardial effusion, MWDs presenting with signs of CHF should be screened for pericardial effusion leading to cardiac tamponade. All MWDs with evidence of a transudate abdominal effusion should be screened for cardiac tamponade. Other clinical signs include tachycardia and jugular venous distension. Treatment consists of pericardiocentesis to relieve the tamponade. Samples should be submitted for cytology.
   - e. Standard treatment guidelines are shown in Table 5-1. MWDs diagnosed with Stage B CHF should be placed in CAT 2, but as previously mentioned, strong consideration should be given to proceeding with disposition in these dogs. Those with Stage C or D CHF should be placed in CAT 4 with limited or no duty and submitted to the MWD disposition process. In reality, stage D patients are those who are refractory to standard outpatient therapy. Humane euthanasia is the most appropriate approach. Contact the supporting 64F or the

DODMWDVS for consultation.
3. Cardiomyopathy. Dilated Cardiomyopathy (DCM) is a potential concern in MWDs. As previously stated, obtaining a current T. cruzi titer and PCR on any DCM suspect is important to assess the possible involvement of this organism as an inciting cause.
4. Clinical Signs. DCM may present due to a wide variety of signs from mild CHF and exercise intolerance, weakness and collapse or syncope, ascites or pleural effusion, or occasionally sudden death. Associated arrhythmias, heart murmur, or abnormal pulse quality may be detected in some dogs prior to onset of other clinical signs. A grade 1-3/6 systolic murmur is typically auscultated over the left and/or right atrioventricular valve(s), a progressive increase in grade may be noted if decreased coaptation of valves secondary to heart enlargement occurs.
    a. Diagnosis. Diagnosis should be made based on radiographic evidence of cardiomegaly with or without pulmonary edema and pleural effusion and echocardiographic evidence of reduced systolic function (decreased ejection fraction, fractional shortening) as well as cardiomegaly (left atrial and ventricular enlargement as well as decreased thickness of interventricular septum/left ventricular free wall). All MWDs with suspected DCM should be evaluated with an ECG study (minimum Lead II but six lead preferred). Arrhythmias noted clinically, or on auscultation and pulse palpation should be better characterized with the ECG. Diagnosis in asymptomatic MWDs must be made with care, and after consultation with a supporting 64F and/or a radiologist at DODMWDVS, as the resting athletic heart may bear some resemblance to mild DCM. Specific radiographic and echocardiographic indices for assessment of MWDs are available to aid in diagnosis.
    b. Treatment and Deployability. Treatment of DCM is directed at improving cardiac contraction with positive inotropes, control of associated arrhythmias, treatment of associated CHF (as above) and treatment of underlying disease (if identified). Any working dog receiving medical care for clinically apparent signs of cardiac disease should be placed in a CAT 4 status and undergo the disposition process. Given the relatively rapid progression of DCM in most dogs, even in the absence of significant clinical signs (i.e., early DCM) MWDs diagnosed with DCM should immediately be placed in a CAT 4 status and undergo the disposition process.

TABLE 2. MWD Treatment and Deployment Guidelines for CHF

Heart Failure Stage	Clinical Signs	Radiographic Changes	Treatment	Deployment Category
A – Asymptomatic (dogs predisposed to cardiac disease)	None; based on signalment	None	None	1
B – Structural heart disease in absence of signs Substage B1: no imaging changes Substage B2: echo/xray changes	Murmur	+/- LA, LV enlargement; generalized cardiomegaly	Substage B1: none; recheck q3-6 months Substage B2: ACEI, +/- beta blocker, special diet	2 or 4
C – Past or current signs present of failure	Same as B + dyspnea, cough,	Same as B +/- pulmonary venous distension	CE, ACEI, diuretic, special diet,	4, initiate disposition

	jugular venous distension, ascites, tachycardia		positive inotrope; light duty	
D - End-stage disease	Same as C, refractory to therapy, require hospitalization	Above plus pleural effusion/ascites	CE, ACEI, diuretic, special diet, positive inotrope, O2 supplementation, topical nitroglycerin; No Duty	4, initiate disposition, or more likely humane euthanasia

Key: LA = left atrium,
LV = left ventricle, RV = right ventricle, Diuretic = Furosemide
CE = client education, tell handler what they should look for if the condition is progressing, ACEI = Angiotensin Converting Enzyme Inhibitor,
Inotrope = Pimobendan
Special Diet = mildly sodium restricted; adequate protein

RESPIRATORY TRACT DISEASE

Respiratory tract disease is not common in the MWD (less than 5% of expected sick call and less than 2% of historic mortality), but deserves mention due to its potential severity and because it must be differentiated from CHF as a cause of weakness, exercise intolerance, and cough. Remember that these two disease conditions may occur together, as one predisposes to the other. Potential causes of respiratory tract disease include infection (bacterial, viral, mycotic, parasitic), neoplasia, conformational problems (i.e. laryngeal paralysis, bronchiectasis, collapsing trachea), and allergic bronchitis.

1. Upper Respiratory Tract (URT) Disease. Diseases of the nares and nasal passages, mouth, nasopharynx, larynx, trachea and bronchi may occur in MWDs due to trauma (e.g. heat injury or excessive use of a choke chain), infection, neoplasia, or due to anatomic abnormality. These problems are rare in MWDs as those with predispositions are generally excluded from purchase and training at the DOD Dog Center, and because infectious upper respiratory disease is uncommon in adult healthy dogs. Kennel cough (Bordetella) and canine influenza vaccinations of MWDs are not authorized at the time of this writing. It is not uncommon to be presented with a working dog with harsh upper airway sounds associated with working on the collar/choke chain. Some dogs (especially Labrador Retrievers) experience transient laryngeal paralysis due to presumed damage to the recurrent laryngeal nerve with either excessive pulling on the lead or overzealous corrective measures on the part of the handler. Absence of signs off lead are supportive of this problem. Attempts to utilize the dog on a harness may be employed by the handler in an effort to salvage the working dog, however, be advised that most handlers and trainers are loath to switch to this system.
    a. Clinical signs. Dogs with URT disease may have signs including mild to progressive, or acute respiratory distress (especially inspiratory), cough, oculonasal discharge, altered bark, weakness or exercise intolerance, and signs of associated systemic and or lower respiratory tract illness.
    b. Diagnosis. Minimum diagnostic evaluation for the MWD with URT disease includes a good

history, observation of respiratory patterns (generally slow deep obstructive) and auscultation (e.g. stertor, stridor, rhonchus), systemic evaluation with CBC, chemistry panel, urinalysis and heartworm test. Additional workup may include three view thoracic and cervical radiographs, rhinoscopy, larngotracheoscopy, fluoroscopy, transtracheal wash, Baermann sedimentation fecal examination and trial therapy.

c. Treatment and Deployability. MWDs under evaluation or treatment for URT disease should be placed in CAT 3. Permanent reduction to CAT 2 is uncommon except in MWDs with neoplastic or traumatic URT disease. Treatment must address primary and underlying disease.

2. Lower Respiratory Tract (LRT) Disease. Diseases of the small airways and pulmonary parenchyma are uncommon in MWDs for reasons similar to URT disease. General causes of LRT disease include immune mediated, infectious, allergic, cardiac and neoplastic disease. Viral, bacterial, and parasitic pneumonias are of limited concern in MWDs due to aggressive prophylactic care and good general health. Bacterial pneumonia should be of increased concern if MWD was recently anesthetized, has a history of vomiting or regurgitation, or episodes of collapse or syncope.

   a. Clinical Signs. Common signs of LRT disease include mild to progressive or acute severe respiratory distress, coughing, mucopurulent nasal discharge, weakness, and an orthopneic stance with neck extended and forelegs bowed (elbow abduction) to facilitate respiration. Associated signs of systemic or associated URT disease may also be present.

   b. Diagnosis. The minimum evaluation for MWD with LRT disease includes a good history, observation (generally shallow fast restrictive respiratory patterns) and auscultation (e.g. crackles, wheezes, rales), and three view thoracic radiographs. Other diagnostic procedures may include fecal exam (parasite migration), serology (fungal), urine fungal antigen screen, arterial blood gas, transtracheal wash (TTW) or bronchoalveolar lavage with fluid culture and susceptibility plus cytology.

   c. Treatment and Deployability. Treatment is dictated by definitive diagnosis of LRT and underlying diseases and may include special attention to maintaining good hydration; cough suppressants (contraindicated in patients with a productive cough) and bronchodilators, anti-inflammatories and antihistamines, and antibiotics. More acute cases may require confinement, oxygen support, nebulization and coupage. Treatment should continue until adequate oxygenation can be maintained on room air and a minimum of one-week past resolution of clinical signs. MWDs with clinical signs of LRT disease should be placed in CAT 3 during evaluation and treatment. Some with chronic recurrent problems may need to be maintained in CAT 2, or patients with predisposing problems such as bronchiectasis, disposition should be strongly considered.

UROGENITAL DISEASE

1. Cystitis and Prostatitis. Prostatitis, and therefore cystitis, is a common problem in the intact male MWD. Given the anatomic proximity between these two structures, co-infection is common. Etiology is usually bacterial though infections can be secondary to predisposing causes such as calculi, outflow obstruction, infection elsewhere in the urinary/reproductive tract, indwelling catheters, immunosuppressive disease, trauma to the bladder, glucosuria, or anatomic abnormality. Thorough rectal examinations are imperative at all semiannual exams to identify problems early. Normal prostate palpation should reveal a smooth, non-painful, symmetrical organ. With progressive age and development of benign prostatic hypertrophy (BPH), a common disease in intact male dogs, the prostate typically gravitates over the brim of the pelvis and can make thorough digital rectal exam challenging. Utilizing the non-dominant hand to place caudodorsal pressure on the abdomen can

facilitate a caudal displacement of the prostate into the pelvic canal and enhance the clinician's ability to better evaluate the organ via rectal examination.

 a. Clinical Signs. Clinical signs typically consist of lower urinary tract signs such as hematuria, dysuria, stranguria, pollakiuria, polyuria, or systemic illness (acute bacterial prostatitis or pyelonephritis), straining to defecate (secondary to prostatomegaly) and, abdominal pain, that may mimic lower back pain (differential for DLSS) or hind limb lameness.

 b. Diagnosis. Diagnosis is established by a number of methods and tests including physical exam, rectal exam, urinalysis, urine culture and susceptibility, CBC, chemistry profile, abdominal radiographs (with or without contrast), urinary tract ultrasound, thoracic radiographs (neoplasia), ejaculate - cytology, culture, prostatic wash - cytology, culture, fine needle aspirate, biopsy of prostate. It is important to rule out other prostatic conditions such as prostatic adenocarcinoma (fixed, painful, asymmetric, firm), prostatic/paraprostatic cysts, benign prostatic hyperplasia, and abscess. See Table 2.

TABLE 3. Prostatic Conditions and Findings

	Fixed	Painful	Symmetrical	Consistency
BPH	N	N	Y	Normal, but enlarged
Cyst	N	Y/N	N	Fluctuant/Firm
Abscess	N	Y	N	Soft/Firm
Prostatitis	N	Y-acute	Y or N	Normal
		N-chronic		
Adenocarcinoma	Y	N/Y	N	Firm and Irregular Texture

 c. Treatment. For an uncomplicated UTI in a female dog, presumptive therapy with an amoxicillin or other first line antibiotic for 5-7 days is appropriate. For an initial urinary tract infection in an intact male dog, treat with an appropriate antibiotic (based on culture and susceptibility testing) for a minimum of 3 weeks while also verifying that sterile urine is achieved both during therapy and within 5-7 days upon cessation of therapy. If the dog is intact and signs are consistent with acute or chronic bacterial prostatitis, then orchiectomy is indicated concurrent with antibiotic therapy. Dogs with prostatitis should be placed on appropriate antibiotics for at least 4-6 weeks. Antibiotics that penetrate the prostate are indicated (i.e., enrofloxacin, TMS, etc.). Initial drug selection should take into account the blood/prostate barrier and definitive therapy should be based upon urine culture and sensitivity. Prostatic abscessation may be chronic and subtle or can present as an acute life-threatening sepsis. Surgical drainage and "omentalization" of the abscess cavity (or large paraprostatic cysts) appears to offer improved survival over more traditional methods of surgical therapy (marsupialization or drainage through the abdominal wall). Patients with sepsis or a ruptured prostatic abscess are too unstable for transport to DODMWDVS for surgical care. Because they require immediate critical care and skilled surgical intervention, referral to appropriate veterinary specialists in the local area is the preferred course of action. For clinically significant benign prostatic hyperplasia and acute/chronic bacterial prostatitis, neutering is the first line of therapy. According to the MEDCOM MWD Medical Readiness Policy, MWDs will only be neutered for clinically relevant, medically-related problems, such as testicular neoplasia, significant benign prostatic hyperplasia/hypertrophy, intractable scrotal dermatitis, perianal adenoma, or other problems that are clearly and directly attributable to the dog being intact. An enlarged prostate, in the absence of clinical manifestations which degrade the dog's performance or quality of life, is not sufficient reason to perform orchiectomy. VCOs should consult with their supporting 64F regarding cases in which they are uncertain of the appropriate action regarding neutering of MWDs. MWDs will be neutered as part of the final processing for adoption as a pet; however, this may be waived if being transferred to civilian law enforcement or other non-DOD federal agencies. VCOs will not neuter male MWDs as a prophylactic procedure or for surgical practice.

CHAPTER 6

DIAGNOSTIC IMAGING

RADIATION SAFETY

Procedures to minimize radiation exposure for all personnel will follow the ALARA (As Low As Reasonably Achievable) principle and will include the following:

1. All unnecessary personnel will leave the radiology room prior to any radiographic exposures being made.
2. All personnel who are restraining or positioning dogs for radiographic exposures must wear protective clothing. Protective clothing includes lead (0.5 mm thick) aprons, gloves, and thyroid shields.
3. Contact the supporting MTF's health physics/radiation safety officer for guidance regarding need for dosimetry badging. Depending on number of exposures made at a facility, dosimetry may not be deemed necessary; however, that determination must be made by supporting health physics/radiation safety personnel. When required, dosimetry badges must be worn by all personnel in the radiology room during exposures IAW health physics/radiation safety guidance.
4. Under NO circumstance should personnel ever have any part of their body within the primary beam of radiation, whether it is shielded or not. The primary beam is within the area outlined by the collimator light. Gloves and aprons are only designed to protect from scatter radiation and will not protect the wearer from exposure to primary beam radiation. Collimation of the primary beam will be used for every exposure.
5. Prior to an exposure being made, it is the responsibility of all personnel within the radiology room to ensure they and all others are properly protected from radiation. The basic tenets of time, distance, and shielding should be constantly employed.
6. Assistants and animal restrainers will be positioned as far away from the primary beam as possible (preferably at the ends of the table).
7. Radiographic procedures should be performed with adequate restraint (i.e. sedation and/or anesthesia if necessary) to ensure proper radiation safety practices, enable proper positioning, and avoid re-takes.
8. An exposure log (date, person holding animal or cassette, type of procedure, kilovolt peak [kVp] and milliampere second [mAs]) will be maintained for each radiographic exposure to help minimize re-takes and calculate radiation workload or exposure history if necessary. This log also allows the VCO to tailor repeated techniques for an individual patient on follow-up exams.
9. A veterinary facility radiation safety SOP specific to the clinic is required by and helps assure adherence to AAHA practice standards.

DIGITAL RADIOGRAPHY

Few aspects of veterinary medicine have changed more than the development and rapid rise of digital radiography since the early 2000s. Even though film radiography is still a viable option, most veterinary schools do not continue to incorporate film radiography in their curricula. Digital radiography holds several advantages over film radiology, with the largest including faster development, time/patient throughput, the ability to post-process images via software reducing the need to repeat images and overall radiation exposure, and the lack of need for a dark room and hazardous chemical use. The term "digital radiography" incorporates both computed radiography (CR) and digital radiography (DR) systems, and is important to understand the basic fundamentals and differences of each system if involved in purchasing, maintenance, or troubleshooting/development of artifacts involved with image generation of these units. It is beyond the scope of this handbook to discuss individual brands/units as multiple types are currently in use in the Army, each with their own proprietary software and equipment variation. If the VCO has more specific questions regarding the digital radiography equipment that the equipment manuals cannot answer, please contact the local medical maintenance staff and/or digital equipment service representative.

1. Computed Radiography. CR uses a cassette which holds a bendable phosphor plate that captures the latent image after patient exposure. After the x-ray exposure has been made, the plate must be transferred from the x-ray table and placed into a processor to generate the image. Depending on the type of phosphor within the plate, the latent image may only be stable for minutes to hours so it is important to process quickly after exposure to ensure no loss of data occurs. Once the cassette has been placed into the processor, the plate within the cassette is ejected and a laser activates the stored energy within the plate. This stored energy is released as visible light/photons, which is captured by the processor, amplified/enhanced and further transformed into the image displayed on the computer monitor. After the image on the plate has been read, the plate is exposed to white light in order to effectively "erase" any stray energy left within the phosphor and then returned to the cassette for the next image. It is normal for wear and tear to occur on these plates as they are bent over time and can eventually create image artifacts due to this wear and tear. These plates are much less expensive than DR, so if dropped, kicked, or broken are much less expensive to replace. Routine maintenance will need to be performed at least annually on these units as dust/debris accumulation within the processors can lead to artifact formation and/or poor image generation. High radiography throughput is not often a major concern with most of our facilities, CR systems are generally less expensive than DR systems, and if parts break CR systems are usually more cost-effective to replace.

2. Digital Radiography. DR (direct, indirect, and charged coupled detector) uses a plate which directly converts the captured x-rays into an electrical image via semiconducting material, transistors, or detector chips (respectively), which is then transferred to the computer for further initial processing before eventual display on the monitor. These plates are generally similar to CR in terms of image resolution, however, afford greater latitude for image post- processing, require less patient exposure to create a diagnostic image, and do not require the extra step for transfer to a processor as advantages over CR. Dependent on the x-ray system and technique chart, the plate may never have to leave the Bucky of the x-ray table unless special techniques (such as horizontal beam imaging) are employed. The transfer of data from the plate to computer/monitor usually involves a thick cable (however wireless plate transfer is available) which is often the "weak point" of the system, and can be broken if stepped on, therefore this must to be guarded. The plates are fairly durable but also can be broken if kicked/dropped and must be protected as well. As the DR plate processes the image, the plate may need to be routinely calibrated per manufacturer's guidelines in order to account for loss of pixels involved in electrical conversion of the x-rays over time. Additionally, certain types of plates do not function well in high temperature situations, so be sure to discuss this problem before purchase if the unit is planned for deployment use.

3. Digital Imaging Worklist (VTF). All software viewers require the patient data to be entered prior to making an image. As the worklist grows on the computer's hard drive, it is of vital importance that the VTF adopt a standardized format for entering patient data; otherwise it may become difficult to find all of the studies listed for one patient as the case files grow. For MWDs, it has become important to adopt the following standardized protocol for entry: Last Name should be "MWD", First Name should be the actual name of the MWD (i.e. "Rex"), and the Patient I.D. category should contain their tattoo number. The rest of the patient data (sex, date of birth, etc.) still needs to be entered as well. By this means, it will be easier to find the images in the system, easier for the

radiologists to locate on their end if receiving the referral, and easier to transfer over the hospital internet when deployed.
4. Digital Imaging Worklist (MEDCEN/MTF). Many VCOs radiograph, MR, or CT MWDs with the help of the local MTF. DODMWDVS has developed a naming convention to enter MWDs properly into Composite Health Care System (CHCS); this convention should be applied at all MTFs. The exams can then be properly stored in the Picture Archiving and Communication System (PACS) and the non-human patients do not appear on physician's worklists within the hospital. The VCO must communicate with the MTF network or CHCS office personnel to assure that these recommendations are applicable to the local situation. The VCO or the technologists in the department (CR, CT, MRI, etc.), must be given access to the non-human registration (NHR) field within CHCS. Last Name should be "MWDOG", First Name should be the actual name of the MWD (i.e. "Rex"), followed by a space and the tattoo number. Enter sex and date of birth. Under SSN, enter the final 9 digits of the microchip number. Patient Category should be listed as K99 (patient not elsewhere classified). This non-human patient can now be "arrived" and procedures selected as with a normal patient. The study can be entered as "procedure only" so that MWD exams do not appear as "unspecified exams" on radiologist or other physician worklists over the hospital network. Alternatively, an MWD imaging study list can be created in the system by the MTF PACS Manager. Discuss this with the technologist when scheduling the study.
5. Digital Image Processing. Once the image appears on a computer screen, it has already undergone multiple pre-processing and processing protocols in order to display the largest number of shades of grey, improve contrast and spatial resolution, and suppress unnecessary noise. These protocols should have been optimized to work with the x-ray unit by the customer service representative. If the image cannot completely process to diagnostic satisfaction following image generation and the radiographic technique chart was correctly utilized, consulting with the service representative/medical maintenance personnel is indicated.
6. Digital Image Post-Processing. Post-processing an image allows the VCO to further fine-tune/manipulate the contrast and overall brightness of the generated image through a concept called windowing/leveling. Windowing refers to changing the overall numbers of shades of grey available based on the pixel values and leveling refers to the mid-point of those pixel values. The mouse cursor often changes to the shape of a half-moon or curly line when altering these values. Depending on the software available for use with the system, there are numerous other post- processing functions that can use to manipulate the image (common ones include zoom, pan, measuring, labeling, etc.), however are too vast of a topic to include all options here. Refer to the viewing software manual to determine all of the capable functions available for use.
7. Digital Radiography Monitors. The standard of practice for medical imaging is a monochrome or grey-scale LCD monitor display. While medical-grade grey scale monitors are ideal, consumer grade monitors have been found to be adequate for diagnosis if appropriate post-processing techniques are used and are much more cost- effective. Consumer grade monitors are usually color monitors with fewer capabilities (decreased brightness, smaller pixel matrices, and smaller graphics cards) for observing the generated image. Color monitors are also not usually calibrated to the grayscale display function standards set forth by the Digital Imaging and Communications in Medicine (DICOM) standard (further discussed below), however, the service representative may be able to calibrate the monitors. Calibrating the monitors is not required but is a quality assurance measure to conform uniformity of the grayscale within the display and between monitors. Ensure that the area where the images on the monitor(s) are viewed has low, indirect ambient lighting, as light pollution can cause misdiagnoses.
8. Digital Imaging Formats. The raw, unaltered/uncompressed digital image created should be able to be saved in a universally accepted format called DICOM. This format is the appropriate form for saving

the image for medical record documentation and submitting to radiologists for consultation. There are several other formats that images may be saved in (common ones include .jpg, .tiff, .bmp, and .png), but these formats will often compress the actual image which decreases the overall resolution and information is lost which might have been diagnostic. Also, compressible files can also be altered or "photo shopped", which deems them inappropriate for medical documentation. This does not mean that if an image is sent for referral to the DODMWDVS in a .jpg format that it will not be provided a consult (example is a camera picture of a film radiograph), but understand that the DODMWDVS may request the DICOM images to confirm the diagnosis.

9. Digital Storage. Storage of digital images can be performed by several means. The images will be stored on the computer hard drive associated with the digital radiography system, but it is important to backup these files as computer crashes are not uncommon. The most cost-effective method for storage of individual radiographic case files is through the use of CDs/DVDs. CDs/DVDs have a good deal of memory for storage capability; one CD (normally 700 MB capacity) can normally hold all radiographic studies for one patient over the course of their life. Ultrasound, CT and MRI studies are larger and need more memory capacity than routine radiographic studies, but usually one of these studies can be entirely contained on a single CD. DVDs can normally hold up to 4.7 GB of data, so can be used in rare cases when needed. External computer hard drives are also becoming rapidly more affordable and should easily backup all of the images with a 500 GB – 1TB external hard drive capacity.

10. Digital Radiography Technique Chart and Artifacts. It is often incorrectly assumed that a technique chart does not need to be developed for a digital radiography system as post-processing affords the ability to correct the overexposure/underexposure of the image. A radiation safety hazard may be created by not producing a technique chart by unnecessarily overexposing the patient to the primary x-ray beam, and overexposing the personnel handling the dog to scatter radiation. Additionally, artifacts may be generated through underexposure and overexposure of the patient which may not be able to be corrected through post-processing and will require more radiation exposure to create another image. Examples of exposure artifacts and other common digital radiography artifacts can be found in standard radiography texts. The procedure for appropriate development of a technique chart is within section 6-3.

TECHNIQUE CHARTS

A technique chart is a table with predetermined x-ray machine settings for each body part, depending on the thickness of the tissue and the part of the body to be radiographed. Technique charts provide an organized approach to radiography based on anatomy, tissue thickness and specific film/screen cassettes to be used. Use of a technique chart is a radiation safety precaution that prevents unnecessary radiation exposure. Technique charts are also helpful with digital radiography systems to help maintain consistency between studies and limit re-takes due to over- and underexposure.

1. References. The AMEDD C&S uses McCurnin's *Clinical Textbook for Veterinary Technicians* and *Radiography in Veterinary Technology* by Lavin when training 68T Animal Care Specialists. Techniques in *Veterinary Radiography* by Morgan and Thrall's *Veterinary Diagnostic Radiology* texts are also excellent resources.
2. For a concise overview, we recommend Lavin, *The Imaging Chain: Links to High Quality Radiography*. Vet Tech 22(5), May 2001.
3. General rules for technique charts. Technique charts need to be developed for every x-ray unit in order to obtain the highest quality diagnostic radiographs. Many manufacturers have already developed a veterinary technique chart specific for use with their equipment. It is recommended that the manufacturer is contacted before creating a technique chart to aid with the creation of based on

the components of the entire system. Before beginning a technique chart, a medical physicist should calibrate the x-ray equipment and the film processor, if required, should be thoroughly evaluated for proper function (PMCS, quality assurance, consistency). For digital systems, technical support should facilitate initial system settings of protocols and processing algorithms. For body parts measuring over 10 cm, a Bucky or stationary grid should be used to block scatter radiation, which otherwise would severely degrade the quality of the image, potentially rendering them non-diagnostic.

4. Making a technique chart. Once the initial calculations are made, a cooperative animal will be required for several test exposures. An estimate of the proper kVp for the exam is obtained using Sante's Rule: (2 x tissue thickness in cm) + Source-to-Image-Distance (40 in) + grid factor = kVp. Grid factor is the first number in the grid ratio (for example, 10:1) for the machines which can be found in the operator or service manual. If the grid ratio is unknown but x-rays are shot to the bucky then the default grid factor is 10. If a grid is not used with the system (never shoot x-rays to a table bucky or lay a grid on the cassette) then a grid factor is not included in the equation. An estimate of proper mAs is obtained by consulting the reference texts mentioned above. In general, higher mAs settings (5-15) are used for radiography of the abdomen, pelvis and spine. Lower mAs settings (2.5 – 5) are used for exams of the thorax and extremities. Higher mA settings, if adjustable on the x-ray tube, will minimize the length of exposure (seconds) for the same mAs and must be a consideration for procedures prone to motion artifact (e.g. thorax). Now obtain three different exposures (calculated value, +2 to 4 kVp, and –2 to 4 kVp) and select the best of those exposures. If none of these exposures are optimal, the technique must be adjusted using the principles of radiology technique evaluation mentioned below. After determining the best exposure technique for the thickness of the test patient, create a variable kVp technique chart by adding or subtracting 2 kVp for each cm change in thickness up to 80, then add 3 kVp from 80-100, and finally add 4 kVp above 100 until the chart is complete. As the maximum/minimum kVp range for the x-ray equipment is reached, one can also vary the mAs by either doubling the mAs and subtracting 10 kVp or halving the mAs and adding 10 kVp to stay within the limits of the x-ray tube while maintaining the same film density. Use the basic rules above to complete the technique chart within the capabilities of the x-ray tube and required patient exams (e.g. there is usually no need for a 20 cm extremity technique or 2 cm thorax exam).

5. Radiology Technique Evaluation. When evaluating the suitability of the technique used to produce a radiograph, three questions must be answered.

    a. Is the film too light? An underexposed image is defined as an overall lack of or poor gross detail of the anatomic structures on one or more areas of the radiograph due to the image being overall too white or has a more mottled/pixelated appearance. We most commonly see this in obese patients along the thorax where radiographic technique charts were not made to deal with the increased amount of fat along the thoracic walls, or in cases where increased amounts of fluid are present within a body cavity or the surrounding soft tissues like we can see with trauma. The peripheral background of underexposed images may also be more of a hazy gray rather than the typical uniform black appearance we should see. If most of the margins of the soft tissue structures cannot be visualized, then this is likely attributed to the fact that the majority of the x-rays used were not powerful enough to make it all the way through the patient to create a diagnostic image. Attempt to correct this by increasing the kVp value by 10- 15%. If most of the soft tissue anatomic margins can be visualized well and the issue largely extends into the peripheral background of the image where it is more gray in appearance than black, then there is likely not a high enough quantity of x-rays available (mAs) to make a diagnostic image. Attempt to correct this by doubling the mAs value and repeat the image. For some studies, increase both kVp and mAs values in order to obtain a diagnostic image. One final point to make is that some tables have x-ray tubes which allow for manual height adjustment based on whether the plate is either resting on the

tabletop or within the bucky. If the x-ray tube is set to shoot to the tabletop and the imaging plate is underneath the table in the bucky, this may cause an underexposed image to occur.
b. Is the film too dark? This is by far the most common technique issue seen in veterinary radiology where the image(s) are overall far too black with loss of soft tissue detail. For digital radiography, overexposure can also be identified by the presence of planking in the areas surrounding the patient and appears as a rectangular pattern in the background. Additionally, clipping may have occurred such that no amount of image adjustment will bring out an image in the thinnest portions of the patient (e.g. no vascular markings in lung, absent ventral body wall, absent musculature surrounding bones on a limb). If the image is overexposed then assess for any loss of the expected margins of the skin or soft tissues (or even small, thin bones if present in the image). If the margins of these structures are clearly noted but the overall image appears to be too dark, then the mAs is too high as there are too many x-rays bombarding the patient. To correct this, reduce the mAs to half of its original value and retake the image. If, instead, the margins or structure of the skin/soft tissues/small bones are significantly darkened or absent then the kVp is too high with too many high intensity x-rays penetrating through this region of the patient. Reduce the original kVp value by 10-15%. If the image is significantly overexposed reduce kVp and/or mAs multiple times in order to create a diagnostic image.
c. Is adequate contrast present? The gray scale displayed on the film equals contrast. Evaluate the quality of x-rays (kVp) used to create the image and the amount of contrast that is desirable for the exam. The overall contrast of the soft tissue structures in the image can either be too high (image is too "black and white" in appearance) or too low (too many "shades of gray"). As the kVp values decrease between images, the amount of radiographic contrast will increase as the image will appear more "black and white" with less shades of gray. This is due to the fact there is less variety of kV values of the x-rays associated with the primary beam that can penetrate through the patient to reach the imaging plate. If instead the kVp values increase between images, this decreases the overall contrast of the image as it creates more variety of x-ray kV values that can penetrate through the patient in the primary beam, and therefore creates more shades of gray in the image. As opposed to over/underexposure issues, both kVp and mAs will ALWAYS change with contrast issues to keep the same level of radiographic exposure in the image. Therefore, if the image has too much contrast and it needs to decrease, INCREASE the kVp by 10-15% but also HALVE the mAs value at the same time in order to maintain the same level of radiation exposure in the image. If the image needs more contrast as it has too many shades of gray involved then DECREASE the kVp by 10-15% and DOUBLE the mAs value.
d. For a complete review of radiology technique evaluation, we recommend the information contained in the references. In most cases, the answers to these basic questions will lead to the proper adjustments of mAs and/or kVp necessary to produce the highest quality radiograph at the best possible technique.
e. Technique chart failure. In some circumstances, a technique chart that has been established will fail to produce a diagnostic, quality radiograph. Rarely is the x-ray tube malfunctioning (especially if recently calibrated). More often there has been an error in measurement or selection of exposure settings. There also may have been an error in film/screen selection or inconsistent film processing. This may also be the result of a disease process, which produces a greater or lesser radiographic density than expected. For example, these diseases can produce less radiographic density than expected: pneumothorax, megaesophagus, aerophagia, GDV, negative contrast (pneumocolon), focal destructive bone disease or generalized bone disease. Other diseases may produce a greater than expected radiographic

density. Some examples include pleural effusion, pericardial effusion, ascites, pulmonary hemorrhage, pneumonia, or administration of a positive contrast medium. Altering the exposure settings IAW with radiology technique evaluation guidelines mentioned above will assist in producing the best quality image possible without masking naturally occurring signs of pathology in the patient.

ABDOMINAL RADIOGRAPHY OF MWDS

Abdominal radiographs are usually made with the MWD awake when possible. Sedation (tranquilization or general anesthesia) can cause splenomegaly and can potentially cause ileus. However, sedation should be used when required to enable proper positioning and radiation safety in obtaining a diagnostic study. Lack of proper preparation of the abdomen is the most common problem with abdominal radiography. Ingesta, fluid, and fecal material frequently obscure the area of interest in an unprepared abdomen. For routine scheduled exams, the MWD should be fasted for 12 hours prior to making radiographs and enemas administered as needed. If a contrast study such as an upper GI or excretory urogram is being done, preparation of the abdomen is essential, and may include one or more enemas 3-4 hours prior to the procedure. Proper preparation for specials studies should be researched and planned on a per case basis.

1. Emergent situations. In an emergency, preparation is not required or recommended. For example, if GDV is suspected, one right lateral view is likely all that is required. Another example of a situation requiring no preparation is in a dog that has been vomiting or has diarrhea. If the dog is being radiographed to rule out ileus or obstruction, no preparation is necessary. If a positive contrast cystogram is being performed after trauma to rule out bladder rupture, no preparation is necessary.
2. Diagnostic quality radiographs of the abdomen. A minimum of two views are generally required for evaluation of the abdomen. The ventrodorsal and right lateral projections are preferred for most routine studies. The right lateral is usually preferred because it allows gas to move into the fundus of the stomach, permitting good visualization of the stomach and liver. If the pylorus and proximal duodenum need to be evaluated, a left lateral may be also be made. Three view abdominal studies (including both right and left laterals) are recommended in vomiting cases, especially if foreign body ingestion is suspected. The foreign body may only be visible on one view. The ventrodorsal view is diagnostically preferred to the dorsoventral view. Positioning of the radiograph is often determined by the area of interest. In large dogs, two overlapping films will likely be required for each view in order to get a diagnostic study of the entire abdomen. An abdominal study needs to include the entire diaphragm through the pelvic inlet with the legs fully extended caudally. In contrast to the lateral technique, an additional 6-8 kVp needs to be added to the ventrodorsal or dorsoventral view in order to properly expose the radiograph. Poor positioning, overexposure or underexposure can create false results or simulate disease.
3. Presence of abdominal fluid. Depending on the amount of peritoneal fluid, it may be necessary to increase the mAs 50% to produce a quality radiograph. In cases that require a shorter exposure time, the kVp can be increased 10-15% instead of increasing the mAs. Remember, that even with proper exposure, the serosal detail will be poor because of the summation of fluid with soft tissue structures.
4. Presence of free abdominal air (pneumoperitoneum). Positional radiography can be very useful in confirming the presence of a pneumoperitoneum. The x-ray table needs to have the capability to make horizontal beam radiographs. Alternatively, a portable x-ray unit (e.g. MinXray unit) can be used. The patient is placed in left lateral recumbency for 10-15 minutes. Gentle ballotment of the abdomen can be performed during this time to assist in shifting any free air to the dorsal body wall. An image is then made collimated to the dorsal (right) abdominal body wall centered just behind the diaphragm. The cassette or plate is place behind the patient perpendicular to the table. The x-ray beam is directed parallel to the table in a ventrodorsal plane. The abdominal radiographic technique

will need to be decreased. Free peritoneal air will accumulate along the dorsal abdominal wall. Care must be made not to mistake gas located within loops of intestine for free air.

ELBOW RADIOGRAPHY OF MWDS

Radiography of elbow joints of MWDs should be performed under appropriate sedation or general anesthesia. After induction, the dog can be intubated and then maintained on gas anesthesia if necessary. Anesthetic protocols should be tailored to the patient and the clinical situation. Several protocols and recommendations are found in other sections of this handbook.

1. Flexed lateral radiographs of the elbow joints. For diagnostic flexed lateral elbow radiographs, the elbow joint needs to be flexed as much as possible. To avoid rotation of the elbow, keep the elbow joint and the carpus in a true lateral position. The beam center should be directly on the elbow joint. We recommend positioning the dog in lateral recumbency, flexing the elbow on the downside as much as possible, and then tucking the dog's foot underneath his neck to hold it in position. For example, if the left elbow is being radiographed, the dog would be in left lateral recumbency, the left elbow flexed, and the left foot placed underneath the neck. The right leg is held out of the beam (caudally) with a sandbag or by an assistant.
2. Technique problems for flexed lateral elbow radiography. For diagnostic technique in the flexed lateral view, the elbow must be flexed far enough so that the medial epicondyle of the humerus is not superimposed over the anconeal process. Underexposure and obliquity are the most common technical errors.
3. Craniocaudal and oblique radiographs of the elbow joints. Place the dog in sternal recumbency and extend the limb cranially. Raise the head and place it on positioning sponges facing the opposite leg. Measure over the thickest area (distal humerus). Center the beam over the elbow joint. The most common technical problem is incomplete extension of the leg resulting in foreshortening of the humerus and obliquity of the elbow joint. For oblique views, start by positioning the dog the same as for a craniocaudal view. Next, roll the leg approximately 10- 15 degrees medially or laterally depending on which oblique view is being performed.

PELVIC RADIOGRAPHY OF MWDS

Pelvic radiography of MWDs should be performed under appropriate sedation or general anesthesia. The anesthetic protocol should be tailored to the patient's needs and clinical situation.

1. Diagnostic quality radiographs of the pelvis. For diagnostic ventrodorsal pelvis radiographs, the pelvis needs to be well positioned. Both obturator foramina should be of equal size. Both legs should be parallel and fully, equally extended and internally rotated with both patellae centered over the femurs. If the pelvis is tilted, the "up" side will appear to have the larger (or more round) obturator foramen, the narrower ilium and better coverage of the femoral head by the dorsal acetabular rim. Lateral views of the pelvis and lumbosacral junction are discussed below.
2. Techniques for standard pelvic radiography. The VD view must include the lumbosacral junction and stifles. Ideally, the last two lumbar vertebrae are also included. In the VD view, the rims of the acetabula should be visible through the femoral heads. In the lateral view, the ilia and the transverse processes should summate and the "down" leg should be pulled slightly forward. Proper radiographic technique for the lateral pelvis will overexpose the stifles. Specific radiographic examination of the stifles must be performed separately. Underexposure and poor positioning are the most common errors leading to non-diagnostic radiographs or misdiagnoses.
3. Stress radiography of the lumbosacral junction. Lateral views of the lumbosacral junction obtained

with the hind limbs in flexed, neutral and hyperextended positions will aid in the identification of intervertebral disc space collapse and subluxation of the first sacral vertebra. Dynamic positioning has also been used in multiple imaging modalities (radiography, myelography, epidurography, computed tomography, magnetic resonance) to assist in the diagnosis of intervertebral disc protrusion or extrusion and identify the site of extradural compression.

THORACIC RADIOGRAPHY OF MWDS

MWDs should be awake if possible for thoracic radiography. If adequate restraint is not possible while the MWD is awake, general anesthesia or sedation, if deemed safe, may be used. If general anesthesia is used, several additional procedures need to be followed to obtain diagnostic radiographs (see section below on radiographing the thorax while under anesthesia).

1. Standard thoracic study. A minimum of two views are required for evaluation of the thorax. A right lateral and ventrodorsal (VD) view are preferred. However, a dyspneic patient should not be placed in dorsal recumbency. A dorsoventral (DV) projection should be made instead. Three view thoracic studies are ideal and recommended. Making both the right and left lateral projections improves detection of focal pulmonary abnormalities, including pneumonia and nodules. If the study is being performed to assess for pulmonary metastasis, a three view study including both laterals and a VD is imperative. Remember, as with abdominal studies, our MWDs often have long bodies. Two overlapping images may be required to include the entire thorax in the study for each view. Images need to include the thoracic inlet to the caudal margin of the lungs (a portion on inflated lung is usually superimposed over the cranial liver) and from the dorsal margin of the thoracic vertebrae to the ventral aspect of the sternum.

2. Diagnostic quality radiographs of the thorax. Thoracic radiographs should be made at full inspiration. In an awake dog, films should be made as close to the end of inspiration as possible. Radiographs made at full expiration superimpose the diaphragm on the caudal border of the heart, creating the false appearance of cardiac enlargement and increased pulmonary opacity. Atelectic lung can mimic pneumonia. Therefore, it is always important to evaluate the phase of respiration when interpreting thoracic radiographs. If an MWD is panting, blowing into the nose or placing an alcohol-soaked cotton ball close to the nose may briefly stop the panting. If panting is not interrupted during the exposure, the resulting radiograph must be interpreted with consideration given to artifacts produced by patient motion and the expiratory phase of respiration. Some conditions of the trachea require that both inspiratory and expiratory views be made. Timing of exposures is important to achieve a maximum difference between the two films.

3. Exposure times and techniques. In order to adequately stop motion, exposure times should be 1/30 of a second or less. The need for a relatively low mAs necessitates a high kVp technique. A grid will be needed for any dog whose thorax measures more than 10 cm. High kVp techniques and thicker patients produce more scatter radiation, so a grid is necessary to reduce the amount of scattered radiation reaching the film. A tabletop technique can be used for dogs that measure 10 cm or less. Pulmonary disease may be magnified by underexposure or masked by overexposure.

4. Thoracic radiography while under anesthesia. Several additional procedures need to be followed in order to achieve diagnostic quality films. There will always be some amount of collapse of the "down" lung lobes if the dog lies on one side for 3 to 5 minutes or longer. The anesthetized MWD will need to be bagged several times prior to an exposure being made in order to better inflate the "down" lungs. The anesthetist should pause at the apex of the inspiratory "breath" while the exposure is being made to simulate a deep inspiration. Bagging while under general anesthesia will deepen the plane of anesthesia of the patient. Diligent monitoring of the patient and proper adjustment of the inhalant anesthetic agent is imperative. The bag should not be held at an abnormally deep inspiration

during the exposure or the lungs may appear abnormally radiolucent due to overinflation. If the MWD is not bagged prior to taking the radiograph, the lung lobes on the "down" side will have less volume (from mild atelectasis) and a mediastinal shift of the cardiac silhouette will result. Occasionally, even after adequate bagging, a mediastinal shift to the side of the thorax that was previously down will be seen. If this occurs, the dog should be rolled over to the other side of the thorax for approximately three minutes. Following this, the dog should again be rolled into position for a ventrodorsal view and then bagged several times.

5. Positioning for thoracic radiographs. The most common positioning artifact in the lateral view is oblique positioning (rotation of the thorax). This is caused by failure to elevate the sternum from the table-top. One wedge-shaped sponge placed under the sternum is usually sufficient to straighten the thorax. Positioning for the ventrodorsal or dorsoventral view is much more difficult in an awake dog. Use of a padded positioning trough will be helpful. The x-ray beam should be centered just behind the caudal border of the scapula for most thoracic views. Special projections can also be done, such as the skyline view of the trachea at the thoracic inlet or oblique views to investigate a rib mass.

6. Presence of pleural fluid. Increase mAs 50% or kVp 10-15%. In severe cases, an exposure similar to the abdominal techniques as measured from the clinic's technique chart may provide the best quality radiograph for the situation. Radiography needs to be performed with care. Make an effort to minimally stress the dog. If the MWD is dyspneic, pleural fluid should be removed prior to radiographing the thorax. A ventrodorsal view will provide the most diagnostic information (when choosing between a VD or DV view). The DV view can be used to detect a small amount of fluid, but when a large amount of fluid is present, the cardiac silhouette will be obscured in the DV view. Remember that dyspneic patients should not be placed in dorsal recumbency. A DV projection will be used in these cases until the patient's respiratory status has improved.

SPINE RADIOGRAPHY OF MWDS

Radiography of the spine of MWDs should be performed under general anesthesia or appropriate sedation. Emergent, acute spinal injuries are exceptions where heavy sedation and patient stabilization (back-board) may necessitate altered, positional views or horizontal beam radiography. If the dog is going to be radiographed at a site other than a Veterinary Treatment Facility, an intravenous catheter should be placed and the dog may need to be pre-medicated prior to transport. The dog can then be induced with a rapid-acting intravenous drug combination at the other location. After induction, the dog can be intubated and then maintained on gas anesthesia if necessary.

1. Indications for spinal radiography in the MWD. Radiography of the spine of MWDs is often performed to rule out several disease conditions. Degenerative Lumbosacral Stenosis is commonly diagnosed in both the Belgian Malinois and the German Shepherd Dog, and the initial diagnostic work-up includes good lumbar spine radiographs. Neoplasia, degenerative myelopathy and discospondylitis are also potential rule-outs that are occasionally diagnosed in MWDs. Degenerative myelopathy is generally diagnosed only after ruling out other diseases of the spine. There is a genetic screening test available for DM which will identify carrier status, however, definitive confirmation of degenerative myelopathy is only possible through examination of spinal cord sections submitted at necropsy.

2. Diagnostic quality radiographs of the spine. Accurate positioning is essential. Various positioning aids are necessary to properly position the spine: roll cotton, foam sponges, foam wedges, tape and sandbags. As an example, for proper lateral cervical spine positioning, a foam wedge needs to be placed under the nose to straighten the head, and another flat sponge under the middle part of the neck to prevent sagging of the neck toward the table. Layered, roll cotton works very well in lieu of positioning sponges. For lateral thoracic and lumbar spine radiographs, a foam wedge under the

sternum and foam blocks between the upper and lower front and hind limbs will help prevent rotation.
3. Techniques for spinal radiography. For diagnostic technique, the x-ray beam should be centered on the area of interest. The beam should be collimated as closely as possible. A complete spine study will made in at least five views: cervical, cervicothoracic, thoracic, thoracolumbar, and lumbar spine. Underexposure is one of the most common technical errors. Improper positioning also results in diagnostic errors. For example, in a lateral film that is not positioned properly, intervertebral disc spaces will appear to be narrower than normal. This can usually be recognized because all of the disc spaces are affected, not just one or two spaces. Assessment of intervertebral disc space narrowing cannot be made accurately on radiographs made on the non-anesthetized patient.
4. Myelography of the spine. A myelogram should not be performed on MWDs without first consulting with the supporting 64F or the DODMWDVS staff. There are many patient considerations that determine the diagnostic necessity of this procedure.

RADIOGRAPHIC CONTRAST/SPECIAL PROCEDURES

Contrast procedures often require special equipment and planning in order to make a diagnostic study. Contrast procedures should only be done after the appropriate clinical examinations, radiographs, and other diagnostic tests have been performed.
1. Local imaging studies vs. MWD/Handler team referral. The advantages of coordinating special procedures at the installation is the ability to use telemedicine consultation to provide learning and mentoring opportunities and unequaled medical care for MWDs. This will save time and money that would otherwise have been expended to transport the MWD/Handler Team to a District/Region VTF or the DODMWDVS. However, we do not recommend the performance of specialized, invasive procedures without absolute medical necessity, proper training, and prior consultation with a 64F or the DODMWDVS staff (e.g. myelography).
2. Myelography and epidurography. The necessity of these invasive procedures must be tempered by good clinical judgment and consultation with a 64F. In most cases, we recommend referral to DODMWDVS or coordination with the local MTF or local veterinary specialty practice to obtain Magnetic Resonance Imaging (MRI) and/or Computed Tomography (CT).
3. Barium enema. This procedure is not recommended due to severe complications (rupture of the colon) that can occur. The barium enema has been replaced by endoscopy/colonoscopy/ultrasonography.
4. Esophagram. Esophagography is the radiographic examination performed to evaluate the morphology and function of the esophagus. Esophagrams are performed without anesthesia or sedation to evaluate the motility of the esophagus and generally require fluoroscopy. If an MWD will not allow administration of barium sulfate or other contrast materials without sedation, do NOT do the esophagram. If the study is done with sedation or anesthesia, it likely will be non-diagnostic. In the worst possible case, aspiration and death can occur. If an esophagram is indicated, but cannot be done because of the dog's temperament, call the DODMWDVS to discuss further diagnostic options. Contrast agents used include liquid barium sulfate, barium sulfate paste, and barium sulfate liquid or paste mixed with dry and soft food. Iohexol, a non-ionic iodinated contrast medium, is the contrast agent of choice for a dog with a suspected esophageal rupture. Gastrografin (an iodinated contrast media) should not be used. In cases where aspiration occurs during administration, severe pulmonary edema and death can occur.
    a. Indications for an esophagram. Indications include regurgitation of undigested food, acute gagging or retching, dysphagia, excessive salivation, suspected esophageal foreign body, mediastinal mass, and esophageal dysfunction.

b. Preparation. Survey radiographs are required to evaluate for a radiopaque foreign body, fluid-filled esophagus, diverticulum, megaesophagus, or pneumomediastinum. If the esophagus is distended and filled with food or evidence of aspiration pneumonia already exists, do not administer barium or other contrast materials due to the increased danger of aspiration. No patient preparation is required for most esophagrams.

c. Technique. Usually an esophageal study is done in a sequential manner, starting with liquid agents and proceeding to thicker agents (or barium solution mixed with canned food) that require and will demonstrate normal esophageal distention for the bolus to reach the stomach. Place a 10-15 mL bolus of commercial liquid preparation of barium into the buccal pouch with a dose syringe while the MWD is in lateral recumbency. Some disorders (dysphagia, altered motility) are difficult to diagnose without fluoroscopy, but an esophagram can still be done without fluoroscopy in some cases. Several radiographs will need to be taken during the swallowing process after passage of the bolus of contrast medium through the esophagus. With radiographs alone, it is impossible to diagnose esophageal disease caused by different forms of megaesophagus. Following administration of liquid barium, linear streaks of barium can be seen extending the length of the esophagus in normal dogs. Paste should be given after liquid barium if more mucosal detail of the esophagus is needed. 5-10 mls of barium paste should be given orally to the MWD via syringe, and the dog given one to two minutes to swallow the paste. Lateral and ventrodorsal radiographs of the cervical and thoracic region should then be obtained. The paste can then be followed by a small amount of food mixed with the barium paste, which most MWDs will eat voluntarily.

d. Complications. Aspiration of barium into the alveoli can cause granulomatous pneumonia but generally, aspiration of a small volume of barium will not cause respiratory disease aside from any compromise caused by the aspiration of the volume of liquid. Aspiration of hypertonic water-soluble iodinated contrast agents (Gastrografin) into the alveoli can cause rapid, fulminate pulmonary edema and death. Perforation of the esophagus may be present, which can allow barium to leak into the mediastinum. This can cause mediastinal granuloma formation and may require surgical intervention if it occurs. Cases of perforation should only be pursued if non-ionic, iodinated contrast agents (e.g. Iohexol) are available.

5. Upper Gastrointestinal (GI) Study. The upper GI study should be conducted when diagnosis or appropriate treatment cannot be determined from survey radiographs and other clinical information. The upper GI is generally reserved for chronic or persistent disorders, like those listed under the specific indications section. The upper GI study must be performed without anesthesia or sedation to evaluate the motility of the GI tract. If an MWD will not allow administration of barium sulfate or other contrast materials without sedation, do NOT do the upper GI study. If the study is done with sedation or anesthesia, GI motility will not be able to be evaluated. Evaluation for obstruction may still be possible in these cases but a 64F should be consulted first. If the upper GI study is indicated, but cannot be done because of the dog's temperament, call the DODMWDVS for further diagnostic options. Contrast agents used include liquid barium sulfate suspensions, barium mixed with food and Iohexol.

a. Suspected GI perforation. Iohexol (Omnipaque; 300 mg Iodine/mL) is the contrast agent of choice for a dog with a suspected GI perforation. Gastrografin (an iodinated contrast media) was used for these cases previously. However, in many cases Gastrografin causes intestinal distention and worsening of dehydration due to its hypertonicity.

b. Indications for an upper GI study. Indications include recurrent non-responsive vomiting, abdominal pain, abdominal masses, abdominal distention, small bowel diarrhea, melena, weight loss, suspected GI foreign body or obstruction (from history or survey radiographs),

abdominal organ displacement, and hernia.
c. Preparation. Unless emergent, fast for 12-24 hours prior to study. Enemas are recommended at least 2-4 hours prior to the upper GI study to ensure removal of all residual ingesta. Large-volume warm water enemas are adequate to empty the digestive tract without causing bowel distention by gas. Enemas should be administered the night before the procedure if possible. Survey radiographs prior to the study are required to ensure the abdomen has been properly prepared and to evaluate for a radiopaque foreign body or obvious radiographic signs of gastrointestinal obstruction that would eliminate the need for the exam.
d. Technique. The dose rate for barium sulfate is 6 ml/lb. The dose rate for Iohexol (Omnipaque; 300 mg Iodine/ml) is 5 ml/lb, using Iohexol diluted with sterile water at a 1:1 dilution rate. Iohexol should be used as the contrast agent in cases of suspected GI perforation as barium will cause a granulomatous reaction in the peritoneum. Administration of the full dose is essential to fully distend the stomach and to stimulate gastric emptying. If a gastric foreign body is suspected, a negative or double contrast gastrogram should be considered as an alternative study. This is to avoid obscuring the foreign body in a large pool of barium. The form of barium used should be a commercial grade liquid that is already in suspension. Barium should be administered preferably by a stomach tube. Assure proper placement of stomach tube prior to contrast administration. A dose syringe can be used to give barium orally, but aspiration can also occur with this method. A Kong with a portion of the small end cut off makes a great MWD mouth speculum.
e. Timing of sequential radiographs. For barium, take films immediately after administration, 15 minutes, 30 minutes, 1 hour, 2 hours, 4 hours, etc. until contrast reaches the colon. When Iohexol is used as the contrast agent, radiographs should be taken immediately, at 15 minutes, 30 minutes, and 1 hour after administration. An upper GI study is not complete (i.e. images should continue to be made at regular time intervals) until a diagnosis is obtained and/or the contrast medium has reached the colon and the stomach is empty.
f. Positioning. Ventrodorsal, dorsoventral, right and left lateral views should be made immediately after contrast administration for best evaluation of the barium-filled stomach. Ventrodorsal and right lateral projections should be made at each following time interval with additional views made as indicated. Additional DV and oblique views, as well as fluoroscopy, may be helpful in evaluating the pyloric antrum and proximal duodenum.
g. Transit times. When the stomach is well distended with barium, gastric emptying is stimulated. Exact time of stomach emptying varies but is considered normal if there is a steady and uninterrupted progression of barium into the small intestine. With liquid contrast medium (no food), the stomach should be empty in 4 hours. The small intestine should appear as a continuous radiopaque ribbon. Most of the jejunum should be filled at one hour. The leading edge of barium usually reaches the cecum in one and a half to two hours. Much of the barium will be in the colon within 3-4 hours. The uniform progression of barium through the GI tract is a more important assessment of normal GI motility than exact transit time. Iohexol has a much more rapid transit time of 30-60 minutes; however, mucosal coating is not as good.
h. Contraindications. Do NOT use barium sulfate suspension in cases of suspected perforation, rupture, or laceration of the stomach or intestine. Do not use oral organic iodine solution (Gastrografin, oral Hypaque). Dehydration, electrolyte imbalance and shock have occurred following usage of these hyperosmolar agents. Diluted non-ionic iodinated contrast medium (i.e. Iohexol) is less hypertonic and much safer. Do not use any contrast agents if the clinical examination or survey radiographs are diagnostic for a specific disease or show the need for immediate surgery. In the event an upper GI study is performed and a perforation is

discovered, DO NOT PANIC. Although micropulverized barium particles can result in a granulomatous reaction, the real threat to the patient is the bowel contents. Copious peritoneal lavage during surgery is required with or without the presence of barium.
6. Excretory Urography. An excretory urogram is a qualitative test of renal function that allows for comparison of function between kidneys. There are now test methods for quantitative analysis of Iohexol excretion (plasma clearance = estimated Glomerular Filtration Rate) as well.
    a. Indications for excretory urography. Chronic hematuria or pyuria, abnormal findings detected during abdominal palpation and suspected hydronephrosis. Excretory urography enhances visualization of the size, shape, and location of each kidney and allows visualization of the size and shape of the renal pelvis. It also identifies the location, patency, and size of the ureters and the position of the urinary bladder as well as providing a rough estimate of renal function.
    b. Preparation. Patient preparation includes 12-24 hour fast, but do not withhold water and cleansing enema given 2-4 hours prior. Renal function must also be determined (contrast agent dose increases if renal function is reduced). It is important to assess hydration status. Always obtain survey films prior to contrast administration.
    c. Technique for excretory urography. Give the full dose as a rapid IV bolus through an indwelling catheter. Any of the water-soluble contrast agents are suitable due to the fact that they are excreted through the urinary system after IV administration (i.e. Conray, Conray 400, Hypaque 50, Renovist, Renografin-76, Iohexol). Routine study: 400 mg Iodine/lb (800 mg Iodine/kg). The entire bolus should be given within 1-3 minutes. Maximum dose is 35 grams. With impaired renal function, 800 mg Iodine/lb is administered.
    d. Timing of sequential radiographs. Immediately after administration, at 5 minutes, 15 minutes, 30 minutes, and 40 minutes. Animals with poor renal function may require additional radiographs at 45, 60, 90 and 180 minutes due to delayed urinary system opacification. VD and lateral projections are made at each time period. Oblique lateral or VD projections are made as necessary. Abdominal compression can be used if necessary but should be performed with caution.
    e. Contraindications. Dehydration is the primary risk factor for contrast-induced acute renal failure. Proper physiologic hydration of the patient must be performed prior to excretory urography.
    f. Complications. Perivascular injection of contrast media can cause sloughing of the tissues. Nausea and emesis immediately following the contrast injection can occur, so MWDs should not be muzzled or be prepared to remove the muzzle rapidly. Dogs under anesthesia must have an endotracheal tube with a fully inflated cuff in place. Anaphylaxis is reported in humans, but is considered to be rare in the dog.
7. Retrograde Contrast Cystography. A fast, simple, and relatively safe procedure that allows evaluation of bladder size, shape or location.
    a. Indications for contrast cystography. Evaluation of abnormal bladder shape or location. Non-visualization of urinary bladder after trauma. Evaluation of caudal abdominal masses adjacent to the urinary bladder (prostate, paraprostatic cyst, neoplasia, etc.). Frequent urination or dysuria. Intermittent or chronic hematuria. Hematuria that occurs throughout or in the later stages of voiding. Persistent post-traumatic hematuria. Urinary incontinence.
        i. For bladder rupture or urinary bladder localization, perform positive contrast cystography.
        ii. For urinary bladder mucosa and wall evaluation, assessment for cystic calculi and evaluation of cystitis, perform double contrast cystography.
    b. Preparation. Fast the patient 12-24 hours prior to the procedure. Do not withhold water.

Administer a cleansing enema 2-4 hours prior to the procedure. Take survey radiographs. Equipment needed includes sterile lubricant, sterile urinary catheters, syringes, speculum for female dogs, positive and negative contrast media.
- i. Positive contrast media include any of the water-soluble iodinated contrast medium (i.e. Iohexol, Conray, Hypaque) diluted to a 20-33% iodine concentration. If bladder rupture is suspected, positive contrast cystography using undiluted iodinated contrast medium is recommended (i.e. Iohexol 240 mgI/ml). Retrograde urethrography can also be performed at the same time if urethral rupture is suspected. Barium should NEVER be used.
- ii. Negative contrast agents include nitrous oxide and carbon dioxide (CO_2). Room air is occasionally used; however, nitrous oxide and CO_2 are preferred due to the decreased risk for air embolism.

c. Technique for contrast cystography. Many references are available with detailed techniques for these procedures. The following is meant only as a basic guide and refresher. Contact the supporting 64F and/or a radiologist for guidance prior to performing the study.
- i. Sedation or anesthesia is strongly recommended, but is not required.
- ii. Preliminary ventrodorsal and lateral caudal abdominal radiographs need to be performed to ensure adequate abdominal preparation. If fecal material remains present in the colon or within loops of intestine overlying the urinary bladder, additional enemas should be administered and survey radiographs repeated.
- iii. Clean the external genitalia. A sterile urinary catheter is aseptically placed. The urinary bladder is emptied. A sterile urine sample should be collected. Once iodinated contrast medium is placed in the urinary bladder, urine culture results will be altered. If a retrograde urethrogram is to be performed, contrast medium is infused after passing the urinary catheter into the tip of the urethra – before advancing the catheter into the urinary bladder and removing urine.
- iv. In awake or sedated dogs with dysuria and/or stranguria, infusing 3-5 mL 2% lidocaine (without epinephrine) into the bladder via the urinary catheter is recommended to reduce pain and spasms.
- v. Place the patient in left lateral recumbency.
- vi. For positive or negative contrast cystography, inject contrast medium slowly and with constant palpation of the urinary bladder to avoid over distention. An estimated 4-10 mL/kg can usually be administered for full bladder distention. Be cautious about bladder distention in known severe and/or chronic cystitis cases as bladder wall integrity may be decreased.
- vii. Obtain lateral, VD, and 45 VD oblique views once bladder distention is achieved. Sequential lateral radiographs can be made during bladder distention to assess progress if necessary. Increase mAs 50% from the survey radiographs for positive contrast studies.
- viii. For double contrast cystography, a negative contrast cystogram is followed by administration of 5-10 mL undiluted iodinated contrast medium. Five mL is recommended as a starting volume. Roll the patient from side to side to coat the bladder mucosa with positive contrast. Obtain at least right and left lateral and a VD view. A DV and 45 VD oblique views should be obtained if the initial images are within normal limits. Administer an additional 5 mL of positive contrast is mucosa coating is poor or the contrast pool is minimal, and repeat all images.

d. Technical errors during cystograms. Incomplete bladder distention. Excessive concentration of positive contrast medium which obscures intraluminal-filling defects. Creating air bubbles

in contrast media. Failure to remove urine before instilling positive contrast. Kinked or knotted catheter.
- e. Contraindications. Negative contrast should not be used for cases of suspected bladder rupture. A positive contrast cystogram should not be used in cases of suspected calculi or other free luminal filling defects; double contrast cystography should be performed instead.
- f. Complications.
    - i. Air embolism can be fatal and results from air entering the venous system and travelling to the main pulmonary artery causing a block in pulmonary circulation. Patients are always placed in left lateral recumbency so air will be trapped in the right ventricle. Prevent by injecting slowly, avoiding over distention, and using CO_2 or nitrous oxide.
    - ii. Suspect if systemic BP falls and/or pulse becomes rapid and weak. Air may be visible in caudal abdominal veins on images. A rumble may be audible on cardiac auscultation.
    - iii. Immediately place the patient in left lateral recumbency and lower the head. Clamp the urinary catheter. Maintain this position for 60 minutes.
    - iv. Additional therapy: Intubate and administer 100% oxygen if respiratory distress and/or hypoxemia occur. If circulatory collapse is present, external chest compressions may help disperse the air from the pulmonary outflow tract. Administer IV fluids and beta-adrenergic agents (epinephrine) as indicated.
    - v. Rupture of the urinary bladder or traumatic catheterization.
    - vi. Iatrogenic infection.
    - vii. Anaphylaxis or allergic reactions due to iodine administration are rare.

ULTRASOUND

Diagnostic medical ultrasound is only second to radiography in terms of imaging studies produced in veterinary medicine, and is of greatest benefit in assessing soft tissue structures which are not surrounded by bone or gas; primarily the abdominal organs and ligaments/musculature in our MWDs. However, most VCOs lack the training and experience to optimally use ultrasound and many times will miss/not recognize significant findings or will incorrectly ascribe importance to normal findings. Obtain training to be able to comfortably use and interpret ultrasound images. It is also imperative that once training and some familiarization has been gained, the VCO must regularly perform sonograms to maintain what skills they have. It is recommended that VCOs perform scans when MWDs are presented even if not indicated in an attempt to maintain some competency.
1. Transducer Selection. In order to be able to perform basic conventional (B mode) ultrasound in MWDs, two multi-frequency transducers are primarily utilized for imaging. A curvilinear or sector transducer with a frequency range of approximately 5-8 MHz is recommended for abdominal scanning. A linear transducer with a frequency range of approximately 5-12 MHz is recommended for assessing musculoskeletal soft tissue structures, and may also be used in the abdomen for higher frequency scanning if required. With echocardiography, a 1-5 MHz sector probe with the ability to perform continuous Doppler is recommended (usually only performed by experienced ultrasonographers).
2. Image optimization. Diagnostic ultrasound is all about being able to perform constant, continual image optimization in order to be able to produce an effective diagnostic study. One must be able to continually monitor multiple factors within the image being created by the ultrasound beam in order to be able to produce the image to standard. Being able to appropriately adjust each of these components: frequency (spatial resolution), focus (lateral resolution), gain, depth, angle of incidence,

and degree of manual pressure is critical. Also remember that appropriately labeling images is extremely important for documentation and for consultants to provide feedback on the organ/structure imaged. If any of these terms are unfamiliar, consult a standard veterinary ultrasound text for review.

3. VCO Expectations. Veterinary schools greatly differ on the degree of ultrasound experience they provide to their students during their training. For this reason, most VCOs are not expected to be able to competently perform a complete abdominal ultrasound examination. It takes a great deal of practice and/or mentoring to become proficient. However, there are some basic ultrasound examinations that every VCO is expected to be able to provide for MWDs. These studies include ultrasound-guided cystocentesis and Focused Assessment with Sonography for Trauma of the thorax and abdomen (FAST exams).

4. Ultrasound-Guided Cystocentesis. In order to perform cystocentesis, the urinary bladder must first be located either by manual palpation or ultrasound guidance. The patient may be placed in dorsal recumbency, lateral recumbency, or standing. The normal ultrasound appearance for the urinary bladder is to have a thin, echogenic wall (typically less than 2 mm thick when distended) and the lumen distended with anechoic fluid. It should be fairly easy to find this structure adjacent to midline within the caudoventral abdomen when distended. If the urinary bladder subjectively appears very small and has a thick, undulating wall then it is likely that the patient has recently urinated and is usually prudent to place the MWD in a cage and wait a couple hours until the urinary bladder is distended again prior to attempt. Use of a 22 gauge, 1" to 1.5" needle with an attached 5- or 10-mL syringe is recommended for urine aspiration/collection. Prior to needle insertion into the abdomen, ensure there are no organs (usually small intestinal loops or spleen) between the urinary bladder and abdominal wall on the image. If organs are present, move the transducer to another site where the organs are not present. Aligning the needle with midline of either end of the transducer, place the needle tip through the skin adjacent to (but not directly on) the head of the transducer. Extend the needle through the abdominal and urinary bladder walls into the bladder lumen. One should be able to see the needle on the image (the tip being most important) in the bladder lumen if on midline of the transducer. If using a curvilinear transducer, insert the needle more parallel to the transducer to see the needle tip. If using a linear transducer, angle the needle underneath the transducer head after skin penetration in order to be able to see the needle enter the lumen. If the needle tip cannot be seen and the needle is through the abdominal wall, stop any movement of the needle and re-align the transducer with the needle before proceeding. After the lumen is entered, aspirate enough urine and release the pressure on the syringe before pulling the needle out of the abdomen.

5. Common errors with US-Guided cystocentesis. One would think ultrasound-guided cystocentesis to be a fairly benign procedure but common errors include: not visualizing the needle during insertion and extending through the opposite bladder wall, laceration of the bladder wall or other organs while attempting to find the needle tip, or inserting the needle too close to the transducer head, creating costly damage to the equipment. Use of gelatin molds containing fruit, pasta, or other similar items to practice ultrasound-guided needle insertion and tracking of the needle can be an effective training tool prior to performing in a live patient if needed.

6. FAST Examinations. Thoracic and abdominal FAST (Focused Assessment with Sonography for Trauma) examinations (TFAST and AFAST, respectively) have been developed for veterinary medicine in order to have a fast, sensitive and reliable method for early detection of free intra-abdominal or intrathoracic fluid (hemorrhage, peritonitis/pleuritis, ascites, etc.) and pneumothorax. These ultrasound techniques have been found to be very beneficial for expediting diagnosis and prompting life-saving procedures for patients with internal injuries, are relatively simple to perform, and can be effectively completed within minutes so are important techniques for every VCO to learn. These exams are not meant to replace more comprehensive ultrasound exams, but to provide

guidance with early resuscitation efforts and patient management.
- a. AFAST Exam – Technique. The AFAST exam is based in the fact that there are four primary sites within the peritoneal space which small accumulations of fluid will initially gravitate towards and accumulate. These sites are (listed in order of significance): the diaphragmatico-hepatic region (DH), the cysto-colic region (CC), the hepato-renal region (HR), and the spleno-renal region (SR). The DH region is located along the ventral diaphragm and adjacent liver lobes, just caudal to the xiphoid process (subxiphoid). The CC region is located on the caudoventral abdominal midline at the apex of the urinary bladder. The HR and SR regions are located along the right and left abdominal walls (respectively), just caudal to their adjacent costal arches where the organs they are named after are located. For each of these four sites, the patient is scanned from medial to lateral in the craniocaudal plane (transducer oriented longitudinally) and then scanned from cranial to caudal in the lateromedial plane (transducer oriented in transverse). While scanning, the patient can be placed in right or left lateral recumbency, whichever is safer or more comfortable for the patient. Right lateral recumbency has been advocated more than left as it is the standard position for ECG evaluation and echocardiography. When scanning these four sites, always start with the DH site (most common for fluid accumulation), and after completion proceed to scan the remaining sites either in a clockwise or counterclockwise manner with the last scanned site being the most gravity-dependent to allow for fluid to accumulate during the exam (either HR or SR). After performing the initial AFAST exam, at least one more serial AFAST exam should be conducted four hours later in order to prevent missing a serious, life-threatening injury that may have been slow to develop.
- b. AFAST Exam – Aspiration. If peritoneal fluid is detected and the fluid pocket is large enough for the comfort level of the ultrasonographer conducting the exam, it should be aspirated in order to determine the fluid type (see cystocentesis section above on how to perform fluid aspiration).
- c. AFAST Exam – Scoring System. A scoring system has been developed to assist with demonstrating progression of fluid accumulation (0=negative and 1=positive per site). An abdominal fluid score (AFS) of 0 equals negative for all quadrants, and an AFS of 4 is the maximal score possible. This scoring system may be of benefit for demonstration of progression and/or resolving cases during serial FAST exams q 4-12 hours, with higher scores clinically associated with severity of injury.
- d. TFAST Exam – Technique. TFAST exams were similarly developed using four primary regions along the thorax to come up with a rapid, effective method for detection of pneumothorax, pleural fluid, or pericardial fluid. There are only two names for these four sites as they are bilaterally symmetric. The chest tube sites (CTS) are defined as the 7th-9th intercostal space on the dorsolateral thoracic wall. The pericardial sites (PCS) are defined as the 5th-6th intercostal space on the ventrolateral thoracic wall. In contrast to the AFAST exam, the patient is initially placed in either lateral recumbency for examination of the upwards CTS site and both PCS sites but is then moved to sternal recumbency for examination of the previous downward or opposite CTS site. For the CTS sites, a curvilinear transducer is placed and held in longitudinal orientation into one of the intercostal spaces at this level in order to observe the appearance of the gas within the thorax for a minimum of 5 respiratory cycles. Normally, the pleural space is only a potential space with negative pressure and absence of gas. Therefore, the gas interface appreciated is actually due to gas within the lungs and this gas-pleura interface should glide forwards and backwards along the thoracic wall during normal respiration. If this "glide sign" does not appear to be present, this is diagnostic of pneumothorax as gas has now accumulated within the pleural space,

preventing visualization of the lung margin. In order to semi quantitate the degree of pneumothorax, the transducer is then moved ventrally until the "glide sign" is appreciated. If a "glide sign" is initially present, but does not have a normal linear to mildly curved appearance to the lung-pleura interface, this is considered to be associated with probable thoracic injury and is referred to as a "step sign". For evaluation of the TFAST PCS sites, the curvilinear transducer is placed in both longitudinal and transverse views sweeping through this region, similar to the sites of the AFAST exam. Becoming proficient at TFAST exams is considered more difficult than AFAST exams. Practice the TFAST examination on normal patients to gain a better appreciation of normal appearances (don't forget the global utility of radiology).
   e. TFAST Exam – Aspiration. If sufficient quantities of fluid are found that are deemed to be large enough for aspiration, thoracocentesis and/or pericardiocentesis may be considered, keeping in mind the importance of the structures adjacent to these sites (lungs, heart, etc.).

COMPUTED TOMOGRAPHY (CT) VS. MAGNETIC RESONANCE IMAGING (MRI)

1. Often the question is posed as to whether a patient needs a CT or MRI conducted for further advanced imaging workup. In general, CT is often superior and used for assessment of margins of osseous/mineralized structures compared to MRI. CT can assess soft tissue changes/differences fairly well by narrowing windows and levels under standard algorithms to see differences of attenuation of the x-rays, but cannot manipulate the soft tissues due to their molecular structure as MRI can in order to enhance or null their differences. Therefore, MRI is often far superior to CT at assessing for subtle changes within soft tissues due to the dramatic contrast enhancement. MRI is most often utilized in veterinary medicine and is the modality of choice when trying to assess soft tissue structures not easily accessed by an ultrasound probe or are looking for diseases that may not be appreciated via any other modality. MRI is used primarily for neurologic (brain and spine) imaging and joint imaging concerning cartilage, ligaments, and/or menisci. Keeping those general statements in mind, either study may be adequate for diagnosis (DLSS, for example). Ultimately, when in doubt as to whether a CT or MRI is needed contact the supporting 64F for further guidance. In the event the supporting 64F is unavailable, contact the DODMWDVS. For GOA patients obtaining advanced imaging studies at MTFs, CT should always be utilized first whenever both modalities are likely to be equally useful in obtaining the suspected diagnosis.
2. If the VCO has a case that requires a CT or MRI, consultation with at least the supporting 64F is indicated to ensure they concur with the case workup and assessment. Sometimes the MWD may need to wait for weeks before the local MTF is able to schedule/coordinate the CT or MRI, so it is important to confirm with a 64F that the study needs to be done (e.g. MRI is not required to make a diagnosis of cruciate tear/rupture).
3. Over the past decade, Army veterinary radiologists have commonly received MRI studies for interpretation that were either non-diagnostic (inappropriately performed) or likely would have also resulted in a diagnosis utilizing CT. This consequently results in excessive or wasted efforts and time on all sides and/or unnecessarily placing the patient under anesthesia in an MRI suite which is often a compromising situation due to limited monitoring capabilities available. Overall, CT is a much safer and easier advanced imaging modality to obtain diagnostic studies at MTFs for our MWDs due to the following factors:
   a. Most MWD CT protocols only require heavy sedation of the patient instead of general anesthesia; converse is true with MRI.

    b. The time needed to complete a CT study is typically much shorter than it is to complete an MRI, resulting in less time the patient is under sedation/anesthesia.
    c. Numerous incompatible VTF anesthetic and monitoring equipment limitations within MRI suites exist, compromising our ability to adequately monitor MWDs.
    d. MTFs may lack capabilities or willingness to provide MRI-compatible anesthetic and monitoring equipment for our MWDs.
4. Due to the above facts, relative inexperience of the vast majority of 64As and VTF staff with conducting MRI studies, and complexity of the situation involved with safely performing TIVA in a foreign location (MTF) while concurrently obtaining a diagnostic study, MRIs are only allowed to be performed for MWDs at an MTF while under the direct supervision of a 64F. The 64F will validate the need that the study is absolutely indicated as well as ensure that all requirements for a safe anesthetic event are met. For cases where the supporting 64F agrees that MRI is indicated but the study cannot be performed at the MTF, coordination with a local specialty referral center or DODMWDVS will be performed. If the study may be performed locally, most MTFs are able to work the patient in within a week or two from the request. If unable to schedule an appointment with the MTF for over 6 weeks from the date it was requested, then consultation with the radiologist at the DODMWDVS is indicated in order to refer the MWD to JBSA-Lackland or a local civilian facility to have the study performed. If the case has a more urgent or emergent need, the 64F and/or the DODMWDVS will do everything they can to assist with expediting the case or referral to a civilian facility.

COMPUTED TOMOGRAPHY

CT is similar to radiography in that x-rays are used to generate the images made within the study. The main difference between CT and radiography is that instead of generating a 2D image with superimposition of all osseous and soft tissue structures on top of one another due to a stationary x-ray tube as in radiography, the x-ray tube now rotates around the patient in the transverse plane. The patient is able to be divided up into separate individual 3D transverse slices of data. With each slice through the patient being assigned a finite distance (varies between 0.5 – 8 mm thick). The computer is then able to take this raw data within each slice and process/filter the data through different assigned "algorithms" to enhance the margins and contrast levels to make a certain tissue type stand out compared to the others. These algorithms are named by the tissue types they are trying to best enhance; bone algorithms enhance bone, standard algorithms enhance soft tissues, lung algorithms enhance lung tissue, and so on. The concept of windowing and leveling (previously discussed in the digital radiography section) is also important in these algorithms in order to make each tissue type stand out, and the window and level can be altered as in digital radiography during post-processing of a study to assist with diagnoses.
1. Sedation/Anesthesia. Just as in radiography, patients must lay perfectly still while CT images are being generated. Therefore, the patient must be either heavily sedated or anesthetized while the study is taking place. Many CT exams can be conducted quickly. While someone may suggest attempting to complete the study on an awake MWD, this is not possible and not authorized under any circumstance. The noise of the gantry and table movement will startle the MWD sufficiently to result in a non-diagnostic study and risks injury to the dog. Placing a handler in the room during the study also constitutes unnecessary human exposure to ionizing radiation. Patient motion becomes even more important during a study of the thorax and abdomen, as respiratory motion will blur/alter the margins of several soft tissue structures if not controlled. Therefore, CT studies of the thorax and abdomen often require anesthesia and intubation of the patient with use of the pop-off valve and manual respiration to create a temporary breath-hold during the study. Depending on the type of CT machine and slice thickness required for the study, this may or may not be a problem for the patient

as the breath hold may have to last for seconds to minutes. It is important to coordinate and discuss with the CT technician prior to arrival at the hospital to conduct the study. This is also important in order to determine what supplies and equipment may need to be brought to the hospital to assist with anesthesia and patient monitoring.
2. Contrast Administration. Intravenous iodinated contrast may be used during a CT study in order to further enhance margins of soft tissue structures or enhance pathology. If a CT is being conducted to assess an abnormal soft tissue mass or structure, intravenous iodinated contrast should be administered after acquisition of routine images for comparison purposes. This contrast administration allows for further characterization of the abnormal soft tissue as only the vascular portions of the structure will enhance. The current standard for use of contrast during CT is non-ionic iodinated contrast media, with the two most common types being Iohexol and Iopamidol. The DODMWDVS and most MTFs use and have the most experience with use of Iohexol. For a vial of Iohexol at a concentration of 240mg/mL, the intravenous contrast dose is 400 mg/kg (rule of thumb is 1 mL per lb of body weight, not to exceed 60 mls). IV catheterization of the patient is required for contrast administration, and the contrast is a thick, sticky solution which needs to be bolused to the patient, so use of 18-gauge catheters and syringe needles is recommended. After bolusing the contrast to the patient, only the study in the standard algorithm needs to be repeated. If the VCO has doubts/concerns as to whether IV contrast is necessary for the CT study or if the patient has had any evidence of renal disease during its lifetime, contact the supporting 64F and/or radiologist at the DODMWDVS to discuss how to best handle and monitor the case. If the patient is dehydrated, the patient should be rehydrated prior to the CT study if possible or at least on IV fluids to correct the problem if unavoidable. Adverse/side effects are rare with non-ionic contrast media in correctly hydrated patients but familiarization with them is necessary prior to injection.
3. CT Protocols. CT protocols will vary per region being imaged; patient positioning, slice thickness, algorithms, and whether or not contrast will be used are all key factors to consider and discuss with the CT technician prior to arrival at the hospital to conduct the study. It cannot be stressed enough that each of these factors are critical to producing a diagnostic study, and the most commonly overlooked factor is patient positioning. Ensuring the region of the patient being imaged is straight and symmetrically positioned on midline of the CT table is very important (have the CT tech use the laser guides), as subtle changes in obliquity may make structures appear abnormal when they are not. Use positional aids/sponges or troughs if needed, and ensure that all metallic or other unnecessary objects (collars, ECG leads, etc.) have been removed from the imaging region. Place the patient either head-first or hind limb-first into the gantry depending on which will be closest to the region for imaging. The following are commonly used protocols at the DODMWDVS for different body regions based on common problems we may see in MWDs. If additional protocols are needed on a case-by-case basis, please contact the radiologist at the DODMWDVS for further guidance.
   a. CT Skull. Patient positioning should be in sternal recumbency with the hard palate parallel to the CT table. Studies should extend from the tip of the nose to C2-C3. Images should be acquired in bone and standard algorithm with a 1.25 mm slice thickness. The bone algorithm images need to be reconstructed (or acquired) in 0.625 mm slices as well (if available). Sagittal and dorsal reconstructions should also be made.
   b. CT Nasal. Patient positioning should be in sternal recumbency, with the hard palate parallel to the CT table. Studies should extend from the tip of the nose to larynx. A bone algorithm with slice thicknesses of 2.5 mm and 0.625 mm (or equivalent) and a standard algorithm with slice thickness of 1.25 mm should be performed. IV contrast should be administered and the standard algorithm with 1.25 mm thick slices repeated. Dorsal reconstructions are required. Sagittal reconstructions should be made as needed.
   c. CT Brain. Patient positioning should be in sternal recumbency, with the hard palate parallel

to the CT table. Studies should extend from mid-muzzle to C2-C3. Bone, standard, and brain algorithms with slice thicknesses of 2.5 mm, 1.25 mm, and 1.25 mm should be performed, respectively. IV contrast should be administered and brain and standard algorithms repeated. Sagittal and dorsal reconstructions of the standard algorithms are required.

d. CT Tympanic Bullae. Patient positioning should be in sternal recumbency, with the hard palate parallel to the CT table. Studies should extend from the orbits to C2-C3. Bone and standard algorithms with slice thicknesses of 0.625 mm (or equivalent) and 1.25 mm should be performed, respectively. Sagittal and dorsal reconstructions should be made as needed.

e. CT Spine. Patient should be positioned in dorsal recumbency, with the hind limbs maximally extended caudally (like for a hip-extended VD pelvic view in radiography). Study should extend through necessary vertebral regions based on pain and/or neurolocalization. More specifically for the hind limbs, if UMN signs are present extend from T8-T9 through sacrum and if LMN signs present, from T12-T13 through sacrum. CT slices should be acquired perpendicular to vertebral canal (may require gantry rotation). Bone and standard algorithms with slice thicknesses of 2.5 mm and 1.25 mm each should be performed, respectively. Additionally, for suspect lumbosacral disease, a bone algorithm with 0.625 mm (or equivalent) thick slices should be included to better visualize the neuroforamina. Sagittal and dorsal reconstructions of bone and standard algorithms are required.

f. CT Thorax. Anesthesia and breath holds required (see above). Patient should be positioned in ventral recumbency. Study should extend from thoracic inlet through caudal aspect of liver (ensure extent of all lungs imaged). Bone, standard, and lung algorithms should be performed with slice thicknesses at 5.0 mm, 2.5 mm, and 1.25 mm, respectively. Sagittal and dorsal reconstructions of lung and standard algorithms are required.

g. CT Abdomen. Anesthesia and breath holds required (see above). Patient should be positioned in dorsal recumbency. Study should extend from caudal margin of cardiac silhouette through pelvic canal (or prostate if male). Bone and standard algorithms should be performed with slice thicknesses at 5.0 mm and 2.5 mm, respectively. Sagittal and dorsal reconstructions of bone and standard algorithms are required.

h. CT Extremity/ Joint: Patient positioning dependent on whether imaging forelimbs of hind limbs. For forelimbs, the patient is in ventral recumbency. The forelimbs should be extended cranially, resting the forelimbs and paws on the table and elbows and shoulders bent at a normal resting position. If the hind limbs are the focus of the study, the patient is usually placed in dorsal recumbency. The hind limbs should be placed in maximal caudal extension. Keep both limbs symmetric and include both in the study for comparison purposes (use tape, sponges, or other positional aids). CT slices should be acquired perpendicular to joint spaces (may require gantry rotation) if the joint is the focus of the study. Bone and standard algorithms should be performed along the affected regions/joints with slice thicknesses each of 1.25 mm. If a joint is the focus of the study, conducting an additional bone algorithm sequence with a slice thickness of 0.625 mm (or equivalent) is required. Sagittal and dorsal reconstructions of the affected limb only are required.

MAGNETIC RESONANCE IMAGING

It is far beyond the scope of this technical guide to discuss the theory and physics behind MRI and those interested should consult a text on the subject. This modality is based on the magnetic properties of every molecule containing hydrogen (and other) atoms within the body, which boils down to manipulation/alteration of these properties in order to achieve various T1-weighted and T2-weighted sequences for interpretation and eventual diagnosis. Of the commonly used imaging modalities, the overall spatial resolution of generated images is worst with MRI, but it is this ability to detect changes on the molecular level and high soft tissue contrast that allows us to see diseases or anatomical details that we could not otherwise appreciate via other modalities. T1-weighted imaging sequences are typically considered "anatomy scans" (lesions often iso- to hypointense) and T2-weighted imaging sequences are typically considered "pathology scans" (lesions usually more hyperintense) as the majority of soft tissue lesions found within the body are considered to be associated with fluid, regardless of whether this fluid is at intra- or extracellular locations.

1. Although not all inclusive, our current protocols are overall adequate in assessing for the majority of diseases we are attempting to find. MRI is most often utilized in veterinary medicine, and is the modality of choice, when trying to assess soft tissue structures not easily accessed by an ultrasound probe or are looking for diseases that may not be appreciated via any other modality (primarily for central nervous system and joint imaging). This does not mean that MRI should not be used at a later point if an ultrasound or CT examination is unremarkable and an abnormality persists, as MRI may be able to detect changes the other modalities could not readily find.

2. MRI Coordination. MRIs are only allowed to be performed for MWDs at an MTF while under the direct supervision of a 64F. Once the 64F has confirmed an MRI study is required, coordination where and when the MRI is to take place will be required. After scheduling, communicate with the MRI technician about how anesthesia will be performed/monitored and what MRI protocol, sequences, and patient positioning will be indicated for the case. This is of paramount importance as MRI studies take much longer to complete compared to CT. Each MRI sequence needs its own individual study performed and they cannot be further created from initial scans like CT reconstructions. MRI appointments have a finite amount of time available and therefore only a limited number of scans can be run, so prioritize what is necessary. Having basic protocols set up and in place are of great benefit as there will likely be less time involved repeating studies/modifying protocols and less overall anesthetic time for the patient. If the MRI study will take place at an MTF, entering the MWD into the hospital records system, discussing what coils will be available for use, and patient positioning are additional factors that may need to be discussed as all of the equipment is designed for human use. Bring positional aids from the VTF. Patient positioning is still important in the MRI suite, but largely depends on whether the area of interest has been appropriately positioned within the coil. Despite this, there is recommended positioning which should be followed (especially for the spine; see listed protocols below).

3. Anesthesia. As the MTF is unlikely to have an MRI-safe anesthetic machine available for use in MWDs, be prepared to perform total intravenous anesthesia (TIVA) in order to complete the study. The VMSB Anesthesia/Pain Management guidelines contain guidance regarding TIVA procedures and protocol/monitoring recommendations. It is prudent to have the animal technician accumulate all of the necessary medications and equipment needed to take the day before the MRI appointment in order to ensure everything is on hand. It is also critically important to prepare for any and all anesthetic complications that may arise and have classic "crash cart" medications and equipment readily on hand as most MTFs will not have these items available in MRI suites. See Appendix D for a stepwise list of the typical steps performed on the day of leading up to the exam and the necessary equipment to bring to the MTF. Patient monitoring presents challenges in the MR gantry due to increased noise, greater chance of hypothermia, and overall decreased patient accessibility, making proper training imperative. Possessing an ability to provide supplemental oxygen via flow by, BVM or MRI-compatible anesthesia machine is absolutely paramount in order to intervene if the patient becomes hypoxemic due to hypoventilation. At a minimum, all MWDs will be intubated while anesthetized and provided supplemental oxygen during MRI studies. Additionally, monitoring the patient's ventilatory status, ETCO2, and circulatory status are critical in ensuring that the patient is adequately supported. The above recommendations are based on VMSB Anesthesia/Pain

Management Standards. Lastly, it is important to familiarize oneself with the layout of the MRI suite prior to the day of the procedure. Appreciating the limitations that may exist may result in abandoning the procedure if it cannot be done safely. In these circumstances, outside referral (civilian or military) to an experienced team would be superior to performing this elective procedure when the patient cannot be adequately monitored or supported.

4. MRI Safety. Ensure that whenever anyone enters the MR suite, they have removed all metal objects from their person or have been approved by the MR tech for entry. It is easy to forget a needle that rolled underneath the dog's body or thermometer left on the table. These objects become dangerous projectiles flying into the magnet in the MR suite. Other considerations of MR safety on include whether any stray metal, metallic implants (plates, screws, pins), or pacemakers are present in the patient or on the patient (e.g. collar/harness). If any anesthetic monitoring equipment is available for use, ensure these wires are not placed in a coiled state as the magnet can induce currents and burn patients. Make sure everyone in the MRI suite is provided hearing protection to include the MWD.

5. MRI Technician Assistance. It is very important for the VCO to be with the MR tech outside of the suite during image acquisition at MTFs, helping the MR technician determine the beginning and end points (range) of the study in each plane as they are not familiar with canine anatomy (humans have five lumbar vertebrae compared to dogs seven, for instance). Defining the start and end points is very important as less time will be needed for each sequence, allowing for additional sequences or reduce patient anesthesia time. For example, the whole thoracic and lumbar spine need not be imaged in every thoracolumbar spine case; the beginning and end points for the study should be based off of the neurolocalization findings (UMN vs. LMN signs). As a quick comparative anatomy terms review: axial (human) = transverse (veterinary), coronal (human) = dorsal/ventral plane (veterinary), and sagittal = sagittal. Review the scans with the MR tech as they are completed, otherwise the scan may need to be repeated later after a radiologist reviews the images and deems them inadequate for diagnosis. It may help to look at images of MR studies before the day of the exam to know how these images should be appropriately centered and collimated; even bringing an example to the MR tech may be of benefit. Let the animal technician monitor the anesthetic depth unless the patient really needs a VCO right there in the MR suite due to the complexity of the case.

6. MRI Contrast Administration. Paramagnetic contrast agents are commonly used during MRI. Contrast agent administration is always required when imaging the brain, and may be necessary for other exams dependent on the case. For example, if neoplasia or discospondylitis of the spine is suspected, then administration of contrast during a spinal exam is warranted. The MTF should be able to supply this contrast agent, but please ensure it is available prior to committing to the procedure. All pre-contrast sequences must be performed prior to contrast bolus administration. The contrast agent most often used in our MTFs for MRI is gadolinium-based, and the dose for IV bolus use in the dog is 0.1 mmol/kg (0.2ml/kg).

7. MRI Protocols. The basic MRI protocols commonly used by the DODMWDVS are listed below. However, if a veterinary radiologist is contacted prior to the MRI they can also help fine-tune what sequences should be performed as one case will vary to the next. Diagnoses may be unfortunately missed as a consequence of not consulting with a radiologist prior to study completion. For instance, if hemorrhage is suspected a gradient echo study may be added to the protocol, but it does not have to be included in every study if trauma or infarction is not on the differential list. If a case requiring MRI of another body region not listed below, consultation with the DODMWDVS for protocol development is indicated.

   a. MRI Brain. The patient should be positioned in dorsal or ventral recumbency depending on the coil used. The head is often encased within a head coil but an alternative may be used. The MRI technician will be the best guide in this decision. Within the coil, it is best if the hard palate is parallel to the gantry and table with the tip of the nose and occiput in a

horizontal line with each other along a standard imaging axis. Studies should extend from the most cranial limit of the orbits/eyes to the level of C2-C3. Slice thicknesses of 3-5 mm should be used; dependent on how many sequences are performed. The following sequences in each respective plane should be performed:
  i. Axial/Transverse Plane. T1-weighted, T2-weighted, FLAIR, T1-weighted with contrast.
  ii. Sagittal Plane. T1-weighted, T2-weighted, T1-weighted with contrast.
  iii. Coronal/Dorsoventral Plane. T2-weighted, T1-weighted with contrast (T1-weighted pre-contrast also if time allows).
b. MRI Spine. The patient should be positioned in dorsal recumbency, and the coil within the table will likely be used. Study should extend through necessary vertebral regions based on pain and/or neurolocalization. More specifically for the hind limbs, if UMN signs are present extend from T8-T9 through sacrum and if LMN signs present, from T12-T13 through sacrum unless otherwise directed. Slice thicknesses of 2-4 mm should be used; dependent on how many sequences performed. The following sequences within each respective plane should be performed:
  i. Axial/Transverse Plane. T1-weighted, T2-weighted (T1-weighted with contrast if indicated).
  ii. Sagittal Plane. T1-weighted, T2-weighted, STIR (T1-weighted with contrast if indicated).
  iii. Coronal/Dorsoventral Plane. T2-weighted (T1-weighted pre and post- contrast administration if indicated).
c. MRI Stifle/Joint Imaging. The patient should be placed in lateral recumbency (affected limb up) with the stifle placed in neutral to moderate extension. Study should at least extend from distal femoral diaphysis to the proximal tibial diaphysis, distal to the tibial crest. A wrist coil is preferable, however if the joint/region to be imaged is too large then cardiac or other similar coils may be used. Slice thicknesses of 2-3 mm should be used; dependent on how much time is available to complete the study. The following sequences within each respective plane should be performed:
  i. Axial/Transverse Plane. Proton Density (PD)-weighted (+/- fat sat).
  ii. Sagittal Plane. PD-weighted (+/- fat sat), T1-weighted, T2-weighted (+/- fat sat).
  iii. Coronal/Dorsoventral Plane. PD-weighted (=/- fat sat), T2-weighted (+/- fat sat).

RADIOGRAPHIC REFERRAL PROCEDURES AND PRACTICAL TELERADIOLOGY

Email dog.consult@us.af.mil or call DODMWDVS at (210) 671-3992/3 or DSN 312-473-3992/3 for questions. All consults should be sent to the following address:

DOD MILITARY WORKING DOG VETERINARY SERVICE
ATTENTION: DIAGNOSTIC IMAGING DEPT
1219 KNIGHT STREET, BLDG 7602
JBSA-LACKLAND, TX 78236-5519

1. Referrals via mail. All referral materials (films, CDs) must be accompanied by a DODMWDVS Consultation Form and a completely filled out SF 519B (Radiologic Consultation Request) as well as the referring VCO's interpretation. (*NOTE: DODMWDVS is not intended to be every VCO's

personal radiologist and it is expected that VCOs endeavor to interpret their own imaging studies. If the VCO needs assistance, their supporting 64F should be engaged first. If the 64F cannot comfortably interpret the images, the VCO should then contact DODMWDVS for consult.) In the absence of access to these standard forms, provide a letter detailing MWD signalment, relevant clinical history, and contact information for the referring VCO, supporting 64F, and any other applicable POCs. When sending follow-up images on a case, be sure to include copies of prior correspondence and previous images for comparison, if available. All radiographs need to be clearly labeled to include MWD name and tattoo, date, positional markers and radiology facility. When the images are received at the DODMWDVS, the referring VCO will typically receive an email or phone call with a response. A copy of the completed report will be emailed to the referring VCO for inclusion in the permanent veterinary medical record. If sending films, a complete address should be included so that the completed SF 519B and films can be mailed back to the sending unit to be placed in the MWD's permanent record. Privately-owned animal images can also be referred, but MWDs and other government-owned animals have priority.

2. Teleradiology – Referrals via email and internet. Telemedicine enables each VCO to provide unequaled medical care to MWDs worldwide through informal and formal consultations. Telemedicine also facilitates learning, mentoring and networking within the Veterinary Corps and can save time and money while working up difficult cases at remote duty sites.
   a. DICOM is the industry standard for transfer of radiologic images and other medical information between computers for diagnostic purposes. If using a digital imaging system, there should be a method for exporting the images in DICOM format and packaging them for writing to a CD or storing on a hard drive. These files can then be mailed or emailed for consultation. DICOM images should be submitted for consultation whenever possible. DICOM files will be large (several MBs each) so may not be transferrable with all email accounts. See Appendix E for information on AMRDEC Safe Access File Exchange, a military website for the sharing of large electronic files. (https://safe.amrdec.army.mil/SAFE/)
   b. An alternative method for sending images is to export them from the digital system as a JPEG or PNG file (the format of most digital photographs). These images are no longer true diagnostic quality due to compression and data loss but are often still sufficient to consult on a case. If this is the only option available, these images can be submitted for consultation.
   c. If consultation is needed on radiographic films, the best method will always be to mail the actual films. The local MTF may have a digitizer/scanner which can convert traditional films into digital images for sending/viewing as above. High quality radiographs will often scan/digitize in sufficient quality for diagnosis. As a last resort, photographs of the films can be made using a digital camera.
      i. High contrast images are often effectively photographed and transmit well (i.e. musculoskeletal radiographs). Photographs of thoracic and abdominal radiographs may not be as diagnostic. In particular, interpretation of digitized thoracic radiographs for detection of pulmonary metastasis has been shown to be of limited accuracy. Poor quality radiographs will not be made better through photographic manipulation!
      ii. When photographing radiographs, darken the room, block the excess light from the view box with cardboard, and set the camera for "black & white" photography. Disable the automatic flash and select the macro option if available. Also, check the owner's manual for high-resolution settings that may be included as menu options. Images should be saved in JPEG or PNG format.
      iii. Provide one photo of the entire radiograph for orientation and magnified photos of

specific areas of interest. These and any additional photos (i.e. gross anatomical lesions) can be sent as email attachments.
3. Equipment
   a. Imaging equipment information and recommendations are available through the Veterinary Medical Standardization Board (VMSB). These standards should be reviewed prior to equipment purchase for further information.
   b. When purchasing or upgrading the digital camera, the number of megapixels, lens quality, optical zoom, and dynamic range are the most important factors in overall image quality.

CHAPTER 7

SURGERY

OVERVIEW OF COMMON SURGICAL PROCEDURES FOR THE MWD

The following chapter lists several elective and emergent surgical procedures that may be encountered when caring for an MWD population. Each procedure is covered in detail in a number of excellent veterinary surgical texts, and the wise surgeon will review the procedure and any associated anatomy prior to undertaking any surgery. This list serves to provide guidance for avoiding some of the most common errors and pitfalls associated with the procedures. Surgeons must consult the most current version of the VMSB Anesthesia/Pain Management guidelines for further information regarding anesthetic aspects of surgery. Any deviation from these guidelines should only be performed after approval from the supporting 64F. All tissue specimens (or a sample thereof) obtained from an MWD during a surgical procedure, elective and/or emergent, should be submitted to the Joint Pathology Center for histopathologic analysis and tissue archiving.

TAIL AMPUTATION (CAUDECTOMY)

1. Indications. Usually performed on MWDs that are "spinners" or otherwise overactive within the confines of a run or kennel. Chronic trauma of the tail tip against walls or fencing often results in open lesions that will not heal. However, every attempt should be made for behavioral and medical management through bandaging to alleviate the lesions prior to surgery being performed. More severe lesions and infections, chronic non-healing fractures, and/or the visualization of bone is grounds for removal in an urgent manner.
2. Preparation. Epidural anesthesia or ring block is mandatory. A wide clip is performed and sterile prep made with the tail hung/elevated. The remainder of the tail is wrapped in sterile self-adherent bandaging material. Be sure to position the patient in a way that will minimize strain on the surgeon and provide good visualization, recommend dorsal recumbency with tail hanging off the table. A purse-string suture and/or gauze sponge in the anus may be useful to minimize contamination. Purse string must be annotated on surgical checklists to ensure that it is removed post operatively. This should be considered a clean-contaminated procedure due to the proximity to the anus, and prophylactic peri-operative antibiotics with increased susceptibility for gram negative organisms (higher generation cephalosporins) are advised.
3. Methods. Make the tail short enough that the dog will not traumatize it further. A good rule of thumb is to place the tail against the perineum and determine the length required to cover the anus and long enough that the tail can be lifted to take a temperature. Amputate between coccygeal vertebrae, not through one. A hypodermic needle can be used as a probe to identify the intervertebral space at which to amputate. A wide Penrose drain (1/2 to 5/8 inch) or sterile self-adherent wrap can be used as a tourniquet at the tail base to help control bleeding. If a tourniquet is used, release it every 30-45 minutes for 5 minutes then reapply. The tourniquet should be released prior to skin closure to ensure all bleeding is controlled. Try to reflect muscle off the vertebra distal to the amputation site to allow for closure over the stump later. Creating a skin and muscular flap that is long enough for a tension-free closure ventral to the vertebrae is the biggest key to success (i.e. the dorsal flap wraps over the end of the stump and meets the ventral flap at a point ventral to the vertebra). The first closure layer is muscle over the vertebra, second is subcutaneous layer and finally skin. A continuous skin suture of non-absorbable monofilament material may be advantageous since it will bring a better seal and

does not have the many knots/suture ends which could irritate the dog and cause licking/rubbing. Along with maintaining a tension-free closure, it is also important to obliterate dead space during closure to help prevent complications later, such as a seroma.
4. Post-operative care. Always use an E-collar, bucket, "no-bite" type collar, side braces or a combination of these to prevent chewing at the tail stump. Some surgeons like to place a soft compressive bandage on the stump for 24-48 hours to minimize edema formation. Analgesics and non-steroidal anti-inflammatory medications should be provided for 3-5 days post-surgery. Use of gabapentin in the pre- and post-operative period has been associated with improved management of so called "phantom pain" and associated self-trauma.
5. Complications. The main complication is dehiscence from chewing or licking the tail stump which can usually be averted by ensuring meticulous closure and using a preventive measure as advised above. Despite best efforts, some dogs will still traumatize the stump by rubbing it against a fence or wall. Hematoma at the surgical site can lead to delayed healing, excessive scar formation or result in dehiscence with or without infection. Also, the tail may have been left too long and further amputation may be required if trauma continues.

SCROTAL ABLATION

1. Indications. Scrotal dermatitis of a chronic nature that is not responsive to medical management. Mature male dogs which have large pendulous scrotums may be subject to increased morbidity from chronic irritation or seroma/hematoma formation if castration is performed without scrotal ablation.
2. Preparation. Similar to a castration, however, include the scrotum and perineum to the ventral aspect of the anus in the clip and scrub. Testicular block can be performed as described in the VMSB Anesthesia/Pain Management guidelines. Epidural anesthesia is advised when the staff is proficient in its application but is not mandatory. A purse-string suture and/or gauze sponge in the anus may be useful to minimize contamination.
3. Methods. This procedure is adequately described in common surgery texts. Once on the table, place a sterile urethral catheter to help identify the penis and urethra and prevent inadvertent disruption during surgery and closure. Use a sterile surgical marker to outline the proposed incision. Exaggerate the curvilinear incisions toward the scrotum as this will help assure enough skin for closure without tension, however, try not to include the dark pigmented portion of the scrotum in the final incision. The scrotum is probably inflamed and making the incisions with electrocautery is useful to control hemorrhage from the skin. Hemostasis in general is important to avoid hematomas. To help control bleeding, make a small incision, control bleeding, incise, control, etc.; this is where the incision outline is helpful. Once the skin is incised full-thickness through the scrotal base, dissect it from the testes, and perform routine orchiectomies. Remember that the dog is upside down, most likely with its hind limbs tied laterally and caudally; this adds tension to the surgical site. Do not panic if the incision is under too much tension at first; simply have an assistant untie the hind limbs and continue the closure. Alternatively, attempt surgery without having the limbs tied down. Make sure to obliterate as much dead space as possible, particularly at the cranial aspect of the incision, but avoid the penis and urethra. Minimize trauma/handling of skin edges, as they are thin and prone to excessive bruising and edema, which can delay healing. Buried intradermal/subcuticular closure of skin is preferable so as to avoid suture knots that might irritate the area and cause the dog to attempt to lick the incision.
4. Post-operative care. No special care is needed, except an E-collar or bucket and appropriate post-operative analgesia.
5. Complications. Dehiscence may occur, and is usually secondary to self-trauma or too much tension. It is usually advisable to allow the incision to heal by second-intention if this situation arises. Substantial bruising and edema can occur if the surgeon leaves excessive dead space.

EXPLORATORY LAPAROTOMY

1. Indications. Exploration of the abdomen may be employed for diagnostic procedures, such as visualization and biopsy of organs or for a variety of therapeutic procedures related to trauma, volvulus, foreign material ingestion, neoplasia or other causes.
2. Preparation. Clip and prep the patient's ventral abdomen generously, expecting to make an incision from xyphoid to pubis if required. Also prep far enough lateral to midline in the event that feeding or drainage tubes need to be placed. In males, do not forget to perform an adequate preputial prep and flush. Depending on the reason for the laparotomy it could be considered a clean-contaminated or contaminated procedure and prophylactic peri-operative antibiotics are advised. Ensure biopsy supplies (formalin, cassettes, biopsy instruments, etc.) are ready and available prior to procedure. Biopsy of target organs should always be performed.
3. Methods. Perform sponge/gauze count prior to the procedure and reconcile prior to closure. Ensure that the linea alba is visualized well prior to entry into the abdominal cavity to avoid injury to the rectus abdominus muscle. It is most apparent at the umbilicus, and tapers to a small strip caudally. The falciform ligament will need to be removed with electrocautery and/or ligated cranially. In males, the skin and subcutis incision are curved 1-2 centimeters (cm) lateral to midline just cranial to the prepuce; the preputialis muscle and vascular branches from the caudal superficial epigastric vessel will be encountered. Perform the exploration in a systematic and consistent manner every time to avoid missing lesions or abnormalities. Use moistened laparotomy sponges to prevent tissues from drying and for packing off organs. After the procedure(s) are performed, lavage the abdomen with 1 liter (L) warm, sterile saline solution per 10 kilograms body weight and evacuate the flush solution. Adequate closure of the abdominal wall depends on appropriately sized and spaced bites within the linea and/or external rectus sheath, and on adequate sized suture with appropriate knot construction.
4. Post-operative care. Post-operative care is generally dictated by the underlying cause for the abdominal exploration. Appropriate post-operative analgesia, including local incisional blocks are paramount for a speedy recovery.
5. Complications. Major complication is dehiscence of the body wall closure, most commonly related to suture pull-through due to inappropriate technique. Seroma formation due to dead space in the subcutis is a common complication for novice surgeons and can be mitigated by minimal dissection of the subcutaneous tissue off the external fascia and meticulous closure. Dehiscence of biopsy sites can also occur when poor techniques (inappropriate needle choice, suture spacing, inappropriate vessel ligatures, etc.) are utilized.

INTESTINAL RESECTION AND ANASTOMOSIS

1. Indications. Removal of perforated, ischemic, neoplastic, or necrotic bowel. Causes of ischemic or necrotic bowel include intestinal obstruction, intussusception, adhesions, and segmental bowel strangulation/volvulus.
2. Preparation. Same as for exploratory laparotomy. Considered a clean-contaminated or contaminated procedure and prophylactic peri-operative antibiotics should be used.
3. Methods. Common surgical texts are replete with descriptions. Ensure ligation sites of vasa recta and jejunal vasculature are chosen wisely to avoid hindering vascular flow to the site of anastomosis. Eversion of mucosa is a common problem that can lead to poor apposition of sutured edges of bowel. Everted mucosa can be trimmed with curved Metzenbaum scissors prior to anastomosis. Use 3-0 or smaller suture on a taper needle, spacing sutures 2-3 millimeters (mm) from cut edge and 2-3 mm apart. Continuous or interrupted techniques have both been shown to be appropriate as long as the

submucosa is incorporated in the bite. "GIA" (GastroIntestinal Anastomosis) and "TA" (ThoracoAbdominal) staplers may be useful for this procedure. Stapling can significantly decrease surgical time and are especially useful if the dog is not doing well under anesthesia. Once the anastomosis is complete check its integrity by occluding the bowel about 3-4 cm from the surgical site and inject saline or lactated Ringer's solution via 25-gauge needle. Carefully close the defect in the mesentery to avoid damaging the vascular supply to the anastomosis site. Copiously lavage (1L+/10kg) the abdomen and suction, then wrap the repair in omentum and close.

4. Post-operative care. Most uncomplicated procedures performed in dogs that were not particularly compromised do very well after surgery and require little special care. Care is generally dictated by the underlying condition. Feeding can begin immediately after surgery, but start with small meals of enteric-formulated canned food frequently. Current literature cautions that judicious use of anti-microbials and anti-emetics is indicated post-operatively as these drug therapies may obscure signs of acute complications such as peritonitis. All tissues that are removed should be submitted to JPC for histological evaluation.

5. Complications. Peritonitis is a concern in dogs with a perforated bowel or with major intra-operative contamination. Patients generally decline in clinical status (inappetant, vomiting, lethargy, etc.) 2-5 days after surgery if the repair has dehisced. Longer-term complications can include adhesions creating an obstruction, abscessation, short-bowel syndrome and neoplastic recurrence.

GASTROPEXY

1. Indications. Until the implementation of prophylactic gastropexies for MWDs, multiple MWDs died each year as a result of GDV. Performing a gastropexy either as a prophylactic measure or at the time of an abdominal exploration incited by GDV occurrence is paramount for any VCO working with MWDs. GDV is most likely encountered on deployment as many MPCs, CWDs, or allied nation MWDs are not gastropexied. It is recommended to gastropexy MWDs at the time of abdominal exploration performed for any reason.

2. Preparation. Pre-operative evaluation and stabilization of patients with GDV should be performed rapidly and aggressively as described elsewhere in this text. Evacuation of air and ingesta from the stomach is performed with an orogastric tube or via trocharization. Research has proven that proper hemodynamic stabilization prior to anesthesia and surgery improves outcomes, and surgery should not be rushed in an unstable patient.

3. Methods. Rapid surgical decompression and derotation of the stomach is the main goal of surgical therapy. A ventral midline laparotomy is performed carefully to avoid injury to the gas-distended stomach. The stomach is returned to its normal position by grasping the stomach wall adjacent to the left body wall (pyloric antrum) with right hand and pulling while pushing dorsally on the stomach wall that lies adjacent to the right body wall (fundus). An orogastric tube can be passed once under general anesthesia to aid in evacuating the stomach and accessing gastric viability. Initial assessment of gastric integrity is performed including the cardia; a complete abdominal exploration is performed, followed by re-evaluation of the stomach. Partial gastrectomy, short gastric artery ligation, and/or splenectomy may be required (see following sections). The next step is to perform a gastropexy. An incisional gastropexy is the preferred method due to its ease, rapid application, strength, and minimal specialized supplies required to perform. A 4-6 cm incision is made in the ventral pyloric antrum with a correspondent incision in the transversus abdominus muscle just caudal to the last rib. The incisions are then apposed and closed in two suture lines with slowly-absorbing monofilament suture material on a taper needle (2-0 size). The gastropexy should not alter the normal gastric axis location, pull the stomach too far caudally as evidenced by excessive tension on the gastro-splenic ligament, or

encroach upon the diaphragm.
4. If the gastropexy is performed in a non-emergent situation such as a prophylactic procedure, it should be accomplished using a right lateral paracostal, laparoscopic-assisted technique, or traditional incisional gastropexy. Additional training and credentialing are required before performing the right lateral paracostal technique. An instructional DVD showing the right lateral paracostal approach is available from the Defense Visual Information Directorate.
5. Post-operative care. Immediate post-operative care is dictated on the indication for performing the gastropexy. Post-GDV patients require moderate to intensive post-operative care and monitoring to include continuous ECG. Elective patients require standard incisional care.
6. Complications. Arrhythmias, disseminated intravascular coagulopathy (DIC), sepsis, hypokalemia, hemorrhage, and peritonitis are all very common post-surgical complications for dogs recovering from GDV. Therapy and monitoring are dictated by clinical findings. It has been noted that seroma formation is common with surgeons that are initially learning to perform the right paracostal gastropexy technique. This can be mitigated by meticulous closure of all tissue layers, and in particular the space between internal and external abdominal oblique muscles.

PARTIAL GASTRECTOMY

1. Indications. Resection of a portion of the left margin of the fundus and body may be required in association with GDV. Partial gastrectomy may also be performed from extensive gastric trauma or in association with neoplasia.
2. Preparation. Pre-operative evaluation and therapy are similar for all GDV patients. Free intra-abdominal gas (pneumoperitoneum) may be evident on pre-operative radiographs in patients with gastric necrosis and rupture. No proven objective evaluation measure for determination of viability of the gastric wall has been reported; clinical assessment is the most valuable tool. Color of green to black, palpable thinness of the wall with loss of the characteristic mucosal "slip", absence of peristalsis, absence of hemorrhage when serosal surface is incised with scalpel, and loss of pulsatile flow from gastric and gastroepiploic arteries are all indicators of likely segmental necrosis. Allow 5-10 minutes after de-rotation to make a final determination, as restoration of vascular supply can improve the character of the stomach wall. Fifty to eighty percent of the stomach may be removed, but if the cardia is non-viable, resection is not possible and euthanasia should be elected.
3. Methods. Partial gastrectomy requires a scrubbed surgical assistant for retraction, and extreme care to avoid contamination of the peritoneal cavity with ingesta. The procedure can either be performed with the cut-and-suture method, or with the aid of a linear stapling device (TA 55 or 90). Incorporation of a stapling device will generally decrease surgical time, as well as the risk of contamination of the abdominal cavity and is advisable, particularly for novice surgeons. Gastric invagination of necrotic portions of the stomach wall is another technique that is less technically dependent but is not recommended and the supporting 64F should be consulted as this technique is considered as a last option.
4. Post-operative care. As for GDV patients, patients with gastric necrosis will always require intensive post-operative therapy and monitoring. Transfer to a 24-hour care facility post-operatively is appropriate when possible. Mortality of patients surgically treated for GDV increases with the presence of gastric necrosis.
5. Complications. Arrhythmias, DIC, sepsis, hypokalemia, hemorrhage, and peritonitis are all common post-surgical complications for dogs recovering from GDV. Therapy and monitoring are dictated by clinical findings.

SPLENECTOMY

1. Indications. Neoplasia, loss of vascularity (thrombi) secondary to GDV, splenic torsion, trauma, generalized splenic disorders.
2. Preparation. Splenectomy is commonly performed as an emergent procedure, with concomitant hemoabdomen and persistent intra-abdominal blood loss due to a (often large) bleeding splenic mass. It is advisable to be familiar with the anatomy of the spleen in normal patients to help recognize vascular structures in these emergent patients. Peri-operative blood product administration may be required.
3. Methods. Arcade ligation of the splenic artery and vein, short gastric arteries, left gastroepiploic artery, and omental attachments provides a method for rapid and safe removal of the spleen. Mass ligation of segments of omentum and specific ligation or stapling (LDS stapler) of larger individual vessels is the preferred technique for most surgeons. Care must be taken to avoid excessive manipulation or trauma to the distal aspect of the left limb of the pancreas due to its close association with the splenic artery and vein. Splenic torsions should not be derotated prior to splenectomy due to release of thrombi and cellular breakdown products. Liver biopsy should always be performed in cases of suspected splenic hemangiosarcoma. Prophylactic gastropexy using an incisional method should be performed at time of splenectomy secondary to large splenic masses if the patient is stable.
4. Post-operative care. Dictated by the reason for performing the splenectomy, and the post-operative condition. Continuous ECG monitoring is advisable for the first 24-48 hours.
5. Complications. Hemorrhage, arrhythmias, and DIC are the most common complications. Arrhythmias (VPCs) may not occur for 12-24 hours post-operatively, and only need to be treated if they are hemodynamically significant.

GUIDE TO ORDERING MWD VIDEOS

MWD instructional videos are available through the Defense Imagery Management Operations Center (DIMOC). The website is: http://www.dimoc.mil/customer/contact.html. The website no longer allows searching for individual videos. Videos can be ordered using the online contact form, select "Digital Fulfillment" as the subject and then complete the required information. In the comments section, include the video name(s) and pin(s), number required and physical address for shipping as orders are shipped via commercial carrier and not the United States Postal Service.

1. The following surgical videos are available:
   a. PIN 615365 - COMMON MILITARY WORKING DOG SURGICAL PROCEDURES (Includes Right Paracostal Gastropexy, castration with scrotal ablation and caudectomy made by DODMWDVS)
   b. PIN 615356 - CANINE RIGHT-SIDED PARACOSTAL GASTROPEXY
   c. PIN 615360 - CANINE CAUDECTOMY
   d. PIN 615361 - CANINE SCROTAL ABLATION
2. The following exam videos are also available:
   a. PIN 614575 - MILITARY WORKING DOG NEUROLOGIC EXAM
   b. PIN 614576 - MILITARY WORKING DOG ORTHOPEDIC EXAM
3. DIMOC contact information:
   Toll free: 1-888-PH-DIMOC (743-4662)
   DSN: 795-9872
   Commercial: 570-615-9872
   Email: dvicustomerservice@defense.gov

CHAPTER 8

DENTISTRY

OVERVIEW OF DENTAL CARE FOR MWDS

Dental disease is common in MWDs due to the nature of these animals and their work. If untreated, dental disease can lead to performance degradation, tooth loss, and systemic illness. Severe dental disease can require the retirement of a dog from active service. The most common conditions encountered are dental attrition, dental fractures, and periodontal disease. Because of safety concerns, a complete oral exam is often impossible without sedation or general anesthesia. In addition, follow up treatments, whether by veterinary or kennel personnel, are difficult to provide. Therefore, careful considerations must be given when formulating a dental treatment plan. If an MWD requires advanced dental procedures (i.e. endodontics or oral surgery) consultation with the DODMWDVS or supporting 64F is recommended. Often excellent dental support for MWDs can be obtained through interaction with the local military dental activity and it is highly recommended that a good working relationship be established with these personnel. Importantly, the attending VCO remains entirely responsible for making therapeutic decisions regarding the MWD patient and IAW veterinary policies and the VMSB Comprehensive Oral Health Assessment and Treatment (COHAT) Guidelines.

DENTAL EXAMINATIONS

An oral exam should be performed at least twice yearly in conjunction with the semi-annual physical examination. Every time an MWD is anesthetized, a careful dental/oral exam should be performed. A complete dental prophylaxis should be performed as needed which is typically about once a year and cleaning should be considered any time an MWD is anesthetized. Special priority should be given to MWDs prior to deployment. Routine and prophylactic procedures should be done by supporting home station personnel prior to deployment of MWD. Although a dental prophylaxis should be performed prior to deployment, it should be noted that dental calculi without associated periodontal disease does not equate to dental disease. Significant dental disease or oral conditions which render the dog otherwise not deployable must be addressed prior to deployment.

DENTAL RECORDS

Any dental problems should be annotated in the record and on the master problem list (e.g. fractures, missing teeth, advanced gingival recession). However, calculus that accumulates between cleanings and prophylactic procedures should not be placed on the master problem list. All dental treatments, including routine prophylaxis should be recorded in the MWDs medical record (SF 600, or equivalent) and on an attached or separate dental chart in accordance with American Veterinary Dental College (AVDC) standards. A standardized dental chart is available in the VMSB COHAT Guidelines and within the electronic veterinary medical record system.

DENTAL FRACTURES

Dental fractures are frequently noted in military working dogs. Because of their large size and rostral positioning, the canine teeth are most frequently affected. Common causes of coronal fractures include aggression training, kennel vices (pan or fence chewing), and overzealous reward retrieval. Clinical signs of bite avoidance, oral bleeding, reluctance to eat or facial swelling are occasionally reported. However, the majority of coronal fractures are identified as incidental findings during an oral exam or dental prophylaxis. Canine teeth may be partially avulsed from the alveolus. In these cases, the tooth is intact but the surrounding bone is fractured. Such teeth can be salvaged by timely and appropriate therapy. Avulsed teeth require a root canal and some form of intra-oral support during healing of the alveolar bone. Consultation with the supporting 64F, local military dentists, and/or the DODMWDVS is recommended.

1. Treatment Decisions. A tooth with a fractured crown should be treated endodontically if the pulp chamber is exposed. These teeth must be distinguished from viable teeth with chronic wear, which have produced tertiary restorative dentin. The latter teeth will have a brownish spot where the pulp has receded but will not allow penetration of a dental probe and the surface shines and feels as smooth as glass when the surface is probed with a dental explorer. Over time, an open pulp chamber may fill in with necrotic debris, dental calculi or other foreign material. In that case, the surface will appear dull and feel rough when probed with a dental explorer; these latter teeth require endodontics or extraction. After a tooth fracture, bacteria from the oral cavity contaminate the pulp. This infection leads to pulpitis and then death of the tooth. (A tooth may be illuminated with a transilluminator, a viable tooth will light up, while a dead tooth will be noticeably dark in the area of the pulp cavity). The infection can spread through the apex causing a periapical abscess, which can progress to osteomyelitis, severe pain, and tooth loss. Because of the morbidity that can occur when fractured teeth are not treated, all teeth with coronal or enamel fractures should be treated endodontically or extracted. Bonded dental sealants should be used for protection of recently exposed dentin secondary to dental fracture that does not involve the pulp chamber. The canines, third maxillary incisors and carnassial teeth are saved whenever possible. Radiographs may further document necrosis with the pulp cavity of a dead tooth appearing wider on radiographs than a viable tooth. Likewise, there may be concurrent widening of the periodontal ligament space and/or resorption of the alveolar bone. If tooth extraction is performed, the entire tooth root needs to be elevated and removed and verified by radiography.

2. Endodontic Therapy (Root Canal). Endodontic therapy is treatment of the tooth pulp. The pulp includes the blood vessels, nerves, and connective tissues that internally support each tooth. Because the periodontium has an independent neurovascular supply from the pulp, it is possible for a mature tooth to be dead and yet remain fully functional and firmly supported. This is the basis of endodontic therapy. The purpose of a root canal procedure is to remove the necrotic pulp from a tooth and seal that tooth to prevent apical spread of bacterial infection. This procedure will eliminate the source of pain and preserve the function of the tooth. Hands-on training of VCOs in endodontic therapy continues to be a part of the Basic Officer Leadership Course (BOLC) and Veterinary Services in Theater of Operations (VSTO) Course. With the proper equipment (listed in the COHAT Guidelines), and a little practice, one can master the techniques. Contact the supporting 64F or DODMWDVS for consultation in specific cases. The following steps are followed when performing a standard root canal:
    a. Dental Prophylaxis if needed
    b. Pre-operative Radiography
    c. Endodontic Access
    d. Canal Debridement
    e. Canal Irrigation/Disinfection
    f. Drying
    g. Obturation (filling of the pulp chamber with an inert substance i.e. IRM, Gutta Percha, etc.)
    h. Restoration of the Access Site (amalgam or light-cured resin)

i. Post-Operative Radiography
3. Dental Restoration. As a general rule, dental restorations (crowns) are discouraged in military working dogs. Most MWDs will continue to have an effective bite as long as the source of pain is eliminated by endodontic therapy. In addition, when a crown is placed, the remaining tooth structure is weakened, and thus the failure rate for these implants is high in working dogs and may result in more serious injury.

PERIODONTAL DISEASE

Periodontal disease is inflammation and/or infection of the tissues that support the teeth. Clinical signs of periodontal disease vary from patient to patient and from mild to severe. Common signs include inflammation of the gingiva (gums) with or without recession, halitosis, ulceration, bleeding, pyorrhea, tooth mobility, and tooth loss.
1. Periodontal disease is staged based on clinical evaluation, which coincides with the pathologic state. Periodontal probing and dental radiography (where available) are important diagnostic techniques that assist in staging periodontal disease. Healthy gingiva is pink or pigmented in color. The gingival sulcus is shallow and the gingival edge is firm and tapered.
    a. Stage I periodontal disease is gingivitis. This stage is recognized by gingival edema and inflammation without deterioration of the support structures.
    b. Stage II is advanced gingivitis. The gums bleed easily on probing and the inflammation is increased. These teeth remain stable.
    c. Stage III patients have established periodontitis. In addition to the above clinical signs, these patients have deep periodontal pockets (>3mm probe depth) with 10-30% loss of bone support. Stage III teeth are slightly mobile.
    d. Stage IV, or advanced periodontitis is an advanced breakdown of the periodontium with deep pockets and >30% loss of alveolar bone and significant tooth mobility. When staging a patient's periodontal disease, each tooth is considered individually. An average score can then be given for the entire mouth.
2. Most MWDs will fall into Stage I or II periodontal disease when evaluated during a dental prophylaxis. Most dogs will not advance beyond advanced gingivitis with regular and thorough dental examinations and cleanings. Attempts should be made to save Stage III teeth with careful, but complete cleaning, paying special attention to the subgingival component with root planing, subgingival curettage, and the application of barrier sealants. Doxycycline gel can be instilled subgingivally into the pocket after cleaning and slowly releases antibiotic locally to help stem further bone destruction and allow repair. Stage IV periodontitis requires heroic procedures to save the tooth and may require placement of an osteoconductive bioglass or graft material after surgical exposure and debridement. Oral antibiotics (clindamycin and others) can also be given to treat alveolar bone infection. Extraction is typically preferred; however, every effort is made to save canine, third maxillary incisor, and carnassial teeth. As continued oral health maintenance is difficult in MWDs, Stage III and IV treatments can easily fail so it is best to conduct regular oral examinations and thorough prophylaxis.

DENTAL PROPHYLAXIS

A complete dental prophylaxis is important to maintain general health. Every MWD should have a complete prophylaxis performed annually or semi-annually as needed. Depending on the handler's rapport with the dog, he or she should attempt monthly oral checks even if it is only a quick look at the buccal surfaces of the teeth and any changes should be reported to the VCO or 68T. Dogs with Stage III or IV periodontitis need more than a routine prophylaxis. These teeth need periodontal therapy directed at the specific lesion. Periodontal therapy techniques include barrier sealants, subgingival curettage, root planing, periodontal surgery, or extraction. Most MWDs can function with missing teeth. In fact, due to the difficulty in providing oral treatments in MWDs, the decision is sometimes made to sacrifice a nonessential tooth in an MWD. It is important to annotate procedures and findings in the dental chart and medical record.

1. A complete dental prophylaxis includes the following steps:
    a. General anesthesia (using VMSB guidelines)
    b. Examination and dental charting
    c. Dental scaling
        i. Rinse the mouth with a very dilute chlorhexidine solution (0.12%).
        ii. Thick calculus can be broken off the teeth (usually most heavy on the maxillary 4th premolars) with extraction forceps or rongeurs, but be careful not to fracture the tooth.
        iii. Proceed to the ultrasonic scaler.
        iv. Use a hand scaler to remove subgingival calculus.
    d. Periodontal probing
    e. Dental polishing
    f. Dental radiographs
    g. Additional procedures as necessary to treat dental disease.
    h. Application of a barrier sealant product should be considered.
2. Antibiotics with efficacy against anaerobic bacteria (lincosamide or aminopenicillin with or without β- lactamase inhibitor) should be initiated several days prior to a dental cleaning in any dog with a heart murmur, kidney or other heart disease, severe oral infection, or if concurrent surgery is planned or possible. Dogs not meeting these criteria generally do not require antibiotics for routine dental cleaning. When indicated, antibiotics should be continued for several days after the dental cleaning.

HANDLER LEVEL DENTAL CARE

The best treatment is prevention. MWD Handlers should be trained in how to open their MWD's mouth for oral exam, how to do a brief visual oral exam, and how to brush their MWD's teeth or utilize an oral rinse. As with human dental care, brushing daily is paramount in preventing periodontal disease and tartar/calculus build-up. If a handler is able to brush the MWD's teeth no less frequently than every other day, there should be significant improvement in overall dental health and the interval at which prophylactic cleanings are needed can be increased in order to prevent repeated anesthetic events. For MWDs that are too aggressive to allow brushing, a viable alternative is a daily rinse with chlorhexidine solution.

CHAPTER 9

PHYSICAL CONDITIONING

OVERVIEW

Police dogs and MWDs are career athletes presented with a unique set of performance challenges. Stakes are high for these dogs as their safety and that of many people depends on their ability to carry out their duties with speed and agility. The dogs must often be called upon in a moment's notice to engage in pursuit at sprinting speeds or to navigate varied terrain in a search exercise. Furthermore, intensive resources are involved in the training of these specialized dogs, so there is much incentive to maximizing the time at which they are at peak performance. Ensuring these dogs are appropriately conditioned is a critical aspect of their care and of preparation for any event that may call upon their services. The following is a discussion of the nature of police and military working dog duties, as well as recommendations for conditioning based on the evidence existing in human exercise physiology.

PHYSICAL DEMANDS ON MWDS

The development of an appropriate conditioning program for military and police dogs requires a thorough understanding of the physiological and biomechanical demands placed on them in their regular activities. Most MWDs are certified to perform a combination of patrol and detection duties. These activities fall in between high-intensity sports such as greyhound racing and extreme endurance events like sled-dog competitions. Patrol activities are conducted mainly for the purpose of pursuing a suspect or intruder. Therefore, dogs will be required to sprint, jump obstacles, turn sharply at top speed, scale walls and fences, and withstand potentially severe compressive and bending forces to the spinal column when apprehending an individual. Detection of either explosives or narcotics requires searching of rooms, vehicles and other areas, sometimes in places that may require crawling or navigating unstable terrain without fatiguing. Therefore strength, endurance, flexibility, proprioception and balance are necessary for peak performance of patrol and detection activities. Additionally, MWDs in particular, may be asked to conduct their duties in environmental extremes, presenting a risk of heat or cold injury.

MUSCULOSKELETAL INJURIES

Knowledge of the types and frequencies of injuries sustained by military and police dogs in the line of duty allows incorporation of preventative strategies into a training program. There is information in the literature with regard to musculoskeletal injuries sustained by police and MWDs, although some of the evidence has relied on handler recall rather than documented diagnosis by a VCO.
1. Musculoskeletal Injuries in MWDs. 14.3% of non-combat related injuries or illness occurring in MWDs in a combat zone were musculoskeletal related (Takara, 2014). Evans and others (2007) retrospectively evaluated 245 military working dog records to determine reasons for discharge from service. Dogs were separated into two age groups: 1 to less than 5 years of age and 5 years of age or older. The most common cause of discharge by far in the younger group was behavior (82.3% of dogs under 5 years), distantly followed by heat injury (8.2%). Spinal cord diseases (30%) were the most common causes of discharge in dogs 5 years of age or older, followed by behavior (14.4%), degenerative joint disease (DJD, 13.8%) and a combination of spinal cord diseases and DJD (12.5%).

Similarly, in an earlier retrospective study of records from 927 MWDs, appendicular DJD (19.2%) and spinal cord/cauda equina disease (15.6%) were two of the top three reasons for death or euthanasia, along with neoplasia (Moore, 2001). The musculoskeletal problem most commonly responsible for MWD discharge from duty appears to have shifted from hip dysplasia/osteoarthritis to degenerative lumbosacral stenosis in the past several decades, but current prevalence among working dogs is unknown for either condition. Regardless, musculoskeletal injuries and diseases appear to play a key role in early release from duty of MWDs.

2. Musculoskeletal Injuries in Police Dogs. In a comparison between police and pet German Shepherd Dog emergency visits, the study found that police dogs were more likely to be seen for orthopedic injuries than the pet population, comprising over 25% of the reasons for police dog emergency visits. Most orthopedic injuries among police dogs were appendicular rather than axial. Police dogs were seen at a younger age than pets; orthopedic injuries were thus postulated to be work-related. Authors indicated the data is suggestive of a need for preventative conditioning programs in police dogs, though specific orthopedic injuries were not discussed (Parr, 2013). Another study investigating 151 police dogs in Egypt found a lower prevalence of orthopedic diseases than in the police dogs of the previous study, with 2.6% having skeletal disorders and an additional 1.4% having muscular disorders (Haithem, 2011).

PHYSIOLOGICAL RESPONSES TO CONDITIONING

The body's response to conditioning is multi-systemic, and can be manipulated to some degree in order to develop physiological changes optimized to a particular sport or activity. A great deal of information exists about conditioning of human athletes, which contributes substantially to the practice of veterinary sports medicine. There is a limited amount of evidence available in dogs as well, allowing the practitioner to develop an understanding of some of the key differences between the species. The following discussion highlights the human physiological responses to training, addressing specific differences in canine athletes when known.

1. Musculoskeletal System. The human muscular system is comprised of two main muscle fiber types. Type I, commonly referred to as "slow twitch" fibers, are muscles designed to sustain persistent, low-level activation. These fibers predominate in postural muscles and in those required to perform prolonged endurance activities, particularly in trained athletes. Type I fibers are thus resistant to fatigue, containing higher levels of oxidative enzymes mitochondria and myoglobin to support aerobic metabolism. Type II, or "fast-twitch", fibers, are more suited to anaerobic metabolism, have low resistance to fatigue, and predominate in muscles of individuals trained in high-intensity strength-related exercises. These fibers contain higher numbers of glycolytic enzymes, and are capable of achieving higher tensile strength and shortening velocity. Dogs, however, have a muscle type and distribution more suited to endurance activity. Their "fast-twitch" fibers (Type IIA, Type IIX and several hybrid) fibers differ substantially from human Type II fibers in that they are capable of much greater oxidative metabolism. The only highly anaerobic fibers known to exist in the canine body are within laryngeal muscles. As a result, canine skeletal muscles do not appear to make significant adaptations in response to endurance training regarding capillary content or mitochondrial number and efficiency. However, resistance training can elicit hypertrophy or reverse atrophy in the dog as in the human, as well as altering the distribution of muscle fiber types. There are also breed-related differences in muscle fiber type distribution. Greyhounds, for example, have a larger proportion of Type II muscle fibers than other breeds, which facilitates their high-power, high-speed sprinting activity.

2. Cardiovascular System. The cardiovascular system of both humans and dogs also undergoes a number of adaptations in response to aerobic training, though large species differences exist as with

the muscular system. In humans, endurance training lowers the heart rate during rest and at a given intensity of submaximal exercise. Bradycardia and cardiac hypertrophy, induced by training, allow for an increased end-diastolic volume and greater contractility via the Frank-Starling mechanism, therefore enhancing stroke volume and cardiac output.
   a. Aerobic conditioning in humans also increases arteriolar oxygen extraction at the level of working muscles (McArdle, 2015). In people, cardiac output and oxygen extraction contribute nearly equally to enhancing maximum oxygen consumption (VO2 max), the most reliable indicator of an individual's fitness. Cardiac hypertrophy and lower heart rate at rest and submaximal exercise are induced by training in canine athletes as with humans. Dogs in one study demonstrated a drop of approximately 14 beats per minute after a period of conditioning (Musch, 1985). Unlike humans, however, increase in VO2 max as a result of endurance training in dogs is mostly due to cardiac output (96%) and stroke volume in particular, rather than oxygen extraction (4%) (Musch, 1987). This is supported by the lack of substantial evidence for muscle biochemical and histochemical adaptations to endurance training in dogs. Conditioning may increase a dog's VO2 max by anywhere from 31% in foxhounds running on a treadmill (Musch, 1985) to almost 300% in trained endurance sled dogs (Pierce, 2013).
   b. As athletes' performance and resistance to fatigue increase with VO2 max, conditioning contributes substantially to both. Training also improves canine lipid oxidation and efficiency of substrate utilization to support prolonged endurance activity. This may increase efficiency of nutrient use from the higher-fat performance diet that is standard for most MWDs (Pierce, 2013).
   c. Thermoregulation. Conditioning improves the ability of an individual to thermoregulate, by reducing the proportion of energy produced as heat and increasing the proportion utilized for work, otherwise known as the energy efficiency. The energy efficiency of an untrained dog is less than 17%, which means that 83% of the energy spent is lost as heat. A conditioned dog can have an energy efficiency of up to 27%, with 73% produced as heat, which is very similar to the efficiency level of certain machines such as car engines. The decreased amount of metabolic energy lost as heat means that the core body temperature will not rise as readily with exercise. This is critical in the MWD, in which heat injury can have significant adverse effects ranging from loss of performance to death. Providing adequate conditioning programs to working dogs may reduce the incidence of heat injuries, and also improve detection performance by reducing the threshold for panting, which interferes with sniffing ability.

PRINCIPLES OF CONDITIONING

1. Overload. The principle of overload describes that the intensity of exercise must be above a certain threshold in order to effect physiologic changes, such as increased VO2 max and muscle hypertrophy (ACSM, 2013). Individual factors such as age, genetics, concurrent illness, and level of fitness influence this threshold. Training will increase the threshold required to elicit changes in physiologic parameters; an elite human athlete requires exercise at intensities of 95-100% VO2 max in order to achieve further alterations in physiologic responses. Interval training is one technique that may assist an individual in producing physiologic gains beyond those achieved by high intensity exercise alone. Interval training for up to 3 months may be equivalent or superior to purely high-intensity activity for the healthy human adult (ACSM, 2013).
2. Specificity. The principle of specificity defines that, in order to improve performance in a given activity, training must involve specific recapitulations of that activity. Therefore, if a working dog

needs to be able to navigate unstable terrain or leap while turning in a chase, training should include exercises that address balance on unstable surfaces and jumping power during a change in direction. Repetition of the activity to be trained is commonly the extent of preparation among individuals participating in canine sports and in the MWD training community. However, exclusively focusing on skills-specific training falls short of ultimate performance improvement as it overlooks other components of the complete athlete. The five most important components of a balanced exercise program include: endurance, strength, preparation and recovery, proprioception and balance, and skill-specific training. Examples of exercises in each category (with some overlap) that are beneficial to MWDs are included in this document.

3. Strength/Power. Measurement of strength of individual muscles or muscle groups is very difficult or would require invasive procedures in dogs. There are proposed strength tests for core, pelvic limbs and forelimbs in dogs, but these are highly subjective and generalized. The most clinically applicable estimation of muscle strength in dogs can be achieved by indirect assessment of muscle mass. When muscle hypertrophy is the desired outcome, the practitioner must understand the timeline along which this type of physiological adaption can take place. This has not been specifically assessed in dogs, but in people there is an initial period of neuromuscular adaptation in which the motor unit coordination improves execution of commands from the CNS, allowing for an early increase in muscle activation efficiency and strength that precedes hypertrophy of muscle fibers. In human kinesiology, it is generally accepted that muscle hypertrophy requires an 8-12 week program consisting of exercises that elicit muscle overload. Muscle mass changes can be estimated with evaluation of circumference of thighs and other areas. Subjective strength assessments can be made at intervals as well. Similar to humans, it must be understood that as dogs age, muscle tissue is gradually replaced with fat, in conjunction with age-induced muscle atrophy (sarcopenia).
    a. The use of resistance bands and asymmetric weight loading are useful in building muscle mass and strength preferentially on a specific limb or with a specific group. Keep in mind that more distal placement of a resistance band will lengthen the moment arm of the limb, thereby increasing the torque and increasing the muscle's workload. Working dogs can be trained to perform a variety of maneuvers, with or without additional weight or resistance, to strengthen specific muscle groups.
    b. Table 1 lists examples of strengthening exercises for the thoracic limbs, pelvic limbs and core muscles designed to lead to improved performance of required duties of working dogs.
4. Endurance. MWDs are considered "intermediate-level" athletes and are not truly engaging in endurance activities as are sled dogs undergoing many miles of running for multiple days in a row. However, it's important to build physical endurance within the range of activities that MWDs are expected to perform, and improving physical endurance also reduces olfactory fatigue for dogs performing detection duties. Aerobic endurance can be helpful in preventing heat injury, as dogs that are aerobically conditioned are more energy-efficient and produce less body heat for a given amount of work performed, as described above. Building endurance requires exercise at a submaximal level (less than 80%-90% maximal effort) for a given duration, generally at least 20-30 minutes. However, interval training with high-intensity intervals at near-maximum effort may actually be more effective than continuous submaximal exercise in building endurance. A 1:1 or 2:1 ratio of lower to higher intensity activity is recommended. Having a land treadmill designed for dogs (at least 6 feet of working belt length for the average MWD) is more suited to a graded endurance conditioning program, as the speed and intensity (incline) can be controlled and altered within accurate interval periods. An endurance program should build over 7-8 weeks at a frequency of 4-5 times per week before reducing to a maintenance level of 3 times per week.

Table 1. Strengthening Exercises

Thoracic Limbs	Pelvic Limbs	Core Muscles
"Shake a paw" with reach at various heights, with or without weights on the carpus	Sit-to-stand. Sit with rump only on an elevated surface and feet on ground (easy) to entire hind end on an unstable surface (hard). Facing downhill (easier) to facing uphill (harder)	Balancing with forelimbs, hindlimbs or whole body on one or more unstable objects (peanut, physioroll, donut, balance disk)
"Pushups" or sit/stand to down facing downhill shifting weight to forelimbs	Pivoting around in a circle with hindlimbs (with or without resistance band hobbles, or with or without stepping over obstacles in between) while forelimbs remain on a small target area	Walking with hindlimbs on a treadmill while forelimbs are in front of the treadmill balancing on an unstable object (or vice-versa)
Stepping up and down (shoulder and elbow flexors and extensors) and off the sides (shoulder adductors and abductors) of an aerobic step with weights above the carpus.	Walking in tall grass, sand or snow (strengthens thoracic and pelvic limbs and their stabilizers)	Navigating over a series of unstable objects (trampoline, balance balls, discs, physiorolls and peanuts, swaying bridges on a child's playground, balancing and turning on a plank)
Digging (contraindicated for explosives detection dogs)	Jumping up to place forelimbs or whole body on an elevated surface. Can alternate with crawling or have the dog explode up from a sit for a more plyometric exercise when safe to challenge	Three-legged standing (easy, best if elevates limb voluntarily to touch a target) to "supermans" with contralateral forelimb and hindlimb elevated. Even more challenging if performed on an unstable surface
Tunnel crawl or "limbo"	Tunnel crawl or "limbo"	Transitions (e.g. sit to stand, sit to down) with forelimbs, hindlimbs or whole body on an unstable surface (balance discs or a physio-peanut)
Cavaletti Rails with or without weighted forelimb(s)	Cavaletti Rails with or without weighted pelvic limb(s)	Planks or plank pushups with forelimbs on a physioball/peanut
Balance with forelimbs on an unstable object and forelimbs elevated (easy) to hindlimbs elevated (challenging)	Balance with hindlimbs on an unstable object and hindlimbs elevated (easy) to forelimbs elevated (challenging)	Standing on a raft floating in water or on a wagon or other wheeled object (always being spotted by a handler) rolled over uneven terrain
Wheelbarrowing	Dancing or walking forward/backward with forelimbs (antebrachii or feet) on a physioroll or rolling stool	Repetitions moving from lateral to sternal recumbency on an unstable surface such as a mattress (targeting transversus abdominus)
Ascending Stairs	Descending Stairs	Sit-to-beg position and hold.

5. Proprioception and Balance. Proprioception and balance can be greatly enhanced by improving core stability, so there is considerable overlap in the exercises for each. Navigating obstacles such as ladder rungs, tires, Cavaletti rails, and unstable terrain will improve proprioception. These exercises

are best performed slowly, allowing the dog time to make adjustments and shift weight, without relying as much on momentum to adjust to the change in position. In MWDs with poor core strength and balance, weight shifting may be performed with the dog in a static standing position. The handler can rock the patient's shoulders or flanks to one side or to both sides, allowing the dog to adjust. Additionally, applying some dorso-ventral motion to the dog's body elicits rhythmic stabilization of the muscles to maintain standing posture, contributing to standing strength and balance as well. Whenever possible, normal posture should be encouraged such that the forelimb-to-hindlimb distance and left-to- right limb distance approach that achieved on a normal, flat surface. Standing weight-shifting can be performed on surfaces of gradually increasing instability (wobble boards, discs, Bosu balls) as the MWD's proprioception improves, in conjunction with exercises performed while the dog is in motion. One advantage of proprioceptive exercises is that they are ideally suited to begin employment in young puppies. These activities are not high-impact and thus minimal risk to growth plates. In working dog puppies, introducing them to unfamiliar and varied surfaces will improve proprioception and environmental confidence which are both desirable in dogs that perform any type of search and rescue, tracking or detection. Neuromuscular adaptation programs in young human athletes have been shown to reduce the rate of injury in a variety of sports activities.

6. Flexibility and Agility
    a. Flexibility can be improved passively or actively through stretching and range of motion activities. Passive range of motion and stretching are performed with the MWD in a relaxed state and without their voluntary muscle movement. This type of range of motion is performed by the trained handler or veterinary personnel, and can be provided globally for a limb or may target a specific joint. Active stretching and range of motion of joints is elicited by the MWD's own voluntary muscle contractions, and may involve either closed-kinetic-chain or open- kinetic-chain activity. Closed-chain activity typically occurs in weight-bearing and the range of motion of one joint is connected to that of adjacent joints on the limb segments. For example, moving from a stand to a sit-position addresses range of motion of the major joints of the pelvic limbs; appropriate sitting posture requires considerable flexion of the hip, stifle and tarsus. Open-chain active range of motion occurs in non-weight-bearing and may or may not involve multiple joints. Stepping over Cavaletti rails and "shake a paw" are examples of open-chain active range of motion exercises. A high "hup" provides an excellent active stretch for the hip and stifle flexors. Having the dog stand with the hindlimbs on an elevated surface such as a stair step and flexing down to a reward between the front legs can replicate a "forward bend" in humans and provide a stretch to the hamstrings. Range of motion and stretching exercises can also be introduced for the spinal column. These maneuvers (dorsal, ventral, and lateral flexion) are likely most effective when the dog voluntarily performs them, such as in following a treat up, down, or to touch the nose to the ribs, flank, limbs, etc.
    b. In order for MWDs to be comprehensive athletes, they must be equally conditioned and capable to move through multiple planes. Often the sagittal plane is the specific focus of training, which consists of movement in a cranial-caudal direction and mainly involves flexion and extension of the limbs. However, it's also critical to ensure MWDs are equally functional in the transverse plane (within which the torso rotates and limbs adduct and abduct) and in the dorsal plane (within which the body laterally flexes and limbs rotate internally and externally). The agile dog is able to move fluidly from plane to plane with greater skill and reduced risk of injury, so training in all planes and with transitions is important. MWDs will frequently move through various planes during patrol and detection work.

EXERCISE PRESCRIPTION: DURATION, FREQUENCY, INTENSITY AND PROGRESSION

The following are determinants of exercise program progression from the American College of Sports Medicine Exercise Testing and Prescription Guidelines, as well as recommendations tailored to canine athletes.

1. Exercise Prescription in MWD Athletes. There is little published information about recommendations for intensity, frequency and duration of exercise for dogs. From one study (Tipton, 1974), 20 minutes of aerobic exercise per day for five days per week (100 minutes per week) appears to induce a trained state in dogs, characterized by a lower heart rate at a given exercise intensity as is seen in humans. Most of the adaptations were lost after 4-5 weeks of de-conditioning. Another evaluation of Australian Herding Dogs demonstrated that success rates were significantly influenced by the frequency of exercise provided to the dogs during off-peak season times. As exercise frequency during these time periods decreased, the percentage of owners reporting success rates of 80% or greater decreased, with a large drop in success rate between dogs that exercised once weekly compared to twice weekly (Arnott, 2014). Additionally, puppies professionally exercised for five days per week had significantly higher scores for tasks evaluated by the TSA (e.g., retrieve, possession, hidden search, energy) than those exercised once per week under the same circumstances (Otto, 2012). The following recommendations for MWDs are extrapolated from the ACSM guidelines for humans and from the limited research evaluating exercise programs in dogs.
2. Aerobic Exercise:
    a. 5 days per week aerobic exercise of moderate intensity, minimum 40 minutes per session (McArdle, 2015, ACSM consensus)
    b. Intensity: Should be fast walking pace (3-3.5 mph) or intervals with walking (2.5 mph) and trotting (4.5-
    c. mph)
    d. Moderate intensity = brisk walking or trotting pace, centerline drills/ball play at a lope but not maximum- intensity sprinting
    e. 5-minute warm-up and 5 minute cool-down required within each aerobic exercise session
    f. 5 days per week, 20 minutes per day of aerobic exercise increased dogs to a trained state (decreased heart rates at a given exercise intensity, decreased post-exercise lactate) – Tipton et al 1974
    g. 3 days per week endurance, 2 days per week power-related (sprints, low grades)
3. Strengthening and Flexibility Exercises:
    a. 2 days per week for each major region (core, forelimbs, pelvic limbs); minimum 48 hours between sessions for a given muscle group necessary except for core.
    b. 12 reps, 2 sets
    c. Stretching 2 days per week or after intense activity
    d. 3 sets X 10-15 second holds for each major muscle group, for a total of 60 seconds of stretching time for each muscle group.
4. Neuromuscular Training:
    a. 2 days per week of neuromuscular training
    b. Includes exercises that stimulate proprioception, plyometrics, agility, balance, dynamic stability and core stability
    c. 20 minutes per session
5. Exercise Monitoring in MWD Athletes. Evaluation of markers of fatigue and the approach of maximal aerobic and anaerobic effort have guided exercise prescriptions for specific individuals as

well as general recommendations for human athletes. Markers of fatigue may be subjective, such as the record of perceived exertion reported by the athlete, or objective, such as lactate, oxygen consumption, and heart rate. These measures have been less reliable indicators (as is the case with heart rate) or are very challenging to obtain in dogs. Additionally, there is a significant psychological component of fatigue in humans, which may also be true in dogs. However, many MWDs will ignore physiological cues in order to keep on task as a result of their high drive. Research is underway to further investigate markers of fatigue in dogs, but current qualitative cues that can be evaluated include reduced interest in work or in reward, slowing down voluntarily, panting with heavy respiratory effort, decreased alertness and elevated heart rate.

6. Exercise Progression in MWD Athletes.
    a. Frequency, intensity and duration are the main factors.
    b. Increase duration by 5-10 min per session every 1-2 weeks over 4-6 weeks initially.
    c. Physiologic adaptations will plateau after this time without progression of intensity and frequency.
    d. Increase intensity and frequency q 1-2 weeks additionally after this initial period.
    e. Resistance/strength training: increase load by 2-10% after two consecutive sessions of comfortable performance at 1-2 reps above current level. Weights on distal limbs of dogs should begin at 1-3% of body weight. Initial dragging weight should be equal to about 10% of the weight of the dog.
    f. Individuals with higher fitness levels can benefit from longer, less frequent sessions.
    g. Intensity of exercise is highly dependent upon individual factors, including cardiorespiratory fitness status, genetic profile, presence or absence of concurrent diseases, and age.
    h. Moderately-trained athletes may require training at 70-80% VO2 max to achieve physiological gains, based on the overload principle.
    i. Highly-trained athletes may require training at the near-maximal level (95-100% VO2 max).

CONDITIONING AND INJURY PREVENTION IN MWDS

The two most common serious orthopedic and neurologic injuries in MWDs evaluated at DODMWDVS are cranial cruciate ligament rupture and degenerative lumbosacral stenosis. Limited information is available to specifically demonstrate the effects of conditioning on working dogs to prevent these injuries; however, some evidence is beginning to emerge. There is significant evidence suggesting a role of conditioning in prevention of similar conditions in humans, although one must take pathophysiological differences between the species into consideration. Evidence demonstrates that conditioning may improve and prevent reoccurrence of low back pain in humans. Core strengthening exercises also were shown to improve function at specific working tasks and reduce pain in MWDs with mild lumbosacral pain (Henderson, 2014). Additionally, muscle involvement and conditioning has been an effective means of preventing other injuries in human athletes.

CHAPTER 10

BEHAVIORAL MEDICINE

BACKGROUND

Although behavioral medicine is a relatively new addition to specialty diagnosis and treatment in animals, behavioral pathology and treatment are by no means "new" or of minor significance clinically. For example, it has been estimated that of all dogs surrendered for euthanasia by pet owners, over 50 percent cited behavior problems as the major factor in their decision. Nationwide, this accounts for over 4,000,000 canine deaths annually, making behavioral pathology the single most significant cause of canine mortality. From another perspective, consider that eighty percent of dog owners polled reported behavioral problems with their pet.
1. Behavioral Problems in MWDs. Behavioral problems are one of the greatest causes of death and disability in MWDs. During the years 1990 through 1994, 131 MWDs were euthanized for the primary complaint of behavioral problems (cause of death cited on DD Form 1743). This accounted for over 10 percent of all euthanasia (greater than mortality attributed to all cancers). It is interesting to note that during this period, another 316 dogs were euthanized because of primary complaints of "age" and or "performance". It might be noted that "age" is not a disease, and "performance" often did not accompany fatal or debilitating medical disease demonstrated at necropsy.
2. Lost Service Attributable to Behavioral Problems. In addition to mortality, behavioral complaints also produce losses in availability of MWDs, in decrements and unreliability of MWD performance, and in increased training and retraining requirements for affected dogs. The scope of this loss has not yet been reliably estimated, but would include (for example) losses due to non-medically related self-trauma, prolonged kenneling of an MWD due to inability to safely handle a dog, and restriction of duty due to loss of certification or inability to work in a particular situation due to fearfulness, over-aggression, or inability to focus on task.

OVERVIEW OF DIAGNOSIS AND TREATMENT OF BEHAVIOR DISORDERS

Like other medical problems, behavioral problems may be diagnosed and treated with varying degrees of success, and just as there are preventive medical procedures available for infectious and environmentally related disease and parasitism, there are also predictive tools and preventive techniques available to decrease the incidence of behavioral pathology. For the purposes of an MWD, behavioral problems may be divided into four major categories. These categories are useful because they suggest etiology, diagnostic techniques, and potentially successful treatment options based on the category to which the behavioral difficulty belongs.
1. Normal behaviors which are unacceptable to people. Behaviors of this kind are species-typical and appropriate for the animal in context. An example of this type of behavioral problem would be an intact male dog, which displays urine marking inside a building. Urine marking is a normal behavior for an intact adult male dog and requires no contact with people or significant learning in order for it to be displayed. Behaviors, which fall into this category, are often sexually dimorphic, but almost always reflect strategies, which would be expected to be adaptive for survival, procreation, and/or feeding in a "wild" state (and so might be described as "instinctual" or "prepared" behaviors). These behaviors are often "released" (produced) by a particular stimulus or situation, but may be significantly strengthened, weakened, or modified through learning and experience. Diagnosis for

these problems would rule-out any medical condition modifying the expression of normal behaviors (an example would be testicular tumors or prostatitis affecting aggression or urine marking).

2. Behaviors, which occur as the result of a social learning and/or incomplete, ineffective, or inappropriate task- related training. These animals learn unacceptable behavioral strategies other than those, which would be expected as the norm. An example of a behavior problem, which might be the result of learning, would be "hand shyness", where an MWD would be presented for "fearfulness" of being touched or handled (may be the result of an association of handling with pain). Another example would be an MWD, which appeared to be able to detect a trained target odor, but would not reliably sit when it appeared to detect that odor (this behavioral problem might be produced by confusion produced during the initial training of the task or by insufficient training of the task to a point of mastery). Diagnosis for these problems would emphasize sensory or motor dysfunction, neurological or systemic disease that could all affect the performance of learned behavior or interfere with learning. Treatment for aberrant social behavior is often slow, and unrewarding (because of the presumed influence of inborn factors and the special nature of very early social learning). However, incomplete or unusual task-related learning may often be reversed with a slow, systematic retraining of the desired behaviors in conflict with the unacceptable response.

3. Behaviors produced by the presence of a primary medical disease. This third category of behavioral complaints would include primary neuroanatomical (trauma, vascular, mass-lesion), neurochemical (toxic, other), and neurophysiological (epileptiform, infectious) diseases, which would produce typical behavioral changes (especially changes in level of consciousness, motor activity, sensory ability, performance of learned behaviors, temperament), and might have localizing (lateral) signs. Other primary medical disease processes which could affect performance and produce typical or exaggerated behaviors would include metabolic disease, endocrinopathies, functional liver, kidney, or pancreatic disease, neoplasia, sensory degeneration, musculoskeletal disease (any painful process), nutritional and gastrointestinal diseases. A classic example is hepatic encephalopathy that can produce temperament changes, decreased level of consciousness, bizarre behavioral patterns, and apparent loss memory and recognition of familiar people, places, and tasks. Diagnosis for these problems involves a complete systemic evaluation with ancillary studies as indicated. Prognosis varies with the etiology and ability to treat or ameliorate the primary medical problem(s).

4. Atypical behaviors. There are two sub-categories of atypical (or pathological) behaviors: those, which occur secondarily to another behavioral problem, and those, which are "primary" in nature (have no identifiable medical or behavioral cause). Although these behaviors are often identified by exclusion from the other three categories, there are some general similarities in these behaviors. Pathological behaviors are usually not seen with any regularity in the "normal" dog, and would not normally be considered to be adaptive to survival, reproduction, or feeding. However, these behaviors may have an increased presence in a particular breed or line of dogs (suggesting an inherited component). Self-traumatic biting of an animal's flank in the absence of undercurrent medical disease or reinforced practice might be considered a pathological behavior. It might be primary, or it could be secondary to some other behavioral process such as boredom or anxiety. Likewise, spontaneous episodic non-selective aggression in the absence of epilepsy or other medical condition might also be included as a pathological behavior. Like idiopathic medical disease, it is reasonable to assume that most primary unlearned non-medical behavioral pathology probably is the result of real, but unidentified processes that are different in affected and unaffected animals. Pathological behaviors may be static, progressive, or episodic. Primary pathological behaviors are usually not significantly modified by experience or learning, and often have a guarded to poor prognosis. Secondary pathological behaviors may benefit significantly from training, medical therapy, and environmental changes which alter the primary behavioral problem and teach the animal new coping strategies.

COMMON PROBLEMS

Behavior problems in MWDs can be similar in many ways to the behavioral problems seen in a pet dog. However, some behavior problems appear to be more frequently encountered than others in MWDs. Common behavioral complaints with working dogs include:
1. Self-trauma to tail, lick granulomas, injured teeth (from chewing), self-trauma to skin.
2. Environmentally destructive behaviors such as digging and destructive chewing.
3. Reactivity, escape and avoidance (fearfulness) in response to sounds, situations, people, things.
4. Over-aggressiveness on task, to the handler, at kennel or other location or indiscriminate aggressiveness.
5. Under-aggressiveness during controlled aggression.
6. Performance failure (examples include poor behavioral control, poor basic obedience, poor control while on task, poor response to reward, poor substance discrimination.
7. Repetitive behaviors (may overlap self-trauma and over-activity) such as circling, pacing, and barking.
8. Over-activity affecting patient well-being and/or task performance.
9. Under-activity affecting patient well-being and/or task performance.
10. Poor attention negatively impacting task performance.
11. Adverse behavioral or cognitive changes such as loss of ability to perform tasks with previously demonstrated proficiency.
12. Failure to release reward objects or bite equipment on command.
13. Forging or excessive pulling on leash.
14. Canine Post-Traumatic Stress Disorder (C-PTSD). This collection of behavior problems is named separately, even though elements of the condition may include a range of behavioral problems. This diagnosis was created to account for adverse behavioral changes occurring during or after prolonged deployment to a combat environment; this factor is inclusionary. Excluded from the diagnosis of C-PTSD are those MWDs that either have behavioral signs historically before deployment or those that develop signs in the absence of deployment and a combat environment. Inclusionary behavioral signs are hyper-reactivity to environmental events (such as sounds, locations, people) and hyper-vigilance, attempts to escape and/or avoid situations that were previously neutral or positive, changes in rapport with the handler (positive or negative), and disruption of normal task performance. These behavioral signs are usually static or progressive; the presence of signs that improve significantly over time is normally an exclusionary factor. Please note that all patients suspected of having C-PTSD need to be referred to DODMWDVS Behavioral Medicine Service for evaluation, but this does not obviate the need for timely treatment.

EVALUATION OF BEHAVIORAL DISORDERS

These behavior complaints, like any physical complaint should first be evaluated medically. The minimum database for a behavioral complaint should include a medical and behavioral history (including a documented interview with the handler and supervisor, and review of the training record), a complete description (brief narrative, onset, progression) of the problem behavior(s), a current physical examination (including a mental status evaluation), complete neurological examination, and current hematology and blood chemistries. Behavioral history and descriptions of problem behaviors are best kept at a descriptive level. When possible, avoid using diagnostic terms or "jargon" to describe behaviors and the observations (e.g., "patient bit handler on hand when removed from home kennel" is much preferred for our use than, "kennel-protective behavior" - the latter does not specify the object of the aggressive behavior or the time of occurrence but does imply a diagnosis which may or may not be accurate).

MEDICAL CAUSES FOR BEHAVIOR PROBLEMS

Remember that unless proven otherwise, it is always wise to assume a medical condition underlies behavioral pathology. The following list is by no means exhaustive, but is presented to provide a starting point for behavioral diagnosis. Medical conditions that may produce behavioral changes include:
1. Neuroanatomical disease: traumatic, vascular, degenerative, neoplastic
2. Neurophysiological disease: epileptiform, neurochemical, functional
3. Toxicities: especially lead
4. Trauma: cranial, muscular
5. Endocrine disorders: thyroid, pancreatic, adrenal (e.g. hyperglycemia, hypoglycemia)
6. Hepatic disease
7. Renal disease
8. Meningoencephalopathies: especially steroid-responsive
9. Neoplasia
10. Metabolic and storage diseases
11. Infectious disease: bacterial, fungal, viral
12. Musculoskeletal disorders.
13. Any painful process

DIAGNOSIS AND INITIAL TREATMENT

Creating a working diagnosis and creating an initial treatment plan may or may not be beyond the scope of non-specialty care. However, case management for any behavioral case is usually accomplished by the attending VCO, so understanding of the basic principles of case management is highly beneficial. The working diagnosis usually identifies problem behavior(s) and desired behaviors for a problem. Case management involves four main principles.
1. Behavior modification involves identifying problem behaviors and making them less possible and less attractive, while identifying specific desired behaviors and increasing the probability of their production by selective reinforcement. A special case of behavior modification is Desensitization and Counter-Conditioning (DSCC), used to replace escape behaviors with rewarded alternatives. One example of a behavior modification program would be the use of "Clicker Training" to better gain and maintain an MWD's attention and increasing the reward behavior of a targeted trained behavior (such as, "heel").
2. Environmental changes (often enrichment) are physical steps taken to reduce the production and attractiveness of undesirable behaviors while at the same time making desired alternative behaviors more attractive. An important environmental management change is one that modifies the facility or interaction in order to mitigate any safety risks or welfare issues to the MWD or anyone interacting with the MWD. Examples of environmental change include the simple addition of environmental enrichment to MWD housing to help redirect destructive behavior and the use of taste and odor attractants and repellants to alter MWD focus on items in its environment.
3. Medical and adjunctive treatments are often used in a behavioral plan to address internal motivation of an MWD. For example, benzodiazepine and non-benzodiazepine anxiolytics may be used acutely to reduce apparent distress in an MWD experiencing moderate to severe signs of C-PTSD. For a moderate to severely distressed MWD that is incompletely managed by an anxiolytic, the use of a drug such as a beta blocker (e.g. propranolol) may benefit the patient by blunting the physiological component of a distress response. Less severely distressed patients may be treated with other anxiolytics and may also benefit from adjunctive therapy with nutraceutical products such as L-

Theanine or pheromone products such as Dog Appeasing Pheromone. Likewise, chronically distressed patients and those displaying non-adaptive repetitive behaviors may benefit from the use of a tricyclic antidepressant (TCA) or selective serotonin reuptake inhibitor (SSRI). Dispositionally overactive and inattentive MWDs may see marked improvement using CNS stimulants, and reactively aggressive MWDs may benefit from a serotonin reuptake inhibitor. A chart of commonly used medications for behavioral care along with indications and dosage guidance follows.

4. Follow-up and treatment modification. It is most beneficial to establish a desired outcome when the treatment plan is developed, using the increase or decrease of observable behaviors as indicators of progress. The use of progress sheets completed by the MWD handler serve not only to monitor progress but also to remind the handler of the specific objectives and training and environmental modifications in effect and why they are being used. Regular rechecks and review of progress are recommended. Treatment plan modifications and transition from active treatment to maintenance can better be accomplished if more objective behavioral outcomes are used to assess progress.

PREVENTATIVE STRATEGIES

Behavior problems or disorders may not be preventable, but there are strategies that can be incorporated into the daily schedule of an MWD with the purpose of increasing overall well-being and welfare, as well as take a proactive approach to some commonly seen issues. The kennel environment is not a natural, species-typical situation for a canine, nor are the tasks that MWDs are asked to perform. Additionally, MWDs receive a lot of

Table 1. Some Drugs Commonly used in the Treatment of Behavioral Problems in MWDs

Generic Name	Trade Name	Drug Class	Dosage
Antidepressants- Depression, reactivity, repetitive behavior, chronic distress			
Amitriptyline	Elavil	Tricyclic Antidepressant	1.0-2.0 mg/kg PO q12h
Buspirone	Buspar	Azapirone	0.5-2.0 mg/kg PO q12h to start
Clomipramine	Anafranil, Clomicalm*	Tricyclic Antidepressant	1.0-3.0 mg/kg PO q12h
Fluoxetine	Reconcile*	Selective Serotonin Reuptake Inhibitor	1.0-2.0 mg/kg PO q24h
Paroxetine	Paxil	Selective Serotonin Reuptake Inhibitor	1.0-1.5 mg/kg PO q24h
Sertraline	Zoloft	Selective Serotonin Reuptake Inhibitor	0.5-4.0 mg/kg PO q24h
Trazodone	Desyrel	Serotonin Antagonist & Reuptake Inhibitor	3.0-5.0 mg/kg PO q12h or PRN 1h before stressor exposure
Venlafaxine	Effexor	Selective Serotonin & Norepinephrine Reuptake Inhibitor	4.0-6.0 mg/kg PO q24h, then q 12h
Anxiolytics- Moderate to severe distress; panic episodes			
Alprazolam	Xanax	Benzodiazepine	0.02-0.1 mg/kg PO q4h (not to exceed 4mg q24h)
Lorazepam	Ativan	Benzodiazepine	0.02-0.5mg/kg q8-12h

Flumazenil (REVERSAL)	Anexate	Benzodiazepine antagnonist	0.5 mg/kg IV

CNS Depressants- Adjunctive for agitation, distress, neuropathic pain, phantom limb, seizure-related behavior problems

Gabapentin	Neurontin	Alpha-2 Ligand	3-10 mg/kg PO q 8-12h
Phenobarbital	Luminal	Barbiturate	2.0-6.0 mg/kg PO q8-12h
Pregabalin	Lyrica	Anticonvulsant	2.0 mg/kg PO q12h

CNS Stimulants-Overactivity with inattention

d-Amphetamine	Dexedrine		0.5-1.5 mg/kg PO am and noon
Methylphenidate	Ritalin		0.5-1.5 mg/kg PO am and noon

Cognitive Agents- Adjunct for compulsive disorder, Pain, Cognitive Dysfunction/Impairment

Memantine	Namenda	NMDA receptor antagonist	0.5 mg/kg q24h
Selegiline	Anipryl	MAOI	1.0 mg/kg PO q24h
Cyproheptadine (REVERSAL)	Periactin	Anticholinergic, antihistamine, antiserotonergic	0.3-2.0 mg/kg q12h

Supplements- Mild distress, Situational stress and environmentally-induced problems, Adjunct

Dog Appeasing Pheromone	Adaptil	Pheromone	As directed per collar, diffuser or spray
Alpha-casozepine	Zylkene	Nutraceutical	15 mg/kg divided, up to 25-30 mg/kg q24h
L-Theanine	Anxitane	Nutraceutical	100 mg/MWD PO q12h
L-Theanine and magnolia/philodendron/whey protein concentrate	Solliquin	Nutraceutical	10 mg/kg q12h
S-Adenosyl Methionine (SAMe)	Novifit	Nutraceutical	100 mg PO q24hr to q12h

Other Adjuncts- Decrease motor activity, reduce physiological distress, other

Acetylpromazine	Acepromazine	Phenothiazine neuroleptic	0.1-0.2 mg/kg PO q12h
Clonidine	Catapres	Alpha-2 Agonist	0.01-0.05 mg/kg PO PRN 1h before stressor exposure
Dexmedetomidine	Sileo*	Alpha-2 Agonist	125 mcg/m$_2$ (syringe dose by weight) to buccal mucosa 1h before stressor exposure
Diphenhydramine	Benadryl	Antihistamine	1.0-2.0 mg/kg PO q12h PRN
Hydroxyzine	Atarax	Antihistamine	1.0 mg/kg PO q8h PRN
Propranolol	Inderal	Beta-Blocker	10-20 mg/MWD PO q8-12h

*FDA Approved Medications for: Canine Separation Anxiety (Clomicalm®, Reconcile®), Canine Cognitive Dysfunction (Anipryl®), Canine Noise Phobia (Sileo®)

handling and veterinary care, whether it is biannual physicals, health certificates, specialty care, or general husbandry through the MWD kennel. Due to the frequency of these interactions, and the history of how we train and house the MWDs, it is important not to become complacent with these practices and to continually

strive to assess and address MWD well-being and welfare. The following information serves to provide AVS personnel with strategies for prevention or reduction of behavior problems specific to the MWD environment and exposure.
1. Environmental Enrichment. The ASPCA defines enrichment as "additions to an animal's environment with which the animal voluntarily interacts and, as a result, experiences improved physical and/or psychological health." Keeping this definition in mind, designing an enrichment program for an MWD kennel must be specific to each MWD's preferences and personality, which may take trial and error and creativity to develop an appropriate plan. Aside from MWD preference, key factors when considering enrichment items are safety, sanitation, appropriateness, and novelty. An enrichment item must be safe for the MWD to manipulate and interact with, and is not going to cause a physical injury or medical emergency. For example, some MWDs can chew through a Jolly Ball, and they can cause cuts and scrapes from the chewed edges as well as foreign body obstruction when the pieces are swallowed. Sanitation is also a key consideration. Enrichment items that are used for tactile manipulation by MWDs must be adequately sanitized between uses and between MWDs. Appropriateness of the enrichment item relates to safety, but also to the age and personality of the MWD. For example, a highly focused MWD should not have a laser pointer used as an enrichment item. Laser pointers are not appropriate because they build frustration and fixation in an already high-drive canine, and historically have caused MWDs to develop compulsive disorders. Additionally, a MWD with a history of food sensitivity should have any gustatory enrichment items approved as appropriate through their veterinarian. The last consideration is novelty. Rotation of enrichment strategies and combinations is important, to maintain the MWD's interest as well as provide cognitive challenges. Infrequent rotation or lack of novel item introduction will result in lack of interaction or interest in the enrichment. The main categories of enrichment and some examples of each are listed below. These are not all-inclusive, and many can be combined:
    a. Social: Handler interaction through exercise, physical conditioning, and husbandry training. Conspecific interaction (dog to dog) is not a typical practice currently, but is possible if care and supervision is performed with any introductions or interactions (*Conspecific interaction as enrichment MUST be approved through appropriate veterinary and kennel chains of command, and should not be performed without a thorough safety assessment).
    b. Cognitive: aka "Brain Games". Cognitive enrichment includes any task-related games, such as Find It, commercial puzzle toys or feeders, as well as the MWDs daily working tasks.
    c. Sensory
        i. Olfactory: Use of spices, scents/extracts, or synthetic animal scents as distractors during training or in the kennel are interesting for MWDs and can amplify the difficulty level of their training tasks by requiring that they continue to search for aids despite the interesting scents. Scents can also be used for calming effects, such as peppermint, lavender, or chamomile.
        ii. Pheromone: Synthetic pheromones are available to promote calming, and come in multiple forms (collars, diffusers, wipes, sprays).
        iii. Visual: Bubbles, animations, wall colors, and even the kennel setup and how the MWD visualizes their surroundings and neighbors can be used as enrichment. As stated before, avoidance of reflections or focused light is recommended.
        iv. Auditory: Music or structured sounds can be used for desensitization, to drown out external noise (e.g., nighttime exercises on the installation when the MWD needs rest), and for general relaxation. Examples include soft classical music, canine-specific music, nature sounds, etc.
        v. Gustatory: Dental chews (brittle, crumbly and easily digestible), food-stuffed tactile objects, ice-blocks (layered frozen treat items), frozen popsicle treats (canned food

or other approved items such as peanut butter, yogurt, canned pumpkin, appropriate fruits or vegetables), and food-reward training. Be creative for patients with motility issues or ingredient-specific diets. Many times, mini marshmallows, carrots, toasted oat cereal, or specialty commercial treats can be used and are palatable.

      vi. <u>Tactile</u>: Balls, tugs, tires, pools, digging pits, brushes, and petting

2. Cooperative Care. The idea of cooperative care is not new, and is widely used throughout zoo and marine mammal medicine, as well as with the Fear FreeSM movement in veterinary practices. The overall purpose is to improve the way we handle MWDs to reduce fear, anxiety, and stress in the veterinary clinic. The reduction of the physiological and emotional arousal in the MWDs leads to reduced aggression, increased safety, and overall improvement in MWD and personnel welfare. Knowledge of canine body language, how to mitigate our human body language, and tools and techniques to make veterinary care positive, predictable, and low-stress are all important aspects of cooperative care. Examples of cooperative care techniques are training staff to recognize fear and stress, creating a pre-visit plan for historically fearful/aggressive MWDs, using safe but low-stress restraint, and teaching voluntary procedures that aid in husbandry tasks and veterinary procedures. Husbandry tasks include voluntary muzzle placement, offering specific body parts for nail trims or ear cleanings, or simply a relaxed "wait" during a bath. Veterinary procedures, such as blood draws, ultrasound, and physical exams can be facilitated by teaching body targeting and voluntary presentations, such as presenting a leg for blood draw or opening the mouth for visual exam.

3. Cruelty, Abuse, or Neglect of a MWD. Veterinary personnel are advocates for the humane care of animals, and MWDs are no exception. Animal abuse, neglect, abandonment, and bestiality are punishable under UCMJ.

    a. The primary recommended method for MWD training is inducive training (encouragement of desirable behaviors) and is not compulsive training (verbal or physical force to coerce a desirable behavior or to discourage an undesirable behavior). The MWD Handler training program does, however, include the use of compulsive training methods. These rules are outlined for MWD Handlers in their curriculum, and it is important for them to understand what that entails and when its use is not appropriate, and veterinary personnel can use our knowledge of canine behavior and welfare, to assist in advocating for the MWDs if these rules are not followed.

    b. If a Veterinary Services employee (Active Duty, NAF, GS, etc) witnesses or highly suspects an act of intentional cruelty, abuse, or neglect in an MWD, it must be reported through the appropriate channels. For minor concerns regarding poor husbandry, inappropriate handling, failure to comply with veterinary care, inappropriate feeding or housing, etc., the VCO should be notified in order to attempt resolution of the issue directly with VTF staff, handlers, or Kennel Masters. For major concerns, or for lack of resolution with minor concerns, the commander and supporting 64F should be notified, as well as the MWD chain of command. For urgent and severe incidents, the commander and installation law enforcement should be immediately contacted.

    c. If there is ever a question regarding appropriate handling or care of a MWD, or possible handling-related injuries, keep in mind that as veterinary professionals, you are mandated to take action on any suspicion of neglect, abuse, or mistreatment of any animal.

CONSULTATION AND REFERRAL INFORMATION

Consultation for behavior problems may be accomplished with the Behavioral Medicine Section at the DODMWDVS (dog.consult@us.af.mil) or individually through a 64F Veterinary Behaviorist.

1. Consultation. The consultation service provides diagnostic assistance and the setup of a field treatment plan for a behavioral problem. The diagnostic plan might include further medical

evaluation and ancillary studies which may be performed by the referring VCO. The process involves review of the above materials, interview with the referring VCO, handler, and KM, assessment and recommendations for further medical evaluation and or treatment, and a written behavioral plan for incorporation in the medical records, the patient's training record and for use by the handler and KM. Behavioral consultation should be considered an ongoing process. Documentation of diagnosis, treatment plans, ability to implement the plans, and efficacy estimates are all crucial in providing feedback to improve the process.
2. Referrals may be accepted for select behavior problems which cannot be resolved in the field, and which require further evaluation and/or treatment attempts at JBSA Lackland. Referrals are accepted only with pre- approval on a TDY basis. The primary reason for referral is to obtain ancillary studies not available in the field, better observational diagnosis and evaluation by medical and training staff, and for the evaluation of more complex treatment modalities. Coordination with training staff at the 341 TRS and TDY for the handler is normally required for referrals. Referrals to 64F Veterinary Behaviorists in other locations can be coordinated based on local policies.
3. In order to expedite the process, it is useful to provide the following information before the consultation is accomplished:
    a. DA Form 7593 with behavioral history summary for MWD from dog handler and KM with a listing of problems, duration and progression of each, correction attempts and detail of success and failure.
    b. Pertinent e-notes/SF 600s
    c. Digital video of problem behavior, if possible
    d. Copy of last periodic physical.
    e. Copies of recent blood work, to include CBC, blood chemistry profile, baseline cortisol, thyroid profile.
    f. Copy of Master Problem List.
    g. Copy of the recent SF 600 entries regarding consultation with history, diagnostic steps, treatment attempted and evaluation, working assessment, patient status and current plan.
4. Point of contact for further information is:

  Chief, Behavioral Medicine
  LTC Daniel E Holland MWD Hospital 1219 Knight Street, Bldg 7602
  JBSA-Lackland, TX 78236-5631
  Phone: (210) 671-7101
  Fax: (210) 671-2308
  DSN Prefix 473
  E-mail: dog.consult@us.af.mil

CHAPTER 11

DISPOSITION

DEFINITION

Disposition encompasses all aspects of evaluating an MWD to determine if it should be declared excess to the needs of the DOD. An MWD may be declared excess because of training deficiencies, medical problems, or both. If an MWD is declared excess to DOD requirements, it will be adopted, transferred to a non-DOD law enforcement agency, or euthanized. Elimination of MWDs from DOD service requires careful evaluation of the reasons for elimination by the owning unit commander, KM and supporting VCO. Disposition requires a detailed physical examination of the MWD, diagnostic testing as appropriate to confirm clinical suspicions, detailed documentation of existing medical problems by the supporting VCO, formal review of medical documents by the supporting 64F, and timely submission of the disposition packet through all echelons involved.

PROCESS

Applicable regulations for MWDs are AFI 31-126(IP)/AR700-81/OPNAVINST 5585.3A/ MCO 10570.1A (Military Working Dog Program) and AR 40-905/AFI 48-131/SECNAVINST 6401.1A (Veterinary Health Services). Implementation of these regulations was modified by Public Law 106-446, amendment to Title 10 United States Code Section 2583, which requires evaluation of excess MWDs for possible adoption or law enforcement transfer.

1. Initiation of the disposition process is the responsibility of the KM. Veterinary Corps Officers and supporting 64Fs have key roles and are required to provide medical evaluations for all MWDs under consideration for elimination, even when the MWD is being submitted for non-medical reasons.
2. Training related dispositions can be evaluated and initiated at any time during an MWD's service. This is initiated by the KM and does require VCO evaluation to ensure there is not an underlying medical condition likely causing the training failure.
3. When a VCO identifies a medical condition that they feel requires medical disposition, they should consult their supporting 64F. After it is determined that a recommendation for medical disposition is warranted, the attending VCO will, in writing, notify the KM and owning unit commander of the recommendation and make the MWD CAT 4. The kennel is generally expected to begin the disposition process once an MWD has been designated as CAT 4. There are rare instances when an MWD that is CAT 4 may be retained in service such as at locations where there is a shortage of MWDs or at installations from which MWDs do not deploy (e.g., USMC dogs not assigned to Marine Expeditionary Forces). If there is a health and welfare concern for continued service, this will be discussed with the owning unit command.
4. Age-related performance decrement. Evaluation of aging MWDs with performance decrement is challenging. As expected, as MWDs age, they become less capable of performing at the same level of energy and stamina. VCOs must objectively evaluate aging MWDs to determine if there are bona fide medical reasons for performance decrement or if performance is deteriorating simply because the dog is aging. Note that MWDs are never eliminated from DOD service simply based on age. Recent changes within the DOD MWD program now permit KMs to submit MILSTRIP requisitions for any MWD when it reaches 9 years of age. However, this is not equivalent to downgrading a medical deployment category or for automatically beginning the disposition process. It is simply a logistical

tool to alert Service and major subordinate command Program Managers of possible replacement needs (this change led to cessation of use of the "12- month veterinarian memorandum"). As it is more difficult for KMs to remove dogs with training issues than for medical reasons, a common practice is for MWD unit personnel to convince a VCO to recommend medical elimination for an MWD that is developing problems detecting or completing patrol duties. To mitigate this 'short cut' tendency, evaluate MWDs carefully over time and objectively. If definitive medical issues develop that truly make an MWD unfit for duty or warrant changing its medical deployment category to CAT 4, initiation of medical elimination is warranted. Proceed with medical elimination if the VCO diagnoses the performance decrement as due to specific medical issues (e.g., heart disease, degenerative lumbosacral disease). Recommend the KM consider training elimination for dogs that have performance decrement believed due to aging, but that lack bona fide medical issues as the cause. Do not support requests for medical elimination simply because the dog is not performing to standard unless true underlying medical causes are detected.

5. The decision to begin the disposition process should be made after discussion and agreement between the owning unit commander, KM and supporting VCO, though such mutual consent is not a requirement. Note that VCOs may not impede the disposition process if they do not agree with the KM or accountable unit commander. There will be times when a KM and VCO disagree as to fitness for duty. In such cases, VCOs will simply provide their required portions to the KM for submission, ensuring their duty to reflect their professional objective medical opinion in their memorandum to the commander and other supporting documents. VCOs are expected to objectively evaluate MWDs medically, and are the sole authority for assessing medical fitness for duty. VCOs should not be unduly influenced by KMs or handlers when making medical assessments. Objectively evaluate the dog, in conjunction with the history from the dog's handler and KM, and make a determination of fitness for duty based on this information.

6. Regardless of the underlying reason for elimination, there is a standardized process for routing disposition requests.
    a. Initially, at the unit level, the KM and VCO prepare specific documents, defined in section 11-3.
    b. These documents are then forwarded and reviewed by the supporting 64F, who assesses suitability for adoption and completes a 64F disposition MFR.
    c. All supporting disposition documents are then returned to the KM, who forwards the packet through the MWD unit's chain of command and program managers.
        i. The Major Command (MACOM/MAJCOM) MWD Program Manager (e.g., Pacific Command, Central Command) reviews the request and forwards approved recommendation for elimination to the Service MWD Program Manager (Army, Air Force, Navy, Marine Corps).
        ii. The Service Program Manager then forwards approved requests for elimination to the DOD MWD Disposition Board for review.
    d. The Disposition Board evaluates the packet, and forwards its recommendation to the 341 TRS Commander for review. An MWD can only be declared excess to DOD requirements by the 341 TRS Commander. The 341 TRS Commander will declare the MWD:
        i. Excess to DOD requirements (unable to perform in any capacity as a military working dog),
        ii. Not excess to DOD requirements (retained by the unit or transferred to another DOD unit that may be able to use the dog)
        iii. Suitable for use as a Training Aid (returned to the 341 TRS for use in training student handlers).

7. Once an MWD has been declared excess, the accountable MWD unit commander is authorized to

make final disposition decision (i.e., adoption, transfer, euthanasia). VCOs must understand that the final decision for adoption, law enforcement transfer, or euthanasia is made by the accountable MWD unit commander.

DOCUMENTATION REQUIREMENTS

Disposition packet requests must contain the following documents, provided by the responsible parties listed as follows:
1. Kennel Master:
    a. Behavioral Testing Video (formerly Bite Muzzle Video). Part 1 is required of all MWDs and part 2 is required of aggression trained MWDs.
    b. Observation Form for Video Behavioral Testing
    c. Adoption Suitability Checklist (completed in conjunction with the VCO).
    d. Disposition Recommendation Letter signed by the Accountable Unit Commander.
2. Supporting Veterinary Corps Officer:
    a. Training elimination. The only document required from the VCO to support a training elimination is a formal memorandum for record addressed to the MWD unit commander. This memorandum must: 1) state the current fitness for duty (e.g., fit for duty, unfit for duty) and deployment category of the MWD, 2) include an assessment of adoptability based on experiences in the VTF when handling the MWD, 3) list all active medical problems (whether contributing to training elimination or not), 4) summarize training deficiencies based on input by the KM, and 5) include contact information for the supporting VCO, to include a valid e-mail address. They must also get a SF 513 (modified), Bite Muzzle Video/Adoption Suitability Consult Form from their supporting 64F. If medical problems are identified that could reasonably be expected to contribute to training deficiencies in any major way, then the VCO will submit all documents required for medical elimination, as described below, even if the KM is submitting the elimination request due to training deficiencies. Note that MWDs with confirmed or suspected C- PTSD or other atypical behavior problems will be processed as medical eliminations.
    b. Medical elimination.
        i. Memorandum for Record. This memorandum will contain the following information: 1) statement clarifying reasons for medical elimination, with specific diagnosis listed and results of major medical diagnostic procedures that support elimination; 2) statement of fitness for duty and medical deployment category; 3) assessment of adoption suitability based on VCO's experience; 4) listing of all active medical problems (whether or not they contribute to the overall medical problem for which dog is being recommended for elimination); 5) a statement that they have consulted with a 64F (with that specialists' name included); and 6) a valid .mil email address for the VCO. See Appendix F for an example memorandum.
        ii. DD Form 1829, Report of Physical Examination or electronic equivalent. Once a decision is made between the KM and the supporting VCO that medical elimination will be requested, a formal elimination medical examination will be performed and documented on DD Form 1829, with Block 5 checked for OTHER and MEDICAL ELIMINATION entered in the block as the purpose of the exam. VCOs will examine the MWD to document the full extent of all medical problems and to provide an overall assessment of medical fitness for duty and suitability for adoption. Note that only this DD Form 1829 should be included; prior DD Forms 1829 are no longer required. All medical problems must be clearly addressed on the

form, especially the problem for which medical elimination is being recommended.
   iii. DD Form 2619, Master Problem List or electronic equivalent. The MPL will list all active problems, especially the problem for which medical elimination is being recommended.
   iv. SF Form 600, Chronological Record of Medical Care or e-notes. Only from the 6-month period preceding packet submission. SF 600s describing working bite quarantines throughout the MWDs service are also required.
   v. Any relevant supporting laboratory tests, imaging reports, pathology reports, behavior consults, or other significant diagnostic test results. Only those reports with direct relevance to the active problem for which medical elimination is being recommended should be included. Do not include other documents.
3. Veterinary Clinical Specialist (64F):
   a. SF 513 (modified), Adoption Suitability Consult Form based on the Behavioral Testing Video.
   b. Memorandum for Record (for dogs being recommended for medical elimination only). This memorandum will contain the following information: 1) statement clarifying reasons for medical elimination, with specific diagnosis listed and results of major medical diagnostic procedures that support elimination; 2) statement of fitness for duty and medical deployment category; 3) assessment of adoption suitability based on VCO's experience; 4) a statement concurring or not concurring with the supporting VCO's recommendation and for or against elimination for medical reasons; and 5) a valid .mil email address for the 64F. See Appendix G for an example memorandum.
4. Disposition packet submission:
   a. VCOs should not send their portions of the packet directly to the Disposition Coordinator or the DODMWDVS. It is incumbent upon the VCO to work closely with the KM to ensure all required parts of the packet are assembled and forwarded in a single submission through the owning MWD program chain of command.
   b. VCOs, supporting 64Fs, and KMs should utilize the AMRDEC SAFE website (https://safe.amrdec.army.mil/safe2/Default.aspx) to forward information to each other.
5. Suspenses. Once the decision has been made to initiate disposition proceedings on an MWD, veterinary personnel must promptly complete the following requirements. The VCOs will be consulting with supporting 64Fs during the medical evaluation for elimination such that delays for additional diagnostics will not be necessary once the decision is made to recommend medical elimination.
   a. Supporting VCO recommended medical elimination to owning unit and/or received notification from the KM of request for elimination, within 15 calendar days:
      i. Conduct an examination of the MWD and complete a DD 1829.
      ii. Prepare the Memorandum for Record to the unit commander.
      iii. Complete the veterinary portion of the Adoption Suitability Checklist.
      iv. Review all required forms and videos for completeness.
      v. Upload MFR and Adoption Suitability Checklist to the electronic VHR.
      vi. Forward all documents and videos to the supporting 64F.
   b. Veterinary Clinical Specialist (64F), upon receipt of documents from the supporting VCO, within 15 calendar days:
      i. Prepare the Memorandum for Record and upload into the electronic VHR.
      ii. Review the Behavioral Testing Video and prepare the Adoption Suitability Consult Form.
      iii. Upload MFR and Consult Form to the electronic VHR.

  iv. Forward all documents to the supporting VCO.
 c. Supporting VCO, upon receipt of the SF 513 (modified), Adoption Suitability Consult Form and Memorandum for Record from the supporting 64F will forward all documents to the KM within 5 calendar days.
 d. Supporting VCO or 68T follow-ups with KM monthly on routing status of medical elimination packet.

MWD TRANSFER/ADOPTION GUIDELINES

MWD transfer and adoption was authorized by legislation late in 2000, known as "The Robby Law." Now as part of Title 10, United States Code, Section 2583, the DOD may declare excess MWDs available for adoption to former handlers of particular MWDs or other individuals capable of humanely caring for these animals or for transfer to law enforcement agencies outside DOD.

1. To be eligible for transfer/adoption, an MWD must first be declared excess to the needs of DOD as determined by the 341 TRS commander, not just the local installation.
2. In order to assist the local commander's decision to transfer/adopt or not transfer/adopt a dog out, the supporting VCO completes the veterinary portion of the Adoption Suitability Checklist. This checklist allows the VCO and KM to make an overall assessment as to the adoptability of the MWD. The KM forwards the completed checklist to the unit commander for their review to assist in making a determination regarding adoptability.
3. MWDs are considered medically ineligible for transfer or adoption when they have a condition that is substantially debilitating and/or threatens life or limb. Mild to moderate degenerative arthritis, mild ataxia/discomfort associated with lumbosacral stenosis or compensated renal, cardiac or hepatic disease are not disqualifying. MWDs are considered behaviorally ineligible if they exhibit aggressive behavior that poses an obvious and substantial threat to people or other animals. Consult supporting 64Fs or DODMWDVS for clarification in specific cases.
4. The owning unit commander or designee interviews potential transferring/adopting individuals to ensure that they understand the responsibility for proper and humane care for a former MWD. This includes but is not limited to: medical care, proper feeding, housing, animal husbandry and adequate supervised exercise. The transferring/adopting individual must also be able to physically control the dog for its own safety and that of other animals and humans. Prospective transferring/adopting persons must understand the potential for an MWD to inflict severe physical injury with minimal warning due to a lifetime of training. The individual must then sign a liability release (covenant not to sue) taking full responsibility for any and all actions of the former MWD and accepting financial responsibility for veterinary medical care of any existing and future conditions.
5. Once the owning unit commander authorizes transfer/adoption of the MWD, the VCO:
 a. In case of adoption only, neuters the MWD; transfers to law enforcement can waive the neuter.
 b. Completes a dental prophylaxis if needed.
 c. Administers or dispenses one month's worth of heartworm and flea & tick control treatment/products.
 d. Updates immunizations if necessary.
 e. Prepares one month's worth of medication (if dog is on chronic administration, i.e. thyroid supplement, anti-inflammatory prescription drug, etc.) for new owner. These medications will be considered the same as for an active MWD (i.e. reimbursement to NAF from appropriated funds). A written prescription may also be given to allow for refills if clinically indicated.
 f. Close out the medical record. The VCO enters the transferring agency or adopter identity,

address and telephone number as the final entry to the SF 600. In addition, copies of all supporting disposition documentation should be placed in the medical record.

    g. Prepares a transfer/ adoption medical record for the new owner. At a minimum, it should include copies of the most current: DD1829, at least the previous six months SF 600, DD 1741 (Immunization Record), and DD 2619 (Master Problem List) or electronic equivalents. Also include, any medical documentation regarding the MWDs pertinent medical condition to include the latest diagnostic results and radiographic images. The deployment VHR can be used as the adoption medical record.

    h. Mails the Permanent VHR and supporting radiographs/media to the DODMWDVS immediately. DOD MWD Record Repository, 1219 Knight Street, Bldg 7602, JBSA-Lackland, TX 78236. Shipment of records via routine/ground methods. Transfers the completed electronic medical record to DODMWDVS.

6. Former MWDs belonging to eligible DOD health care beneficiaries (i.e. personnel that may be cared for within DOD MTFs) are eligible to receive the same level of care as other POAs through US Army VTFs. Charges will be applied and become due just as occurs in the care of other POAs. Former MWDs belonging to persons not eligible for DOD health care within DOD MTFs are not eligible for care at VTFs. If euthanasia is performed on a retired MWDs within a VTF it is highly recommended that a complete or cosmetic necropsy be performed and the samples submitted to JPC as outlined in chapter 12. This will allow the Veterinary Corps the ability to gather valuable information from these canine heroes that could be utilized for future medical developments to enhance care for both MWDs as well as Service members.

7. Disposition and adoption inquiries to veterinary personnel. The responsibility for the overall disposition and adoption process lies within the owning MWD unit and branch of service. As such, veterinary personnel receiving questions regarding MWDs and adoptions should redirect queries to the 341 Disposition Coordinator at JBSA- Lackland, TX, mwd.adoptions@us.af.mil or 210-671-3153 (DSN: 473).

CHAPTER 12

NECROPSY AND PATHOLOGY SUPPORT

ACTIONS PRIOR TO NECROPSY

Regardless of cause (e.g, naturally, due to disease, or via euthanasia) MWDs will undergo a complete necropsy as soon as possible IAW AR 40-905 and TB MED 283. MWD necropsy and surgical specimens will be submitted to the Joint Pathology Center (JPC) for diagnosis, database entry and archiving; all samples must be submitted with a Veterinary Consultation Request Form. Prior to elective/non-emergent euthanasia the Veterinary Health Record MUST document appropriate workup and assessment of problems to support euthanasia. Prior to non-emergent euthanasia the supporting 64F MUST be consulted. Documentation of the 64F consult should be placed in the VHR. Ensure the final SF 600 or e-note entry states the specific reason for death or euthanasia and also list this as the final entry on the Master Problem List.

1. MWD necropsy and surgical specimens must be submitted to the JPC or Public Health Command-Europe, Laboratory Sciences, Biological Analysis Division. Should a civilian veterinarian perform an MWD necropsy, the protocol described in the TB MED 283 should be followed. Relevant clinical information and/or treatments, medications, and summaries provided by the civilian veterinarian will be transferred into the electronic VHR as soon as possible following death.
2. Know what to look for before starting the necropsy. A thorough review of the clinical findings and history are prerequisites for an intelligently planned necropsy. Enter all clinically relevant data to include laboratory test results, radiographic interpretations, and a medical summary into the DD Form 1626. When applicable, gross necropsy lesions should be captured via digital photography and images submitted along with the tissues.
3. A list of instruments, equipment and supplies for an MWD postmortem examination is located in TB MED
4. 283. Timely necropsy and specimen collection cannot be performed without the proper equipment (e.g. bone saw for spinal cord removal). Acquire this equipment through the appropriate chain of command or arrange for use of equipment through the local MTF. It may be possible to establish a MOU with the local MTF to use their fully equipped autopsy room for MWD necropsies. Otherwise, select an adequate facility and/or location with the ability to keep formalin fumes to a minimum.
5. Verify the identification of the MWD scheduled for euthanasia. Microchip scan is the most accurate method of identification as tattoos can often become illegible over time.
6. Prepare DD Form 1743, Death Certificate of a Military Dog and DD Form 1626, Veterinary Necropsy Report. Also complete the current JPC Veterinary Consultation Request Form (JPC VET Form), currently available at http://www.jpc.capmed.mil/docs/vet_consultation_request_form.pdf. Enter a summary of the medical or behavioral problems leading to death or euthanasia. "Euthanasia" is NOT acceptable as the only cause of death on the death certificate. In addition to euthanasia, the condition(s) leading to the decision to euthanize the dog must also be listed in the cause of death area of the DD Form 1743.
7. Blood and urine specimens must be taken prior to any euthanasia IAW TB MED 283. Process these samples locally, as with any other clinical specimen. Do NOT send fluids (e.g., whole blood, serum, urine), fecal samples, bacterial culture samples, uro/choleliths (stones), and the like for processing at the JPC. Do NOT send brain tissue for rabies testing to JPC. Rabies testing is performed at the FADL and most state veterinary diagnostic laboratories.
8. Enclose a copy of the laboratory findings with the necropsy report. For animals found dead, enclose a

copy of the most recent ante-mortem laboratory findings. Blood and urine may be sampled and evaluated from recently dead animals, although it must be clearly noted in the record that the samples were taken post-mortem.
9. If the MWD is euthanized, verify death. Compliance with the most recent set of AVMA Guidelines for the Euthanasia of Animals is required. Be mindful of using drugs that may alter clinicopathologic data prior to necropsy. Do not euthanize an animal in the same room that necropsies or autopsies are routinely performed as the residual smell of blood and formalin may cause undue distress to the animal.

NECROPSY

TB MED 283 is the guideline for prescribed necropsy method. A necropsy is performed to identify cause of death and to identify incidence and severity of disease processes in all MWDs.
1. Forms. The forms used and regulations governing necropsy of the MWD are:
    a. TB MED 283, Veterinary Necropsy Protocol for Military Working Dogs and Submission Guidelines for Necropsy and Surgical Biopsy Specimens.
    b. DD Form 1626, Veterinary Necropsy Report.
    c. DD Form 1743, Death Certificate of a Military Working Dog.
    d. JPC VET Form/or online entry form, Joint Pathology Center Veterinary Consultation Request Form.
    e. Downloadable versions of current forms are available at the JPC website, http://www.jpc.capmed.mil/consultation.asp.
2. Equipment and supplies required for necropsy.
    a. Necropsy instruments, equipment and supplies - see TB MED 283 for complete list.
    b. Approximately 12 liters of fresh 10% neutral buffered formalin.
    c. Always wear appropriate personal protective equipment (PPE) to include gowns, gloves, and eye protection; avoid exposure to formalin fumes via the use of fume hoods and/or portable respirators (e.g.; PAPR).
3. Specimen Collection. The proper handling of the animal and tissues before, during, and after the necropsy is imperative to ensure accurate histopathologic results. Refrigerate the carcass if necropsy will be delayed more than 1-2 hours after death. Freeze remains as a last resort and only if refrigeration is not an option. Be prepared to collect and submit to the appropriate laboratory a variety of specimens for histology, cytology, microbiology, and toxicology.
    a. Regardless of the type of specimen collected, all specimen containers must be properly labelled with the MWD's name and alphanumeric tattoo identification.
    b. Collection and fixation of tissue specimens for histologic examination.
        i. Collect a complete set of tissues for histology (see TB MED 283 for list of tissues).
        ii. In addition to tissues listed, collect tissue specimens from all lesions and/or suspected lesions. Note additional tissues collected in the Remarks section of block 36 of the DD 1626.
        iii. Avoid mishandling tissues which may result in artifacts.
        iv. Collect thin (0.5 cm thick) tissue specimens to ensure adequate fixation. Bread loaf larger specimens to allow thorough fixation while retaining overall tissue architecture.
        v. Collect and fix eyes, brain, spinal cord and heart in their entirety. Open the chambers of the heart as outlined in TBMED 283 to allow for proper fixation. At minimum, perfuse the right cranial lung lobe (along with any other affected lobes) with formalin and submit (see TB MED 283 for instructions on specific tissues).

vi. Collect eyes and bone marrow samples early in the necropsy procedure as these tissues are especially sensitive to autolysis. A small amount of formalin (0.25 mL) may be injected into the vitreous humor to aid in fixation.
4. Cytology
    a. Bone marrow smears and cytology specimens must be thoroughly air dried before methanol fixation. If methanol fixation is not available, unfixed, air-dried specimens should be submitted.
    b. Always prepare and submit at least two stained and two unstained specimens.
    c. Never expose cytologic specimens to formalin, as artifactual alteration will result which may preclude definitive diagnoses.
    d. When submitting bone marrow specimens for evaluation, it is helpful to include cytological specimens of peripheral blood (i.e. blood smears) collected at the same time as the bone marrow.
5. Microbiology and Toxicology
    a. If applicable, collect samples for culture and/or toxicologic analysis IAW TB MED 283.
    b. Samples collected for culture and toxicological analysis must be processed by civilian veterinary diagnostic laboratories.
    c. Do NOT send samples for microbiology or toxicology to the JPC as delays may strongly influence
6. results.
7. Photography. All necropsies should be accompanied with digital photographs. Photographs taken during the necropsy with a digital camera can be submitted through ROVR, on CD/DVD, or printed in color.
8. Tissue fixation procedures.
    a. Fix all tissues in large, wide-mouth containers.
    b. It is not necessary to separately label all submitted tissues; however, small tissues and/or tissues with similar appearances (e.g.; lymph nodes), tissues requiring left and right identification (e.g.; kidney), and other tissues requiring specific identification (masses) should be labeled separately.
    c. Use a ratio of 10 times the volume of fixative to volume of tissue.
    d. Change formalin after 24 hrs. Formalin fix tissues for a minimum of 48 hours, prior to packaging for shipment to the JPC; formalin fix brain samples for a minimum of 1 week prior to shipping.
9. Tissue packaging and shipment procedures. Package the specimens IAW TB MED 283 to prevent leakage or breakage. Do not ship tissues immersed in formalin inside plastic (e.g., ziplock bags) or glass (e.g., food jars) containers.
    a. After adequate fixation, wrap tissues in formalin-soaked gauze sponges, and double-bag in heavy-duty plastic bags and, if available, vacuum/heat-seal wrapped tissue specimens. Ensure proper vacuum sealing to prevent the crushing of tissue.
    b. Ship materials in a sturdy cardboard box lined with two heavy-duty plastic bags. Use adequate packing material to ensure that specimens remain stable during shipment and do not contact the walls of the box. Close each plastic bag securely and seal the box with strapping or shipping tape.
    c. Label all specimens IAW TB MED 283. When shipping specimens from more than one dog, ensure that each specimen is clearly labeled and correlates with the respective included paperwork.
    d. Do not ship cytological specimens (e.g. bone marrow smears, fine needle aspirates) with formalin-fixed tissues. Formalin fumes may render cytological samples non-diagnostic. Ship

samples in a separate package using cardboard or plastic microscope slide mailers. Ensure to annotate on the JPC VET Form, Veterinary Consultation Request that two separate packages have been sent (i.e. part 1 or 2 and part 2 of 2). Include a copy of the paperwork (tracking numbers) for both shipments on the Veterinary Consultation Request Form.

e. Send fixed tissue specimens, the completed and signed Necropsy Report (DD Form 1626), a Veterinary Consultation Request Form (JPC VET Form), photocopies of any lab work or photos taken at time of necropsy, and a photocopy of the dog's master problem list and assignment history to the JPC Veterinary Pathology Service immediately upon fixation of the tissues. Do NOT send fluids (e.g., whole blood, serum, urine), fecal, culture, uro/choleliths (stones), and/or culture samples to the JPC for processing. Do NOT send brain tissue for rabies testing to JPC. It is strongly recommended that specimens are shipped so they do not arrive on a weekend or holiday using private couriers (e.g. UPS, FEDEX, DHL) and that the courier's reference tracking number is retained, to locate the sample, in the event it is misdirected.

Address: Joint Pathology Center
ATTN: Veterinary Case Accessioning 606 Stephen Sitter Avenue
Silver Spring, MD 20910

f. Personnel in EUCOM, CENTCOM, and AFRICOM may submit specimens to the Public Health Command-Europe, Laboratory Sciences, Biological Analysis Division following the same protocol listed above for JPC. The only exception is that the Biological Analysis Division does accept brain tissue for rabies testing. Shipping can also be done through military transport, but prior telephonic communication must be made to ensure planning for receipt, DSN 314-590-9710.

Military Address: US Army, Public Health Command-Europe
(WK4UPX) Laboratory Sciences
ATTN: MCHB-RE-LS Laboratory Operation Division CMR 402
or APO AE 09180

German Address: US Army, Public Health Command-Europe
(WK4UPX) Laboratory Sciences
ATTN: Laboratory Operation Division
Kirchberhg Kaserne, Gebaude 3809, Raum N202
D-66849 Landstuhl, Germany

g. Send the MWD's complete medical record, any radiographs, the signed death certificate (DD Form 1743) and a copy of the Necropsy Report (DD Form 1626) to the DOD Military Working Dog Veterinary Service; do not wait for receipt of the finalized JPC Pathology Consult report before forwarding. The JPC Veterinary Pathology Service will send the finalized pathology consultation report to the referring VCO and to the DODMWDVS at dog.consult@us.af.mil. Records should be shipped within one week of death; however, overnight or other rush method is not required nor should be utilized except in extraordinary circumstances. The MWD's record held in ROVR should be marked "inactive" upon death.

Address: Central Records Repository
DOD Military Working Dog Veterinary Service

1219 Knight Street, Bldg. 7602
JBSA-Lackland, TX 78236-5631

JPC Diagnostic Services and Pathology Support

The JPC Veterinary Pathology Service offers no-cost diagnostic histopathologic and cytopathologic services for all government-owned animals, and for privately-owned animals belonging to individuals who are authorized to receive DOD veterinary services. The JPC Veterinary Pathology Service also offers second-opinion consultation services for both federal and civilian veterinary pathologists as an integral part training for Army veterinary pathology residents in the DoD Veterinary Pathology Residency Program.

1. Diagnostic materials accepted by the JPC. Accepted materials include formalin-fixed tissue specimens, paraffin-embedded tissue specimens, stained histologic sections, cytologic samples (i.e. glass slide preparations), radiographs and photographs. Do NOT send fluids (e.g.; whole blood, serum, urine), fecal, culture, uro/choleliths (stones), and/or culture samples to the JPC for processing; receipt of the aforementioned samples will be discarded immediately.
2. Surgical biopsy and cytology diagnostic material.
    a. Fix tissues and prepare for shipment as previous described.
    b. Complete one copy of JPC VET Form (Veterinary Consultation Request) and forward with case material. A link to this form is located on the JPC website, http://www.jpc.capmed.mil/docs/vet_consultation_request_form.pdf.
        i. Include complete signalment (animal identification, species, breed, sex and age).
        ii. Include pertinent clinical information to include the anatomic location from which the specimen was collected, clinical history (including clinical signs, treatments, response to treatments, distribution of lesions, etc.) and pertinent laboratory findings.
        iii. Include a telephone number, fax number and an e-mail address where the results should be directed. Include a phone number that is answered outside of normal clinic hours.
    c. Correct packaging of specimen containers is essential to prevent breakage, environmental contamination, and tissue dehydration.
    d. Do NOT ship tissues immersed in formalin.
3. Case priority and turn-around times. Final JPC Pathology Consult reports will be sent to the contributor indicated on JPC VET Form Veterinary Consultation Request within the number of days after receipt of case materials as listed below. If special situations justify faster case processing; annotate "rush" on the request. The cases that may warrant rush include: public health issues (e.g.; zoonoses), unexplained sudden death, and/or criminal investigations.
    a. Surgical biopsy cases. Seven (7) duty days for routine cases; additional time may be required if advanced diagnostics (histochemical or immunohistochemical stains) are warranted. A resident and/or staff pathologist will contact the contributor if additional processing time is required.
    b. Cytology cases. Four (4) duty days.
    c. Necropsy cases. Sixty (60) calendar days.
4. Contacting the JPC veterinary pathology service. Questions regarding any aspect of the JPC pathology services or the MWD necropsy should be addressed to JPC, Chief, Veterinary Diagnostic Services; COM (301) 295- 6200; Fax (301) 295-9971; DSN 312-295-6207. E-mail: dha.ncr.ncr-medical-dir-jpc.askvetpath@mail.mil.

APPENDIX A

REFERENCES

SECTION I
REQUIRED PUBLICATIONS

Army regulations (AR) are available from the U.S. Army Publishing Directorate (APD) Web site: http://www.armypubs.army.mil.

AR 40–905/SECNAVINST 6401.1B/AFI 48-131
Veterinary Health Services

SECTION II
RELATED PUBLICATIONS

A related publication is a source of additional information. The user does not have to read it to understand this publication. Air Force publications are available at http://www.e-publishing.af.mil. Except as noted below, Army publications are available online from the U.S. Army Publishing Directorate Web site: https://armypubs.army.mil/.

AFI 31-126
DOD Military Working Dog Program

ATP 4-02.7
Multi-Service Tactics, Techniques, and Procedures for Health Service Support In A Chemical, Biological, Radiological, and Nuclear Environment

ATP 4-02.8
Force Health Protection

ATP 4-02.83
Multiservice Tactics, Techniques, and Procedures for Treatment of Nuclear and Radiological Casualties

ATP 4-02.84
Multiservice Tactics, Techniques, and Procedures for Treatment of Biological Warfare Agent Casualties

ATP 4-02.85
Multi-Service Tactics, Techniques and Procedures for Treatment of Chemical Warfare Agent Casualties and Conventional Military Chemical Injuries

SECTION III
REFERENCED FORMS

Unless otherwise indicated, DD Forms are available on the Office of the Secretary of Defense (OSD) Web site https://www.esd.whs.mil/Directives/forms. SF Forms are available on the United States General Services Administration (GSA) Web site: https://www.gsa.gov/reference/forms. DA forms are available from the APD Web site: https://www.armypubs.army.mil.

DD Form 1741
Immunization Record

DD Form 1829
Record of Military Dog Physical Examination

DD Form 2208
Rabies Vaccination Certificate

DD Form 2209
Veterinary Health Certificate

DD Form 2341
Report of Animal Bite

DD Form 2619
Master Problem List

SF 512
Weight Plotting Chart

SF 515
Tissue Examination

SF 516
Operation Report

SF 519
Radiographic Reports

SF 519-B
Radiological Consultation Request

SF 545
Laboratory Report Display

SF 600
Chronological Record of Medical Care.

AF Form 2110A
Health Record Outpatient

DA Form 7389
Anesthesia Record

WHMC Form 3381
Military Working Dog Procurement Physical Examination

SECTION III
SELECTED BIBLIOGRAPHY

Armbrust LJ, Hoskinson JJ, Biller DS, et al. *Comparison of digitized and direct viewed (analog) radiographic images for detection of pulmonary nodules.* Vet Radiol Ultrasound 2005;46:361–367.

American College of Sports Medicine (2013-03-04). *ACSM's Guidelines for Exercise Testing and Prescription* (Kindle Locations 4742-4744). LWW. Kindle Edition.

American College of Sports Medicine. American College of Sports Medicine position stand. *Progression models in resistance training for healthy adults.* Med Sci Sports Exerc. 2009;41(3): 687– 708.

Arnott ER, Early JB, Wade CM, McGreevy PD. *Environmental factors associated with success rates of Australian stock herding dogs.* PLoS One 2014; 9(8): 1-13.

Burghardt WF. *Behavioral considerations in the management of working dogs.* Vet Clin Small Anim 2003;33:417-446.

Charles, RP. *Contrast studies of the urogenital system. Veterinary Clinics of North America.* Vol. 23, No. 2, March 1993.

Evans RI, Herbold JR, Bradshaw BS, Moore GE. *Causes for discharge of military working dogs from service: 268 cases (2000-2004).* J Am Vet Med Assoc. 2007; 231(8): 1215-20.

Fletcher DJ, Boller M, Brainard BM, et al. *RECOVER evidence and knowledge gap analysis on veterinary CPR. Part 7: Clinical guidelines.* J Vet Emerg Crit Care. 2012;22(S1): S102-S131.

Garber CE, Blissmer B, Deschenes MR, et al. American College of Sports Medicine Position Stand. *The quantity and quality of exercise for developing and maintaining cardiorespiratory, musculoskeletal, and neuromotor fitness in apparently healthy adults: guidance for prescribing exercise.* Med Sci Sports Exerc. 2011;43(7): 1334– 59.

Haithem AMF, Wael MK, Ebada M. *Field survey on most common medicinal and surgical diseases in police guard and explosive dogs from 11/2007-2/2010.* J Amer Sci 2011; 7(4): 816-26.

Henderson AL. Master's Thesis: *Effect of a Core Conditioning Program on Lumbar Paraspinal Area, Asymmetry and Pain Score in Military Working Dogs with Lumbosacral Pain.* University of Tennessee

Knoxville; 2014.

Jenkins EK, Lee-Fowler TM, Angle TC, Behrend EN, Moore GE. *Effects of oral administration of metronidazole and doxycycline on olfactory capabilities of explosives detection dogs.* Am J Vet Res 2016;77:906-912.

McArdle WD, Katch FI, Katch VL. *Exercise Physiology: Nutrition, Energy and Human Performance,* 8th edition. Philidelphia: Lippincott Williams and Wilkins; 2015. Moore GE, Burkman KD, Carter MN,

Park DE, Wrigley RH: *Contrast cystography.* In Thrall DE, editor: *Textbook of Veterinary Diagnostic Radiology,* 5th ed., St. Louis, MO, 2007, Saunders Elsevier Inc., pp 709-724.

Park, RD. *Radiographic Contrast Studies of the Lower Urinary Tract.* Veterinary Clinics of North America, Vol. 4, No. 4, 1974.

Peterson MR. *Causes of death or reasons for euthanasia in military working dogs*: 927 cases (1993-1996). J Am Vet Med Assoc. 2001; 219(2): 209-14.

Millis, DL. In: Millis DL, Levine D, editors. *Canine Rehabilitation and Physical Therapy,* 2nd edition. Philadelphia: Elsevier; 2014. p. 92-153.

Musch TI, Haidet GC, Ordway GA et al. *Dynamic exercise training in foxhounds. I. Oxygen consumption and hemodynamic responses.* J Appl Physiol 1985; 45:169-89.

Musch TI, Haidet GC, Ordway GA et al. *Training effects on regional blood flow response to maximal exercise in foxhounds.* J Appl Physiol 1987; 62:1724-32.

Parr JR, Otto CM. *Emergency visits and occupational hazards in German Shepherd police dogs* (2008-2010). J Vet Emerg Crit Care 2013; 23(6): 591-7.

Pierce, BP. D*OD Military Working Dog Physical Conditioning Program Overview and Conditioning Protocol.* 2013.

Takara MS, Harrell K. *Noncombat-related injuries or illnesses incurred by military working dogs in a combat zone.* J Am Vet Med Assoc. 2014; 245(10): 1124-1128.

Tipton CM, Carey RA, Eastin WC, Erickson HH. *A submaximal test for dogs: evaluation of effects of training, detraining, and cage confinement.* J Appl Physio 1974; 37(2): 271-5.

Wallack, ST. *The Handbook of Contrast Radiography.* 2003; 123-4.

Zink MC and Van Dyke JB. *Canine Sports Medicine and Rehabilitation.* Ames, Iowa: Wiley-Blackwell; 2013.

APPENDIX B

SEQUENCE OF FORMS FOR MWD VETERINARY HEALTH RECORD

Record Jacket: The four-part record jacket is AF Form 2110A, Health Record Outpatient (Supplied by DODMWDVS)

Front Cover:

1. Label with Dog's Name, Tattoo, Breed, and Whelp date on top right corner
2. AVID Microchip Number – sticker, handwritten, and centered.
3. Label with "Procurement pelvic and elbow radiographs are on permanent file at the Department of Defense Military Working Dog Veterinary Service. Inquiries concerning them should be addressed: DODMWDVS, 1219 Knight St, Bldg 7595, JBSA-Lackland, TX 78236-5631
4. Label with "WORKING DOG" in space provided for military service and grade

Inside Back Cover:

1. Label with Dog's Name, Tattoo, Breed, and Whelp date on top right corner
2. Semiannual Identification – Red and Yellow sticker over the number corresponding to the month of the Red and Yellow Semiannual Physical Exam
3. Photo of Dog-Side view with head turned toward camera. Name & Tattoo written on photo
4. Certification – i.e. Patrol, Patrol/Drug, Patrol/Explosives

Inside record: Sections 1 – 4, left to right. Forms are listed from top to bottom. Forms are filed in proper sections, chronologically, with newest on top. All forms and documents must be clearly labeled with MWD Name and Tattoo number

Section 1:

1. SF 600, Chronological Record of Medical Care. Section 2:
2. DD Form 2619 (or equivalent), Master Problem List
3. DD Form 1741 (or equivalent), Immunization Record
4. DD Form 1829, Record of Military Dog Physical Examination
5. WHMC Form 3381 (or equivalent), Military Working Dog Procurement Physical Examination.
6. Clinical History from previous owner (if any)

Section 3:

1. SF 512 (or equivalent), Weight Plotting Chart (each large block is equivalent to one month; with each vertical line representing 3 days and each horizontal line representing one half (½) or one (1) pound)
2. SF 545, Laboratory Report Display (or equivalent/local form) and Clinical Pathology Reports. File lab reports in order by date, not by type of test. Smaller reports should be photocopied onto a full size paper and not attached with staples to allow for scanning. Cytopathology is filed here. Serology and infectious disease (Serology) reports. Histopathology reports are not filed here.

Section 4:

1. Deployment History Form
2. SF 519 or SF 519-B (or equivalents), Radiographic Reports and Radiological Consultation Request.
3. SF 516 (or equivalent), Operation Report. This section will also include any type of correspondence dealing with oral and dental procedures, and videoscopic procedures.
4. DA Form 7389 (or equivalent), Anesthesia Record.
5. SF 515 (or equivalent/local form), Tissue Examination. Gross and Histological Pathology reports are included here.
6. Electrodiagnostic procedures – to include ECG, EEG, and all other neurological procedures.
7. DD Form 2209, Health Certificate. Any other import or export documents necessary for travel.
8. Miscellaneous correspondence – will include all correspondence that does not identify with any of the areas listed above (i.e., referral memorandums, rabies certificates, etc.)

NOTE: When an MWD is transferred to the DODMWDVS, the referral memorandum should be temporarily placed on the top of the SF 600s in Section 1.

9. Sequence of Forms Memorandum

APPENDIX C

CARDIOPULMONARY RESUSCIATATION (CPR) ALGORITHM FOR MWDS

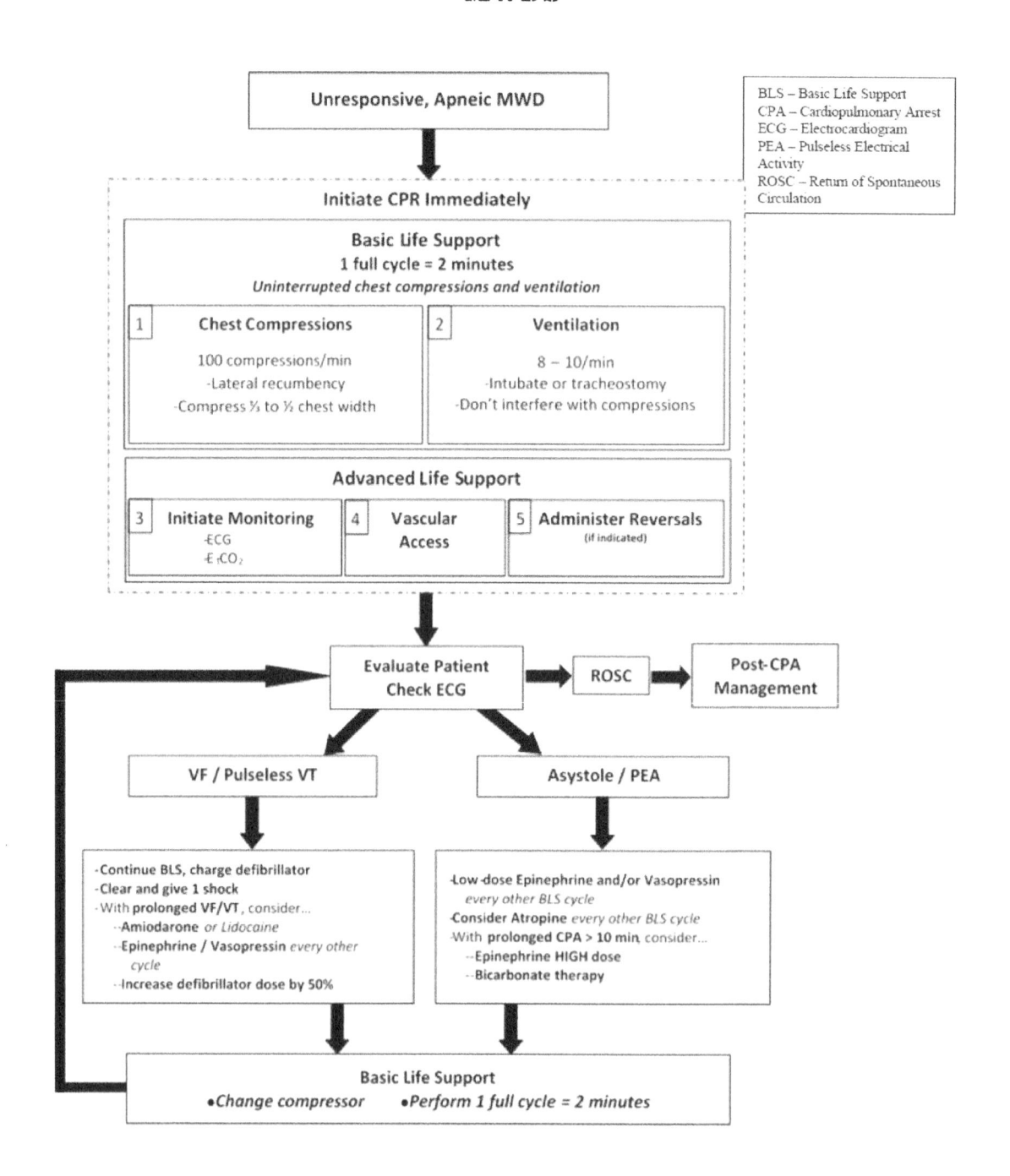

Abbreviations:
- BLS – Basic Life Support
- CPA – Cardiopulmonary Arrest
- ECG – Electrocardiogram
- PEA – Pulseless Electrical Activity
- ROSC – Return of Spontaneous Circulation

Unresponsive, Apneic MWD

Initiate CPR Immediately

Basic Life Support
1 full cycle = 2 minutes
Uninterrupted chest compressions and ventilation

1. Chest Compressions
- 100 compressions/min
- Lateral recumbency
- Compress ⅔ to ½ chest width

2. Ventilation
- 8 – 10/min
- Intubate or tracheostomy
- Don't interfere with compressions

Advanced Life Support

3. Initiate Monitoring
- ECG
- E_tCO₂

4. Vascular Access

5. Administer Reversals (if indicated)

Evaluate Patient / Check ECG → **ROSC** → **Post-CPA Management**

VF / Pulseless VT
- Continue BLS, charge defibrillator
- Clear and give 1 shock
- With prolonged VF/VT, consider...
  - Amiodarone or Lidocaine
  - Epinephrine / Vasopressin every other cycle
- Increase defibrillator dose by 50%

Asystole / PEA
- Low-dose Epinephrine and/or Vasopressin *every other BLS cycle*
- Consider Atropine *every other BLS cycle*
- With prolonged CPA > 10 min, consider...
  - Epinephrine HIGH dose
  - Bicarbonate therapy

Basic Life Support
- Change compressor
- Perform 1 full cycle = 2 minutes

APPENDIX D

STEP-BY-STEP MRI GUIDELINES

1. MRI studies must be directly supervised by a 64F. When considering whether or not an MRI is indicated, consult directly with the supporting 64F. The actual performance of the study must be performed under the direct supervision of a 64F in order to ensure:
    a. That an MRI is absolutely indicated. Radiologists from DODMWDVS indicate that subjectively over 90% of advanced imaging required for MWD workups may be performed satisfactorily with CT alone.
    b. Safety of the MWD is preserved. Historically we have lost an unacceptable number of MWDs to anesthesia-related deaths during MRI studies. Involvement of a 64F helps ensure that safe performance of anesthesia is accomplished as well as mentoring the 64A in the fundamentals of TIVA.
2. Perform a site visit to the MRI suite PRIOR to the scheduled procedure date. This allows the VCO to consult with the technician(s) and/or radiologist to discuss the technical requirements for a diagnostic scan as well as to ensure that requirements for a safe anesthetic event can be met.
3. Assemble required equipment prior to performing the scan:
    a. Syringe pump; ideally a syringe pump will be utilized to precisely deliver propofol at the recommended dosage rate. Ensure the machine is MRI compatible IAW manufacturer guidance and compliance with the facility's safety guidelines. Ensure that the pump is secured outside the 150 Gauss line in the magnet room. Alternately, a non-MRI compatible syringe pump can be used from the control room and several extension sets daisy chained through the port to the patient.
    b. Endotracheal tube, ties/gauze, and laryngoscope; it is of paramount importance that the MWD be intubated in order to preserve a patent airway, implement ventilation, and to provide supplemental oxygen during the procedure.
    c. Oxygen line; if oxygen is unavailable in the magnet room, coordinate with the staff to take an E-tank and regulator yoke. The tank may be maintained in the control room and the oxygen line can be pushed through the control port to the patient. If supplemental oxygen cannot be provided for the patient, the procedure should not be performed.
    d. BVM
    e. Esophageal stethoscope (MRI compatible); a technician should be present during the procedure to monitor heart rate and respiratory rate during the procedure
    f. IV fluids and drip sets; a crystalloid such as lactated ringer's solution (LRS) should be delivered during the procedure at a rate of 5-10 ml/kg/hr
    g. Syringes of various sizes, needles of various sizes
    h. IV catheters, flush, tape, vet wrap, scrub/alcohol, clippers, etc. for placing IV catheter
    i. Eye lubrication
    j. Thermometer
    k. Pulse oximeter (only for use outside MRI suite, unless MRI compatible)
    l. Emergency drugs. Resuscitation and reversal medications is primarily indicated.
    m. Anesthesia chart with emergency drug dosages pre-calculated
    n. Positioning equipment such as V-trough
    o. Litter/stretcher
    p. Additional drugs such as propofol, IV fluids, etc.

4. It is extremely important that all personnel involved with the scan understand that no metallic objects should be brought into the MRI suite. MRI staff may assume that veterinary personnel are also medical and understand this concept. Reiterating with all personnel that metallic objects (pens, needles, laryngoscope, implants such as bone plates, etc.) can become dangerous projectiles causing severe injury or even death to the patient or attending personnel.

APPENDIX E

INFORMATION FOR UPLOADING FILES FOR TRANSFER TO VIA AMRDEC SAFE

1. Save the files in one folder and create a .zip file to upload.
    a. Find the folder on the computer hard drive.
    b. Right click on the folder name.
    c. Scroll down to "send to" and select "compressed (zip) folder."
    d. Save the file as a .zip folder on the desktop.
2. Upload the file for delivery.
    a. Go to the following website: https://safe.amrdec.army.mil/SAFE/default.asp
    b. The following screen will come up:

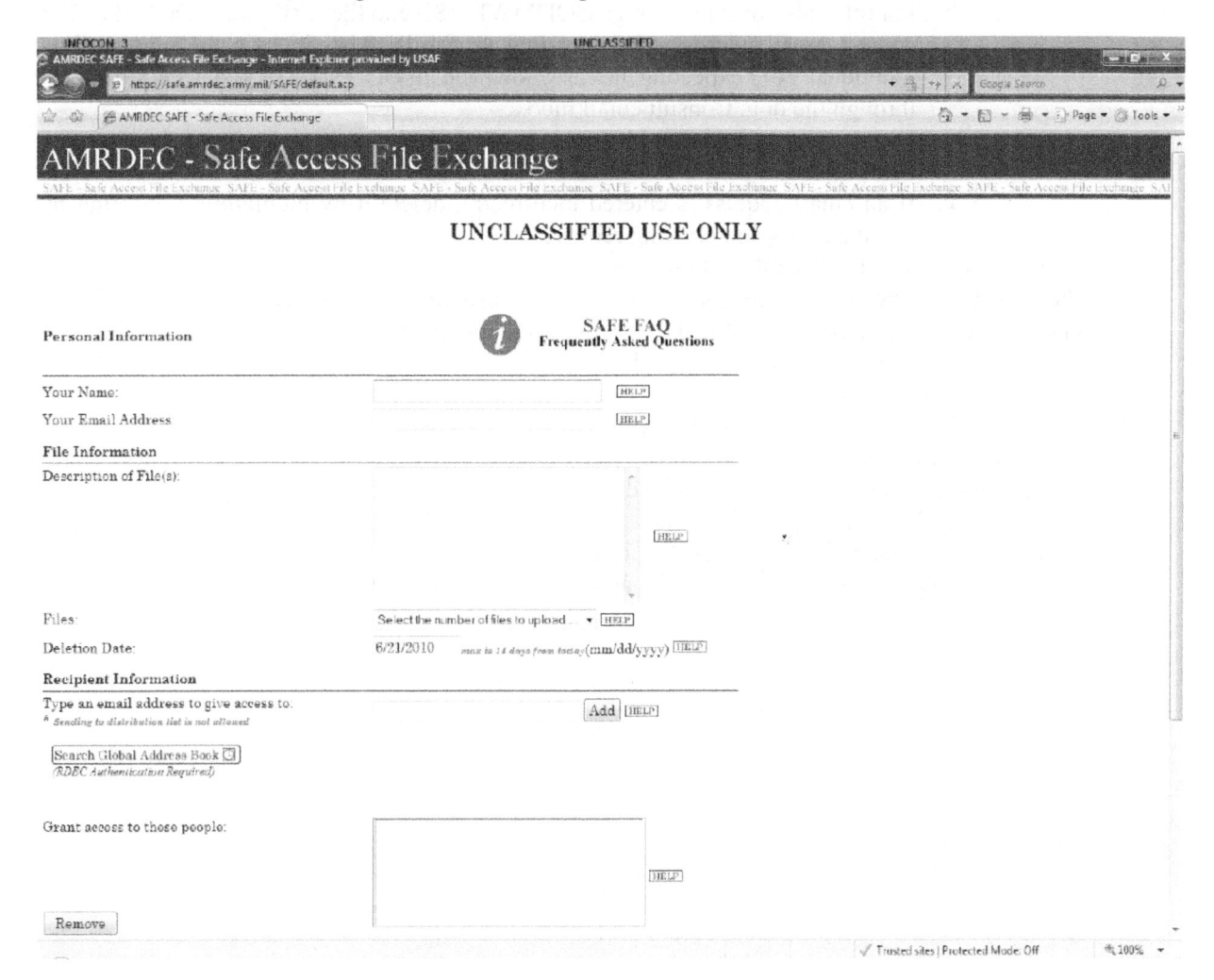

    c. Type in your name and email address.
    d. Type in a short description of the file.
        i. Make the description something that will alert the person to what the files are that are waiting for download. This description will show up in the email the receiver gets in their inbox.
        ii. For imaging consults, be sure that the description includes the patient's name, tattoo number, type of images, and a list of who the consult is being sent to.
    e. Select the number of separate files to upload (25 max).
    f. Click on Browse next to "File1."
        i. Find the .zip file saved on the desktop and select it.
        ii. Click Open at the bottom of the window.
        iii. The file with the complete path (i.e. C:\users....) will now be in the File1 box.
    g. Select a deletion date (up to 14 days max) or leave as the default date.
    h. Type an email address to send to and click Add.
        i. The email address will show up in the "grant access to these people:" box.
        ii. Military and civilian addresses can be used.
        iii. For referrals/consults through DODMWDVS, send files to the main DODMWDVS consult email address (dog.consult@us.af.mil). Also include the email of the individual VCO expecting the case; however, all DODMWDVS consults are tracked through the dog. Consult email inbox.
        iv. Use this site to consult with the supporting 64F by entering their email address(es) here instead.
        v. If an email address is entered incorrectly, delete it by highlighting/selecting the email address and clicking remove.
    i. Click Upload under File Submission.
3. The files are in route to the recipients selected. Each email address entered will receive an email with a link to the pick-up website, the file description, and a unique password.
4. To retrieve a file once an email is received:
    a. Click on the website link.
    b. Paste the password into the password box on the website.
    c. Click Submit.
    d. Select the first file in the download list.
    e. Select Save and choose a location.
    f. When the download is complete, click Close.
    g. For .zip file, right click on the file and Extract all to open files.

APPENDIX F

EXAMPLE OF ATTENDING VCO DISPOSITION MEMORANDUM

DEPARTMENT OF THE ARMY
MOODY AIR FORCE BASE VETERINARY TREATMENT FACILITY
4997 BURRELL STREET
MOODY AIR FORCE BASE, GEORGIA 316995

MCHB-RS-GSY   13 May 2019

MEMORANDUM FOR Commander, Commander, 23d Security Forces Squadron

SUBJECT: Veterinary Corps Officer Disposition Request for Military Working Dog (MWD) Benga V160

1. **History:** Military Working Dog (MWD) Benga V160 is an 8 year-old male neutered German Shepherd Dog certified in patrol and explosives detection. He is currently in deployment Category IV status due to lumbosacral stenosis (LSSD) and elbow dysplasia. Benga was evaluated on 13 March 2019 for lameness of all four limbs. Radiographs, computed tomography (CT) and magnetic resonance imaging (MRI) were performed revealing degeneration and stenosis of the lumbosacral junction leading to compression of the spinal cord and spinal nerves. Benga also has a history of otitis externa that is managed with routine ear cleaning.

2. **Diagnosis:** Benga has been diagnosed with LSSD and elbow dysplasia. Due to these medical conditions he is unable to perform his required duties as an MWD.

3. **Prognosis:** Benga's prognosis for utility as an MWD is poor. He is unable to perform both patrol and detection duties due to pain and neuro logic deficits of his hind end as a result of LSSD and pain in his forelimbs from elbow dysplasia. Benga's prognosis for retirement is good with medical pain control.

4. **Fitness for Duty:** I recommend that Benga V160 be declared excess to the needs of the DoD and considered for adoption at the discretion of the unit commander and IAW Public Law 106-446. Review of his records describe Benga's personality as friendly making him an excellent candidate for adoption.

5. I have consulted with MAJ Iam A. Specialist (64F), and they concur with the clinical assessment, prognosis, and fitness for duty recommendation for Benga. It must be noted that the replacement of any MWD is also a logistics and supply function that must be completed through the kennel master's chain-of-command and in conjunction with their MWD Program Manager.

6. POC is the undersigned at (229) 000-0000 or starr.veterinarian.mil@mail.mil.

                                                                                STARR VETERINARIAN
                                                                                CPT, VC
                                                                                OIC, Moody AFB Section

APPENDIX G

EXAMPLE OF 64F DISPOSITION MEMORANDUM

DEPARTMENT OF THE ARMY
PUBLIC HEALTH COMMAND-ATLANTIC
4411 LLEWELLYN AVENUE, BLDG 4550, STE 204A
FORT GEORGE G. MEADE, MD 20755-5225

MCHB-RN-VSD   3 June 2019

MEMORANDUM FOR Commander, 341st Training Squadron, ATTN: Disposition Board Members, 1239 Knight Street, Lackland Air Force Base, Texas 78236-5631

SUBJECT: Disposition Board Request for Military Working Dog (MWD) Benga V160

1. Benga V160 is an 8 year old, male, neutered, German shepherd, military working dog that has been trained as a patrol and explosives detection dog (P/EDD). I have reviewed his medical records, physical exam findings, imaging reports, and other pertinent records pertaining to the disposition. Benga V160 has a history of lameness in multiple limbs. During his medical work-up, Benga V160 was diagnosed with degenerative lumbosacral stenosis (DLSS) with nerve root compression at L7-S1 and bilateral elbow degenerative joint disease. He is on multimodal pain management but continued work will only exacerbate his clinical signs. Medical disposition is warranted.

2. I recommend Benga V160 be declared excess to the needs of the DoD. There are no indicators of aggression in his medical record or adoption suitability checklist. He has one bite that occurred during patrol training. Both the Veterinary Corps Officer (VCO) and accountable unit commander recommend adoption. Based on medical record, adoption suitability checklist, and bite muzzle video review, I have assessed Benga V160 as a fair candidate for adoption.

3. If adopted, his owners should be counseled on his current medical conditions. He will need routine veterinary check-ups and daily medications to maintain his current quality of life. He may need further medical care, including surgery, if his condition declines. Strenuous physical activity should be avoided, and he would benefit from regular, controlled exercise, physical therapy, and other pain management modalities. In addition, Benga V160 requires a special diet to manage his allergic dermatitis.

4. Point of contact is the undersigned at (301) 000-0000 or iam.a.specialist.mil@mail.mil.

IAM A. SPECIALIST
MAJ, VC
Clinical Consultant, PHC-A

APPENDIX H

EXAMPLE OF MWD MEDICAL DEPLOYMENT CATEGORY MEMORANDUM

01 November 2017

MEMORANDUM FOR RECORD

SUBJECT: Deployment Status for 802nd SF MWD Kennels

1. Listed below are the Medical Deployment Categories for the MWDs:

Name	Tattoo	Age	Deployment Status	Cat III ERD	WDMS Registry Comment	Meal 1a	Meal 2a
ARES	P669	8 Y	Cat I		Conus	2c SDA	2c SDA
BONO	P589	8 Y	Cat II		Mild OA	2c SDA	2c SDA
FANDO	R364	7 Y	Cat I		Deployed	2c SDA	2c SDA
JANY	N544	10 Y	Cat IV		Pending Dispo	3c SDA	2.5c Z/D
LUIGI	T260	8 Y	Cat I			2c SDA	2c SDA
SONJA	P307	9 Y	Cat I			2c SDA	2c SDA
VVENICE	N772	9 Y	Cat III	01-Dec-17	RR Lameness	2c SDA	2c SDA
VVIPER	N714	9 Y	Cat I			2c SDA	2c SDA
ZUSA	N098	10 Y	Cat I			2c SDA	2c SDA

Note: Chart generated utilizing ROVR Registry Report

2. Deployment category definitions are as follows
    a. CAT 1 - Unrestricted Deployment: MWD is medically fit for any contingency or exercise, can handle extreme stresses and environments (very hot weather, prolonged physical activity, etc.) and has no limiting or compromising factors (lack of stamina, etc.). MWD will have no existing or recurring medical problems that limit performance or will worsen by stress or increased demands. Note: Medical problems may exist or be under treatment but do not limit performance.
    b. CAT 2 - Restricted Deployment: MWD is medically fit for regions/missions with minimal requirement for acclimation to heat or physical stress, no significant limiting or compromising factors. MWD may have medical problems which exist that slightly limit performance but are controlled. The reason for restriction must be reported in the Veterinary Health Record (VHR).
    c. CAT 3 - Temporarily Nondeployable: MWD has a medical condition exists that impedes daily duty performance and is under diagnosis, observation, or treatment. The reason for nondeployability must be reported in the VHR. The Estimated Release Date (ERD) from

CAT 3 must be reported in the VHR and be no longer than 90 days.
d. CAT 4 - Nondeployable: MWD has unresolved medical or physical problems exist that frequently or regularly impede daily duty performance and ERD cannot be given. Medical or physical conditions warrant submission to the

MWD Disposition Process with subsequent replacement. The reason for nondeployability must be reported in the VHR.

3. Point of contact is the undersigned at   .

                                      JOHN SMITH
                                      CPT, VC
                                      Camp Swampy VTF

DISTRIBUTION
Kennel Master (Squad Leader, 1st Line Supervisor)
Local File

                                    Date _____

Receipt of Notice of Medical Deployment Status for Military Working Dogs (MWD).

Receipt acknowledged. I understand that the medical deployment category as defined above.

                                  _____
                                              (Signature)

                                  _____
                                            (Printed Name)

APPENDIX I

CANINE – TACTICAL COMBAT CASUALTY CARD (CTCCC)

Can be found on the Joint Trauma System (JTS) Web site:
https://jts.amedd.army.mil/index.cfm/documents/forms_after_action

CANINE-TACTICAL COMBAT CASUALTY CARE CARD (cTCCC)

EVAC CAT: ☐ Urgent ☐ Priority ☐ Routine

EVAC TYPE: ☐ Fixed ☐ Rotary ☐ Ground ☐ MEDEVAC ☐ CASEVAC

UNIT: _____ **NAME:** _____ **TATTOO:** _____

DATE: (DD-MM-YY) _____ **TIME:** _____ **GENDER:** ☐ M ☐ F

Mechanism of Injury: (Mark X all that apply)
☐ IED ☐ GSW ☐ MINE ☐ BURN ☐ GRENADE ☐ ARTILLERY ☐ FALL
☐ OTHER: _____

Injury: (Mark all injuries that apply with an X)

Signs and Symptoms: (fill in the blank)

Time					
Pain Score (0-10)					
Temperature (99-102.5)					
Pulse Rate/Location (60-80)					
Respirations (16-30)					
Blood Pressure (120/80)					
Pulse Ox% (> 95%)					
Capillary Refill (< 2 sec)					

NOTES: _____

02 May 2019 version 4.0   (Send card to dog.consult@us.af.mill)

CANINE-TACTICAL COMBAT CASUALTY CARE CARD (cTCCC)

Treatments: (Mark X all that apply) and fill in the blank)   **Location:**

M: Dressing - ☐ Hemostatic ☐ Pressure ☐ TQ   Other:

A: ☐ Intact   ☐ ET-Tube   ☐ Tracheostomy

R: ☐ O^2 ☐ Needle-D   ☐ Chest-Tube   ☐ Chest-Seal

C:

Total Crystalloid Shock Volume of fluids is 90 mls/kg:
Administer 20ml/kg over 10-20 min. Reassess (as with human casualty):
If lack of response after 2-3 boluses consider adjunct therapy (HES/HTS.)

CRYSTALLOID	Volume	Route	Time
HYDROXYETHYL STARCH (HES): 5mls/kg over 5 - 10 min. After ½ shock crystalloid not effective.			
HYPERTONIC SALINE (HTS): 4mls/kg (If two or three ¼ shock boluses and 1-2 boluses of HES not effective)			
TXA: 10 mg/kg IV in 100ml NaCl or LRS given in first 3hrs. Followed by a 10-15 mg/kg CRI over 8 hours.			

C: ☐ Splint   ☐ Other Bandage

H: ☐ Hypothermia-Prevention   ☐ Hyperthermia-External Cooling

H: ☐ Head Injury

Pain Meds and Antibiotics (Circle if given and write the time in the notes.)

DRUG (conc)	DOSE	RTE	60lb/ 27.3kg	70lb/32kg	80lb/36.4kg
Ketamine (100mg/ml)	2-5mg/kg	IV/IM	1 ml	1.5 mls	2 mls
Midazolam (5mg/ml)	0.1-0.3mg/kg	IV/IM	3 mls	4 mls	5 mls
Morphine (10mg auto inj.)	0.2-0.5 mg/kg	IM	1 *auto*	1 *auto*	2 *auto*
Meloxicam	0.1-0.2mg/kg	IV/SQ/PO	5 *mg*	6 *mg*	7 *mg*
Cefazolin/Ceftriaxone	25 mg/kg	IV/IM	600 *mg*	800 *mg*	900 *mg*
Cefotaxime	25 mg/kg	IV/IM/SQ	600 *mg*	800 *mg*	900 *mg*
Ertapenem (100mg/ml)	15mg/kg	IV/SQ	4 mls	5 mls	6 mls

NOTES:

FIRST RESPONDER:
Name (Last, First):   AOC/MOS:

02 May 2019 version 4.0   (Send card to dog.consult@us.af.mill)

GLOSSARY

SECTION I
ACRONYMS

341 TRS
341st Training Squadron

64B
US Army Veterinary Corps Officer, Veterinary Preventive Medicine Specialist Area of Concentration

64F
US Army Veterinary Corps Officer, Veterinary Clinical Specialist Area of Concentration

AAHA
American Animal Hospital Association

AFAST
Abdominal Focused Assessment with Sonography for Trauma

AFI
Air Force Instruction

AR
Army Regulation

ATP
Army Techniques and Procedures

AVS
US Army Veterinary Service

BVM
Bag Valve Mask (Ambu® bag)

CBP
Customs and Border Protection

CBRN
Chemical, Biological, Radiological and Nuclear

ccSOAP
Chief Complaint, Subjective, Objective, Assessment, Plan

CDC
Centers for Disease Control

COHAT
Comprehensive Oral Health Assessment and Treatment

CPG
Clinical Practice Guidelines

CPR
Cardiopulmonary Resuscitation

c-PTSD
canine – Post Traumatic Stress Disorder

CWDs
Contract Working Dogs

DHAVS
Defense Health Agency, Veterinary Services

DHS
Department of Homeland Security

DLA
Defense Logistics Agency

DOD
Department of Defense

DODMWDVS
Department of Defense Military Working Dog Veterinary Service

DV
Dorsoventral

EA
Executive Agent

ECG
Electrocardiogram

ERD
Estimated Release Date

FADL
DOD Food and Animal Diagnostic Laboratory

FDA
U.S. Food and Drug Administration

FYGVE
First Year Graduate Veterinary Education

GDV
Gastric Dilatation Volvulus

GOA
Government Owned Animal

GVMP
Global Veterinary Medical Practice

IAG
Interagency Agreements

IAW
In Accordance With

IWR
Ideal Weight Range

JPC
Joint Pathology Center

JSMWDC
Joint Services Military Working Dog Committee

KM
Kennel Master

MEDCOM
US Army Medical Command

MPL
Master Problem List

MOA
Memoranda of Agreement

MOS 68T
US Army Animal Care Specialist

MOU
Memoranda of Understanding

MTF
Medical Treatment Facility

MWD
Military Working Dog

NAF
Non-Appropriated Fund

NATO
North Atlantic Treaty Organization

NCMI
National Center for Medical Intelligence

PHA
Public Health Activity

PM
Program Manager

POA
Privately Owned Animal

SAPE
Semi-Annual Physical Examination

TFAST
Thoracic Focused Assessment with Sonography for Trauma

TSA
Transportation Security Agency

USAF
United States Air Force

USDA
United States Department of Agriculture

USMC
United States Marine Corps

USSS
United States Secret Service

VCO
Veterinary Corps Officer

VETAC
Veterinary Activity

VETCEN
Veterinary Center

VD
Ventrodorsal

VHR
Veterinary Health Record

VMO
Veterinary Medical Officer (GS Civilian)

VMSB
Veterinary Medical Standardization Board

VTF
Veterinary Treatment Facility

WDMS
Working Dog Management System

09 MAY 2019

By Order of the Secretary of the Army:

MARK A. MILLEY
General, United States Army
Chief of Staff

Official:

KATHLEEN S. MILLER
Administrative Assistant
to the Secretary of the Army

DISTRIBUTION:
Distributed in electronic media only (EMO).

PIN: 107252-000

Made in the USA
Monee, IL
18 September 2023